THE MINSTER

THESAURUS

OF ENGLISH WORDS

THE MINSTER

THESAURUS

OF ENGLISH WORDS

MINSTER BOOKS

First published in 1979 by
The Hamlyn Publishing Group Limited
Published in 1984 by Newnes Books,
Michelin House,
81 Fulham Road,
London SW3 6RB

This 1992 edition reprinted exclusively for MINSTER BOOKS

ISBN 0 600 38779 8

Printed at Thomson Press (India) Ltd.
Faridabad (Haryana)

Introduction

A thesaurus is a book of words arranged according to ideas. You use it when you can think of an idea but cannot find the exact word to express it or when you have a word in mind that isn't close enough to the one you really want. This is where a thesaurus comes in: it gives words in lists according to the ideas they stand for.

This thesaurus covers the central part of the vocabulary of English – the 'core' of the language we all use most of the time – and groups this under 990 categories, each representing a different idea. It does not include highly technical words, but does reflect the fact that the English language used today is becoming more colloquial. By looking up a word in the index and referring to one of the categories in the book you will find a list of words with a similar meaning and you will then be able to choose the one you want.

The first thesaurus was written by Peter Mark Roget (1779–1869), and published in 1852. Its full original title was *The Thesaurus of English Words and Phrases Classified and Arranged so as to Facilitate the Expression of Ideas and Assist in Literary Composition*. It has since been published in many editions and the concept has been taken over and used for other languages. Many changes have been made in writing this thesaurus: categories have been re-ordered, many have been given more intelligible names, and there is a thorough coverage of new words that have entered the language. A large number of older words and phrases have been rejected as no longer used.

This thesaurus is written for those who use language – those who speak and write English and want to use a variety of words, for those who solve crosswords, and for those who just like browsing through its pages to pore over the richness of the language. After all, the word 'thesaurus' itself comes from the Greek word for 'treasure', and we hope that something of the deep resources of the language will be discovered in these pages.

M. H. Manser

How to use this thesaurus

Imagine that you have a word in mind, let us say, 'beautiful'. You have used this word already and don't want to use it again, or you want something more expressive. The first thing to do is to look up this word − 'beautiful' − in the index. The index is arranged in alphabetical order. Every entry in the index consists of a word or words, a part of speech, and a number or numbers. Parts of speech have been abbreviated as follows: *n.* = noun; *adj.* = adjective; *vb.* = verb; *adv.* = adverb; *prep.* = preposition. The numbers refer to categories. The entry for 'beautiful' looks like this:

beautiful *adj.* 844

If you turn to category **844** in the main part of the book and look under the appropriate part of speech − here *adj.* − you will find a list of alternative words that you can use: beautiful, attractive, good-looking, . . . Some of the entries in the index have numbers printed in a darker, bold type. These show the main references for particular words.

The words listed have slightly different meanings from each other. If you are not familiar with a word it would therefore be advisable to look up the word in a good modern dictionary before using it. Otherwise you may risk using the word in the wrong context. Two further abbreviations are used. Informal or colloquial words are marked as (*inf.*) and slang words (*sl.*). At the end of many entries there are cross-references to other categories (e.g. see also **56, 112**). These can usefully be followed up to find further lists of related words. You should also consult the words given at the other parts of speech in an entry, as some words there may suggest others to you.

If you look at the adjacent categories, too, you will find further help or perhaps the possibility of using a word meaning something opposite, e.g., the categories **534 resolution, 535 perseverance, 536 irresolution.**

A list of the 990 categories is given after the index and you can check that the number of the category you are looking up is the one you want.

Plan of categories

Thesaurus

I Abstract Relations

A Existence

1 existence

n. existence, being, essence, self-existence, reality, actuality, presence; subsistence, givenness, historicity, factuality; actualization, creating, becoming, potentiality, possibility; ontology, existentialism, metaphysics, realism.

fact, truth, *fait accompli*, real thing, entity, vital principle.

adj. existing, being, in being, in existence, afoot, given, uncreated; ontological, metaphysical; extant, living, current, present, standing, surviving; subsisting, subsistent, obtaining, prevailing, prevalent; real, actual, true, authentic, genuine, mere, objective; essential, substantial, substantive, self-existing, self-existent, intrinsic, factual.

vb. be, exist, have being, live, breathe, abide, remain, stay, prevail, be so, be the case; subsist, obtain; consist in, inhere in, reside in; stand, find itself, lie, be situated, be found; occur, take place, happen, continue, go on, endure, last.

adv. actually, really, in fact, in reality.

2 non-existence

n. non-existence, inexistence, non-being, nonentity, nothingness, nullity, nihility, neverness; vacuum, vacuity, emptiness, void, blank; extinction, destruction, abolition, obsolescence.

adj. non-existent, void, vacuous, blank; extinct, dead, obsolete, vanished; unreal, wrong, untrue, false, specious, imaginary, fictitious, hypothetical, groundless, unfounded.

vb. come to nothing, pass away, die, vanish, disappear, dematerialize, evaporate, dissolve; bring to nothing, nullify, destroy, abolish, kill.

3 material existence

n. materiality, substantiality, actuality, essentiality, reality, objectivity, substantivity, corporeity, corporality, concreteness, solidity, tangibility.

substance, thing, body, solid, stuff, matter, entity, flesh and blood (*inf.*).

adj. material, substantial, actual, solid, corporeal, objective, substantive, concrete, physical, real, natural; visible, tangible.

see also 327

4 non-material existence

n. immateriality, insubstantiality, inessentiality, intangibility.

shadow, token, dream, vision, apparition, spirit, illusion, optical illusion, mirage, breath, mist, vapour, wisp.

adj. immaterial, insubstantial, abstract, intangible, imponderable, airy, vaporous, ethereal, spiritual, ghostly, spectral, bodiless, disembodied, visionary, shadowy, vague.

see also 328

5 being according to internal form

n. intrinsicality, inherence, inwardness, internality, essentiality, immanence.

essence, substance, basis, being, soul, fundamental, principle, quality, quintessence, essential, heart, core, character, nature, constitution, structure, make-up, bearing, framework, frame; attribute, element, aspect, quality, feature, manner, temper, temperament, mood, humour, disposition, personality, particularity, idiosyncrasy, endowment, heredity, gene.

adj. intrinsic, essential, inherent, inward, central, fundamental, immanent, implicit, internal, original, integral, innate, distinctive, specific, characteristic, particular, peculiar, unique; native, genetic, hereditary, inborn, congenital, ancestral.

vb. inhere, be intrinsic; internalize.
see also 223, 224

6 being according to external form

n. extrinsicality, externality, objectivity, outwardness, transcendence, projection, extrapolation; accessory, external.

adj. extrinsic, external, objective, transcendent, exterior, outward, extraneous, foreign, independent, additional, outside.

vb. be extrinsic, transcend, surpass; make extrinsic, objectify, project, extend, extrapolate.
see also 222, 825

7 absolute state

n. state, standing, condition, station, status, case, position, stand, rank, class, degree, estate, style, fashion, mode, aspect, facet, posture, attitude.

8 circumstance

n. circumstance, circumstances, situation, environment, surroundings, setting, background, backdrop, *milieu*, context, how the land lies, ambience, atmosphere, climate; conditions, factors, details, items, features, particulars, requirements, necessities; cause, reason, motives, grounds.

adj. circumstantial, modal, surrounding, environmental, contextual, incidental, background, contingent; detailed, itemized, particular.

adv. under the circumstances, this being the case, incidentally, under these conditions, in the event of.

B Relation

9 relation

n. relation, relatedness, association, relationship, arrangement; connection, link, dependence, involvement, implication, bearing; relativity, correspondence, analogy, correlation; relevance, suitability, appositeness.

adj. relative, related, connected, involved, arranged, linked, bearing upon, concerning, belonging, appertaining; reciprocal, mutual; analogous, comparable; relevant, suitable, apposite, appropriate, proper, applicable, pertinent.

vb. be related to, concern, refer to, touch upon, bear upon, deal with, treat, have to do with, apply, hold true for, be a factor in; relate, associate, link, refer; correspond to, be analogous to; belong, pertain.

adv., prep. concerning, regarding, as regards, on, about, with reference to, with respect to, on the subject of, in the matter of, à propos, re, in re.

10 absence of relation

n. irrelation, dissociation, unrelatedness, non-involvement, independence, arbitrariness; disproportion, difference, misfit, irreconcilability, irrelevance, unsuitability, inconsequence.

adj. unrelated, independent, unconcerned, uninvolved, unconnected, inappropriate, incongruent; isolated, arbitrary, free, unallied, unilateral; irrelevant, unsuitable, inapplicable, inapposite, inconsequential.

vb. be unrelated to, have no relation with, not concern, have no bearing upon, have nothing to do with, not be one's business.

adv. by the way, incidentally.

11 kindred relations

n. consanguinity, blood relationship, blood, ties of blood, kinship, kindred, relations, relatives, kith and kin; ancestry, parentage, antecedents, forbears, patrimony, heritage, lineage; descent, descendants; affiliation; children, offspring, issue, progeny; sibling, brother, sister, twin, cousin, uncle, aunt, nephew, niece, parent, father, mother; kinsman, clansman, fellow, compatriot; family, matriarch, patriarch, fatherhood, paternity, motherhood, maternity, brotherhood, fraternity, sisterhood, sorority; in laws; household, one's folks (*inf.*), home, family circle; race, stock, generation, strain, breed, line, side, clan, tribe, stirps.

adj. related, akin, kindred, consanguineous; parental, maternal, paternal, brotherly, fraternal, sisterly, sororal, cousinly, avuncular; collateral, allied; ethnic, racial, minority, tribal.

vb. be related to, be akin, generate, adopt, affiliate.

12 correlation

n. correlation, relation, correspondence, mutuality, reciprocity, interchange, interrelation, interdependence, interaction, interplay, exchange, alternation, equivalence.

adj. correlative, reciprocal, reciprocating, mutual, relative, corresponding, equivalent, interchangeable.

vb. correlate, interrelate, interconnect, interplay, interact, reciprocate, correspond, alternate.

adv. correlatively, mutually, reciprocally, alternately.

13 identity

n. identity, identicalness, oneness, sameness, selfsameness, equality, unity, homogeneity, uniformity, invariability, interchangeability.

adj. same, identical, one, very, constant, invariable, unchangeable, unvarying, homogeneous; like, alike, indistinguishable; equivalent, duplicate, equal, twin.

vb. be identical, coincide, coalesce, equate; not distinguish, not know from Adam.

14 absolute difference

n. contrariety, inequality, inequity, contrariness, oppositeness, adverseness; incompatibility, irreconcilability; contradiction, inconsistency, polarity, antithesis.

adj. contrary, different, contrasting, inconsistent, contradictory, mutually exclusive, opposite, reverse, diametrical, adverse, opposing.

vb. be contrary, differ, contrast, contradict, oppose, go against the grain; clash.

adv. on the other hand, on the contrary, contrariwise, conversely, in the opposite way.

15 variance

n. variance, difference, variation, unlikeness, heterogeneity, diversity; disparity, deviation, divergence, deflection, discrepancy, disagreement; differentiation, discrimination.

variant, irregularity, special case.

adj. different, unlike, unidentical, dissimilar, variable, changeable, varying, variant; heterogeneous, diverse, indiscriminate; changed, modified; contrasting, incongruous, contrary, deviating, divergent, disparate, incompatible.

vb. differ, vary, change, modify; diverge, deviate; differentiate, discriminate, distinguish.

16 uniformity

n. uniformity, homogeneity, constancy, sameness, invariability, stability, regularity; symmetry, evenness, unity, congruity; conformity; monotony, routine, ritual, standardization, stereotype.

adj. uniform, homogeneous, same, consistent, invariable, steady, stable, regular, symmetrical, even, unchanging, unvarying; monotonous, routine, standardized, stereotyped.

vb. be uniform, accord, conform; make uniform, characterize, standardize, normalize, level, smooth.

17 non-uniformity

n. non-uniformity, heterogeneity, inconstancy, variability, diversity, instability, irregularity, asymmetry, unevenness, disunity, incongruity.

adj. non-uniform, heterogeneous, inconsistent, variable, diversified, motley, unsteady, irregular, asymmetrical, uneven, changing, varying, incongruous.

18 similarity

n. similarity, likeness, resemblance, affinity, analogy, similitude; disguise, camouflage; correlation, comparison,

equivalent, correspondence; counterpart.

adj. similar, like, alike, resembling, twin, analogous, à la, equivalent, typical, representative; lifelike, realistic, faithful, true, exact, simulating, imitative; camouflaged, disguised, mock.

vb. be similar, look like, seem, pass for, take after, approximate; liken, assimilate to, imitate; answer to the description of.

19 dissimilarity

n. dissimilarity, difference, unlikeness, dissimulation, diversity, disparity; variety, variation.

adj. dissimilar, different, unlike, disparate, incongruent; atypical; unrealistic, inexact.

vb. be unlike, differ from, bear no resemblance, have nothing in common with.

20 imitation

n. imitation, imitativeness, copying, representation, portrayal, mimicry, impersonation, caricature, parody; simulation, patterning; likeness, replica, reflection, portrait, echo, copy, reprint, facsimile, counterpart; translation, paraphrase, interpretation; cribbing, plagiarism; counterfeit, forgery, fake, sham.

imitator, simulator, ape, copycat (*inf.*), parrot, conformist, sheep, mimic, impersonator; translator, paraphraser, interpreter; plagiarist; forger, counterfeiter, faker.

adj. imitative, apish, parrot-like, counterfeit, pseudo-, sham, fake, mock, phoney (*sl.*); modelled on, based on.

vb. imitate, emulate, portray, depict, represent, simulate, do likewise, take after, follow suit, take a leaf out of someone's book; parrot, take off (*inf.*), send up (*inf.*), mimic, parody, caricature; repeat, mirror; pretend, disguise; copy, quote, reproduce, paraphrase, translate; crib, plagiarize; counterfeit, fake.

21 non-imitation

n. originality, creation, creativeness, inventiveness, ingenuity, independence, newness, novelty, individuality, authenticity, genuineness; real thing.

adj. unimitative, uncopied, underived, authentic, primary, genuine, creative, inventive, original, independent, first hand, incomparable, unique, rare, exceptional.

22 copy

n. copy, reprint, facsimile, reproduction, transcript, translation, paraphrase, interpretation, crib, forgery; semblance; study, representation, portrait, echo; parody, caricature, travesty; counterpart, duplicate, replica, reflection, likeness, impression, dummy, cast, tracing, model, transfer; analogue, correlate.

23 prototype

n. prototype, archetype, type, primitive form, original; precedent, first occurrence; principle, basis, standard, pattern, frame of reference, criterion; blueprint, design, plan, example, instance, illustration; dummy, mockup; model, poser, sitter, mannequin; die, stamp, mould, shell, negative, plate, mint.

vb. be an example, set an example; act as a mould; model for, sit, pose; typify, exemplify.

24 agreement

n. agreement, understanding, harmony, unity, integration, uniformity, unanimity, consensus, unison, accord, concord, correspondence, concurrence, consonance; coincidence, congruity; reconciliation, sympathy; treaty, contract.

adj. agreeing, like-minded, unanimous, agreed, corresponding, conforming, concurrent, coinciding, concerted, harmonious, unifying, consonant, concurring, united, collective, undisputed, in step, in concert, of one accord, with one voice, sympathetic, reconcilable, compatible, consistent.

vb. agree, concur, assent, accord, tally, harmonize, match, reconcile, coincide, correspond, fit in with, dovetail, square with, synchronize, adapt, adjust, go hand in hand with, say yes to, see eye to eye, get along with, get on with, click (*inf.*), hit it off (*inf.*); keep in with (*inf.*), keep on the right side of (*inf.*).

see also **643**, **699**

25 disagreement

n. disagreement, discord, misunderstanding, division, tension, dissidence, argument, dispute, contention, quarrel, disunion, dissension, strife; discrepancy, dissonance, dissimilarity, disparity, incongruence.

adj. disagreeing, differing, disputing, contradictory, inconsistent, incongruous, out of character, disproportionate, at odds, at variance, at loggerheads, out of step; hostile, inimical, factious, dissenting, non-conformist.

vb. disagree, object, not accept, say no to, speak against, contradict, defy, reject; oppose, fight, quarrel, dispute, come into conflict with, come up against; not conform, be contrary to.

see also **642**

C Quantity

26 quantity

n. quantity, amount, number, sum, extent, scope, expanse, size, dimensions, measure; length, breadth, width, height, depth, volume, capacity, area; mass, bulk, weight; mouthful, handful, spoonful, dose, portion, lot, batch, deal, whole, heaps (*inf.*), masses (*inf.*), load (*inf.*), abundance, profusion, greatness, magnitude, largeness.

adj. quantitative, quantified, measured, some, any.

vb. quantify, measure.

see also 32

27 relative quantity

n. degree, level, grade, point, stage, measure, rate, proportion, ratio, scale, measure, standard, comparison, criterion; extent, scope, range, intensity, frequency, size, speed, shade, nuance, tint; gradation, graduation, calibration, measurement.

adj. graded, graduated, calibrated, measured, scaled, comparative, proportional, relative; gradual, tapering, shading off, fading.

vb. graduate, grade, measure, calibrate; compare, rank, classify; taper off, shade off, fade, narrow, reduce, lessen, thin out.

adv. gradually, in stages, little by little, step by step.

28 equality

n. equality, parity, uniformity, sameness, equivalence, equalization, equation, adjustment, equilibrium, balance, symmetry, steadiness, synonymity, six of one and half a dozen of the other (*inf.*), six and two threes (*inf.*).

equivalent, draw, tie, dead heat, stalemate, no decision; counterpart, opposite number, equal, complement, twin, double, peer; synonym.

adj. equal, equivalent, equilateral, regular, symmetrical, fifty-fifty, on equal terms, even, level, flush, parallel, reciprocal, uniform, comparable, commensurate, proportionate, coextensive, tantamount, synonymous.

vb. be equal, agree with, coincide, suffice, rank with, match, rival, meet, touch, live up to, measure up to, come up to, be the equivalent of, keep pace with, come to the same thing, go halves; tie, draw, balance.

equalize, make equal, adjust, square.

29 inequality

n. inequality, disparity, non-uniformity, unlikeness, disproportion, dissimilarity, deviation, divergence, dissemblance, inferiority, shortcoming, deficiency; unevenness, imbalance, lopsidedness, unsteadiness.

adj. unequal, disparate, non-uniform, uneven, odd, inferior, deficient, insufficient, inadequate; disproportionate, lopsided, top-heavy, crooked, overbalanced.

vb. be unequal, outclass, outstrip, have the advantage, fall short of, not come up to, not hold a candle to (*inf.*).

30 mean

n. average, mean, golden mean, medium, happy medium, median, balance, norm, par, middle term, middle point, midpoint, centre, halfway, middle, compromise.

adj. mean, average, median, middle, grey, intermediate, halfway, lukewarm, middling, fair to middling, medium; typical; mediocre, run of the mill.

vb. average out, take the average, split the difference, strike a balance, go halfway.

31 compensation

n. compensation, weighting, equalization, balance, counterbalance, ballast, allowance, amends, costs, damages, remuneration, reimbursement, indemnification, indemnity, reparation, restitution, recompense, repayment, refund, offset, satisfaction, atonement, requital.

adj. compensatory, indemnificatory, restitutory, balancing.

vb. compensate, make amends, balance, neutralize, equalize, counterbalance, counteract, overcompensate, pay costs, indemnify, remunerate, recompense, reimburse, redeem, refund, recoup, satisfy, make up for, make reparation, allow for, set off, offset, take back.

32 greatness

n. greatness, largeness, bigness, vastness, enormity, immenseness, magnitude, size, bulk; spaciousness; might, mightiness, power, strength, intensity; amplitude, fullness, plenitude.

great quantity, profusion, abundance, masses, lots, quantities, oodles (*inf.*), stacks (*inf.*); excess, redundance, superfluity, superabundance.

adj. big, large, great, considerable, numerous, massive, enormous, vast, colossal, huge, sizeable; tall, lofty, high, towering; strong, mighty, powerful, energetic; ample, plentiful, abundant, profuse, plenteous, copious; noble, sublime, high, stately, exalted; remarkable, notable, unspeakable; extensive, far-reaching, widespread, prevalent, sweeping, universal, worldwide; marvellous, exceptional, surpassing, wonderful, overwhelming, unbelievable, stupendous, astounding.

vb. be great, be big, be large; mount, soar, tower, exceed, rise above, transcend.

adv. enormously, vastly, highly, on a big scale, in a big way; heavily, strongly, mightily, powerfully, actively; greatly, very, much, in a great measure, extremely, exceedingly, considerably; plenteously, plentifully, abundantly, immeasurably, unspeakably, ineffably, awfully (*inf.*), tremendously; excessively, inordinately, immoderately; unbelievably, exceptionally.

see also 75

33 smallness

n. smallness, littleness, tininess, diminutiveness, minuteness; shortness, slightness, slenderness; meagreness, scantiness, paucity, scarcity, fewness, sparseness, rareness.

small quantity, dash, trace, soupçon, shade, morsel, crumb, iota, jot, tittle; point, dot, spot, fleck, speck, grain, atom, particle, modicum, chip, flake, shred, bit, rag, fragment, trifle.

adj. small, little, diminutive, minimal, infinitesimal, imperceptible, tiny, minute, miniature; slim, slender, thin, slight, scanty, meagre, insufficient, few, sparse, rare, inconsiderable, minor, trifling; modest, poor, pitiful.

adv. slightly, little, to a small extent, faintly, on a small scale, in a small way; humbly, modestly; scarcely, hardly, barely, pitifully.

see also 76

34 superiority

n. superiority, supremacy, dominance, transcendence, excellence, perfection, nobility, sublimity, eminence, pre-eminence; advantage, privilege, prerogative, favour, upper hand, head start, start.

superior, better, elder, master, overlord, chief, boss, management, senior, top dog (*inf.*).

adj. superior, eminent, upper, higher, greater, major; better, preferred, surpassing, exceeding; supreme, pre-eminent, greatest; first, chief, principal, main, capital, leading, mainline, cardinal, paramount; best, excellent, superlative, first-class, matchless, unrivalled, unsurpassed, beyond compare.

vb. be superior, rise above, tower, transcend, exceed, excel, surpass, eclipse, top, cap, overshadow, outmatch, get the better of, lord it over; prevail, predominate; have the advantage, have the edge on (*inf.*).

adv. eminently, superlatively, prominently, above all, *par excellence*, principally, especially, particularly.

35 inferiority

n. inferiority, deficiency, imperfection, shortcoming; mediocrity, poorness; lowliness, subordination, subjection, back seat (*inf.*).

inferior, subordinate, servant, slave, junior, auxiliary, accessory, workers, poor relation, underdog (*inf.*).

adj. inferior, low, lower, junior, minor, lesser, subordinate, secondary, accessory, auxiliary, ancillary, unclassified; lowly, humble, menial, subject, obedient; deficient, mediocre, substandard, imperfect, worse, worst, common, below par, not a patch on (*inf.*).

vb. be inferior, fall short of, not come up to, not compare with, not come near, want, lack, not hold a candle to (*inf.*); take a back seat (*inf.*).

see also 571

36 increase

n. increase, rise, augmentation, growth, progression, development, spread, proliferation, build-up, prolongation, extension, expansion, enlargement, escalation, magnification, heightening, swelling, incorporation, merger, cumulative effect, snowball (*inf.*).

adj. increasing, rising, growing, progressing, developing, proliferating, expanding, escalating, enlarging, intensifying, cumulative, crescent.

vb. increase, grow, rise, gain; thrive, flourish; multiply, enlarge, magnify, amplify, aggrandize; develop, escalate, boost, build, build up, expand, swell, add, compound, upsurge, strengthen, intensify, accumulate, accrue, snowball (*inf.*); prolong, lengthen, broaden, widen, thicken, deepen, heighten; enhance; exacerbate, aggravate.

37 decrease

n. decrease, decline, fall, drop, reduction, wane, restriction, restraint, curtailment, paring, pruning, squeeze; fade-out, regression, depression, depreciation, shortening.

adj. decreasing, falling, declining, reducing, dwindling, fading, on the wane.

vb. decrease, lessen, fall, drop, diminish, moderate, subside, decline, abate, recede, dwindle, wane, shrink, ebb, drain away, tail off; peter out, taper off; deteriorate; reduce, restrain, limit, check, curb, curtail, cut back, economize, consume, use up, shorten, trim, squeeze, compress, erode, dilute, quell.

38 numeration

n. numeration, numbering, enumeration, counting, count, census, figuring, reckoning, calculation, computation; mathematics, arithmetic, algebra, geometry, trigonometry, calculus, analysis; addition, subtraction, multiplication, division; statistics, figures, data, tables, measurements; abacus, ready reckoner, computer, electronic brain, microprocessor, calculator; addent, subtrahend, product, quotient.

adj. numerable, countable, calculable, computable, statistical, numbered, mathematical, arithmetical, algebraical, geometrical, analytical.

vb. number, count, tell, score, tally, cast, enumerate, poll; calculate, add, total, subtract, multiply, divide, compute, figure, work out, reckon, estimate; inventorize, list; classify; measure.

39 number

n. number, numeral, figure, digit, cipher, integer, whole number, prime number, symbol, character, sign, notation; function, variable, expression, formula; fraction, denominator, numerator, decimal, power, root.

adj. numerical, arithmetical, even, odd, prime, whole, positive, negative, rational, irrational, transcendental, exponential, integral, digital, decimal, binary; multiple, reciprocal, fractional.

40 addition

n. addition, summation, total; increase, enlargement, annexation, accession, accretion, accruing, supplement; prefixion, suffixion, affixation.

adj. additional, additive, adopted, extra, new, further, added, fresh, other, extraneous, accessory, auxiliary, supplementary.

vb. add, add up, sum, total; append, annex, attach, tack on, clap on (*inf.*), slap on (*inf.*), join, insert, contribute, supplement, increase, accumulate; accrue; affix, suffix, prefix, infix.

adv. in addition, moreover, furthermore, further, besides, as well, also, additionally, extra, and, too, over and above, in conjunction with.

41 thing added

n. adjunct, addition, attachment, fixture, extension, accretion, accession, accessory, appurtenance, increment, rise, interest, bonus, contribution, supplement; qualification, rider; annexe, wing; *addendum*, appendix, appendage, postscript, note; prefix, suffix, infix.

42 subtraction

n. subtraction, deduction, removal, withdrawal, curtailment, reduction, decrease, cutback, deletion, discount; amputation; abbreviation.

vb. subtract, deduct, take away, detract from, remove, exclude, withdraw, withhold, cut back; unload, unpack; shorten, abbreviate, delete; sever, amputate.

adv., prep. minus, without, with the exception of, bar, excepting, save.

43 thing subtracted

n. deduction, decrement, cut, decrease, reduction, rebate, discount, allowance, credit, depreciation, remission, forfeit, write-off; loss, shortcoming, defect.

44 remainder

n. remainder, rest, remnant, vestige, remains, residue, relic, hangover; result; balance, surplus, excess, margin; left-overs, waste, garbage, rejects, salvage, debris, sediment, dregs, slag, scum, leavings, clippings, crumbs, pairings, trimmings, castoffs.

adj. remaining, left, left over, over, residual, surviving; outstanding, carried over; surplus, unused, spare, to spare, superfluous; outcast.

45 mixture

n. mixture, mingling, combination, fusion, infusion, amalgamation, merger, integration; adulteration, transfusion.

blend, compound, composite, composition, conglomeration, amalgam, alloy, tincture, admixture; medley, miscellany, patchwork, pastiche, jumble, tangle, pot-pourri, mélange, mishmash, gallimaufry; hybrid, mongrel.

adj. mixed, composite, fused, merged, combined, united, amalgamated, half-and-half; stirred, blended, heterogeneous, adulterated, hybrid, mongrel; miscellaneous, assorted, motley, varied, jumbled, hotch-potch.

vb. mix, mix up, join, fuse, alloy, merge, combine, unite, amalgamate, conjoin, mingle, intermingle, stir, transfuse, shake, scramble; adulterate, water down; jumble; be mixed, permeate, infect, infiltrate; interbreed, cross with.

46 freedom from mixture

n. simpleness, purity, homogeneity, simplicity, plainness, purification, sifting, elimination.

adj. simple, pure, clean, clear, plain, uniform, absolute, homogeneous, uncomplicated, unadulterated, unqualified; mere, only, sheer.

vb. simplify, purify, unmix, unscramble, disentangle, eliminate, sift, winnow.

47 junction

n. junction, joining, connection, union, reunion, contact, tying, fastening, coupling, merging, fusion, bonding, marriage, concatenation; assemblage, structure, tie-up.

adj. joined, connected, linked, coupled, allied, married, wed, attached, fixed, secure, tied, hooked, stuck, firm, fast, close, rooted; tight, inextricable, inseparable; united, together, whole.

vb. join, attach, fix, stick on, affix, bolt, nail, screw; connect, link, make contact, span, bridge; put together, merge, fuse, combine, marry, juxtapose, cement; secure, tie, hook, couple, fasten, bind, splice, yoke, harness, knit, string, tether, clamp, clinch, twist; assemble, confederate, band together; dovetail, fit, set; unite, become one, meet, converge; unify, associate, ally with.

48 separation

n. separation, disconnection, dissociation, disjoining, detachment, segregation, disunion, disengagement, removal, withdrawal, dislocation, dismemberment, severance, division, cut, parting, divorce; dissolution, disintegration, break-up, dissection, breakdown, analysis; rupture, fracture, cleavage; burst, puncture, blowout.

adj. disjoined, discontinuous, unattached, unconnected; separable, detachable, divisible; apart, distinct, discrete, detached, divorced, isolated, alone, broken, fractured, in pieces, interrupted, torn, rent, cut, split, dismembered.

vb. separate, part, disunite, detach, disengage, break away, set apart, keep apart, disconnect, partition, demarcate, hive off, divide, subdivide, dissociate, divorce, isolate; disintegrate, decompose; fracture, rupture, break, fragment; unravel, disentangle; uncouple, unhitch, dislocate, unbind, loose, free, set free, release; tear, undo, rend; cut, dissect, hew, fell, reap, dice, chop, snip, slit, split, burst, puncture, sever, saw, chip, dissect, behead, carve; distribute, disperse; diverge; decollate.

49 bond

n. bond, link, connection, channel, passage, bridge; line, cable, string, rope, cord, chain, thread, ribbon, band, bandage, ligature, strip, girdle, belt, harness, lace, braid, tie, plait; knot, fastening, zip, hook, hook and eye, nut, bolt, screw, clasp, coupling; joint, junction, nexus, node, weld, seam, splice, swivel, hinge; adhesive, fixative, glue, paste, cement, epoxy, sticky tape.

50 coherence

n. coherence, cohesion, cohesiveness, consistency, adhesiveness; continuity, attachment, solidarity, inseparability, indivisibility.

adj. cohesive, adhesive, sticky, clinging, tenacious; inseparable, indivisible, inextricable, close, compact, solid.

vb. cohere, hold, hold fast, hold together; congregate; fit tight; adhere, stick, cleave, cling, fasten, unite, glue, gum, paste, weld, solder; hug, embrace, grasp, clasp, grip, clinch.

see also 332

51 incoherence

n. incoherence, non-coherence, nonadhesion, separability, divisibility, looseness, laxity.

adj. non-adhesive, slippery, loose, disconnected, lax, runny, inconsistent.

vb. unstick, unglue, detach, disjoin, disunite, peel off; come unstuck, fall apart, shake.

52 combination

n. combination, coalescence, fusion, mixture, synthesis, amalgamation, merger, integration, union, incorporation, embodiment, association, affiliation.

adj. combined, linked, integrated, connected, synchronized, harmonious, unified.

vb. combine, join, link, integrate, fuse, put together, merge, consolidate, unify, compound, group, incorporate, embody, coalesce, amalgamate; mix, blend, absorb; harmonize, synchronize; affiliate, cooperate, work together; kill two birds with one stone; make the best of both worlds, have one's cake and eat it.

see also 639

53 decomposition

n. decomposition, resolution, dissolution, analysis, breakdown, disintegration; decentralization; destruction; decay, putrefaction, corrosion, rottenness, putrescence, mould, rot, blight, mildew.

adj. decomposed, rotten, off, bad, rancid.

vb. decompose, resolve, break down, analyse, reduce, simplify, dissolve, dissect, atomize; decentralize, disband; disintegrate, break up; degenerate, waste away, decay, erode, corrode, rust, rot.

see also 588

54 whole

n. wholeness, completeness, entirety, totality, unity, comprehensivity, inclusiveness, panorama, catch-all; all, everyone, everybody, everything, total, whole, aggregate, sum, ensemble.

adj. whole, all, every, entire, full, complete, single, integral, total, universal, aggregate, gross, outright, inclusive, undivided, indivisible, inseparable, indissoluble; comprehensive, all-inclusive, all-embracing, sweeping, extensive, widespread, far-reaching, omnibus, wholesale, indiscriminate, blanket, catch-all, compendious, encyclopedic; intact, solid, perfect, safe, good, unbroken, undamaged, unblemished, unimpaired, flawless.

adv. wholly, entirely, completely,

altogether, a hundred per cent, all in all.

55 part

n. part, portion, share, cut, division, section, sector, segment, compartment, department, class, group, family, branch; genus, phylum; piece, fragment, bit, scrap; detail; splinter, sliver, chip, chunk, lump, wedge, slice; instalment, part payment, foretaste, downpayment, deposit; excerpt, extract; constituent, component, factor, element, member, ingredient, integral part; aspect, facet, feature.

adj. in parts, fragmentary, broken, in bits and pieces, defective; partial, incomplete, half-finished; constituent, integral, inherent, built-in, inclusive.

vb. part, divide, separate, allot, share.

adv. partly, piecemeal, in part, bit by bit.

see also 73, 717

56 completeness

n. completeness, wholeness, fullness, plenitude, saturation, one's fill, replenishment, refill; entirety, universality, comprehensivity, nothing lacking, nothing to add, integration; perfection, integrity, soundness; last touch, finish.

adj. complete, full, utter, entire, whole, plenary, all, gross, replete; comprehensive, exhaustive; absolute, extreme, thorough, thoroughgoing, radical, sweeping, wholesale, unqualified, unconditional; integral, perfect; abounding, profuse, brimful, saturated, swamped, drowned, sated, laden.

vb. be complete, come to maturity, culminate; overflow, bulge; make complete, consummate, add, perfect; conclude, fulfil; fill, replenish, top up, soak, overwhelm, saturate, swamp,

drown; cloy, glut, gorge, sate, cram, pack, stuff.

adv. completely, wholly, entirely, fully, utterly, perfectly, altogether, quite, undividedly, exclusively, absolutely, out and out; hook, line, and sinker; with a vengeance, from beginning to end.

see also 659

57 incompleteness

n. incompleteness, defectiveness, deficiency, shortcoming, deficit, shortage, shortfall, omission, defect, want, need, lack, break, decrease.

adj. incomplete, defective, imperfect, deficient, short, lacking, not enough, sparing, depleted; superficial, unfinished, half-done, under construction, in preparation, in progress; imperfect, sketchy, meagre, skimpy, scrappy, rough.

vb. be incomplete, lack, want.

adv. incompletely, partially, imperfectly, inadequately.

see also 660

58 composition

n. composition, constitution, organization, make-up; nature, character, condition, quality, personality; design, pattern; compilation.

vb. constitute, compose, form, make up, comprise, consist, comprehend, include, incorporate, belong to, be a component of; arrange, mix, organize, systematize, construct, compile, assemble, devise, design, plan, write.

59 unity

n. unity, oneness, wholeness, homogeneity, unification, integration, uniqueness, singularity, individuality, singleness, isolation, solitude, indivisibility.

unit, item, bit, piece, one, point,

entity, whole, entirety; assembly, system.

adj. one, singular, individual, peculiar, specific, special; sole, single, only, unique, unprecedented, unequalled, *sui generis,* indivisible; lone, alone, lonely, lonesome, homeless, rootless, on one's own, single-handed, unaccompanied.

60 accompaniment

n. accompaniment, togetherness, concomitance, coexistence, society, association, partnership, cooperation, fellowship.

concomitant, accessory, adjunct, attachment, appendage, belongings, appurtenance, attendant, complement; satellite; *sine qua non;* coincidence; consequence.

adj. accompanying, concomitant, coexistent, attendant, accessory, connected, related, associated, belonging, attending, coincidental, incidental, ancillary; contemporary, concurrent, synchronous, simultaneous; symptomatic; united.

vb. accompany, be found with, exist with, happen with, coexist, belong, characterize, coincide, be connected with, go hand in hand, go together, be related, follow.

adv. together, hand in hand, collectively.

61 duality

n. duality, dualism, doubleness, double-sidedness, couple, pair, couple, couplet, twosome, tandem.

adj. dual, duple, dualistic, binary, both, twin, paired, duplex, bilateral, bipartite, bipartisan, bi-.

vb. pair, couple, match, mate, dualize; combine.

62 duplication

n. duplication, doubling, reduplication, repetition, iteration, encore, copy.

adj. double, duplicate, twofold, twin, second.

vb. double, repeat, twin, duplicate, reduplicate, copy.

adv. twice, again, once more.

63 bisection

n. bisection, halving, forking, bifurcation; half, hemisphere, dichotomy; dividing line, equator.

adj. bisected, half, bifurcated, semi-, demi-, hemi-.

vb. bisect, halve, cut in two, divide, split, sunder, bifurcate; go halves; diverge, fork.

64 triality

n. triality, trinity; three, triad, threesome, trio, triplet, trilogy, triangle.

adj. three, tertiary, tripartite, trilateral, triangular, triplex, triform, tri-; triune.

65 triplication

n. triplication, triplicity, hat trick.

adj. treble, threefold, triplicate, third.

vb. treble, triple, triplicate.

66 trisection

n. trisection, tripartition, third, trichotomy.

vb. trisect, cut in three.

67 quaternity

n. quaternity; four, tetrad; square, quadrilateral, quadrangle; quartet, foursome, quadruplet, tetragon.

adj. four, quaternary, quaternal; quadratic, biquadratic, square, quadrilateral, quadri-, tetra-.

68 quadruplication

n. quadruplication, quadruplicity.

adj. fourfold, quadruplicate, fourth, quadruple.

vb. quadruple, quadruplicate.

69 quadrisection

n. quadrisection, quadripartition; fourth, quarter, quart.

vb. quadrisect, quarter, cut in four.

70 five and over

n. five, fiver, pentad, quintuplet, pentagon, quintet, quincunx, Pentateuch; six, half a dozen, hexad, sextuplet, hexagon, sextet; seven, heptad, septuplet, heptagon, septet; eight, octad, octagon, octet, octave; nine, ennead, nonagon, enneagon, nonet; ten, decade, decagon; double figures; eleven, endecagon; twelve, dozen, dodecagon; thirteen, baker's dozen; teens; twenty, score; hundred, century, centenary; three figures, treble figures; gross; thousand, grand, millenium; ten thousand, myriad; million; billion; trillion.

adj. five, quintuple; six, sextuple; seven, septuple; eight, octuple; ten, decimal; twelve, duodecimal; -fold.

71 multisection

n. multisection, quinquesection.

vb. multisect, quinquesect.

72 plurality

n. plurality, plural, number, multiplicity, variety, abundance, some; majority.

adj. plural, pluralistic, pluralistical, multiple, many, some, numerous; more.

73 fraction

n. fraction, fragment, part, section, portion, segment.

adj. fractional, partial, fragmentary, constituent, sectional.

see also 55, 717

74 zero

n. zero, nil, nought; nothingness, nullity, void; nothing, none, no one, nobody; no score, duck, love.

adj. zero, null, not one.

75 multitude

n. multitude, numerosity, multiplicity; great amount, quantity, lot; great number, hundreds, thousands, myriads, millions; crowd, mob, army, throng, flock, legion, host, posse; plenty, a great deal, abundance, profusion, bonanza (*inf.*); majority, main part, mass, bulk, main emphasis, weight.

adj. many, not a few, several, considerable, numerous, manifold, countless, legion; much, sufficient, enough, ample, galore (*inf.*); profuse, abundant, overflowing, prevalent, plentiful; crowded, populous, peopled; dense, teeming with, alive with, thick.

vb. be many, crowd with, throng with, flock, mass, swarm with, teem with, crawl with; overflow with; pack, stuff; outnumber.

76 fewness

n. fewness, paucity, scarcity, sparseness, thinness, rarity; a few, handful, smattering, sprinkling; remnant, minority, insufficiency, absence, lack.

adj. few, not many, sparse, scant, thin, inconsiderable, negligible, infrequent, few and far between.

vb. diminish, reduce, lessen; lack, need.

77 repetition

n. repetition, recurrence, repetitiveness, reappearance; reproduction, copy, duplication; renewal, resumption; reiteration, rehearsal, recapitulation.

repeat, encore, replay; reprint, reissue, rehash.

adj. repeated, reiterated, restated, reworded, retold; reproduced, remade, redone, copied; repetitious, repetitive, boring.

vb. repeat, reiterate, restate, reword, retell, iterate; recite, say after, echo; rehearse, go over, take it from the top (*inf.*); recapitulate; redo, remake, renew, rework, remodel; rehash, revive; reissue, republish, copy; reoccur, reappear.

adv. again, over again, anew; ditto, encore; repeatedly.

78 infinity

n. infinity, endlessness, limitlessness; eternity; infinitude, perpetuity.

adj. infinite, immense, vast, untold, boundless, endless, immeasurable, unexhaustible, interminable; countless, numberless, unnumbered; eternal, perpetual.

vb. go on and on, know no bounds.

adv. infinitely, *ad infinitum*, without end.

D Order

79 order

n. order, organization, arrangement, array, state of order; tidiness, orderliness, neatness; method, pattern, regularity, system; uniformity, routine, habit; discipline.

adj. orderly, organized, methodical, systematic, regular, harmonious; under control, businesslike; neat, tidy, shipshape, well-ordered.

vb. order, organize, harmonize; take shape, fall into place.

adv. in order, all right, all correct, O.K., orderly, systematically, methodically.

80 disorder

n. disorder, disarrangement, muddle, clutter, mess, disarray, disharmony, disorderliness, untidiness; chaos, crisis; confusion, disturbance, shambles, Bedlam, mix-up.

turmoil, tumult, turbulence, agitation, to-do, ferment, storm, upheaval, *mêlée*, *fracas*, uproar, hullaballoo, frenzy, row, riot; anarchy, unruliness.

adj. orderless, out of order, unorganized, disorganized, in disarray, out of order, untidy; unsystematic, unmethodical, irregular, non-uniform; incoherent, muddled, confused, mixed up (*inf.*), disconnected; chaotic; tumultuous, turbulent; anarchical, lawless.

adv. confusedly, anyhow, irregularly, in disorder, higgledy-piggledy, upside down.

81 arrangement

n. arrangement, ordering, reduction to order, composition, preparation, organization, reorganization, regulation, marshalling, disposal, distribution; plan, method, system.

adj. arranged, well-arranged, ordered, organized, well-organized, methodical, regular, systematic, well-regulated, classified, sorted; coordinated, connected, disposed; disciplined; disentangled, unravelled, straightened out.

vb. arrange, plan, prepare, compose, put in order, set in order, reduce to order, array, dispose; assign, set, establish, formulate, coordinate, line up, regulate, marshal, range; organize, systematize, standardize, formalize, coordinate, connect; collocate; classify, pattern; disentangle, unravel, untwist, uncoil, straighten out; put one's own house in order.

82 disarrangement

n. disarrangement, derangement, disorganization, dishevelment, discomposure; irregularity, tangle, entanglement.

adj. disarranged, discomposed, disorganized, disorderly.

vb. disturb, disorganize, disorder, jumble, shuffle, mix up, muddle, derange, upset, unsettle; agitate, disconcert, discompose; ruffle, dishevel; confuse, perturb, confound, trouble; disperse, scatter; destroy, disrupt, dislocate; disband; overturn, overthrow; stir up, put the cat among the pigeons (*inf.*).

83 list

n. list, enumeration, classification, record, register, catalogue, directory, file; statement, schedule, agenda, table; roll, roll-call; roster, rota; enrolment; inventory, stock list, checklist; programme, prospectus, syllabus, synopsis; index, table of contents, bibliography, thesaurus, dictionary, glossary, lexicon.

vb. list, enumerate, catalogue, itemize, classify; enter, register, book, inscribe, record, file, log; enrol, enlist, matriculate; schedule.

84 precedence

n. precedence, antecedence, priority, precedency, previousness; coming before, anteriority; pre-eminence, precedent, preference, superiority.

adj. preceding, precedent, antecedent, anterior; previous, earlier, former, foregoing, prior, aforementioned.

vb. come before, go before, go ahead, precede, have precedence, take pre-

cedence; lead, be in front, head, place before; herald, pioneer, forerun, blaze the trail (*inf.*), clear the way, show the way, set the fashion; preface, introduce, prelude, preamble, usher in.

adv. before, in advance, above.

85 sequence

n. sequence, going after, following, placement, succession; successiveness, consequence; order, series, progression, set, string, row, chain, train, flow, concatenation.

adj. following, succeeding, ensuing, resulting, subsequent, successive, consequent; next, later, posterior; sequential, consecutive, serial; connected.

vb. come after, go after, go behind; ensue, follow, result; place after, append; succeed, come next, supersede, displace, supplant, become heir to.

adv. after, afterwards, behind, subsequently.

86 precursor

n. precursor, predecessor; pioneer, herald, vanguard, scout, pathfinder, forerunner, harbinger; parent, ancestor, forbear.

precedent, antecedent; prelude, preliminary, introduction, prologue, foreword, preface, exordium, prolegomena, preamble; prefix; authoritative example; preparation.

adj. precursory, preliminary, prefatory, introductory; exploratory, preparatory.

87 sequel

n. sequel, consequence, effect, result, end, issue, outcome, upshot, aftermath; after-effect, by-product, spin-off; inference, deduction, conclusion; afterthought, second thoughts; follow-up; continuation, tail, tailpiece, supplement, postscript, epilogue, appendage; suffix.

88 beginning

n. beginning, start, commencement, outset, onset, outbreak; foundation, establishment, origination, invention, birth, origin, genesis, cause, source, root, spring; infancy, primitiveness, youth; starting-point, square one.

inauguration, initiation, début, coming out, unveiling, *première*, opening, inception.

preliminaries, introduction, prelude, foreword, preface; rudiments, first principles, ABC, primer, basics.

adj. beginning, first, starting, initial, maiden; introductory, precursory, opening, inaugural; foundational, elementary, fundamental, basic, rudimentary; original, embryonic, primitive.

vb. begin, start, commence, go ahead, make a beginning, make a start, kick off (*inf.*); come into existence, arise, break out, burst forth, rise, be born, see the light of day; make one's début, come out; undertake, do, set about, tackle, enter upon, set in motion, start up, get under way, start the ball rolling, activate; take the first step, break the ice; begin again, go back to square one (*inf.*).

initiate, conceive, introduce, found, establish, institute, inaugurate, open, originate, invent.

adv. initially, in the first place, first, *ab initio*, at the outset, to begin with, for a kick-off (*inf.*).

see also 605

89 end

n. end, conclusion, close, termination, ending, finish, stop, cessation, completion, closure, adjournment, dissolution; expiration, death, decease, demise; retirement; finale, swan song, last word, death blow, curtains (*inf.*), *finis*, end of the line (*inf.*).

extreme, extremity, terminus, terminal, furthest point, achievement; consummation, perfection, culmination, climax, *dénouement;* goal, limit, point, boundary, top, peak, summit, head, bottom, base, tail; postscript, epilogue, appendage.

adj. ending, final, last, ultimate, terminal, concluding, consummate, ended, settled, concluded; extreme.

vb. end, finish, stop, conclude, terminate, cease, discontinue, desist, refrain, come to an end; expire, breathe one's last, die; run out, run its course, come to a close, draw to a close, break off; settle, determine, bring to an end, put an end to, dispose of, suspend, postpone, cancel, bring to a standstill, arrest, quell; switch off, wind up; end up.

adv. finally, lastly, at last, in conclusion, ultimately.

see also 144

90 middle

n. middle, midpoint, centre, middle distance, equidistance, halfway house; pivot, heart, kernel, core; focus, focal point; average, mean, median; midst, thick of things.

adj. middle, centre, central, mid, equidistant, halfway, medial, intermediate; focal; mean, average; moderate, neutral, compromising.

adv. in the middle, midway, halfway, in between.

91 continuity

n. continuity, continuousness, consecutiveness, progression, continuance, one thing after another, constancy, flow, succession, endlessness, perpetuation, perpetuity; routine, daily round, monotony; sequence, queue, crocodile, procession, march, cortège, column, train, suite, retinue, single file, tail, tailback.

adj. continuous, consecutive, running, serial, successive, progressive, constant, endless, perpetual, sustained, persisting, unbroken, uninterrupted; regular.

vb. continue, carry on, maintain, sustain, remain, succeed, follow in a line; file, march, parade, queue; endure.

adv. continuously, in succession, successively, in file, in train.

92 discontinuity

n. discontinuity, disconnectedness, disjunction; interruption, intervention, break, interval, intermission, pause, breather, rest, stop-over; gap, missing link.

adj. discontinuous, disconnected, unconnected, interrupted, broken; intermittent, irregular, infrequent, few and far between; spasmodic, jerky, uneven, desultory.

vb. discontinue, break, interrupt, pause, stop over; disconnect.

adv. at intervals, irregularly, in fits and starts, discontinuously.

see also 200

93 position in a series

n. term, serial position, order, rank, grade, station, position, situation, status, standing, footing, level, tier, rung, degree.

94 assemblage

n. assemblage, bringing together, juxtaposition, mobilization.

gathering, assembly, association, collection, company, society; circle, clique; meeting, reception, party; council, committee, conference, congress, commission, convention, congregation, convocation, symposium.

group, body, mass, crowd, throng, mob, crush, huddle, band, gang, troop, horde; team, cast, crew, squad; swarm, colony, herd, flock, pack, brood, shoal, school; set, cluster, bunch, lot, batch, bundle.

adj. gathered, assembled, met, convened; crowded, dense, swarming.

vb. gather, assemble, meet, come together, associate, congregate, converge, rendezvous; group, crowd, throng, rally, flock in, pour in; swarm, huddle, bunch; accumulate, pile up, amass; collect, bring together, call up, summon, convene, muster, round up.

95 dispersion

n. dispersion, dispersal, scattering, dissemination, broadcasting, dissipation, diffusion, divergence, decentralization.

adj. dispersed, scattered.

vb. disperse, scatter; disseminate, broadcast, sow, seed; sprinkle, strew, spread, dissipate; separate, divide; shed, distribute, propagate, dispense, dole out, dispel, diffuse, decentralize, disband; evaporate; sprawl, diverge.

96 focus

n. focus, focal point, centre; meeting place, forum, market, club, rendezvous; heart, hub, centre of interest, headquarters, nerve centre; Mecca, promised land.

vb. focus, converge, concentrate, centre, attract, draw attention.

see also 224

97 class

n. class, sort, kind, type, category, section, division, group, grouping, department, branch; mark, brand, make; strain, breed, line, family, genus, species, phylum, caste; hierarchy, rank.

classification, categorization, specification, taxonomy, systematization, list.

adj. classificatory, taxonomic.

vb. class, sort, classify, categorize, hierarchize, rank, grade, group, divide.

98 inclusion

n. inclusion, admission, reception, incorporation, embodiment, composition.

adj. inclusive, comprehensive, all-inclusive, all-embracing, overall, wholesale, sweeping.

vb. include, admit, incorporate, embody, comprehend, comprise, consist of, constitute, contain, involve, take in, entail, embrace, enclose, subsume.

99 exclusion

n. exclusion, exclusiveness; omission, rejection, ejection; prohibition, boycott, embargo, blockade; eviction, dismissal, suspension, expulsion, excommunication, ostracism, segregation, apartheid; bar, ban, closed shop, lock-out.

adj. exclusive, restrictive, segregated, prohibitive.

vb. exclude, omit, leave out, remove, eliminate, except, disregard; disqualify, reject, dismiss, suspend, deport, banish, expel, excommunicate, send to Coventry, ostracize; feel left out, feel out of things; restrict, forbid, prohibit, bar, segregate, ban, black, blacklist, boycott; prevent, preclude, obviate.

prep. except, excluding, apart from, save, bar.

100 extraneousness

n. extraneousness, foreignness; outsider, foreigner, alien, stranger, immigrant, expatriot, migrant, emigrant, refugee; newcomer, guest, visitor; squatter, interloper, invader.

adj. extraneous, extrinsic, external, outward, outside; foreign, alien, strange, immigrant; exotic, imported, borrowed, adopted, introduced, naturalized; alienated, estranged.

101 generality

n. generality, universality; ubiquity; broadness; generalization, abstraction, observation, simplification, overview; average man, man in the street, everybody, every mother's son (*inf.*), all the world and his wife (*inf.*).

adj. general, overall, universal, global, catholic; worldwide, international, cosmopolitan; typical, representative, generic; broad, wide; comprehensive, widespread, ubiquitous, blanket, average.

vb. be general, prevail, predominate; generalize, expand, broaden; conclude, infer.

102 speciality

n. speciality, particularity, originality, individuality, peculiarity, distinctiveness, uniqueness, idiosyncrasy, characteristic.

particulars, specifications, details, minutiae.

adj. special, particular, peculiar, especial, distinct, unique, original, *sui generis*, individual, individualistic, characteristic, idiosyncratic; specific, precise.

vb. specify, define, particularize, itemize, designate, enumerate, go into detail; single out, isolate, put one's finger on (*inf.*).

103 rule

n. rule, regulation, law, direction,

instruction, ordinance, code, order, precept, norm, principle, maxim, proposition, formula, guide, criterion, model, standard, procedure, system, convention.

adj. regulated, normative, prescriptive; legislative; formulaic, conventional.

see also 626, 954

104 diversity

n. diversity, variation, variousness, heterogeneity, multiformity, variability, difference; medley, mixture, variety, miscellany.

adj. diverse, diversified, various, manifold, heterogeneous, multifarious, motley, irregular; different, disparate, variable, changeable.

see also 45

105 conformity

n. conformity, correspondence, congruity, consistency, coincidence, compatibility, agreement, affinity, resemblance, similarity, adjustment, acclimatization.

conformist, conventionalist, traditionalist, loyalist, conservative.

adj. conforming, agreeing, harmonious, corresponding, appropriate, applicable, consonant; similar, resembling, well-matched, conformable, adaptable, adjustable, compatible, consistent.

vb. conform, comply, agree, accord; accommodate, adapt, adjust, fit, suit, integrate, bend, square, accustom, acclimatize, harmonize, reconcile; follow, obey, observe, fall into line, toe the line, adhere to.

106 unconformity

n. unconformity, difference, contrast, dissimilarity, disagreement, incon-sistency, incongruity, incompatibility; nonconformity, unorthodoxy, heresy, schism; eccentricity, peculiarity, unconventionality, abnormality, irregularity.

nonconformist, dissenter, rebel, angry young man, separatist, demonstrator, maverick; eccentric, crank; homosexual, queer (*sl.*), gay (*sl.*), lesbian.

adj. unconformable, different, dissimilar, inconsistent, incongruous, incompatible, inappropriate, inapplicable; nonconformist, unorthodox; heretical, dissident, unconventional, eccentric, peculiar, abnormal, irregular, unusual, unfamiliar.

E Time

107 time

n. time, duration, continuance, extent, life, span, season, date.

adj. temporal; dated.

vb. elapse, pass; continue, last; spend time, employ, fill, occupy oneself, use, what do with oneself, while away, idle, fritter, squander; happen, occur, transpire.

adv., prep. during, when, while, whilst, in the course of, throughout, in the process of; meanwhile, in the meantime, in the interim.

see also 109

108 absence of time

n. timelessness, neverness, nothingness, eternity.

adv. never, at no time, never again, nevermore.

109 period

n. period, era, epoch, time, season, interval, phase, age, generation; term, span, spell, stint, stretch; cycle, second, minute, hour, day, week, fortnight, month, year, leap year, decade, decennium, jubilee, centenary, millenium, aeon.

adj. periodic, seasonal, recurring, recurrent, cyclic, regular.

110 course of time

n. course of time, lapse of time.

vb. elapse, pass, lapse; flow, proceed, run, fly.

see also 109

111 contingent duration

adv., prep. as long as, provisionally, for the present, for the time being.

112 long duration

n. lifetime, ages, eternity, month of Sundays (*inf.*), prolongation, permanence; endurance.

adj. long-term, long-standing, long-lasting, abiding, lasting, durable, permanent; enduring, steadfast, unyielding, persistent, surviving.

vb. last, endure, continue, stay, persist, remain, abide, never end, prevail, persevere; survive, outlive, outlast, outstay, live on, linger.

113 short duration

n. transience, ephemerality, evanescence, impermanence; brief period, flash in the pan (*inf.*), nine days' wonder (*inf.*).

adj. transient, transitory, brief, temporary, quick, short, short-term, momentary, short-lived; fading, passing, fleeting, cursory, ephemeral, evanescent, impermanent, perishable, before one can say Jack Robinson (*inf.*).

vb. be transient, pass, pass away, fly, fleet, flit, fade, vanish, disappear.

114 endless duration

n. perpetuity, endlessness, eternity, infinity, everlastingness, timelessness, immortality, constancy, endurance.

adj. perpetual, eternal, endless, interminable, continual, unceasing, incessant, unremitting, infinite, everlasting, enduring, around-the-clock, timeless, ageless, immortal, incorruptible, imperishable; perennial.

vb. perpetuate, immortalize, eternalize, preserve, keep alive; never end, go on forever.

adv. always, forever, on and on, perpetually.

115 point of time

n. instantaneousness, suddenness, abruptness; instant, second, moment, flash, jiffy (*inf.*), twinkling, point of time.

adj. instantaneous, immediate, spontaneous, sudden, abrupt, prompt, punctual.

adv. instantaneously, instantly, immediately, at once, directly, forthwith, without delay, promptly, suddenly, abruptly, at the drop of a hat, on the spur of the moment.

116 chronometry

n. chronometry, horology, chronology, timing, timekeeping, dendrochronology; date, day, time; local time, summer time, daylight saving.

timepiece, timekeeper, chronometer, clock, alarm clock, digital clock, watch, wristwatch, digital watch, stopwatch, hour-glass, sun-dial, egg-timer; time-signal, pips, siren, hooter; calendar, schedule, timetable, diary, journal, register, almanac, chronicle, annals, log, memoirs.

adj. chronological, horological, temporal, horometrical, chronometrical.

vb. time, date; put the clocks back, put the clocks forward, set the alarm, wind up, keep time, gain, lose; clock in, clock out.

117 anachronism

n. anachronism, wrong date, misdating, mistiming, parachronism, prochronism.

adj. anachronistic, misdated, undated; early, beforehand; late, overdue.

vb. misdate, antedate, predate, postdate.

118 priority

n. priority, antecedence, anteriority, previousness; pre-existence, pre-occurrence; precedent, antecedent, foretaste, preview.

adj. prior, earlier, before, preceding, previous, anterior, past, antecedent, ahead of; pre-existing; one-time, ex-, retired, former; foregoing, above-mentioned, above, aforesaid.

vb. go before, come before, precede, forerun, antecede, herald.

see also **84, 124**

119 posteriority

n. posteriority, succession, subsequence; sequel, follower, successor.

adj. following, subsequent, later, after, coming after, next, posterior; designate, elect, to-be; consequential, resulting.

vb. come after, go after, succeed, ensue, follow, result.

see also **85, 123**

120 present time

n. contemporaneity; present time, present moment, present, the time being, this day and age, modern times, today.

adj. present, contemporary, modern, current, present-day, latest, newest, actual, contemporaneous, existent.

adv. now, at present, at the moment, today, nowadays, right now, at this moment in time.

121 different time

n. different time, not now, other time.

adv. not now, yesterday, earlier, tomorrow, later, sometime, sooner or later, at one time or other, at a different time.

122 synchronism

n. synchronism, simultaneousness, coexistence, concurrence, coincidence, contemporaneity; same age; contemporary, own generation, peers, fellows, year, class, set.

adj. synchronous, contemporary, concurrent, coincident, coexistent, simultaneous, contemporaneous; accompanying.

vb. synchronize, coexist, exist together, coincide; accompany.

adv. at the same time, simultaneously, concurrently, in phrase, in step.

123 future

n. futurity, future, tomorrow, time to come; prospect, fate; the shape of things to come; afterlife, world to come, next world, hereafter.

adj. later, future, coming, to come, approaching, unfolding, at hand; prospective, designate; imminent, impending; likely, expected, inevitable.

vb. lie in the future, be near, draw near, approach; impend, threaten.

adv. tomorrow, in the future, in the course of time, hereafter.

124 past

n. past, history, antiquity, prehistory, archaism; retrospection, memory; olden times, yesterday good old days (*inf.*).

adj. past, historical, ancient, prehis

toric, primitive, proto-; gone, bygone, lost, forgotten, no more; former, late, old, once, one-time, ex-, retired, sometime, erstwhile.

vb. be past, have run its course, have had its day (*inf.*), be a thing of the past.

adv. yesterday, formerly, in the past, ago, of old.

125 newness

n. newness, modernity, renovation, modernization, novelty, innovation.

fad, craze, passing fancy, vogue, fashion, the latest thing (*inf.*), all the rage (*inf.*), the last word (*inf.*), the in-thing (*inf.*); innovator, pioneer, leader, futurist, trendsetter, pacesetter, *avant-garde*, upstart, fledgling.

adj. modern, new, novel, current, topical, recent, original; contemporary, present-day, up-to-the-minute, up-to-date, brand-new, just out, hot off the press (*inf.*); newfangled (*inf.*); untraditional, in fashion, in vogue, stylish, chic, smart, modish, trendy (*inf.*), in (*inf.*), *à la mode*, *avant-garde;* advanced, forward-looking, progressive, ultra-modern, streamlined, futuristic, space-age; convenient, automatic, electronic; fresh, virgin, budding, inexperienced.

vb. modernize, bring up to date, adapt, renew, reissue, republish, refurbish, renovate, streamline, update; innovate.

adv. recently, newly, lately, afresh, anew, of late.

126 oldness

n. oldness, antiquity; obsolescence, extinction, decay, deterioration, decline; maturity, ripeness; tradition, footsteps; old age, senility, infirmity.

adj. old, archaic, prehistoric, antique, ancient, primitive, primeval,

aboriginal, extinct; time-worn, time-honoured, venerable, forgotten, antediluvian, distant, former, unrecorded, of earliest time; old-fashioned, antiquated, obsolete, obsolescent, outmoded, discarded, disused, unstylish, *passé*, out of date, old hat (*inf.*), out of fashion, behind the times, anachronistic, dated, outdated; traditional, handed down, established, customary, Victorian; dilapidated, secondhand, used, decrepit, decayed, faded; patched, mended, in holes, rusty, moth-eaten.

see also **30**

127 morning; spring; summer

n. morning, morn, a.m., sunrise, dawn, daybreak, break of day, cock-crow, the small hours, forenoon, matin, matins, aurora; noon, midday, meridian; spring, springtime, spring-tide, flowering, budding; summer, summertime, summertide, midsummer, Indian summer, St. Luke's summer, St. Martin's summer.

adj. morning; spring, springlike, vernal; summer, summery, aestival.

128 evening; autumn; winter

n. p.m., afternoon, evening, eventide, eve, evensong, vesper, vespers; sunset, sundown, twilight, dusk, dimness, half-light, gloaming, curfew, night, nightfall, nighttime; midnight, witching time of night, dead of night; autumn, fall, harvest; winter, wintertime, wintertide, midwinter.

adj. afternoon, vespertine, evening; crepuscular; night, nocturnal; autumn, autumnal; wintry, winter, brumous.

129 youth

n. youth, youthfulness, young blood, juniority, juvenility; infancy, tender age, childhood, adolescence, puberty, pubescence, boyhood, girlhood, school-going age, teens, boyishness, girlishness, next generation; freshness, salad days, awkward age, growing pains, younger generation, immaturity, inexperience, callowness, greenness, prime, spring, springtime; minority, wardship, nonage, pupilage.

adj. young, youthful, boyish, girlish, childlike, teenage, adolescent, pubescent, in one's teens; formative, budding, flowering, unwrinkled, ageless, tender, developing; childish, unripe, green, callow, awkward, raw, unfledged, immature, inexperienced, puerile, juvenile; minor, under-age, infant, younger, minor, junior, youngest.

see also 131

130 age

n. age, oldness, old age, senility, second childhood, senescence, seniority, dotage, infirmity; middle age, middle years, older generation; responsibility, experience, wisdom, maturity, caution.

adj. old, aged, elderly, advanced in years, senile, senescent, matured, seasoned, grey, balding, wrinkled, toothless; superannuated; inactive, infirm, debilitated, feeble, enfeebled, doddery, decrepit, moribund, dying, with one foot in the grave; experienced, qualified, expert, respected, venerable; major, senior, older, elder, oldest, eldest, first-born.

vb. age, grow old, decline, progress, advance in years, have seen better days, show one's age; superannuate; mellow, develop, mature.

see also 132

131 infant

n. baby, babe, infant, suckling, mite, toddler, tot, bairn; child, youngster,

kid, brat (*sl.*); young person, juvenile, pupil, schoolchild, minor, teenager, adolescent, student; boy, schoolboy, lad, junior, master; young man, youth, stripling, fellow; girl, schoolgirl, young lady, lass, miss.

adj. baby, newborn, childlike; infantile, babyish, childish, puerile, juvenile; boyish, girlish; adolescent, youthful, teenage, pubescent; immature, naive, innocent, spontaneous.

132 veteran

n. old person, elder, senior, retired person, old age pensioner, senior citizen, dependant; veteran, patriarch, old hand (*inf.*), old timer (*inf.*), grand old man, elder statesman; old woman, matriarch.

133 adulthood

n. adulthood, years of discretion, manhood, womanhood, maturity, age of majority, majority.

adult, grown-up, man, woman.

adj. adult, grown-up, manly, womanly, mature, responsible; marriageable.

vb. come of age, grow up, attain majority; mature.

see also 380, 381

134 earliness

n. earliness, primitiveness, anticipation, presentiment, recency, immediacy, punctuality, promptness, promptitude, prematurity; foresight, hunch; early riser, early bird (*inf.*).

adj. early, prior, previous, recent, primitive; new, fresh, budding; premature, in advance, precocious, preceding, anticipatory, preparatory, advanced, prevenient; immediate, precipitant, speedy; imminent; punctual, prompt, timely, on time, sharp.

vb. be early, anticipate, foresee,

forestall, prepare for; precede, take precedence, get a head start, pre-empt, jump the queue.

135 lateness

n. lateness, belatedness, tardiness, retardation, slowness, dilatoriness, backwardness; late hour, high time, last minute; delay, deferment, postponement, adjournment, discontinuation, suspension, procrastination, cooling-off period, moratorium, respite, days of grace, stay, reprieve, remission, wait and see, filibuster; slow starter, late riser.

adj. late, advanced, tardy, dilatory; too late, overdue, belated, delayed, behind, behindhand; last-minute; unready, unpunctual.

vb. be late, stay up, burn the midnight oil; tarry, be slow, linger, saunter, dawdle, dally, shilly-shally, delay, defer, postpone, procrastinate, retard, stay, adjourn, put off, suspend, withhold, hold back, wait and see, play for time, filibuster; put in cold storage, mothball (*inf.*), put in mothballs (*inf.*), put on ice (*inf.*), shelve.

136 timeliness

n. timeliness, opportuneness, opportunism, expediency, fortuity.

opportunity, chance, occasion, right time; crisis, emergency, turning point, dilemma, eleventh hour, nick of time, moment of truth, hour of decision.

adj. opportune, fortuitous, timely, well-timed, punctual, on time, propitious, auspicious, providential, suitable, expedient, advantageous, convenient; critical, crucial, decisive, momentous, significant, key, urgent.

vb. grasp the opportunity, use to the full, take advantage of, cash in on, exploit, capitalize, make capital out of,

opportunize, play on, profit by; hang in the balance.

see also 577, 915

137 untimeliness

n. untimeliness, inopportuneness, inexpediency, mistiming; disturbance, interruption, intrusion.

adj. mistimed, ill-timed, untimely, unpunctual, too early, premature, too late; wrong, ill-chosen, improper, untoward, unseemly, intrusive, interrupting, disturbing, inconvenient, disadvantageous, unsuitable, inappropriate, unseasonable, unfavourable, inopportune, inauspicious.

vb. mistime; interrupt, disturb, intrude, break in on (*inf.*); miss an opportunity, let an opportunity slip, miss the boat, fail to exploit.

see also 578, 916

138 frequency

n. frequency, recurrence, reoccurrence, regularity, constancy, oftenness.

adj. frequent, regular, recurrent, successive, reiterated, rhythmic; common, commonplace, customary, not rare, familiar, habitual, general, expected, usual, periodic; incessant, non-stop, perennial, constant, monotonous, continual, steady.

vb. recur, repeat; go on, continue, occur regularly.

adv. often, frequently, usually, generally, as a rule, commonly, regularly, repeatedly; sometimes, now and again, occasionally, at times, from time to time.

see also 140

139 infrequency

n. infrequency, rarity, uncommonness, scarcity, intermittence, unpredictability, irregularity.

adj. infrequent, occasional, rare, sparse, scarce, few, few and far between, scanty, sporadic, meagre, precious; unique, single, individual; uncommon, unusual, bizarre; intermittent; casual, chance, incidental.

adv. infrequently, scarcely, hardly, hardly ever, occasionally, uncommonly, now and then, rarely, seldom.

see also 141

140 regularity

n. regularity, recurrence, periodicity, repetition, frequency; stabilization, evenness, steadiness, constancy; timing, phasing, alternation, oscillation; current, wave, rota, cycle, rotation, swing, circuit, pulsation, beat, rhythm, pulse; routine, daily round; anniversary, birthday, commemoration.

adj. periodical, regular, routine, periodic, systematic, methodical, organized, steady, constant, uniform, serial, cyclic, rotational, pulsating, rhythmic, alternating.

vb. recur, repeat, reiterate, come round again, alternate, undulate, regulate, revolve, throb, beat, pulsate, swing.

adv. periodically, systematically, regularly, at regular intervals, like clockwork; hourly, daily, weekly, monthly, annually.

see also 138

141 irregularity

n. irregularity, fitfulness, jerkiness, unsteadiness, inconstancy, unevenness, variability; jerk, fits and starts, spasm, stop, break, bump.

adj. irregular, sporadic, off and on, fitful, jerky, spasmodic, irregular, uneven; unsteady, shaky; inconstant, random, fluctuating, faltering, waver-

ing, flickering; capricious, changeable, casual.

vb. fluctuate, come and go.

see also 139

F Change

142 change

n. change, variation, alteration, modification, adjustment, qualification, transformation, refinement, evolution, alternation; fluctuation, wavering, modulation; exchange, transference, substitution, mutation, permutation, conversion; transition, diversion, deviation; renewal, innovation, novelty, reconstruction, improvisation, reformation, revision, rearrangement, reorganization, readjustment, metamorphosis, vicissitude, transmutation; deterioration, withdrawal, removal.

modifier, changer, converter, transformer, catalyst, agitator, leaven, adapter.

adj. variable, varying, changeable, modifiable, qualifiable, alternating, inconstant, mutable, plastic, transformable, movable, mobile.

vb. change, alter, vary, modify, qualify, transform, adapt, adjust, improvise; exchange, transfer, substitute; turn, shift, veer; convert, commute; renew, revise, rearrange, reorganize, reform, translate, reconstruct, renovate; refine, moderate, temper; evolve; alternate, fluctuate, waver, modulate.

143 permanence

n. permanence, constancy, invariability, continuity, steadiness, stability; immobility, solidity, consistency; durability, endurance; conservatism, *status quo*, traditionalist, conservative, reactionary, die-hard, stick-in-the-mud.

adj. permanent, immovable, unchangeable, changeless, certain, fixed, uninterrupted, unchanging, continual, constant, lasting; enduring, unwavering, abiding; stable, unremitting; strong, robust, firm, steady, steadfast; conservative, traditional, unprogressive, reactionary, conventional; obstinate, stubborn.

vb. stay, remain, abide, persist; stabilize, maintain, preserve, uphold, sustain, support.

144 cessation

n. cessation, discontinuation, discontinuance, expiration, termination, conclusion.

stop, halt, standstill, closure, interruption, suspense, lapse; industrial action, stoppage, shut-down, strike, go-slow, work-to-rule, sit-in, walkout, unofficial strike, wildcat strike, general strike, lock-out; deadlock, confrontation; ceasefire, armistice, truce; rest, pause, holiday, vacation, respite, lull, breathing space, remission, recess; intermission, interlude, interval, interim, interregnum.

vb. cease, terminate, stop, discontinue, desist, refrain, finish, knock off (*inf.*), break up, quit, shut down, close down, shut up shop, call it a day (*inf.*), pack it in (*inf.*), knock it off (*sl.*); halt, check, restrain, put a stop to, arrest, stall, interrupt; strike, down tools, come out, go out, walk out, lock out, picket, boycott; pause, break, take five (*inf.*), rest, relax, let up (*inf.*); fizzle out (*inf.*)

see also 89

145 continuance

n. continuance, continuation, perpetuation, maintenance, persistence, duration, prolongation.

adj. continual, uninterrupted, unbroken, connected, steady, constant, unceasing, incessant, ceaseless, sustained, inexhaustible.

vb. continue, carry on, keep on, go on, maintain, sustain, uphold, keep at it; stay, remain, last, survive, abide; endure, progress, persist, persevere, stay the course.

see also 535

146 conversion

n. conversion, convertibility, processing, development, change-over, transformation, alteration; regeneration, new birth, rebirth, evangelization; convert, disciple, follower, believer, proselyte, catechumen.

adj. converted, altered, changed, transformed; regenerate, born again.

vb. convert, turn into, alter, transform, transmute; evangelize, proselytize, save, redeem; camouflage, disguise, mask, hide, conceal, obscure; remodel, improve, mend, reconstruct, reshape, reform, mould, metamorphose.

see also 142

147 reversion

n. reversion, return, regress, regression, reaction, rebound, flashback, boomerang, recoil, backfire, backlash; restoration, restitution, re-establishment, reconditioning, refreshment, rejuvenation, recovery, reopening; atavism, throwback; resurrection, renewal, revival, comeback; reversal, *volte-face*, about-turn, backsliding, apostasy, lapse, relapse.

adj. reverted; atavistic; apostate, degenerate.

vb. revert, go back, return, turn

back, reverse; recur, reappear, restore, restitute, reinstate, replace; recoil, rebound; regress, retrogress, throw back; backslide, fall away, lapse, relapse, degenerate.

148 revolution

n. revolution, disaster, *débâcle*, explosion, eruption; *coup*, shake-up, overthrow, upheaval, revolt, rebellion, insurrection, anarchy, plot, subversion.

radical, revolutionary, extremist, fanatic, demonstrator, agitator, rebel, anarchist, guerrilla, freedom fighter, insurrectionist, traitor.

adj. revolutionary, radical, progressive, extreme, thorough, deep, complete, rabid; earth-shaking, catastrophic, cataclysmic, shattering; militant, rebellious, revolting, anarchistic, insurgent, underground, subversive, seditious.

vb. revolutionize, subvert, overthrow, upset, shake up; rise up, revolt.

149 substitution

n. substitution, exchange, transference, alternation, commutation, shift, shuffle, switch, rearrangement, transposition, vicariousness.

substitute, transfer, alternative, replacement, understudy, proxy, ghostwriter, locum, reserve, stand-in, standby, relief; deputy, agent, delegate; double, dummy, stopgap, makeshift; scapegoat, whipping boy.

adj. substitutional, alternative, vicarious, reserve, provisional, temporary, makeshift; dummy, mock, imitation.

vb. substitute, exchange, transfer, replace, commute, transpose, shuffle, shift, switch, act for, stand in for, cover for, fill in, relieve, fill in for, put in the place of, ghost, double for, serve in one's stead; take it out on (*inf.*), work off.

adv. instead, in the place of, in lieu.

150 interchange

n. interchange, exchange, transfer, reciprocation, swap, mutuality, interrelation, interchangeability, tit for tat; barter, trade, commerce, correspondence, give and take (*inf.*).

adj. in exchange, mutual, reciprocal, reciprocating, interchangeable, commutable.

vb. interchange, exchange, swap, commute, interact, trade, barter, correspond; give and take (*inf.*).

151 changeableness

n. changeableness, changeability, variability, mutability, irregularity, instability, inconstancy, mobility, fluctuation, vacillation, wavering; fickleness, indecision, unreliability, erraticness, waywardness.

adj. changeable, variable, irregular, inconstant, mobile, vacillating, wavering, fluctuating, volatile, many-sided, versatile, flexible, malleable, adaptable, plastic, unstable, unsteady, protean; fickle, flighty, indecisive, fidgety, capricious, unreliable, erratic, wayward.

vb. vary, range, mutate, chop and change, waver, shift, vacillate, fluctuate, variegate, differ, depart, diverge, dissent.

152 stability

n. stability, immutability, invariability, firmness, permanence, constancy, irreversibility, immobility, immovableness, solidity; regularity; reliability, resoluteness, endurance; stabilization, equilibrium, balance, homeostasis.

fixture, establishment, constant,

invariant; rock, pillar; stabilizer, ballast, counterbalance, counterweight, sandbags.

adj. unchangeable, invariable, changeless, stable, constant, steady, immovable, immobile, stationary; unwavering, inflexible, unadaptable; resolute, reliable, steadfast; stereotyped, uniform; fixed, fast, set, sure, established, entrenched, inveterate.

vb. stabilize, fix, set, steady, secure, sustain, support, fasten; balance; establish, entrench, anchor, transfix.

see also 535

153 present events

n. eventuality, incidence; event, occurrence, incident, episode, happening, situation, circumstance, development, chance, proceeding, transaction, phenomenon, adventure, experience, triumph, celebration; affair, matter, concern; predicament, accident, misadventure, misfortune, mishap, calamity, emergency, catastrophe.

adj. happening, current, present, afloat, in the air, in the wind, about, prevailing.

vb. happen, take place, occur, come about, follow, ensue, arrive, transpire, fall on, befall, arise, come up, turn up, crop up; be realized, come off, turn out, feel, undergo, experience, meet.

154 future events

n. prospect, outlook, forecast, prediction, approach, promise; fate, destiny; imminence, threat, menace.

adj. impending, approaching, coming, near, close, forthcoming, imminent; threatening, brewing, ominous, certain, inevitable, inescapable, unavoidable, fateful, destined, fated; in prospect, in store, to come, in the offing, on the horizon.

vb. impend, approach, draw on,

near, advance, hover, be in store; loom, threaten, hang over, overshadow, menace; forecast, prognosticate; anticipate, expect.

see also 902

G Causation

155 cause

n. causation, causality, origination, motivation, authorship.

cause, origin, source, root, spring, foundation, seed; beginning, birth, derivation, nativity, genesis; means, basis, grounds, ground, agent, occasion, influence, mainspring, determinant, antecedent; first cause, prime mover, producer, creator, author, originator, inventor, discoverer, founder; motive, inducement, activation; factor, element, rudiment, principle; reason, explanation.

adj. causal, original, determinant; basic, fundamental, primary, radical, initial.

vb. cause, make, create, produce, originate, effect, determine, bring about, provoke, generate, evoke, elicit, induce, call forth, give rise to, arouse, occasion, motivate, suggest, influence, lead to; conduce, contribute to, involve.

156 effect

n. effect, result, consequence, end, outcome, upshot, issue, product; consummation, after-effect, aftermath, repercussion, wake, reaction, backlash, sequel, fruit, harvest, emanation; by-product, spin-off.

adj. caused, consequent, consequential, resultant, resulting, following, ensuing, subsequent, derivative.

vb. result, follow, ensue, spring from,

157

proceed from, derive from, emanate from, originate in; become of, come of.

157 assignment of cause

n. assignment, attribution, imputation, reference, ascription; association; explanation, theory, hypothesis, rationale.

adj. attributable, assignable, referable, imputable, derivable, culpable; linked, associated; explanatory.

vb. attribute, assign, ascribe, impute, refer, charge, blame, trace, credit with, derive from, lay at; connect, associate, link; explain, account for, solve.

158 chance

n. chance, fortuity, randomness, unpredictability; odds, risk-taking, probability; fate, lot, fortune, luck, good luck, bad luck, pot luck; fluke (*inf.*), gamble.

adj. casual, chance, accidental, coincidental, fortuitous, random, haphazard, unthinking, hit-or-miss, aimless, fluky (*inf.*); unmotivated, inexplicable, unintentional.

vb. chance, fall to one's lot; chance upon, stumble on, venture, happen on, gamble, risk; stand a chance.

adv. by chance, by accident, unexpectedly, unintentionally, fortuitously, randomly, casually, perchance.

see also 553

159 power

n. power, potency, might, strength, energy, vigour, life, liveliness, dynamism; dominance, domination, omnipotence; sway, control, teeth, muscle, influence; ability, capability, skill, potentiality, competence, efficiency, capacity, faculty, efficacy; force, potential, thrust, pressure, horse-power, steam, electricity, juice (*sl.*),

gas, nuclear power, solar energy, hydro-electricity; power station, grid, pylon.

adj. powerful, mighty, energetic, vigorous, strong, lively, dynamic, empowered, forceful, dominant, potent; omnipotent, almighty; able, capable, up to (*inf.*), equal to, potential, competent, efficient, effective.

vb. be able, be up to (*inf.*), be capable of, lie in one's power; be powerful, perform, operate, accomplish; empower, confer, enable, power, charge, invest, arm, strengthen, electrify.

see also 161

160 impotence

n. impotence, lifelessness, powerlessness, ineffectuality, ineffectivity, helplessness; inability, incapability, incompetence; unproductiveness, infertility, barrenness; eunuch, gelding.

adj. powerless, unenergetic, unable, incapable, incompetent, inefficient, ineffective, inadequate, disabled, incapacitated, inept; infirm, helpless, unprotected, defenceless; spineless, nerveless, feeble; impotent, sterilized, sterile, barren, infertile, frigid.

vb. not be able, cannot, not find it in oneself to; disable, impair, exhaust, wear down, run down, incapacitate, disarm, unman, paralyze, put out of action, throw a spanner in the works; disqualify, invalidate; castrate, emasculate, spay, geld.

161 strength

n. strength, might, energy, vigour, force, vitality, toughness, stamina, hardness, brawn, muscle; invincibility.

adj. strong, mighty, powerful, forceful, energetic, firm; unyielding, unresisting, persistent; brawny, muscular, stout, hardy, tough, robust, stalwart, strapping, burly, beefy, big, solid, hefty, virile, athletic; secure, durable.

vb. strengthen, fortify, confirm, reinforce, establish, substantiate, empower, energize, stimulate, build up, brace, refresh, invigorate.

see also 535, 537

162 weakness

n. weakness, feebleness, frailty, faintness, fragility, flimsiness, delicacy, tenderness; infirmity, debility; effeminacy, femininity.

weakling, coward, cry-baby, sissy (*sl.*), pansy (*sl.*).

adj. weak, powerless, helpless, delicate, puny, frail; fragile, flimsy, brittle, insubstantial, makeshift, unsteady; effeminate, womanly; weakminded, spineless, anaemic (*inf.*), fainthearted, insipid, diluted, wishy-washy (*inf.*); worn, rotten, decrepit.

vb. faint, sicken, languish, crumble, decline; weaken, exhaust, enfeeble, impoverish, debilitate, enervate, disable, handicap; dilute, water down, blunt, sap; fade, give way, fizzle out (*inf.*).

163 production

n. production, productivity, output, performance, through-put; foundation, manufacture, establishment, construction, fabrication, processing; propagation, generation, procreation, fertility, reproduction, breeding, copulation.

product, creation, work, article, piece, goods, merchandise, handiwork, fruit, harvest, produce, yield, result, opus; edifice, building, structure, erection, invention, concoction, brain-child (*inf.*), baby (*sl.*), thing (*sl.*).

adj. productive, generative, creative, manufacturing; fruitful, rich, prolific, fertile; pregnant, expecting, with child,

with young, in the family way (*inf.*), in the club (*sl.*).

vb. produce, create, make, manufacture, put together, make up, fabricate, construct, build; devise, compose; furnish, effect, perform, return, render, provide; invent, concoct, cook up; carve, chisel; yield, blossom, flower; reproduce, generate, procreate, propagate, multiply, conceive, beget, breed.

164 destruction

n. destruction, annihilation, elimination, liquidation, extirpation, disintegration, demolition, eradication, obliteration, nullification, abolition, dissolution, suppression; slaughter; waste, overthrow, subversion, desolation, havoc, wreckage, sabotage, ruin, ravage, downfall, collapse, ruination.

adj. destructive, hurtful, troublesome, harmful, detrimental, ruinous, deadly, fatal, lethal, poisonous, venomous, toxic, internecine, shattering, annihilative.

vb. destroy, terminate, nullify, abolish, suppress, eradicate, wipe out, blot out, obliterate, wipe off the face of the earth, dissolve; annihilate, eliminate, liquidize, extirpate, exterminate, atomize, pulverize, decimate, decapitate; demolish, break, dismantle, knock down, pull down; crush, overthrow, overturn; blitz, bombard, smash, shatter, mutilate, undo; damage, lay waste, devastate, raze, plunder, ruin, pillage, ravage, despoil, sack.

be destroyed, perish, disintegrate, deteriorate, decay, crumble, go to rack and ruin.

165 reproduction

n. reproduction, reconstruction,

remaking, renovation, reforming; regeneration, resurrection; rediscovery, revival, renaissance; duplication, reduplication, reprinting.

adj. reproductive, regenerative, renascent.

vb. reproduce, reconstruct, rebuild, remake, redo, refashion, remould, reform, renovate, renew, revive, rediscover, regenerate, repeat; propagate, multiply; proliferate, duplicate, reprint, copy.

166 producer
n. producer, creator, maker, instigator, mover, manufacturer, constructor, builder, architect, composer, author, writer, originator, inventor, discoverer.

167 destroyer
n. destroyer, breaker; anarchist, terrorist, desperado, gunman, murderer; disrupter, ravager, vandal, defacer, wrecker, iconoclast, nihilist, abolitionist.

plague, pestilence, moth, locust, erosion, rust, cancer, poison, virus, fungus, mildew, blight; demolition expert, demolisher.

see also 370

168 productiveness
n. productiveness, productivity, generative capacity; prolificness, fruitfulness, fertility, proliferation, fecundity; lushness, luxuriance, exuberance, profusion, richness, abundance, wealth, plenty, horn of plenty, cornucopia, bounty, plethora, hotbed, warren; prosperity, boom.

adj. productive, fruitful, prolific, profuse, fertile, rich, fecund; bounteous, spawning, abundant, plenty, copious, lush, luxurious, fulsome,

exuberant, booming; prosperous, wealthy.

vb. be fruitful, blossom, prosper, thrive, flourish, proliferate, grow, swarm.

see also 163

169 unproductiveness
n. unproductiveness, stagnation, unprofitability, incapacity, barrenness, desolateness, infertility; sterilization, contraception; slump, recession, depression, austerity.

adj. unproductive, unprofitable, fruitless, profitless; desolate, barren, poor, unfruitful; ineffectual, ineffective; infertile, unbearing, sterilized, sterile, impotent, frigid, childless, celibate.

vb. stagnate, vegetate, fail; exhaust; castrate, emasculate, spay, geld.

170 parenthood
n. parenthood, ancestry, origin, genealogy, parentage, line, lineage; fatherhood, paternity; parent, progenitor, procreator, begetter; father, dad, daddy, pop (*sl.*); motherhood, maternity; mother, mum, mummy.

adj. generative, procreative, lifegiving; ancestral, genealogical; family, familial; parental, paternal, fatherly, maternal, motherly.

171 offspring
n. offspring, issue, progeny, posterity; lineage, generation, next generation; adoption; descent, sonship, filiation; family, child, son, daughter; heir, descendant; bastard.

adj. descended, familiar, lineal; filial, daughterly; bastard, illegitimate; adopted.

172 operation
n. operation, agency, action, execution, application, performance, run-

ning, management, conduct, function, process, instrumentality, means.

adj. operative, active, functioning, in operation, in action, in force; live, running, working, effective; executive, operational, functional, agential.

vb. operate, function, work, go, move, run; act, behave, perform, handle; produce, bring about.

see also **564, 565**

173 vigour

n. vigour, energy, power, dynamism, vehemence, strength, lustiness, élan, dash, verve, vitality, get-up-and-go (*inf.*), go (*inf.*), zest, pep, bounce, zip; drive, push, thrust, enterprise, initiative, aggression.

stimulant, invigorator, activator, incentive, stimulus, fillip, pick-me-up, catalyst, booster, drug, shot.

adj. vigorous, powerful, potent, dynamic, strong, vehement, intense, lively, brisk, energetic; enterprising; aggressive, pushy (*inf.*), self-assertive; stimulating, invigorating, activating.

vb. invigorate, energize, activate, strengthen, fortify, reinforce, stimulate, animate, enliven, vitalize, drive, push, intensify.

see also **159, 161**

174 inertness

n. inertness, inertia, inactivity, motionlessness, lifelessness, immobility, dullness, passivity, indolence, idleness, lethargy, listlessness.

adj. inert, lifeless, immobile, motionless, dead, inactive, idle, languid, torpid, lethargic, listless, indolent, passive, slow, still, pacific, dull, sluggish, dormant.

vb. slumber, languish, idle, stagnate, vegetate.

see also **267**

175 violence

n. violence, force, boisterousness, turbulence, destructiveness; outburst, outbreak, uproar, explosion, eruption, disruption, clash, clammer, assault, onslaught; disorder, disturbance, turmoil, ferment, fury, frenzy, tumult; storm, blizzard, gale, hurricane, tornado, thunderstorm, hailstorm, cloudburst, tempest.

savage, barbarian, brute, beast, monster, animal, maniac, fiend, terrorist, bully, ruffian.

adj. violent, extreme, severe; vehement, forceful, boisterous, turbulent; rough, raging, wild, stormy, furious, outrageous, rampageous, destructive; aggressive; brutal, brutish, savage, fierce, barbarous.

vb. run wild, rush, mob; erupt, explode, blast, break out; roar, fume, boil, seethe; incite, stir up, whip up, lash; force, coerce; provoke.

176 moderation

n. moderation, assuagement, alleviation, pacification, placating, soothing; reduction; gentleness, calmness, mildness; control.

moderator, balm, consolation, relief, cure, tranquillizer, restraint.

adj. moderate, modest, reasonable; calm, gentle, tranquil; restrained, temperate.

vb. be moderate, be at peace, keep a low profile; keep a happy medium; moderate, restrain, temper, alleviate, reduce, decrease, abate, tone down, cushion, soften the blow, mitigate, mollify, soothe, relieve, console, assuage, pacify, placate, still, quieten; relax, let up.

177 influence

n. influence, weight, dominance,

power, control, force, pressure, sway, authority, pull (*inf.*); significance; prestige, reputation.

adj. influential, weighty, dominant, powerful, forceful, controlling, prevailing, authoritative, important, significant, momentous; prominent, reputable.

vb. influence, determine, affect, convince, persuade, sway, compel, turn, dominate, govern, control, lobby, bring pressure to bear, put pressure on, carry weight with, pull strings (*inf.*), get in with (*inf.*).

see also 420

178 tendency

n. tendency, trend, direction, bent, drift, aim; tenor, thrust, spirit; inclination, bias, leaning, propensity, proneness, predisposition, predilection, penchant, fondness, liking, preference, weakness, proclivity.

adj. tending, conducive, predisposed.

vb. tend, lean, incline, drift, predispose, point to, aim, gravitate towards.

179 liability

n. liability, liableness, susceptibility, amenability; subjection, responsibility.

adj. liable, apt, inclined, disposed, prone, likely to, subject to; answerable, responsible, amenable.

vb. be liable, run the risk of, incur, fall on, be subject to, succumb to, fall prey to, expose oneself to, lay oneself open to.

180 concurrence

n. concurrence, collaboration, co-operation, partnership, working together, joint action; union, concert.

adj. concurrent, combined, allied, united, joint, cooperative; mutual.

vb. concur, cooperate, collaborate,

work together, unite, combine; agree, harmonize, accord.

see also 639

181 counteraction

n. counteraction, opposition, polarity, antagonism, contradiction; retroaction, offsetting, neutralization; friction, resistance, drag, counterweight, cross-current, countermeasure; antidote, cure, medicine, relief, preventive, antibiotic, injection.

adj. counter, counteractive, neutralizing, retarding.

vb. counteract, work against, militate against, run counter to; neutralize, cancel out, invalidate, hinder, prevent, frustrate; interfere, oppose, contradict; drag; counterbalance, countervail.

II Space

A Space in general

182 indefinite space

n. space, expanse, extent, expansion, span, area, surface; range, scope, compass, reach, sweep, stretch, gamut, spread; room, open space, clearance, elbow-room, breathing space, latitude, margin, leeway.

adj. spatial; spacious, ample, extensive, roomy, capacious, vast, expansive, deep, broad, wide, long, far-reaching, widespread.

vb. reach, extend, spread, stretch, sweep, flow, range, encompass, span; open, expand, widen.

183 definite space

n. region, area, district, zone; patch, section, sector, quarter, square.

territory, country, state, kingdom,

realm, principality, duchy, province, county, shire, community, city, capital, centre, borough, town, village, hamlet; constituency, ward; diocese, parish; conurbation, metropolitan county, metropolitan district, metropolis, suburb, suburbia; locality, surroundings, environment, neighbourhood, environs, locale, milieu.

adj. territorial, regional; provincial, local, municipal, urban, suburban, rural; parochial, insular.

184 limited space

n. place, spot, position, point, stand, locus, corner; enclosure, field, compound, pen, close, sty, pound, paddock, plot, zone, square, quadrangle, yard, patio, precinct; niche, groove, socket.

185 situation

n. situation, position, location, station, setting, site, place, scene, scenery; whereabouts, bearings.

adj. situated, located, placed, positioned, sited, set, situate.

vb. be situated, be, be found, lie, be there, stand, sit, be located.

186 location

n. location, position, site, place, seat, station, locus, stand, scene, placing, placement, emplacement; encampment, mooring, lodging.

adj. located, positioned, entrenched, installed, settled, encamped.

vb. locate, position, establish, determine, set, place, unearth, discover, search out, come across, find; park, encamp, set up, install, settle, entrench, camp, moor, lodge.

187 displacement

n. displacement, dislocation, derangement, misplacement, shift, unloading, unpacking; loss, mislaying.

adj. displaced, disturbed; dislocated,

uprooted, homeless, rootless; out of place, uncomfortable.

vb. displace, disarrange, disturb, confuse; dislodge, dislocate, disestablish, unseat, uproot, unsettle, derail; shift, move, remove, replace, transpose, transport; discharge, unload, unpack, extract, withdraw, evacuate, vacate; misplace, lose, mislay; feel out of place.

188 presence

n. presence, attendance, participation; occupancy, residence, inhabitance, habitation; ubiquity, omnipresence.

adj. present, in attendance, attendant, resident; available, at one's disposal, at hand, ready, on call, on tap.

vb. be present, be there, be, be around, kick around (inf.); attend, visit; haunt, hang around (inf.), frequent; live, inhabit, occupy, reside; appear, make an appearance, turn up, show up (inf.), present oneself.

189 absence

n. absence, disappearance, nonappearance; absenteeism, non-attendance, truancy, defection, desertion; non-residence, inexistence; emptiness, vacuity, vacuum, bareness, void, loss, vacancy; lack, need, deficiency.

adj. absent, not here, away, missing, lost, out, not in, elsewhere, not at home, moved, removed, vanished, disappeared; wanting, lacking, minus, unavailable, omitted; empty, vacant, bare, vacuous, unoccupied, uninhabited.

vb. be absent, stay away, be missing, lack, want; absent oneself, take no part in, play truant, play hooky (sl.), take French leave.

190 inhabitant

n. inhabitant, native, national; citizen, resident, house-dweller; householder; tenant, lodger, paying guest, incumbent, boarder, occupier, squatter; tax-payer, commuter, voter; city-dweller, townsman, town-dweller, suburbanite; denizen; population, populace.

settler, colonist, pioneer; immigrant, foreigner, guest worker; aborigine, autochthon, primitive, ancient.

adj. native, vernacular, common, popular, national, indigenous, domestic, home, local, domesticated, naturalized, aboriginal.

191 habitation

n. habitation, abode, habitat, accommodation, dwelling, residence, residency, domicile, establishment.

house, address; mansion, country house, hall, lodge, grange, manor, castle, villa, chalet, cottage, bungalow; flat, apartment, suite, maisonette, pad (*sl.*), penthouse, bedsitter, block of flats, tenement, mews, skyscraper, high-rise flats; shelter, hut, shanty; home, fireside, hearth, homestead; lodgings, rooms, quarters, billet, berth, barrack, camp, digs (*inf.*), diggings (*inf.*).

inn, hotel, guest house, boarding house, bed and breakfast, hostel, motel, pension; public house, pub (*inf.*), local (*inf.*), tavern, hostelry, club; bar.

restaurant, café, cafeteria, snack bar, buffet, canteen, refreshment room, tearoom, teashop, coffee-bar, ice-cream parlour, take-away; pull-up.

vb. live, dwell, inhabit, people, populate; settle, colonize; reside, abide, stay, visit, sojourn, stop (*inf.*); settle down, take up residence, put

down roots; occupy, rent, lodge, keep, squat.

192 contents

n. contents, items, pieces, ingredients, parts, elements, constituents, components; equipment, material, implements, accessories, articles; load, cargo, freight, stuffing.

vb. load, charge, store, freight, ship, weight, pile, mass, take on, pack.

193 container

n. container, receptacle, holder, cover, envelope; depository, reservoir; packet, package, parcel; bag, sack, purse, wallet, pouch, case, suitcase, trunk, briefcase, grip; box, carton, tin, can, chest, coffer, locker, capsule, canister, crate, bin, hopper, bunker, granary, basket, hamper, pannier; pot, jug, glass, beaker, cup, bucket, pail, bowl, plate, vessel, jar, pitcher, urn, basin, boat, crock, vase; bottle, flask, flagon; cauldron, vat; cistern.

B Dimensions

194 size

n. size, proportions, dimension, measurement, distance, area, extent, mass, weight, volume, capacity; largeness, greatness, hugeness, bigness, enormity, vastness, amplitude, immensity, capaciousness, solidness, bulkiness, corpulence, plumpness, obesity, fleshiness, stoutness.

giant, monster, colossus, leviathan, whale.

adj. big, large, great, huge, enormous, vast, jumbo; fat, obese, stout, plump, podgy, corpulent, fleshy, beefy, pot-bellied; overgrown, larger-than-life; bulky, heavy, solid.

see also 32

195 littleness

n. littleness, shortness, smallness, minuteness, tininess, slightness, scantiness, exiguity, diminutiveness, brevity.

dwarf, pigmy, midge, midget; atom, particle; reduction, miniature.

adj. little, small, tiny, slight, miniature, limited, puny; dwarfed, stunted, squat, dumpy; minute, microscopic, diminutive, atomic, infinitesimal, wee.

see also 33

196 expansion

n. expansion, increase, growth, spread, enlargement, augmentation, extension, supplementation, reinforcement, development, escalation, elaboration, amplification, intensification; dilation; inflation.

adj. expanded, expansive, dilated, stretched, swollen, tumescent.

vb. expand, grow, spread, increase, develop, boost, enlarge, blow up, extend, augment, supplement, reinforce, escalate, elaborate, amplify, intensify, magnify; dilate, distend, let out, gather, swell, bloat, stretch, protract; inflate.

197 contraction

n. contraction, reduction, lessening, decrease, shortening, abridgment, curtailment, compression, confinement, narrowing; shrinkage, constriction, recession, deflation; compressor, roller, constrictor.

adj. contracted, shrunken, shrivelled, astringent, wizened.

vb. contract, weaken, lessen, reduce, decrease, decline, abate, subside, dwindle; curtail, abridge, shorten; shrink, shrivel, wrinkle; constrict, confine, compress, squeeze, pinch, nip.

198 distance

n. distance, length, reach, extent, range, space, way, mileage; horizon, skyline, background; farness, remoteness, back of beyond, world's end, outpost, foreign parts, outskirts, limit; aloofness, reserve.

adj. distant, far, far-away, far-flung, far-off, furthest, farthest, furthermost, long-distance, long-range, out of range, out of sight, ultimate, hindmost; remote, inaccessible, out-of-the-way, God-forsaken; unapproachable, aloof.

vb. distance, outstrip, outpace, outrun, outspeed; keep one's distance, keep out of the way of.

adv. far, away, at a distance, to the ends of the earth, to the back of beyond; out of reach, out of range, out of bounds.

199 nearness

n. closeness, proximity, vicinity; adjacency, juxtaposition, contiguity.

near place, foreground, neighbourhood, locality; close quarters, close range, short step, stone's throw, earshot, spitting distance, hair's breadth.

adj. near, close, nearest, nearby; local, neighbouring; adjacent, adjoining, next; short-distance, short-range; intimate.

vb. be near, approach, approximate; adjoin, abut, connect, border, neighbour; juxtapose.

adv. nearby, in the neighbourhood, locally; at close quarters, at hand, close at hand; within hearing, within range, within earshot.

nearly, almost, approximately, virtually, practically, nigh; tantamount to, to all intents and purposes, substantially, in effect, all but.

200 interval

n. interval, space, separation, clearance, margin, leeway, gap, hole, ditch, cleft, break, crack, chink, rift, fault, passage, pass, gorge, ravine, gulf, chasm, valley, leap, interstice.

vb. space, keep apart, separate, split, intervene, interspace.

201 contact

n. contact, juxtaposition, contiguity, tangency, junction, connection, meeting, touching.

adj. contiguous, in contact, tangential.

vb. contact, touch, meet, brush, graze, kiss; adjoin, abut, border; juxtapose, bring together; unify.

202 length

n. length, space, measure, span, reach, extent; line, mark, stroke, strip, row, file, string, channel; longness, linearity, longimetry, linear measure; lengthening, extension, prolongation, elongation.

adj. long, lengthy, extensive; high, tall, lofty; lengthened, extended, outstretched, elongated, stretching, drawn out, long drawn out, protracted, enlarged; interminable, limitless, boundless, unending.

vb. be long, stretch out; lengthen, extend, stretch, elongate, draw out, prolong, spin out, protract, enlarge, expand.

203 shortness

n. shortness, briefness, brevity, abridgment, curtailment, reduction, shortening.

adj. short, small, low, slight, little, stunted, dwarf, compact, tiny, stunted, dumpy, stubby, chunky, thickset; curt, concise, succinct, terse.

vb. shorten, abbreviate, abridge,

condense, abstract, summarize, telescope, epitomize, concentrate, boil down; curtail, cut back, truncate, slash; contract, reduce; cut down, shave, prune, shear, trim, strip, clip, nip, pare, whittle, crop, stunt.

204 breadth; thickness

n. breadth, broadness, width, wideness, expanse, latitude, amplitude; bore, calibre, diameter, girth; thickness, plumpness, density, solidity, crassitude; bulk, mess, body.

adj. broad, wide, extended, large, spacious, extensive, roomy, bulky, massive, full, thick, thickset, stout, compact, squat, dumpy, chunky, stubby.

vb. broaden, widen, thicken, fatten.

205 narrowness; thinness

n. narrowness, confinement, restriction, contraction, thinness, slimness, emaciation, leanness, tenuity, shallowness, delicacy; neck, strait, narrows, bottleneck.

adj. narrow, confined, limited, restrained, close; thin, slender, slim, meagre, lanky, lean, threadlike, fine, delicate, skinny, scraggy, weedy, emaciated, bony, spindly, flimsy, wasted, withered, haggard, shrivelled, wizened.

vb. make narrow, taper, confine, straiten; make thin, attenuate, compress; slim, reduce weight, lose weight, take off weight, diet, go on a diet, bant, watch one's weight, starve; shrink, contract.

206 layer

n. layer, stratum, thickness, bed, course, band, substratum, fold, overlap, overlay; row, tier, level, class, zone, storey, floor; coat, coating, ply, seam, laminate, lamina, sheet, slab, foil, panel, slate, plate, scale, flake, squama; lamination, stratification.

adj. layered, laminated, laminate, flaky, scaly, squamous, laminar, lamellar, lamellate, lamelliform, lamellose, laminose.

vb. laminate, layer, overlay, overlap, cover, stratify, scale, flake; veneer.

207 filament

n. filament, wire, thread, cord, strand, string, rope, cable, twine, twist, wisp, lock, shred, hair, whisker, fibre, tendril, eyelash, gossamer; sinew, tendon; strip, tape, band, ribbon, belt, sash, bandage, scarf, strap.

adj. fibrous, threadlike, wiry, stringy, hairy, capillary, sinewy, tendinous.

208 height

n. height, elevation, altitude; loftiness, highness, tallness, stature; uplands, hill, mountain, rise, slope, escarpment, fell, moor; tower, spire, steeple, mast, skyscraper, pillar, column; summit, top.

adj. high, giant, towering, soaring, elevated, sky-high; multi-storey, high-rise; tall, lanky; eminent, distinguished, sublime, exalted, lofty.

vb. tower, soar, extend above, mount, look over, look out on, overlook, command, dominate, overshadow.

adv. high, up, aloft.

209 lowness

n. lowness, depression, netherness, debasement; lowlands, valley, hollow; depths, floor.

adj. low, low-lying, depressed, sunken, nether; lesser; inferior; underlying, lesser; inferior.

vb. be low, lie low, crouch, squat, grovel; lower, depress, debase, sink.

adv. under, underneath, beneath, below, down; underfoot, underground.

210 depth

n. depth, lowness, profundity; drop, depression, bottom, abyss, gorge, pit, space, charm, hollow, trench, mine, chamber, ravine; deeps.

adj. deep, low, profound; deep-seated, deep-rooted; bottomless, fathomless; sunken, buried, immersed; submerged, underwater, deep-sea; subterranean, underground; yawning, gaping.

vb. deepen, hollow, dig, excavate, scrape out, sink, plunge.

adv. deeply, out of one's depth.

211 shallowness

n. shallowness, superficiality; shallow, shoal; covering, veneer, gloss, façade, surface.

adj. shallow, superficial, surface, skin-deep; cosmetic; light, inconsiderable, cursory, slight.

vb. skim, brush, touch on, scratch the surface.

212 summit

n. summit, top, peak, apex, zenith, pinnacle, tip, vertex, acme; consummation, maximum, limit, climax; crown, head, crest, brow, cap, spire.

adj. top, topmost, uppermost, highest, maximal, tip-top; apical, acmic, zenithal; head, capital.

vb. crown, top, tip, head, cap; culminate.

213 base

n. base, root, foundation, support, prop, stand, stay, pier, rest, bottom, basement, floor, basin, substratum, bed, channel, ground, understructure, shaft, substratum, groundwork; foot, toe, pedestal.

214

adj. bottom, undermost, fundamental, basic, underlying.

214 being vertical

n. verticality, uprightness, perpendicularity, erectness, plumbness, straightness, sheerness, steep, cliff, precipice.

adj. vertical, perpendicular, upright, erect, upstanding, plumb, on end, straight up; steep.

vb. be vertical, stick up, rise; make vertical, erect, raise, elevate.

215 being horizontal

n. horizontality, planeness, flatness, evenness; level, plane.

adj. horizontal, plane, level, even, flush; prostrate, prone, supine, recumbent.

vb. be horizontal, lie down, recline, repose; flatten, level, even out, smooth, plane, squash, prostrate, roll out, straighten.

216 hanging

n. pendency, suspension, hanging; pendant, locket, earring; curtain, hangings; pendulum, stalactite.

adj. hanging, suspended, pendent, dangling, drooping, swaying, pendulous, stalactitic, overhanging.

vb. hang, suspend, fall, hover, float, poise, dangle, drape; droop, sag, swing, sway, oscillate, flap.

217 support

n. support, sustenance, maintenance, reinforcement, back-up; supporter, guide, backing, stiffener, strengthener, sustainer; foundation, base, carriage, bearing, undercarriage, underframe, chassis, bogie, truck, stilt, stay, mainstay, buttress, pole, post, prop, stake, boom, column, pillar, corner-stone, pier, pile, timber, brace, beam, rafter, girder, strut, joist; breakwater, pier,

wall; splint, crutch, truss; back, rest, headrest, backrest, backbone; wedge, chock; pivot, lever, hinge, axis, fulcrum; stand, board, table, seat, saddle, cushion, pillow; shelf, ledge, rack; backer, provider, patron.

adj. supporting, sustaining.

vb. support, hold up, prop, sustain, maintain, carry, bear, keep up; bolster, shore, brace, stay, truss, underpin, undergird, back, buoy up, shoulder; uphold, establish, promote, advance, further, encourage, confirm, strengthen, corroborate, back up, stand by, stick by (*inf.*), stand up for, stand behind, stick up for (*inf.*).

see also 636

218 parallelism

n. parallelism, equidistance, coextension; likeness, correspondence, similarity, affinity; parallelogram; parallelopiped.

adj. parallel, equidistant, not meeting, not converging, coextensive; corresponding, similar, uniform.

vb. parallel, correspond, be equal; match, equate, compare.

219 being oblique

n. obliqueness, obliquity, skewness, curvature, asymmetry; curve, bend, twist, squint, divergence, diagonal; slope, inclination, slide, acclivity, decline, declivity.

adj. oblique, inclined, leaning, angled, skew, askew, skew-whiff (*inf.*), asymmetrical, awry, crooked, askance; sloping, upward, acclivitous, downward, declivitous; divergent, sideways, slanted, bent, curved, twisted, contorted; cross-wise, diagonal, transverse.

vb. incline, lean, slope, tilt, angle, bend, curve, twist, warp; diverge, deviate, slant.

220 inversion

n. inversion, transposition, reversion, reversal; palindrome, about-turn, *volte-face*; upset, capsizal, somersault.

adj. inverted, inverse, opposite, upside-down, back-to-front, topsy-turvy.

vb. invert, transpose, rearrange, exchange, reverse, revert, put the cart before the horse (*inf.*); turn over, overturn, overthrow, turn upside down, stand on its head, tip, topple, tilt, capsize, keel over, somersault; turn inside out.

221 crossing

n. crossing, junction, intersection, confluence, crossroads, crossover; cross, crux, crucifix, cruciform, swastika; network, system, intercommunication; wickerwork, lattice, grid, grill, web, net, netting, mesh, textile, fabric, weave, loom, plait.

vb. cross, intersect, interlink, cut, pass across, mesh, weave, loom, knit, sew, plait, twist, interlace, spin, twine, intertwine, interlock, tangle, entangle.

222 being exterior

n. exteriority, extraneousness, externality, outwardness; outside, exterior, surface, top, front, face, appearance, façade, covering.

adj. exterior, outside, external, outward, outer, outermost, outlying; extrinsic, foreign.

vb. be outside; externalize, extrapolate, project, objectify, embody.
see also 825

223 being interior

n. interiority, internality, inwardness; inside, interior; substance, contents, heart, centre, soul.

adj. interior, inside, internal, inward,

inner, innermost; intrinsic, inborn, innate; central, integral; inland.

vb. be inside; internalize.
see also 5, 224

224 centrality

n. centrality, centralization; centre, middle, bull's eye; focus, concentration, convergence; nucleus, core, heart, hub, nub, gist, kernel, marrow, pith.

adj. central, centre, middle, inner, focal, pivotal.

vb. centre, centralize, concentrate, focus, converge, draw, attract.
see also 96

225 covering

n. covering, superimposition, cover, lid, flap, box, wrapping; ceiling, roof, shelter, dome, awning, tent, marquee, tarpaulin, canopy, mask, hood, shade, film, blind, umbrella, parasol, sunshade, sheath; sheet, blanket, robe, carpet, rug, mat; coating, varnish, paint, veneer, lacquer, glaze, enamel, wash, polish, stain, distemper, gloss; skin, peel, shell, rind, coat, husk, hull, pod, jacket, integument, tegument.

adj. covered, sheltered, hooded, wrapped, enveloped, veiled, varnished, painted, surfaced.

vb. cover, put on, lay over, protect, shield, shelter, wrap, envelop, enshroud, enclose, veil, superimpose, superpose; roof, carpet, pave, paper; coat, surface, varnish, paint, plate, gloss, glaze, spray, veneer, wax; mask, hide, conceal.

226 lining

n. lining, insulation, interlining; inner surface, inside; filling, stuffing, wadding, padding, quilting, inlay.

vb. line, insulate, interline, inlay,

stuff, wad, pad, fill, quilt, reinforce, overlay, face, encrust.

227 dressing

n. dressing, toilet; dress, clothing, wardrobe, outfit, vesture, garb, gear, guise, raiment, apparel, attire; clothes, garment, vestment, costume, suit, dress; uniform, livery.

adj. dressed, well-dressed, dressed-up, clad.

vb. dress, clothe, turn out, deck out (*inf.*), equip, fit out; wear, have on, be dressed in; put on, get dressed, don, slip on, throw on, assume; dress up, get dressed up, smarten oneself up; change into; wrap up.

228 undressing

n. undressing, divestment; bareness, undress, nakedness, nudism, nudity, naturism, *déshabillé*, stripping, striptease; nude, nudist, naturist; baldness, alopecia, shaving, tonsure.

adj. bare, exposed, unveiled, uncovered, unprotected; revealing, *décolleté*; undressed, naked, nude, stark naked, stripped, in one's birthday suit (*inf.*), in the altogether (*inf.*), starkers. (*sl.*); bald, hairless, bald-headed, balding, shaven, tonsured, shining, smooth; threadbare, denuded.

vb. uncover, expose, unveil, reveal; remove, take off, cast off; undress, unclothe, strip, disrobe, divest; pluck, peel, pare, shed, bare, skin, flay, scalp, shell, stone, excoriate, decorticate; denude, ravage.

229 being around

n. environment, ambience, circumstances, surroundings; circumjacence; scene, *milieu*, background, setting, habitat, situation; atmosphere, climate; environs, suburbs, vicinity.

adj. environmental, ambient, surrounding, background, situational.

vb. surround, circle, enclose, close in, envelop, girdle, encompass.

adv., prep. around, about.

see also 8

230 being between

n. interposition, intermediacy, intercurrence, intervention, interruption, interjection, interpolation; mediation, intercession; partition, wall, watershed, fence, hurdle; insert, inset, wedge.

adj. intermediary, intermediate, intervening.

vb. place between, mediate, interpose; insert, intersperse; interrupt, interject, intervene.

prep. between, among.

see also 653

231 circumscription

n. circumscription, encircling, circumnavigation; limitation, demarcation, boundary, restriction.

vb. circumscribe, encircle, ring, encompass, surround, circumambulate, circumnavigate, circumvent; surround, limit, restrict, bound, mark off, confine.

232 outline

n. outline, perimeter, periphery, outside, circumference, circuit, border, boundary, contour; sketch, skeleton, silhouette, profile, framework, tracing, delineation.

vb. outline, sketch, trace, delineate.

233 edge

n. edge, extremity, end, limit, verge; border, frontier, boundary; threshold, brink, brim, rim, side, corner, point, tip, margin, skirt; edging, skirting, fringe, hem.

vb. border, verge, edge, skirt; rim, hem, margin, fringe.

234 enclosure

n. enclosure, confinement; envelope, wrapping; area, ground, pitch, arena; plot, court, yard, garden, park; cell, prison, dungeon, den; pen, cage, pound, aviary, coop, warren.

fence, wire, wall, hedge, fencing, paling, rail, railing, balustrade, barrier, ditch, moat, trench, ha-ha.

vb. enclose, envelop, wrap, enfold, confine, contain, blockade, shut in, shut up, lock up, fence, impound, hedge in, hem in; package, parcel; bottle; jail, imprison.

235 limit

n. limit, end, utmost, extremity, destination, terminus, conclusion; limitation, delimitation, restriction, definition, control; hurdle, barrier, frontier, boundary, border, borderline; threshold, upper limit, ceiling; demarcation line, mark, fringe, edge.

adj. limited, set, defined.

vb. limit, set, settle, define, delimit, demarcate, bound, confine, restrict, draw the line at, curb.

236 front

n. front, frontage, exterior, façade, anterior, foreground, face, head, forehead, vanguard, front line; visage, countenance, physiognomy; semblance.

adj. front, forward, fore, foremost, frontal, frontmost, head, obverse, anterior, leading, advance.

vb. face, front, look out on; border; head, lead; meet, confront, encounter, come face to face with.

adv. in advance, ahead; in the foreground.

237 rear

n. rear, back, tail, end, reverse, posterior, backside, bottom, dorsum; wake, rearguard; background, hinterland, backstage.

adj. rear, back, hind, tail, posterior, after, terminal, final, bottom, dorsal, backmost, hindmost, rearmost, background, backstage.

vb. be behind, follow, back on to; bring up the rear.

adv. at the rear, behind, in the background.

238 sidedness

n. sidedness, laterality; juxtaposition, adjacency; side, hand, flank, shoulder.

adj. side, lateral, sidelong, sidewise, sideways, flanking; adjacent.

vb. be side by side, flank, skirt; juxtapose.

adv. laterally, sideways, abreast, alongside, side by side.

239 being opposite

n. opposition, contraposition, polarity; opposite, converse, reverse, contrary, contrast, contradiction, antipode, antipole.

adj. opposite, contrary, opposing, contradictory.

vb. be opposite, oppose, confront, face.

adv., prep. opposite, over against, facing, *vis à vis*.

240 right side

n. right-handedness, dexterity, dextrality; right, right hand; right-hander, dextral; starboard.

adj. right, right-hand, right-handed, off, offside, dextral, dextrorse.

241 left side

n. left-handedness, sinistrality; left, left hand; left-hander, sinistral; port.

adj. left, left-hand, left-handed, near-side, sinistrorse.

C Form

242 form

n. form, shape, style, look, appearance, fashion, design, outline, profile, contour; structure, construction, formation; morphology.

adj. formed, shaped, developed; formative, impressionable, plastic, mouldable.

vb. form, make, create, fashion, pattern, model, mould; cast, stamp, impress, carve, cut; arrange, construct, build, assemble; take shape, develop, express, grow, materialize.

243 absence of form

n. formlessness, shapelessness, amorphism, fuzziness; chaos, liquid; fluid.

adj. formless, shapeless, amorphous; vague, unclear, indistinct, blurred, fuzzy; indeterminate, indefinite; chaotic, misshapen, unshapely, deformed.

244 symmetry

n. symmetry, regularity, conformity, proportion, equality, evenness, balance, harmony, arrangement, order; shapeliness.

adj. symmetrical, balanced, even, proportioned, harmonious, shapely, regular, well-proportioned.

245 asymmetry

n. asymmetry, disproportion, lopsidedness, irregularity, distortion, contortion, twist, deformity, malformation.

adj. asymmetrical, disproportionate, irregular, misproportioned, uneven, unshapely, grotesque, ugly, hideous, distorted, deformed, malformed, dis-figured, crippled, mangled, hunch-backed, crooked, awry, askew.

vb. distort, contort, twist, pervert, deform, misshape, disfigure, buckle, cripple; writhe, scowl, grimace.

see also 845

246 angular form

n. angularity, pointedness, serration; angle, crotch, elbow, fork, corner, point, zigzag; right angle, acute angle, obtuse angle, reflex angle; triangle; quadrilateral, parallelogram, rhomboid, rectangle, oblong, square, diamond, lozenge, rhombus, rhomb, polygon, pentagon, hexagon, heptagon, octagon, nonagon, enneagon, decagon, endecagon, dodecagon; polyhedron, cube, tetrahedron, pyramid, prism, wedge.

adj. angular, pointed, sharp-cornered, scraggy, jagged, serrated, zigzag, wedge-shaped, cuneiform, cuneate; triangular, rectangular, multilateral.

vb. angle, bend, intersect, serrate, zigzag.

see also 259

247 curved form

n. curvature, bending, flexion, flexure, arcuation; curve, bend, sweep, bow, curl, camber, arc, chord, arcade, rainbow, arch, crook, trajectory; catenary, parabola, hyperbola, circle, ellipse, epicycle; crescent, half-moon, lune, lunula, meniscus, lens, lunate.

adj. curved, bent, rounded, arched, vaulted, crescent, lunate.

vb. curve, turn, arch, bow, curl, crook, buckle, twist, warp, flex; waver, meander, swerve, deviate, veer.

248 straight form

n. straightness, rectilinearity; verticality, perpendicularity; horizontality; bee-line.

adj. straight, even, level, direct; upright, vertical, perpendicular, erect; horizontal; unbroken, uninterrupted.

vb. straighten, order, make straight; untwist, unbend, uncoil, disentangle, unravel, uncurl, unfold.

adv. in a straight line, as the crow flies.

249 round form

n. rotundity, roundness; round, globe, sphere, orb, ball, marble, balloon, bubble, drop, droplet, globule; cylinder, barrel, roll, drum.

adj. round, rotund, rounded, spherical, globular, orbicular, globe-shaped, globoid, globose, cylindrical.

vb. round, ball, roll, coil up.

250 simple circularity

n. circularity, roundness; circle, orbit, circuit, ring, loop, halo, crown, corona, aureola, circus, bowl, hoop, quoit, wheel, disc, equator; ellipse, oval, egg; band, belt, wreath, garland; circumference, perimeter, rim, periphery.

adj. round, circular, cyclic, orbicular; oval, elliptical.

vb. encircle, go round; make round.
see also 322

251 complex circularity

n. convolution, intricacy, twisting, sinuosity, torsion; coil, turn, twine, twist, plait, kink, loop, spiral, helix, screw, curl, tendril, scroll.

adj. convoluted, intricate, involved; winding, spiral, coiled, helical, flexuous, sinuous, tortuous; serpentine, snake-like; meandering, undulating, wavy.

vb. turn, wind, curl, loop, twist, twirl, fold, twine, plait, intertwine, entwine, sinuate, wrinkle, contort, wreathe; crimp, ripple; meander, undulate; wriggle, squirm, wiggle.

252 convexity

n. convexity, protuberance, bulginess, outgrowth.

swelling, growth, bump, hump, lump, ridge, protuberance, rising, bulge; tumour, cancer, corn, boil, inflammation, carbuncle, bunion, wart, pimple, bulb; dome, cupola, vault.

adj. convex, arched, raised, curved, bent; bulbous, swollen, bloated; bulging, swelling, excrescent, tumescent, tumid.

vb. swell, bulge, rise, project, protrude, jut.

253 prominence

n. prominence, salience; projection, protuberance, protrusion, extension, spur, spit, promontory, tongue, headland, relief; leader, figure-head, model, example.

adj. prominent, conspicuous, protuberant, extended, jutting, protruding, projecting, salient, obtrusive.

vb. protrude, extend, jut, project, stand out, stick out.

254 concavity

n. concavity, hollowness; hollow, hole, aperture, opening, depression; pit, abyss, mine, shaft, well, trench; corner, niche, recess, alcove, indentation, pocket; valley, dale, bowl, drop, gulf, basin, glen, ravine, crevasse, fissure, crater, gorge, canyon, gully, chasm; dip, dent, dimple, cave, burrow, cavern, grotto, furrow, covert, warren, pothole; excavation, tunnel, passage, retreat, dug-out, dig (*inf.*).

adj. concave, hollow, depressed, excavated, sunken, carved out, indented.

vb. hollow out, excavate, dig, spade,

gouge, delve, mine, tunnel, bore; indent, depress; cave in, fall in, collapse.

255 sharpness

n. sharpness, acuteness; point, tip, prick, thorn, sting, spike, nail, pin, needle, fork, prong; barb, thorn, bramble, prickle, brier, spine; tooth, edge, scissors, shears, knife.

adj. sharp, acute, pointed, fine, keen, cutting, biting, piercing, incisive, trenchant; spiked, spiky, spiny, prickly, thorny, needle-pointed, barbed; pronged, tapered, tapering, acuminate.

vb. be sharp, prick, sting, taper; sharpen, grind, edge, file, hone, whet, strop; barb, point; puncture.

256 bluntness

n. bluntness, obtuseness, flatness.

adj. blunt, unsharpened, unpointed, dull, unsharp, obtuse; toothless.

vb. blunt, dull, take the edge off, round, turn, obtund; be blunt, not cut.

257 smoothness

n. smoothness, flatness, levelness, regularity; stillness, glossiness, silkiness; glass, ice, marble; gloss, varnish, polish, finish.

adj. smooth, flat, plane, level, even, uniform, steady, stable, continuous; quiet, still, sleek, polished, glossy, glassy, lustrous, silky, soft, slippery, oily.

vb. smooth, even, level, plane, scrape, shave, flatten, iron, sand, file, press; polish, shine, burnish, glaze, gloss, varnish; glide, slide, float, skim, drift, stream.

258 roughness

n. roughness, asperity, unevenness, coarseness, harshness, bumpiness, brokenness, irregularity, jaggedness, corrugation.

adj. rough, uneven, coarse, harsh, bumpy, broken, jagged, rugged, choppy, ruffled; bristly, prickly, hairy, hirsute.

vb. roughen, coarsen, break, notch, serrate, crumple, ruffle.

259 notch

n. notch, indentation, cut, zigzag, cleft, trench, trough, gouge, saw, nick, incision, depression, serration.

adj. notched, jagged, saw-toothed, serrated.

vb. notch, serrate, cut, tooth, cog, indent, nick.

260 fold

n. fold, gather, pleat, lapel, overlap, tuck; crease, crimp, wrinkle, corrugation, turn.

adj. folded, gathered, creased, wrinkled, corrugated, pleated, puckered, overlapping.

vb. fold, double, crease, lap, overlap, plicate, pleat, curl, crimp, wrinkle, ruffle, pucker, gather, corrugate.

261 furrow

n. furrow, groove, slit, slot, trench, rut, gouge, moat, channel, canal, ditch, gutter; corrugation.

adj. furrowed, grooved, ribbed, fluted, corrugated, ridged.

vb. furrow, groove, slot, flute, corrugate, channel, plough.

262 opening

n. opening, aperture, orifice, hole, gap, hollow, slit, perforation, slot, break; mouth, throat, gullet; outlet, vent; window, porthole; door, doorway, gate, exit, entrance, hatch, hatchway, channel, passage.

adj. open, unlocked, unfastened, unsealed; clear, accessible; ajar, gaping, wide, yawning; torn, rent.

vb. open, unlock, unbolt, unbar,

unfasten, undo; clear, admit, free, loosen; expose, reveal, unfold; gape, yawn.

see also 264, 462

263 closure

n. closure, occlusion, stoppage, blockage, obstruction.

adj. closed, unopened, shut, fastened, bolted, blocked, sealed.

vb. close, shut, lock, fasten, bar, bolt.

see also 265

264 perforator

n. perforator, sponge, sieve, strainer, colander; borer, awl, gimlet, drill, lancet, needle, pin, punch; perforation, porosity.

adj. perforated, porous, pervious, permeable, penetrable, spongy, absorbent, holey.

vb. cut, perforate, pierce, prick, slit, puncture, crack, stick, inject, drill, stab, lance, spear, spike, skewer, impale, bore, mine, tunnel; hole, riddle.

265 stopper

n. stopper, plug, cork, bung, tap, valve, stopcock, wedge, rammer, stuffing, filling, stopping.

adj. stopped up, blocked, obstructed, sealed, impenetrable, impervious, watertight.

vb. block, obstruct, blockade, stop, choke, clog, stuff, ram, fill, dam, seal, cork, plug, bung, occlude, obturate.

D Motion

266 motion

n. motion, mobility, movableness, movement, action, activity, unrest, restlessness, move, passage, progress, advance, ascension, descension; velocity, speed.

adj. moving, in motion, transitional, movable, mobile, restless, nomadic.

vb. move, go, run, progress, proceed; push, impel, stir, set in motion, activate, propel.

267 rest

n. rest, immobility, motionlessness, cessation, stillness, standstill, stop; discontinuance, interval, pause; silence, calm; quiet, calmness, peace, tranquillity.

adj. quiet, peaceful, still, quiescent, asleep; immovable, immobile, motionless, unruffled, peaceful, placid, serene.

vb. rest, stand still, pause, halt, stop, cease; not stir, keep quiet; still, soften, quiesce, relax, lull, becalm, hush.

see also 174

268 transference

n. transference, transferal, conveyance, movement, removal, shift, relay, conduct, remittance, dispatch, delivery, hand-over; transport, transportation, transit, carriage, shipment, trans-shipment, haulage, freight, consignment.

adj. transferable, transmittable, transmissible, conveyable, movable, portable.

vb. transfer, move, remove, conduct, carry, take, convey, shift; send, direct, remit, relay, dispatch, forward, deliver, hand over, consign; ship, cart, truck, haul, load, post, mail; convoy, escort; import, export; transmit, communicate; relocate, transplant, ply, shuttle.

see also 714

269 land travel

n. travel, tourism, touring, sightseeing, globe-trotting, roaming; journey, tour, trip, outing, expedition, excursion, day out, picnic; pilgrimage;

venture, adventure; visit, sojourn; exploration, quest, safari.

walk, step, pace, stride, gait, march; stroll, hike, jaunt, saunter, amble, ramble, wayfaring, tramp; promenade, constitutional, perambulation; peregrinations, wanderings.

riding, horse-riding, horsemanship, horse-racing, equestrianism, show-jumping, dressage; cycling, spin, ride; drive; driving, motoring; itinerary, route, course, circuit, direction, map.

adj. journeying, travelling, visiting; peripatetic.

vb. travel, journey, tour, rove, visit, cruise, explore, traverse; walk, step, pace, march, tread, amble, ramble, wander, hike, trek, stroll, ambulate, perambulate, promenade; gad about (*inf.*), gallivant about (*inf.*); ride, cycle, bike (*inf.*); drive, motor.

270 traveller

n. traveller, tourist, sightseer, globe-trotter, holiday-maker, daytripper, visitor, voyager, explorer, adventurer; itinerant, wanderer, roamer, pedlar, vagabond, vagrant, tramp, hobo; migrant, emigrant, immigrant, refugee, gypsy, nomad, bedouin.

pedestrian, walker, foot-passenger, hiker, trekker, rambler, pilgrim, wayfarer, runner, athlete; rider, horse-rider, jockey, show-jumper, hitch-hiker; passenger, commuter, season-ticket holder; motorist, driver.

271 water travel

n. navigation, sailing, cruising, circumnavigation; seamanship, seafaring, exploration; voyage, cruise; water sports, aquatics, sailing, yachting, boating, rowing, canoeing, swimming, diving, surfing.

adj. navigational, sailing, nautical, naval, marine, maritime.

vb. sail, cruise, voyage, ply, run, ferry; set sail; launch, cast off; navigate, steer, pilot, make for, head for, set a course; drop anchor, moor; swim, bathe, dive, dip, paddle, wade, surf, water-ski.

272 mariner

n. mariner, sailor, seaman, seafarer, pilot, boatman, marine, crew, captain, boatswain, navigator, helmsman.

273 air travel

n. air travel, aeronautics, aviation, flying, gliding, flight.

pilot, airman, aviator, flier, aeronaut.

adj. flying; aerial, aeronautical, aerodynamic.

vb. fly, pilot, taxi, take off, climb, rise, soar, zoom; spin, loop, roll; glide, dive, dart, shoot; plunge, plummet; parachute, bail out; touch down, land, come down, crash-land; talk down.

274 space travel

n. space travel, astronautics, cosmonautics; countdown, space flight, space walk; grand tour; re-entry, splashdown.

astronaut, spaceman, cosmonaut, space traveller.

adj. astronautical, cosmonautic, cosmonautical.

vb. take off, orbit, splash down.

275 carrier

n. carrier, bearer, porter, messenger, runner; basket, bag, container; horse, packhorse, llama, beast of burden.

vb. carry, transport, move, convey, transfer, bear.

276 vehicle

n. vehicle, conveyance; cycle, bike bicycle, pushbike (*sl.*), velocipede, tandem, tricycle; moped, scooter, motor scooter, motorcycle, motorbike; car, automobile, motor, saloon, sports car, G. T., coupé, hard-top, convertible, hatchback, estate car, station wagon, shooting-brake, minibus; taxi, taxicab, minicab, cab, hackney carriage, rickshaw; bus, coach, motor bus, tram, trolley-bus; van, lorry, pick-up, dump truck; train, underground, rapid transit; engine, locomotive, diesel locomotive, electric locomotive, steam engine.

cart, trolley, pram, barrow, trailer; carriage, wagon, buggy, trap, gig, hansom.

adj. vehicular, locomotive, wheeled.

277 ship

n. ship, boat, vessel, craft; motorboat, steamer, steamboat, steamship, freighter, barge, lighter, packet, ferry, mail-ship, tanker, supertanker, liner; pilot, tug, launch; destroyer, warship, frigate, battleship, aircraft carrier, submarine; sailing ship, clipper, yacht, rowing boat, paddle boat, canoe, kayak, gondola, junk, galleon.

adj. nautical, marine, maritime, naval, seagoing, seaworthy.

278 aircraft

n. aircraft, aeroplane, plane, airliner, jet, jumbo jet, turbo-prop, shuttle, glider, bomber, seaplane; hovercraft, hydrofoil, helicopter; airship, balloon, Zeppelin.

adj. aviational, aeronautical.

279 spaceship

n. spaceship, spacecraft, capsule, module, space shuttle, space probe; space station, satellite, sputnik; flying saucer, UFO; rocket.

280 velocity

n. velocity, speed, quickness, rapidity, hurry, haste, rush, expedition,

celerity; acceleration, hastening, quickening, speeding up, spurt, burst charge.

adj. quick, fast, speedy, brisk, swift; nimble, agile, deft, spirited; light-footed, prompt, expeditious.

vb. go fast, speed, hurry, hasten, quicken, race, tear, fly, dash, rush, run, sprint, dart, whiz, zip, pelt, bomb, run like mad, go all out, do a ton (*sl.*), go full pelt (*inf.*); accelerate, go faster, speed up, spurt, put on speed, step on it (*inf.*), put one's foot down (*inf.*), get a move on (*inf.*), get one's skates on (*inf.*), make it snappy (*inf.*); overtake, gain on, catch up, reach, pass, overhaul, go after, outstrip, outpace, outdistance, capture, beat; run for dear life.

adv. fast, quickly, speedily, swiftly, at full speed, flat out, at full pelt.

see also **613**

281 slowness

n. slowness, sluggishness, lethargy, apathy, hesitation, reluctance; deceleration, retardation, slackening, delay, go-slow, brake, curb, restraint.

slowcoach, tortoise, snail, dawdler, lingerer, loiterer, loafer, idler.

adj. slow, slow-moving, dawdling, lingering; sluggish, listless, lethargic, apathetic, inactive, leisurely, hesitant, reluctant.

vb. go slowly, idle, stroll, saunter, dawdle, linger, tarry, take one's time, loiter, loaf, crawl, inch, falter, limp, hobble, shuffle, plod; decelerate, slow down, reduce speed, slacken, relax, let up, ease off, delay, retard, brake, put on the brakes; curb.

282 impulse

n. impulse, thrust, impetus, charge, rush, drive, pressure, momentum, impulsion; bump, shove, shock, jolt, impact, brunt, clash, crash, collision, pile-up, smash-up; hit, knock, rap, blow, smack.

vb. impel, push, drive, press, propel, move, set in motion, activate, get going, start; collide, crash, run into, bump into, smash, dash, meet, encounter, touch, impinge, clash, butt, bump, jog, shove, jolt, force, scrape, jar.

hit, strike, beat, smite; tap, rap, jab; slap, thump, clout, smack, pummel, thrash, whip, whack, wallop (*sl.*), sock, clap, box, punch, club, cudgel; hammer, pound, bash, slosh (*sl.*), flail; bang, knock, bruise; kick, knee.

283 recoil

n. recoil, reaction, rebound, spring, bounce, repercussion, echo, reverberation, boomerang, backlash, rebuff, answer, reply.

vb. recoil, react, respond, rebound, bounce, spring, kick back, backfire, echo, reverberate; shrink from, draw back, pull back, wince, flinch.

284 direction

n. direction, bearing, orientation, point of the compass, cardinal point, north, south, east, west; destination, aim, object, intention; tendency, thrust, tenor; outlook, standpoint, point of view.

vb. orientate oneself, take one's bearings, locate; direct, signpost, lead, aim for, go for, head for, make for, point to, steer; tend.

adv. towards, in the direction of, via, heading for, on the way to.

285 deviation

n. deviation, misdirection, disorientation, deflection, divergence, turning, departure, diversion, detour; digression, tangent; irregularity, deterioration.

adj. deviating, aberrant, deviant, divergent, misguided, mistaken, lost; tangential, off-beam.

vb. deviate, deflect, swerve, bend, wander, stray, err, depart from, veer, shift, lose one's bearings, turn aside; disorientate, misdirect; digress, get sidetracked, go off the point, go off at a tangent.

286 precedence

n. precedence, priority, leading, heading, vanguard.

vb. precede, go before, come first, take precedence, herald, go in advance, lead, lead the way, head, take the lead.

adv. in advance, ahead, before.

see also **84**, **118**

287 following

n. following, succession; follower, disciple, hanger-on, attendant, dependant, adherent, supporter, recruit.

vb. follow, go after, come after, ensue, succeed, attend, wait on; shadow, chase, pursue, track, tail (*sl.*), dog; lag behind, trail.

see also **85**, **119**

288 progression

n. progression, progress, advance, headway, gain; development, growth, furtherance, advancement, improvement.

adj. forward, progressive, tolerant, broad-minded, forward-looking, enterprising; ongoing.

vb. progress, advance, proceed, move on, forge ahead, press on, strive forward, push ahead, make progress, make headway, gain ground, never look back (*inf.*); further, promote, develop, grow, evolve, become, mature, improve, move with the times.

adv. forward, onward, on, in progress.

289 regression
n. regression, retreat, withdrawal, retirement, return; regress, retrogression, reversal; departure; escape; about-turn, *volte-face*, about-face, U-turn.

adj. backward, backward-looking, reactionary, narrow-minded, reverse, retrograde, retrogressive.

vb. go backwards, regress, recede, retire, back out, withdraw, retreat, draw back, secede, fall back, lose ground; retrogress; go back on one's word, turn around.

290 propulsion
n. propulsion, impulsion, impetus, drive, push, thrust, pressure; missile, projectile, bullet, shell, torpedo, arrow, dart, propellant, shot.

vb. propel, push, move, impel, drive, direct, thrust, press, shove; launch, throw, cast, pitch, toss, chuck (*inf.*); shoot, discharge.

291 pulling
n. pulling, traction, drawing, tow, haul; tug, tractor, traction engine, draught animal; trailer, caravan, train.

vb. pull, draw, haul, drag, heave, tow, tug, take in tow; attract, magnetize; trail.

292 approach
n. approach, advance, arrival, coming; nearness, approximation.

adj. approaching, nearing, forthcoming, coming, looming, drawing near; accessible, get-at-able, approachable, obtainable, available, attainable, convenient, at one's disposal.

vb. approach, draw near, come near, advance, come forward, come into sight, close in on, sidle up to, loom up; approximate, verge on, near.

293 retreat
n. retreat, recession, withdrawal, departure, escape, retirement, removal, evacuation, flight.

vb. retreat, recede, withdraw, back out, depart, run away, fall back, evacuate, escape, retire, remove; fade, die away, sink.

294 attraction
n. attraction, drawing power, gravitation, affinity, pull, draw, influence; magnet, gravity, bait, lure, decoy.

adj. attracting, appealing, magnetic, charismatic.

vb. attract, pull, drag, draw, bring; interest, fascinate.

see also 547

295 repulsion
n. repulsion, rebuff, snub, beating off, dismissal.

adj. repulsive, offensive, repelling.

vb. repel, repulse, drive back, put to flight, beat off, hold off, push back, throw off, turn away, drive away; dismiss, send packing; rebuff, snub; resist.

see also 892

296 convergence
n. convergence, concurrence, confluence, concentration, confrontation, collision course, focalization; union, meeting, encounter.

adj. convergent, concurrent, converging.

vb. converge, come together, focalize, unite, gather, concentrate, meet, tend, narrow the gap, come to a point.

297 divergence
n. divergence, radiation, ramification; fork, bifurcation; fan, spoke, ray.

adj. divergent, deviating, radiating; centrifugal.

vb. diverge, radiate, branch, fork, bifurcate, diffuse, spread, fan out, disperse, scatter, ramify, divaricate.

298 arrival

n. arrival, coming, approach, entrance, entry, appearance, emergence; start, onset; reaching, attainment; return, homecoming; landing, touchdown, disembarkation, alighting, dismounting, docking, mooring.

destination, goal, terminus, journey's end, objective, resting place, harbour, port, dock, berth, landing place, airport.

vb. arrive, come, reach, get to, enter, approach, appear, show up (*inf.*), turn up, return, come home; land, touch down, disembark, alight, dismount, get down, set foot on, dock, moor, drop anchor.

299 departure

n. departure, going, leaving, setting out, exit, withdrawing, abandonment, removal, retreat, flight, take-off, embarkation, sailing; leave-taking, parting, separating, farewell, send-off, dismissal, valediction, parting shot, *congé*; exodus; emigration.

vb. depart, go, leave, move, quit, retire, withdraw, evacuate, go away, take one's leave, make tracks, set out, start out, be off, push off (*inf.*), push along (*inf.*), shove off (*sl.*); rush off, run away, beat it (*sl.*), scram (*sl.*).

300 entrance

n. entrance, entry, ingress, incoming, induction, initiation, immigration; admittance, admission; introduction, influx, intrusion, infiltration, incursion, penetration, invasion, raid.

vb. enter, come in, step in, go in, set foot in, make one's way into, visit, drop in; intrude, invade, trespass, gatecrash; force into, break in; wriggle in, worm in; insert, put in, admit, introduce, implant, penetrate, infiltrate, percolate.

301 emergence

n. emergence, egress, outflow, emanation, issue, discharge, outflow, effluence, flow; escape, gush, spout, welling, oozing, outpour, leakage, seepage, eruption, secretion.

vb. emerge, go out, come out, come out into the open; emit, eject, discharge, expel, flow out, run out, effuse, give out, exhale, send forth, pour out, gush, spurt, shoot, secrete, seep, erupt, squirt; bleed, leak, empty, weep; exude, ooze.

see also 312

302 reception

n. reception, admission, admittance, acceptance, receptivity; access, welcome, open arms, hospitality, registration, enlistment, enrolment; initiation, baptism, barmitzvah; incorporation, assimilation, absorption, digestion.

adj. admissible, acceptable, receivable; suitable; receptive, sympathetic.

vb. admit, receive, accept, take in; allow in, accommodate, welcome, make welcome; initiate, baptize, introduce, induct, install; assimilate, incorporate, swallow, absorb, digest.

see also 716

303 ejection

n. ejection, expulsion, eviction, removal, elimination; dismissal, discharge, sack (*inf.*), push (*sl.*), deportation, exile, banishment, extradition;

ejector, bouncer (*sl.*), chucker-out; nausea, sickness, vomiting.

vb. eject, emit, expel, remove, exclude, eliminate, eradicate, wipe out, evict; dismiss, get rid of, dispose of, discharge, sack (*inf.*); depart, exile, banish, extradite, relegate; urinate, excrete; be sick, vomit, bring up (*inf.*), throw up (*inf.*), spew, retch, heave.

304 eating; drinking

n. eating, ingestion, nourishment, feeding, nutrition, consuming, partaking; feasting, devouring, banqueting; digestion, chewing, mastication; drinking, imbibation, potation; gastronomy, epicurism, gourmandise, gluttony.

eater, partaker, consumer, nibbler, chewer, glutton; drinker, sipper, drunkard; connoisseur, gourmet, gourmand, epicure.

vb. eat, consume, feed on, partake; chew, masticate, champ; bite, digest, swallow; gorge, gobble, bolt, put away (*inf.*), eat up, tuck into (*inf.*), polish off (*inf.*); devour, dispose of; breakfast, lunch, sup; eat out, dine out, wine and dine, feast, banquet, gourmandize; stuff, eat one's fill.

nourish, feed, satisfy, provide, maintain, nurture, strengthen, sustain, tend, gratify; suckle, breast-feed, give suck, nurse.

drink, gulp, take in, imbibe, wash down (*inf.*); tipple, guzzle.

305 provisions

n. provisions, food, stores, sustenance, stock, foodstuffs, groceries, subsistence, rations, board; fodder, feed, pasture, pasturage, roughage, provender; portion, helping, share, slice, quota, division, ration; larder, pantry, refrigerator, freezer.

306 food

n. food, meat and drink, foodstuffs, edibles, comestibles, provisions, nutrition, aliment, nutriment, cooking, grub (*sl.*), tuck (*sl.*); victuals, pabulum, viands; delicacy, delicatessen, luxury, delight.

portion, mouthful, piece, bite, morsel, spoonful.

meal, refreshment, fare; repast, refection; breakfast, brunch, elevenses, lunch, luncheon, packed lunch, tea, afternoon tea, high tea, dinner, supper; snack, sandwich, bite, nibble, buffet, tiffin; feast, banquet, orgy, blow-out (*inf.*), beanfeast, beano (*sl.*); picnic, barbecue; menu, bill of fare, table, cover, spread; dish, course, hors-d'oeuvre, appetizer, soup, broth, pottage, aperitif, entrée, main course, sweet, dessert, afters (*inf.*), pudding, savoury.

meat, flesh, game, poultry, fowl; egg; flour, starch; fish, sea-food; milk product, butter, cream, cheese; oil, fat, grease, blubber, margarine, vegetable fat, vegetable oil; bread, staff of life, loaf, roll; pastry, patisserie, biscuit, wafer, cracker, cake; fruit, soft fruit, berry, jam, conserve, spread, extract, jelly, gelatin; vegetable, herb, edible root, greens, tuber, root; cereal, grain; nut, dried fruit, seed, stone, kernel, pip; sweet, confectionery, sweetmeat, confections; cookery, cuisine, catering, domestic science, home economics.

adj. edible, eatable, comestible, digestible, nutritious, delicious, succulent, palatable, appetizing, satisfying, tempting, scrumptious (*inf.*); culinary; prandial, pre-prandial, postprandial.

vb. cook, prepare, fix, heat up, warm up; simmer, steam, boil, coddle; stew, casserole, braise; bake, roast, spit; grill, barbecue, broil; fry, sauté, sizzle; poach, scramble; toast, crisp, dry; curry, fricassee; dice, mince; lard, baste.

307 condiment

n. condiment, flavouring, seasoning, additive, sauce, relish, herb, plant, pickle, salt, pepper, mustard.

vb. season, flavour, spice, salt, pepper, bring out the flavour.

308 tobacco

n. tobacco, nicotine, snuff, cigarette, cigar, pipe.

vb. smoke, smoke a pipe, inhale, puff, draw, suck; take snuff.

309 drink

n. drink, beverage, potion, liquid, fluid, juice, sap, whey; infusion, decoction; soft drink, water, milk, tea, coffee, thirst-quencher, nightcap; alcóholic drink, beer, wine, champagne, toast, cocktail; sip, gulp, drop; draught, dram.

310 excretion

n. excretion, urination, evacuation, voiding, discharge, secretion, defecation, expulsion, ejection, excrement, exudation; faeces, excreta; waterworks (*sl.*); urine; bowel movement, diarrhoea, dysentry; offal, dung, droppings, manure; ordure, stool; smegma; perspiration, sweat.

adj. excretive, excretory, secretory; faecal.

vb. excrete, expel, defecate, discharge, evacuate, urinate, secrete, pass, spend a penny, go to the lavatory, be excused.

311 insertion

n. insertion, injection, infusion, introduction, insinuation.

vb. insert, put in, inject, infuse,

introduce, interpolate, include, insinuate, pour in, impregnate, stick in, throw in; force in, drag in (*inf.*), embed, install, fix, implant, bury, sink, immerse.

312 extraction

n. extraction, removal, withdrawal, expulsion, discharge, ejection, extrication, pulling; quarrying, mining; scoop, digger, chisel, extractor, gouge, excavator, dredger.

vb. extract, remove, withdraw, pull out, draw out, pluck, wrench, extricate, cut out, extort, dislodge, uproot, displace, lever out; quarry, mine, excavate, dredge, gouge, chisel; get money out of a stone (*inf.*).

313 passage

n. passage, crossing, journey, trek, voyage; way, thoroughfare, traffic, flow; traffic control, traffic regulation, rule of the road, highway code.

vb. pass, cross, traverse, go through, penetrate, emerge, proceed, drive, weave, thread, ford, span.

314 overstepping

n. overstepping, overrunning, infestation, invasion; transcendence; encroachment, violation, transgression.

vb. go beyond, overstep, encroach, go too far, exceed the limit, overrun, overshoot; invade, infest, plague, swarm, ravage; excel, surpass, outdo, transcend, rise above, eclipse; outdistance, outstrip; trespass, violate, infringe, transgress.

315 shortcoming

n. shortcoming, inadequacy, imperfection, falling short; loss, deficit, shortfall, shortage, dearth, default; need, lack, requirement, deficiency, fault, weakness, lapse, weak point; privation, destitution.

adj. short, deficient, missing, lacking, inadequate, not up to scratch; imperfect, incomplete.

vb. fall short, come short, be deficient, fail, need, miss, lack; lag behind, lose ground; collapse, come to nothing.

316 ascent

n. ascent, ascension, climbing, rise, mount, lift, jump, surge, towering, soaring; ladder, step-ladder, steps, stairs, staircase, escalator, moving staircase, travelator, lift, elevator; hill, mountain, acclivity.

adj. ascending, rising, upward.

vb. ascend, go up, rise, tower, soar, rocket, surge, grow, sprout; take off; climb, mount, scale, surmount, progress, top, scale, conquer, scramble, clamber, creep, work one's way up.

317 descent

n. descent, drop, fall, lapse, swoop, sinking, plunge, downfall, tumble; slump, recession, reduction, declination; subsidence, landslide, hole, cave, chasm.

adj. descending, downward.

vb. descend, go down, fall, drop, subside, decline, swoop, plunge, slump, sink, droop, land, come down, touch down; parachute; crash-land; splash down; topple, push over; tumble, overbalance, lose one's balance, stumble, capsize, turn over, tilt, lurch.

318 elevation

n. elevation, lift, raising, erection; exaltation, ennoblement, sublimation.

adj. raised, lifted, elevated, high, aerial, tall, erect, upstanding, upraised; exalted, noble, sublime, lofty.

vb. lift, elevate, raise, pick up, pull up, help up, uplift, hoist, heave, erect;

support, prop; leaven; boost; glorify, heighten, enhance, exalt.

get up, stand up, get to one's feet, arise; jump up, spring to one's feet.

319 depression

n. depression, lowering, dip; hole, cavity; curtsy, bow, genuflexion; debasement.

adj. depressed; smoothed; even; sitting, sedentary, settled, inactive; prostrate.

vb. depress, lower, press, squash; settle, sink, dip, sag, droop, decline; push down, bring low, ground; fell, cut down, chop down, topple, pull down, demolish, raze to the ground.

drop, let fall, shed, loosen, release, let go, spill; fall, drip, dribble, leak, ooze, seep, drain, permeate, percolate, filter.

sit down, be seated, squat, crouch, kneel, genuflect; perch, roost; bend over, stoop, incline, hunch, bow, curtsy.

320 leap

n. leap, jump, dance, spring, vault, bound, hop, rise, pounce, hurdle, leapfrog, saltation.

adj. lively, frisky, saltatory.

vb. leap, jump, spring, vault, dance, hop, bounce, skip, leapfrog, surge, rise.

321 plunge

n. plunge, jump, rush, dive, drop, fall, plummet, leap, pitch, dip, swoop; ducking, immersion, submergence.

vb. plunge, dive, dip, jump, fall, pounce, cast down; duck, submerge, immerse, drown, souse, dunk; go down, sink, go under; splash down; crash-land; go to the bottom.

322 circulation

n. circulation, circumnavigation; spiral; compass, lap, course, circuit, loop, round trip, orbit, ambit, full circle; by-pass, ring road, detour, diversion.

vb. circle, circulate, go around, revolve around, circumnavigate, circumscribe, circumambulate, lap, tour, ring, gird, wind; by-pass.
see also **250**

323 rotation
n. rotation, revolution, turn, circle, spin, cycle, roll, circuit, whirl, twirl, gyration, pirouette; spiral, orbit; whirlpool, eddy, whirlwind, cyclone, tornado, vortex.

adj. rotary, gyratory, rotating, revolving.

vb. rotate, revolve, twist, circle, circulate, spin, cycle, roll, whirl, twirl, loop, swing, spiral; swivel, pivot, swirl, eddy; pirouette.

324 evolution
n. evolution, development, growth, unfolding, unfurling; disentanglement; evolutionism, Darwinism; missing link.

adj. evolving, evolutionary.

vb. evolve, develop, grow, emerge; advance, progress, mature; unfold, open out, unfurl, unroll, unwind, uncurl, uncover, unwrap; unravel, disentangle, free, release, straighten.

325 oscillation
n. oscillation, fluctuation, vacillation, wavering, undulation, quiver, shake, swing, lurch, roll; vibration, tremor, thunder; faltering, hesitancy, uncertainty.

pulse, pulsation, throb, beat, drumming, pound, surge, palpitation, flutter, ripple, wave; earthquake, seismology.

pendulum, oscillator, vibrator, shuttle, see-saw, cradle, rocking-chair, rocking-horse.

adj. oscillating, fluctuating, throbbing, pulsatory; seismic; vacillating, hesitant, undecided, irresolute.

vb. oscillate, alternate, fluctuate, vacillate, vibrate, pulse, throb, beat, pound, surge, flutter, wave, waver, undulate, librate; nod, swing, sway, see-saw, wobble, totter, lurch, roll, rock, quake, quiver, teeter, zigzag; ebb and flow, back and fill; hesitate, falter.

adv. back and forth, to and fro, up and down, from side to side.

326 agitation
n. agitation, disturbance, vibration; jar, jolt, jog, bump, bounce; shudder, quake, tremble, wobble, tremor, jerk; shakes, jitters (*inf.*), shivers, heebie-jeebies (*sl.*), butterflies (*inf.*), apprehension; fit, convulsion, spasm, palsy, seizure, fever, attack, stroke; itch, twitch.

confusion, tumult, turmoil, turbulence; excitation, melodrama, emotion, commotion, fuss, bother, flap (*inf.*), dither (*inf.*), tizzy (*sl.*).

adj. agitated, shaking, unsteady, wavering, shaky, tremulous; jelly-like, itchy, twitching, nervous, apprehensive, jittery (*inf.*).

vb. shake, tremble, vibrate, quiver, quake, shiver, chatter, shudder, palpitate, flap, toss, flutter, totter, stagger; itch, twitch; twinkle, flicker, glimmer, sparkle.

agitate, sway, rock, swing, beat, disturb, jolt, jar, jerk, bounce; convulse, seize, throw a fit; go out of control.

III Matter

A Matter in general

327 materiality

n. materiality, substantiality, concreteness, corporeality, corporality, tangibility; materialism, Marxism, dialectical materialism.

matter, body, material, stuff, mass, flesh and blood, flesh; thing, object, something, article, commodity, item, being; element, atom, molecule; component, part, ingredient, factor.

adj. material, substantial; corporeal, bodily; physical, concrete, tangible, real, objective, somatic; materialistic, unspiritual, worldly, mundane.

vb. materialize, realize, become real, take form, become flesh, take flesh, objectify, substantialize.

328 immateriality

n. immateriality, insubstantiality, dematerialization, intangibility, disembodiment; spirituality, otherworldliness; shadow, ghost.

adj. immaterial, incorporeal, insubstantial, bodiless, disembodied, intangible, ethereal, shadowy, ghostly, unreal; otherworldly, spiritual.

vb. dematerialize, disintegrate, disembody; spiritualize.

329 universe

n. universe, creation, space, outer space, cosmos, galaxy; world, earth, sphere, globe, orb, nature; heavenly body, celestial body, planet, planetoid, asteroid, moon, satellite, falling star, shooting star, meteor, meteorite, star, sun, constellation, nebula, quasar, pulsar, black hole; heavens, firmament, vault; atmosphere, air, ether, sky, night sky; astronomy, astrophysics, stargazing; observatory, planetarium, telescope; astrology, horoscope, signs of the Zodiac; cosmology, cosmogony, cosmography, geography; map, atlas.

adj. universal, cosmic, galactic; terrestrial, earthly, worldly, mundane; heavenly, celestial, empyrean; extraterrestrial, planetary, solar, astral, lunar; astronomical; geographical.

330 weight

n. gravity, gravitation, attraction; weight, heaviness, pressure, force, mass, bulk; ballast, load, freight, sinker, counterweight, paperweight, stone, rock, sandbags, anchor, plumb; burden.

balance, scales, weighing machine, weighbridge.

adj. heavy, weighty, ponderous, bulky, cumbersome, top-heavy; burdensome, oppressive, troublesome.

vb. weigh, balance, poise, measure, put on the scales, counterpoise, counterbalance; weigh down, weight, load, overload; burden, overwhelm, saddle.

331 lightness

n. lightness, levity, weightlessness, imponderability; buoy, cork; leaven, lightener, ferment, yeast.

adj. light, insubstantial; underweight; weightless; feathery, dainty, airy, fluffy; gentle, delicate, soft; floatable, buoyant, unsinkable; lightweight, summerweight; small, portable.

vb. be light, float, surface, swim; levitate, defy gravity; lighten, raise, ferment; unburden, take off, remove, unload, disencumber, jettison.

B Inorganic matter

332 density

n. density, solidity, thickness, compactness, concreteness, heaviness, concentration, congestion, substantiality; incompressibility, impenetrability, impermeability; consolidation, crystallization, coagulation, solidification, thickening, stiffening; mass, solid, body, substance, lump, conglomerate.

adj. dense, solid, thick, compact, close, heavy, impenetrable, impermeable, condensed, compressed; clotted, curdled; frozen; indivisible, insoluble.

vb. solidify, thicken, coagulate, freeze, clot, fix, crystallize, harden, stiffen, set, congeal, jell (*inf.*), curdle; petrify, ossify; compress, condense, compact.
   see also 50

333 rarity
n. rarity, thinness, fineness; low pressure, vacuum, emptiness; rarefaction, attenuation.

adj. rare, thin, light, rarefied, fine, attenuated, airy, ethereal; weak, tenuous, sparse, shrill, flimsy, fragile, insubstantial, subtle; empty, void.

vb. rarefy, lessen, reduce pressure, purify, refine, thin, attenuate.

334 hardness
n. hardness, stiffness, firmness, toughness, rigidity, solidity, impenetrability, inflexibility; hardening, stiffening.

adj. hard, solid, thick, dense, compact; rigid, firm, stiff, taut, tight; tough, unyielding, unbreakable, impenetrable, unbending, inflexible, inelastic, unmalleable, impermeable.

vb. harden, toughen, strengthen, set, stiffen, temper; concentrate, consolidate, solidify, crystallize, freeze,

coagulate, congeal, fossilize, ossify, petrify, starch.
   see also 537

335 softness
n. softness, penetrability, flexibility, plasticity, tractability, suppleness, pliancy, litheness; looseness, laxity.

adj. soft, smooth, fluffy, spongy, mellow; gentle, delicate; flimsy, limp; tender, pliant, flexible, plastic, elastic, supple, pliable, lithe, limber, mouldable.

vb. soften, ease, modify, temper, tenderize; subdue, assuage, mollify, appease; knead, mash; give, yield, relax, relent.

336 elasticity
n. elasticity, flexibility, pliability, springiness, spring, bounce, resilience, buoyancy; stretch, extensibility, tensility.

adj. elastic, flexible, pliant, resilient, buoyant; stretching, extensile, tensile.

vb. stretch; spring, bounce.

337 toughness
n. toughness, durability, strength, tenacity, cohesion; bone, gristle, cartilage.

adj. tough, durable, hard, firm, solid, robust, strong, stiff, enduring, unbreakable, tenacious; impervious, unyielding, resistant; fibrous, gristly, sinewy.

vb. toughen, strengthen, stiffen, harden.

338 brittleness
n. brittleness, frailty, fragility, delicacy.

adj. brittle, delicate, frail; breakable, fragile; crispy, crumbly; flimsy, frangible; shaky, unsteady; friable.

vb. break, break easily, split, snap,

shatter, fragment, burst, fall to pieces, splinter, crumble.

see also 48

339 texture

n. texture, pattern, weave, organization, composition, constitution, make-up, form, structure; feel, sense, taste, shape, mould, fibre, fabric, web, weft, tissue.

adj. structural, organizational, constructional, tectonic; textural, granular.

340 powderiness

n. powderiness, pulverulence; crumbling, pulverization; powder, dust, grain, particle, granule, crumb, flake, pollen.

adj. powdery, fine, granulated, pulverized, pulverulent; dusty; impalpable; crumbling, friable.

vb. grind, crush, pulverize, granulate, pound, beat, grate, scrape, crunch, crumble, atomize.

341 friction

n. friction, rubbing, abrasion, erosion, wearing away, grinding, filing, irritation; massage, polishing; stroke.

adj. frictional, abrasive, rubbing.

vb. rub, abrade, scour, grate, graze, rasp, chafe, grind, file, scrape, scrub; wear away, erode; polish, shine, smooth, massage; burnish; brush, clean, wipe.

342 lubrication

n. lubrication, anointment, unction; lubricant, grease, oil, wax, fat, ointment, cream, lotion, balm, salve, unguent; petrol, juice (*sl.*).

vb. lubricate, grease, oil, cream, daub, smear, coat, rub, anoint.

343 fluidity

n. fluidity, liquidity, wateriness, juiciness, solubility, dilution; fluid, liquid, liquor, vapour, solution, solvent, drink, flow.

adj. fluid, liquid, running, flowing, molten, liquefied, watery, juicy, liquescent.

vb. flow, run, pour, stream, swell; liquefy.

344 gaseity

n. gaseity, gaseousness, vaporousness, aeration; gas, vapour, steam, fume, air, smoke, fluid.

adj. gaseous, vaporous, vapory, gassy, gas-like, steaming, aeriform, airy, light, windy, volatile.

vb. gasify, aerate.

345 liquefaction

n. liquefaction, solubility, dissolution, thawing; solvent, dissolvent.

adj. runny, molten, liquefied, melted, thawed, disintegrated; liquefacient, soluble.

vb. liquefy, dissolve, melt, run, thaw, defrost, fuse, flux, condense, fluidify, fluidize, deliquesce, disintegrate.

346 vaporization

n. vaporization, evaporation, condensation, sublimation, gasification, volatilization, distillation; vapour, moisture, exhalation, mist, smoke, sublimate.

adj. vaporous, steaming, steamy, gassy, volatile.

vb. vaporize, evaporate, sublimate, distil, diffuse, dissipate, gasify, exhale, smoke, fume, steam.

347 water

n. water, liquid, rain, wet, dampness; ice, steam, water vapour.

adj. watery, aquatic, aqueous,

hydrated, liquid, fluid, wet, moist, hydrous, aqua-, hydro-.

see also 349

348 air

n. air, oxygen, fresh air; airing, exposure, ventilation, air conditioning, aeration; atmosphere, stratosphere, ozone, ether, sky; pneumatics, aerodynamics.

weather, climate, elements; meteorology, forecasting.

adj. airy, aerial; exposed, ventilated, open, aerated; draughty, breezy, windy; pneumatic, aero-; metereological.

vb. air, aerate, ventilate, open, refresh, freshen, cool, aerify, purify, fan.

see also 359

349 moisture

n. moisture, humidity, dampness, wetness, precipitation; drip, damp, dew, rain, wet; moistening, saturation, wettening, humidification.

adj. moist, damp, wet, humid, muggy, dank, misty; saturated, soaked, sodden, waterlogged, awash, drowned, drenched, wet through, like a drowned rat.

vb. moisten, dampen, wet, humidify; sprinkle, dabble, shower, dip, sponge, splash; saturate, drench, soak, bathe, souse, steep, stream, seep, sog; duck, immerse, submerge; waterlog, drown, flood, swamp, inundate, deluge.

350 dryness

n. dryness, aridity, aridness, parchedness, desiccation, dehydration; thirst, drought.

adj. dry, arid, parched, unmoistened, rainless, sapless, evaporated; barren, desert, dusty, baked, scorched,

bleached; dried, dehydrated, thirsty; waterproof, rainproof, watertight.

vb. dry, dehydrate, freeze-dry, dripdry; desiccate, parch, bake, scorch, torrefy; air, evaporate; shrivel, wither; soak up, absorb.

351 ocean

n. ocean, sea, deep, brine, high seas; oceanography.

adj. oceanic, marine, maritime, pelagic; oceanographical.

352 land

n. land, terrain, *terra firma*, mainland, continent; inland, interior; peninsula, neck, isthmus; ground, soil, earth, gravel, sand, rock, pebble; fields, pasture; shore, beach, seaside, strand, bank, coastline, seaboard.

adj. terrestrial, earthy; inland, interior, landlocked, central; coastal, seaside, littoral, riverside, riparian.

353 gulf

n. gulf, inlet, bay, estuary, bight, mouth, creek, lagoon, sound, fiord, firth, loch, strait, narrows, arm, kyle; cove, cave.

354 lake

n. lake, tarn, loch, lagoon, pool, pond, creek, mere, inland sea, reservoir, basin; puddle.

355 marsh

n. marsh, fen, swamp, mire, bog, quagmire, quicksand, morass, slough, moor, mud.

adj. marshy, soft, fenny, swampy, boggy, wet, waterlogged, squelchy, slushy, muddy, miry, paludal.

356 plain

n. plain, expanse, open country, flat, lowland, champaign, grassland; meadow, field, grass, pasture; steppe, prairie, savannah, pampa, llano; moor, moorland, common, heath, wold; upland, plateau, tableland, downs; tundra, veld.

357 island

n. island, isle, islet, holm, eyot, ait, archipelago; reef, atoll, ridge, sandbank, cay, key.

358 water in motion

n. river, watercourse, waterway, tributary, branch, fork, effluent; stream, brook, rivulet, beck, runnel, rill, runlet, bourn, creek.

tide, current, flow, course, undercurrent; spring, fountain, spout, gush, rush, jet, outpouring, uprising; whirlpool, eddy, vortex, swirl, maelstrom; wash, backwash.

wave, billow, swell, roller, surge, crest, ripple, undulation, breaker, tidal wave, white-caps, white horses; waterfall, cataract, fall, shoot, cascade, torrent, rapids, weir.

rain, rainfall, precipitation, drizzle, shower, downpour, thunderstorm, cloudburst, flood, deluge, inundation, monsoon; mist.

adj. runny, streaming; rainy, moist, wet, showery, cloudy, thundery, stormy; torrential.

vb. flow, run, stream, sweep, rush; gush, well, spurt, squirt, jet, spout, issue, flood, inundate; wave, undulate, billow, swell, ripple, ebb; swirl, eddy, surge, roll, whirl, tumble; dash, break, splash; drop, drip, seep, leak, trickle, dribble, gurgle; spill, overflow, spew, exude; fall, cascade; drain, empty, clear, tap, expel, deplete, decant, bleed.

rain, pour, patter, spit, drizzle, shower.

359 air in motion

n. wind, draught, current, breeze, whisk, whiff, puff, flutter, waft, zephyr;

gust, blast, flurry, flaw; gale, storm, squall, blizzard, whirlwind, cyclone, typhoon, tornado, hurricane, tempest; trade wind, mistral, föhn.

breathing, respiration, inhalation, expiration, exhalation, afflatus; breath, gasp, sigh, pant, cough, sneeze, wheeze.

adj. windy, open, exposed, fresh, blustery, squally, gusty, stormy, tempestuous; draughty, well-ventilated; wheezy, asthmatic.

vb. blow, breeze, whiff, waft, flutter, flap, buffet, sweep, whisk, fling; blast, rush, roar, howl, wail, stream, whirl; breathe, respire, inhale, exhale, expire, puff, pant, gasp; sigh; cough, sneeze, wheeze; pump, inflate, blow up, swell, fill.

360 water channel

n. conduit, channel, way, passage, bed, ditch, trench, trough, moat; course, canal, aqueduct; tunnel, pipe, pipeline, tube, main, duct, culvert; spout, tap, funnel, siphon; drain, drainpipe, gutter, sewer; flume, gully, cloaca.

361 air-pipe

n. air-pipe, shaft, tube; vent, chimney, flue, ventilator.

362 semiliquidity

n. semiliquidity, viscosity, glutinousness, stickiness, adhesiveness; semiliquid, glue, paste, size, colloid, emulsion, syrup.

adj. semiliquid, semifluid, gelatinous, viscous, viscid, glutinous, coagulated, slimy, syrupy, creamy, sticky, tacky, slushy, gummy, colloid.

363 bubble; cloud

n. bubble, globule, sac, froth, foam, spray, surf, spume; fizz, head; lather, suds; effervescence, fermentation, bubbling.

cloud, haze, haziness, mist, fog, smog, pea-souper (*inf.*), film.

adj. bubbly, foaming, bubbling, soapy, effervescent, sparkling, fizzy, spumous, spumy; cloudy, overcast, dull, grey, unclear, murky, gloomy, dim, misty, hazy, foggy, nebulous.

vb. effervesce, bubble, boil, fizz, foam, ferment.

364 pulpiness

n. pulpiness, sponginess, softness, succulence; pulp, mash, sponge, paste, pap, mulch, mush, jelly, dough, batter, poultice.

adj. pulpy, mushy, doughy, soggy, spongy, pulpous, ripe, fleshy, succulent; thick, smooth.

vb. pulp, mash, crush.

365 unctuousness

n. unctuousness, oiliness, greasiness; oil, fat, grease, blubber; unction, oil, unguent, embrocation, salve, nard, ointment, lubricant, balm, emollient, remedy, cream; resin, gum, pitch, varnish, lacquer, shellac, asphalt, bitumen.

adj. unctuous, oily, greasy, fatty, unguent, creamy.

vb. grease, oil, lubricate; resin, varnish; anoint.

C Organic matter

366 animate matter

n. creation, nature, animals, plants, fauna, flora; creature, organism, cell, protoplasm; biology, natural history, nature study, ecology, genetics, evolution, biochemistry, anatomy, physiology, botany, zoology.

adj. animate, organic, biological.

367 inorganic matter

n. mineral, rock, deposit, ore, metal, coal; geology, mineralogy, metallurgy.

adj. inorganic, inanimate, mineral, metallurgical.

368 life

n. life, existence, being; organism, human, body, creature, man, person, individual, personage, mortal.

soul, spirit, life-blood, breath, heart; élan, verve; vivification, animation, liveliness, vigour, vitality, force, energy.

adj. living, alive, surviving, in the flesh, vital; lively, animated, vigorous, vivacious, forceful, energetic, spirited, alive and kicking, active.

vb. live, exist, be, have life, breathe, respire; move, subsist; be spared, survive.

be born, come to life, come into the world, see the light; bear, beget, conceive, give birth to, bring to life.

vivify, quicken, animate, reanimate, vitalize, enliven, revive, breathe life into.

369 death

n. death, mortality; decease, dying, passing, departure, end, expiration, exit, extinction, parting, separation, release, homecall; loss, bereavement; fatality; demise, dissolution.

last hour, death bed, last breath, swan-song; death list, death toll, casualty list; obituary; the dead, departed, deceased, ancestors, forefathers, those gone before.

adj. mortal, sick, perishing, deathly, moribund, at death's door, on one's last legs; dead, deceased, departed, late, lamented; lifeless, breathless; defunct, extinct, cold, extinguished; terminated, ended, exterminated, lost.

vb. die, depart, go, expire, pass away, give up the ghost, breathe one's last, go the way of all flesh, be taken, kick the bucket (*sl.*); perish, succumb, come to nothing, be no more; be killed, lose one's life; push up daisies (*inf.*).

370 killing

n. killing, slaying, slaughter, destruction, assassination, murder, homicide, manslaughter; bloodshed, carnage, massacre, genocide, butchery, holocaust, liquidation, extermination, annihilation, decimation; shooting, knifing, lynching, poisoning, execution, hanging, strangulation, electrocution, crucifixion, burning, drowning, vivisection; euthanasia, mercy killing; abortion; suicide, self-destruction, hara-kiri, kamikaze.

killer, murderer, assassin, slayer, butcher, cut-throat, poisoner, strangler; gunman, terrorist, gangster, homicidal maniac; hangman, executioner.

adj. killing, lethal, fatal, mortal, deadly, destructive; homicidal, murderous, internecine; suicidal.

vb. kill, murder, slay, destroy, take life, put to death, bump off (*sl.*), knock off (*sl.*), do in (*sl.*), do away with (*inf.*), slaughter, assassinate, massacre, butcher, mow down (*inf.*), gun down (*inf.*), liquidate, annihilate, decimate, exterminate; execute, behead, guillotine, decapitate, shoot, gun, knife, hang, lynch; poison; strangle, suffocate, choke, asphyxiate; put to sleep (*inf.*), put down, put away.

kill oneself, commit suicide, take one's life, do oneself in (*sl.*), blow one's brains out, shoot oneself, cut one's throat.

371 corpse

n. corpse, remains, body, carcass, skeleton, relics, ashes, dust, mummy, cadaver, stiff (*sl.*).

adj. cadaverous, corpse-like, deathlike, deathly, pale.

372 burial

n. burial, funeral, interment, entombment, sepulture; cremation, incineration; embalment, mummification.

burial service, funeral rites, last rites, mourning, obsequies; requiem, elegy, last post, knell, passing bell; epitaph, obituary, in memoriam, RIP; coffin, urn, sarcophagus, pall, mummy case.

mortuary, morgue; undertaker, funeral director; gravestone, headstone, tombstone, monument, memorial; tomb, grave, sepulchre, vault, crypt, mausoleum, barrow; burial ground, graveyard, churchyard, God's acre, cemetery, catacomb, necropolis; pyre, crematorium; war memorial, cenotaph; exhumation, disinterment.

adj. buried, interred; funereal, funeral, mourning, mournful, sad.

vb. bury, inter, inhume, entomb, enshrine, embalm, lay out, lay to rest, sepulture; cremate; exhume, disinter, unearth.

373 animality; animal

n. animality, fauna, zoology; animal, creature, beast, vertebrate, invertebrate; quadruped, biped, man; mammal, marsupial; carnivore, herbivore, omnivore; fish, amphibian, mollusc, crustacean; bird, fowl, bird of prey, waterfowl; insect; reptile; cattle, herd, livestock, poultry, game; pet, domestic animal; rodent, vermin, parasite.

adj. animal, zoological, mammalian; piscine, fishy, amphibian; avian.

374 vegetability; plant

n. vegetability, vegetation, botany;

plant, shrub; plantation, shrubbery, undergrowth, corn, grain, cereal, crop, field; flower, bloom, bud, petal, blossom; flower-bed, garden; foliage; foliation, leafage; grass, pasture, verdure, sod, turf, lawn; herb; weed; tree, sapling, scion; branch, limb, bough, twig, sprig, spray, shoot, stem, stalk, leaf; wood, forest, bush, jungle; copse, spinney, coppice, woodland, thicket, covert, arboretum; forestry, dendrology, conservation; seed, root, bulb.

adj. vegetal, vegetative, botanical, horticultural, floral, verdant, grassy, weedy, arboreal.

375 zoology
n. zoology, life science, anthropology, anatomy, physiology, ichthyology, ornithology, bird-watching, entomology, embryology, taxonomy.
adj. zoological, ornithological.

376 botany
n. botany, plant science, horticulture, ecology, phytology.
adj. botanical, horticultural.

377 management of animals
n. animal husbandry, breeding, stockbreeding, grazing, taming, domestication.

farm, ranch, homestead; fishery, aquarium; zoo, zoological gardens; veterinary science, vet; shepherd, herdsman, herd, cattleherd, cowherd.

vb. keep, husband, breed, rear, raise, herd, drive, ranch, farm, tend, shepherd; feed, fodder, graze, fatten, market; shear, chip, fleece; milk; tame, domesticate, train; groom.

378 agriculture
n. agriculture, farming, cultivation, horticulture, gardening, growing, crop raising, husbandry; strip farming, rotation crops, contour ploughing; landscape gardening.

farm, ranch, homestead, holding, smallholding, grange; kibbutz; farmland, meadow, grassland, farmstead, estate, croft, enclosure, land, field, soil, patch, plot, allotment, plantation; garden, orchard, nursery; greenhouse, vineyard, arboretum.

farmer, husbandman, agriculturalist, cultivator, tiller, planter, grower, rancher, homesteadman, peasant, serf, hiredman, labourer, farmhand; gardener, nurseryman, horticulturalist, landscape gardener.

adj. agrarian, farming, agricultural, rustic, rural, peasant; horticultural, garden.

vb. cultivate, till; fertilize, manure; water, irrigate; dig, plough, harrow; seed, sow, broadcast, disseminate, plant, drill, bed, transplant; weed, hoe; graft; harvest, reap, gather in, glean, winnow, thresh, mow, cut, scythe, bind, stack, pick, pluck.

379 mankind
n. mankind, humanity, human race, human beings, populace, population, the world, flesh; person, man, human being, individual, creature, mortal, body, earthling, *homo sapiens*, Adam, anthropoid; people, public, folk.

society, community, civilization, politics; nation, state, body politic, nationality, statehood; chauvinism, nationalism, imperialism; anthropology, social anthropology, ethnology, sociology.

adj. human, mortal; individual, personal; social, civilized; political, national, state, general, public, civil, federal, social, communal, societal, civic; nationalistic, chauvinist, racialist.

380 male

n. male, man, gentleman, sir; chap, fellow, guy (*sl.*), bloke (*inf.*), boy; virility, masculinity, manliness, manhood.

male animal, cock, drake, gander, dog, tom-cat, hart, stag, stallion, billygoat, ox, bull; gelding.

adj. male, masculine; manly, virile; gentlemanly.

381 female

n. female, woman, lady, girl; madam, miss; fair sex, weaker sex; femininity, womanliness, girlishness, womanhood; feminism, women's lib; effeminacy; womankind.

female animal, hen, duck, goose, bitch, she-dog, filly, ewe, sow, hind, doe, mare, nanny-goat, cow.

adj. female, feminine, girlish, womanly, lady-like; effeminate.

IV Intellect

1 Formation of ideas

A Intellectual operations in general

382 intellect

n. intellect, mind, brain, consciousness, mentality, intelligence, intellectuality, instinct, faculties; perception, conception, capacity, judgment, understanding, reasoning, genius, wisdom; psychology, behaviourism; psychiatry, psychotherapy.

soul, spirit, psyche, heart, individuality, personality, conscience,

self, ego, id, superego, unconscious, subconscious.

adj. mental, intellectual, conceptional, abstract, perceptual, critical, rational, conscious, cognitive, cerebral, intelligent; psychological, psychic, subconscious, subliminal; spiritual.

vb. conceive, cognize, perceive, reason, judge; realize, sense, mark, note.

see also 434

383 absence of intellect

n. unintellectuality, unintelligence, imbecility, stupidity, shallowness, mindlessness, brainlessness.

adj. unintellectual, unintelligent, empty-headed, mindless, brainless.

see also 435

384 thought

n. thought, cogitation, concentration, brain-work; reflection, meditation, rumination, contemplation, thoughtfulness, brooding, pondering, absorption, preoccupation, deliberation; consideration, perception, appreciation, discernment, observation, reasoning, concluding.

adj. thoughtful, pensive, contemplative, reflective, studious; absorbed, engrossed, wrapped up in, dreamy; introspective; discerning, penetrating, intellectual.

vb. think, cogitate, consider, give thought to, concentrate, reflect, meditate, deliberate, ponder, muse, ruminate, contemplate, brood, turn over in one's mind, mull, study, examine, bear in mind, put on one's thinking cap (*inf.*), have on one's mind, take it into one's head (*inf.*); esteem, appraise, weigh up; philosophize, reconsider.

occur to, come to mind, strike, suggest itself, enter one's head.

385 absence of thought

n. thoughtlessness, irrationality, incomprehensibility, folly, senselessness, ignorance, inattention, inconsideration, carelessness, neglect.

adj. thoughtless, irrational, unreasoning, incomprehensible, foolish, blank, vacant, switched off (*inf.*).

vb. not think about, ignore, forget, dismiss, get off one's mind, get out of one's mind, get out of one's head; think no more of, not give another thought to, not give a second thought, not enter one's head.

386 idea

n. idea, notion, concept, conception, thought, mental impression, image, impression; conjecture, fancy, guess, theory, hypothesis, postulate; observation, opinion, assessment, plan.

see also 420

387 topic

n. topic, subject, problem, matter, question; argument, theme, burden, concern, thesis, proposition, thrust, *leitmotif*, issue, point, point in question, moot point.

B Preliminary conditions and operations

388 curiosity

n. curiosity, interest, concern, regard; thirst, quest, desire, eagerness, inclination; inquisitiveness, intrusiveness, nosiness (*sl.*), prying.

questioner; busy-body, snoop, intruder, meddler, Nosy Parker (*sl.*); gossip, backbiter, chatterbox, scandalmonger.

adj. curious, interested, concerned, into (*inf.*), questioning; inquisitive, searching, poking, scrutinizing; intrusive, prying, snooping, meddlesome, nosy (*sl.*).

vb. enquire, question, investigate, seek; show interest, be into (*inf.*), have a thing about (*inf.*); intrude, pry, snoop, meddle, gossip, chatter, backbite.

389 incuriosity

n. incuriosity, apathy, dislike, disinclination.

adj. incurious, unconcerned, inattentive, apathetic, indifferent, uninquisitive, uninterested, bored.

vb. ignore, disregard, be blind to, dismiss, take no interest in, not care less.

390 attention

n. attention, regard, notice, observation, inspection; consideration, study, attentiveness; assiduousness, diligence; mindfulness, heed, heedfulness, vigilance; concentration, preoccupation.

adj. attentive, mindful; heeding, wary, vigilant; considerate, observant; studious, assiduous, diligent.

vb. pay attention, listen, catch, give heed to, observe, notice, take notice, mind, heed, look to, regard, note, take into account; consider, study, inspect, examine, mark, scrutinize, concentrate on; drink in (*inf.*), lap up (*inf.*), hang on someone's every word; lose oneself in; keep one's ear to the ground (*inf.*); attract, draw, pull, focus.

391 inattention

n. inattention, carelessness, inconsideration, unconcern, heedlessness, thoughtlessness; slackness, indolence; neglect, disregard; indifference, coolness, coldness, detachment; absent-mindedness, wandering.

adj. inattentive, careless, inconsiderate, thoughtless, heedless, unobservant; negligent, indifferent, cool, cold, detached; absent-minded, distracted.

vb. be inattentive, dream, daydream, let one's mind wander; not catch, miss, disregard, overlook, neglect; go in one ear and out the other; distract, divert, draw away, turn away, call away, detract, attract from, beguile; upset, disconcert.

392 care

n. care, concern, regard, thought, heed, consideration, solicitude, thoughtfulness, pains; carefulness, scrupulousness, prudence, judiciousness, wisdom; watchfulness, vigilance, alertness; forethought, precaution, caution.

exactness, particularity, thoroughness, meticulousness, neatness, fastidiousness, conscientiousness; economy, conservation, frugality, management, husbandry, stewardship.

oversight, direction, surveillance, supervision, inspection, protection, guarding.

adj. careful, concerned, thoughtful, considerate, courteous, kind, solicitous; prudent, judicious, wise, discreet, unobtrusive, self-possessed, watchful, sober, alert, awake, circumspect, vigilant; diplomatic, politic.

thorough, rigorous, particular, precise, exact, exacting, discriminating, conscientious, meticulous, punctilious, scrupulous; neat, tidy, fussy, finicky; pedantic, fastidious, religious; assiduous, diligent, painstaking, dependable, faithful; economical, sparing, frugal, thrifty (*inf.*).

vb. be careful, mind, heed, tend, look after, take care of; watch, observe; superintend, supervise, direct, manage, stand over; baby-sit, chaperon; keep vigil; keep tabs on, follow up, protect, support, guard.

393 neglect

n. neglect, carelessness, unconcern, disregard, inconsideration, negligence, neglectfulness, apathy, indifference, omission, dereliction, failure, procrastination; imprudence, rashness, hastiness.

adj. negligent, careless, inconsiderate, unthinking, thoughtless, unmindful, forgetful, oblivious; remiss, lax, inattentive; lackadaisical, imprudent, unguarded, hasty, rash, unwary, reckless, unheeding, injudicious, unwise; apathetic, indifferent, casual, slipshod, lazy; wasteful, extravagant, immoderate.

vb. neglect, omit, miss, forget, dismiss, reject, leave undone, lose sight of, evade, gloss over, skip, skimp; disregard, ignore, overlook, not look at, pass over, make light of, brush aside, laugh off, pooh-pooh, shut one's eyes to, give the go-by, turn a blind eye to.

see also **920**

394 enquiry

n. enquiry, inquiry, examination, investigation, study, analysis, search, probe, quest, perusal; checking, scrutiny, review, inspection; question, query, request, invitation, petition, challenge, feeler; experiment, quiz, test, exam, viva, questionnaire; interrogation, interview, dialogue, cross-examination, grilling, catechism.

questioner, examiner, enquirer, interrogator, interviewer, researcher, investigator, canvasser, pollster.

adj. inquiring, inquisitive, curious, nosy (*sl.*); exploratory, fact-finding.

vb. enquire, ask, put a question, pose, put it to; call upon, request, invite, challenge, charge, bid, petition, canvass; question, interrogate, quiz, cross-examine, interview, grill; seek, look for, search, hunt, turn inside out, peruse; sniff out (*inf.*), smell out; investigate, examine, study, inspect, analyse, probe, scrutinize, check, review, monitor; try, hear; pry, snoop, spy.

395 answer

n. answer, reply, response, acknowledgement; comeback, feedback, rebuttal, rejoinder, retort; repartee, backchat, retaliation.

answerer, replier, correspondent, examinee, candidate.

adj. answering, responsive.

vb. answer, reply, respond, come back to, write back, acknowledge, remark, rejoin, retort, answer back, rebut.

396 experiment

n. experiment, test, research; observation, analysis, inspection, operation, diagnosis, exercise; check, verification, proof, sifting; rehearsal, practice run, trial run, test case, pilot, pilot scheme; feeler, probe; speculation, guess, conjecture, trial and error, hit and miss, shot in the dark, hypothesis; sounding board, guinea pig.

researcher, research worker, scientist, boffin (*sl.*), back-room boy, experimenter, experimentalist, speculator.

adj. experimental, hypothetical; tentative, trial, provisional, temporary, probationary, preliminary, preparatory, unproved, speculative, trial, test.

vb. experiment, investigate, study, examine, scrutinize, explore, research,

search, sound out, prove; analyse, diagnose; check, verify, prove; guess, speculate, hypothesize; put out a feeler, see which way the wind is blowing, spy out the land.

397 comparison

n. comparison, juxtaposition; weighing, estimation, measurement; relation, connection, association, balance, match, parallel, parallelism, correspondence, equation; identification, resemblance, similarity, likening, analogy, illustration, example, picture, metaphor, simile, allegory; contrast, opposition.

vb. compare, juxtapose, parallel, draw a parallel between, put side by side; measure, weigh, confront, collate; liken, relate, associate, link, balance, match, equate; contrast, oppose, separate.

398 discrimination

n. discrimination, discernment, acumen, astuteness, keenness, shrewdness, penetration; distinction, nicety, differentiation; diagnosis, appreciation, critique, judgment, sense, sensitivity, tact, feel, refinement, taste, selection, choice.

adj. discriminating, careful, selective, particular, exacting, choosy (*inf.*), judicious, tactful, discerning, perceptive, sensitive, critical, tasteful, refined.

vb. discriminate, differentiate, discern, tell apart, tell from, distinguish; compare and contrast; choose, pick carefully, select, separate, set apart.

399 indiscrimination

n. indiscrimination, uncriticalness, insensitiveness, tastelessness.

adj. indiscriminate, undiscriminating, unselective, uncritical, undiscerning, careless; mixed, blanket, promiscuous; random, haphazard; aimless, chaotic, confused.

vb. not discriminate, draw no disctinction, disregard differences, lump together; confuse, confound, mix, muddle, jumble together.

400 measurement

n. measurement, mensuration; quantification; estimation, determination, computation, calculation, assessment, evaluation, reckoning; graduation, calibration; measure, dimension, distance, degree, pitch, time; size, length, depth, height, width, breadth, thickness; area; mass, weight, density, volume, capacity, pressure, intensity, speed, strength, calibre, viscosity; quantity, magnitude, range, extent; amplitude, frequency, ratio, diameter, radius; temperature.

meter, gauge, scale, rule, ruler, tape-measure, slide-rule, calculator, computer; scales, balance, mark, grade, step, point, limit, standard, criterion; weights and measures, imperial system, avoirdupois, apothecary, troy, metric system, SI unit; metrication.

adj. mensural, dimensional; measurable, assessable, calculable, computable.

vb. measure, quantify, estimate, compute, assess, count, reckon, determine, evaluate, appraise, calculate, survey; gauge, calibrate, graduate; take a reading; level, square; survey, map; average; check; go metric, metricate.

C Materials for reasoning

401 evidence

n. evidence, fact, clue, reason, justification, explanation, grounds, data, case; support, foundation, backing;

sign, indication, trace; document, documentation, information; testimony, witness, statement, plea, assertion, allegation, attestation, exhibit, reference, affidavit; confirmation, corroboration.

adj. suggestive, indicative, symptomatic, corroborative, supporting.

vb. evidence, show, suggest, indicate, evince, illustrate, demonstrate, document, manifest, imply; confirm, verify, support, substantiate, attest, corroborate; testify, bear witness to, witness, affirm; speak for itself (*inf.*), speak volumes (*inf.*).

see also **413**

402 counter-evidence

n. counter-evidence, counterclaim, defence, rebuttal, answer, reply.

adj. rebutting, defending, conflicting; uncorroborative, countervailing; contradictory, contrary, answering, replying.

vb. weigh against, contradict, rebut, refute, squash, deny; be contrary to; cancel out.

see also **414**

403 qualification

n. qualification, modification, limitation, restriction; proviso, exception, reservation; allowance.

adj. qualifying, qualificatory, provisional, contingent, conditional, mitigating, extenuating.

vb. qualify, modify, adjust; limit, restrict, restrain, moderate, mitigate, lessen, temper; condition, colour, make exceptions, exempt, allow for, make allowances for.

see also **700**

404 possibility

n. possibility, potentiality, practicability, feasibility, plausibility, reasonableness, virtuality.

adj. possible, likely, probable; virtual, potential; able, capable, viable, feasible, plausible, practical, practicable, available, attainable, within reach, obtainable, within the bounds of possibility; conceivable, thinkable, imaginable, credible.

vb. be possible, can, may, might, stand a chance; make possible, enable, admit of.

see also 406

405 impossibility

n. impossibility, impracticability, unavailability, inaccessibility; unreasonableness, no hope, hopelessness, no chance.

adj. impossible, unbelievable, inconceivable, unimaginable, unthinkable, prohibited; insoluble, difficult; unable, implausible, unpracticable, unavailable, insurmountable, insuperable, inaccessible, unobtainable, out of the question, beyond the bounds of possibility.

vb. be impossible, defy possibilities; not dream of (*inf.*); make impossible, exclude.

adv. no way (*inf.*).

see also 407

406 probability

n. probability, likelihood, likeliness, expectation; prospect, promise, chance, possibility, good chance, hope, opportunity.

adj. probable, likely, expected; reasonable, presumable, on the cards, supposable; promised, well-founded, seeming; feasible, practicable, workable, plausible, credible.

vb. be probable, may well happen, show signs of; make likely, increase the chances of, hope for.

adv. probably, likely, no doubt, in all probability, quite possibly, most likely, to be expected, to be supposed, as likely as not, everything being equal.

407 improbability

n. improbability, unlikelihood, implausibility, inconceivableness, unreasonableness, rarity, infrequency; bare possibility, million to one chance.

adj. improbable, unlikely, unexpected, unreasonable, impracticable, unworkable, implausible, unbelievable, hardly possible, unheard of, doubtful, dubious, questionable; absurd, extraordinary.

vb. be improbable, probably not happen.

408 certainty

n. certainty, certitude; conviction, assurance; reliance, confidence, trust; truth, accuracy, genuineness; dogmatism; unambiguity, conclusiveness; necessity, inevitability, inexorability.

foregone conclusion, safe bet, sure thing (*inf.*), dead cert (*sl.*).

adj. certain, settled, decided, final, definite; absolute, sure, conclusive, solid, irrefutable, indubitable, indisputable, unquestionable, unmistakable, incontrovertible, unassailable, undisputed; reliable, unfailing, unshakable, inerrant, infallible, sound, authoritative, unerring, trustworthy; unambiguous, unequivocal, incontestable; unconditional; ascertained, certified, verified, attested, confirmed, ratified; self-evident, axiomatic.

vb. make certain, guarantee, authenticate, certify, check, confirm, test, prove, verify, corroborate, ratify; ensure, secure, settle, attest, endorse, clinch; commit, engage, take sides; seal, sign, shake hands.

adv. certainly, without doubt, of

course, definitely, at all events, sure thing (*inf.*); in the bag (*inf.*).

409 uncertainty

n. uncertainty, incertitude; unreliability, questionableness, unpredictability, untrustworthiness, ambiguity; vagueness, obscurity; inconclusiveness, indeterminateness, improbability, unlikelihood.

doubt, disbelief, unbelief, suspicion, misgiving, scepticism, agnosticism, faithlessness, doubtfulness, incredulity; indecision, equivocalness, wavering, hesitancy, suspense; perplexity, bewilderment; puzzle, problem, maze, dilemma, quandary, enigma; fog, haziness; anybody's guess.

adj. uncertain, doubtful, undecided; unsure, inconclusive, ambiguous, vague, unclear, indeterminate, unpredictable, unlikely, possible; risky, chancy, insecure; haphazard, random, casual; questionable, unreliable, fallible, erring; shakable, precarious; puzzling, perplexing.

controversial, open, debatable, contentious, problematical, moot; uncertified, unverified, unattested, unconfirmed, unratified.

doubting, unbelieving, suspicious, sceptical, faithless, distrustful, agnostic.

vb. be uncertain, doubt, flounder, grope, fumble; suspect, smell a rat; not know where one stands, not know which way to turn; sit on the fence, waver; fall between two stools; puzzle, bewilder, perplex.

adv. in the air, in question, open to question.

D Reasoning processes

410 reasoning

n. reasoning, rationalizing; judgment, argumentation; reason, rationality, logic, rationalism; thinking, brainwork, cogitation, knowing, realizing; insight, discernment, acumen, penetration, understanding, comprehension, grasp; reflection, deliberation; concluding.

conclusion, inference, deduction, induction, derivation; syllogism; problem, proposition, premise, postulate, thesis, theorem.

discussion, conversation, exchange, dialogue, interview, disputation, argument, dispute, debate, controversy, symposium; apologetics.

adj. rational, reasoning, logical, sound, rationalistic, reasonable; thoughtful, deliberate, collected; arguing, discursive, controversial, polemical; argumentative.

vb. reason, argue, discuss, converse, dispute, talk about, explain; defend, justify, plead, make out a case, support, contend; philosophize; conclude, put two and two together (*inf.*), deduce, infer, derive, syllogize; be reasonable, add up (*inf.*), make sense, hold water.

411 intuition

n. intuition, instinct, sentiment, feeling, sense; insight, inspiration, extra-sensory perception, ESP, sixth sense; automatic reaction, reflex action, hunch, presentiment, premonition, impression.

adj. intuitive, instinctive; involuntary, reflex, automatic, mechanical, unthinking; spontaneous, inspired, impulsive.

vb. feel, sense, feel in one's bones,

guess, just know, have a funny feeling, have the feeling, follow one's nose.

412 false reasoning

n. sophistry, irrationality, unreasonableness, unsoundness, invalidity; delusion, deceit, deception, erroneousness, speciousness, evasion.

fallacy, sophism, ambiguity, solecism, illogicality, paralogism; inconsistency, *non sequitur*, contradiction; circular argument, vicious circle; misinterpretation; miscalculation; preconception; perversion, prejudice, deviation, aberration.

adj. sophistic, fallacious, illogical, specious, inconsistent, loose, contradictory, ambiguous, solecistic; irrational, unreasonable, unsound, untenable, inconsistent, invalid, deceptive, erroneous, heretical.

vb. reason falsely, evade the issue, beat about the bush, miss the point, beg the question; cavil.

413 demonstration

n. demonstration, proof, verification, justification, establishment, affirmation, validation, corroboration; averment; explanation, elucidation, interpretation, illustration; exhibition, presentation, display.

adj. demonstrative; demonstrated, clear, evident, conclusive, certain, decisive; established, concluded, upheld, valid; demonstrable, verifiable, deducible, inferable.

vb. demonstrate, prove, show, verify, make evident, establish, confirm, substantiate, bear out, affirm, authenticate, attest, validate, test, check; declare, testify, witness, document; have a case; settle, determine; justify; explain, illustrate, describe; manifest, exhibit, display.

414 disproof

n. disproof, confutation, refutation, invalidation, rebuttal, contradiction, denial; upset; exposure; clincher.

adj. disproved, confuted, invalidated; shown up, exposed; contradicted.

vb. disprove, prove false, rebut, invalidate, repudiate, contradict, deny; contend, debate, argue, oppose, dispute; show up (*inf.*), discredit, expose; overthrow, overturn, defeat, finish, confound, overwhelm, crush, floor, silence; knock the bottom out of (*inf.*), cut the ground from under one's feet, get the better of.

E   Results of reasoning

415 judgment

n. judgment, consideration, contemplation, appraisal, examination, review, weighing, sifting, assessment, estimation, appreciation, evaluation, determination; adjudication, arbitration; report, opinion, view, belief, idea, decree, decision, finding, recommendation, pronouncement, verdict, ruling, resolution.

judge, assessor, examiner, valuer, surveyor, adjudicator, arbitrator, referee, umpire.

adj. judicial, judicious; critical; unprejudiced, unbiased.

vb. judge, consider, contemplate, size up (*inf.*), examine, review, appraise, survey, analyse, weigh, sift, assess, evaluate, estimate, appreciate; decide, conclude, find, recommend; pronounce, rule, decree, settle, adjudicate, arbitrate.

416 misjudgment

n. misjudgment, miscalculation, misconception, misunderstanding, misinterpretation, distortion, overestimation, preconception; underestimation; prejudice, bias; narrow-mindedness, pettiness, narrowness, bigotry.

adj. misjudging, wrong; uncritical, unrealistic; injudicious, unwise, ill-judged; partial, unfair, one-sided, biased, prejudiced, intolerant; narrow-minded, petty, mean, narrow, short-sighted, bigoted, insular.

vb. misjudge, miscalculate, misconceive, misconstrue, misapprehend, misunderstand, bark up the wrong tree (*inf.*); undervalue, overvalue, overrate; prejudge, presume, suppose, preconceive, jump to conclusions; prejudice, bias, jaundice, twist, sway, warp, influence.

see also **916**

417 overestimation

n. overestimation, overvaluation, overrating, exaggeration, overstatement; optimism.

adj. overestimated, exaggerated.

vb. overestimate, exaggerate, overvalue, overrate; maximize, emphasize, make a mountain out of a molehill, make too much of, paint in glowing colours.

see also **481**

418 underestimation

n. underestimation, undervaluation, understatement, minimization; pessimism.

adj. underestimated, understated; deprecatory; modest.

vb. underestimate, underplay, play down, underrate, understate, minimize; depreciate, disparage, slight; make light of, not do justice to, think too little of.

419 discovery

n. discovery, finding, disclosure, uncovering; manifestation, revelation; detection, identification, catching; invention; exploration.

adj. on the right track, near, close, warm (*inf.*).

vb. discover, find, hit upon; realize, see, perceive, understand, become aware of, get wise to, get on to, twig (*inf.*); meet, come across, happen upon; expose, disclose, detect, spot, lay bare, reveal, uncover, unearth, bring to light, run to earth (*inf.*), run to ground (*inf.*), track down; catch in the act, catch red-handed.

420 belief

n. belief, credence, trust, acceptance, faith, credit; reliance, dependence, conviction, confidence, persuasion; certainty, surety, assurance, hope; admission, confession, avowal.

creed, doctrine, dogma, credo, revelation; tenet, canon, principle; articles of faith, catechism.

opinion, thought, view, sentiment, idea, notion, conception, impression, assumption; attitude, way of thinking; point of view, position, outlook, angle, stand, stance.

adj. believing, accepting, reliant, dependent, convinced, persuaded, certain, confident; believable, credible, tenable, plausible, trustworthy, reliable, unfailing.

vb. believe, accept, hold, trust, depend, rely, be convicted of, be persuaded of, take at one's word, take on trust, take one's word for; think, consider, regard as, suppose, presume, surmise, fancy, assume, deem, conclude; come round to, change one's views, be converted; have faith in, be a believer, profess, confess.

convince, persuade, bring round, prove, argue, assure, satisfy, make realize, bring home to; teach; captivate, have a way with (*inf.*).

see also 854

421 unbelief

n. unbelief, disbelief, doubt, uncertainty, incredulity, scepticism, misgiving, suspicion, mistrust, distrust, qualm, hesitation, reservation, apprehension, irresolution; faithlessness, rejection; agnosticism, atheism.

adj. unbelieving, disbelieving, doubting, questioning, sceptical, distrusting, incredulous; unbelievable, untenable, unreliable, doubtful, dubious, suspicious, questionable, implausible.

vb. disbelieve, doubt, hesitate, waver, not believe, give no credence to, lack confidence in, set no store by; mistrust, suspect, question, challenge.

422 gullibility

n. gullibility, credulity, simpleness, unsophistication.

adj. gullible, credulous, simple, naive, unsophisticated, inexperienced, guileless, simple, green.

vb. be gullible, fall for (*inf.*), be easily persuaded.

423 incredulity

n. incredulity, suspicion, scepticism; sophistication.

adj. incredulous, unbelieving, sceptical, unresponsive, ungullible, sophisticated.

vb. refuse to believe, distrust, doubt; reject, turn a deaf ear to.

see also 421

424 assent

n. assent, affirmative, yes; approval, agreement, acceptance, support, approbation; authorization, permission, consent, empowering, legalization, authority, sanction, guarantee, warrant, authentication, ratification, endorsement, affirmation, go-ahead (*inf.*), green light (*inf.*), nod (*sl.*).

like-mindedness, unanimity, consensus, general agreement; supporter, follower, assenter, signer, subscriber, ratifier, signatory, aye.

adj. assenting, acquiescent; approved, accepted, voted, carried, passed; unanimous, of one mind.

vb. assent, say yes to, agree, concur, affirm, accept, support, subscribe to, approve, vote for, pass, rubber-stamp (*inf.*), put up with (*inf.*), go along with, tolerate, stand for (*inf.*), bear, endure, acquiesce; acknowledge, admit, concede, grant, yield, recognize, defer to.

authorize, grant permission, empower, legalize, ratify, sign, endorse, authenticate, seal.

425 dissent

n. dissent, disapproval, disagreement, dissidence, disapprobation; difference, variance, discord, dissension, protest, controversy, vendetta, animosity, division; non-conformity; non-acceptance, withdrawal, secession; objection, reservation, negative, no.

dissenter, objector, protester, rebel, non-conformist, caviller; interrupter, heckler; separatist; recusant.

adj. dissident, disagreeing, differing; protesting, objecting.

vb. dissent, disagree, disapprove, differ, agree to differ, protest, object, oppose, challenge, heckle, shout down, take exception; reject, refuse, contradict; withdraw, secede.

426 knowledge

n. knowledge, knowing, awareness, consciousness, recognition, realization, understanding, grasp, cognition; intelligence, education, instruction; learning, erudition, scholarship, culture, bookishness; accomplishments, attainments; facts, information, encyclopedia; expertise, know-how, skill, proficiency; wisdom, maturity, experience.

adj. knowing, conscious, mindful, aware, cognizant; discerning, perceptive; acquainted, familiar, well versed in, well grounded in, *au fait;* clever, intelligent, informed, instructed, trained, knowledgeable, educated, well-taught, well-read, learned, erudite, scholarly, cultured, intellectual; mature, wise, experienced.

known, widely known, common, proverbial, commonplace, household name, hackneyed; infamous, notorious.

vb. know, realize, understand, grasp, see, perceive, realize, apprehend, be aware of, discern, appreciate, recognize; experience; be well-informed, be well up on, be into (*inf.*), know backwards, know inside out, know like the back of one's hand.

see also 434, 460

427 ignorance

n. ignorance, unawareness, unconsciousness, unknowingness, nescience; unenlightenment, incomprehension, darkness, fog, haziness, vagueness; inexperience, immaturity, greenness, naivety, simplicity, empty-headedness, stupidity; unlearnedness, unintellectuality, illiteracy; unskilfulness, awkwardness.

smattering, shallowness; unknown, unknown quantity, unexplored ground,

virgin territory, mystery, closed book, sealed book.

adj. ignorant, unaware, unknowing; unmindful, unconscious, disregarding; inexperienced, immature, green, inept, simple, stupid, thick, dense; unenlightened, in the dark, unfamiliar with, not conversant, a stranger to, none the wiser; untaught, illiterate, uneducated, untrained, backward, unscholarly, unlearned, uncultivated, unread, uncultured, Philistine, unintellectual; unknown, untold, unseen, mysterious, secret, undiscovered, virgin, uncharted.

vb. not know, be ignorant, be in the dark, not have any idea, not have the foggiest idea (*inf.*); pass (*inf.*).

see also 435

428 student

n. student, scholar, schoolchild, learner, disciple; philosopher, scientist, researcher, expert, man of letters, wise man, savant, sage; professor, don, teacher, doctor; bookworm, intellectual, egghead (*inf.*); genius, brain, know-all, mine of information, walking encyclopedia.

see also 473, 474

429 ignoramus

n. ignoramus, know-nothing, dunce, fool, blockhead; greenhorn, raw recruit, babe, simpleton.

see also 437

430 truth

n. truth, fact, reality, the case, gospel truth, plain truth, real thing, real McCoy (*inf.*).

trueness, verity, correctness, exactitude, accuracy, precision, perfection, rectitude, faithfulness, sincerity, honesty; authenticity, infallibility, genuineness, validity.

adj. true, truthful, veracious, real,

right, factual, correct, objective, actual; historical; genuine, authentic, original, official, veritable; unadulterated, unmixed; attested, valid, guaranteed; undisputed, conclusive, final; accurate, exact, precise, faithful, infallible; sincere, honest, upright.

vb. be true, be the case· ring true; hit the nail on the head (*inf.*); come true, come about, happen, occur.

see also **476**

431 error

n. error, mistake, fault, blunder, failure, fall, flaw, lapse, omission, lie, untruth, wrong, deviation, sin; *faux pas*, slip, slip-up (*inf.*); misjudgment, misunderstanding, misconception, inaccuracy, mismanagement; misprint, literal; bloomer (*sl.*), clanger (*sl.*), howler (*sl.*).

erroneousness, falsity, inaccurateness, inexactness.

adj. wrong, incorrect, unreal, untrue; unauthentic, unoriginal, spurious; inaccurate, inexact, imprecise; erroneous, mistaken, lying, untruthful, in error; unfaithful, disloyal, deceitful, corrupt, unsound; deceptive, fallacious, misleading, pretended, sham, counterfeit, faked, mocked; misunderstood; fallible.

vb. go wrong, make a mistake, err, blunder, slip up (*inf.*), bungle; be wrong, be mistaken; misconceive, misunderstand; not hold water, fall down, fall to the ground; mislead, lead astray, lead up the garden path (*inf.*), pervert, deceive, trick, hoax.

see also **477, 478**

432 maxim

n. maxim, proverb, saying, truth, text, dictum, motto, slogan, watchword, moral, aphorism, adage, axiom; banality, truism, platitude, commonplace, cliché; epigram, witticism.

adj. aphoristic, proverbial, epigrammatic; brief, concise, pithy, terse; trite, commonplace.

433 absurdity

n. absurdity, ridiculousness, ludicrousness, outrageousness, folly, silliness, stupidity, nonsense; spoonerism, malapropism; jest, trick, practical joke, prank, farce, buffoonery, clowning, wildness; extravaganza.

adj. absurd, ridiculous, crazy, farcical, nonsensical, senseless, inane, wild, foolish, silly, stupid, bizarre, extravagant, fantastic.

vb. be absurd, talk nonsense, fool around; play tricks.

see also **451**

434 intelligence; wisdom

n. intelligence, understanding, brightness, cleverness, brilliance; genius, talent, brains, grey matter, intellect, sense, common sense, wit.

wisdom, experience, erudition, sagacity, sapience; shrewdness, discernment, judgment, acumen, insight, perspicacity, sharpness, acuteness, penetration, prudence, foresight.

adj. intelligent, clever, bright, brilliant, able, knowledgeable; wise, sagacious, shrewd, prudent, knowing, contemplative, reasoning, thoughtful, sober, sensible, judicious, circumspect, discreet, considerate, astute, perceptive, perspicacious, far-sighted, discerning, quick, acute, sharp, penetrating, keen, discriminating, having one's wits about one, not born yesterday (*inf.*).

vb. be wise, understand, discern; have one's head screwed on the right way (*inf.*).

see also **426**

435 unintelligence; folly

n. unintelligence, stupidity, dullness, slowness, heaviness; foolishness, folly, weakness, shallowness, silliness, simplicity, childishness, puerility, imbecility; imprudence, short-sightedness, indiscretion.

adj. unintelligent, unthinking, unreasoning; stupid, dull, slow, weak, shallow, superficial, vacant, simple, dumb, thick, dense, empty-headed, slow-witted, feeble-minded, simple-minded, weak-minded, half-witted, blockish, oafish, feather-brained, doltish; foolish, crazy, silly, insane, inane, idiotic, imbecile, puerile, childish; backward, retarded, handicapped, subnormal, deprived; unwise, imprudent, short-sighted, undiscerning.

vb. be foolish, act the fool, fool around, lark about (*inf.*).

see also 427

436 sage

n. sage, wise man, man of learning, savant, pundit, expert, doctor, scholar, master, great thinker, authority, oracle, elder statesman, connoisseur, luminary; wiseacre, know-all, sciolist.

see also 428, 473

437 fool

n. fool, simpleton, dunce, idiot, ignoramus, scatterbrain, half-wit, fathead, thickhead, blockhead, nitwit, nincompoop, moron, cretin, imbecile, numskull, bore, dolt, ass, buffoon, chump (*sl.*), lout, oaf, ninny, jerk (*sl.*), twit (*sl.*).

see also 429, 630

438 sanity

n. sanity, saneness, balance, normality, clearmindedness, lucidity, wholesomeness, *mens sana*, rationality, reason.

adj. sane, normal, sound-minded, healthy-minded, sound, right-minded, sober, lucid, in one's right mind, self-possessed, all there (*inf.*).

439 insanity

n. insanity, insaneness, madness, lunacy; imbecility, cretinism, idiocy; phobia, mania, craze, passion, obsession, infatuation, fixation, compulsion; mental illness, nervous breakdown, nervous disorder; nervousness, nerves; hysteria, frenzy, fever, attack, fit, rage; peculiarity, eccentricity, abnormality, oddity.

adj. insane, mad, unsound, unbalanced, crazy, deranged, confused, demented, rabid, berserk, out of one's mind, off one's head, off one's rocker (*sl.*); obsessed, infatuated; frenzied, wild, raging, furious; eccentric, odd, cranky, peculiar.

vb. be mad, wander, ramble; go mad, lose one's sanity, take leave of one's senses, go out of one's mind, crack up (*inf.*), go off one's rocker (*sl.*); madden, drive mad, unbalance.

440 madman

n. madman, lunatic, mental case, loony (*sl.*), bedlamite; maniac, psychopath, psychotic, paranoid, hysteric, neurotic, manic-depressive, melancholic, hypochondriac, kleptomaniac; imbecile, idiot, moron, cretin, mongol; fool, crank, nut (*sl.*), eccentric, freak, weirdo (*inf.*), crackpot (*inf.*).

F Extension of thought

441 memory

n. memory, recollection, reminiscence, retrospection, recall, review, flashback, afterthought, hindsight, reconsideration, reflection, thought; retention, good memory, photographic memory, *déjà vu*.

memorandum, memo, reminder, record, note, jotting, scribble, mark; notes, summary, agenda, minutes; mnemonic, aid to memory; souvenir, memento, token, keepsake, relic, trinket; testimonial, memorial, monument, trophy, commemoration; warning, advice, suggestion, hint; prompt, prompter; memoirs, reminiscences, recollections, memories, memorabilia; diary, journal, album, scrapbook, notebook.

adj. remembered, recalled, retained, unforgotten, fresh, vivid; half-remembered, at the back of one's mind; reminiscent, reminding, evocative; memorable, unforgettable, indelibly fixed on one's mind; commemorative, memorial.

vb. remember, recollect, recall, bring to mind, be reminded of, think of, not forget; review, retrace, go back, flash back, look back, turn one's thoughts back, reminisce, call up, revive, rake up the past, drag up (*inf.*), dredge up (*inf.*); recognize, identify, know again, make out.

come to mind, ring a bell, stay in the memory, never be forgotten, haunt, recur, penetrate, stay in one's mind, not leave one's thoughts, not get out of one's mind.

memorize, learn, commit to memory, know by heart, learn by rote, master, impress, retain, fix in the mind; keep always, hold dear, treasure, cherish, commemorate, enshrine in the memory, keep the memory alive.

remind, prompt, suggest, hint, bring back, make one think of, jog one's memory, refresh one's memory; warn, throw the book at (*inf.*).

442 oblivion

n. oblivion, forgetfulness, unmindfulness, absent-mindedness, amnesia, memory like a sieve, loss of memory, blankness, complete blank, mental block; insensibleness, indifference, carelessness.

adj. forgotten, unremembered, lost, out of one's mind, clean forgotten, unrecalled, unretained, in one ear and out the other; out of sight, out of mind; almost remembered, on the tip of one's tongue.

oblivious, forgetful, unmindful, heedless, inattentive, preoccupied, distracted, absent-minded.

vb. forget, fail to remember, have no recollection, put out of one's mind, have a short memory, think no more of, not give another thought, one's memory be a blank, escape one; be forgotten, sink into oblivion, fade from one's memory.

443 expectation

n. expectation, expectancy, looking forward, contemplation, anticipation, prospect, outlook; confidence, trust, hope, high hopes; preparedness; suspense, apprehension, pessimism.

adj. expectant, waiting, in anticipation, looking forward to, in suspense, on tenterhooks, itching, on edge, with bated breath; hoping, hopeful, confident; eager, watchful, vigilant, prepared; apprehensive, pessimistic.

expected, awaited, anticipated, foreseen, predicted, prophesied, longed for, looked for; on the cards, prospective.

vb. expect, look forward to, promise oneself, hope for, anticipate, contemplate, foresee, long for, bargain for (*inf.*), predict, prophesy, forecast, see coming, take for granted; wait for, await, bide one's time, mark time, hold one's breath, be in suspense; rely on, bank on, count on; be expected, lead one to expect, not put it past (*inf.*), be just like one.

444 non-expectation

n. inexpectation, unpreparedness, unexpectedness; surprise, shock, start, jolt, blow, bombshell, bolt from the blue, thunderbolt; turn-up for the book (*sl.*).

adj. unexpected, unforeseen, sudden, surprising, astonishing, staggering; unheralded, unpredicted, uncontemplated; unheard of, not thought of; more than one bargained for, not on the cards, without warning, out of the blue.

surprised, startled, thunderstruck, off one's guard, unready, unprepared, caught napping.

vb. not expect, not bargain for; surprise, take by surprise, catch unawares, catch in the act, catch red-handed, make one jump, startle, astonish, bowl over (*inf.*), knock down with a feather, come unexpectedly, turn up.

445 disappointment

n. disappointment, foiling, bafflement; discouragement, despondency, dissatisfaction, unfulfilment, discontent, frustration, disillusionment, regret, distress, displeasure.

bad news, setback, adversity, defeat, failure, anti-climax, miscarriage, let-down (*inf.*).

adj. disappointed, discouraged, dissatisfied, thwarted, baffled, unsuccessful, defeated, foiled, let-down (*inf.*), disconcerted, depressed, frustrated, disillusioned, full of regrets, despon-

dent; disappointing, unsatisfactory, inadequate, insufficient, not up to expectations.

vb. disappoint, fail, let down (*inf.*), thwart, foil, baffle; come short of, dash one's hopes, not come up to expectations, leave much to be desired; frustrate, disconcert, disillusion, dissatisfy, let the side down (*inf.*).

446 foresight

n. foresight, second sight, foresightedness, anticipation; forethought, premeditation, preconsideration, preconception.

adj. foreseeing, foresighted, looking ahead, anticipatory.

vb. foresee, prophesy, forecast, anticipate; see ahead, look into the future, have a premonition, feel in one's bones.

447 prediction

n. prediction, forecast, foretelling, prophecy, prognostication, prognosis, foresight, forethought, foreknowledge, precognition, prescience, prevision; augury, divination, vaticination, astrology, clairvoyancy, soothsaying, fortune-telling, crystal-gazing, palmistry, casting lots; parapsychology, extra-sensory perception; telepathy, telesthesia.

omen, sign, indication, symptom, portent, clue, hint, auspice, writing on the wall; warning, forewarning, foreboding, presentiment; guess, estimate, conjecture, budget; foretoken; presage; horoscope, fortune; herald, harbinger.

oracle, forecaster, prognosticator, prophet, prophetess, seer; fortune-teller, soothsayer, clairvoyant, augur, diviner, palmist, astrologer, crystal-gazer, gipsy; witch, wizard, medium; sibyl, haruspex; thought-reader, mind-reader, telepath, parapsychologist; weatherman, meteorologist.

adj. predicting, predictive, prognostic, divinatory, clairvoyant, portentous, significant; auspicious, favourable; ominous, foreboding; psychic, second-sighted; supernatural, paranormal, parapsychological; predictable, foreseen, expected, likely; divinable.

vb. predict, forecast, prognosticate, foresee, foretell, prophesy, vaticinate; forewarn; promise; bode, forebode, betoken, portend, foreshadow, presage; divine, augur, tell the future, tell fortunes, cast lots, read one's hand, read one's palm, read tea leaves.

see also 984

G   Creative thought

448   supposition

n. supposition, guesswork, speculation, theorizing, postulation.

guess, surmise, notion, fancy, conjecture, inkling, hint, intimation, shrewd idea, vague idea, sneaking suspicion, rough guess, wild guess, shot in the dark.

premise, presupposition, postulate, proposition; inference, deduction, conclusion; thesis, hypothesis, working hypothesis, theory.

theorist, scientist, theorizer, academic, thinker, speculator, backroom boy, boffin (*sl.*).

adj. suppositional, unproved, tentative, speculative, conjectural, hypothetical, theoretical; supposed, assumed, presupposed, presumed, reputed, alleged, postulated, putative.

vb. suppose, believe, imagine, think, fancy, deem, guess, venture a guess, conjecture, speculate, estimate, divine, surmise, suspect, gather, assume, presume, presuppose; postulate, posit; infer, imply, deduce, theorize.

449   imagination

n. imagination, inventiveness, creativity, originality, visualization; fantasy, diversion, whimsy, daydreaming, castle-building, pipe-dreaming, wishful thinking, escapism; utopia, paradise, world of fantasy, cloud-cuckoo land, dream world.

idea, figment of the imagination, invention, notion, fancy, whim, caprice, vagary, chimera, will-o'-the-wisp, vision, appearance, day-dream, castles in the air, romance, flight of fancy, dream, nightmare.

visionary, prophet, seer, idealist, escapist, Quixote, dreamer, day-dreamer.

adj. imaginative, inventive, creative, resourceful, inspired, visionary, idealistic, with one's head in the clouds, quixotic, impractical, unrealistic; imaginary, fanciful, fantastic, capricious, whimsical, chimerical, dream-like, ideal, utopian, fictitious, pretended, make-believe, illusory, fabulous.

vb. imagine, picture, conjure up, envisage, conceive, suppose, visualize; invent, create, make up, think of, devise, fabricate, coin, hatch; dream, muse, fancy, fantasize, idealize, romanticize, build castles in the air, daydream, pretend, make believe.

2   Communication of ideas

A   Nature of ideas communicated

450   meaning

n. meaning, sense, significance, interpretation, implication, explanation; intent, aim, import, drift, tenor, thrust, purport; substance, essence, content.

meaningfulness, expressiveness; signification, connotation, denotation, reference, referendum, definition; unambiguity, equivalence, synonymity; synonym, related word.

adj. meaningful, significant, indicative, expressive, suggestive, evocative; substantial, pithy, full of meaning, pregnant; unambiguous; literal, verbal, word for word, verbatim, exact, faithful, true; semantic, linguistic.

vb. mean, signify, designate, refer to, drive at (*inf.*), denote, connote, indicate, symbolize, suggest, express, convey, declare, state, assert, spell; intimate, hint, betoken, bode, purport, import; imply, involve, speak of, touch on, point to.

451 meaninglessness

n. meaninglessness, senselessness, inexpressiveness, expressionlessness, nonsensicalness; misinterpretation, illogicality, ambiguity.

nonsense, balderdash, rubbish, twaddle, blather, rot (*sl.*), poppycock (*sl.*), trash, inanity, drivel, bunkum, prattle, baloney (*sl.*), bunk (*sl.*), ballyhoo, piffle (*sl.*); hot air (*sl.*), empty talk, humbug; cliché, truism, platitude.

adj. meaningless, insignificant, unindicative, inexpressive, unevocative; insubstantial, empty, void, vacant, blank; irrelevant, unimportant, senseless, aimless, purposeless; vague, ambiguous, tautological; trite, trivial, absurd, nonsensical, foolish; unintended, misinterpreted.

vb. be meaningless, mean nothing;

talk nonsense, babble, prattle, blather, twaddle; talk through one's hat (*sl.*).

452 intelligibility

n. intelligibility, comprehensibility; recognizability, cognizability; lucidity, clarity, transparency; precision, plainness, explicitness, unambiguousness; readability, legibility, decipherability; audibility; plain speech; plain English.

adj. intelligible, comprehensible, understandable; clear, obvious, lucid, precise, plain, explicit, clear-cut, distinct, unambiguous, unequivocal; simple, straightforward, popular, made simple, for the beginner, made easy, without tears, for the million; recognizable, readable, legible, decipherable; audible.

vb. understand, apprehend, comprehend, grasp, follow, take in, figure out (*inf.*), catch on (*inf.*), get the meaning of, get the hang of (*inf.*), twig (*inf.*); fathom, penetrate, get to the bottom of, read between the lines, get the idea, get the gist of; know, have knowledge of, realize, perceive, appreciate; discern, distinguish, make out (*inf.*), work out (*inf.*); conceive, be aware of, recognize, sense, be conscious of.

be intelligible, make sense, be clear, click (*sl.*); make clear, put in plain English, put in words of one syllable.

see also 502

453 unintelligibility

n. unintelligibility, incomprehensibility, meaninglessness, unrecognizability, unsearchableness, impenetrability; unclearness, obscurity, illegibility, ambiguity, indecipherability, unreadability; inaudibility; gibberish, incoherence, double Dutch, Greek; puzzle, mystery, enigma, sealed book, closed book.

adj. unintelligible, incomprehen-

454

sible, meaningless, beyond one's
comprehension; indistinct, vague,
indefinite, hazy, inexact, ill-defined,
loose, unclear, ambiguous, equivocal;
incoherent, mixed up; obscure,
puzzling, hard, complicated, intricate,
profound, academic, over one's head,
abstruse, recondite; concealed,
mysterious, hidden, enigmatic,
esoteric; illegible, indecipherable,
unreadable; inaudible; unrecognizable,
impenetrable, unsearchable, inexplicable; inscrutable, unfathomable,
unutterable, ineffable.

vb. not understand, not have the
first idea, not get the hang of (*inf.*),
not make head or tail of, be baffled, be
beyond one, get hold of the wrong end
of the stick (*inf.*); be unintelligible,
talk above someone's head; not make
sense, escape one, be all Greek to one.

see also 503

454 ambiguity
n. ambiguity, equivocalness;
vagueness, uncertainty; ambivalence,
equivocation, incongruity, incon-
sistency, prevarication; play on words,
pun, *double entendre.*
adj. ambiguous, ambivalent,
equivocal, uncertain, vague, vacillating, prevaricating; two-edged, back-
handed; incongruous.
vb. cut both ways; play on words,
pun; quibble, equivocate, prevaricate.

455 figure of speech
n. figure of speech, metaphor, transference, figurativeness; symbolism,
imagery; rhetoric; comparison, simile,
likeness, allegory, trope, fable, parable,
allusion, personification; euphemism,
irony, satire; understatement; onomatopoeia.
adj. figurative, metaphorical, extended, transferred, allusive; rhetorical;

symbolic; comparative, allegorical,
parabolic; euphemistic, euphuistic,
ironical, satirical.

456 interpretation
n. interpretation, explanation,
exposition, commentary, elucidation,
clarification, illumination, explication;
background, reason; analysis, diagnosis, review, criticism, critique, survey,
investigation, appraisal, evaluation;
significance, importance; annotation,
note, comment; example, illustration,
instance.

translation, equivalent, dynamic
equivalent, paraphrase, rendering,
rendition, adaptation, rewording,
restatement, gloss, transcription,
transliteration, version, reading.

interpreter, commentator, reviewer,
critic, analyst, exponent, writer, editor,
annotator, expositor, preacher,
exegete; translator, linguist, polyglot;
hermeneutics, exegetics, homiletics.
adj. interpretive, explanatory,
expository, explicatory; analytical,
diagnostic, critical, evaluatory; defining, descriptive, illuminating, discursive, exegetical; exemplary, illustrative; editorial, glossarial; literal, faithful, word-for-word; free, rough.

vb. interpret, explain, account for,
give reasons for, give reasons why,
make sense of; expound, lay bare the
meaning, give an account of, state the
significance of, read between the lines;
make clear, elucidate, make plain,
clarify, illuminate, throw light on, cast
light on; simplify, expand on,
emphasize; demonstrate, illustrate,
exemplify, show by example; set forth,
reveal, expose, lay bare, unfold, spell
out.

translate, render, put in other words,
put into, reword, restate, rephrase,

paraphrase; transliterate, transcribe; decipher, decode, crack, solve; annotate, comment on, remark on, edit, gloss.

457 misinterpretation

n. misinterpretation, misreckoning, misconception, misunderstanding, misconstruction, falsification, distortion, perversion, delusion, error, mistake; mistranslation.

vb. misinterpret, misunderstand, get hold of the wrong end of the stick (*inf.*), misquote, falsify, distort, pervert, read into, misconstrue, not give a true account of, give a false impression of.

see also 453

B Modes of communication

458 manifestation

n. manifestation, revelation, showing, demonstration, disclosure, expression, presentation, exhibition; publishing, telling, announcement; divulgence, betrayal.

appearance, vision, apparition; exhibit, show, layout, example, specimen, showpiece; parade, procession, pageant; evidence, sign, miracle, theophany.

adj. manifest, apparent, clear, visible, perceptible, observable, obvious, patent, open, evident, self-evident, unmistakable, crystal-clear, staring one in the face, written all over one, express, explicit, conspicuous, noticeable, prominent, bold, striking, pronounced, flagrant, glaring, salient.

vb. manifest, appear, reveal, show, disclose, express; present, produce, publish, tell, announce, proclaim, betray, divulge, demonstrate, exem-

plify, indicate, show signs of, evince; make manifest, make plain, lay bare, expose, show forth; display, exhibit, set out, uncover, unfold, unmask, parade; promote, publicize.

see also 462, 823

459 latency

n. latency, secrecy, subtlety, dormancy; insidiousness; undercurrent, implication, suggestion, hint, allusion, connotation, inference, more than meets the eye, snake in the grass.

adj. latent, hidden, veiled, dormant, quiescent, lurking, subtle, insidious, beneath the surface, between the lines, underlying, undercover; underdeveloped, potential, possible; implied, inherent, inferred, suggested, intimated, hinted, supposed, tacit, understood, unmentioned, unspoken, unexpressed; suggestive, indicative, provocative.

vb. be latent, be beneath the surface, lurk, lie low; imply, indicate, infer, suggest, mean, intimate, hint, insinuate, involve, provoke, entail.

see also 461

460 information

n. information, knowledge, facts, info (*inf.*), gen (*sl.*), low-down (*sl.*); briefing, run-down (*inf.*); proof, evidence, notes, details, results, figures, tables, statistics, data; intelligence; news, message, report, notice, communication, notification, declaration, presentation, proclamation, broadcast, transmission; narration, account, description, story, tale, paper; tidings, discovery, revelation, enlightenment; dispatch, release, hand-out, announcement; telephone call, telex, telegram, cable, wire, teletext.

hint, mention, advice, aside, wink, whisper, word in one's ear, tip-off (*inf.*), warning, intimation, suspicion, glimmer, indication, suggestion.

informant, spokesman, narrator, story-teller, messenger, newsman, reporter, authority, announcer, broadcaster, correspondent, journalist; dispatcher, courier, herald, emissary, envoy, ambassador, carrier; guidebook, manual, chart, itinerary, map, timetable.

informer, spy, secret agent, observer, wire tapper, snoop, grass (*sl.*), squealer (*sl.*); gossip, tell-tale, eavesdropper, newsmonger, tattler, scandalmonger.

adj. informative, instructive, enlightening, educational, enriching, newsy (*inf.*), chatty (*inf.*), communicative.

vb. inform, speak, say, tell, notify, let know, communicate, give the facts, put over, put across, get across, get over, present, give to understand, convey, declare, announce, express, proclaim; relate, narrate, recite, report, describe, set forth, make known, let in on, tip off (*inf.*), have a word in someone's ear; enlighten, put in the picture; broadcast, spread the news, circulate, disseminate, promulgate; telephone, ring, call, telex, cable, wire; report back, debrief (*inf.*).

bring up to date, fill in on (*inf.*); keep up with, keep tabs on (*inf.*), keep track of, keep one's finger on the pulse, keep up to date, keep posted; hint, suggest, get at, insinuate, intimate, advise, warn; tell on, inform on, betray, grass on (*sl.*), squeal (*sl.*).

see also **464, 597**

461 concealment

n. concealment, covering, hiding, confinement, burying, secretion; suppression, evasion; seclusion, privacy, isolation, solitude; camouflage, disguise, shroud, veil, curtain, screen, mask, cloak, purdah; cabal.

adj. concealed, hidden, out of sight, behind the scenes, covered, eclipsed, buried, obscured, unseen, unexposed; disguised, camouflaged, incognito; furtive, stealthy, secret, hush-hush, clandestine, underhand, sly.

vb. conceal, hide, cover, bury, suppress, screen, cloak, shroud, veil, curtain, evade, withhold, pull the wool over someone's eyes (*inf.*), keep secret, lie low, keep in the dark, keep under one's hat (*inf.*), sweep under the carpet (*inf.*), secrete; cloud, obscure, envelop, ensconce, store, harbour, cache, shelter, stash (*inf.*); close, seal, lock.

sneak, prowl, creep, lurk, steal, slink.

see also **463, 466, 826**

462 disclosure

n. disclosure, exposure, opening, uncovering, revelation, apocalypse; show-down; betrayal, manifestation, give-away; acknowledgement, admission.

adj. disclosed, uncovered, exposed, conspicuous, open; indicative, betraying, tell-tale.

vb. disclose, reveal, give away, expose, divulge, lay open, lay bare, make plain, uncover, unfold, unveil, unfurl, unmask, take the wraps off; not contain oneself for, bring into the open; declare, make known, spit it out (*inf.*); put one's cards on the table, nail one's colours to the mast, show one's colours; open up (*inf.*), unburden oneself, unbosom, confide, get out of one's system (*inf.*), get off one's chest (*inf.*); come out of one's shell.

confess, admit, acknowledge, concede, grant, own up (*inf.*), come clean, avow, plead guilty, make a clean breast of; one's sins will find one out.

betray, not keep a secret, blurt out, let on, let out, blabber, leak, let the cat out of the bag (*inf.*), spill the beans, come out with, talk out of turn, give the game away.

see also **458, 460**

463 hiding

n. hiding, deceit, faking, deception; hiding place, hide-out, hidey-hole, refuge, retreat, covert, den, shelter.

disguise, camouflage, mask, blind, masquerade, cloak, cover, veil, guise, façade, envelope, shade, blackout, masking; ambush, snare, trap, pitfall, net, noose.

vb. ambush, trap, ensnare, waylay, lay in wait, set a trap for, decoy.

see also **459, 801**

464 publication

n. publication, announcement, communication, revelation, disclosure, notification, proclamation, declaration, promulgation, broadcasting, dissemination.

broadcast; book, booklet; newspaper, periodical, magazine, journal; publicity, promotion, canvassing, advertisement, poster, sign, bill, placard, notice, broadsheet, leaflet, folder, brochure, pamphlet, circular, hand-out, handbill, flysheet, blurb, plug (*inf.*).

adj. published, in print, available, obtainable, in circulation; current, public.

vb. publish, issue, bring out, put into circulation, print, distribute; reissue, reprint; be published, come out, circulate, get around.

make known, announce, notify, proclaim, declare, pronounce, impart, send forth, communicate, reveal, disclose, spread, broadcast, diffuse, pass the word round, put about, blazon, promulgate, disseminate; publicize, promote, advertise, canvass, circularize, sell, plug (*inf.*), tell the world.

465 news

n. news, tidings, information, facts, events, current affairs; headlines, front-page news, stop press, newsflash, scoop, sensation; description, account, report, story, bulletin, message, release, communiqué, press release, announcement, hand-out, dispatch.

rumour, gossip, hearsay, scandal, whisper, popular report, fabrication, tale, chit-chat; grapevine, bush telegraph.

vb. report, tell, broadcast, publish, circulate, spread; make news, hit the headlines.

466 secret

n. secret, mystery, puzzle, riddle, brain-teaser, enigma, arcanum; code, cipher, cryptogram, hieroglyph; confidence; skeleton in the cupboard; suppression, blackout, censure.

adj. secret, strange, mysterious, hidden, unknown, puzzling, mystical, cryptic, enigmatic; private, confidential, classified, top secret, hush-hush; secretive, reticent, taciturn; secluded.

vb. keep secret, keep to oneself, not tell, hide, conceal, keep mum (*inf.*), suppress, stifle, sit on (*inf.*), hush up, censor.

adv. in secret, in private, confidentially, under one's breath, between ourselves; between you, me, and the bedpost.

see also **461**

467 messenger

n. messenger, dispatcher, dispatch bearer, carrier, courier, runner, crier, bearer, office-boy, message-boy, errand-boy, page-boy, buttons; spokesman, intermediary, go-between, ambassador, envoy, emissary, internuncio; herald, forerunner, precursor, harbinger, trumpet; minister, angel, prophet.

post, mail, correspondence; post office; telecommunications, telephony, telegraphy; broadcasting, radio, transistor, wireless, television, the box; telephone, phone, receiver; radio set, two-way radio, intercom (*inf.*), pocket radio, walkie-talkie, field radio; telegram, wire, cable, cablegram, telegraph; teleprinter, telex, teletext, semaphore, flag, beacon, smoke-signal.

468 affirmation

n. affirmation, assertion, statement, declaration, proposition, profession, pronouncement, explanation, answer, report, observation, expression, formulation; admission, acknowledgement, attestation, avowal; agreement, ratification, endorsement.

swearing, asseveration; oath, vow, testimony, sworn statement, affidavit, promise, contract, pledge.

adj. affirmative, assertive, affirmatory, declarative; emphatic, strong, forceful, dogmatic, positive, assured, solemn, sworn, on oath.

vb. affirm, assert, state, declare, profess, pronounce, express, explain, maintain, contend, submit, asseverate, aver; confirm, endorse, ratify; admit, acknowledge; emphasize, stress, underline, highlight, impress, urge, reinforce, rub in (*inf.*), make much of, plug; speak out, have one's say, put one's foot down (*inf.*); swear, vow, promise, pledge, testify, attest, assure, guarantee,

vouch; swear in, put on oath, charge, adjure.

see also 514, 698

469 negation

n. negation, denial, contradiction, repudiation, refusal, renunciation, disclaimer, disavowel; abnegation, recusance.

adj. negative, denying, contrary, contradictory, disavowing, recusant, repugnant.

vb. negate, deny, belie, give the lie to, contradict, contravene, gainsay, renounce, repudiate, disown, disavow, disclaim, abjure, abnegate; refuse, reject; cancel, nullify, invalidate.

see also 694

470 teaching

n. teaching, education, pedagogy, pedagogics, didactics; instruction, training, study, schooling, direction, guidance, tuition, tutoring, coaching, tutelage; preparation, discipline, cultivation, enlightenment, edification; indoctrination, brainwashing, inculcation, conditioning, propagandism, proselytism; spoon-feeding.

course, curriculum, class, lesson, lecture, talk; catechism, sermon; homework, prep (*inf.*), assignment, exercise, task, work.

adj. educational, informative, instructive, enlightening, edifying; academic, pedagogical, didactic, scholastic.

vb. teach, educate, instruct, impart, inform, acquaint, familiarize, direct, guide, discipline, advise, counsel; convince, explain; prepare, initiate; school, coach, cram, prime, put through the mill (*inf.*); enlighten, edify; cultivate, nurture, train, exercise, practise, groom, drill, ground, bring up, foster, rear, breed, lick into shape (*inf.*); indoctrinate, inculcate, din into, force down someone's throat, ram down someone's throat (*inf.*), instill, imbue, condition; proselytize; catechize; hold classes, lecture, hold forth, expound, preach, sermonize, moralize.

471 misdirection

n. misdirection, misguidance, misinstruction, misteaching, misrepresentation, falsification, perversion, mistake, error, blind leading the blind.

vb. misdirect, misinform, mislead, misrepresent, pervert, distort, deceive.

472 learning

n. learning, knowledge, scholarship, training, erudition, lore; self-improvement, self-education, self-instruction; attainments, study, reading, application, studiousness, industry; lesson, class, course, classwork, homework, prep (*inf.*), assignment; revision, refresher course.

adj. knowledgeable, academic, studious, well-read, learned, industrious, scholarly, erudite; self-taught, self-instructed, self-made.

vb. learn, acquire, pick up, attain; experience, understand, grasp, discover, appreciate; master, become familiar with, get off pat (*inf.*), get the hang of (*inf.*); memorize, learn by heart; study, read, go into, go in for, specialize; absorb, assimilate, digest, drink in, imbibe; read up on, revise, review, refresh oneself, cram, prepare, get up, brush up, improve; pore over, bury oneself in; contemplate; burn the midnight oil; browse, scan, thumb through, flick through (*inf.*), dip into; improve one's mind, teach oneself; study under, sit at the feet of.

see also **426**

473 teacher

n. teacher, educator, advisor, guide, counsellor; school-teacher, headmaster, principal, head; professor, lecturer, don, reader, fellow, doctor, dean; tutor, instructor, pedagogue, coach, trainer, guru, governess.

see also **436**

474 learner

n. learner, pupil, scholar, student, schoolchild; undergraduate, fresher, freshman, graduate, postgraduate; swot, bookworm; follower, disciple, adherent; apprentice, trainee, probationer, novice, beginner, recruit, newcomer, tyro; class, set, form, grade, stream.

see also **428**

475 place of learning

n. school; nursery, kindergarten, crèche; college, polytechnic, university, academy, institute, institution, seminary, varsity (*inf.*), *conservatoire*, *lycée*, *gymnasium*; classroom, schoolroom, study, lecture theatre, auditorium; library, carrel.

476 truthfulness

n. truthfulness, veracity, integrity, frankness, openness, candour, straightforwardness, forthrightness; accuracy, honesty, reliability, sincerity, uprightness, guilelessness, impartiality.

adj. truthful, veracious, sincere, guileless, impartial; frank, open, candid, unreserved, plain, direct, straight, straightforward, forthright, blunt, ingenuous.

vb. be truthful, not lie; speak plainly, tell someone straight, not hesitate, make no bones about, speak one's mind, paint in its true colours, call a

spade a spade, tell all; not to put too
fine a point on it (*inf.*).
   see also 430, 508

477 falsehood

n. falsehood, fraudulence, falsification, fabrication, inaccuracy, deception, dishonesty, lying, mendacity,
perjury; misrepresentation, distortion,
perversion; double dealing, two-faced-
ness, duplicity, hypocrisy, insincerity,
guile; mockery, pretence, make-
believe, façade.

adj. false, lying, untruthful, men-
dacious; fabricated, inaccurate, misre-
presented, distorted, put on (*inf.*),
make-believe, counterfeit, bogus,
pretended, fake, invented, spurious;
fraudulent, dishonest, insincere,
hypocritical; double-dealing, two-
faced; roguish, corrupt, oily, smooth,
disingenuous, perfidious.

vb. falsify, lie, fib, exaggerate, understate, tell a white lie, bear false witness,
perjure oneself, forswear; prevaricate,
equivocate, deceive, mislead, misrepresent, distort, manipulate, doctor,
adulterate, make up, invent, concoct,
construct, contrive, fabricate, hatch,
get up (*inf.*), trump up, spin a yarn;
fake, counterfeit, forge; feign, put on
(*inf.*), put on a brave face, go through
the motions, play, pretend, make
believe, sham, simulate, dissemble;
laugh off (*inf.*).
   see also 431

478 deception

n. deception, misleading, deceit,
misrepresentation, cheating, trickery,
craftiness, treachery, fraudulence,
dishonesty, lying, guile, furtiveness,
beguilement, betrayal, treason; hoax,
crying wolf, delusion, self-deception,
wishful thinking, hallucination,
illusion.

trick, dodge, ruse, trap, artifice,
stratagem, subterfuge; fraud, swindle,
fiddle, rip-off (*sl.*), bamboozle (*inf.*),
skulduggery (*inf.*), underhand dealing,
sharp practice, sleight of hand, legerdemain.

adj. deceiving, deceptive, illusory,
false, sham, fake, fraudulent, dishonest,
underhand, behind someone's back,
furtive, treacherous, crafty, wily,
cunning, shifty.

vb. deceive, mislead, delude, fool,
trick, trap, trip up, catch, entrap,
ensnare, hoodwink, beguile, dupe, pull
the wool over someone's eyes (*inf.*);
outwit, outmanoeuvre; go behind
someone's back.

cheat, trick, defraud, swindle, fleece,
rip off (*sl.*), bamboozle (*inf.*), chisel
(*sl.*), cozen; go down (*inf.*), diddle
(*sl.*), cross (*sl.*), double-cross, pull a
fast one (*sl.*), stack the cards against,
put one over on (*inf.*), victimize; take
advantage of, get the better of, take for
a ride (*inf.*); hoax, cry wolf; play a
joke on, kid (*sl.*), pull someone's leg,
have on (*inf.*), trifle with, cajole;
betray, commit treason.

479 dupe

n. dupe, fool, victim, sucker (*sl.*),
sitting duck, simpleton, greenhorn,
gull.

480 deceiver

n. deceiver, beguiler, dodger, trickster, swindler, crook, cheat, rogue,
impostor, con man (*sl.*), phoney (*sl.*),
wolf in sheep's clothing, charlatan,
chisel (*sl.*), knave, cozener, sharper;
hypocrite, actor, dissembler, Tartuffe;
liar, fibber, story-teller; betrayer,
traitor, quisling, rat (*sl.*), informer,
double-crosser, victimizer; underground, fifth columnist, saboteur,
terrorist.

481 exaggeration

n. exaggeration, overstatement, extravagance, hyperbole, misrepresentation, misjudgment, stretching; storm in a teacup, much ado about nothing, stretch of the imagination, fantasy, tall story.

adj. exaggerated, extravagant, preposterous, fabulous, hyperbolic, excessive, superlative, overdone, out of all proportion, coloured, high-falutin, boastful, bombastic.

vb. exaggerate, overstate, overestimate, overplay, hyperbolize, make too much of, overdo, strain, misrepresent; amplify, enlarge, magnify, emphasize, highlight, maximize, heighten, intensify, aggravate; colour, embroider; make a mountain out of a molehill, stretch a point, lay it on thick, pile it on (*inf.*), out-herod Herod.

see also 417

C Means of communicating ideas

482 indication

n. indication, calling, identification, designation, symbolization, signification; sign, badge, emblem, figure, design, symbol, representation, type, token, logo; colophon, flag, banner, pennant, standard, ensign, colours, pendant, bunting, streamer, Union Jack, Stars and Stripes; coat of arms, crest, insignia, medal, regalia.

label, ticket, name, card, notice, bill, stub, counterfoil, docket, form, voucher, counter, chip, tab, tag; indicator, marker, pointer, needle, arrow, index, gauge; stamp, seal, imprint, impression, fingerprint, footprint; signature, autograph, initials, monogram.

signal, gesticulation, gesture; wink, nod, wave, call, shout, whistle, nudge; alarm, siren, hooter, bell; light, beacon.

evidence, hint, suggestion, note, explanation, proof, clue, intimation, symptom, hallmark.

adj. indicative, suggestive, symptomatic, symbolic, typical, representative.

vb. indicate, call, mean, signify; identify, designate, show, name, specify, appoint, assign, symbolize, point to; manifest, express, imply, bear the marks of, evince, intimate, denote, betoken; mark, point, gauge, brand, score, scratch, spot.

label, tag, docket, tab, earmark; stamp, seal, print, punch, impress, emboss, emblazon; sign, initial, autograph; annotate, number, letter, paginate.

gesticulate, gesture, signal, motion, wave, beckon, wink, nod, hoot, ring, shout, whistle, nudge.

483 record

n. record, register, catalogue, account, document, report, statement; brief, memo, memorandum, note; newspaper, bulletin, gazette, almanac; diary, journal, log; certificate, ticket; archives, public records, proceedings, minutes, annals, chronicle, scroll, inscription, manuscript; tape-recording, photograph, film, videotape.

souvenir, memento; relic, mark, trace, remains, evidence; trail, footprint, impression, scent; wash, wake; monument, testimony, witness, memorial, statue, column, cenotaph, remembrance, testimonial, mausoleum, shrine.

adj. recorded, documented, noted, reported.

vb. record, note, mark, report,

account, write down, take down, jot down; register, write in, enter, fill in, insert, inscribe, enrol, matriculate; document, list, catalogue, minute, chronicle; tape, tape-record, photograph, film.

adv. on record, in black and white, in writing, on the books.

484 recorder

n. recorder, registrar, secretary, clerk, accountant; diarist, chronicler, annalist, historian, biographer, journalist, archivist, scribe, amanuensis.

tape-recorder, stereo-recorder, cassette-recorder, video-recorder; record, disc.

485 obliteration

n. obliteration, deletion, erasure, effacement, blotting out, eradication, cancellation, expunction; eraser, rubber, sponge, duster.

vb. obliterate, wipe out, rub off, delete, efface, erase, blot out, black out, strike out, write out, leave no traces, remove, iron out, raze, cancel, expunge.

486 representation

n. representation, description, depiction, illustration, portrayal, exemplification, enactment, personification; reproduction, copy, imitation, image, likeness; picture, sketch, diagram, chart, map, model; art, painting, sculpture; photography, photograph, photo, snapshot, slide, transparency.

adj. representative, characteristic, typical, illustrative.

vb. represent, stand for, stand in the place of, serve as; render, realize, draw, depict, describe, portray, illustrate, picture, reproduce, delineate; reflect, mirror; exemplify, typify, embody, symbolize; designate, express.

487 misrepresentation

n. misrepresentation, distortion, perversion, twisting, falsification, exaggeration, understatement; caricature, parody, travesty, burlesque, counterfeit; misinterpretation.

vb. misrepresent, distort, twist, garble, warp, pervert, falsify, caricature, parody, give the wrong impression; misinterpret, misstate.

488 painting

n. painting, art, graphics, fine art; picture, illustration, mural, depiction, canvas, fresco, wall-painting, collage; work, study, sketch, drawing, outline, silhouette, cartoon, representation, copy, composition, likeness; abstract painting, landscape, portrait, self-portrait, still-life; watercolour, oil painting, miniature, masterpiece, old master.

technique, treatment, design, pattern, atmosphere, tone, shadow, values, perspective.

adj. graphic, visual, pictorial, picturesque, scenic.

vb. paint, portray, depict, compose, illustrate, draw, sketch, design, represent, copy, crayon, pencil, silhouette, ink, shade, tint, limn.

489 sculpture

n. sculpture, carving, stone-carving, cutting, casting, moulding; ceramics, pottery; statue, bust, cast, embossment, relief, marble, plaque, cameo; figure, representation, image.

adj. carved, sculptured, glyptic, glyphic.

vb. sculpture, sculpt, carve, chisel, cut, hew, shape, fashion, model, mould, emboss, cast.

490 engraving

n. engraving, etching, carving, chiselling, incising, printing, photogravure, lithography; inscription, print, lithograph, block, woodcut, linocut, plate.

vb. engrave, etch, inscribe, cut, carve, chisel, incise, chase, print, impress, stamp.

491 artist

n. artist, creator, composer, painter, designer, draughtsman, architect, drawer, sketcher, cartoonist, photographer, cameraman; sculptor, carver, modeller, statuary, lapidary; potter, ceramist; engraver, etcher, lithographer, printer, typographer.

492 language

n. language, communication, speech, tongue, talk, style, diction, parlance; utterance, expression, voice, articulation; idiom, dialect, provincialism, *patois*, jargon, pidgin, *koine*, *lingua franca*; mother tongue, vernacular, common speech, British English, American English, Standard English, Queen's English, Received Pronunciation; artificial language, world language, Esperanto; Babel, confusion of tongues.

linguistics, grammar, syntax, semantics, phonetics, phonology, historical linguistics, comparative linguistics, etymology, philology, dialectology, lexicography; linguist, polyglot, philologist, grammarian, lexicographer.

adj. linguistic, lingual, grammatical, standard, current, vernacular, idiomatic.

see also 514

493 letter

n. letter, symbol, consonant, vowel; capital, upper case, large letter, majus-

cule; small letter, lower case, minuscule; rune, cuneiform, hieroglyph; syllable, character, ideogram, pictogram; alphabet, ABC; orthography, spelling, spelling-pronunciation.

adj. literal, alphabetical, orthographic, syllabic.

vb. spell, letter, form letters; syllabify.

494 word

n. word, expression, term, name, designation, vocable, sound, syllable, utterance, phrase, construction, locution; neologism, slang, colloquialism, jargon, provincialism, cliché, vogue word, catch phrase, slogan; archaism; root, derivative, derivation; synonym, antonym, homonym.

vocabulary, lexicon, wordlist, dictionary, glossary, thesaurus, concordance, index; lexicology, lexicography, etymology, terminology.

adj. verbal, literal, lexical, lexicographical.

495 neologism

n. neologism, new word, new usage, coinage, neology; formation, translation, loan-word, borrowing, calque, portmanteau, blend, hybrid; corruption, barbarism, nonce word; cliché, vogue word, slang, vulgarism, argot, cant, colloquialism, informal usage, journalese, Americanism, Anglicism, Briticism.

adj. newly-coined, newfangled, colloquial, informal, slang, foreign, borrowed, translated, nonce, vogue.

496 nomenclature

n. nomenclature, naming, calling, appellation, designation, identification, terminology, classification.

name, title; Christian name, first name, given name, forename; surname, last name, family name, signature; sign, style, label, tag; nomen, denomination; nickname, description, epithet.

adj. nominal, titular; named, known as.

vb. name, call, designate, identify, specify, term, title, dub, label, tag, style; classify, characterize, describe, define, nominate, denominate; christen, baptize; be known as, be called, go by the name of, go under the name of.

497 misnomer

n. misnomer, misnaming, malapropism; nickname, pet name, pen name, pseudonym, fictitious name, assumed name, alias, *nom de plume*, stage name, sobriquet, *nom de guerre.*

anonymity, namelessness; what's-its-name, thinggamy (*inf.*), thingumabob (*inf.*), what-d'you-call-it, so-and-so, A. N. Other, Mr. X.

adj. misnamed, in name only, professed, pretended, pseudo-, quasi-, self-styled, so-called, *soi-disant;* anonymous, unknown, unidentified, nameless, unknown.

vb. misname, nickname, dub, mislabel, mistake.

498 phrase

n. phrase, clause, sentence, group of words; idiom, figure of speech; expression, utterance, locution; slogan, maxim, saying, formula, cliché.

vb. phrase, word, reword, express, state, put into words, formulate, verbalize.

499 grammar

n. grammar, usage, syntax, word order, sentence structure, analysis, parsing; inflection, case-ending, morphology, accidence.

part of speech, noun, substantive, proper noun, collective noun, mass noun, count noun, case, gender, number, declension; pronoun; verb, participle, gerund, copula, infinitive, split infinitive, person, tense, active, passive, conjugation; adjective, qualifier, modifier, comparative, superlative, comparison; adverb, particle; preposition; interjection; conjunction; article, definite article, indefinite article, determiner; subject, predicate; affix, prefix, suffix, infix.

adj. grammatical, syntactic, correct, proper, well-formed, acceptable, appropriate.

vb. parse, analyse, inflect, conjugate, decline.

500 solecism

n. solecism, ungrammaticalness, bad grammar, misusage, mistake, error, barbarism, blunder; mispronunciation, slip of the tongue; malapropism, spoonerism, cacology, catachresis.

adj. ungrammatical, incorrect, solecistic; slovenly, slipshod, loose; inappropriate, unacceptable, badly-formed.

vb. use bad grammar, make a mistake, murder the language.

see also 511

501 style

n. style, manner, characteristics, presentation; command, fluency, mastery, skill; manner of speaking, diction, phrasing, phraseology, wording, composition, writing; usage, mode of expression, expression, vocabulary, word-power, parlance, choice of words, way of putting it, feeling for words, *sprachgefühl;* mannerism, idiosyncrasy, intonation.

see also 510, 514

502 lucidity

n. lucidity, clearness, clarity, perspicuity, transparency, unambiguousness, intelligibility, directness, plain speech, simplicity, exactness, precision.

adj. lucid, clear, perspicuous, unambiguous, distinct, obvious, direct, plain, intelligible, explicit, easily understood, limpid, pellucid.

see also 452, 802

503 obscurity

n. obscurity, imperspicuity, vagueness, opaqueness, ambiguity, imprecision, unintelligibility, complexity, abstruseness.

adj. obscure, cloudy, blurred, fuzzy, vague, unclear, imperspicuous, imprecise, indistinct, ambiguous, unintelligible, incomprehensible, complicated, involved, intricate, abstruse.

see also 453, 803

504 conciseness

n. conciseness, succinctness, brevity, terseness, curtness, pithiness, laconism; contraction, ellipsis.

adj. concise, brief, succinct, condensed, compressed, shortened, short, precise, pithy, terse, compact, summary, laconic, sententious; elliptic, telegraphic.

vb. be concise, condense, compress, shorten, abridge, abbreviate, summarize, come to the point, put in a nutshell.

adv. in short, in brief, in a nutshell, to the point, to cut a long story short.

505 diffuseness

n. diffuseness, profuseness, abundance; wordiness, verbosity, discursiveness; digression, departure, deviation, excursus; tautology, redundancy, verbiage, repetition, padding, circumlocution, periphrasis, pleonasm.

adj. diffuse, discursive, wordy, lengthy, long-winded, verbose, tedious, rambling, digressive, redundant, repetitious, protracted, prolix, pleonastic, roundabout, periphrastic, circumlocutory.

vb. amplify, enlarge on, develop, expatiate; digress, ramble, wander, deviate, go off at a tangent, go off the subject, get off the point, get sidetracked, beat about the bush (*inf.*); go on and on, talk at length, repeat oneself.

see also 516

506 vigour

n. vigour, power, strength, intensity, force, effectiveness, forcefulness, urgency, piquancy; sparkle, spirit, punch (*sl.*), fervour, vehemence, verve, animation, vitality, fire, glow, warmth.

adj. vigorous, powerful, strong, forceful, trenchant, incisive, bold, tough, lively, inspired, sparkling, racy, fervent, vehement, insistent, impassioned, fiery, ardent, passionate, persuasive; vivid, graphic; pointed.

see also 173, 755

507 feebleness

n. feebleness, weakness, faintness, frailty, flaccidity, enfeeblement, pauperism, barrenness, lifelessness.

adj. feeble, weak, faint, frail, thin, poor, limp, lifeless, flaccid, insipid, meagre, scant, slight, shallow, diluted, wishy-washy, uninspired, stale, flat, tame, forced.

see also 162

508 plainness

n. plainness, simplicity, plain speech, naturalness, straightforwardness, modesty, unpretentiousness, severity.

adj. plain, simple, natural, unaffected, artless, naive, straightforward, modest, ordinary, undramatic, severe, restrained, unadorned, unpretentious, unsophisticated, common, homely, homespun, unimaginative, matter-of-fact; direct, frank, open, blunt.

vb. speak plainly, call a spade a spade, come straight to the point.

  see also 476

509 ornament

n. ornamentation, adornment, embellishment, elaboration, enrichment, enhancement, decoration, embroidery, floweriness.

ornament, colour, frills, rhetoric, metaphor, euphemism, verbosity, grandiloquence, bombast, fustian.

adj. ornate, adorned, embellished, grand, rich, lofty, elaborate, lavish, grandiose; vivid, dazzling, scintillating; fancy, extravagant, pretentious, showy, flashy, loud, flaunting, boastful, big, high-falutin, high-flown, big-sounding, magniloquent; rhetorical, voluble, pompous, flowery, euphemistic, euphuistic, grandiloquent.

vb. embellish, adorn, enrich, colour; talk big, lay it on (*inf.*).

  see also 846

510 elegance

n. elegance, tastefulness, style, grace, graciousness, dignity, beauty, correctness, refinement, propriety, polish, finish; harmony, balance, proportion, rhythm; artificiality, affectation.

adj. elegant, tasteful, gracious, graceful, dignified, artistic, delicate, refined, pure, stylized, polished; proper, appropriate, happy, well-expressed, right, correct, felicitous, seemly; harmonious, balanced, well-proportioned, well-turned, mellifluous; affected, artificial.

  see also 848

511 inelegance

n. inelegance, tastelessness, bad taste, gracelessness, impropriety; barbarism, coarseness, vulgarity; incorrectness, stiltedness, formality, awkwardness, clumsiness.

adj. inelegant, tasteless, graceless, unseemly, improper, incorrect, laboured, stilted, forced, heavy, stiff, formal, ponderous, clumsy, awkward, inappropriate; coarse, crude, vulgar, rude, uncouth.

  see also 849

512 voice

n. voice, sound, speech, language, utterance; vocal organs, vocal chords, tongue, lips, larynx, lungs, breath; articulation, pronunciation, vocalization, enunciation, delivery, inflection, intonation, pitch, rhythm, tone, accent, timbre, stress, emphasis; vowel, consonant, phoneme; phonetics.

adj. vocal, expressed, uttered, spoken, oral, lingual, vocalic, phonetic, voiced, sonant, sounded; clear, distinct, articulate.

vb. voice, speak, express, sound, pronounce, utter, articulate, get one's tongue round, vocalize, enunciate; nasalize, palatalize, aspirate; roll, trill, burr; stress, emphasize.

513 muteness

n. muteness, aphonia, voicelessness, inarticulation, dumbness, silence.

adj. mute, voiceless, speechless, tongueless, unsounded, unvoiced, unvocal, surd, inarticulate, tongue-tied, dumb, silent, mum, inaudible.

vb. mute, silence, dumbfound, strike dumb, still, soften, deaden, muffle, suppress, smother.

  see also 517, 779

514 speech

n. speech, language, talk, discourse, utterance, articulation, expression, pronunciation, communication; eloquence, fluency, expressiveness, facility, vivacity, style, poise, delivery, rhetoric, vigour, force, gift of the gab (*inf.*).

speaker, talker, conversationalist; public speaker, orator, lecturer, after-dinner speaker, expositor, rhetorician, declaimer, preacher; spokesman, mouthpiece.

adj. speaking, talking, verbal, oral; articulating; eloquent, fluent, voluble, expressive, forceful, meaningful.

vb. speak, say, talk; vocalize, pronounce, voice, enunciate; express, utter, tell, affirm, converse, communicate, chat; repeat, rattle off, trot out (*inf.*).

address, discuss, lecture, teach, instruct, plead, argue, make a speech, give a talk, deliver a lecture, have the floor, hold forth, preach, speechify (*inf.*), rant, spout.

see also **468, 516**

515 imperfect speech

n. imperfect speech, speech defect, aphasia, impediment, stammer, stutter, faltering, hesitation, mispronunciation, lisp, twang, nasalization, drawl.

adj. inarticulate, indistinct, throaty, shaking, stuttering, stammering, hesitant.

vb. stammer, stutter, hesitate, pause, falter, stumble, lisp, drawl, slur, speak through one's nose, mispronounce, mumble, mutter, garble, swallow one's words.

516 talkativeness

n. talkativeness, gift of the gab (*inf.*), loquacity, garrulity, verbosity, long-windedness.

chatter, chat, jabber, babble, prattle, blather, prittle-prattle (*inf.*), chit-chat,

idle talk, chinwag (*sl.*), palaver, small talk; nonsense, drive, twaddle, hot air (*sl.*), yap (*inf.*), yackety-yack (*sl.*); gossip, scandal.

chatterbox, prattler, jabberer, tattler, windbag (*inf.*), gasbag (*si.*); gossip, muckraker (*inf.*).

adj. talkative, chatty, voluble, loquacious, garrulous; chattering, babbling; glib, eloquent, fluent; long-winded, verbose; gossipy.

vb. chat, keep on, go on about (*inf.*), chatter, talk idly, waffle, ramble on; babble, jabber, prattle, gabble, yackety-yack (*sl.*), yack (*inf.*); gossip, tell tales.

see also **505**

517 taciturnity

n. taciturnity, reserve, reticence, silence, uncommunicativeness, no comment, curtness, brusqueness; modesty, hesitance.

adj. taciturn, reserved, reticent, silent, dumb, mute, quiet, uncommunicative, secretive, tight-lipped, close-lipped, mum, restrained, hesitant, modest, retiring; curt, brusque, laconic; aloof, distant.

vb. say nothing, refuse to comment, keep quiet, keep one's mouth shut, hold one's tongue, save one's breath; stand aloof.

see also **779**

518 address

n. address, speech, talk, lecture, oration, discourse, reading, recitation, recital, exhortation, paper, pep talk (*sl.*), spiel (*sl.*), appeal, invocation, homily, sermon, allocution; harangue, tirade, declamation.

inaugural address, opening; greeting, salutation; farewell address, goodbye, valediction.

oratory, rhetoric, speech-making,

public speaking, elocution, preaching, homiletics.

519 conversation

n. conversation, chat, talk, discussion, interview, exchange of views, interchange, expression, repartee, colloquy, interlocution; chatter, chit-chat, prattle; *tête-à-tête*, heart-to-heart.

conference, debate, dialogue, consultation, conflab (*inf.*), powwow, summit conference, summit, congress, symposium, convention, seminar, parley, council, audience, hearing.

vb. converse, chat, discuss, hold a conversation, communicate, counsel, confer, exchange views, debate, negotiate, put one's heads together, confabulate.

520 monologue

n. monologue, soliloquy, monody; apostrophe, aside.

vb. soliloquize, talk to oneself.

521 writing

n. writing, script, lettering, calligraphy, stroke, flourish; handwriting, hand, fist, longhand; graphology, chirography; mark, scribble, scrawl; transcription, inscription, printing, copying, shorthand, stenography, typing; correspondence, letter-writing; journalism, reporting.

written matter, copy, work, composition, document, paper, manuscript, transcript, typescript, parchment, scroll.

writer, calligrapher, scribe, copyist, transcriber, secretary, stenographer, typist; author, novelist, journalist.

adj. written, graphic, in writing, handwritten, in black and white, roman, italic.

vb. write, pen, compose, prepare, draft, write out, report, document,

write down, record, put pen to paper; scribble, scrawl; transcribe, inscribe, copy, engrave, print, type.

522 printing

n. printing, typography; composition, typesetting; publishing; print, impression, stamp, page, sheet, copy, printed matter; type, lead, leading, rule, letter, fount, space; galley, proof, slip, bromide.

printer, typographer, typesetter, compositor; proofreader, reader; copy editor.

adj. printed, in print, typographical.

vb. print, impress, imprint, stamp, engrave; compose, set type, set up; run off, go to press, put to bed; publish, issue, bring out.

523 correspondence

n. correspondence, communication, exchange of letters, post, mail; letter, postcard, note, message, report, missive, dispatch, epistle, chit, acknowledgement, reply, answer; business letter, love letter, valentine, fan letter, poison pen letter, chain letter, round robin, circular; address, destination.

correspondent, letter-writer, penfriend, pen-pal (*inf.*), addressee, recipient.

adj. epistolary, postal.

vb. correspond, write to, communicate, exchange letters, drop a line, send, post, mail, dispatch.

524 book

n. book, publication, work, volume, tome, copy, text, manuscript, bestseller, paperback, hardback, booklet, edition, reprint, offprint; study book, course book, textbook, set book, primer, workbook; reader, companion volume, selected readings; complete works, omnibus edition.

magazine, periodical, journal, review, gazette; back number, back issue.

reference book, encyclopedia, cyclopedia, handbook, manual, dictionary, bible, guidebook; index, concordance; bibliography, reading list.

library, collection of books, lending library, public library, mobile library, inter-library loan.

writer, author, novelist, biographer, essayist, reporter, ghost-writer, hack; editor, publisher, reviewer, critic; man of letters, man of learning, bookworm, scholar, book-collector, bibliophile.

525 description

n. description, account, report, statement, record, summary, information, explanation, characterization, specification; portrayal, sketch, portrait, representation, illustration, picture, image, profile; narrative, story, tale, yarn, anecdote, saga, epic; fiction, myth, legend, fairy-tale, fairy story, fantasy, fable, parable, allegory; plot, story-line, subject, argument.

narrator, reciter, story-teller, novelist, raconteur, anecdotist, fabricator.

adj. descriptive, narrative, expressive; graphic, vivid, true-to-life, lifelike, telling, detailed, pictorial; fictional, made-up, legendary, mythical, fabulous, parabolic, allegorical.

vb. describe, portray, sketch, set forth, represent, outline, trace, illustrate, picture, draw, paint, imagine, delineate, characterize, define, specify, mark out, express; account, report, state, record, explain, summarize; narrate, tell, recount, relate, recite, rehearse.

526 dissertation

n. dissertation, essay, paper, composition, commentary, exposition, thesis, treatise, monograph, discourse, disquisition; survey, review, analysis, examination, enquiry, investigation, study, discussion, story, comment, write-up, critique.

essayist, expositor, commentator; critic, reviewer.

vb. discuss, treat, handle, concern, deal with, consider, comment; analyse, survey, examine, explain, interpret; review, criticize, write up.

527 compendium

n. compendium, summary, resumé, precis, abridgment, abstract, summing up, syllabus, survey, outline, synopsis, skeleton, reduction, analysis, conspectus, epitome; core, essence; digest, miscellany, anthology, selections, readings.

adj. compendious, concise, brief, succinct, abbreviated.

vb. summarize, sum up, abstract, abridge, condense, reduce, shorten, digest, outline, survey; boil down to.

528 poetry; prose

n. poetry, song, rhyme, poem, verse, stanza, sonnet, ode, lyric, idyll, epic, ballad, jingle, limerick; chorus, refrain; prosody, versification, scansion, rhythm, metre, stress, beat, foot; prose, writing, literature, composition, story.

poet, writer, composer, versifier, poet laureate, bard, minstrel, troubadour.

adj. poetic, rhythmic, lyrical, idyllic, tuneful.

vb. poetize, sing, versify; rhyme, scan; write, conceive, imagine, compose.

529 drama

n. theatre, the stage; hall, opera

house, cinema, playhouse; play, drama, show, opera, melodrama, tragicomedy, tragedy, comedy, farce, slapstick, pantomime, mime, variety, cabaret, pageant, revue, spectacle, carnival; presentation, appearance, exhibition, production; dramatics, stagecraft, showmanship, acting, performance, histrionics.

actor, actress, performer, player, role, part, character, Thespian, lead, star, understudy, extra; cast, characters, *dramatis personae*.

adj. dramatic, theatrical; impressive, spectacular.

vb. dramatize, direct, produce, present, stage, produce, put on, perform, enact, play.

V Volition

1 Individual volition

A Volition in general

530 will

n. will, volition, intention, resolution, power, mind, conviction, determination, willpower, choice, free will, discretion, conation; desire, wish, inclination.

adj. volitional, willing, minded, voluntary, free, intentional, wilful, deliberate, wished, premeditated, conative.

vb. will, wish, want, desire, incline, choose, resolve, make a decision, decide, make up one's mind, determine, purpose, see fit, take it into one's head to (*inf.*), have one's own way; conclude, come to the conclusion.

adv. at will, at pleasure, as one thinks, of one's own accord.

531 necessity

n. necessity, compulsion, obligation; inevitability, unavoidability, certainty, inexorableness, inescapableness; determinism, predestination, foreordination, fatalism; involuntariness, spontaneity, reflex action, instinct, intuition.

no choice, no alternative, Hobson's choice, six of one and half a dozen of the other; must (*inf.*), essential, prerequisite; fate, the inevitable, whatever will be shall be, *che sara, sara*.

adj. necessary, inevitable, unavoidable, inescapable, inexorable, certain, sure, foreordained, predetermined, destined, predestined, irresistible; essential, indispensable, imperative; compulsory, obligatory; deterministic, fatalistic; involuntary, unintentional, instinctive, unconscious, automatic, reflex, mechanical.

vb. necessitate, compel, oblique, constrain, force, dictate; destine, foreordain; need, require, cry out for.

adv. of necessity, necessarily, inevitably, certainly, willy-nilly.

532 willingness

n. willingness, readiness, disposition, inclination, compliance; eagerness, enthusiasm, zeal, earnestness.

adj. willing, prepared, ready, disposed, inclined, game, desirous, compliant, eager, enthusiastic, zealous; voluntary, uninvited, unasked, unprompted.

vb. be willing, like to, want, desire, choose, feel like, show willing (*inf.*), be inclined towards; volunteer, take on the responsibility, offer oneself; be eager, enthuse, jump at, leap at, lean over backwards (*inf.*), fall over oneself to (*inf.*); gush over, go overboard about (*inf.*), go to town on (*inf.*).

adv. willingly, gladly, eagerly, readily; voluntarily, of one's own accord; off one's own bat.

see also 611

533 unwillingness

n. unwillingness, disinclination, unreadiness, hesitation, reluctance, scruple, qualm, aversion, demur; non-cooperation, protest, abstention.

adj. unwilling, unready, disinclined, reluctant, hesitant, averse, opposed, loath, not in the mood, unenthusiastic, indifferent, half-hearted.

vb. be unwilling, not feel like, not want to, would rather not, refuse, hesitate, hold back, balk at, shirk, demur, fight shy of, shy away, shrink, dodge, evade; force oneself.

adv. unwillingly, without enthusiasm, against one's will, against one's better judgment, under protest, grudgingly.

see also 612

534 resolution

n. resolution, determination, resolve, certainty, persistence, constancy, doggedness, conviction, perseverance, boldness, tenacity, fortitude, steadfastness; firmness, willpower, strength of will, mettle; self-control, self-reliance, self-possession.

adj. resolute, determined, steadfast, firm, steady, strong, certain, serious, strong-willed, iron-willed, inflexible, bold, persistent, tenacious, constant, dogged; single-minded, wholehearted, committed, decided; unyielding, unhesitating, unflinching, unwavering, unswerving, unbending.

vb. be resolute, determine, resolve, decide, be bent on; have one's heart set upon, stand fast, take one's stand, hold one's ground, not give in, stick to one's guns, stand no nonsense, put one's foot down; take the bull by the horns; commit oneself, dedicate, put one's heart and soul into.

535 perseverance

n. perseverance, tenacity, steadfastness, firmness, persistence, continuance, constancy, endurance, indefatigability, undauntedness, doggedness; stamina, guts (*inf.*), staying power, backbone, stickability (*sl.*), moral fibre, stiff upper lip.

stayer, bulldog.

adj. persevering, persistent, determined, tenacious, steadfast, constant, steady, firm, unmoved, undaunted, indefatigable, untiring, obstinate, enduring, continuing; diligent, industrious, assiduous.

vb. persevere, remain, persist, endure, continue to the end, go on, carry on, have what it takes, keep at it, keep going (*inf.*), stick at it (*inf.*), soldier on, plod (*inf.*), plug away (*inf.*), slog away, see it through (*inf.*), stick it out (*inf.*); stick out for, hold out for; hold a job down (*inf.*).

536 irresolution

n. irresolution, indecision, vacillation, wavering, fluctuation; inconstancy, hesitation, fickleness, instability.

adj. irresolute, indecisive, undecided, fluctuating, wavering, vacillating, fickle, hesitant, in two minds, unstable, infirm, inconstant, changeable.

vb. be irresolute, vacillate, waver, fluctuate, hesitate, falter, shilly-shally.

537 obstinacy

n. obstinacy, stubbornness, inflexibility, rigidity, tenacity, hardness, relentlessness, obduracy, intransigence, intractableness; bigotry, dogmatism, narrow-mindedness, intolerance, fanaticism.

dogmatist, bigot, fanatic, die-hard, mule, intransigent; pedant, stickler.

adj. obstinate, stubborn, inflexible, tenacious, uncompromising, intransigent, unyielding, unrelenting, hardened, hard, intractable, headstrong, self-willed, set in one's ways; stiff-necked, pig-headed, recalcitrant, refractory, obdurate, pertinacious; dogmatic.

vb. be obstinate, not give in, stick to one's guns; resist, oppose, dig one's heels in.

see also 534, 535

538 change of mind

n. change of mind, second thoughts, afterthought, change of heart, *volte-face*, repentance; retraction, withdrawal, backing out, reversal, abandonment, desertion, defection, renunciation, recantation; tergiversation, backsliding, apostasy.

turncoat, time-server, rat, renegade, traitor, deserter, apostate.

adj. fickle, irresolute, unfaithful, inconstant.

vb. change one's mind, have second thoughts, think beter of, change one's tune; take back, withdraw, back out, back down, climb down (*inf.*), disown, deny, retract, revoke, recant, disclaim; nullify; trim; apologize, eat humble pie, eat one's words; fall away, apostasize.

539 caprice

n. caprice, whim, fancy, vagary, notion, quirk, prank, crotchet, freak, craze, whimsy, whim-wham, flash; jest,

witticism; capriciousness, whimsicality; fickleness, inconstancy.

adj. capricious, whimsical, fanciful, inconstant, fickle, changeable, flighty, frivolous, freakish, crotchety, unpredictable, erratic, fitful.

540 choice

n. choice, option, decision, determination, selection, adoption; alternative, preference, substitute.

vote, ballot, poll, election, representation, referendum, plebiscite; suffrage, franchise; voter, elector, electorate, constituency, ward.

adj. optional, elective, selective, discretional, discriminating, choosy (*inf.*), fastidious; electoral, voting.

vb. choose, pick, decide on, opt, adopt, sort, prefer, take up, go for, plump for (*inf.*), like, fancy, favour, appoint, co-opt, elect, nominate, commit oneself; separate, select, isolate, segregate, cull, glean, sift, winnow, divide the sheep from the goats, separate the wheat from the chaff; weigh, judge, discriminate, make up one's mind; vote, cast votes, poll, ballot, draw lots, vote in, return.

541 absence of choice

n. no choice, Hobson's choice, first come first served; impartiality, neutrality, no preference, indifference; abstention, don't know.

adj. choiceless, neutral, impartial, disinterested, unbiased, indifferent.

vb. be neutral, abstain, not commit oneself, sit on the fence, not take sides.

542 rejection

n. rejection, dismissal, repudiation, denial, refusal, renunciation, rebuff, disownment, disapproval, exclusion, expulsion.

adj. rejected, repudiated, excluded, renounced, spurned.

vb. reject, not accept, dismiss, exclude, repudiate, renounce, deny, refuse, disapprove, rebuff, spurn, decline, disown, disclaim, despise, turn up one's nose at (*inf.*), expel, jettison, discard, brush aside, have nothing to do with, turn one's back on, laugh in someone's face (*inf.*).

see also **556, 694**

543 predetermination

n. predetermination, predestination, preordination, inevitability, necessity, finality; prediction, forecast; doom, fate; premeditation, predeliberation, foregone conclusion.

adj. predetermined, planned, proposed, designed, fixed, deliberate.

vb. predetermine, foreordain, predestine, appoint, destine, predestinate; predict, forecast, foretell, determine beforehand; premeditate, preconceive.

544 spontaneity

n. spontaneity, spur of the moment; improvisation, extemporization; involuntariness, reflex action; impetuosity, impulsiveness, hastiness, suddenness, rashness; impulse buying.

adj. spontaneous, impulsive, unpremeditated, unthinking, unconsidered; involuntary, automatic, instinctive, reflex; extempore, impromptu, improvised, ad lib (*inf.*); hasty, sudden, rash, precipitate; casual, offhand, throwaway.

vb. act impulsively; blurt out, say the first thing that comes into one's mind; improvise, extemporize, ad lib (*inf.*), play by ear.

adv. on impulse, on the spur of the moment, impulsively, rashly, instinctively, automatically.

see also **613, 859**

545 habit

n. habit, custom, mode, practice, wont, usage, fashion, style, rule, procedure; tendency, propensity, bent, disposition, predisposition, weakness, bias, penchant, second nature, instinct; routine, ritual, rut, groove, treadmill, regularity; convention, precedent, tradition, etiquette, protocol, the done thing; conditioning, accustoming, adaptation, familiarization, training, acclimatization.

addict, habitué, fiend, creature of habit, devotee, client, patron, regular (*inf.*).

adj. usual, customary, normal, common, general, accepted, expected, prevalent, current, conventional, orthodox, established; habitual, frequent, regular, routine, stereotyped; mechanical, seasoned, inveterate; confirmed, ingrained, deep-seated; besetting, clinging, persistent; accustomed, used to, adapted.

vb. accustom, get used to, take to, adapt, adjust, accommodate, condition, train, familiarize, orientate, acclimatize, harden, season, inure, habituate; catch on.

be wont to, be in the habit of, make a practice of.

adv. usually, as is usual, generally.

546 absence of habit

n. disuse, unaccustomedness, desuetude, cessation, relinquishment; decay, neglect, deterioration.

adj. unused, unaccustomed, not used to, not in the habit of; unskilled, inexperienced.

vb. break a habit, abandon, neglect, relinquish, discard, discontinue, rid

oneself of, throw off, wean from; not
get used to, not take to; not catch on.
see also 607

547 motive

n. motive, cause, reason, purpose,
ground, basis, spring, spur, impetus,
urge, prod, goad, carrot, lure, bait;
influence, stimulus, incentive, inspiration, prompting, instigation; persuasion, inducement, coaxing, cajolery,
wheedling; charm, attraction, glamour;
enticement, temptation, bribery.

motivator, instigator, prompter,
animator, coaxer, wheedler; pressure
group, lobby, lobbyist.

adj. motivating, persuasive, convincing, impelling, forceful; provocative,
stimulating, rousing; fascinating,
alluring, charming, captivating,
enthralling, enticing, tantalizing.

vb. motivate, cause, inspire, stimulate, prompt, instigate, insist,
induce, drive, push, egg on, spur, urge,
prod, goad; provoke, elicit, call forth,
evoke; influence, encourage, support;
persuade, sway, prevail on, talk into,
win over, wear down resistance, brainwash (*inf.*), twist round one's little
finger (*inf.*), pull strings; coax, cajole,
wheedle; captivate, fascinate, charm,
attract, interest, entice, tempt, tantalize, beguile, enrapture; lobby, put
pressure on; bribe, buy, get at (*inf.*),
oil, corrupt.

548 dissuasion

n. dissuasion, discouragement, hindrance, deterrent, disincentive, dam-
per, restraint, cold water, wet blanket;
spoilsport, killjoy.

adj. dissuasive, discouraging.

vb. dissuade, deter, hinder, prevent,
advise against, discourage, talk out of,
wean from, dampen, stifle, disparage,
pour cold water on.

549 pretext

n. pretext, excuse, plea, apology,
justification, pretence, show,
guise, veil, cloak, mask, appearance,
alibi.

adj. ostensible, alleged, specious.

vb. allege, pretend, claim, profess,
excuse; apologize, make excuses, bluff.

550 good

n. good, benefit, gain, profit, success,
advantage, service, boon, windfall,
godsend, pennies from heaven, providence, blessing, good turn; well-
being, welfare, prosperity, fortune,
happiness, weal; improvement, betterment, edification, progress.

adj. good, beneficial, advantageous,
helpful, useful, edifying.

see also 899, 935

551 evil

n. evil, misfortune, ill, harm, ruin,
nuisance, disadvantage, bane, accident,
tragedy, disaster, catastrophe,
calamity, affliction, trial, crying shame,
raw deal; foul play, wrong, injury,
pain, anguish, hurt; wickedness,
corruption.

adj. evil, bad, wicked; unfortunate,
ill, tragic, catastrophic, disastrous,
painful, distressing, hurtful.

see also 900, 936

B Prospective volition

552 intention

n. intention, purpose, aim, intent,
meaning; goal, object, end, objective,
mark, destination, target; plan, design,
idea, proposal; dream, desire, aspiration, expectation, ambition.

adj. intended, designed, planned,
proposed, deliberate; intending, pur-
poseful, teleological.

vb. intend, aim, go for, attempt, try for, pursue; plan, propose, project, design, purpose, mean; dream, expect, hope, aspire, have designs on (*inf.*); consider, think about, contemplate, study, have in mind, have in view, calculate, work out, decide, determine, resolve.

553 chance

n. chance, randomness, uncertainty, fortuity; fate, fortune, luck, coincidence, fluke, toss-up (*inf.*); speculation, venture, risk, hazard; bet, gamble, wager, stake, flutter, draw, lottery.

speculator, gambler, better, backer, punter; bookmaker, turf accountant, bookie (*inf.*).

adj. chance, lucky, fortuitous, unintentional, haphazard, aimless, random, risky, hazardous, touch-and-go.

vb. chance, risk, venture, hazard, speculate, gamble, bet, wager, back.

see also **158**

554 pursuit

n. pursuit, hunt, chase, race, pursuance, quest, search, tracking; hunter, chaser, pursuer, seeker, quester, follower.

adj. pursuing, following.

vb. pursue, look for, search, follow up, seek, quest, prosecute; hunt, go after, chase, give chase, hound, tail, trail, stalk, shadow, track, sniff out (*inf.*), smell out, dog.

prep. after, in pursuit of, on the track of.

555 avoidance

n. avoidance, evasion, escape, flight, withdrawal, retreat, shunning, abstinence, circumvention; shirker, fugitive, runaway, absconder, eloper, deserter, refugee, truant.

adj. avoiding, evasive, elusive.

vb. avoid, escape, evade, elude, keep away, keep off, boycott; flee, shrink, flinch; get out of, shun, shirk, dodge, flunk, turn away, duck, hedge; steer clear of, keep one's distance, take no part in, leave alone, not get involved in, disregard, give the go-by; abstain, refrain; retreat, withdraw.

556 relinquishment

n. relinquishment, abandonment, giving up, surrender, renunciation, discontinuance, withdrawal, desertion, quitting.

vb. relinquish, abandon, give up, renounce, forgo, abdicate, waive, surrender, throw in the towel; turn over to, turn in; leave, quit, withdraw, back out, go back on, retreat, secede, forsake; discontinue, break with, break off with, drop, let go, throw away, cast off, discard, part with, shed, desert, chuck (*inf.*), ditch, jilt; leave in the lurch, have done with (*inf.*), walk out on (*inf.*).

see also **542, 713**

557 business

n. business, affairs, dealings, trade; job, employment, post, appointment, position, situation, engagement, incumbency; vocation, calling, pursuit, occupation, profession, line of business, speciality, *métier*, craft; career, life-work, life, mission; work, task, undertaking, activity, assignment, affair, concern; function, office, role, capacity, responsibility, duty, charge, commission, terms of reference, scope, area, field, realm, province, portfolio.

adj. businesslike, efficient, professional, official, prompt; busy, tied up with (*inf.*).

vb. employ, occupy, appoint, select, recruit, engage, contract, take on, give

558

a job to, commission, enlist, hire, rope in (inf.), take on the payroll; work, undertake, be busy, be occupied with, be engaged on, be about.

558 plan

n. plan, scheme, project, design, programme, proposal, schedule; scope, outline, sketch; method, procedure, guidelines, principles; policy, course of action, strategy; representation, chart; master-plan, long-range plan; blueprint, draft, rough draft, pilot scheme, dummy run; plot, conspiracy, intrigue, cabal, little game (inf.).

planner, director, designer, organizer, architect, engineer, administrator; conspirer, plotter, schemer.

adj. planned, projected, prospective, on the drawing board, procedural.

vb. plan, design, work out, draw up, organize, arrange, propose, devise, create, dream up (inf.), frame, undertake, proceed, outline, sketch, draft; forecast, project, think ahead, phase; scheme, plot, conspire, concoct, hatch.

559 way

n. way, manner, fashion; method, means, procedure, process; tactics, measures, steps; direction, passage, entrance, access, approach, route, itinerary, course.

path, track, footpath, walk; road, street, avenue, lane, drive, crescent, close, alley, terrace, park, garden, green, hill, grove, boulevard, square, place, court, circus, arcade, piazza, market, mall, embankment; ring-road, by-pass, arterial road, motorway, dual carriageway, clearway, primary route, trunk road, highway.

railway, underground, tube; main line, branch line, feeder.

560 mid-course

n. centre, mean, middle course, middle of the road, half-way house.

adj. middle, central, medial, neutral, middle-of-the-road, unextreme, moderate, intermediate, midway, half-way.

561 circuit

n. circuit, detour, by-pass, roundabout way; digression, deviation.

adj. circuitous, roundabout, indirect, out-of-the-way.

see also **250**

562 requirement

n. requirement, requisite, stipulation, need, want, demand; condition; essential, imperative, necessity, must (inf.); desideratum; needfulness, obligation, compulsion, indispensability, emergency, urgency, matter of life and death, essentiality.

adj. necessary, essential, imperative, indispensable, vital, needful, urgent; wanted, in demand.

vb. require, need, want, wish; lack, be in need of, miss; demand, call for, ask, invite, cry out for; necessitate, force, compel.

563 instrumentality

n. instrumentality, mediation, subservience, intervention; help, aid, assistance, agency, medium, vehicle, intermediary, organ.

adj. instrumental, intermediate, conducive, assisting, subsidiary, auxiliary, subservient, contributory, helpful; effective.

vb. be instrumental, help, aid, mediate.

see also **172**

564 means

n. means, wherewithal, resources, ways and means, equipment, supplies, assets, reserves, provisions; power, potential; factor, agent, medium, channel, organization.

vb. find the means, provide, equip, supply.

565 instrument

n. instrument, implement, apparatus, equipment, appliance, gadget, device, invention, contrivance, contraption; machine, mechanism, machinery, engine; tool, utensil; computer, robot, automaton.

adj. instrumental, mechanical, automatic.

566 materials

n. materials, resources, supplies, assets, means, wherewithal, stuff, raw materials.

567 store

n. store, collection, accumulation, heap, pile, stack, load, mass, stock, hoard, bulk, deposit, bundle; crop, harvest; hoard, treasure, reserves, savings, nest-egg; backlog; fountain, well, spring, gold-mine, reservoir; abundance, profusion, fullness.

storage, safekeeping; warehouse, stockroom, storeroom, depot, depository; library, museum, archives.

adj. stored, accumulated, saved, kept.

vb. store, keep, put away, put aside, put by, stow away, stash away (*inf.*); accumulate, pile up, heap, stack, amass, bulk, bundle, stockpile, lay in; collect, save, deposit, invest, hoard, salt away (*inf.*); harvest, gather; put by for a rainy day.

adv. aside, in store, in reserve, in stock.

568 provision

n. provision, equipment, supply, furnishings, fittings, fixtures, reserve, store, facilities, belongings, accessories,

accompaniments, outfit, paraphernalia, apparatus, appliance; catering, purveying.

adj. provided, furnished, equipped, well-equipped.

vb. provide, equip, supply, furnish, fit, prepare, rig, dress, assemble, deck; give, afford, lend, invest, endow; maintain, stock, cater; supplement, complement; replenish, fill up.

569 waste

n. waste, ruin, decay, devastation, desolation, dilapidation, deterioration, erosion, wear and tear, loss, exhaustion, depletion, decline; consumption, disuse, misuse, squandering, uselessness, dissipation; extravagance, wastefulness, prodigality; excess.

adj. wasteful, extravagant, prodigal, squandering, spendthrift; wasted, squandered, depleted, worthless.

vb. waste, consume, expend, eat up, eat away, exhaust, reduce, deplete, empty, drain, devour, dissipate; squander, lavish, abuse; destroy, erode, decay, dry up, dwindle, wither, run dry, wear out; be of no avail, come to nothing.

570 sufficiency

n. sufficiency, adequacy, enough to go on with; right amount.

adj. sufficient, adequate, enough, satisfactory, acceptable; plenty, abundant, generous, liberal, full, complete, replete.

vb. be sufficient, suffice, be enough, avail, do, comply with, qualify, fill the bill, come up to, live up to, satisfy requirements, make the grade, prove acceptable; lick into shape (*inf.*).

571 insufficiency

n. insufficiency, inadequacy, deficiency, scarcity, meagreness, scantiness, slightness, poverty, paucity, dearth, lack.

adj. insufficient, inadequate, not enough, unacceptable, meagre, thin, slight, scanty, poor, bankrupt, sparing, unsatisfactory, wanting, lacking, missing, failing, disappointing; miserly, parsimonious.

vb. be insufficient, not come up to, fall short, come short, fail, want, need, lack, require.

prep. without, in want of, short of.

see also 35

572 excess

n. excess, redundance; exorbitance, inordinacy, superfluity, oversufficiency, abundance, plenty, lavishness, plethora, profusion, glut, surfeit, surplus, over-supply, saturation, exuberance, superabundance, inundation, flood, deluge, torrent, avalanche, bounty, bonanza, cornucopia, congestion; enough and to spare, more than enough; luxury, extravagance, too much of a good thing.

adj. excessive, inordinate, exorbitant, extravagant, immoderate, unreasonable, saturated, plentiful, superfluous, overfull, congested, surplus, redundant, to spare, extra; plenty, abundant.

vb. abound, teem, swarm; overdo; saturate, glut, inundate, flood, overwhelm, choke, drench.

573 importance

n. importance, significance, consequence; seriousness, gravity; substance, matter, weight, moment, import; prominence, eminence; be-all and end-all, priority, urgency.

adj. important, significant, momentous, decisive, critical, relevant, consequential, crucial, considerable, valuable; great, extensive; serious, grave, weighty, ponderous, heavy, solemn; famous, well-known, eminent, notable, distinguished, prominent, impressive, imposing, influential, illustrious, extraordinary, outstanding, exceptional, top-notch (*inf.*), heavyweight (*inf.*), mainline (*inf.*); basic, essential, fundamental; chief, main, primary, principal, foremost, leading, paramount, salient.

vb. be important, carry weight, influence, matter, deserve attention; make important, emphasize, underline, stress; value, prize, set great store by, think much of.

574 unimportance

n. unimportance, insignificance, triviality, worthlessness, immateriality, paltriness, irrelevance; red herring, trifle, nothing to speak of, nothing to write home about, nonentity, drop in the ocean.

adj. unimportant, insignificant, immaterial, worthless, inconsequential, irrelevant, trivial, worthless, paltry, petty, trifling, inconsiderable, slight, common, ordinary, superficial.

vb. be unimportant, not matter; play second fiddle, make light of, play down, make nothing of.

575 utility

n. utility, usefulness; utilization, employment, helpfulness, efficacy; suitability, applicability, practicability, serviceableness.

advantage, benefit, profit, worth, value, merit; service, application, convenience.

adj. useful, valuable, beneficial, profitable, advantageous, suitable, practicable, convenient, helpful, handy, available, 'applicable; utilitarian, functional, sensible, pragmatic.

vb. be useful, help, serve a purpose, perform a function, come in handy; profit, benefit, stand one in good stead, avail.

use, employ, have the use of, exploit, exercise, utilize, take advantage of, turn to, take up, adopt, practise, apply, avail oneself of; handle, operate; spend, consume.

see also **606**

576 inutility

n. inutility, uselessness, worthlessness, fruitlessness, ineffectiveness, unsuitability, impracticability; futility, hopelessness, vanity.

lost labour, waste of time, wild-goose chase; dead wood; waste, refuse, rubbish, waste-product, litter, dregs, dust, muck.

adj. useless, of no use, worthless, purposeless, futile, vain, pointless, empty, ineffective, incompetent, counter-productive; thankless, unrewarding; unusable, unsuitable, impracticable, inconvenient, unhelpful, disadvantageous, unavailable; out of order, broken down, inoperative; unnecessary, uncalled for.

vb. be useless, be of no help, come to nothing; flog a dead horse, labour in vain, have no future, beat the air.

577 expedience

n. expedience, suitability, appropriateness, fitness, rightness, advisability, propriety, desirability, advantageousness, usefulness.

adj. expedient, advantageous, suitable, fitting, appropriate, apposite, desirable, advisable, seemly; practical, useful, convenient; wise, politic.

vb. suit, fit; help, do, benefit.

see also **136, 915**

578 inexpedience

n. inexpedience, unsuitability, inappropriateness, inadvisability, undesirability, unfitness, impropriety, inconvenience, disadvantage, prejudice.

adj. inexpedient, unsuitable, inappropriate, undesirable, inadvisable, unfitting, unseemly, unwise, inopportune, imprudent, unfavourable, detrimental, disadvantageous, inconvenient.

vb. not do, not help; inconvenience, put out, embarrass, bother, trouble, hinder.

see also **137, 916**

579 goodness

n. goodness, excellence, fineness, greatness, magnificence, superiority; quality, value, price, worth, merit.

top people, elite, cream, pick of the bunch, salt of the earth, treasure, gem, one in a million, champion, corker (*sl.*).

adj. good, excellent, fine, great, superb, splendid, magnificent, marvellous, wonderful, attractive, lovely; masterly, skilled, competent, praiseworthy, commendable; admirable, desirable, enticing, surprising, astonishing; super, terrific, out of this world (*inf.*), cool (*sl.*), neat (*sl.*), magic (*sl.*).

best, first-class, first-rate, optimum, premium, prime, highest, supreme, superlative, A-1, top-notch (*inf.*), tops; exceptional, incomparable, surpassing, incredible, unbelievable, excelling, exemplary; choice, select, exquisite, superior, capital (*inf.*); valuable, priceless, inestimable.

fair, pretty good, not bad, all right, O.K., passable, tolerable, adequate, middling, fair to middling.

vb. be good, have value, have quality; do good, benefit, help, edify.
see also 550, 844

580 badness

n. badness, nastiness, wickedness, vileness, foulness; inferiority, unsatisfactoriness, mediocrity; bane, ill wind, woe, spanner in the works, fly in the ointment.

adj. bad, wrong, awful, nasty, terrible, horrid, horrible; inferior, imperfect, defective, worthless, poor, second-rate, below average, deficient, unsatisfactory, mediocre, ordinary, unwholesome, shoddy, trashy, crummy (*sl.*), shabby; lousy (*sl.*), rotten; pitiful, contemptible, paltry.

harmful, damaging, detrimental, hurtful, destructive, fatal, deadly, corrupting, poisonous, corroding, toxic, venomous, subversive.

vb. be bad, have no value; do bad, harm, injure, hurt, wound, ruin, destroy, corrupt, subvert; vex, trouble, wrong.

see also 551

581 perfection

n. perfection, excellence, impeccability, faultlessness, stainlessness; maturity, completion, culmination, consummation.

ideal, standard, model, paragon, summit, ultimate, height, acme; showpiece, masterpiece, *pièce de résistance*.

adj. perfect, faultless, pure, flawless, impeccable, immaculate, untainted, unblemished, untarnished, stainless, spotless, unstained, uncontaminated, unadulterated, irreproachable, beyond compare, brilliant; supreme, ideal.

whole, sound, complete, entire, finished, developed, fulfilled, completed, accomplished, consummate.

vb. perfect, develop, complete, finish, bring to fruition, get down to a fine art, consummate.

582 imperfection

n. imperfection, impurity, defectiveness, inadequacy, immaturity; disfigurement, defacement, deformity, discoloration.

blemish, flaw, stain; fault, mistake, defect, lack, drawback, snag, loophole, weak spot, weak link in the chain.

adj. imperfect, flawed, defective, deficient, malformed, distorted, tainted, adulterated, blemished, damaged, injured, impaired.

incomplete, unfinished, unsound, uneven, unsatisfactory, faulty, inadequate, fallible.

vb. be imperfect, show faults, fall short, not come up to, be found wanting.

see also 847

583 cleanness

n. cleanness, cleanliness, pureness, spotlessness, whiteness; neatness, tidiness, orderliness, trimness; cleaning, washing, scrubbing, scouring, sprinkling; sterilization, disinfection; cleansing, purification, purgation, ablution.

adj. clean, tidy, neat; immaculate, white, spotless, stainless, untarnished, unblemished, unstained, unsullied, unpolluted, unsoiled, dirtless, spick and span, starched, laundered, polished; germ-free.

vb. clean, tidy, clear; wash, lather, shampoo; bathe, scrub, scour, sponge, mop, swab; brush, sweep; freshen, ventilate; disinfect, fumigate; sterilize, pasteurize; launder, starch, iron; cleanse, purify, sprinkle, purge, expurgate.

584 uncleanness

n. uncleanness, impurity, untidiness, disorderliness, muckiness, filthiness, pollution, defilement.

dirt, filth, spot, stain, smear, smudge, blot, muck, grime, grease, slime; squalor.

adj. unclean, dirty, soiled, polluted, tarnished, sullied, spotted, smeared, daubed, smudged, besmirched; filthy, grimy, greasy, muddy, sooty; squalid, foul, mucky; contaminated, decayed, rotten, rancid, putrid; sloppy, untidy, messy, slovenly, dishevelled, bedraggled, unkempt, like something the cat brought in (*inf.*), unwashed; defiled, unrefined, unpurified.

vb. be dirty, rust, decay, rot, collect dust; dirty, soil, sully, tarnish, daub, bedaub, smudge, blot, pollute, foul; mess up, untidy; corrupt, defile, debase, taint, contaminate, infect.

585 health

n. health, wholeness, soundness, healthfulness, healthiness, salubrity, wholesomeness, balance, vitality; sanity; fitness, strength, well-being, good health, rosy cheeks.

hygiene, sanitation, public health, cleanliness.

adj. healthy, well, sound, whole, wholesome, fit, strong, robust, vigorous, energetic, hale, hearty; all right, rosy-cheeked, flourishing, never feeling better, in fine fettle, in good shape, fighting fit.

healthful, invigorating, stimulating, bracing, beneficial, salubrious; nutritious, nourishing, body-building, restorative, therapeutic, corrective; good for one, what the doctor ordered; hygienic, sanitary.

vb. be healthy, flourish, feel fine; be good for.

586 ill health

n. ill health, poor health, bad health, frailty, weakness, infirmity, invalidity, unhealthiness, indisposition.

illness, disease, ailment, malady, sickness, complaint, disability, affliction, condition, disorder, breakdown, collapse, relapse; fever, infection, virus (*inf.*), bug (*sl.*), pain; bout, spell; stroke, fit, attack, seizure, spasm, convulsions.

lack of hygiene, insalubrity, uncleanliness, contagiousness, infectiousness.

adj. ill, unwell, ailing, weak, unhealthy, poorly, frail, infirm, sick; suffering, down with, indisposed, disabled; drooping, languishing, declining, bedridden, laid up, confined; run down, exhausted; under the weather (*inf.*), out of sorts, seedy (*inf.*), groggy (*inf.*).

unhygienic, insanitary, polluted, bad for, insalubrious; infectious, contagious, endemic; poisonous, toxic, deadly.

vb. be ill, be down with, suffer; fall ill, catch, become ill with, contract, go down with, get, be stricken with; show symptoms of, sicken for; waste away, droop, languish; be bad for, disagree with.

587 improvement

n. improvement, betterment, change, advance, development, refinement, progress, reformation, face-lift, amelioration; enrichment, promotion, furtherance, reform, modernization; revision, correction, amendment.

adj. improved, corrected, amended, revised, reformed, touched up; progressive, reformatory.

vb. improve, develop, further, better, reorganize, promote, reform, straighten out, mend, ameliorate; revise, update, upgrade, correct, rectify; polish, refine, enrich; decorate, beautify, touch up, refurbish; progress, make progress, get better, advance, profit; pick up, come on, rally; pull one's socks up (*inf.*); mellow, mature.

see also **288**

588 deterioration

n. deterioration, impairment, degeneration, decay, rotting, decomposition, erosion, rust; dilapidation, ruin, collapse, decadence, disintegration; impoverishment, adulteration, defilement, corruption, spoiling, detriment, pollution; retrogression; damage, injury, wound, lesion, cut, gash, sore, bruise.

adj. deteriorated, impaired, spoiled, decadent, ruined; damaged, harmed, desolate, ravaged, plundered, robbed, marred, mutilated; decayed, decomposed, rotten, putrified, foul, putrid; worn away, wasting away, emaciated, depleted; ramshackle, tumbledown.

vb. deteriorate, worsen, degenerate, decay, decline, slide, fall, slump, sink, go downhill, fall away, depreciate; go bad, rot, wither, crumble, the rot set in (*inf.*); wither, shrivel; spoil; go to pieces, break up, decompose, fade away, waste away, die; collapse, break down, founder, go to wrack and ruin, go to the dogs (*inf.*), go to pot (*inf.*); go off the rails (*inf.*).

impair, pervert, ruin, corrupt, distort; lower, pull down, reduce, degrade, dehumanize, adulterate, defile, deprave, infect, contaminate; eat away, erode, corrode.

harm, damage, injure, wound, savage, cripple, lame; maltreat, misuse; disgrace, dishonour, discredit; exacerbate, aggravate; hold against (*inf.*), count against; confuse, mess up (*inf.*).

589 restoration

n. restoration, healing, cure, recovery, convalescence, recuperation; renovation, repair, reconditioning, refurbishing, reconstruction, remaking; rehabilitation, re-establishment, resumption, reinstatement, return, getting back to normal; reparation, restitution, amends; reclamation, salvage, rescue.

revival, renewal, reawakening, reinvigoration, resuscitation, rebirth, regeneration, resurrection, renaissance, resurgence, rejuvenation; Indian summer, face-lift, new look, comeback.

adj. restored, repaired, re-established, back to normal; restorative, corrective, remedial, recuperative, therapeutic, soothing, curative.

vb. restore, rebuild, reconstruct, remodel, refashion, reorganize, recondition, reform, remake, revamp, renovate, modernize; repair, mend, fix; refurbish, touch up; darn, patch, sew.

put right, correct, rectify, amend, redress; return, recompense, refund, make amends, make restitution, reinstate, put back, reinstall, re-establish, resume, return to normal; reclaim, salvage, rescue, retrieve, redeem.

revive, refresh, renew, recreate, reanimate, regenerate, resurrect, resuscitate, rejuvenate, reawaken, revitalize, rekindle.

cure, heal, treat, minister to, nurse, rehabilitate, put on one's feet again.

be restored, recover, convalesce, recuperate, get well, get better, fall on one's feet (*inf.*); pick up, rally, pull through, gain strength, get back into circulation (*inf.*); come up smiling (*inf.*).

see also **618**

590 relapse

n. relapse, return, reversion, retrogression, regression; deterioration, declension; apostasy.

vb. relapse, regress, retrogress, deteriorate, degenerate, sink back, slip back, revert, suffer, relapse; backslide, fall from grace, apostasize.

see also 289

591 remedy

n. remedy, cure, relief, assistance, treatment, medication; medicine, medicament, preparation, prescription, pharmaceutical, drug; mixture, dose, potion, linctus; pill, tablet, capsule, lozenge; vaccine, injection, inoculation, jab (*inf.*), shot (*inf.*); lotion, ointment, balm salve; tonic, pick-me-up, stimulant, restorative, refresher, tranquillizer. sedative; panacea, cure-all, elixir; operation, surgery.

adj. remedial, therapeutic, healing, medicinal, corrective, curative, restorative.

vb. remedy, cure, heal, restore; treat, attend, practise; relieve, support, help, mitigate, soothe, palliate; send for the doctor, send to hospital, dial 999, hospitalize, operate; undergo treatment, take pills, take one's medicine.

592 bane

n. bane, curse, plague, evil, scourge, affliction, trial, cross, thorn in the flesh; pain in the neck (*inf.*); weakness, besetting sin; poison, venom, virus; blight, mildew, rust, mould, rot, fungus, gangrene, cancer.

adj. baneful, evil, pestilent; deadly, poisonous, venomous; harmful, destructive.

593 safety

n. safety, security, surety, impregnability, invulnerability, immunity; protection, defence, safekeeping, custody, guardianship, supervision, care; law and order.

protector, guard, defender; custodian, warden, curator, keeper, trustee; life-guard, bodyguard, guardian; patrol, lookout, scout, night watchman, watchdog, vigilante, sentry, policeman.

adj. safe, secure, impregnable, invulnerable, unassailable; protected, guarded, safeguarded, defended, shielded, sheltered; unharmed, unhurt, safe and sound, unscathed; waterproof, bulletproof.

vb. make safe, safeguard, protect, keep, guard, defend, shelter, screen, shield, harbour; supervise, care for, mind, look after, take charge of, keep an eye on, attend to, take under one's wing; keep order, patrol, police, be on the lookout, keep vigil, keep cave (*sl.*); hide, lie low, go to earth.

adv. out of danger, in the clear, out of harm's way, in safe hands, under one's wing, under lock and key.

see also 595

594 danger

n. danger, peril, risk, hazard, jeopardy; menace, threat; dangerousness, perilousness, riskiness, insecurity, precariousness, vulnerability, exposure, openness, helplessness; weak spot.

adj. dangerous, perilous, hazardous, risky, insecure, precarious, alarming, unsafe, treacherous, slippery, shaky, unstable; unsheltered, unshielded, vulnerable, exposed, open, naked, unfortified; menacing, threatening, ominous; critical, serious, delicate, explosive.

vb. endanger, jeopardize, put in jeopardy, expose, lay open to, risk, run the risk of, render liable to, court disaster, tempt providence.

595 refuge

n. refuge, shelter, sanctuary, asylum, retreat; home, ivory tower, port, harbour, haven; den, lair, nest, covert; castle, fortress, stronghold; safeguard, protection, defence; cover, screen, shade, shield, umbrella, wind-break; escape, way out, recourse, last resort.

see also 593, 646

596 pitfall

n. pitfall, trap, snare, ambush, booby-trap; reef, rock, sandbank, quicksand, undercurrent; danger spot, black spot, trouble spot; trouble-maker, wrecker, snake in the grass.

597 warning

n. warning, caution, lesson, example, advice, counsel, caveat; alert, hint, intimation, admonition, tip-off (*inf.*), early warning, writing on the wall, symptom, sign, omen, augury; foreboding, premonition; notice, indication, notification; call, cry, shout.

adj. warning, cautionary, advisory, instructive.

vb. warn, caution, advise, alert, admonish, counsel, encourage, exhort, hint, prompt, suggest; forewarn, tip off (*inf.*); notify, inform, give notice, apprise.

see also 460

598 indication of danger

n. alarm, alert, bell, alarm bell, fire alarm, siren, horn, fog-horn, klaxon, tocsin; light, red light, warning light; red alert; SOS, distress signal; beacon; war-cry, drum-beat; false alarm, hoax, scare.

vb. give the alarm, raise the alarm, dial 999, alert, put on the alert; cry wolf.

599 preservation

n. preservation, protection, maintenance, saving, keeping, conservation; storage, canning, freezing, refrigeration, dehydration.

adj. preservative, protective; preserved, kept, intact, protected; fresh, well-preserved.

vb. preserve, maintain, keep, protect, look after; conserve, keep fresh, bottle, can, tin, season, cure, salt, dry, smoke, freeze, refrigerate, freeze-dry, dehydrate, pickle, spice, marinade; embalm, mummify.

600 escape

n. escape, flight, departure, getaway; evasion, avoidance, abdication, desertion, disappearance; freedom, release, deliverance, rescue; retreat, withdrawal; narrow escape, close shave, near miss, near thing.

exit, way out, overflow, vent, waste-pipe, exhaust, leak, leakage, life-line, loophole.

escaper, runaway, truant, dodger, fugitive, refugee.

adj. escaped, free, out, at large, at liberty, missing, wanted.

vb. escape, flee, take flight, abscond, leave, depart, break loose, break out, decamp, free, get clear of, get away with, make one's getaway, make oneself scarce, give the slip, slip through one's fingers, elude, avoid, evade, elope, play truant; emerge, issue, burst out.

see also 921

601 deliverance

n. deliverance, saving, rescue, release, freeing, liberation, relief; extrication, unbinding, loosening, disentanglement; ransom, forgiveness, pardon; remission, discharge, acquittal, reprieve, exoneration; emancipation, affranchisement, manumission.

vb. deliver, rescue, release, free, discharge, relieve; remit, acquit, let off (*inf.*), exonerate; extricate, loosen, untie; emancipate, liberate; salvage, retrieve; save, redeem, ransom, pardon, forgive.

see also 680, 911

602 preparation

n. preparation, plan, step, arrangement; outline, draft, scheme, foundation, groundwork, spadework; rehearsal, practice, training, dummy run; approach, run-up (*inf.*); preparedness, readiness, fitness, experience, all systems go (*inf.*); red alert.

adj. preparatory, introductory, initial; prepared, ready, alert, waiting, on call, standing by, all set; experienced, skilled, qualified, versed, seasoned, broken in.

ready-made, prefabricated, ready-mixed, treated; frozen, pre-cooked, processed, dehydrated, ready-to-eat, oven-ready, instant; off-the-peg.

vb. prepare, get ready, arrange, plan, make preparations; settle, decide; adapt, adjust, fit, equip, supply, deck out, fit out, provide; take steps, take measures; practise, rehearse, train, study, hold in readiness; clear the decks, lay the foundations, prepare the ground, pave the way, smooth the way, blaze a trail, do the groundwork, do one's homework, break the ice.

see also 558

603 non-preparation

n. non-preparation, unpreparedness, lack of training, inexperience; immaturity, rawness, naivety.

adj. unprepared, unready, napping, surprised, taken aback, unguarded, off one's guard, with one's pants down (*sl.*); unorganized, makeshift, hasty, rush (*inf.*); thoughtless; inexperienced,

unskilled, uninstructed, untrained, unqualified, unequipped; new, naive, raw, immature; undeveloped, half-baked; backward, developing; fallow, virgin.

vb. be unprepared, be taken unawares, be caught napping; not plan, make no provision for; improvise.

604 attempt

n. attempt, try, effort, trial, experiment, endeavour, essay, undertaking, enterprise, venture.

adj. experimental, probationary, tentative, trial.

vb. attempt, try, have a try, make an effort, endeavour, venture, seek, aim for, strive, contend, risk, aspire, contest, have a go, lift a finger, put oneself out, have a crack at (*inf.*), have a shot at (*inf.*), have a stab at (*inf.*).

605 undertaking

n. undertaking, enterprise, project, plan, programme, cause, pursuit, campaign, operation, exercise, venture, exploit, feat; occupation, business, job, task, work, concern, matter in hand, proposition, engagement, commitment, obligation.

adj. enterprising, adventurous, venturesome, daring, go-ahead, pioneering, progressive, up-and-coming; ambitious, aspiring.

vb. undertake, engage in, go in for, do, take part in, participate in, devote oneself to; manage, engage, promise, contract; take upon oneself, put one's hand to, commit oneself to, take on, assume, shoulder, bear the burden of, tackle, embark on, enter upon, get down to (*inf.*), launch into, plunge into, commence, begin, start, set to, broach, set about; get down to business, get one's teeth into (*inf.*), take the bit between the teeth (*inf.*), get down to brass tacks (*inf.*), get to grips with.

adv. in hand, under control, in order.
see also **88**

606 use

n. use, usage, application, practice, exercise, employment, management, conduct, realization, adoption, conversion, treatment, handling, performance, control; method, technique; utility, usefulness.

adj. used, applied, utilized, adopted, accepted, practised; in use, in service, in force; old, second-hand.

vb. use, employ, apply, utilize, put to use, put into service; realize, adopt, draw on, take advantage of; adapt, convert, relate, bring to bear, resort to, have recourse to, fall back on; manage, conduct, deal with, treat, handle; exploit, use to the full, get the most out of, cash in on (*inf.*), capitalize, get the benefit of.
see also **575**

607 disuse

n. disuse, non-use, discontinuance, suspension, abolition, rejection, relinquishment, abandonment, unemployment, abeyance; obsolescence.

adj. disused, neglected, abandoned, idle, abolished, deserted, derelict; unused, unemployed, unspent; out of order, out of service, inactive; extra, spare.

vb. disuse, suspend, abolish, put aside, have done with, reject, get rid of, throw out, jettison, discard, scrap, throw on the scrap-heap, neglect, abandon, desert, relinquish.

608 misuse

n. misuse, abuse, misapplication, misemployment, mishandling, mismanagement, misappropriation; per-

version, debasement, degradation, prostitution, desecration, defilement, profanation, pollution; outrage, violation; error, mistake.

vb. misuse, abuse, mistreat, ill-treat, maltreat, mishandle, misemploy, misappropriate; pervert, prostitute, debase, desecrate, defile, violate, deprave, profane; wrong, insult, injure, hurt, harm, malign; squander, waste.

C Voluntary action

609 action

n. action, doing, execution, commission, operation, management, handling.

act, deed, thing, work, job, activity, feat, exploit; performance, achievement, undertaking, accomplishment; move, step, measure; blow, stroke.

doer, performer, worker, workman; instrument.

adj. doing, in operation, in process, operative.

vb. act, do, conduct, operate, work, function.

achieve, accomplish, complete, fulfil, carry out, bring about, execute, realize, effect, perform, dispose of, commit, transact, put into effect, put into action, put into operation.

take action, take steps, do something about, specialize in, concern oneself with, make it one's business, go in for; persist, persevere, keep going.
see also **611, 615**

610 inaction

n. inaction, rest, waiting, inertia, suspension, abeyance; laissez-faire, dormancy, neglect, stagnation.

adj. inoperative, idle, unemployed; suspended, in abeyance.

vb. not act, wait, pause, hang fire, bide one's time, twiddle one's thumbs, hold your horses (*inf.*); wait and see, do nothing, abstain, refrain; leave alone, have nothing to do with, let sleeping dogs lie.

see also **612**

611 activity

n. activity, liveliness, agility, nimbleness, alertness, alacrity, readiness, keenness, eagerness; energy, life, vigour, spirit, verve, zest, dynamism, enthusiasm, get-up-and-go (*inf.*); hurry, bustle, flurry, rush, commotion, rat-race.

industry, diligence, assiduousness, perseverance, resolution, determination, application, concentration; enterprise, initiative; activism, militancy, aggressiveness.

busy person, enthusiast, zealot, activist, fanatic, militant, live wire.

adj. active, lively, energetic, dynamic; busy, hard at it, eventful, bustling, dashing, raring to go; alert, agile, nimble, sharp, spry, wire, alive; restless, fidgety.

enthusiastic, keen, zealous; pushy (*inf.*), ambitious, aggressive, forceful, activist, militant, go-ahead, enterprising; industrious, diligent, hardworking, studious.

vb. be active, be busy, rush around, bustle about, have one's hands full, have a finger in every pie; have many irons in the fire; busy oneself in, stir oneself, rouse onself; persevere, keep going, keep at it; work hard, not have a moment to spare, never stop, overwork, overdo it, have no time to call one's own.

see also **532, 609**

612 inactivity

n. inactivity, stillness, inertia, lethargy, slackness, sluggishness, torpor, lifelessness, listlessness; apathy, indifference, carelessness; idleness, laziness, indolence, sloth.

fatigue, tiredness, weariness, sleepiness; sleep, slumber, rest, doze, nod, snooze, shut-eye, catnap, forty winks, siesta, repose, dormancy; breather, pause, holiday, vacation.

lazy person, idler, loafer (*inf.*), good-for-nothing, lazy-bones, bum (*sl.*), tramp, sluggard, wastrel, parasite, sponger.

adj. inactive, still, stable; unemployed, unoccupied, fallow, barren; idle, lazy, slothful, indolent, lethargic, slack, sluggish, listless, torpid, languid; unadventurous, unenterprising, stay-at-home; apathetic, indifferent, uninterested.

tired, weary, drowsy, sleepy, fatigued, somnolent, dormant; exhausted, run down, overworked, worn out, washed out, drooping, faint, weak, stale.

vb. be inactive, rest, relax, pause, bide one's time; drift, vegetate, stagnate.

idle, loaf about (*inf.*), mooch about (*sl.*), loiter about, hang about (*inf.*), bum around (*sl.*); dilly-dally, shilly-shally, languish; kill time, waste time, while away the time.

sleep, slumber, doze, drowse, snooze, take a nap, nod off, have forty winks, yawn, dream; go to bed, turn in, kip down (*sl.*), hit the sack (*sl.*).

see also **533, 617, 841**

613 haste

n. haste, rush, hurry, scramble, scurry, flurry, hurly-burly; dash, spirit, spurt, run, burst, sprint, bolt, race;

hurriedness, hastiness, urgency, promptness, precipitation, rashness, impulsiveness, impetuosity.

adj. hasty, quick, fast, swift, speedy, hurried, dashing; impetuous, impulsive, rash, inconsiderate, reckless, foolhardy, precipitate, headlong, impatient.

vb. hasten, quicken, speed up, accelerate, expedite, dispatch, stimulate, fillip, urge, goad, whip, incite, push through, rush through, railroad through (*inf.*).

rush, sprint, spurt, scurry, scuttle, dash, bustle, zoom, tear, bomb (*inf.*), go all out (*inf.*), step on it (*inf.*).

see also 280, 544, 859

614 leisure

n. leisure, free time, spare time, time off, recreation, relaxation, rest, respite, breather, break, pause, lull, recess; holiday, leave, leave of absence, vacation, sabbatical, furlough, home leave.

adj. leisurely, resting, unoccupied.

vb. have time to spare, be off, take one's ease, relax, rest.

adv. off, off duty, on holiday; at leisure, at one's convenience, at an early opportunity.

see also 281, 840

615 exertion

n. exertion, effort, panic, trouble, toil, labour, work, travail, strife, strain, tension, elbow grease, drudgery; hard work, handful (*inf.*), uphill task, sweat (*sl.*), drudge.

adj. laborious, arduous, hard, difficult, strenuous, onerous, painstaking, gruelling, punishing, uphill, back-breaking.

vb. exert oneself, try, attempt; take pains, work, labour, fight, toil, contend, struggle, strive, sweat blood; knuckle

down (*inf.*), get down to it (*inf.*), buckle down (*inf.*); drudge, grind, plod (*inf.*), plug away (*inf.*), slog away, sweat one's guts out (*sl.*); make heavy weather of, make a meal of; put oneself out, do one's best, do one's utmost, go to all lengths, go all out, leave no stone unturned, move heaven and earth, pull out all the stops (*inf.*); overdo it, have one's work cut out.

see also 535, 611

616 repose

n. repose, rest, relaxation, inaction; breather, break, pause, coffee-break, tea-break, lunch-break, lunch-hour, rest period; day of rest, Sabbath, Lord's Day; ease, quiet, quietness, tranquillity.

adj. restful, tranquil, quiet, calm, peaceful; sabbatical.

vb. rest, be quiet, stop, halt; take a rest, take it easy, let up, ease off, slow down, stretch one's legs, have a break; get away from it all (*inf.*).

see also 610, 618

617 fatigue

n. fatigue, tiredness, weariness; sleepiness, heaviness, drowsiness, doziness, somnolence; faintness, weakness, exhaustion, collapse, staleness, jadedness; lassitude, languor.

adj. tired, weary, exhausted, run down, fagged out (*inf.*), worn out, ready to drop (*inf.*), dog-tired, dead beat, all in, whacked (*inf.*); heavy, dozy (*inf.*), drowsy, sleepy; weak, faint, dropping, haggard; washed out, drained, stale, jaded.

vb. be tired, drop, collapse, flag, jade, peg out (*inf.*), flake out (*sl.*); faint, pass out (*inf.*), lose consciousness; work too hard, overdo it.

weary, tire, fatigue, wear out,

exhaust, take it out of (*inf.*), fag out (*inf.*), strain; bore.

see also **612, 841**

618 refreshment

n. refreshment, enlivenment, invigoration, recovery, restoration, convalescence, recuperation, relief.

adj. refreshing, restoring, invigorating, exhilarating, bracing, stimulating, arousing, refreshed, invigorated, like a new man.

vb. refresh, restore, arouse, revive, enliven, animate, strengthen, stimulate, invigorate, renew, reawaken, bring round, give new life to, energize, improve, relieve, resuscitate, vivify; encourage, cheer.

recover, recuperate, pick up, perk up, recharge one's batteries, get one's breath back.

see also **589, 616**

619 agent

n. agent, doer, actor, performer, participant, instrument, medium, practitioner, executor; worker, workman, operator, mechanic, labourer, operative, craftsman, skilled worker; apprentice; hack, drudge, slave, fag.

workforce, employees, staff, personnel, labour, payroll, manpower, resources.

620 workshop

n. workshop, workplace, establishment, installation, institution, plant, factory, works, foundry, yard; shop, house, office, bureau, branch, station, laboratory; firm, company, concern, industry.

621 conduct

n. conduct, behaviour, manner, deportment, demeanour, air, carriage, bearing, posture, attitude, comportment, mien, delivery, appearance, guise; guidance, control, oversight, supervision, superintendence, execution, government, management, organization; strategy, tactics, policy, campaign, programme.

adj. behavioural; tactical, strategical.

vb. behave, act, conduct; acquit oneself, bear oneself, comport oneself, pose, appear, seem; behave oneself, mind one's manners, mind one's P's and Q's, be on one's best behaviour; manage, guide, supervise, direct, regulate, administer.

622 management

n. management, conduct, guidance, direction, control, order, charge, power, execution, government, organization, administration, decision making, handling, regulation, legislation, jurisdiction; oversight, supervision, superintendence, surveillance, command, authority, leadership; stewardship, husbandry, housekeeping, economics.

adj. directive, managerial, controlling, supervisory; executive, administrative, governmental, gubernatorial, legislative; official, bureaucratic.

vb. manage, conduct, run, guide, direct, lead, control, regulate, order, govern, command, steer, point the way, decide; handle, execute, administer, organize, legislate; supervise, superintend; steward.

623 director

n. manager, director, controller, leader, executive, governor, politician, minister, legislator, commander; dictator; superintendent, supervisor, inspector, overseer, foreman; steward; administrator, official, bureaucrat, functionary, secretary; guide, organizer.

see also 34, 675

624 advice

n. advice, suggestion, opinion, view, counsel, guidance, encouragement, information, instruction, recommendation; warning, admonition, criticism, dissuasion; caution, notice; notification.

advisor, counsellor, right-hand man, friend, confidant, teacher, informant, helper, consultant; think-tank.

adj. advisory, consultative.

vb. advise, guide, direct, tell, have a word with, suggest; exhort, urge, prompt, encourage, persuade, recommend, counsel; warn, admonish, dissuade; inform, notify, acquaint.

consult, ask, discuss, talk over, seek the opinion of, seek advice, turn to, confide in.

625 council

n. council, cabinet, committee, government, parliament, board, directorate, board of governors; congress, conference, assembly, convention, synod, convocation, diet; panel, forum, brains trust.

councillor, minister, member of parliament, back-bencher, parliamentarian, statesman, senator, congressman; delegate, representative, officer.

626 precept

n. precept, maxim, command, direction, instruction, prescription, principle, law, statute, commandment, rule; canon, doctrine, law, charge, mandate, injunction, edict; formula, recipe.

see also 103, 954

627 skill

n. skill, capability, proficiency, competence, skilfulness, expertness, ability, aptitude, talent, gift, genius, endowment, flaw, strong point, forte, what it takes, knack; experience, practice, training, qualifications, expertise, know-how, judgment; adeptness, deftness, adroitness, facility.

adj. skilful, capable, able, proficient, competent, effective, clever; experienced, trained, qualified, fit, suited, cut out for (*inf.*), accomplished, well-versed, expert, veteran; gifted, endowed; handy, adept, deft, adroit, agile, dexterous; all-round, versatile; enterprising, inventive.

vb. be good at, shine at, have what it takes; be expert, know backwards, know the ropes (*inf.*), know the ins and outs (*inf.*).

628 unskilfulness

n. unskilfulness, inability, ineptitude, inexperience, greenness, weak point, incompetence, inefficiency, mismanagement; awkwardness, clumsiness; botch-up, hash, mess, cock-up (*inf.*).

adj. unskilful, inexperienced, uneducated, unqualified, incompetent, amateur, unsuited, unused to, lay, amateurish, unprofessional, do-it-yourself, scratch; butterfingers; awkward, clumsy, heavy-handed, bungling, maladroit; impracticable, home-made, Heath Robinson; unwieldy, cumbersome, bulky.

vb. be no good at (*inf.*), spoil, bungle, ruin, botch, mismanage, mishandle, make a mess of, make a hash of, mess up (*inf.*), louse up (*sl.*), screw up (*sl.*), cock up (*sl.*), put one's foot in it; misfire.

629 expert

n. expert, master, adept, proficient,

handyman, Jack-of-all-trades, man of many parts, man of many talents; professional, authority, specialist, scholar, genius, whizz-kid (*inf.*), veteran, old hand; man of the world.

see also **436**

630 bungler

n. bungler, fumbler, botcher, muddler, dunce, idiot, blockhead, scatterbrain, ignoramus; butterfingers; beginner, novice, greenhorn; amateur, layman; lout, lubber.

see also **437**

631 cunning

n. cunning, craftiness, intrigue, deceit, guile, artfulness, craft, subtlety, slyness, wiliness, cleverness, shrewdness, chicanery, finesse.

stratagem, artifice, trick, deception, plot, scheme, ruse, wile, dodge, trap, little game (*inf.*), con (*sl.*), hoax, fabrication, double-dealing, casuistry.

artful dodger, hypocrite, fraud, cheat, plotter, con-man (*sl.*), trickster, slippery customer (*inf.*), smooth talker (*inf.*).

adj. cunning, shrewd, crafty, artful, sly, wily, deceptive, subtle, dishonest, fraudulent, unscrupulous, underhand, shifty, smart, shady, smooth, slippery, sharp, clever (*inf.*), too clever by half (*inf.*).

vb. be cunning, trick, deceive, fraud, cheat, trap, hoax, con (*sl.*), plot, scheme, contrive, pull a fast one (*sl.*), put one over on (*inf.*), put one across (*inf.*), outwit, get the better of.

632 artlessness

n. artlessness, simplicity, innocence, naivety, simple-mindedness, guilelessness, ingenuousness; child, babe.

adj. artless, innocent, simple, naive,

simple-minded, guileless, unaffected, natural, uncomplicated, straightforward, ingenuous, childlike, unsophisticated, genuine, frank, open, candid, forthright.

vb. be natural, wear one's heart on one's sleeve; speak one's mind, not mince words.

D Antagonism

633 difficulty

n. difficulty, problem, headache, trouble, tall order, handful, heavy going; dilemma, predicament, quandary, strait, plight, embarrassment, fix, pickle (*inf.*), scrape, tight spot (*inf.*), hole (*sl.*); hardship, arduousness, laboriousness, troublesomeness; perplexity.

adj. difficult, hard, tough, laborious, arduous, uphill, strenuous; awkward, burdensome, trying, troublesome, bothersome, wearisome; unclear, obscure, knotty, thorny, baffling, perplexing, complicated, intricate.

vb. be in difficulties, flounder, have a hard time, strike a bad patch, make heavy weather of, make a meal of, not keep one's head above water; get into difficulty, get into hot water; put one's foot in it (*inf.*); beset, trouble, harm, disconcert, discourage, inconvenience, embarrass; baffle, perplex, put on the spot (*inf.*).

adv. in deep water, in difficulty, on the horns of a dilemma, in a quandary, in a spot, in hot water, in trouble.

see also **615, 635**

634 ease

n. ease, facility, straightforwardness; child's play, plain sailing, piece of cake (*inf.*), nothing to it (*inf.*), walk-over (*inf.*), push-over (*inf.*), cinch (*sl.*).

adj. easy, simple, cushy (*inf.*), manageable, facile; obvious, apparent; pleasant, comfortable; clear, uncomplicated; effortless.

vb. be easy, require no effort, present no difficulties, give no trouble, run smoothly, go like clockwork; take in one's stride.

ease, facilitate, smooth the way, free, relieve, rid, get rid of, lighten, release, disentangle; take a weight off someone's mind (*inf.*).

635 hindrance

n. hindrance, impedance, intervention, interruption; restriction, prohibition, restraint, check, blockage; retardation, curb, arrest, drag; inconvenience, hitch, setback, hold-up, bottleneck, catch, snag, spanner in the works (*inf.*), encumbrance, chain, menace.

obstacle, obstruction, barrier, impediment, interference, stumbling-block, barricade, hurdle, bar, impasse, cul de sac.

adj. hindering, restraining, preventive.

vb. hinder, prevent, thwart, frustrate, hamper, trammel; stop, check, restrain, foil, confine, retard, arrest; deter, prohibit, restrict, bar, forbid, encumber, burden, chain, fetter, shackle; interfere, meddle; obstruct, block, impede, barricade; spoil, gum up the works (*sl.*).

see also **633, 665**

636 aid

n. aid, help, assistance; helping hand, leg up; encouragement, comfort, relief, succour, alleviation, mitigation; favour, benevolence, service; advice, backing, guidance.

financial aid, giving, support, maintenance, charity; compensation, allowance, grant, subsidy, benefit, stipend, honorarium, expenses; patronage, sponsorship, promotion, advancement.

adj. helpful, beneficial, assisting; auxiliary.

vb. help, aid, assist, cooperate; encourage, stand by, back up, sustain, bolster, relieve, comfort, succour, save, rescue, abet; lend a hand, play one's part; befriend, advise, serve, minister to, take under one's wing.

patronize, finance, support, keep, maintain, promote, subsidize, foster, shoulder, sponsor, sanction.

see also **217, 639**

637 opposition

n. opposition, antagonism, confrontation, repugnance, defiance, hostility, abhorrence, aversion, incompatibility, polarity; dislike, dissension, contradiction.

adj. opposing, antagonistic, defiant; hostile.

vb. oppose, counter, conflict with, fly in the face of, run counter to; confront, fight, combat, hinder, obstruct, thwart; object, dispute, contradict; resist, defy; deny, not have any part in, part company with, disapprove, disagree.

see also **648, 883**

638 opponent

n. opponent, antagonist, adversary, enemy, foe, the opposition, competitor, challenger, candidate, entrant, rival, contestant.

see also **883**

639 cooperation

n. cooperation, collaboration, participation, partnership, fellowship, brotherhood, harmony; give and take, teamwork, solidarity; amalgamation, merger, fusion, affiliation, membership; help, assistance.

adj. cooperative, collaborative, participatory; associated.

vb. cooperate, collaborate, give and take, help each other out, play ball with; contribute, help.

join, combine, unite, merge, club together, affiliate, join forces, pool together, pool resources, stand together, stick together (*inf.*), pull together; share, take part in, participate, throw in one's lot, go along with, team up with, take sides; gang up against (*inf.*); put one's heads together (*inf.*).

see also 180, 709

640 auxiliary

n. auxiliary, helper, assistant, aid, ancillary, collaborator, helping hand, partner, associate, colleague, fellow-worker, co-worker, team-mate, sidekick (*inf.*); accomplice, confederate; friend, companion, ally, comrade; follower, adherent, disciple; hanger-on; patron, backer, supporter; right-hand man, stalwart, tower of strength.

see also 636

641 party

n. party, group, movement, organization, society, band, body; council, congress, alliance, association, confederation, federation, league, coalition, union; community, fellowship, brotherhood; company, firm, establishment, concern, cooperative, cartel, syndicate.

faction, sect, denomination, tradition, splinter-group, clique, coterie, inner circle.

adj. federal, allied, confederate, cooperative; exclusive, cliquish, partisan, sectarian.

vb. join, enrol, become a member of, affiliate, subscribe; associate with, side with.

642 discord

n. discord, dissension, trouble, difference, disagreement, misunderstanding, cross purposes, variance, ill feeling, tension, friction; divisiveness, troublesomeness, quarrelsomeness, rivalry.

dispute, quarrel, row, fight, argument, squabble, bickering, tiff, vendetta, feud; schism, split, rift, parting of the ways.

adj. discordant, disagreeing, divisive; contradictory; quarrelsome, troublesome, violent, factious, pugnacious, harsh, uncooperative, bolshie (*sl.*).

vb. differ, clash, conflict, dissent; fall out with, part company with; break up.

dispute, contend, fight, struggle, strive, come to blows, complain, object, argue, disagree; quarrel, wrangle, squabble, bicker; have a bone to pick with, have words with, take issue with; look for trouble (*inf.*), ask for it (*inf.*), rub up the wrong way (*inf.*), tread on someone's toes.

adv. at loggerheads, at odds, at variance, at sixes and sevens, not on speaking terms.

see also 25, 893

643 concord

n. concord, agreement, harmony, conformity, understanding, consonance, rapport, goodwill, friendship, amity, concert, accord, consensus, unanimity, unity, *détente*, *rapprochement*, entente, entente cordiale.

adj. agreeing, harmonious, friendly,

peaceful, amicable, reconciled, unanimous, united.

vb. agree, get on with, get along with, hit it off (*inf.*), see eye to eye, be at one with; come to an understanding.

see also **24, 699**

644 defiance

n. defiance, disobedience, rebellion, insubordination, insolence, obstinacy; mutiny, revolt, revolution; challenge, dare.

adj. defiant, bold, daring, proud; unruly, rebellious, disobedient, insubordinate; independent, lawless, anarchistic, militant.

vb. defy, confront, brave, challenge, dare, fling down the gauntlet, call one's bluff; resist, disobey, oppose, disregard, flout, spurn, laugh at, scorn, taunt; rebel, revolt, insult, protest, kick against, kick against the pricks.

see also **648**

645 attack

n. attack, assault, onslaught, aggression, advance, charge, push, thrust, drive, outbreak, outburst, raid, offensive, storm, skirmish, foray, sally, sortie; invasion, intrusion, inroad, incursion, encroachment; siege, barrage, bombardment, blitz; mugging, rape.

attacker, aggressor, assailant, fighter, raider, stormer, invader, enemy, intruder, sniper, ravager; mugger, rapist.

adj. attacking, assaulting, aggressive.

vb. attack, assault, advance, charge, rush, push, thrust, assail, fight; raid, invade, storm, sally, sortie, foray; intrude, encroach; besiege, lay siege to, blockade; ravage, lay waste; fire, shoot, snipe; bomb, bombard; beat up, do over (*sl.*), smash somone's face in (*inf.*), mug, rob, rape.

646 defence

n. defence, protection, guarding, security; fortification, castle, fort, fortress, stronghold, keep, bastion, citadel, garrison; trenches, ditch, moat; embankment, rampart, battlement, earthworks; armour.

defender, guard, watch, sentry; protector, champion.

adj. defended, guarded, safe; defensive, armed, watchful.

vb. defend, protect, guard, keep, keep safe, safeguard, secure, shield, shelter, screen; withstand, beat off, ward off, fend off, drive back, take evasive action; spring to someone's defence; strengthen, reinforce, fortify; arm, cover, camouflage.

see also **593**

647 retaliation

n. retaliation, reprisal, revenge, reaction, backlash, counterattack, counterinsurgence, second-strike capability; measure for measure, an eye for an eye, tit for tat, just deserts; requital, repayment, vengeance, punishment, retribution; recrimination; retort, riposte.

adj. retaliatory, retributive, reciprocal.

vb. retaliate, hit back, strike back, fight back, get back (*inf.*), defend oneself; requite, avenge, revenge, punish, return, repay, vindicate, pay back, settle up, get square, get one's own back, give tit for tat, get even with; reciprocate, return the compliment, give someone a dose of his own medicine; retort, counter, recriminate.

see also **912**

648 resistance

n. resistance, withstanding, defence, stand, check; steadfastness, renitence.

adj. resisting, recalcitrant, hard-hearted.

vb. resist, withstand, not give in, not submit, repel, stand up to, not take lying down, stand fast; stay, defend, hold off, oppose, prevent, thwart, foil, frustrate, obstruct, attack; counteract, neutralize; endure, suffer, tolerate; persevere, hold out, stick it out (*inf.*); maintain, take one's stand, stand one's ground, stick one's heels in (*inf.*), stick to one's guns, hold one's own.

see also 535, 644

649 contest

n. contest, engagement, fight, battle, war, encounter, confrontation, action, skirmish, feud, *mêlée*, set-to, tussle, scrap (*sl.*), brush, affray, altercation; duel, joust, warfare, hostilities; conflict, strife, struggle, bloodshed, onslaught, carnage.

game, match, event, rally, race, challenge, competition, round, tournament; sport, recreation.

adj. contending, contestant; competitive.

vb. contend, fight, oppose, combat, confront, challenge, encounter, engage in battle, campaign, battle, brush with, dispute, strive, struggle, scrap (*sl.*), set to, take on, tussle, joust, assert oneself; compete, contest, race, vie with.

see also 651, 655

650 peace

n. peace, absence of hostilities, armistice, truce, treaty; pacification, conciliation, reconciliation, love, friendship, agreement, harmony, accord; cold war, peaceful coexistence.

adj. peaceful, quiet, tranquil; bloodless, nonaggressive; pacifist; appeasing, conciliatory, peace-making.

see also 24, 652

651 war

n. war, hostilities, combat, fighting, warfare, attack, battle, campaign, operation, mission, action, contention.

aggressiveness, warlikeness, belligerence, militancy, warmongering, pugnacity.

adj. warlike, aggressive, militant, pugnacious, belligerent, martial, threatening, contentious, warmongering, unfriendly, bellicose, up in arms, on the warpath; fighting, warring.

vb. wage war, engage in hostilities, attack, invade, contend, strive; declare war, go to war; mobilize, call up, recruit, enlist, conscript, muster.

see also 645, 649

652 pacification

n. pacification, peace-making, appeasement, conciliation, reconciliation, reparation, satisfaction, assuagement, alleviation, mollification, soothing, calming; propitiation, atonement.

peace-offering, sacrifice, placation, gift; white flag, olive branch.

adj. pacificatory, placatory, propitiatory; irenic.

vb. pacify, conciliate; appease, satisfy, sacrifice, atone, propitiate; quiet, calm, still, moderate, quell, soften, alleviate, assuage, mollify, placate, tranquillize; reconcile, harmonize, bring together, bring to terms, settle one's differences, accommodate; make peace, bury the hatchet; make it up, shake hands.

see also 650

653 mediation

n. mediation, arbitration, interposition, intervention, shuttle diplomacy.

mediator, arbitrator, go-between, intermediary, arbiter, negotiator, peace-maker, trouble-shooter, intercessor, third party; judge, referee, umpire; adjudicator, assessor; neutral, independent.

adj. mediatory, intercessory.

vb. mediate, arbitrate, negotiate, reconcile, hear both sides, intercede, interpose, intervene; judge, umpire, rule; interfere, meddle.

see also 230

654 submission

n. submission, yielding, obedience; acquiescence, resignation, deference; submissiveness, docility, meekness, humility, passivity.

adj. submissive, obedient; compliant, amenable, tractable, mouldable; resigned, subdued; acquiescent, reconciled, patient; docile, humble, lowly, tame.

vb. submit, give in, yield, surrender, capitulate, resign, relinquish, give up, throw in the towel, admit defeat.

obey, defer, bow to, comply, acquiesce; take the line of least resistance.

see also 673, 679

655 combatant

n. combatant, fighter, contender, opponent, serviceman, soldier, conscript, recruit, pressed man; casual, irregular; mercenary, hireling; warrior, veteran.

armed forces, services, troops, forces, military force, army, infantry, cavalry, artillery; navy, air force; unit, group, division, section, squad, troop, patrol, party; task force; formation, column, line, array.

656 non-combatant

n. non-combatant, pacifist, conscientious objector, neutral, dove, flower people, conchie (*sl.*); peace-maker.

657 arms

n. arms, weapons, armament, munitions; armour, mail, panoply; small arms, firearm, gun; revolver, rifle, shotgun, machine gun, automatic; cannon, mortar; bazooka; hand-grenade bomb, explsoive, dynamite, gunpowder; atomic bomb, hydrogen bomb, H-bomb, neutron bomb; armoury, arsenal; ballistics.

658 arena

n. arena, battlefield, battleground, scene of action, field of action, theatre of war, trenches, front; field, ground, centre, scene, sphere, track, court, course; stadium, gymnasium, playground, campus, coliseum, amphitheatre, circus, forum, pit.

E   Results of action

659 completion

n. completion, finish, end, conclusion, achievement, performance, accomplishment, fulfilment, perfection, realization, execution.

finishing touch, crown, *coup de grâce;* last straw, limit (*sl.*).

adj. complete, finished, accomplished, fulfilled, perfect, entire, whole; conclusive, final, last.

vb. complete, finish, end, conclude, terminate; achieve, perform, carry out, implement, bring off (*inf.*), pull off (*inf.*), succeed; knock off (*inf.*), polish off (*inf.*), wrap up (*inf.*); get over with (*inf.*), get over and done with (*inf.*); accomplish, work out, hammer out, see through, go through with, realize, effect, fulfil, discharge, settle; be resolved, things work out, perfect, consummate, ripen, mature; culminate, come to a head.

see also 56, 609

660 non-completion

n. non-completion, failure, non-performance, neglect, defeat; fault, blemish, deficiency, defect.

adj. uncompleted, failed, neglected, incomplete, half-done, partial, imperfect, deficient.

vb. not complete, leave undone, neglect, miss, fail, drop out, leave, not stay the course.

see also 57, 582

661 success

n. success, completion, achievement, attainment, accomplishment; successfulness, happy ending, favourable outcome, prosperous issue; triumph, victory, conquest, push-over (*inf.*), walk-over (*inf.*); breakthrough, advance, progress; prosperity, luck, happiness, bed of roses; success story, hit, smash hit (*sl.*).

winner, victor, champion, hero, title-holder, conqueror.

adj. successful, winning, victorious, triumphant, champion, in the lead, unbeaten, invincible; beneficial, advantageous; fruitful, prosperous, fortunate, thriving, flourishing.

vb. succeed, make a success of, achieve, attain, accomplish, reach, complete, fulfil, obtain, get, capture, gain, pull off (*inf.*), bring off (*inf.*); be successful, come off (*inf.*), do the trick (*inf.*); advance, get on, make it (*inf.*), make a go of (*inf.*), make a breakthrough, proceed, progress, benefit, reap, profit, prosper, flourish, thrive, prevail, score a hit, hit the jackpot.

win, beat, conquer, defeat, get the better of, gain the upper hand, clobber (*sl.*), overcome, ride out the storm, crush, overwhelm, win hands down, walk away with (*inf.*), come out on top (*inf.*), come off with flying colours; survive, get by, hang on.

662 failure

n. failure, misadventure, breakdown, collapse, fiasco, disaster, débâcle, disappointment, flop (*inf.*), wash-out (*inf.*); defeat, overthrow, downfall, ruin, landslide; unsuccessfulness, ineffectiveness, defectiveness; neglect, omission, shortcoming; no-go (*inf.*), wild goose chase, utter defeat, clobbering (*sl.*), rout.

loser, underdog, has-been (*inf.*), also-ran (*inf.*), non-starter, dud.

adj. unsuccessful, futile, vain, useless, fruitless, profitless; unfortunate, disastrous; inadequate, ineffective, abortive; overthrown, defeated, fallen, outmatched, thwarted, frustrated, foiled, pipped at the post, outvoted.

vb. fail, go amiss, fall down, let one down; abandon, neglect, miss; thwart, frustrate; fall short, break down, fall through (*inf.*), miscarry, come to nothing, flounder, falter, go on the rocks, flop (*inf.*), fizzle out (*inf.*); lose, be defeated, suffer defeat, go down, go under; bark up the wrong tree (*inf.*), not get to first base (*inf.*); get no change out of (*inf.*).

663 trophy

n. trophy, prize, reward, award, honour, medal, badge, cup, memorial, decoration, ribbon, order, crown, palm, laurel, accolade, mention, citation; consolation prize, booby prize, wooden spoon.

booty, loot, spoil, plunder, premium, capture.

see also 724

664 prosperity

n. prosperity, good fortune, happiness, welfare, well-being, successfulness, luckiness, affluence, wealth, riches, luxury, benefits, blessings; golden age, good old days, heyday, boom, bed of roses, halcyon days, summer.

adj. prosperous, flourishing, thriving, successful, well-to-do, well-off, comfortable, rich, auspicious; up-and-coming, born with a silver spoon in one's mouth; golden, glorious, cloudless, sunny, halcyon.

vb. prosper, thrive, flourish, increase, blossom, be successful, fare well, turn out well; get on in the world, make one's mark, be rich, make a fortune; Fortune smile upon.

see also 661

665 adversity

n. adversity, misfortune, trouble, hardship, unluckiness, bad luck, hard times, bad patch, ill wind, deep water, difficulty, misadventure, unhappiness; disaster, distress, catastrophe, crisis, calamity, burden, pressure, affliction, blight, curse, plague, scourge.

adj. adverse, unfavourable, hostile, unfriendly, sinister; disastrous, catastrophic; afflicted, troubled, wretched, stricken; unfortunate, unlucky, unhappy, ill-starred, ill-fated, down on one's luck, in a bad way, in the wars.

vb. be in trouble, hit a bad patch, be in for it (*inf.*), have a hard time of it, feel the pinch, fall on hard times, decline, sink, stew in one's own juice, go under, get out of one's depth, fall flat on one's face (*inf.*), fall by the wayside.

see also 633

666 mediocrity

n. mediocrity, commonness, ordinariness, averageness, passableness, tolerableness.

adj. mediocre, average, ordinary,

indifferent, middling, fair, poor, feeble, common, commonplace, dull, monotonous, stale, insipid, wishy-washy, tolerable, fair-to-middling, passable, humdrum, run of the mill, so-so, nothing to write home about, much of a muchness.

vb. make do, just exist, struggle along, muddle through, scrape through, manage somehow, get by, just keep one's head above water, stagnate, vegetate.

2 Intersocial volition

A General

667 authority

n. authority, power, control, right, prerogative, command, rule, sway; dominion, sovereignty, ascendancy, upper hand, supreme authority, last word; influence, prestige, power behind the throne, arm of the law.

government, democracy, *vox populi*, officialdom, bureaucracy, administration, establishment, them, powers that be; open government, devolution.

adj. authoritative, commanding, dominant, lawful, powerful, sovereign; in office, in power; official, executive, administrative, bureaucratic, governmental, democratic, gubernatorial, political.

vb. rule, govern, control, direct, dominate, lord it over, domineer, command, sway, reign; assume control, take over, take the reins, have power, rule the roost; authorize, empower, back, devolve, decentralize.

see also 671

668 laxity

n. laxity, slackness, looseness, flexibility; anarchy, lawlessness, mob rule, disorder, chaos, turmoil.

adj. lax, slack, loose, remiss, soft, flabby, relaxed, flexible; anarchic, uncontrolled, lawless, chaotic, rebellious.

vb. be lax, tolerate, not enforce, stretch a point; misrule, misgovern; give a free hand to, give free rein to; take the law into one's own hands, do what is right in one's own eyes.

see also 670

669 severity

n. severity, strictness, austerity, firmness, rigidity, inflexibility, rigour; hardness, cruelty; firm hand, strong hand, heavy hand, rod of iron, tight rein, pound of flesh, letter of the law.

tyranny, oppression, despotism, fascism; tyrant, dictator, despot, autocrat, taskmaster, authoritarian, disciplinarian.

adj. severe, stern, strict, harsh, hard, austere, extreme, puritanical; firm, rigid, unbending, inflexible, immovable, unchanging; rigorous, exacting, uncompromising, stringent; grim, cruel, forbidding; unfeeling, hard-hearted; tyrannical, overbearing, domineering, despotic, totalitarian, authoritarian, oppressive, heavy-handed.

vb. be severe, be hard on, discipline, come down on (*inf.*), deal harshly with, insist, crack down on (*inf.*), clamp down on (*inf.*), put one's foot down (*inf.*), keep a tight rein on, rule with an iron hand, domineer, lord it over, dominate, oppress, tyrannize.

see also 963

670 lenience

n. lenience, softness, tolerance, mildness, forbearance; mercy, clemency,
forgiveness, pardon; kindness, compassion, favour.

adj. lenient, soft, gentle, mild, kind, compassionate, loving, soft-hearted, tender, sympathetic, easy-going; tolerant, forbearing, long-suffering; merciful, forgiving, clement.

vb. be lenient, go easy on, spare the rod; pass over, forbear, refrain; forgive, pardon; tolerate, bear.

671 command

n. command, direction, rule, charge, ordinance, mandate, directive, dictate, injunction, behest; bidding, call, summons; decree, ruling, law, act, fiat, canon, edict, bull, proclamation; writ, warrant, subpoena; demand, claim, request, requirement; final demand, ultimatum.

adj. commanding, powerful, authoritative.

vb. command, rule, direct, dictate, order, charge, decree, proclaim, ordain; lay down, prescribe; demand, claim, request, ask, require, exact; bid, call, summon, invite, send for.

see also 667, 954

672 disobedience

n. disobedience, violation, disregard, neglect, non-observance, infringement, transgression, sin; misbehaviour, naughtiness; waywardness, stubbornness, insubordination, defiance, intractableness, unruliness; mutiny, revolt, rebellion, revolution, desertion, riot, insurgence.

rebel, revolutionary, radical, anarchist, reactionary, extremist, insurrectionist, insurgent, rioter, terrorist, mutineer, deserter; trouble-maker, brawler.

adj. disobedient, insubordinate; naughty, misbehaving; defiant, refractory, unsubmissive, disloyal, rebellious, intractable, unruly, lawless, uncontrollable, obstreperous; stubborn, wayward, insolent; revolutionary, mutinous, riotous, anarchistic, dissident, factious, insurgent.

vb. disobey, defy, fly in the face of, disregard, neglect, ignore, pay no attention to, not heed, violate, infringe, transgress, sin, break rules; misbehave; revolt, rebel, mutiny.

673 obedience

n. obedience, submission, compliance, loyalty, devotion, faithfulness, fidelity, constancy; meekness, docility.

adj. obedient, submissive, complaisant; law-abiding, well-behaved, good; devoted, loyal, faithful, respectful, dutiful, subservient, docile, acquiescent; round one's little finger (*inf.*), at one's beck and call, on a string, henpecked.

vb. obey, submit, do, keep, observe, follow, pay attention to, bow to, heed, comply, fulfil, agree, behave, do what one is told, do one's duty, do what is expected of one.

see also **654, 679**

674 compulsion

n. compulsion, force, drive, necessity, need, obligation, pressure, constraint, coercion, violence, strong arm, duress; urgency; conscription.

adj. compelling, compulsive, necessary, driving, pressing, coercive, unavoidable, irresistible, compulsory, urgent.

vb. compel, force, drive, coerce, constrain, impel, dictate, necessitate, oblige, require, urge, bring pressure to bear on, inflict.

675 master

n. master, mistress, chief, leader, head, superior, principal, lord; director, manager, supervisor, boss, management, overseer, authority, officer, official, mayor, mayoress; governor, governess, ruler, president, executive, sovereign, king, queen, prince, princess, emperor, empress, regent; captain, commander, lieutenant; big Chief (*sl.*), bigwig.

see also **34, 623**

676 servant

n. servant, dependant, assistant, right-hand man, subordinate, employee, worker, staff, personnel; slave, serf, vassal, captive, bondman, fag; orderly, menial; drudge, hack; chauffeur, butler, domestic, housekeeper, maid, nurse; porter, janitor, doorman; steward, stewardess, waiter, waitress, barman, barmaid; charwoman, cleaner.

adj. serving, ministering, attending, helping.

vb. serve, work for, be in the employment of, minister, aid, help, wait upon, care for, look after, nurse, mother; attend, do for (*inf.*).

677 sign of authority

n. badge of office, insignia, symbol, emblem, livery, uniform, regalia, rod, sceptre, mace, crown, staff, wand, rod, sword, stripe, decoration, flag.

678 freedom

n. freedom, liberty, independence, autonomy, democracy, self-determination; freedom of choice, free will; immunity, exemption, privilege, *carte blanche*, blank cheque, unrestraint; range, scope, play, field, room, leeway, latitude, opportunity, full play, free rein, elbow room.

adj. free, released, liberated, freed, at liberty, at large, let out, scot free; clear, extricated, unshackled, unfettered, unattached, unengaged, unconfined, unimpeded, unhindered, unrestrained; independent, autonomous, self-governing, democratic, enfranchised.

vb. free, have a free hand, have the run of; be independent, please oneself, do as one wishes, fend for oneself, stand on one's own two feet, go it alone.

see also **680**

679 subjection

n. subjection, subservience, servitude, dependence, subordination, inferiority; allegiance, service; bondage, slavery, serfdom, servility, thrall.

adj. subject, dependent, subordinate, submissive, inferior, junior, accessory, subsidiary, satellite, auxiliary; accountable, answerable, liable, contingent.

vb. subject, enslave, dominate, subordinate, master, rule, hold captive, conquer, tame, subdue, subjugate, hold under one's thumb; repress, suppress, sit on.

be subject to, depend on, lean on; be at the mercy of, serve.

see also **35**

680 liberation

n. liberation, release, discharge, deliverance, rescue; extrication, disengagement, unravelling, loosing, unfettering, loosening, untying; emancipation, enfranchisement, manumission.

adj. freed, liberated, released, loose.

vb. liberate, free, release, discharge, deliver, save, rescue, set at liberty, restore, let out; extricate, loose, remove fetters, unfetter, untie, remove, unbind, undo, cut loose, disengage, unravel, let slip; ransom, pardon, dismiss, acquit; emancipate, enfran-

chise; shake off, free oneself of, get rid of, lose.

see also **601**, **961**

681 restraint

n. restraint, control, constraint, discipline, self-control, self-discipline, self-restraint, reticence, reserve, caution; repression.

restriction, limitation, barrier, check, hindrance, impediment, obstacle, block, bar, curb, blockade, embargo, ban, veto; curfew; closed shop; censorship, news blackout; monopoly, cartel, protectionism.

custody, detention, imprisonment, confinement, impounding; chain, bond, irons, fetter, shackle.

adj. restraining, restrictive, controlling, limiting, strict, narrow, repressive; restrained, under control, in check, controlled, disciplined, reserved, cautious, calm, reticent, withdrawn, repressed, pent-up, bottled-up.

in custody, under arrest, imprisoned, detained, confined, in prison, in detention, behind bars, inside (*sl.*), in jug (*sl.*), in clink (*sl.*).

vb. restrain, control, limit, govern, check, arrest, curb, keep in check, hold back, narrow; discipline, bridle; repress, suppress, keep back, bottle up, muzzle, gag, subdue, quell, quash; hinder, impede, restrict, hamper; control oneself, pull oneself together, take a grip on oneself (*inf.*), sort oneself out (*inf.*), get organized.

take into custody, apprehend, help police with their inquiries, run in, turn in (*inf.*), turn over to, pick up, arrest, convict, take prisoner; imprison, detain, confine, put into prison, put away (*inf.*), shut up, lock up, put behind bars, intern, impound; tie, bind, chain, fetter, manacle.

682 prison

n. prison, gaol, jail, lock-up, nick (*sl.*), clink (*sl.*), jug (*sl.*), maximum-security prison, police station; cell, cage, guardroom; dungeon; detention camp, internment camp, concentration camp; Borstal, detention centre, approved home, remand centre.

683 keeper

n. keeper, custodian, warden, curator, attendant, official, guard; caretaker, porter, janitor, concierge, housekeeper, gatekeeper; watchman, lookout, patrol, scout; baby-sitter, governess, nurse, nanny, guardian; escort, bodyguard; gamekeeper, ranger; jailer, warder, prison governor, screw (*sl.*).

see also 593

684 prisoner

n. prisoner, convict, culprit, con (*sl.*), inmate, star, gaolbird, young offender, captive, prisoner of war, internee; defendant, the accused, detainee; criminal, rogue.

see also 906, 940

685 vicarious authority

n. commission, delegation, deputation, representation, authorization, committal, trusteeship; appointment, nomination, assignment; mission, embassy, envoy, legation, agency; devolution, decentralization; inauguration, installation, investiture, induction, ordination, coronation; accession.

trust, charge, mandate, authority, warrant; task, duty, errand, employment.

adj. commissioned, delegated, vicarious, deputed.

vb. commission, delegate, appoint, empower, grant authority to, authorize, charge, commit, assign, entrust; devolve, decentralize; name, nominate; inaugurate, invest, induct, ordain, install, place, establish; crown, enthrone; employ, engage, hire, contract.

represent, deputize, act on behalf of, stand in for.

686 annulment

n. annulment, cancellation, abrogation, dissolution, revocation, retraction, invalidation, nullification, reversal, repeal, abolition, countermand.

dismissal, removal, displacement, the sack (*inf.*), the boot (*sl.*), the push (*sl.*); retirement, lay-off, redundancy, natural wastage; deposal, dethronement, impeachment.

demotion, downgrading, degradation.

adj. annulled, cancelled, null and void; rained off, abandoned, postponed.

vb. annul, cancel, abolish, repeal, revoke, dissolve, rescind, quash, render void, nullify, invalidate; refute, counteract, reverse, repudiate, countermand.

dismiss, oust, overthrow, unseat, remove from office, discharge, depose, dethrone, displace, suspend, sack, fire, give the push to (*sl.*), give the boot to (*sl.*), give papers to, show the door to, strike off the register, write out, pension off; relieve, replace, recall; impeach, unfrock; demote, degrade, downgrade.

687 resignation

n. resignation, abdication, retirement, relinquishment, renunciation, withdrawal, departure, leaving, surrender, desertion; pension, golden handshake, leaving gift, leaving present, gratuity, superannuation.

adj. resignatory; retired, former,

previous, outgoing, one-time, sometime, emeritus.

vb. resign, quit, leave, depart, vacate office, relinquish, abandon, step down, stand down, stand aside, retire, abdicate, give up office, walk out of, hand in one's notice, tender one's resignation, hand in one's papers.

688 consignee

n. consignee, delegate, representative, substitute, deputy; trustee, executor, nominee, proxy; intermediary, middleman, negotiator, broker; committee, board, panel, group, organization, deputation, cabinet, decision maker.

ambassador, envoy, commissioner, delegation, emissary, diplomat, consul, attaché, plenipotentiary, nuncio; embassy, consulate, mission.

see also 619, 689

689 deputy

n. deputy, assistant, second-in-command, right-hand man; delegate, substitute, representative, proxy, surrogate, stand-in, agent, proxy, vicar; ambassador, commissioner; spokesman, mouthpiece.

adj. deputy, deputizing, vice, pro, acting.

vb. deputize, substitute, represent, stand in for, act on behalf of.

B Special

690 permission

n. permission, liberty, leave, freedom, consent; authorization, legalization, confirmation, endorsement, affirmation, sanction; authority, permit, grant, charter, licence, certificate, concession, allowance; pass, passport, visa, pass-

word; letter of commendation; go-ahead, green light (*inf.*), all-clear, clearance, nod; free hand, free rein, *carte blanche*, blank cheque.

adj. permitting, allowing; tolerant, lenient, permissive; permitted, granted, allowed, authorized, approved.

vb. permit, let, allow, grant, give permission; consent, approve, favour, have no objections; authorize, warrant, legalize, sanction, certify, charter, franchise, license; give the go-ahead, give the green light (*inf.*), give clearance, rubber-stamp (*inf.*); tolerate, concede, bear, suffer.

691 prohibition

n. prohibition, forbiddance, obstruction, suppression, repression, refusal, interdiction, injunction, disallowance, countermand, ban, veto, embargo, boycott, taboo.

adj. prohibiting, forbidding; prohibitive, excessive, restrictive; prohibited, forbidden, illegal, illicit, unlawful, taboo, impermissible.

vb. prohibit, forbid, refuse, withhold, deny, disallow, prevent, hinder, hamper, preclude, restrain, interdict; ban, veto, boycott, say no to, debar, exclude, shut out; obstruct, oppose, suppress, repress, restrict, stop, halt.

692 consent

n. consent, acceptance, agreement, allowance, permission, approval, assent, concurrence, acquiescence, compliance.

adj. consenting, agreeable, willing, acquiescent.

vb. consent, accept, allow, agree, approve, assent, say yes to, be in favour of, concur, acquiesce, accede; concede, grant, yield, acknowledge, vouchsafe.

see also 690

693 offer

n. offer, tender, bid, submission; approach, advance, overture; proposal, proposition, presentation, suggestion.

adj. on offer, available, for sale, advertised.

vb. offer, hold out, present, suggest, propose, submit, extend, move, put forward, put forth, tender, bid, approach; make overtures, make advances; lay at one's feet, sacrifice, proffer.

volunteer, offer oneself, come forward, stand for.

694 refusal

n. refusal, rejection, denial, declension; rebuff, snub, slap in the face, insult; veto, ban, exclusion.

adj. refusing, unwilling, uncompliant, resisting, hard-hearted, reluctant.

vb. refuse, reject, not want, decline, resist, ignore, turn down, say no to, not hear of, exclude, disallow, shun, repudiate, repel, spurn, rebuff, scorn, snub, repulse, turn one's back on, turn a deaf ear to, set one's face against, wash one's hands of, harden one's heart against; slam the door in someone's face (*inf.*); withhold, deny, hold back.

see also **469, 542**

695 request

n. request, call, petition, invitation, bid, application, demand, appeal, plea, address; inquiry, question; offer, proposal, proposition; prayer, entreaty, intercession, invocation, supplication; importunity, urgency.

adj. requesting, petitioning, supplicatory, imprecatory, invocatory, prayerful, begging, on bended knees; urgent, importunate, persistent, clamorous.

vb. request, call, ask, express a wish, apply for, summon, demand, implore, beseech, beg, appeal, entreat, pray, call on, petition, crave, plead, adjure; inquire, invite.

urge, ply, press, persist, pester, bother, coax, clamour.

canvass, solicit, importune, tout, hawk; appeal for money, pass the hat round (*inf.*), have a whip-round (*inf.*), make a collection.

696 protest

n. protest, deprecation, disapproval, objection, complaint, dissent, expostulation, remonstrance.

demonstration, demo (*inf.*), rally, sit-in, mass meeting, march, protest march, strike, hunger strike.

adj. protesting, deprecatory, expostulatory, remonstrative.

vb. protest, depreciate, speak against, lodge a protest, ask not to, disapprove, object, disagree, oppose, criticize, demur, remonstrate, expostulate; groan, jeer, murmur, heckle, sneer; demonstrate, march, strike, go on strike, picket.

see also **144**

697 petitioner

n. petitioner, supplicant, suppliant, applicant, claimant, candidate, bidder; inquirer, advertiser; lobby, lobbyist, pressure group, canvasser, hawker, tout, pedlar, vendor; beggar, scrounger, cadger, sponger, loafer, idler, vagabond, tramp, down-and-out.

C Conditional

698 promise

n. promise, covenant, pledge, contract, pact, undertaking, commitment, consent, word, vow, word of honour; gentleman's agreement.

engagement, betrothal; fiancée, fiancé, intended (*inf.*).

adj. promised, committed, pledged, bound; engaged, betrothed.

vb. promise, agree, undertake, commit, declare, covenant, pledge, contract, consent, vow, swear; warrant, guarantee; bind onself, give one's word, pledge one's honour; become engaged, betrothe.

699 contract

n. contract, agreement, covenant, undertaking, pact, concordat, promise, pledge, understanding, arrangement, settlement, transaction, bargain, deal (*inf.*); negotiation, compromise, give and take; treaty, convention, alliance, league, charter, entente; gentleman's agreement.

adj. contractual, conventional, promissory.

vb. contract, agree, covenant, undertake, pledge, promise, arrange, bargain, deal, negotiate, hammer out, stipulate; sign, sign on the dotted line, agree on terms, settle, come to an agreement, accept an offer, shake on it (*inf.*); ratify, confirm.

see also 24, 643

700 conditions

n. conditions, terms, provisions, specifications, frame of reference, strings, proviso, contingencies, arrangements, limitations, restrictions, reservations, exceptions, escape clause, *sine qua non*.

adj. conditional, provisional, contingent, with strings attached, granted on certain terms, dependent on, subject to.

vb. negotiate, discuss; propose

conditions, postulate, stipulate, attach strings, insist on, impose.

see also 403

701 security

n. security, surety, warranty, covenant, bond, promise, pledge, earnest, token, certainty; deposit, caution money, money in advance, forfeit, stake, insurance, bail, pawn, mortgage, collateral; liability, responsibility; hostage, captive, prisoner.

adj. guaranteed, pledged, pawned, on deposit.

vb. give security, guarantee, pledge, sign for, insure, assure, underwrite, mortgage, stake, pawn; give bail, go bail; stand surety, bail out; stand for, back.

702 observance

n. observance, attention, performance, doing, carrying out, keeping, heeding, practice; obedience, compliance, devotion.

adj. observant, practising, professing; diligent, conscientious; exact, scrupulous, pedantic; dependable, responsible; loyal, faithful, devoted, obedient.

vb. observe, heed, keep, do, carry out, follow, adhere to, perform, discharge, practise, adopt, conform to, fulfil, comply; keep on the right side of the law; hold fast, stand by, embrace, profess, give allegiance to, be loyal to.

703 non-observance

n. non-observance, neglect, disregard, omission; breaking, infringement, violation, transgression, trespass, breach, sin; disobedience, disloyalty, infidelity; inattention, carelessness, indifference, irresponsibility.

adj. non-observant, negligent,

careless, indifferent; unfaithful, disobedient.

vb. not observe, not practise, not keep; break, disobey, violate, infringe, transgress, breach, contravene; neglect, disregard, omit; break faith, be faithless.

704 compromise

n. compromise, bargaining, agreement, understanding, settlement; give and take, concessions, mutual concessions; middle course, middle ground, half-way house; composition; *modus vivendi.*

vb. compromise, make concessions, give and take, meet half-way, go fifty-fifty, steer a middle course, split the differences; negotiate, come to an agreement, come to an understanding, reconcile, settle, adjust, agree to differ.

D Possessive relations

705 acquisition

n. acquisition, getting, obtainment, procuration; recovery, retrieval, redemption.

gain, benefit, advantage, reward, income, earnings, wages, salary, grant, profit, receipts, proceeds, emolument; collection, gathering, produce, output, yield, fruit, harvest, crop; addition, accrual, accumulation.

adj. obtainable, available; acquisitive, hoarding, grasping.

profitable, fruitful, productive, advantageous, worthwhile, lucrative, paying its way, remunerative.

vb. acquire, get, obtain, take possession of, make one's own, appropriate, lay hold of, procure; force from, grab, seize, capture, pocket, secure, draw, tap; gain, accept, receive, make,

collect, earn, benefit, win, accumulate; gather, harvest, glean, reap.

get back, recover, retrieve, regain, redeem.

buy, purchase; profit, capitalize on, cash in on (*inf.*); inherit, come into, be left.

see also 716

706 loss

n. loss, mislaying, misplacement; dispossession, deprivation, forfeiture, want, bereavement; insolvency, bankruptcy.

adj. lost, missing, misplaced, mislaid, nowhere to be found, hidden, obscured, vanished, strayed, gone; lacking, wanting, deprived of, bereft; overdrawn, insolvent, bankrupt; unprofitable, disadvantageous, wasted, irretrievable, desperate, hopeless, futile.

vb. lose, mislay, misplace, not find; let slip, drop, miss, fail, forfeit; deprive, displace; waste, squander; incur losses, go bankrupt.

707 possession

n. possession, ownership, occupancy, residence, tenancy, tenure; possessorship, proprietorship; hold, mastery, grasp, control, custody; purchase.

adj. possessing, having, owning; possessive, exclusive, monopolistic, selfish; possessed, owned, purchased, enjoyed, in possession of.

vb. possess, own, have, hold, keep, retain, grasp, occupy, control, maintain, use, boast of, enjoy; have title to, have rights to, have claim upon; monopolize, hog (*inf.*), have all to oneself, corner; include, comprise, contain; belong, appertain.

708 non-possession

n. non-possession, loss, deprivation, surrender of rights; lease; no man's land.

adj. not owning, lacking; destitute, poor, impoverished, penniless; unowned, unoccupied, unpossessed, unattached, free, ownerless, virgin, unclaimed, lost, independent, unbound.

see also **706**

709 joint possession

n. joint possession, co-ownership, cooperation, participation, partnership, sharing; socialism, communism, public ownership, nationalization, worker participation, profit-sharing; community, cooperative, collective, kibbutz; joint fund, kitty, pool; share, portion.

participator, partner, member, partaker, shareholder, worker-director.

adj. cooperative, joint, participatory, common, communal, profit-sharing; involved, committed, dedicated, connected with.

vb. participate, share, cooperate, join, take part in, partake, go halves.

see also **639**

710 possessor

n. possessor, owner, holder, master, partner; buyer, purchaser; occupant, occupier, tenant, resident, lodger, lessee, landlord, landlady, landowner, landholder, proprietor, proprietress; heir, heiress, inheritor.

711 property

n. property, land, assets, resources, means, goods, riches, wealth, valuables, inheritance, capital, investment, equity, land, holding, estate.

belongings, equipment, paraphernalia, things, trappings, fixtures, furniture, furnishings, goods and chattels; appurtenances, accoutrements; personal effects, luggage, baggage; burden, encumbrance, impedimenta.

712 retention

n. retention, holding, keeping; hold, grasp, clench, clinch, grip, hug, embrace, clasp; confinement, stranglehold, tight grip, straitjacket.

adj. retentive, holding; retained, held, kept.

vb. retain, hold, keep, keep hold of, grasp, clench, grip, clinch, clasp, clutch, embrace, hug, squeeze, press; cling to, stick to, fasten on, secure, hold fast; contain, restrain, enclose, confine; maintain, preserve; cherish, nurture, harbour; detain, reserve, withhold.

713 non-retention

n. relinquishment, abandonment, renunciation, disposal; exemption, dispensation, release; divorce, dissolution.

adj. abandoned, thrown away, rejected, marooned.

vb. not retain, relinquish, abandon, renounce, let go, part with, dispose of, discard, throw away, jettison, release; waive, lift restrictions, derestrict, exempt.

see also **556, 921**

714 transfer

n. transference, conveyancing, assignation; changeover, change of hands; devolution, delegation; exchange, conversion, interchange; sale, lease; bequest, endowment, legacy.

adj. transferable, negotiable, interchangeable, exchangeable; transferred, made over.

vb. convey, transfer, sell, sign,

consign, assign, change over, deliver, make over; entrust, commit; exchange, convert; devolve, delegate, decentralize; bequeath, will, make a will, pass on, hand down.

see also **268**

715 giving

n. giving, bestowal, conferral, granting, imparting, delivery.

gift, present, donation, grant, award, presentation, prize; allowance, subsidy, aid, assistance; tip, gratuity; bounty, largesse, windfall; leaving present, golden handshake; charity, hand-out, alms; bequest, legacy; blessing, favour, grace, mercy.

sacrifice, offering, worship, dedication, consecration; offering, collection, offertory.

giver, donor, contributor.

adj. giving, charitable, generous, liberal, sacrificial; given, free.

vb. give, donate, grant, award, present, contribute, render, remit, convey, supply, furnish, provide, afford, dispense, hand out, dole out, distribute, administer, deal out, mete out, subsidize, give towards; bestow, confer, endow, invest with, impart, communicate; expend, spend, lavish; offer, sacrifice.

716 receiving

n. receiving, reception, acquisition, acceptance, admission, collection; receipts, proceeds, dues, monies, toll.

recipient, receiver, beneficiary; object, target, victim, guinea pig; customer, client; trustee, payee, addressee, earner; heir, heiress.

adj. receiving, receptive, welcoming, hospitable, sensitive.

vb. receive, accept, admit, be given, get, gain, acquire, collect, obtain, draw, take in, derive, come by, attract, come

in for, be on the receiving end; take up, levy, charge; be received, accrue, come in, fall to one.

see also **302, 705**

717 apportionment

n. apportionment, allotment, sharing, division, distribution, dealing, rationing.

portion, share, allocation, section, piece, part, fraction, fragment; helping, serving, slice, ration; proportion, quota, allowance; cut (*sl.*), split, parcel, lot.

vb. apportion, allot, distribute, divide, share out, hand out, dole out, dish out (*inf.*), farm out, parcel out, deal, assign, dispose, administer, give away, dispense, ration.

see also **55**

718 lending

n. lending; loan, advance, mortgage, allowance, credit, investment, credit card, credit account, hire purchase, never-never (*inf.*).

bank, building society, pawnbroker, pop-shop (*sl.*); banker, bank manager, lender, financier, money-lender, creditor; usurer, shark, angel (*sl.*), Shylock.

vb. lend, let out, allow to borrow, trust with, entrust, hire out, let, lease, charter; loan, finance, support, back, advance, grant, lend on security, put out at interest, give credit, risk.

719 borrowing

n. borrowing, rental, hire, loan; assumption; appropriation, adoption, importation; imitation, copy.

vb. borrow, rent, hire, lease, charter; take on tick (*inf.*), raise money, pawn, cadge; touch for (*sl.*); obtain, use, adopt.

720 taking

n. taking, possession, acceptance, appropriation, requisition; seizure, grab, capture; kidnapping, abduction; dispossession, deprivation, extortion, confiscation; recovery, retrieval.

taker, possessor; seizer, grabber, raider; kidnapper, abductor.

adj. taking, grasping, greedy, rapacious, extortionate, ravenous.

vb. take, possess, accept, receive, get, obtain, win, gain; seize, lay hold of, appropriate, take for oneself, acquire, avail oneself of, adopt, assume; grip, clasp; catch, apprehend, grasp; grab, trap, snatch, capture, raid; take away, steal, kidnap, abduct; confiscate, commandeer; recover, retrieve; take from, remove, deprive of, divest of, dispossess, extort, strip, disinherit.

see also 722

721 restitution

n. restitution, restoration, return, giving back, reinstatement; retrieval, recovery, repossession, repatriation; recompense, repayment, refund, amends, compensation, reimbursement, remuneration, reparation, indemnification, redemption, satisfaction.

adj. restitutive, restoring, compensatory, redemptive.

vb. restore, return, give back, reinstate, reinstall; rehabilitate, repair; recover, get back, retrieve, recoup, regain, retake, reclaim.

make restitution, refund, make amends, reimburse, repay, compensate, indemnify, redeem, ransom.

see also 589

722 stealing

n. stealing, theft, larceny, robbery, burglary, house-breaking, shop-lifting; vandalism, looting, pilfering, ransacking, pillage, plunder, sacking; hijacking, skyjacking (*inf.*); kidnapping, abduction; hold-up, stick-up (*inf.*), mugging (*inf.*), hit-and-run-raid, smash-and-grab-raid, job (*sl.*); embezzlement, misappropriation, extortion, fraud.

adj. thieving, light-fingered.

vb. steal, take, burgle, thieve, rob, remove, go off with, get away with, make off with, run off with, seize, pilfer, pick-pocket, pinch (*sl.*), nick (*sl.*), filch, fleece, nobble (*sl.*), knock off (*sl.*), rip off (*sl.*), screw (*sl.*), shoplift, purloin; abduct, kidnap, mug (*inf.*), hijack, skyjack; embezzle, misappropriate, defraud, swindle, cheat, fiddle, peculate, smuggle; loot, rifle, sack, raid, ransack, plunder, pillage.

be stolen, fall off the back of a lorry (*inf.*).

723 thief

n. thief, robber, stealer; burglar, house-breaker, shop-lifter, mugger, attacker; pilferer, pick-pocket; hijacker, skyjacker (*inf.*), highwayman; safe-blower, safe-cracker; kidnapper, abductor; plunderer, looter; embezzler, swindler, cheater, fiddler; crook, rogue, thug, smuggler, pirate.

see also 684

724 booty

n. booty, prize, haul, loot, swag (*sl.*), takings, plunder, spoil, winnings, stolen goods, goods fallen off the back of a lorry (*inf.*), capture, premium, contraband, prey.

725 business

n. business, trade, commerce, business affairs, traffic; negotiations, bargaining, transactions, marketing, buying and selling; barter, exchange, swap (*inf.*).

adj. business, trading, commercial, mercantile.

vb. transact business, trade, traffic, deal in, handle, market, buy and sell; negotiate, bargain; exchange, barter, swap (*inf.*).

726 purchase

n. purchase, buying, obtaining, acquisition; shopping, payment, investment, marketing.

buyer, purchaser, consumer, shopper, customer, patron, client, clientele, custom, market, patronage.

vb. purchase, buy, get, obtain, gain, acquire; go shopping, pay for, invest, exchange, bargain, sign; patronize; go window-shopping, buy back, redeem.

727 sale

n. sale, disposal, selling, marketing, trading; clearance, sell-out; bazaar, jumble sale, rummage sale; auction, public sale; sales talk, salesmanship, high-pressure salesmanship, sales patter, promotion, advertising.

seller, vendor, retailer, shopkeeper, shop assistant, salesman, commercial traveller, sales rep.

adj. saleable, marketable, in demand; available, on the market.

vb. sell, dispose, market, flog (*sl.*), retail, trade, dump, vend; ask, demand; transfer, transact, exchange; peddle, hawk; reduce prices, sell off; auction, come under the hammer.

728 trader

n. trader, dealer, retailer, shopkeeper, tradesman, middleman, wholesaler, exporter, importer, shipper, trafficker, merchant; businessman, industrialist, capitalist, manager, financier, entrepreneur, tycoon, stockbroker, speculator.

pedlar, hawker, tinker, huckster; tout; rag-and-bone man.

729 merchandise

n. merchandise, commodities, stock, wares, articles, goods, property, product, possessions; things, stuff; line, supplies; consumer goods, consumer durables.

730 market

n. market, mart, square, mall, arcade, shopping centre, shopping precinct, exchange, emporium; shop, store, supermarket, department store, multiple, chain store, boutique, hypermarket; kiosk, stand, stall, booth, barrow, bazaar; place of business, premises, concern, establishment.

731 money

n. money, currency, legal tender, cash, bank notes, bread (*sl.*), dough (*sl.*), lolly (*sl.*); change, small change; cheque, credit card, hire purchase; pay, salary, wages, pocket money, pin money; sum, amount, balance; funds, credit, finance, reserves, capital, wealth, wherewithal.

adj. monetary, pecuniary, financial.

vb. mint, coin, issue, monetize, put in circulation; withdraw, remove from circulation, call in, demonetize.

732 treasury

n. treasury, bank, exchequer, repository, coffer, vault, strongroom, depository, safe, cash box; cash register, till; money-box, piggy bank; wallet, purse, bag.

733 treasurer

n. treasurer, receiver, cashier, banker, purser, bursar, paymaster, accountant, teller, steward, trustee.

734 wealth

n. wealth, riches, money, affluence, luxury, opulence, prosperity, fortune, money to burn; profits, assets, means, resources.

rich man, millionaire, moneybags, man of means, capitalist.

adj. rich, wealthy, affluent, prosperous, luxurious, well-off, in the money, well-to-do, well provided for, made of money (*inf.*), rolling in it (*inf.*).

vb. get rich, make a fortune, come into money, line one's pocket; live comfortably, afford, bear the expense of, make both ends meet.

735 poverty

n. poverty, impoverishment, poorness; destitution, scarcity, privation, penury, pennilessness, pauperism, indigence, insolvency; beggary, mendicancy; poor man, pauper, beggar.

adj. poor, needy, destitute, underprivileged, distressed; impecunious, poverty-stricken, penniless, hard up, broke (*inf.*), bankrupt, insolvent; begging, mendicant; starving, hungry, empty-handed, down-and-out.

vb. be poor, find it hard going, live from hand to mouth, starve; impoverish, ruin, eat out of house and home.

736 credit

n. credit, trust, reliability; loan, account, credit account, credit card; creditor, mortgagee.

vb. credit, charge, charge to an account, credit one's account; give credit, defer payment, lend.

737 debt

n. debt, liability, obligation, claim, commitment, indebtedness, due, duty; debts, bills, amount due, amount owing, accounts outstanding, score, deficit, arrears.

debtor, borrower, purchaser, buyer, mortgagor.

adj. indebted, liable, answerable, responsible, committed, under obligation; owing, in debt, overdrawn, in the red; unpaid, due, outstanding, payable, unsettled, in arrears, overdue.

vb. be in debt, owe, be under obligation, overdraw, run up a bill, fall into debt, be in Queer Street (*sl.*).

738 payment

n. payment, remittance; settlement, clearance, reckoning; recompense, restitution, compensation, reimbursement, refund, subsidy; deposit, instalment, down payment, first payment.

pay, wages, salary, earnings, remuneration, emolument; fee, stipend, allowance, expenses, honorarium; pay packet, pay slip; payroll.

adj. paying, remunerative, not owing; paid, discharged, out of debt.

vb. pay, make payment for; repay, reward, remunerate; settle, discharge, defray, meet, bear the cost of, foot the bill; recompense, reimburse, compensate, recoup, refund; subsidize; pay on the nail; contribute, chip in (*inf.*), fork out (*inf.*), cough up (*sl.*); spend, expend; stand, treat.

739 non-payment

n. non-payment, failure to pay, default, bankruptcy, insolvency, liquidation, crash, ruin; overdraft, overdrawn account; debts.

non-payer, defaulter, bankrupt, lame duck; embezzler.

adj. non-paying, defaulting, insolvent, bankrupt, failed, ruined, on the rocks (*inf.*), bust (*inf.*), liquidated.

vb. not pay, default, fall into arrears, go bankrupt, go into liquidation, go to the wall, fold up (*inf.*), fail, be wound up, go bust (*inf.*), crash, go under; write off; bankrupt, ruin, wind up, put in the hands of a receiver, liquidate.

740 expenditure

n. expenditure, outlay, payment, disbursement, spending, costs, expenses, outgoings, investment.

vb. spend, expend, pay, pay out, lay out, invest, foot the bill; exhaust, discharge, consume; squander, waste, lavish.

741 income

n. income, receipts, revenue, returns, earnings, salary, wages, profit, assets, proceeds, dividends, gains, takings, turn-over, box-office receipts, gate-money.

receipt, acknowledgement, slip, voucher, record.

742 accounts

n. accounts, bookkeeping; account, bill, invoice, reckoning, statement, balance sheet; ledger, log, cash-book; budget.

accountant, chartered accountant, auditor, bookkeeper, actuary, cashier.

adj. accounting, budgetary.

vb. account, keep the books, enter, debit, credit, balance; budget; cook the books (*inf.*), falsify, fiddle (*sl.*).

743 price ·

n. price, cost, expense, amount, charge, toll, fee, fare; rent, rental, hire charge; value, face value, worth; evaluation, valuation, estimate, quotation.

taxation, tax, duty, levy, tariff, inland revenue; excise, custom, impost, tribute, dues; rates, rateable value, assessment.

price control, price freeze, austerity, squeeze; cost of living, price index; price tag, label, ticket.

adj. priced, marked, charged, valued, worth.

vb. price, value, charge, assess, estimate, put a price on, reckon, rate; demand, ask; reduce, mark down; increase, mark up.

cost, be worth, go for, sell for, fetch, come to, amount to.

tax, exact, levy, put a tax on, raise taxes; pay taxes.

744 discount

n. discount, reduction, rebate, allowance, deduction, cut, subtraction, remission, concession; depreciation; subsidy.

vb. reduce, lower, rebate, deduct, cut, take off, knock off, subtract, allow; depreciate.

745 dearness

n. dearness, expensiveness, expense, costliness; exorbitance, excessiveness, extravagance.

adj. dear, expensive, costly, high-priced, pricey (*inf.*); exorbitant, too high, overpriced, excessive, prohibitive, extortionate, immoderate, unreasonable, extravagant, lavish, steep (*inf.*), stiff (*inf.*).

vb. be dear, cost a lot, cost a pretty penny (*inf.*); go up, increase, revalue; overcharge, exploit, bleed, fleece, extort.

746 cheapness

n. cheapness, inexpensiveness, competitiveness, reasonableness; bargain, good value, good buy.

adj. cheap, inexpensive, low-priced, moderate, reasonable, fair, peanuts (*sl.*).

family-sized, economy-sized, economy, bargain, standard; reduced, cut-price, half-price, marked down, dirt cheap.

free, gratuitous, for nothing, without charge, complimentary, gratis, on the house, for love.

vb. be cheap, get one's money's worth; fall in price, decrease, cheapen, depreciate, mark down, devalue.

747 liberality
n. liberality, generosity, benevolence, bounteousness, bounty, largesse; kindness, giving, charity, hospitality, cordiality.

adj. liberal, generous, big-hearted, open-handed, bountiful, lavish, unsparing, unstinting, munificent; kind, benevolent, unselfish, charitable, beneficient.

vb. be liberal, give generously, lavish, heap upon, spare no expense, go beyond what one can afford.

748 economy
n. economy, thrift, care, prudence, housekeeping, stewardship, management, frugality, husbandry, providence; parsimony, stinginess; saving; retrenchment.

adj. economical, economizing, careful, prudent, good, saving, thrifty, frugal, sparing; stingy, mean; convenient, time-saving, labour-saving.

vb. economize, cut back, keep costs down, cut costs, cut corners, tighten one's belt (*inf.*), make ends meet, live within one's means; manage, steward, husband, save, conserve.

749 extravagance
n. extravagance, wastefulness, squandering, prodigality, lavishness, immoderateness; money to burn, shopping spree, spending spree, no thought of tommorow; prodigal, wastrel, spendthrift, squanderer.

adj. extravagant, wasteful, squandering, prodigal, lavish, over-generous, immoderate, exorbitant, reckless, careless, profligate.

vb. waste, squander, throw away, have money to burn, spend money like water, hang the expense, blow (*sl.*), blue (*sl.*); fritter away, dissipate; go too far, overdo it.

750 parsimony
n. parsimony, parsimoniousness, stinginess, scrimping, niggardliness, penny-pinching, cheese-paring, meanness, miserliness, penuriousness; niggard, miser, screw; greed, avarice, covetousness, avidity, voracity, gluttony.

adj. parsimonious, stingy, niggardly, miserly, mean, tight-fisted, close-fisted, penny-pinching, scrimping; sparing, chary,

greedy, avaricious, voracious, possessive, acquisitive, grasping, grabby (*inf.*), itchy (*inf.*), rapacious, covetous, avid.

vb. be parsimonious, scrimp, stint, skimp; over-economize; be greedy, always want more.

VI Affections

A Affections in general

751 affections
n. affections, qualities, character, nature, make-up; personality, psyche, heart, soul, breast, inner self; temperament, disposition, spirit, temper, mood, state of mind, frame of mind, humour; tendency, inclination, bent, bias.

adj. affected, characterized, formed,

752

moulded, disposed, inclined, predisposed.

see also 5, 58

752 feeling

n. feeling, emotion, affection, sentiment, passion; experience, sense, impression, consciousness, sensation, perception, sympathy, warmth, tenderness, sensitivity, empathy; fervour, ardour, enthusiasm.

adj. feeling, emotional, sentimental, romantic, passionate, fervent, intense, impassioned, dramatic, burning, earnest, moving, tender; felt, experienced, heart-felt, thrilled, moved, affected, touched.

vb. feel, sense, experience, go through, enjoy, suffer, undergo, bear, endure.

move, affect, touch, stir, impress, excite, influence, quicken, touch one's heart, touch to the quick; appreciate, respond; thrill, tingle.

753 sensitivity

n. sensitivity, sensibility, susceptibility, awareness, consciousness, responsiveness, excitability.

five senses, sight, hearing, smell, taste, touch; sixth sense, intuition, feminine intuition; extra-sensory perception.

adj. sensitive, aware, conscious of, alive to, awake to, susceptible, impressionable, receptive, sensible; sensory, sentient.

raw, tender, bare, sore, bruised, delicate, painful, oversensitive, hypersensitive; exposed, open, vulnerable.

754 insensitivity

n. insensitivity, insensibility, unawareness, unresponsiveness, inexcitability, impassivness; apathy, indifference, lethargy, aloofness, coldness; hypnosis, numbness, paralysis; dream, trance, coma, stupor; hardness of heart, callousness; stoic, ascetic; iceberg.

adj. insensitive, insusceptible, unimpressionable, unresponsive, inexcitable, unmoved, unaffected, unaware, unconscious, dead to, blind to, oblivious to, lost to, insensible; lethargic, dull, unenthusiastic, apathetic, indifferent, cool, aloof; unfeeling, unemotional, passionless, unresponsive, frigid, cold, numb, paralyzed; blank, poker-faced, dead pan, expressionless; thick-skinned, hard-hearted, callous, cold-blooded.

vb. deaden, numb, paralyze, stupefy, stun, harden, sear, blunt, dull, drug; turn off (*inf.*), switch off (*inf*); be unaffected, leave cold.

755 excitation

n. excitation, stimulation, activation, animation, inspiration, quickening; incitement, provocation, agitation, excitement; captivation, fascination, interest.

adj. exciting, stimulating, inspiring, moving, sparkling, exhilarating, thrilling, delightful; captivating, fascinating, interesting, absorbing, gripping, stirring, tantalizing, compelling, impressive, dramatic, sensational.

vb. excite, stimulate, arouse, activate, move, stir, work up, whip up, incite, influence, affect, provoke, awaken, touch, interest, animate, quicken, inspire; inflame, intensify, kindle, fire, light up; electrify, galvanize, energize.

absorb, fascinate, attract attention, impress, intrigue; tantalize, tease, anger, cause a stir; catch one's attention, come home, arrest, compel, engage; make one's mouth water, whet the appetite; knock for six (*inf.*), take one's breath away; delight, thrill, exhilarate, turn on (*inf.*), switch on (*inf.*).

see also 756, 829

756 excitability

n. excitability, impetuousness, boisterousness, instability, emotionalism, restlessness, agitation, irritability, intolerance.

excitement, exhilaration, thrill, ecstasy, transport; rage, fury, outburst, agony; hysterics, delirium; fuss, big song and dance (*inf.*), hullabaloo, tizzy (*sl.*), tiz-woz (*sl.*), dither (*inf.*), fluster, stew (*inf.*), to-do.

adj. excited, moved, stirred, inspired, thrilled, quickened, enthusiastic, eager, impressed, delighted, pleased, happy, joyful, touched.

excitable, sensitive, highly-strung, nervous, easily excited, emotional; impulsive, quick-tempered, impetuous; moody, temperamental; impatient, irritable, touchy, edgy, jumpy, jittery, restless, fidgety; tense, uptight, all worked up (*inf.*), keyed up, a bundle of nerves (*inf.*); distraught, beside onself; mad, fuming, raging.

vb. be excited, thrill; let oneself go, get carried away, abandon oneself, freak out (*sl.*); tingle, glow, palpitate, pant; tremble, quiver, shake.

get excited, work oneself up; feet, flap (*inf.*), shuffle, fuss; rage, fume, explode, flare up, boil over (*inf.*).

see also 755

757 inexcitability

n. inexcitability, imperturbability, stability, composure, calmness, coolness, level-headedness, even temper, steadiness; peace of mind, serenity, tranquillity; self-possession, self-control, self-restraint, self-assurance; detachment, aloofness; stoicism.

patience, endurance, forbearance, long-suffering, submission, humility, meekness, resignation.

adj. inexcitable, calm, cool, composed, collected, self-possessed, dispassionate, imperturbable, unflappable (*inf.*), unruffled, immovable, stable, level-headed, even-tempered, easygoing, moderate, sedate, serene, tranquil, placid, inoffensive, mild, phlegmatic; patient, forbearing, uncomplaining, meek, submissive, philosophic, stoical; detached, aloof, disinterested, spiritless, nonchalant, blasé, casual.

vb. keep calm, keep one's temper, keep one's cool (*sl.*), keep one's shirt on (*sl.*), not bat an eyelid; calm down, compose oneself, control oneself, relax, take hold of oneself, pull oneself together, cool it (*sl.*), simmer down (*inf.*), cool off.

bear, tolerate, endure, put up with, stomach (*inf.*), stick it out (*inf.*), swallow, brook, resign oneself to, grin and bear it, submit to, make the best of.

B Sensation

758 touch

n. touch, feeling, contact, tactility; feel, touching, stroking, massage, manipulation; tickle, titillation, itching, scratching, pricking, stinging, shivers.

adj. tactile, tactual, tangible, touchable, palpable.

vb. touch, feel, press, squeeze, stroke, rub, finger, paw, smooth, caress, fondle, massage, manipulate, lick, kiss; tap, pat, hit, strike; explore, feel for, grope, fumble; grasp, grip, grab, grapple, clasp, clutch; tickle, titillate, itch; graze, scratch, prick, sting.

759 heat

n. heat, hotness, warmth, tepidity; temperature, thermometer; thermostat, hot weather, summer, heatwave, scorcher (*inf.*), dog days; fire, blaze, glow, light, sparkle, flicker, conflagration; ardour, fervour, zeal, passion, intensity.

adj. thermal; hot, very warm, torrid, parched; burning, fiery, blazing, ignited, lit, alight, on fire, in flames, glowing, incandescent, smoking; heated, molten; sweltering, baking, scorching, sizzling, scalding, grilling, roasting; tropical, humid, sticky, close, sultry, muggy, stifling, oppressive; warm, tepid, lukewarm; temperate, mild, fair, sunny, summery; bright, clear; intense, fervent, vehement, passionate, ardent, excited.

vb. be hot, burn, flame, burst into flames, catch fire, flare up, flicker, glow; smoke, fume, reek, smoulder, smother, suffocate; cook, boil, scald, seethe, fry, sizzle, roast, parch, scorch, bake, swelter.

760 cold

n. cold, coldness, chilliness, frigidity, frozenness, iciness, frostiness, congelation; chill, nip, shivers, shivering; cold snap, arctic conditions; ice, icicle, glacier, iceberg, black ice; frost, rime, hoar-frost; hail, hailstorm; snow, snowflake, snowdrift, snowstorm, blizzard, avalanche, sleet, slush.

adj. cryoscopic, cold, cool, chilly, fresh, crisp, brisk, nippy, frigid; piercing, biting, cutting, numbing, stinging; raw, sharp, keen; wintry, brumal, bleak, Siberian, arctic, polar; freezing, icy, gelid, frosty, hoary.

vb. be cold, freeze, shiver, shudder, quiver; chatter.

761 heating

n. heating, warming; combustion, burning, incineration, flaming, kindling, ignition, scorching, incandescence.

adj. heating, warming, calefactory; combustible, flammable; glowing, incandescent.

vb. heat, warm, heat up, reheat, put on the fire; ignite, kindle, set fire to, strike a light, put a match to, touch off; burn, scorch, consume, scald, incinerate, reduce to ashes, cremate; fire, smelt; thaw, defrost, de-ice, unfreeze, melt, liquefy; insulate.

762 refrigeration; incombustibility

n. refrigeration, cooling, chilling, freezing, glaciation, glacification.

incombustibility, non-flammability; asbestos, safety curtain.

adj. cooled, chilled; frozen, icy.

incombustible, non-flammable, fireproof.

vb. refrigerate, cool, chill, make cold, freeze, deep-freeze, ice, frost, congeal, glaciate.

extinguish, put out, blow out, quench, stifle, smother, damp, choke, snuff, douse, drown.

763 furnace

n. furnace, boiler, kiln, stove, cooker, oven; incinerator; crematorium; fire, heater, radiator; hearth, fireplace, fireside, grate, hob.

764 refrigerator

n. refrigerator, fridge, freezer, deep-freeze, icebox, icepack, cool-bag, cool-box, cooling apparatus, cold storage; air-conditioner, fan, ventilator.

765 fuel

n. fuel, combustible; coal, coke, charcoal, briquette, wood, log, gas, oil, petrol, electricity, juice (*sl.*), hydro-electricity, nuclear power, solar energy.

. match, lighter, firelighter, fuse, touch-paper, vesta, detonator, torch, firebrand, tinder, flint.

adj. combustible, flammable, explosive.

vb. fuel, fire, power; feed, stoke.

766 thermometer

n. thermometer, calorimeter, thermostat, mercury, clinical thermometer, pyrometer, thermocouple, thermopile, thermograph; Fahrenheit, centigrade, Celsius, Réamur, kelvin; degree.

767 taste

n. taste, flavour, relish, savour, smack, sapor; tang, after-taste; tongue, palate, taste buds; gustation.

adj. tasty, palatable, delicious, appetizing, gustatory.

vb. taste, relish, enjoy, eat, smack one's lips; try, sample, sip; taste of, savour of.

768 tastelessness

n. tastelessness, insipidity, flavourlessness, dullness, flatness, staleness.

adj. tasteless, unsavoury, insipid, flavourless, dull, flat, bland, stale, wishy-washy, unseasoned, unspiced, plastic (*inf.*), uninteresting.

see also 507, 843

769 pungency

n. pungency, piquancy, sharpness, keenness, spiciness, tanginess; zest, bite, edge, tang, kick (*inf.*), zing (*sl.*), punch (*sl.*).

adj. pungent, sharp, piquant, penetrating, poignant, strong, tangy,

racy; spiced, curried, hot; tart, sour, bitter.

see also 307

770 savouriness

n. savouriness, palatability, deliciousness, tastiness, richness, lusciousness.

delicacy, luxury, treat, rarity, delight, titbit, dainty, *bonne bouche*, chef's special, dish fit for a king; caviar; ambrosia, nectar.

adj. palatable, delicious, savoury, tasty, nice, dainty, delightful, choice, rich, luscious, delectable, exquisite, heavenly (*inf.*), scrumptious (*inf.*), yummy (*inf.*); fit for a king, fit for the gods; well done, done to a turn.

appetizing, mouth-watering, tempting, inviting, enticing, tantalizing, moreish (*inf.*).

vb. taste good; enjoy, like, relish, savour, appreciate.

771 unsavouriness

n. unsavouriness, unpalatability, unpleasantness, flavourlessness; bread and water, bitter pill, yuk (*sl.*).

adj. tasteless, flavourless, bland, dull, inedible; undrinkable; underdone; gone off; yukky (*sl.*); uninteresting, unappealing, unappetizing, uninviting, disagreeable, horrible, revolting.

vb. nauseate, disgust, turn one's stomach; disagree with, turn off (*inf.*); dislike, loathe.

772 sweetness

n. sweetness, sweetening, sugariness; sweet, sweetener, sugar, honey, molasses, syrup, treacle, saccharin.

adj. sweet, sweetened, sugared; sugary, saccharine, sirupy, rich, luscious, delicious; sticky; bitter-sweet, sweet-and-sour.

vb. sweeten, make sweet, sugar; dulcify.

773 sourness

n. sourness, acidity, bitterness, sharpness; acid, vinegar, gall, wormwood.

adj. sour, acid, tart, bitter, caustic, cutting, pungent, sharp, biting, dry; acidulous, vinegary, acetous; unsweetened, unsugared, unripe.

vb. sour, turn sour, set one's teeth on edge; ferment, curdle, tartarize.

774 odour

n. odour, smell, scent, trace, trail, exhalation, emanation, effluvium; fragrance; stench.

sense of smell, smelling, olfaction, detection.

adj. smelling, scented, odorous; strong, pungent, redolent; olfactory.

vb. smell, smell of, give out, give off, emit, scent, exhale; sniff, whiff, detect, perceive, smell out.

see also 776, 777

775 inodorousness

n. inodorousness, no smell; deodorization, ventilation, fumigation; deodorant, deodorizer; fumigant, fumigator, cleanser.

adj. inodorous, odourless, unscented, scentless.

vb. deodorize, fumigate, aerate, clean, purify.

776 fragrance

n. fragrance, aroma, bouquet, scent, perfume, spice, balm.

adj. fragrant, aromatic, scented, perfumed, spicy, sweet-scented, sweet-smelling, redolent, odoriferous, odorous, ambrosial.

vb. smell, scent, be fragrant; scent, perfume, embalm.

777 stench

n. stench, smell, stink, fetor, reek, fume, mephitis, miasma; foulness, uncleanness, smelliness, mustiness, rancidity; B.O. (*inf.*), body odour; skunk, polecat; stink-bomb.

adj. smelly, stinking, foul, unclean, fetid, strong-smelling, foul-smelling, nasty, vile, repulsive, offensive, rank, noxious, noisome; stale, musty, rancid, putrid, decaying, high, putrescent.

vb. smell, stir k, reek, smell to high heaven (*inf.*).

778 sound

n. sound, noise, vibration, resonance, report, reverberation, echo, ringing; loudness, softness; note, level, accent, cadence, tenor, intonation, tone, timbre; acoustics, phonetics.

adj. sounding, heard, audible, distinct, within earshot; loud, resonant, sonorous; auditory, acoustic, phonetic.

vb. sound, make a noise, give out, emit, produce; hear, listen.

see also 795

779 silence

n. silence, inaudibility, quietness, stillness, noiselessness; peace, quiet, still, hush; loss of signal, blackout, news blackout, security blackout, censorship.

adj. silent, inaudible, noiseless, hushed, quiet, still, soundless, unuttered, unspoken, unvoiced; soundproof.

vb. silence, hush, quiet, still, calm, muffle, reduce to silence, mute, stifle; subdue, deaden, repress, tone down, put the lid on.

see also 513, 517

780 loudness

n. loudness, noisiness, audibility, rowdiness; noise, racket, roar, boom, blast, swell, din, clamour, tumult, outcry, uproar, hubbub, hullabaloo, pandemonium.

adj. loud, noisy, clamorous, vociferous, loud-mouthed; boisterous, rumbustious, rowdy, obstreperous; thundering, deafening, ringing, booming, ear-splitting, resounding, piercing, blaring, crashing, stentorian, enough to wake the dead.

vb. be loud, boom, roar, thunder, fulminate, resound, bellow, blare, peal, crash, rattle, deafen, be unable to hear oneself think.

781 faintness

n. faintness, softness, inaudibility; whisper, breath, undertone, murmur, mutter, sigh, rustle, ripple, hum.

adj. faint, soft, quiet, hushed, inaudible; indistinct, stifled, muted, muffled, deadened, subdued; feeble, weak, low, distant, muttering.

vb. whisper, speak softly, murmur, mutter, sigh, hum, rustle, purr, creak, squeak.

782 sudden and violent sound

n. bang, blast, shot, report, boom, detonation, eruption, explosion; thud, whack, knock, slap, tap, rap, snap; crash, crackle; shout, cry, yelp.

vb. crash, crack, knock, slap, smack, whack, tap, rap, snap; click; plop, plonk, thud; thunder, boom, detonate, bang, pop, slam, burst, explode, blow up, set off.

783 repeated and prolonged sound

n. roll, clang, clatter; rattle, rustle; chuckle, cackle; whistle, hum, whirr, purr, buzz, strum; throb.

vb. roll, clang, clatter; rattle, rustle; ripple, swish, hum, drone, whirr, purr, buzz, strum, whistle, trill; thump, throb, palpitate, tick, beat, pound,

patter; chime, peal, toll; chuckle, cackle; rumble, grumble, growl.

784 resonance

n. resonance, vibration, tintinnabulation; ringing, clanging, echo, resounding, thunder, boom; chime, bell, gong, jingle, tinkle.

adj. resonant, vibrant, reverberating, loud, echoing, ringing, clanging, chiming, deep-sounding.

vb. resound, reverberate, boom, vibrate, echo, re-echo, ring, gong, chime, tinkle, jingle, clang, whirr, buzz, drone, whine, purr, hum.

785 non-resonance

n. non-resonance, thud, bump, plop, plump, thump, plonk, clonk, clunk.

adj. non-resonant, deadened, muffled, dead, heavy, dull.

vb. thud, bump, plonk, plump, plop, thump, clonk, clunk; muffle, stifle, dull, damp, deaden.

786 hissing sound

n. hiss, hissing, sibilance, buzz, swish, rustle, whirr, whistle, splash, squelch, whoosh, zip.

adj. hissing, sibilant.

vb. buzz, hiss, swish, rustle, whistle, splash, whoosh, zip, fizz, whiz, whirr, squelch, sizzle, sneeze, wheeze, effervesce, sibilate.

787 harsh sound

n. harshness, hoarseness, gruffness, discord, dissonance, cacophony; shrillness, whistle, croak, squawk, squeal, screech, shriek.

adj. strident, shrill, high-pitched, piercing, sharp, penetrating; squealing, creaking, grating, scratchy, tinny, metallic; clanging, clashing, screeching, jarring, discordant, dissonant; hoarse, gruff, harsh, raucous, loud, husky, throaty, guttural, dry.

788

vb. clang, clatter, clunk, crash, bang, clash, jangle; croak, quack, squawk, caw, cluck; saw, grind; shrill, whistle, shriek, screech, scream, squeal, yelp, squeak, creak; grate, rasp, irritate, jar, set one's teeth on edge, get on one's nerves.

788 human sound

n. cry, exclamation, utterance, shout, call, noise, shouting, clamour, outcry; scream, shriek, yell, moan, groan, wail, bellow, howl, whimper.

adj. clamorous, noisy, loud, yelling, vociferous.

vb. cry, exclaim, call, speak, utter, shout, scream, yell, shriek, screech, squeal, squeak, caterwaul, bawl, bellow, hoot, vociferate, whoop, hoop, hollo; groan, moan, complain, howl, wail, whine, whimper, sob.

cheer, chant, clamour, support; shout down, hiss, boo, ridicule, disapprove, censure.

789 animal sound

n. call, cry, ululation, barking.

vb. cry, yelp, yap, squeal, squawk; cackle, cluck, quack, caw, crow; screech, croak; coo, cuckoo; gobble, gaggle; chuckle, chirp, chirrup, cheep; tweet, twitter, whistle, pipe, trill, sing, warble; purr, miaow, mew, caterwaul; hum, drone, buzz; bark, bay, howl, woof, roar, bellow, bell; grunt, snort, snap, growl, snarl, whine, oink; neigh, bray, whinny; bleat, baa; moo, low.

790 melody

n. melody, melodiousness, tunefulness, concord, consonance, euphony, harmony, unison, accord, concert, music, blending.

adj. melodious, musical, euphonic, tuneful, rhythmical, melodic, lyrical, harmonious, in tune, accordant; sweet-

sounding, dulcet, soothing, pleasing, mellow, soft, rich; catchy, memorable, singable, popular.

791 discord

n. discord, discordance, unmelodiousness, inharmoniousness, dissonance, atonality; noise, din, racket, cacophony.

adj. discordant, dissonant, atonal, unmelodious, inharmonious, unmusical, untuneful, out of tune, off key, flat, sharp; cacophonous, clashing, jarring, grating.

792 music

n. music, composition, work, opus, piece; arrangement, adaptation, setting, transcription, orchestration, instrumentation; incidental music, background music, accompaniment; record, recording; concert, recital.

classical music, chamber music, light music, country and western, folk music, pop music, electronic music, jazz, blues, reggae, punk, rock, soul, ragtime.

symphony, concerto, suite; overture, prelude; sonata; ballet, dance; opera, operetta; song, air, solo, hymn, strain; tune, chorus, refrain, round; duo, trio, quartet; passage, movement, phrase.

adj. musical, tuneful, pleasing; vocal, choral; scored, arranged, adapted.

vb. compose, write, set to music, arrange, score; perform, render, play, make music, interpret; sing, chant, croon; listen.

793 musician

n. musician, artist, player, performer, virtuoso, soloist, instrumentalist, concert artist; singer, vocalist, chorister, bard, minstrel, artiste, choir, chorus, singing group; orchestra, band, ensemble, symphony orchestra, chamber orchestra; group; dancer, ballerina; composer.

794 musical instrument

n. musical instrument, brass, wood-wind, stringed instruments, percussion; record player, gramophone, stereo, hi-fi, music centre, stereogram, juke-box; record, disc, single, LP; tape-recorder, cassette-recorder; recording tape.

795 hearing

n. hearing, sense of hearing; good hearing, an ear for; earshot, range, carrying distance, sound; listening, auscultation; eavesdropping, wire-tapping.

listener, hearer, auditor, witness; eavesdropper, wire-tapper, peeping Tom; audience, auditorium; audition, interview, reception.

adj. auditory, hearing, auricular.

vb. hear, listen to, catch, take in, pick up, lend an ear, be all ears, give a hearing to, hark; attend to, pay attention to; perceive, detect, get wind of; overhear, listen in, eavesdrop, tap, bug.

796 deafness

n. deafness, inaudibility, deaf-and-dumbness, deaf-mutism; lip reading, deaf-and-dumb alphabet, deaf-and-dumb language, dactylology.

adj. deaf, hard of hearing, stone-deaf, deaf-and-dumb, deaf-mute; deafening, stunning, ear-splitting; deaf to, unaware of.

vb. deafen, stun.

797 light

n. light, illumination, lighting, radiance, brilliance, splendour, brightness, clearness, lightness; luminosity, phosphorescence.

beam, ray, gleam, shaft, streak, laser, pencil, stream, glint, chink; flash,

streak, blaze, flame, flare, glow, spark, sparkle, twinkle, flicker, glimmer, glitter, dazzle, shimmer; glare, gloss, shine, lustre; polish, reflection; daylight, sunshine; sunrise, daybreak, dawn.

adj. luminous, light, bright, clear, shining, brilliant, beaming, glowing, glittering, sparkling, gleaming, dazzling; shiny, glossy, sheeny; illuminated, lighted, lit; cloudless.

vb. shine, burn, glow, blaze, glitter, glimmer, glisten, gleam, sparkle, dazzle, blind; flash, shimmer, flicker, twinkle, scintillate, blink, flare, beam; dance, play, reflect, glare.

illuminate, switch on, lighten, brighten, enlighten, dawn, shed light on, light up, irradiate; polish, burnish.

798 darkness

n. darkness, dark, night, nightfall, Cimmerian gloom, blackness, black-out, eclipse, shade, shadow, umbra, penumbra, adumbration, obscuration; gloom, sombreness.

adj. dark, unlit, unlighted, unilluminated; black, starless, dull, overcast, cloudy; indistinct, obscure, shady, nebulous, shaded, shadowy; tenebrous, obfuscous; dismal, gloomy, sombre, dreary, bleak, desolate, murky, dim.

vb. darken, blacken, black out, switch off, cover, eclipse, obscure, overshadow, becloud, place in shadow, cast a shadow over, obfuscate, adumbrate.

799 dimness

n. dimness, murkiness, shadiness, obscurity; dusk, twilight, half-light, gloaming, gloom.

adj. dim, dull, faint, vague, indistinct, obscure, blurred, opaque, fading, evanescent; grey, cloudy, foggy, hazy, misty, shadowy, gloomy.

vb. dim, dull, fade out, blur, obscure, shade, becloud, cloud over, dull, vanish, wane, evanesce.

800 source of light

n. light, luminary, sun, moon, planet, star, halo, aurora, corona, nimbus; meteor, shooting star; lightning, flash; fireworks.

lamp, torch, bulb, spotlight, searchlight, flashlight, floodlight, headlamp, side-light, indicator; neon light, fluorescent tube, strobe light, lantern; beacon, lighthouse.

candle, wick, spill, taper, wax; match, flame, flare; coal, ember, brand.

801 shade

n. shade, covering, veil, shield, screen, blind, curtain, shutter, drape; sunglasses, blinkers, goggles; visor, hood; shelter, awning, canopy; umbrella, parasol.

adj. shady; screened.

vb. shade, cover, veil, screen, shield, shelter, protect, curtain, blinker.

see also 463, 593

802 transparency

n. transparency, clearness, glassiness, vitreosity, translucence, lucidity.

adj. transparent, translucent, clear, see-through, revealing, unobstructed, glassy, vitreous, crystal, lucid, diaphanous, pellucid, limpid.

vb. be transparent, see through, show, show through.

see also 502

803 opacity

n. opacity, opaqueness, cloudiness, murkiness, obscurity, darkness; smoke, mist, cloud, film.

adj. opaque, non-transparent, absorbing light, impervious, dark, unclear, smoky, misty, cloudy, muddy, blurred,

filmy, dull, murky, dim, darkened, turbid.

vb. make opaque, devitrify, obscure, darken, cloud, smoke, obstruct one's vision.

see also 503

804 semitransparency

n. semitransparency, translucence, pearliness, milkiness; smoked glass, frosted glass, opal glass; dark glasses, sunglasses.

adj. semitransparent, semitranslucid, semiopaque, frosted, pearly, smoked, milky.

805 colour

n. colour, hue, shade, tinge, tone, dash, touch, tint, tincture, cast; paint, pigment, dye, wash, stain, lake; prism, spectrum; glow, brilliance, warmth, intensity; coloration, colouring, pigmentation, complexion, chromatism.

adj. coloured, chromatic, tinted, tinged, touched, dyed, painted, stained; constant, fast.

colourful, bright, warm, glowing, intense, strong, deep, rich, brilliant; garish, glaring, gaudy, loud, showy, flashy, lurid, harsh, clashing, painful.

soft, pastel, subdued, refined, tender, delicate, matt; faded, dingy, dull, drab, cold, uninviting.

vb. colour, shade, tinge, paint, touch up, stain, wash, coat, put on, lay on; contrast, set off, throw into relief; clash, not go with, conflict, grate.

806 absence of colour

n. colourlessness, achromatism, discoloration, fading, paleness, dullness, dimness, faintness, flatness; anaemia, sallowness, whitening, bleaching.

adj. colourless, hueless, toneless, lacklustre, dull, lifeless, cold, dim, faint, weak; faded, washed out, pale, pallid, sallow, ashen, white, anaemic, pasty; transparent.

vb. fade, lose colour, lose brightness, bleach, blanch, wash out, whiten, drain, turn pale, discolour, grow dim, etiolate.

807 white

n. white, whiteness, whitishness, lightness, fairness, paleness; milkiness, chalkiness, silveriness, snowiness.

adj. white, fair, light, blonde, hoary; snowy, snow-white, frosted, milky, lactescent, chalky, silvery, pearly, ivory, albescent; whitish, cream, off-white; pale, ashen, anaemic, sallow, wan; clean, spotless, pure.

vb. whiten, whitewash, bleach, blanch, snow; clean, purify.

808 black

n. black, blackness, darkness, inkiness, sootiness.

adj. black, blackish; jet-black, pitch-black, coal-black; inky, sooty, stained; dark, murky; sable, swarthy.

vb. blacken, ink, ink in, darken, shade.

809 grey

n. grey, greyness, dinginess, drabness, dusk, shade.

adj. grey, greyish, shaded, dull, drab, dingy, sombre, neutral; dusty, smoky; silver-haired, hoary; speckled, pepper-and-salt.

810 brown

n. brown, tan, beige, mahogany.

adj. brown, brownish, beige, khaki, maroon, auburn, buff, bronze, copper, chocolate, coffee, rust-coloured, reddish-brown, bay, chestnut, russet, sepia, ochre, hazel.

811 red

n. red, redness, blush, glow, colour, cochineal, carmine.

adj. red, reddish, ruddy, scarlet, crimson, vermilion, ruby, cherry-red, blood-red, coral, brick-red, maroon, rust, magenta, russet, auburn, pink, salmon-pink, rosy; glowing, warm; blushing, embarrassed, burning.

vb. redden, blush; glow, flush.

812 green

n. green, verdure; iawn, turf.

adj. green, greenish, grassy, verdant, leafy, lime, emerald, sage, olive, beryl, blue-green, aquamarine, sea-green, pea-green; bilious, sickly, pale; fresh, unripe.

813 yellow

n. yellow, cream, tan, lemon; buttercup, daffodil, crocus, jasmine.

adj. yellow, yellowish, cream, saffron, sand, gold, golden, buff, tan, khaki, light-brown; sallow, bilious, jaundiced.

814 purple

n. purple; violet, pansy, lavender.

adj. purple, purplish, reddish-blue, bluish-red, violet, indigo, mauve, lilac, lavender, plum-coloured.

815 blue

n. blue, sky, azure, indigo.

adj. blue, bluish, turquoise, azure, royal blue, navy blue; sapphire, sky-blue, indigo.

816 orange

n. orange, tangerine, apricot, peach, mandarin, carrot, salmon, coral.

adj. orange, orangey, reddish-yellow, gold, old gold, copper, bronze, brass, ginger.

817 variegation

n. variegation, diversification, diversity, motley, spectrum, rainbow, kaleidoscope; chequerwork, tartan, mosaic, parquetry, marquetry.

adj. variegated, kaleidoscopic, many-coloured, multi-coloured; spotted, mottled, motley, patched, piebald, pied, dappled, speckled, freckled; striped, streaked, checked.

vb. diversify, variegate, chequer, checker; stud, mottle, spatter, dapple, speckle, stipple, streak, strip.

818 vision

n. vision, sight, eyesight, perception, recognition; observation, inspection, scrutiny, investigation, notice, once-over (*inf.*); bird's eye view, survey, panorama, overview.

look, view, regard, glance, glimpse, eye; squint, peep, peek; leer; wink, twinkle.

viewpoint, standpoint, position, outlook, perspective, attitude; lookout, observation point, watch-tower, gallery, grandstand.

adj. visual, ocular, opthalmic, optical; observant; watchful, vigilant.

vb. see, look at, view, watch, look on, observe, perceive, discern, recognize, notice, catch sight of, set eyes on, eye; glance, glimpse, catch a glimpse of, peep; blink, wink, twinkle; gaze, gape, stare, fix one's eyes on; leer, ogle, glare, glower.

scrutinize, investigate, survey, inspect; scan, look through, look over, flick through (*inf.*), thumb through (*inf.*).

819 blindness

n. blindness, sightlessness, colour-blindness, night-blindness, snow-blindness; blind spot, blind side, failing, mote in one's eye.

adj. blind, sightless, unseeing, eyeless, colour-blind; blinded, blind-fold, blinkered, hoodwinked, in the dark.

vb. be blind, lose one's sight, strike blind, put someone's eyes out; obscure, hide, mask, screen, blindfold, blinker, hoodwink.

820 imperfect vision

n. imperfect vision, partial vision; shortsightedness, myopia; longsightedness, presbyopia; double vision; colour-blindness; squint, strabism, cross-eye, astigmatism, conjunctivitis, cataract.

adj. dim-sighted, purblind, half-blind; shortsighted, myopic; long-sighted, presbyopic; colour-blind, astigmatic, cross-eyed, squinting, strabismic.

vb. see double, squint, screw up one's eyes, see blurred.

821 spectator

n. spectator, viewer, onlooker, observer, watcher, eye-witness, bystander, passer-by, looker-on, beholder; sightseer; peeper, peeping Tom; spy, snoop, meddler.

spectators, crowd, public, supporters, fans, followers, turn-out, audience.

822 optical instrument

n. glasses, spectacles, bifocals, goggles, specs (*inf.*), contact lenses, monocle, eye-glasses, lorgnette, pince-nez; binoculars, opera glasses, field glasses, telescope; microscope, magnifying glass, lens; camera; mirror, looking glass, reflector, glass, speculum.

823 visibility

n. visibility, perceptibility, clarity, distinctness, plainness, prominence, conspicuousness.

adj. visible, apparent, in view, in sight, observable, perceptible, noticeable, before one's very eyes; evident, clear, plain, obvious, patent; prominent, conspicuous, pronounced, standing out; unmistakable, glaring; open, exposed; distinct, well-defined, definite, clear-cut.

vb. show, show through, show itself, manifest itself, be revealed, come into sight, come into view; stand out, stand out a mile (*inf.*), stick out like a sore thumb (*sl.*), hit in the face, leap to the eye.

see also **458**, **825**

824 invisibility

n. invisibility, concealment, seclusion, latency, obscurity, indistinctness, imperceptibility, indefiniteness, vagueness, indiscernibility, cloudiness, darkness, haziness, fuzziness.

adj. invisible, imperceptible, indiscernible; hidden, out of sight, concealed, obscure; inconspicuous; indistinct, unclear, ill-defined, vague; intangible, unseen, spiritual; cloudy, nebulous, shadowy, mysterious, hazy, blurred, fuzzy.

see also **461**, **826**

825 appearance

n. appearance, look, aspect, feature, shape, form, outline, profile, face; condition, presentation, expression; posture, pose, bearing; mien, countenance, manner, behaviour; externals, appearances, outward show, first impression, face value.

phenomenon, spectacle, display, exhibition, show, demonstration, scene, parade, pageant.

adj. apparent, visible, manifest; seeming, ostensible, supposed, specious, plausible, alleged, outward, superficial, external, to look at (*inf.*).

vb. appear, look, seem, show, take the form of; emerge, arise, come into view, be revealed, turn up, show up, put in an appearance, crop up (*inf.*), pop up (*inf.*), occur, happen, present itself, express itself, manifest itself, materialize, come to light, come into the picture, come onto the horizon, see the light of day.

adv. apparently, to all appearances, superficially, at first sight, on the face of it, for show, to all intents and purposes.

see also **222**, **458**, **823**

826 disappearance

n. disappearance, vanishing, fading, fade-out, evanescence, evaporation, dematerialization; departure, retirement, flight, escape, removal, withdrawal, loss.

adj. disappearing, fading, evanescent; disappeared, vanished, missing.

vb. disappear, vanish, fade, evaporate, dematerialize, dissolve; pass out of sight, leave no trace, disappear into thin air, go up in smoke, vanish from sight, be eclipsed, be swallowed up, be lost to view.

go away, depart, remove, withdraw, retire, escape, flee; cease, be no more, die, perish, sink.

see also **824**

C Personal

827 pleasure

n. pleasure, joy, happiness, gladness, delight, enjoyment, satisfaction, fulfilment; serenity.

enchantment, bewitchment, exultation, relish, gusto, zest, glee, cheer, thrill, kick (*inf.*), ecstasy, elation, bliss, rapture, euphoria, transport; luxury, ease, convenience, comfort, paradise, bed of roses, golden age, halcyon days, lap of luxury.

gratification, indulgence, self-indulgence, revelry, hedonism, sensuousness, sensuality, sexuality.

adj. pleasant, satisfying, enjoyable, delightful, exciting, adorable, welcome; comfortable, snug, cosy, homely, comfy (*inf.*), congenial, convenient, palatial, luxurious; gratifying, pleasurable, sensuous, bodily, physical, hedonistic, voluptuous, self-indulgent, carnal.

happy, pleased, joyful, glad, delighted, joyous, satisfied; thrilled, excited, tickled pink (*inf.*), exhilarated, starry-eyed, bubbling over, in the seventh heaven; smiling, laughing, genial, convivial, delirious; merry, in good spirits, cheery, jolly, blithe, gladsome, blissful; overjoyed, ecstatic, in ecstasies, enraptured, in raptures enthusiastic, carried away; peaceful, contented, at peace.

vb. enjoy, like, take delight in, derive pleasure from, rejoice in, love, fancy, be keen on, appreciate, relish, revel in, get a kick out of (*inf.*), rave about (*inf.*), enjoy oneself, have a good time, tread on air.

see also 829, 836, 840

828 pain

n. pain, hurt, distress, discomfort, affliction, anguish, misery, agony, shock, blow, injury, suffering, unhappiness, sorrow, grief, sadness, regret, melancholy, despair, broken heart, weeping, wretchedness, tribulation, trial, ordeal, torment, torture, martyrdom, crucifixion, hell; bereavement, sense of loss, mourning, grieving; ache, twinge, pang, spasm, stitch, wound, sting, burn, illness, sickness.

worry, anxiety, heartache, vexation, fretting, uneasiness, discontent, disquiet, dissatisfaction; problem, care, burden.

sufferer, victim, prey, scapegoat, wretch, guinea pig.

adj. painful, hurtful, tormenting, excruciating, suffering, writhing, agonizing, harrowing; unpleasant, extreme, sharp, severe, grievous, sore, sensitive.

unfortunate, unhappy, sad, miserable, troubled, afflicted, heavy-laden, burdened, anxious, worried, vexed, uneasy; sorrowful, weeping, mournful, wretched, cut up (*inf.*), heart-broken.

vb. undergo, suffer, go through, bear, endure, put up with (*inf.*), persevere; ache, smart, throb, sting, burn; be tender, be sore, be bruised; regret, despair, mourn, weep.

see also 830

829 pleasurableness

n. pleasurableness, pleasantness, niceness, enjoyableness, loveliness; charm, fascination, glamour, prestige, attractiveness, winsomeness, allurement.

delight, treat, surprise, amusement, fun, gift, joy, honeymoon, benefit, refreshment, titbit, feast, banquet, manna.

adj. pleasant, nice, enjoyable, agreeable, pleasing, lovely, charming, fascinating, attractive, beautiful, picturesque; glamorous, prestigious, appealing, enchanting, winsome, luring, seductive; delightful, exquisite, delicious, luscious, tasty.

vb. please, satisfy, delight, gladden, rejoice, thrill, gratify; turn on (*inf.*), turn on to (*inf.*), switch on (*inf.*), stimulate, excite; interest; attract, charm, enchant, enthrall, captivate, bewitch, enrapture; amuse, tickle, titillate.

see also **755, 827**

830 painfulness

n. painfulness, hurtfulness, unpleasantness, bitterness, disagreeableness; sorrow, pain, disappointment, irritation, annoyance, nuisance, difficulty, problem, care, burden, trouble, load, cross, concern, nightmare, bitter cup, bitter pill; embarrassment.

adj. unpleasant, disagreeable, bothersome, upsetting, disturbing, troublesome, annoying, irritating, trying, tiresome; distressing, awful, grim, shocking, appalling, tragic, extreme, dreadful.

vb. hurt, grieve, injure, wound, afflict, pain; distress, worry, trouble, outrage, bother, upset, disturb, annoy, irritate, vex, needle; torment, harass, pester, tease, pick on (*inf.*), have it in for (*inf.*); harrow, agonize, excruciate, crucify, martyr, torture, obsess, haunt, plague; lose sleep over (*inf.*); discomfort, put out, inconvenience.

see also **828, 893**

831 content

n. content, contentment, peace, peace of mind, happiness, satisfaction; self-satisfaction, complacency; ease, rest, comfort, serenity, solace.

adj. contented, content, pleased, peaceful, satisfied, happy, carefree, without cares, uncomplaining.

vb. be content, be satisfied, sit pretty, have one's wishes granted, have all that one could wish for, have nothing to worry about, have nothing to complain of, can't complain.

satisfy, gratify, indulge, suffice; go down well, put at ease; appease, reconcile.

832 discontent

n. discontent, dissatisfaction, unhappiness, sadness, depression, resentment, regret, unrest, uneasiness, tension, strain; grudge, chip on one's shoulder.

complainer, grumbler, fault-finder, grouch; reactionary, radical, protester, angry young man.

adj. discontented, unhappy, uneasy, restless, disgruntled, dissatisfied, cheesed off (*sl.*), browned off; grumbling, complaining, critical, hyper-critical, hard to please, never satisfied.

vb. be discontented, grumble, criticize, find fault, go on about, pick holes in (*inf.*), speak out against, moan; dissatisfy, disappoint, disconcert, disgruntle, discourage, dishearten.

833 regret

n. regret, sorrow, misgiving, compunction, scruple, qualm, pang of conscience, apology, repentance, change of heart, contrition, penitence, self-reproach, remorse, soul-searching.

adj. regretful, apologetic, penitent, humble, sorry, remorseful, contrite, repentant, broken, conscience-stricken.

vb. regret, apologize, be sorry for, cry over, repent, humble oneself, admit, own up, grieve, weep over, mourn, bewail, bemoan; rue.

834 relief

n. relief, alleviation, mitigation, assuagement; help, aid, comfort, consolation, relaxation, ease, load off one's mind; remedy, cure.

adj. relieving, easing, comforting, consoling, consolatory, soothing, comfortable, breathing easily.

vb. relieve, alleviate, mitigate, ease, soften, comfort, cushion, assuage, soothe, lighten, ease the strain, console, cheer up.

be relieved, feel better, recover; heave a sigh of relief, breathe again.

see also 176

835 aggravation

n. aggravation, exacerbation, worsening, heightening, intensification, sharpening, deepening, strengthening, inflammation; annoyance, irritation, exasperation.

adj. aggravated, worsened, made worse, not improved.

vb. aggravate, worsen, exacerbate, make things worse, complicate, increase, magnify, multiply, heighten, intensify, deepen, go from bad to worse, get worse and worse; annoy, irritate.

836 cheerfulness

n. cheerfulness, good humour, happiness, gladness, joy; high spirits, vitality, animation, sparkle, liveliness, jollity, merriment, mirth, gaiety, glee; laughter, fun and games; light-heartedness, levity, breeziness; stoicism, stiff upper lip.

adj. cheerful, glad, happy, joyful; genial, animated, lively, in good humour, sparkling, vivacious, exuberant, full of beans (*inf.*), in high spirits, high-spirited, on top of the world, jolly, merry, gay, jovial, jocular, playful, sporty; light-hearted, perky, chirpy, breezy, carefree, debonair.

cheering, heartening, encouraging, inspiring, heartwarming.

vb. cheer, gladden, cheer up, perk up (*inf.*); brighten, encourage, comfort; enliven, animate, inspire, uplift; raise the spirits, warm the heart.

be cheerful, take heart, snap out of it (*inf.*); persevere, keep smiling (*inf.*), grin and bear it, keep one's chin up

(*inf.*), keep a stiff upper lip, keep one's end up (*inf.*).

see also 827, 838

837 dejection; seriousness

n. dejection, despondency, melancholy, sorrow, sadness, grief, depression, despair, gloom, misery, heaviness of spirit, low spirits, blues, dumps, doldrums, mopes, *weltschmerz.*

seriousness, earnestness, solemnity, gravity, sedateness, sobriety, coolness; dead pan (*inf.*), straight face.

adj. dejected, unhappy, despondent, downcast, sad, sorrowful, down-hearted, depressed, low, troubled, desolate, dispirited, broken-hearted, crushed, heart-broken, upset, cut up (*inf.*), discouraged, crestfallen, blue, down, moping, down in the mouth, down in the dumps, in the doldrums (*inf.*), out of sorts; melancholy, world-weary, careworn, gloomy, miserable, dismal, forlorn, doleful, wretched, cheerless, dull; suicidal, despairing.

serious, earnest, grave, sober, solemn; thoughtful, pensive; stern, strict; straight-faced, dead pan (*inf.*), expressionless.

vb. be dejected, lose heart; regret, grieve, mourn, sorrow; fret, brood, mope; languish, droop, wilt, pull a long face, beat one's breast.

sadden, oppress, break a person's heart, cut up (*inf.*), discourage, deject, depress, unnerve, dismay, demoralize, get down (*inf.*); cast down; drive to drink (*inf.*); dampen, pour cold water on.

be serious, keep a straight face, take life seriously, not see the joke.

see also 828, 839

838 rejoicing

n. rejoicing, happiness, celebration, congratulation, jubilation, exultation, revelry, festivity, merrymaking, mirth, thanksgiving; cheers, shouts, hurrahs, applause; laughter, laugh, chuckle, chortle, giggle, snigger, cackle, titter, roar, guffaw; smile, grin, smirk, beam.

adj. rejoicing, jubilant, elated, exultant, rollicking.

vb. rejoice, be happy, sing for joy, leap for joy, dance, exult, celebrate, revel, have a party; clap one's hands, applaud, say thankyou to, congratulate.

laugh, chuckle, chortle, guffaw, giggle, titter, snigger; burst out laughing, roar, fall about laughing, double up with laughter, be convulsed with laughter, split one's sides, roll in the aisles (*inf.*), be in stitches (*inf.*); smile, beam, smirk, grin, twinkle; laugh at, ridicule, poke fun at, deride.

see also **840, 842**

839 lamentation

n. lamentation, mourning, grief, sorrow, weeping, sobbing, tears, waterworks (*sl.*); cry, weep, good cry, sob, bawl, wail, whimper; lament, elegy, requiem, dirge, funeral oration.

adj. lamenting, sad, mournful; weeping, sobbing, in tears, tearful.

vb. lament, grieve, sorrow; cry, weep, burst into tears, break down, dissolve into tears, shed tears, turn on the waterworks (*sl.*), sob, cry one's eyes out (*inf.*), sob one's heart out (*inf.*), blubber, snivel, whimper, whine, howl, bawl, wail.

see also **837**

840 amusement

n. amusement, pleasure, fun, good time; leisure; hobby, pastime, diversion, relaxation, entertainment, recreation, sport, play, game; television, radio, cinema, concert, theatre; meal, picnic, party, barbecue, banquet,

feast; fete, fair, carnival, gala, fiesta, festivity; holiday, excursion, outing, pleasure trip, jaunt.

adj. entertaining, amusing, engaging, diverting, pleasant, witty; amused, entertained.

vb. amuse, entertain, delight, cheer, enliven, brighten up.

amuse oneself, enjoy oneself, relax, play games, go out, have fun, have a good time, let off steam (*inf.*), have a ball (*sl.*), let one's hair down (*inf.*), live it up (*inf.*), whoop it up (*inf.*), paint the town red (*sl.*), carouse, revel.

see also **614, 827, 842**

841 weariness

n. weariness, tiredness, exhaustion, fatigue, lassitude; tedium, boredom, apathy, listlessness, world-weariness, ennui, monotony, sameness, humdrum, the same old thing (*inf.*).

misery, wet blanket, drip; pain in the neck.

adj. wearisome, tiresome; tedious, boring, uninteresting, uninspiring, heavy, monotonous, dreary, flat, stale, repetitious, repetitive, soporific; tired, weary, exhausted, drowsy, jaded, worn out.

vb. weary, fatigue, tire, tire out, send to sleep, bore, exhaust, depress, leave cold; flag, droop.

see also **612, 617, 843**

842 wit

n. wit, wittiness, humour, joking, fun; jocularity, whimsicality, facetiousness, flippancy, drollery.

joke, witticism, repartee, pun, play on words, quip, jest, Spoonerism, *double entendre*, whimsy, sally, wisecrack, gag, funny story, shaggy-dog story, chestnut, aphorism, epigram; satire, sarcasm, irony; banter, burlesque, badinage.

humorist, comedian, joker, wag, life and soul of the party, jester, clown, buffoon, satirist.

adj. witty, humorous, funny, amusing, jocular, quick-witted, whimsical, quick, keen, lively, nimble; waggish; clownish; teasing, bantering.

vb. be witty, crack a joke, joke, jest, pun, bring the house down (*inf.*), sparkle, scintillate; tease, pull a person's leg, banter, rib (*inf.*), rag (*sl.*), make fun of, ridicule, kid (*sl.*).

843 dullness

n. dullness, heaviness, tediousness, mediocrity, insipidity, colourlessness, drabness, dreariness, tameness, flatness, dryness, stuffiness, slowness; familiarity, triteness, banality.

adj. dull, heavy, ponderous, tedious, boring, uninteresting, dry, stuffy, stodgy, sluggish, mediocre, flat, uninspired, lifeless, dead, drab, dreary, gloomy; long-winded, prosaic; conventional, stereotyped, common, commonplace, trite, banal, pointless.

844 beauty

n. beauty, elegance, attractiveness, good looks, loveliness, prettiness, fairness, handsomeness, shapeliness, pulchritude; glamour, grace, charm, appeal; magnificence, gloriousness, splendour, brilliance; beautification, face-lift, hair-dressing, adornment; cosmetics, make-up; plastic surgery.

good looker, smasher (*inf.*), stunner (*inf.*), belle, raving beauty, peach (*sl.*), pin-up (*inf.*), dream, Venus; ornament, masterpiece, showpiece.

adj. beautiful, attractive, good-looking, lovely, pretty, swell (*inf.*), smashing (*inf.*), glamorous, fair, handsome, appealing, pleasing, sightly, graceful, elegant, refined, comely, char-

ming; shapely, well-formed, well-proportioned.

splendid, magnificent, brilliant, wonderful, glorious, marvellous, gorgeous, grand, fine, resplendent, excellent, impressive, exquisite.

vb. beautify, improve the appearance of, pretty up (*inf.*), doll up (*inf.*), tart up (*sl.*), dress up (*inf.*), adorn, decorate, ornament, trim, embellish.

see also 579, 846

845 ugliness

n. ugliness, hideousness, unloveliness, uncomeliness, inelegance, disfigurement, offensiveness; mutilation, deformity, distortion.

eyesore, defacement, horror, mess, blemish, blot, graffiti, slum.

adj. ugly, hideous, inelegant, unbecoming, unprepossessing; frightful, horrid, shocking, offensive; unlovely, unseemly, uncomely; disfigured, deformed, misshapen, monstrous, grotesque.

vb. make ugly, disfigure, deface, distort, mutilate.

see also 245

846 ornamentation

n. ornamentation, decoration, adornment, embellishment, enhancement, trimming, frill, foil; embroidery, needlework; illumination, lettering, illustration; jewellery, jewel, gem, stone, precious stone; tinsel, ribbon, lace, gilt, tassel, bunting.

adj. ornamental, decorative, adorning, embellishing, garnishing, cosmetic; florid, dressy, ornate, fancy, gaudy, garish.

vb. decorate, adorn, beautify, enhance, brighten up, embellish, garnish, embroider, deck, bedeck, gild, festoon, array, set off.

see also 509, 844

847 blemish

n. blemish, defect, flaw, stain, smudge, blot, blur, taint, daub, spot, speck, smirch, blotch, tarnish, rust, stigma, dent, impurity, disfigurement, deformity.

adj. blemished, spoilt, disfigured, defective, imperfect.

vb. blemish, stain, smudge, blot, daub, smear, smirch, tarnish, sully, soil, spoil, mar, damage, deface, disfigure.

see also 582, 845

848 good taste

n. good taste, refinement, tastefulness, elegance, grace, polish; discrimination, good judgment, culture, sophistication; decorum, decency, soberness, seemliness, properness, restraint, simplicity, delicacy, daintiness.

good judge, connoisseur, expert, critic, gourmand, *bon vivant.*

adj. tasteful, in good taste, refined, polished, elegant, dignified, graceful, delicate; decent, sober, becoming, seemly, proper, simple, aesthetic; cultured, discriminating, sophisticated, cultivated.

see also 510

849 bad taste

n. bad taste, tastelessness; vulgarity, coarseness, rudeness, barbarism; pretension, artificiality; showiness, gaudiness; ugliness, unloveliness, hideousness; dowdiness, unfashionableness; cad, bounder (*sl.*).

adj. tasteless, in bad taste, unrefined, unpolished; vulgar, coarse, rude, gross, crass, uncouth; pretentious, artificial,

florid, ostentatious, flashy, showy; inelegant, ugly, unsightly, unlovely; dull, tawdry, shoddy, low, common, plebeian.

see also 511

850 fashion

n. fashion, style, mode, trend; new look, latest style, the latest; fad, craze, rage, all the rage, the last word; society, high society, set, right people; upper cut, upper crust.

adj. fashionable, stylish, trendy, latest, in fashion, in vogue, in (*inf.*), all the rage (*inf.*), modern, up-to-the-minute.

vb. catch on (*inf.*), become popular, grow in popularity, find favour; jump on the bandwagon (*inf.*), follow the crowd.

851 ridiculousness

n. ridiculousness, ludicrousness, funniness, outrageousness, absurdity.

adj. ridiculous, funny, comic, droll, amusing, hilarious, farcical, whimsical, side-splitting, too funny for words, rich, priceless (*sl.*), killing (*sl.*), absurd, ludicrous, preposterous, outrageous, fantastic.

vb. be ridiculous; laugh; bring the house down (*inf.*); play the fool, look silly.

see also 853

852 affectation

n. affectation, pretentiousness, pretense; artificiality, unnaturalness; show, sham, foppery, put-on (*sl.*), play-acting, front, façade, act, airs, airs and graces.

pretender, actor; play-actor; charlatan, impostor, humbug, dandy, fop.

adj. affected, pretentious, put-on, tongue in cheek, pretended, assumed, artificial, unnatural, theatrical; showy, for effect; awkward; superficial, shallow, hollow; insincere.

vb. be affected, pretend, assume, put on, feign, simulate, act out the part of, pose, fake, sham, go through the motions of; talk big; put up a front.

853 ridicule

n. ridicule, mockery, contempt, scorn, disdain, derision, sneering, jeering, scoffing; satire, parody, caricature, burlesque; irony, sarcasm.

laughing-stock, target, victim, butt, dupe, fool.

adj. derisory, contemptuous; scoffing; ironical.

vb. ridicule, mock, laugh at, deride, sneer, jeer, scoff, revile, gibe; boo, hiss, hoot; pour scorn on, run down, make fun of, pull a person's leg; banter, taunt; laugh on the other side of one's face (*inf.*); parody, caricature, satirize.

see also **924**

854 hope

n. hope, faith, trust, reliance, confidence, assurance; promise; expectation, anticipation; aspiration, dream, vision, pipe-dream, desire, wish, longing, yearning, ambition; optimism, cheerfulness, high hopes; false optimism, wishful thinking, pious hopes, fool's paradise.

hoper, aspirant, competitor, candidate, optimist, idealist.

adj. hoping, trusting, expecting, hopeful, assured, expectant, optimistic, relying on, confident, sanguine, bold, fearless, ambitious; promising, auspicious, favourable.

vb. hope, trust, believe, have faith in, rely, rest on, depend, lean on, bank on, rest assured, expect, anticipate; aspire, dream, wish, desire, long for, yearn for, contemplate; look on the bright side, see things through rose-coloured spectacles.

raise one's hopes, inspire, promise, lead one to expect, have the makings of, show signs of promise, bid fair, bode well.

see also **420, 836**

855 hopelessness

n. hopelessness, despair, desperation, despondency; irrevocability, irredeemability; defeatism, pessimism; pessimist, Job's comforter.

adj. hopeless, irrevocable, irredeemable, incurable, irreversible, beyond hope, vain, to no avail, futile; unfortunate, bad, disastrous, impossible, helpless, lost, gone; pessimistic, defeatist.

vb. despair, lose heart, give up hope, abandon all hope, give up; dash one's hopes.

see also **837**

856 fear

n. fear, fright, terror, horror, dread, scare, tremor, panic, despair, alarm, blue funk (*sl.*), consternation, awe, trepidation; timidity, fearfulness, timorousness.

anxiety, hesitation, worry, concern, uneasiness; nervousness, apprehension, cold feet, butterflies (*inf.*), nerves, jitters (*inf.*), willies (*sl.*), heebie jeebies (*sl.*), cold sweat.

adj. afraid, frightened, terrified, dreading, scared, scared stiff, shocked, in awe, trembling, panicking, panic-stricken, startled, petrified, shrinking.

uneasy, worrying, anxious, troubled, bothered, disturbed, hesitant, timid, shy, timorous, cautious; nervous, apprehensive, fidgety, jittery (*inf.*), jumpy, edgy, on edge, tense.

terrible, frightful, awful, dreadful, horrifying, ghastly, atrocious, frightening, terrifying, appalling, harrowing, traumatic, inconceivable; disturbing, disquieting.

vb. fear, be afraid, panic; dread, shake, quiver, quake, cringe, tremble, shudder, one's knees be knocking, be scared out of one's wits, break out in a cold sweat; funk, shrink, flinch; go to pieces, crack up (*inf.*), break down.

frighten, scare, terrify, shock, startle, make one jump; intimidate; give cause for alarm, appal, petrify, frighten out of one's wits, make one's hair stand on end, make one's blood run cold; put the fear of God into (*inf.*); disturb, trouble, bother, concern, dismay, daunt, disquiet, unnerve, worry, torment.

see also **858**

857 courage

n. courage, valour, bravery, fearlessness, boldness, intrepidity, audacity, daring, fortitude; pluck, mettle, heart, backbone, guts (*inf.*), what it takes, stamina, staying power, spunk (*inf.*), grit (*inf.*); Dutch courage; gallantry, chivalry, heroism, prowess, manliness, self-reliance, resolution, determination, firmness, strength; enterprise, initiative.

brave person, hero, heroine, stalwart.

adj. courageous, brave, valiant, bold, confident, fearless, intrepid, audacious, daring, dauntless, undaunted, unflinching; determined, resolute, strong, tough, plucky, heroic, chivalrous, gallant; game; enterprising, adventuresome.

vb. be courageous, have what it takes; keep one's chin up (*inf.*); face, brave, encounter, confront, handle, look in the face, face up to, meet face

to face, take the bull by the horns; have the nerve to; make a stand, risk.

pluck up courage, take heart, summon, muster, nerve oneself.

hearten, encourage, strengthen, fortify, inspire, assure, boost.

see also **534, 535**

858 cowardice

n. cowardice, cowardliness, faint-heartedness, weakness, shrinking, funk, cold feet, weak knees, yellow streak; fear, apprehension; shyness, timidity.

coward, scaredy-cat (*inf.*), cry-baby; deserter, shirker, slacker; poltroon, dastard, sneak.

adj. cowardly, craven, faint-hearted, timid, shy, weak, weak-kneed, scared, lily-livered, yellow (*inf.*), chicken (*sl.*); dastardly, pusillanimous.

vb. lose one's courage, get cold feet, back out, chicken out (*inf.*), funk, shrink, quail, show the white feather.

859 rashness

n. rashness, temerity, imprudence, impulsiveness; hurriedness, overhastiness, carelessness, recklessness, foolhardiness; indiscretion; daring, presumption; flippancy, levity; daredevil, harum-scarum (*inf.*).

adj. rash, impulsive, impetuous, hurried, sudden, precipitous, overhasty, premature, breakneck, headlong, frenzied, furious; reckless, foolhardy, careless, thoughtless, imprudent, inconsiderate; headstrong, unthinking, heedless; wild, brash, ill-considered.

vb. be rash, stick one's neck out (*inf.*), jump to conclusions, rush to conclusions, play with fire, burn one's fingers, court danger, court disaster, ask for trouble (*inf.*), ask for it (*inf.*), fools rush in where angels fear to tread, throw caution to the winds, tempt providence.

see also **544, 613**

860 caution

n. caution, prudence, cautiousness, care, heed, alertness, vigilance, wariness, suspicion; discretion, circumspection, deliberation, forethought, precaution, presence of mind, foresight.

adj. cautious, watchful, wary, circumspect, careful, prudent, vigilant.

vb. be cautious, play safe, take precautions, take care, look out, provide for, look before one leaps, watch one's step.

861 desire

n. desire, wish, need, want; liking, fondness, fancy, weakness, predilection, inclination, urge, aspiration, ambition; ardour, longing, yearning, pining; nostalgia, homesickness; craze, frenzy, lust, covetousness.

hunger, thirst, ravenousness, craving, voracity, relish, appetite, famine, drought.

adj. desiring, wanting, wishing, liking, desirous, fond, inclined, partial, longing, yearning, pining, itching (*inf.*); dying; eager, keen, crazy, mad, keen, craving; covetous.

hungry, greedy, ravenous, starving, famished, voracious, dry, parched; unsatisfied; peckish (*inf.*).

vb. desire, want, wish, need; like, be fond of, enjoy, choose, fancy, take a fancy to, incline towards, love, take to, be sweet on, have a soft spot for, go for in a big way, set one's heart on (*inf.*), set one's sights on, prize, esteem; aspire, dream; long for, crave, yearn, pine, hanker; make one's mouth water, lust, covet; relish.

be hungry, hunger, starve, famish; be thirsty, be dry, thirst.

see also **889**

862 dislike

n. dislike, distaste, disinclination, dissatisfaction; hate, hatred, loathing, aversion, repugnance.

adj. disliking, disinclined, averse to, loath to, fed up with, allergic, squeamish.

disliked, objectionable, repugnant, loathsome, abhorrent, abominable, disagreeable, unpopular.

vb. dislike, not feel like, not care for, hate, loathe, detest, not take kindly to, have nothing to do with, avoid, turn up one's nose at (*inf.*), not go for, not stomach.

see also **892**

863 indifference

n. indifference, unconcern, apathy, coldness, insensitivity, neutrality; half-heartedness, lukewarmness; unambitiousness.

adj. indifferent, cold, neutral; lukewarm, half-hearted; unconcerned, impassive, dispassionate, unresponsive, unmoved, uninvolved, lackadaisical, listless, inattentive; isolated, uncommunicative.

vb. be indifferent, not mind, not care, not care less, not give a damn (*inf.*), take no interest in, not matter, be all the same to, leave one cold; take it or leave it.

see also **754**

864 fastidiousness

n. fastidiousness, fussiness, meticulousness, scrupulousness, punctiliousness, pedantry, conscientiousness; perfectionism, idealism.

perfectionist, idealist, stickler, purist, pedant; fuss-pot (*inf.*).

adj. fastidious, particular, exact, precise, meticulous, exacting, scrupulous, rigorous, choosy (*inf.*), discriminating, selective, squeamish, finicky, pernickety (*inf.*), over-scrupulous, overparticular, overprecise, hypercritical; hard to please; pedantic; delicate; nice.

vb. be fastidious, fuss, be hard to please, split hairs, pick and choose; make a fuss about, make a song and dance about (*inf.*).

865 satiety

n. satiety, repletion, saturation, fill, surfeit, glut, plethora, jadedness, too much of a good thing.

adj. sated, satiated, replete, gorged, glutted, cloyed, overfull, overflowing; full, satisfied.

vb. satiate, fill, surfeit, glut, gorge, stuff, cloy, overfill, overfeed, satisfy, gratify; have one's fill, have enough.

866 wonder

n. wonder, surprise, amazement, awe, astonishment, bewilderment, fascination, stupefaction, incredulity.

sensation, miracle, sign, phenomenon, portent, spectacle, freak, marvel, drama, the unbelievable, prodigy, curiosity, oddity, rarity, something to write home about.

adj. surprising, amazing, astonishing, marvellous, fantastic, unbelievable, incredible, dramatic, remarkable, sensational, phenomenal, miraculous, stupendous, unprecedented, unparalleled, extraordinary, unusual, freakish, unique.

surprised, amazed, astonished, lost in wonder, bewildered, flabbergasted, spellbound, speechless, dumbfounded, thunderstruck, aghast.

vb. wonder, marvel, be surprised, be amazed, be taken aback, stare, gape, not believe, not get over.

amaze, astonish, surprise, bewilder, stupefy, dumbfound, flabbergast, overwhelm, take one's breath away.

867 absence of wonder

n. non-wonder, blankness; expectation; ordinariness, just as one thought, nothing much to write home about.

adj. unastonishing, expected, common, ordinary, usual; unamazed, unsurprised, unimpressed.

vb. not wonder, not be surprised, not bat an eyelid, not turn a hair; expect, take for granted, presume.

868 repute

n. repute, good standing, reputation, name, good name, renown, character, credit, respectability, reliability, trustworthiness, dependability; respect, favour, prestige, honour, glory, regard, kudos (*inf.*); fame, distinction, eminence, prominence, popularity; greatness, dignity, superiority, exaltation, majesty; rank, position, station, status.

big name, somebody, celebrity, star, dignitary, VIP, bigwig, big shot (*sl.*), grand old man.

adj. reputable, respectable, reliable, trustworthy, dependable, respected, well thought of, esteemed, acclaimed; renowned, of renown, famous, popular, celebrated, notable, leading, well-known; prestigious, honourable, distinguished, illustrious, eminent, prominent.

dignified, noble, great, grand, superior, high, exalted, elevated, sublime, majestic.

vb. be somebody, have a name, leave one's mark, make a name for oneself, go down in history.

honour, regard, respect, esteem, hold
in high regard, admire, revere, praise,
worship; exalt, glorify, crown,
enthrone, ennoble, knight, immortalize.

869 disrepute

n. disrepute, disfavour, dishonour,
ill-repute, bad name, bad character,
unreliability, poor reputation;
notoriety, infamy; disgrace, disrespect,
reproach, shame, humiliation,
degradation, abasement, ignominy,
contempt.

scandal, gossip, backbiting, slander,
calumny, defamation; slur, slight,
insult, stain, stigma, brand, blot.

adj. disreputable, dishonourable, discreditable, ignominious;
humiliating, lowering, degrading;
notorious, infamous; shady, questionable; disgraceful, scandalous, shameful, outrageous, shocking, contemptible, despicable, corrupt, offensive, flagrant, base, mean, low, shabby,
shoddy.

disgraced, humiliated, unable to
show one's face.

undistinguished, obscure, unknown,
unheard of, unrenowned.

vb. disgrace oneself, lose one's
reputation, lose face, lapse from grace,
fall from grace, fade; condescend,
stoop, descend, lower oneself.

put to shame, disgrace, discredit,
dishonour, expose, mock, show up;
ridicule, embarrass, humiliate, humble;
debase, degrade, snub, confound,
unfrock; stain, tarnish, smear, sully,
blot; take down a peg or two (*inf.*), cut
down to size (*inf.*), drag through the
mire (*inf.*).

870 nobility

n. nobility, dignity, grandeur, greatness, distinction, eminence; rank,
descent, birth, blood, high birth, blue
blood; royalty, majesty, court; aristocracy, gentry, landed gentry, peerage,
ruling class, privileged class, elite,
gentility; society, high society, upper
classes, upper ten thousand, upper
crust (*inf.*), higher-ups (*inf.*).

nobleman; peer, peeress; archbishop; duke, duchess; marquis, marchioness; earl; count, countess; viscount, viscountess; bishop; baron,
baroness; lord, lady; baronet; knight,
dame; life peer; dowager.

adj. noble, dignified, grand, great,
magnificent, lofty, imposing, distinguished; royal, majestic, monarchic,
regal, reigning, princely; aristocratic,
courtly, titled, lordly; highborn, of
gentle birth, born in the purple.

871 common people

n. commonalty, common people,
commons; people, the masses, general
public, rank and file, grass roots; bourgeoisie, middle class; working class,
lower class, have-nots, underdogs,
proletariat; rabble, crowd, herd, riffraff, *hoi polloi*, ragtag and bobtail, the
great unwashed, scum, dregs.

commoner, plebeian, citizen,
civilian, man in the street, Mr.
Average; countryman, rustic, yokel,
country bumpkin, peasant, serf.

adj. common, plebeian, bourgeois,
ordinary, average, lowly, humble, of
low estate, mean, ignoble; rustic.

872 title

n. title, name, designation; courtesy
title, handle (*inf.*), honorific; order,
privilege, honour; decoration, ribbon,
medal, crest, emblem.

873 pride

n. pride, self-respect, self-regard, self-esteem, dignity, self-love; conceit, vanity, haughtiness, vainglory; self-exaltation, self-glorification; ego-trip; arrogance, insolence.

proud person, bighead (*inf.*), swank (*inf.*), boaster, bragger.

adj. self-respecting, pleased with oneself, self-assured, self-satisfied; dignified, lofty, stately, elevated, high-falutin; egotistic, conceited, bigheaded (*inf.*), patronizing.

vb. be proud, hold one's head high; take pride in, pride oneself on, glory in, boast.

see also **875**

874 humility

n. humility, humbleness, self-abasement, self-effacement; submission, obedience, meekness, lowliness, modesty, subservience, subjection; unobtrusiveness.

humiliation; abasement; mortification; come-down (*inf.*), let-down (*inf.*), deflation, crushing, shame.

adj. humble, lowly, meek, submissive, modest, self-effacing, subservient, servile; unassuming, unpretentious; humiliated, humbled, let down (*inf.*), deflated, squashed, crushed, crestfallen, chastened; embarrassed, ashamed.

vb. humble oneself, submit, obey; condescend, stoop, deign; eat humble pie, come down from one's high horse; be humiliated, not dare show one's face, feel small, feel squashed.

humiliate, humble, shame, embarrass, deflate, crush, squash, let down (*inf.*), bring low, put to shame, disconcert, make one feel small, take down a peg or two (*inf.*), teach one his place, reduce to tears.

see also **881**

875 vanity

n. vanity, conceit, self-importance, self-glorification, egotism, vainglory,

self-applause,' boastfulness; self-worship, narcissism; show, ostentation, exhibitionism; futility, emptiness, uselessness.

egotist, show-off, exhibitionist, know-all, smart aleck (*inf.*), toffee-nose (*sl.*), Narcissus.

adj. vain, conceited, haughty, self-centred, self-important, self-glorifying, self-applauding, full of oneself, boastful, cocky, swollen-headed, stuck up (*inf.*), puffed up, too big for one's boots (*sl.*), swanky (*inf.*), snooty (*inf.*), high and mighty (*inf.*), pompous, arrogant, insolent, supercilious, pretentious, snobbish, toffee-nose (*sl.*), stand-offish; showy, exhibitionist.

vb. be vain, be puffed up, get too big for one's boots (*sl.*), have a high opinion of oneself, think too much of oneself, come the high and mighty with (*inf.*), know it all, boast, show off; turn up one's nose at (*inf.*); go to one's head, puff up.

see also **879**

876 modesty; shyness

n. modesty, unassumingness, unpretentiousness, unobtrusiveness, restraint, meekness, retiring nature; chastity, purity, virtue.

shyness, timidity, bashfulness, reserve, reticence, coyness; inhibition, nervousness.

adj. modest, retiring, restrained, meek, unassuming, unobtrusive, diffident, shrinking; restrained, tasteful, undecorated; chaste, pure, innocent.

shy, timid, bashful, quiet, reserved, coy, reticent, reluctant, backward, inhibited, secretive, demure, proper; blushing, embarrassed, red.

vb. hold back, hide one's face, keep in the background, take a back seat, hide one's light under a bushel, retire into one's shell; blush, go red.

877 ostentation

n. ostentation, exhibitionism, showiness, pretension; pomp, pompousness, magnificence, splendour, grandeur, majesty, pageantry; blatancy, flagrancy, flashiness, gaudiness, loudness; flourish, parade, fuss, splurge, showing off; bravado, histrionics, theatricality, sensationalism, effect, showmanship; exhibitionist, show-off, showman.

adj. ostentatious, showing off, proud, pompous, grandiose, extravagant, bombastic, high-flown, fancy, jazzy, showy, garish, gaudy, flashy, flamboyant, flaunting, blatant, flagrant, obtrusive, conspicuous, loud, screaming; spectacular, sensational, theatrical, histrionic, for effect, for show.

vb. show off, flaunt, parade, flourish, splurge, play to the gallery, do for show, make an exhibition of oneself, give oneself airs; sensationalize.

878 celebration

n. celebration, commemoration, honouring, keeping, observance; anniversary, jubilee, birthday, red-letter day, centenary, bicentenary, tercentenary; ceremonial; solemnization; ceremony, function, occasion, festive occasion, do (*inf.*); clapping, applause, praise, acclaim, cheers, hurrahs, cries, ovation, standing ovation, salute.

adj. celebrative, commemorative, anniversary, congratulatory, ceremonial, festive.

vb. celebrate, commemorate, observe, keep, remember,˙ honour, congratulate, crown; throw a party, make merry, kill the fatted calf.

879 boasting

n. boasting, self-glory, self-glorification; boast, brag, empty talk, big talk, hot air, bombast, bluster, braggadocio, gasconade.

boaster, big mouth, swank (*inf.*), gas-bag (*sl.*), braggart, Gascon.

adj. boastful, bragging, big-mouthed, pretentious, inflated, self-glorifying, vaunting.

vb. boast, vaunt, brag, show off, talk big, bounce, exaggerate; blow one's own trumpet, have a high opinion of oneself, pat oneself on the back, congratulate oneself, flatter oneself.

880 insolence

n. insolence, rudeness, boldness, audacity, effrontery, impudence, impertinence, arrogance, presumption, forwardness, shamelessness, officiousness, sauciness, defiance, lip (*sl.*), cheek, nerve (*inf.*), sauce, brass.

upstart, wise guy (*sl.*), pup.

adj. insolent, impudent, impertinent, arrogant, high-handed, disrespectful, insulting, rude, offensive, officious, outrageous, defiant, cheeky, saucy, uppity (*inf.*); presumptuous, forward.

vb. be insolent, have the cheek, have a nerve (*inf.*), get fresh, come the high and mighty with (*inf.*), get on one's high horse (*inf.*), throw one's weight about (*inf.*); give lip (*sl.*), brazen it out, answer back, presume, take for granted.

881 servility

n. servility, obsequiousness, meniality, sycophancy, toadyism; sycophant, toady, back-scratcher, yes-man, sponger, parasite, hanger-on, boot-licker.

adj. servile, menial, beggarly, slavish, subservient, obsequious, cringing, toadyish, boot-licking, ingratiating, fawning, grovelling, snivelling.

vb. be servile, suck up to (*sl.*), crawl (*inf.*), grovel, go down on one's knees, lick the boots of, ingratiate oneself with, toady, fawn, curry favour; flatter.

D Sympathetic

882 friendship
n. friendship, companionship, amity, comradeship, fraternity, intimacy, familiarity; friendliness, affection, amicability, sociability, good terms, neighbourliness, understanding, compatibility, matiness, warmth, cordiality.

friend, companion, mate, pal, chum, buddy, comrade; boy-friend, girl-friend; acquaintance, neighbour; close friend, best friend, bosom friend, confidant, intimate.

adj. friendly, close, familiar, intimate, inseparable, confiding; faithful, loyal, devoted, true, trusted, staunch, firm; amicable, sympathetic, compatible, sociable, affectionate, warm-hearted, brotherly, matey, pally; kind, benevolent.

vb. be friendly, know, be acquainted with, be on good terms with; befriend, get to know, make friends with, get in with (*inf.*), get pally with, chum up with, break the ice; go out with (*inf.*), go with, knock about with (*inf.*), go around with, keep company with, go together, see (*inf.*), run after (*inf.*), go after (*inf.*), chase, try to get, take out, accompany, court, woo, make advances; be just good friends.

see also **889**

883 enmity

n. enmity, hostility, inimicality; antipathy, unfriendliness; hatred, antagonism, dislike, repugnance, animosity; ill-feeling, hard feelings; separation, estrangement, alienation; bitterness, acrimony, coolness.

enemy, foe, antagonist, opponent, adversary, arch-enemy, invader; public enemy; rival, informer.

adj. inimical, hostile, antagonistic, unfriendly, ill-disposed, opposed; irreconcilable, alienated, estranged; at odds, at daggers drawn, at loggerheads, not on speaking terms, on bad terms; cool, cold, chilly, uncordial; opposite, contrary, conflicting; quarrelsome, unsympathetic, grudging, resentful.

vb. be opposed to, differ, be at odds with, conflict, clash; antagonize, provoke, alienate, estrange.

see also **637, 638**

884 sociability
n. sociability, geniality, friendliness, cordiality, gregariousness, conviviality, affability, hospitality, open house, social intercourse.

party, social, get-together, ball, meeting, reunion, rendezvous, reception, at home, soirée; visit, call, appointment, engagement, date, interview, stay; arrangement.

visitor, dropper-in, guest, caller; mixer, good mixer, life and soul of the party; gate-crasher, uninvited guest.

adj. sociable, friendly, genial, cordial, affable, gregarious, neighbourly, hospitable.

vb. be sociable, invite, welcome, receive, entertain, throw a party, keep open house; visit, drop in on, look in, call by.

885 unsociability
n. unsociability, unfriendliness, uncommunicativeness, shyness; dis-

tance, unapproachability, aloofness;
seclusion, privacy, separateness,
isolation, retirement, withdrawal,
solitariness, loneliness; backwater,
back of beyond, backwoods, refuge,
retreat, cloister, ivory tower, shell,
desert island.

recluse, hermit, monk, anchorite,
backwoodsman; loner, stay-at-home;
outcast, castaway; refugee, evacuee;
outlaw, bandit; orphan, leper.

adj. unsociable, unfriendly, distant,
shy, uncommunicative, unapproachable, aloof, stand-offish,
antisocial, inhospitable; lonesome,
solitary, lonely, friendless, desolate,
retiring, withdrawn; secluded, for-
saken, isolated, rustic, out-of-the-way,
remote, God-forsaken, unexplored,
uninhabited, deserted.

vb. be unsociable, stand aloof, keep
oneself to oneself, keep one's distance,
go into seclusion, shut oneself up,
retire into one's shell; seclude, exclude,
expel, excommunicate, repel, cold-
shoulder, keep at arm's length, keep at
bay, beat off.

886 courtesy
n. courtesy, thoughtfulness, consideration, politeness, manners, good
manners, civility, culture, refinement,
breeding, gentility, respect, kindness,
friendliness, generosity, gallantry,
chivalry; condescension, flattery,
oiliness.

good turn, favour, compliment;
greeting, handshake, smile, embrace,
hug, kiss.

adj. courteous, polite, well-man-
nered, civil, amiable, affable, thoughtful, considerate, kind, friendly,
generous, obliging; cultivated, cultured, refined, polished, well-bred;
politic, diplomatic; gentlemanly, lady-

like; gallant, chivalrous; condescen-
ding, obsequious, ingratiating, patronizing.

vb. be courteous, behave oneself,
mind one's P's and Q's, be on one's
best behaviour; give one's regards,
give one's compliments, send best
wishes, pay one's respects, compliment; greet, welcome, hail, exchange
greetings, hold out one's hand, shake
hands, smile, wave, hug, embrace, kiss.

887 discourtesy
n. discourtesy, impoliteness, bad
manners, misbehaviour, incivility, ill
breeding; disrespect, impudence,
unfriendliness, brusqueness; meanness,
nastiness, unpleasantness, rudeness,
vulgarity, boorishness, coarseness,
grossness, shamelessness.

adj. discourteous, impolite, bad-
mannered, uncivil, uncultured, unrefined, unbecoming, misbehaved,
ungentlemanly, rude, unfriendly, unkind, ungracious, unpleasant, nasty,
obstreperous, disrespectful, offensive,
crude, coarse, vulgar, shameless;
loutish, rowdy, disorderly, boorish;
thoughtless, careless, inconsiderate,
tactless, gauche, outspoken; brusque,
abrupt, curt, offhand, rough, gruff,
surly, difficult; audacious, brash;
cheeky, high-handed.

vb. be rude, insult, affront, outrage;
give the cold shoulder; irritate, annoy,
shout down, interrupt; snub, disregard, ignore.

888 congratulation
n. congratulation, felicitation, best
wishes, compliments, happy returns;
applause, appreciation, bouquet,
praise, acknowledgement, toast.

adj. congratulatory, complimentary.

vb. congratulate, compliment, felicitate, pay one's respects, offer one's

congratulations, salute, praise, honour, acclaim, sound the praises of, appreciate, admire, adulate; toast, celebrate; mob.

889 love

n. love, fondness, affection, attachment, devotion, adoration; passion, Eros, ardour, amorousness, lust, infatuation, crush (*sl.*), pash (*sl.*); first love, calf-love, puppy love; emotion, sentiment; attractiveness, charm, winsomeness, appeal, sex-appeal, fascination; love affair, affair, romance, liaison, relationship, flirtation, amour, eternal triangle.

lover, admirer, suitor, wooer, boy-friend, girl-friend, date (*inf.*), steady (*inf.*), blind date; Romeo, Juliet, fiancé, fiancée; mistress; cohabitant.

adj. loving, fond, affectionate, devoted, adoring, attached; emotional, sentimental, tender, soft; yearning, longing, passionate, ardent, amorous, glowing.

enamoured, attracted, enchanted, fascinated, caught, charmed, captivated, enraptured, taken with, sweet on, keen on, infatuated, gone on, crazy, wild, mad, smitten, in love, head over heels in love.

lovable, winsome, attractive, charming, appealing, captivating, irresistible, dear; loved, beloved, cherished.

vb. love, like, be fond of, care for, delight in, adore, fancy; treasure, hold dear, take to one's heart (*inf.*), admire, regard, cherish, appreciate, esteem, value, prize; be in love, dote on, be enraptured by; fall in love, fall for, be crazy about, have it bad (*inf.*); lose one's heart to, have a crush on, be swept off one's feet (*inf.*), be infatuated with; long, yearn; copulate, have intercourse, make love to, have sex with (*inf.*), sleep with (*inf.*), sleep together (*inf.*), go to bed with, have it off with (*sl.*); live with, live together, cohabit, live in sin (*inf.*).

attract, appeal, fascinate, captivate, charm, enchant, allure, draw, rouse, enrapture, infatuate, sweep off one's feet (*inf.*).

see also **861, 882**

890 endearment

n. endearment, affection, attachment, fondness, love, soft nothings, embrace, kiss, cuddle, stroke, fondling, petting, necking (*sl.*); courtship, courting, wooing, pass, advance, dating, flirtation, amorous intentions; love-letter, Valentine; proposal, offer of marriage, engagement.

vb. woo, court, go out with (*inf.*), run after (*inf.*), pursue, chase, date, pay attentions to, make overtures, make advances, make passes, make eyes at (*inf*), ogle, flirt; propose, pop the question (*inf.*).

be fond of, cherish; embrace, hug, clasp, draw close, snuggle, kiss, cuddle; stroke, fondle, caress, pat, pet, neck, smooch (*inf.*).

see also **882**

891 darling; favourite

n. darling, dear, love, beloved, dearest, sweetheart, angel, pet, sweet, sweetie (*inf.*), sweetie-pie (*inf.*), sugar (*inf.*), honey (*inf.*), precious (*inf.*), treasure (*inf.*), jewel (*inf.*); favourite, mother's darling, teacher's pet, blue-eyed boy, apple of one's eye.

892 hate

n. hate, hatred, dislike, antipathy, aversion, loathing, abhorrence, repugnance, repulsion, disgust, scorn, detestation, nasty look.

anathema, abomination, menace, pest, *bête noire*, bitter pill.

adj. detestable, hateful, odious, abominable, abhorrent, loathsome, accursed, offensive, repugnant, disgusting, revolting, repulsive, vile; averse to, hostile, antagonistic.

vb. hate, dislike, loathe, abhor, detest, abominate, denounce, condemn, object to, spurn, spit upon, curse, reject, have it in for (*inf.*).

offend, rub up the wrong way, repel, disgust, shock, alienate, estrange, antagonize, make one's blood run cold.

see also **295, 862**

893 resentment; anger

n. resentment, bitterness, hurt, soreness, malice, grudge, bone to pick; sore point.

anger, indignation, displeasure, antagonism; rage, fury, wrath, vehemence, passion, vexation, exasperation, annoyance, impatience, ire; bad temper, outburst, fit, tantrum, huff, tiff, quarrel, argument, fight.

adj. resentful, indignant, sore, hurt, grudging, bitter, embittered, with a chip on one's shoulder, acrimonious.

angry, cross, irate, furious, raging, fiery, mad (*inf.*), hopping mad (*inf.*), fuming, displeased; antagonized, enraged, exasperated, infuriated, annoyed, irritated, peeved (*sl.*), impatient, irritable, ratty (*sl.*), shirty (*sl.*), provoked, affronted, riled, vexed, worked up, het up (*inf.*), up in arms, in a huff, hot under the collar, foaming at the mouth (*inf.*).

vb. resent, feel bitter towards, take umbrage, take exception, be insulted, bear a grudge, bear malice, have a bone to pick.

get angry, get cross, lose one's temper, blow one's top (*inf.*), hit the roof (*inf.*), fly off the handle (*inf.*), blow up (*inf.*), explode; get worked up, get het up (*inf.*), get hot under the collar, go up the wall, go off the deep end (*inf.*).

be angry, burn, roar, rage, rant and rave, fume, storm, boil, seethe, foam at the mouth (*inf.*); snap, bite someone's head off (*inf.*), jump down someone's throat (*inf.*); criticize, nag, get at.

anger, enrage, incense, infuriate, madden, antagonize, exasperate, provoke, bother, harass, vex, annoy, incite, irritate, needle, nettle, rankle, rile, stir, get someone's back up (*inf.*), get someone's blood up, make one's blood boil, send up the wall, rub up the wrong way (*inf.*), tread on someone's toes (*inf.*), get on someone's nerves, get under someone's skin, get someone's goat (*sl.*), upset, ruffle, discompose, put out.

see also **642**

894 irritability

n. irritability, sensitivity, nervousness, uneasiness, exasperation, impatience, touchiness, bad temper.

adj. irritable, sensitive, susceptible, touchy, oversensitive, prickly, edgy, short-tempered, ratty (*sl.*), shirty (*sl.*), uptight, gruff, grumpy; nervous, anxious, jumpy, jittery (*inf.*); temperamental, moody; irritated, annoyed, needled, riled, rankled, nettled, rubbed up the wrong way, with a chip on one's shoulder; irascible, choleric, querulous, cantankerous.

895 sullenness

n. sullenness, moroseness, glumness, moodiness, unsociability, sourness, bad temper, gruffness, spleen; frown, scowl, grimace, sneer, dirty look (*inf.*), wry face.

adj. sullen, morose, glum, silent,

unsociable; moody, surly, grouchy, churlish, sulky, cross, mopish, ill-humoured, ill-natured, disagreeable, sour, mournful, saturnine; scowling, frowning; gloomy, dismal, sad, dim, dark, cheerless, sombre.

vb. scowl, frown, grimace, make a face, pull a face, glower, growl, sulk, grouch, mope, sneer.

896 marriage

n. marriage, matrimony, wedlock, conjugality, union, match, alliance, marriage tie, marriage bed; wedding, pledging, ceremony, nuptials, espousals; church wedding, civil marriage, registry-office wedding; elopement, abduction; shotgun wedding; reception, wedding breakfast, party, dance; honeymoon, consummation.

man and wife, bride and groom, bridal pair, newlyweds, honey-mooners; partner, spouse, mate; husband, man; wife, helpmeet, better half (*inf.*), the missus (*sl.*).

adj. matrimonial, marital, nuptial, conjugal, married, wed, united, matched; newly-wed; honeymooning, going-away, marriageable, eligible, suitable, of marriageable age.

vb. marry, get married, wed, espouse, take to oneself, lead to the altar, plight one's troth, become one, get hitched (*sl.*), get spliced (*sl.*), make an honest woman of (*inf.*); honey-moon, go away, consummate; run away, leave home, elope; join, unite, pronounce man and wife, marry, give in marriage, give away; marry into, marry out of; marry off, match, match-make, find a match for, find a mate for; catch, find, hook (*sl.*).

see also **889**

897 celibacy

n. celibacy, singleness, bachelorhood, virginity, spinsterhood; celibate, bachelor, confirmed bachelor; spinster, bachelor girl, old maid, virgin.

adj. celibate, single, unmarried, unwed, not the marrying kind; eligible, unattached, free; virgin.

898 divorce; widowhood

n. divorce, separation, annulment, dissolution, decree nisi, desertion; breakdown of marriage.

widowhood; survivor, widow, dowager, relict; widower; grass widow, golf widow.

adj. divorced, parted, separated, living apart.

vb. divorce, get a divorce, annul, cancel, put asunder, sue for a divorce, desert, split up (*inf.*), separate, live apart; widow, bereave; leave, survive.

899 benevolence

n. benevolence, kindness, helpfulness, thoughtfulness, kindheartedness, graciousness, courtesy, charity, altruism, philanthropy, fellow-feeling, the golden rule; service, good deed, good turn, aid, relief, favour, benefit, alms.

kind person, good Samaritan, good neighbour, altruist, humanitarian, do-gooder, philanthropist, heart of gold.

adj. kind, benevolent, charitable, helpful, careful, thoughtful, well-meaning, well-intentioned, well-meant, gracious, good, pleasant, generous, obliging, neighbourly, kindhearted, warm-hearted, compassionate, sympathetic, unselfish, altruistic, humanitarian, philanthropic; merciful, pitying.

vb. be kind, help, do a good turn, do a favour, benefit, support, encourage, comfort, relieve, bless, mean well, wish well, do as one would be done by, bend over backwards to help.

see also 550, 905, 935

900 malevolence

n. malevolence, unkindness, hate, animosity, malice, malignity, spite, bitterness, acrimony; cruelty, inhumanity, wickedness, ruthlessness, relentlessness, harshness, severity, callousness; tyranny, oppression, despotism, intolerance; brutality, beastliness, savagery, barbarousness, brutishness, monstrousness.

ill, harm, misfortune, mischief, blow, outrage, foul play, catastrophe, disaster, atrocity, torture.

adj. unkind, unfriendly, unloving, uncharitable, stepmotherly, inconsiderate, thoughtless; spiteful, malicious, catty, hateful, resentful, bitter, acrimonious, caustic.

cruel, malevolent, malicious, inhuman, wicked, harsh, severe, relentless, fierce, savage, barbarous, brutal, beastly; pitiless, unmerciful, intolerant, ruthless, cold, callous, hardhearted, oppressive, despotic, devilish, diabolical.

vb. be malevolent, hurt, harm, abuse, maltreat, damage, injure, oppress, tyrannize, not tolerate, persecute, torture, torment, victimize, have it in for (*inf.*), take it out on (*inf.*).

see also 551, 906, 936

901 curse

n. curse, malediction, denunciation, execration, abuse, vilification, vituperation, scurrility; profanity, swearing, oath, imprecation, expletive, swearword, naughty word, bad language, blasphemy, sacrilege, profanation.

adj. maledictory, imprecatory, damnatory; abusive, scurrilous, profane,

sacrilegious, blasphemous, blue, naughty, indecent, obscene.

vb. curse, wish on (*inf.*), invoke, summon, call down on; abuse, defame, denounce, pour abuse, call names, revile, vituperate, vilify, damn; swear, swear like a trooper, blaspheme.

902 threat

n. threat, menace, warning, intimidation, blackmail; writing on the wall, danger signal, distress signal; threatening, commination.

adj. threatening, menacing, intimidating, frightening; ominous, imminent.

vb. threaten, menace, intimidate, blackmail, frighten, scare, torment, bully, push around (*inf.*), order about (*inf.*); be brewing, loom, be imminent.

see also 154

903 philanthropy

n. philanthropy, humanitarianism, utilitarianism, altruism, social conscience; welfare state, social services; patriotism, love of one's country, loyalty, public spirit; nationalism, chauvinism; internationalism.

philanthropist, humanitarian, dogooder; idealist, altruist, visionary, man with a vision, missionary; patriot, lover of one's country, loyalist, nationalist, chauvinist; internationalist, citizen of the world, cosmopolitan.

adj. philanthropic, humanitarian, humane, kind, altruistic, patriotic, chauvinistic; public-spirited, reforming.

vb. have a social conscience, be public-spirited, show public spirit; love one's country.

904 misanthropy

n. misanthropy, selfishness, egotism, cynicism, unsociability, incivism;

misanthrope, man-hater, misogynist, woman-hater, cynic, egoist.

adj. misanthropic, antisocial, unsocial, unsociable, inhuman, cynical; unpatriotic.

see also **885**

905 benefactor

n. benefactor, benefactress, helper, good neighbour, do-gooder, giver, donor, contributor; protector, guard, watch, champion, guardian; patron, supporter, backer, rescuer, deliverer, liberator, redeemer; angel, guardian angel.

see also **640**

906 evildoer

n. evildoer, wrongdoer, troublemaker, mischief-maker; criminal, lawbreaker, offender, transgressor, sinner, public enemy; crook, villain, rogue; thief, gangster, con man (*inf.*); murderer, assassin; ruffian, thug, hooligan, layabout (*inf.*), nasty piece of work (*inf.*); beast, brute, monster, vampire, viper.

see also **684, 723, 940**

907 pity

n. pity, compassion, goodness, kindliness, benevolence, understanding, charity; tenderness, soft-heartedness, warm-heartedness; condolence, sympathy, commiseration, fellow feeling, comfort, solace, consolation; mercy, favour, grace, clemency, forbearance, forgiveness, second chance.

adj. pitying, compassionate, kind, tender, gentle, lenient; merciful, gracious, clement, forbearing, forgiving, generous; sympathetic, consoling, commiserating, comforting, sorry; pitiful, pitiable.

vb. pity, show mercy, take pity on, pardon, spare, forgive, reprieve, give a

second chance; relent, relax, repent; put out of one's misery.

sympathize, feel for, feel with, put oneself in someone's shoes, be understanding, express sympathy, commiserate, share another's sorrow, grieve with, weep for, love, console, comfort, support, uphold, encourage, sit by, put one's arm round.

908 pitilessness

n. pitilessness, ruthlessness, mercilessness, relentlessness, cruelty, heartlessness, callousness, hardness of heart; letter of the law, pound of flesh.

adj. pitiless, unpitying, unmerciful, merciless, relentless, unrelenting, unforgiving, barbarous, tyrannical, vindictive, revengeful; rough, harsh, severe; cruel, brutal, savage; cold, unsympathetic, unfeeling, unmoved, inflexible; hard-hearted, stony-hearted, cold-blooded.

vb. show no pity, stop at nothing (*inf.*), harden one's heart, turn a deaf ear to, give no quarter, exact one's pound of flesh; one's heart bleed for (*inf.*).

909 gratitude

n. gratitude, thankfulness, appreciation, gratefulness, sense of obligation; thanks, thank-you, acknowledgement, response, recognition, praise, tribute, vote of thanks, honour, credit; blessing, grace, prayer, benediction; bread-and-butter letter; reward, trip; leaving-present.

adj. grateful, thankful, appreciative, responsive; indebted, obliged, much obliged; pleased, gratified, overwhelmed.

vb. thank, say thank you, show one's gratitude, respond, appreciate, show one's appreciation, acknowledge, recognize, praise, pay a tribute to, never forget, applaud; reward, tip; give thanks, say grace, return thanks.

910 ingratitude

n. ingratitude, ungratefulness, lack of appreciation, thanklessness, no sense of obligation; thoughtlessness, rudeness.

adj. ungrateful, unappreciative, unmindful, forgetful, rude; thankless, unrewarding, unprofitable, worthless; unthanked, unacknowledged, unrewarded.

vb. be ungrateful, not thank, take for granted, presume upon.

911 forgiveness

n. forgiveness, pardon, free pardon, absolution; remission, acquittal, release, discharge; exoneration, exculpation; justification, reconciliation, redemption, atonement; reprieve, amnesty, indemnity; grace, mercy, patience, forbearance.

adj. forgiven, pardoned, excused, absolved, let off, acquitted, free, not guilty, released, reinstated, reconciled, restored, taken back, welcomed home; redeemed, justified, adopted.

vb. forgive, pardon, excuse, remit, reprieve, clear, absolve, discharge, acquit, free, declare not guilty, let off (*inf.*), let go; let pass, disregard, ignore, shut one's eyes to, grant amnesty to; show mercy, tolerate, forbear; redeem, reconcile, justify; purge, blot one's sins out, wipe the slate clean; bury the hatchet, make it up, kiss and make up; forgive and forget, let bygones be bygones.

see also **921, 961**

912 revenge

n. revenge, vengeance, requital, reprisal, retaliation; vindictiveness,

spitefulness, rancour; avenger, vindicator.

adj. revengeful, vengeant, spiteful, retaliatory, unrelenting, rancorous, unappeasable, implacable.

vb. avenge, take revenge, take vengeance, requite, vindicate, retaliate, get even with, get one's own back.

see also **647**

913 jealousy

n. jealousy, resentment, intolerance, distrust, suspicion, green eye, green-eyed monster; rivalry, unfaithfulness, hostility; vigilance, watchfulness, possessiveness.

adj. jealous, green-eyed, resentful, distrustful, suspicious, vigilant, watchful, possessive.

914 envy

n. envy, covetousness, resentment.

adj. envious, covetous, jealous.

vb. envy, covet, lust after, desire, crave, hanker; grudge, begrudge.

E Moral

915 right

n. right, justice, rightfulness, lawfulness, legality, legitimacy, fairness, equity, impartiality, poetic justice; suitability, reasonableness, fittingness; the right thing, what is right, the proper thing, square deal, fair play.

adj. right, correct, precise, true, valid, accurate; appropriate, proper, suitable, apt, fit, on the right track; fair, honest, upright, righteous, just, rightful, lawful, legitimate, equitable, impartial, objective, unprejudiced, unbiased, disinterested, dispassionate, straightforward, plain; fair and square, straight, fair-minded, sporting.

vb. be just, play the game, try to be

fair, do justice to, do the right thing, give the Devil his due.

see also 577

916 wrong

n. wrong, wrongness, injustice, wrongfulness, inequity, unfairness, partiality, partisanship, prejudice, bias, favouritism; foul play, raw deal, irregularity; grievance, injury; preferential treatment, discrimination, reverse discrimination, nepotism.

adj. wrong, unjust, wrongful, unreasonable, unfair, inequitable, partial, biased, prejudiced, partisan, uneven, unbalanced; below the belt, not cricket (*inf.*), unsportsmanlike; erroneous, imprecise, inaccurate, on the wrong track, at fault; injurious, harmful; wicked, sinful; unsuitable, unfitting, inappropriate, improper; unjustifiable, inexcusable, unforgivable; inadmissible, illegal, illicit, illegitimate.

vb. do wrong, break the law, wrong, hurt, injure, harm, treat unfairly, maltreat, cheat; discriminate, favour, prefer, show preference, be biased, show partiality; not play the game properly, not play fair, hit below the belt.

see also 416, 578

917 dueness

n. dueness, due; deserts, comeuppance, just deserts, merits; right, human rights, rights of man, women's rights; dues, fees, levy, contribution; reward, compensation; punishment; privilege, responsibility, prerogative.

adj. due, owing, payable, overdue, outstanding, unpaid, unsettled, in arrears, chargeable; deserved, well-deserved, merited, worthy, just, warranted, entitled, deserving, worthy, needy, rightful, meritorious.

vb. be due, become due, mature, deserve, merit, have the right to, be entitled to; be worthy of, warrant, expect, earn, claim, lay claim to; demand one's rights; have it coming to one (*inf.*), have only oneself to thank, serve someone right.

918 undueness

n. undueness, unfittingness; presumption, assumption, overstepping, arrogation, violation, encroachment; dispossession, disentitlement, forfeiture, disfranchisement.

adj. undue, undeserved, unmerited, unwarranted, uncalled for, improper, unnecessary, immoderate; unworthy, unjust, unfair, undeserving; unentitled, unprivileged.

vb. have no right to, presume, venture, overstep, assume, usurp, violate, not be entitled to, take liberties; not expect; disqualify, invalidate, disentitle, disfranchise.

919 duty

n. duty, obligation, liability, responsibility, burden, onus; accountability; engagement, commitment, pledge, contract, debt; call of duty, sense of duty, moral obligation, conscience, still small voice; loyalty, faithfulness, allegiance.

adj. incumbent, up to one, behoving; obliged, duty-bound, under obligation; liable, responsible, answerable, subject to, accountable; obligatory, binding, compulsory, necessary; dutiful, obedient, submissive, tractable, compliant.

vb. be one's duty, be the duty of, should, ought, had better, behove; be responsible for, rest with, devolve on, rest on the shoulders of, fall to, fall to one's lot; accept responsiblity, commit oneself; do one's duty, do what is

920

expected of one, perform, fulfil, acquit oneself well, meet one's obligations; impose a duty, call upon, enjoin, look to; oblige, bind, saddle with, put under obligation.

920 neglect of duty

n. neglect, disregard, omission, evasion, non-observance, dereliction, negligence; carelessness, slackness, remissness, slovenliness; absence, absenteeism, truancy; defection, desertion, mutiny; disloyalty, unfaithfulness.

adj. negligent, inattentive, careless, slack, undutiful; disloyal, unfaithful; rebellious, mutinous.

vb. neglect, fail, break, violate; pass over, let slip, let go, omit, ignore, evade, shirk; defer, postpone, procrastinate; suspend, discard, dismiss; rebel, mutiny; absent oneself, play truant; let someone down, not trouble oneself.

see also 393

921 exemption

n. exemption, immunity, privilege; freedom, liberation, release, dispensation, exception, absolution; permission, leave; lifting of restrictions; escape-clause.

adj. exempt, free, clear, non-liable, not subject to, not chargeable; immune, privileged; unaffected, unrestrained, uncontrolled, unbound, unrestricted; outside.

vb. exempt, free, clear, release, acquit, discharge; lift restrictions; shrug off, pass the buck (*inf.*); be exempt, be free, enjoy immunity, get away with murder (*inf.*).

see also **680, 961**

922 respect

n. respect, regard, honour, esteem, appreciation, favour, admiration, recognition, high opinion, high regard,

deference, liking, love; praise, reverence, veneration, awe, worship; respects, bow, curtsy, salute, greeting, salutation.

adj. respectful, deferential, courteous, polite, admiring, showing respect for; attentive, reverential; on one's knees, prostrate.

respected, highly regarded, valued, appreciated, esteemed, honoured, time-honoured, important, well thought of.

vb. respect, regard highly, think well of, think a great deal of, have a high opinion of, admire, take off one's hat to (*inf.*), value, appreciate, honour, hold dear; praise, extol, revere, worship; pay one's respects, bow, kneel, curtsy, welcome, greet; scrape, grovel; keep in with (*inf.*), keep on the right side of; stand in awe of.

command respect, impress, overawe, awe, stun, overwhelm, humble.

923 disrespect

n. disrespect, discourtesy, impoliteness, irreverence, dishonour, low opinion, low regard; insult, affront, offence, humiliation, slight, snub, rebuff, slap in the face, backhanded compliment.

adj. disrespectful, discourteous, impolite, irreverent, dishonourable, insulting, offensive, slighting, cutting, humiliating, rude, scornful, impertinent, depreciating, pejorative.

vb. have no respect for, show disrespect for, have a low opinion of, have no time for, underrate, dishonour, offend, insult, affront, slight, snub, rebuff, scorn, despise, look down on (*inf.*), humiliate, interrupt.

924 contempt

n. contempt, scorn, disdain, ridicule, mocking, derision, disrespect, disdainfulness, contemptuousness, scornfulness, snobbishness, haughtiness; sneer, slight, scoff, cold shoulder.

adj. contemptuous, disdainful, scornful, disrespectful, haughty, supercilious, insolent, snooty, snobbish; contemptible, mean, poor, base, worthless, shameful, despicable, beneath contempt.

vb. despise, disdain, spurn, scorn, pour scorn on, turn one's nose up at (*inf.*), sneer at, mock, laugh at, ridicule, deride; pity, look down on (*inf.*), look down one's nose at (*inf.*); disregard, cut dead; avoid, shun, steer clear of; cheapen, belittle, pooh-pooh, not care a fig for.

see also 853

925 approval

n. approval, recognition, acknowledgement; satisfaction; agreement, permission, sanction, adoption, acceptance; admiration, esteem, credit, honour; compliment, bouquet, commendation, citation, write-up; praise, glorification; applause, clapping, ovation, acclaim.

adj. approving, favourable, complimentary, commendatory, laudatory; approvable, commendable, laudable, praiseworthy, creditable, acceptable; approved, popular, praised, uncensored.

vb. approve, recognize, acknowledge; agree, give permission, allow, sanction; accept, adopt, favour; not reject, not sniff at; praise, admire, esteem, compliment, commend, speak well of, write up, crack up (*inf.*), take off one's hat to (*inf.*), give full marks to, must hand it to (*inf.*); find no fault with, have nothing but praises for; sing the praises of, rave about (*inf.*); clap, applaud, cheer, acclaim, hail, give a big hand to.

926 disapproval

n. disapproval, disagreement, non-acceptance, objection, criticism, complaint, opposition, rejection, contradiction, denunciation, censure, fault-finding, reprehension, judgment, blame, reproach, sneer, taunt.

rebuke, reprimand, reproof, admonition, talking to, telling off, lecture, piece of one's mind; brickbat; dissatisfaction, discontent, displeasure.

adj. disapproving, critical, hostile, reproachful, sneering, taunting, reproving, chiding, censorious, condemnatory, defamatory; niggling, fault-finding; unfavourable, uncomplimentary, disparaging; shocked, not amused.

objectionable, blameworthy, reprehensible, not good enough, in person's bad books, not all it is cracked up to be (*inf.*).

vb. disapprove, disagree, not accept, not think much of, not hold with, hold no brief for, frown on; run down, disparage, belittle; object to, oppose, contradict; boo, hiss; blame, reproach, incriminate; snub, taunt, sneer.

criticize, complain, denounce, find fault with, pick holes in; reprehend, reprove, rebuke, reprimand, admonish, upbraid, judge, knock (*sl.*), slam (*sl.*), condemn, censure, punish, put someone in his place; tell off, talk to, tick off (*inf.*), speak to, lecture, have words with (*inf.*), dress down (*inf.*), dust down (*inf.*), tear off a strip (*sl.*), chide, scold, take to task, rap over the knuckles (*inf.*), haul over the coals (*inf.*); give a piece of one's mind to, give a person what for (*sl.*).

927 flattery

n. flattery, adulation, compliment,

soft soap (*inf.*), eyewash (*sl.*), false praise, insincerity, obsequiousness, fawning, cajolery, wheedling.

flatterer, cajoler, wheedler, hypocrite, toady.

adj. flattering, adulatory, blandishing, complimentary, over-complimentary, unctuous, ingratiating, insincere, smooth, smarmy (*inf.*).

vb. flatter, butter up (*inf.*), suck up to (*sl.*), soft-soap (*inf.*), cajole, wheedle, inveigle; lay it on thick (*inf.*), lay it on with a trowel (*inf.*).

see also 881

928 disparagement

n. disparagement, depreciation, detraction, degradation, debasement, vilification, discrediting, belittling; defilement, denigration, smear campaign, whispering campaign, muckraking, mud-slinging, backbiting; slander, libel, calumny, defamation; aspersion, slur, smear, insinuation, innuendo, scandal, gossip.

disparager, critic, slanderer, libeller, backbiter, scandal-monger, muckraker, mud-slinger; mocker, scoffer, cynic, satirist.

adj. disparaging, deprecatory, derogatory, pejorative, denigratory, slanderous, libellous, defamatory, slighting; cynical.

vb. disparage, depreciate, belittle, play down, run down (*inf.*), decry, discredit, cut down to size (*inf.*); denounce, denigrate, blacken; attack, cast aspersions on; criticize, revile, defame, vilify, malign, slight, slur, tarnish, defile, sully, knock (*sl.*), smear; slander, libel; hound; deride, scoff, mock, ridicule.

929 vindication

n. vindication, justification,

establishment, support, plea, defence, excuse, extenuation; ground, right, basis; exoneration, exculpation.

adj. vindicating, justifying, excusing; extenuating; justifiable, arguable, defensible, plausible.

vb. vindicate, justify, establish, support, bear out, uphold, confirm, show, prove, demonstrate, maintain, defend, give grounds for; absolve, acquit, clear, exonerate, excuse, make excuses for, make allowances for.

930 accusation

n. accusation, indictment, prosecution, arraignment, impeachment, charge, censure, incrimination, insinuation, slur, exposé, complaint, denunciation, smear, blame, allegation, action, case; frame-up (*inf.*), put-up job.

accuser, plaintiff, prosecutor.

adj. accusing, denunciatory, incriminating, defamatory.

vb. accuse, censure, charge, bring charges, prefer charges, arrest, arraign, impeach, indict, impute, complain, bring a complaint, find fault with, blame, pin blame on, denounce, incriminate, implicate, involve, reprove, slur, attack, recriminate, slander, libel; point the finger at; frame (*sl.*), trump up, concoct, invent, fabricate, construct, bear false witness.

931 probity

n. probity, uprightness, rectitude, honesty, integrity, fidelity, faithfulness, loyalty, morality, goodness, virtue, reliability, conscientiousness, truthfulness, character, principles, high principles.

adj. honourable, upright, moral, right, fair, good, straight, square, virtuous, honest, law-abiding, reputable, reliable, trustworthy, dependable, conscientious, faithful, loyal, straightforward, sincere, frank, candid, principled, scrupulous.

see also 935, 951

932 improbity

n. improbity, dishonesty, immorality, badness, evil, wickedness, criminality, corruption; cunning, guile; disloyalty, faithlessness, double-dealing, double-crossing, sell-out, duplicity, betrayal, defection, treason, treachery, perfidy, foul play, trick, prank.

adj. dishonest, immoral, bad, wicked, corrupt, evil, criminal, fraudulent; unscrupulous, unprincipled, disreputable; unreliable, undependable, faithless; betraying, treacherous, perfidious, insidious, two-faced, insincere, deceitful, double-dealing; underhand, sly, crafty, devious, shady, dubious, suspicious, questionable, fishy (*sl.*).

vb. be dishonest, lie, cheat, swindle, deceive, betray, double-cross, sell out (*inf.*), two-time (*sl.*).

see also 936, 952

933 disinterestedness

n. disinterestedness, impartiality, indifference, non-involvement, unconcern, detachment, objectivity, neutrality; selflessness, self-sacrifice, self-denial.

adj. disinterested, impartial, indifferent, unconcerned, unbiased, unprejudiced, dispassionate, objective, fair, unselfish, selfless, self-denying, self-sacrificing, self-effacing, self-forgetful; generous, liberal, magnanimous.

934 selfishness

n. selfishness, self-indulgence, greed, meanness, narrowness; self-worship, narcissism, egoism, vanity, self-interest, self-seeking.

self-seeker, egoist, individualist, time-server, narcissist, number one.

adj. selfish, self-centred, self-indulgent, greedy, miserly, mean, narrow; wrapped up in oneself, self-absorbed, self-seeking, egoistic.

vb. be selfish, look after number one.

935 virtue

n. virtue, morality, goodness, uprightness, righteousness, narrow way, sanctity, rectitude; honesty, temperance, kindness, excellence; quality, character, integrity; purity, chastity, innocence; ethics, morals.

adj. virtuous, moral, good, upright, righteous, holy, saintly, angelic; honest, kind, excellent, worthy, proper; perfect, irreproachable, unblemished, immaculate, impeccable; chaste, pure, innocent.

vb. be good, behave oneself, acquit oneself well, keep to the straight and narrow; set a good example.

see also 931, 951

936 vice

n. vice, wickedness, corruption, iniquity, evil, immorality, perversity, baseness, meanness, malignity, malevolence, grossness, wantonness; degeneration, deterioration; unrighteousness, transgression, ungodliness; bad habit, besetting sin, failing, weakness, fault.

adj. wicked, evil, bad, corrupt, immoral, wayward, dissolute, perverse, gross, wanton, base, mean, malevolent, perverted, depraved, degenerate, irreligious, sinful, unrighteous, ungodly, unregenerate.

offensive, shocking, outrageous, scandalous, atrocious, abominable, heinous, repugnant, monstrous, unforgivable.

vb. err, stray, fall, lapse, degenerate, transgress, go off the rails (*inf.*); make wicked, corrupt, demoralize, defile, lead astray.

see also 932, 952

937 innocence

n. innocence, guiltlessness, blamelessness, inculpability, irreproachability, faultlessness, integrity, probity, uprightness, perfection, purity, impeccability; clear conscience, clean hands, clean slate.

adj. innocent, not guilty, above suspicion, in the clear, pure, clean, spotless, unsoiled, untainted, undefiled, blameless, irreproachable, faultless, upright, perfect, impeccable; unoffending, simple, unsophisticated, inexperienced, guileless.

vb. be innocent, have a clear conscience, have nothing to confess.

938 guilt

n. guilt, blame, culpability; responsibility, liability, answerability; criminality, sinfulness; bad conscience, guilty conscience.

crime, offence, transgression, trespass, misdeed, sin, misdemeanour, misconduct, misbehaviour, error, fault, lapse, slip.

adj. guilty, wrong, at fault, offending, to blame, culpable, reproachable; blamed, condemned, judged, incriminated; red-handed, caught in the act.

939 good person

n. good person, good example, model, standard, pattern, ideal, paragon; one in a million, salt of the earth, last word, ultimate; saint, angel, hero, pillar; perfect gentleman; good fellow, good sort, good egg, sport (*sl.*).

see also 905

940 bad person

n. bad person, wrongdoer, evildoer, sinner, transgressor; reprobate; scoundrel, wretch, villain, miscreant, rogue, rascal, blackguard, knave; bully, scallywag, scamp, scapegrace; wastrel, bum (*sl.*), idler, loafer, prodigal, beggar, tramp; ugly customer, nasty piece of work (*inf.*), bad lot, bad egg; good-for-nothing, ne'er-do-well, black sheep; criminal, crook, liar, cheat, traitor, impostor; rat, louse (*sl.*), worm.

941 penitence

n. penitence, repentance, change of heart, confession, contrition; sorrow, regret, remorse; sackcloth and ashes, hair shirt; penitent, convert, prodigal son.

adj. penitent, repentant, confessing, humble, contrite, conscience-stricken, convicted; regretful, sorry, compunctious, apologetic, full of regrets.

vb. repent, confess, acknowledge, plead guilty, humble oneself, own up, admit; feel shame, deplore; be penitent, be sorry, regret, apologize; turn from sin, see the light, be converted.

942 impenitence

n. impenitence, hardness of heart, heart of stone, seared conscience, obduracy; no regrets; hardened sinner.

adj. impenitent, unrepentant, uncontrite; hard, insensitive, callous, stubborn, obdurate, unashamed; incorrigible, irredeemable; dead, lost.

vb. be impenitent, have no regrets, show no remorse; harden one's heart.

943 atonement

n. atonement, satisfaction, amends,

apology, redress, compensation, indemnity, retribution, requital, repayment, restitution, reparation.

propitiation, reconciliation, sacrifice, offering; substitute, representative; scapegoat; expiation; penance; purgatory.

adj. atoning, satisfying, indemnificatory, compensatory; propitiatory, reconciliatory, sacrificial, redemptive; substitutionary, representative, vicarious.

vb. atone, make amends, redress, compensate, indemnify, requite, repay; apologize; propitiate, reconcile, appease, satisfy, redeem.

944 temperance

n. temperance, moderation, abstemiousness, restraint, self-restraint, self-control, self-discipline; self-denial, abstinence, teetotalism; abstainer, total abstainer, teetotaller.

adj. temperate, moderate, restrained, disciplined, careful; self-denying, self-controlled, abstinent; continent; sparing, frugal, plain; abstemious, sober.

vb. be temperate, exercise self-control, control oneself, deny oneself, abstain, refrain; know when to stop, know when one has had enough.

945 intemperance

n. intemperance, excess, extravagance, inordinateness, self-indulgence; sensuality, voluptousness, carnality, flesh; luxury, high living; dissipation, debauchery; hedonism, epicureanism.

adj. intemperate, immoderate, unrestrained, inordinate, excessive, self-indulgent; sensual, sensuous, voluptuous, carnal, bodily, fleshly,

gluttonous, debauched; high-living, pleasure-loving, epicurean, hedonistic.

vb. be intemperate, indulge oneself, have one's fling, sow one's wild oats, paint the town red (*sl.*), not know when to stop, overeat, drink too much.

946 ascetism

n. ascetism, austerity, abstinence, abstemiousness, mortification, plain living.

ascetic, self-denier, recluse, hermit, anchorite, stylite; fakir, dervish, flagellant.

adj. ascetic, austere, plain, severe, rigid, stern, abstemious, puritanical, rigorous.

947 fasting

n. fasting, abstinence, hunger, starvation; fast, bread and water, short commons, diet, slimming; fast-day, Lent, Ramadan.

adj. fasting, abstinent, abstaining, starving, hungry, unfed, famished, Lenten.

vb. fast, eat nothing, go hungry, starve, famish; go on hunger strike; diet, reduce weight, slim, take off weight.

948 gluttony

n. gluttony, greed, voracity, rapacity, unsatiability, intemperance, excess, indulgence.

glutton, pig (*inf.*), guzzler, hog, greedy-guts (*sl.*); gourmand, epicure.

adj. greedy, gluttonous, ravenous, devouring, guzzling.

vb. overeat, stuff oneself, make a pig of oneself (*inf.*), eat like a horse, devour, guzzle, gobble, gulp down, bolt down; eat out of house and home.

949 soberness

n. soberness, sobriety, temperance, abstinence, teetotalism, prohibition.

sober person, abstainer, teetotaller, total abstainer, prohibitionist, Band of Hope, Temperance League.

adj. sober, temperate, abstinent, teetotal, on the wagon (*sl.*), off drink, clear-headed, in one's right mind, in possession of one's senses, unintoxicated, stone-cold sober, dry.

vb. be sober, not drink, sign the pledge; hold one's drink, have a good head for drink; sober up, sleep it off (*inf.*).

950 drunkenness

n. drunkenness, intoxication, inebriety, insobriety, intemperance; alcoholism, dipsomania; a drop too much, tipsiness; drinking-bout, pub-crawl, party, celebration, orgy; pink elephants; hangover, head, headache.

drunkard, drinker, heavy drinker, hard drinker, tippler, boozer, alcoholic, drunk (*sl.*).

adj. drunk, intoxicated, inebriated, under the influence, tipsy, high, lit up (*inf.*); on the bottle; happy, high, lit up (*inf.*); seeing double, glassy-eyed; groggy; the worse for drink, sloshed (*sl.*), tight (*inf.*), stoned (*sl.*), blotto (*sl.*), canned (*sl.*), sozzled (*sl.*), plastered (*sl.*), under the table.

vb. drink, booze, guzzle, tipple, wet one's whistle (*inf.*), hit the bottle, drink like a fish, drown one's sorrows; be merry, be tipsy, have a drop too much, have one over the eight; be drunk, have more than one can hold, see double, get stoned out of one's mind (*sl.*); intoxicate, inebriate, go to one's head.

951 purity

n. purity, cleanness, cleanliness, whiteness; sinlessness, perfection; untaintedness, unsulliedness, spotlessness, immaculateness.

morality, chastity, virtue, decency, abstemiousness, virginity; prudery, primness, prudishness, overmodesty, false modesty, squeamishness; prude, prig, old maid.

adj. pure, clean, perfect, sinless; unsullied, untainted, spotless, undefiled, unadulterated, unc .taminated; decent, demure, abstemious; edifying; chaste, virtuous; continent, celibate, virgin, platonic; prudish, prim, squeamish, shockable, narrow, strict, Victorian, puritanical, strait-laced, old-maidish; simple, innocent, guileless, artless; inexperienced.

see also 931, 935

952 impurity

n. impurity, uncleanness, sinfulness, imperfection, taintedness, sulliedness, contamination, pollution, adulteration.

immorality, unchastity, indecency, looseness of morals, permissive society; lewdness, prurience, profligacy, incontinence, lechery, wantonness, licentiousness, dissoluteness, salaciousness, lasciviousness; lust, sensuality, eroticism; obscenity, filth, dirt, smut, pornography; free love, promiscuity, adultery, wife-swapping (*inf.*), sleeping around (*inf.*), fornication, unfaithfulness, infidelity, affair, relationship, liaison, eternal triangle; seduction, rape, assault, violation, defilement; prostitution, street-walking, harlotry, whoredom; homosexuality, lesbianism, sodomy, incest.

adj. impure, unclean, imperfect, tainted, sullied, contaminated, polluted, adulterated; immoral, unchaste, indecent, loose, slack, of loose morals, easy, fast, wild, promiscuous, of easy virtue, permissive; lewd, profligate, lecherous, licentious, lascivious, wanton, dissolute, salacious, debauched; sensual, erotic; vulgar, coarse, risqué, spicy; obscene, filthy, dirty, smutty, lurid, sexy, pornographic, blue, unprintable, unexpurgated; homosexual, gay (*sl.*), queer (*sl.*), lesbian; extramarital, unlawful, illicit, adulterous, incestuous.

vb. be impure, commit adultery, fornicate, sleep around (*inf.*); seduce, take advantage of (*inf.*), rape, assault, violate; go on the streets, walk the streets, prostitute, adulterate, contaminate; sully, taint, pollute.

see also **932, 936**

953 libertine
n. libertine, profligate, Don Juan, rake, womanizer, lecher, adulterer, seducer, rapist, fornicator; homosexual, homo (*inf.*), queer (*sl.*), gay (*sl.*), fairy (*sl.*), pansy (*inf.*), nancy (*sl.*), butch (*sl.*), transvestite, pervert; lesbian.

adultress, woman of easy virtue, loose woman, flirt, tart (*sl.*), slut, pickup (*inf.*); mistress; prostitute, pro, callgirl, fallen woman, whore, harlot, street-walker, hustler (*sl.*).

954 legality
n. legality, legitimacy, lawfulness, permissibility, validity, constitutionality; legislation, law-giving, lawmaking, authorization, codification, sanction, enactment; right, authority, justice; jurisprudence.

law, statute, decree, ordinance, act, edict, order, code, regulation, rule, bylaw, constitution.

adj. legal, legitimate, lawful, right, just; constitutional; permissible, permitted, valid, sanctioned, codified, authorized, prescribed, within the law, statutory; jurisprudential, nomothetic.

vb. legalize, permit, authorize,

sanction, approve, validate, establish, enforce, pass, license, charter, empower; legislate.

see also **103, 626**

955 illegality
n. illegality, unlawfulness, unconstitutionality, miscarriage of justice, injustice; law-breaking, violation, transgression, trespass, contravention, encroachment, infringement, offence, wrong, crime.

lawlessness, antinomianism, irresponsibility, terrorism, anarchism, mob rule, chaos, disorder, breakdown of law and order.

illegitimacy, bastardy; bastard, illegitimate child, natural child, love child.

adj. illegal, unlawful, illicit, forbidden, prohibited, banned, unauthorized, wrong, against the law, outside the law; stolen, black-market, smuggled, contraband; lawless, wild, chaotic, anarchic, irresponsible; illegitimate, bastard, natural, born out of wedlock, born on the wrong side of the blanket, born without benefit of clergy (*inf.*).

vb. break the law, disobey, commit, violate, transgress, contravene, infringe; take the law into one's own hands, be a law unto oneself; nullify, abrogate, void, annul, cancel.

956 jurisdiction
n. jurisdiction, authority, control, direction, supervision; right, power, responsibility, capacity, competence; executive, corporation, administration; domain, extent, scope, range, territory.

police, police force, constabulary; police officer, policeman, constable, officer, copper (*sl.*), cop (*sl.*), rozzer (*sl.*), fuzz (*sl.*); traffic warden, meter maid.

adj. jurisdictional, judiciary, competent, responsible, judicial, executive.

vb. administer, preside, direct, supervise; judge; police, keep order, control.

957 tribunal

n. tribunal, court, assizes, session, bench, bar; judgment seat, mercy seat, throne; dock, witness-box; courthouse.

958 judge

n. judge, justice, J.P., recorder, magistrate, stipendiary, beak (*sl.*); judiciary; marshal; jury, panel, tribunal; juror, juryman, jurywoman, foreman.

see also 653, 960

959 lawyer

n. lawyer, legal practitioner; the bar, legal profession; defender, counsel, barrister, advocate, bencher; legal adviser, attorney, procurator, solicitor; prosecution; notary, commissioner for oaths; legist, jurist, jurisconsult; pettifogger.

vb. practise law, plead; be called to the bar, take silk; argue, defend, advocate, allege, prosecute.

960 lawsuit

n. lawsuit, case, suit, action, legal proceedings, hearing, indictment; litigation, judicature; summons, writ, subpoena; affidavit, bill; pleadings, argument, prosecution, cross-examination, defence, plea, summing-up; verdict, finding, decision, ruling, pronouncement, sentence, decree, award, precedent; appeal; litigant, party, suitor, plaintiff, defendant.

vb. go to law, prosecute, sue, litigate, bring an action against, bring to trial, file a claim; try, hear, give a hearing to, judge, arbitrate, adjudicate; rest one's case; sum up; rule, find, pronounce, declare, return a verdict, bring in a verdict, pass sentence, sentence, convict, acquit.

961 acquittal

n. acquittal, discharge, reprieve, release, remission, pardon, clearance, dismissal, exoneration, exculpation; innocence; suspended sentence.

adj. acquitted, not guilty, clear, discharged, released, set free, liberated, justified; forgiven.

vb. acquit, declare not guilty, discharge, pardon, absolve, forgive, clear, dismiss, grant remission, reprieve, release, set free, let off (*inf.*), exempt; exonerate, exculpate; justify, vindicate; save, rescue, redeem.

see also 601, 921

962 condemnation

n. condemnation, denunciation, conviction.

adj. condemnatory, damnatory.

vb. condemn, find guilty, sentence, pass sentence on, judge, convict, punish, doom, damn, curse; proscribe, denounce, criticize, find fault with, blame, rebuke.

963 punishment

n. punishment, reproof, discipline, chastisement, correction, reprimand, retribution; penalty, imposition, fine, damages, costs, compensation; exile, banishment; hard labour; bread and water.

corporal punishment, slap, rap, cuff, blow, clout; capital punishment, death sentence, execution, decapitation, beheading, hanging, electrocution, strangling, strangulation, poisoning, crucifixion, impalement, drowning; torture; slaughter, genocide, mass murder, massacre, annihilation.

punisher; executioner, hangman, firing squad; inquisition.

adj. punitive, penal, castigatory, disciplinary, corrective.

vb. punish, reprove, discipline, chastise, correct, sentence, take to task, admonish, rebuke, reprimand, dress down (*inf.*), come down on like a ton of bricks (*inf.*), crack down on (*inf.*); make an example of; retaliate, get one's revenge, get even with.

expel, exile, banish, deport, transport, outlaw, isolate, send to Coventry; imprison, jail; penalize, fine, endorse one's licence.

strike, hit, slap, rap over the knuckles, box on the ears; flog, whip, beat, thrash, scourge, flay; spank, give a good hiding (*inf.*), thrash the living daylights out of (*sl.*), lick (*sl.*), tan (*sl.*), belt, strap, clout, wallop (*sl.*), cane, whack (*inf.*).

kill, put to death, shoot, execute, behead, guillotine, decapitate; hang, lynch; hang, draw, and quarter; crucify, impale; electrocute, gas; strangle; burn at the stake; drown; poison; slaughter, annihilate, massacre; torture, martyr, put on the rack, break on the wheel, tar and feather.

be punished, suffer, pay the penalty, get one's just deserts, have it coming, deserve; face the music, take the rap.

see also **926**

964 means of punishment

n. scourge, birch, whip, lash, belt, cane, rod, stick, switch, cat-o'-nine-tails; pillory, stocks, ducking stool, whipping post; torture chamber, rack, wheel, screw, water torture; axe, guillotine; block, scaffold; cross, stake; gallows, gibbet, noose, rope; electric chair, gas chamber, death chamber; condemned cell.

965 reward

n. reward, pay, payment, compensation, recompense, remuneration, reimbursement, reparation, redress; allowance, expenses, honorarium; tip, gratuity; prize, award, trophy, bonus, premium, bounty, accolade, guerdon.

adj. rewarding, remunerative, compensatory; profitable, advantageous, worthwhile; charitable, liberal, generous, open-handed, unsparing.

vb. reward, pay, recompense, reimburse, redress, compensate; award, recognize, pay tribute, present, give, bestow, confer, grant, thank.

see also **663, 715**

F   Religious

966 divinity

n. divinity, divineness, deity, godhead; God, Spirit, Supreme Being, Creator, prime mover, Providence.

adj. divine, spiritual, godlike, godly; heavenly, celestial, sublime; transcendent, immanent, self-existent; eternal, everlasting, immortal; almighty, omnipotent, all-powerful, infinite, supreme; omniscient, all-knowing; just, merciful, gracious, loving, personal.

967 God

n. God; Trinity; Father, Lord, Yahweh, Jehovah, Almighty, King of Kings; Son of God, Jesus Christ, Son of Man, Immanuel, Word, Messiah, Saviour, Redeemer; Holy Spirit, Holy Ghost, Comforter, Paraclete.

god, goddess, object of worship; idol, false god; golden calf; pantheon; numen; totem, fetish; mumbo-jumbo.

supreme deity, Zeus, Jupiter; goddess of women and marriage, Hera, Juno; goddess of crops, Demeter,

968

Ceres; god of the sun, Phoebus, god of music, medicine, and poetry, Apollo; god of war, Ares, Mars; god of commerce, eloquence, and cunning, Hermes, Mercury; god of the sea, Poseidon, Neptune; god of metalworking, Hephaestus, Vulcan; god of wine and revelry, Dionysus, Bacchus; god of the underworld, Hades, Pluto, Dis; god of agriculture, Kronos, Saturn; god of love, Eros, Cupid; goddess of love and beauty, Aphrodite, Venus; goddess of the moon and hunting, Artemis, Diana; goddess of wisdom, Athena, Minerva; god of the countryside, Pan, Faunus.

Allah; Brahma, Atman, Vishnu, Shiva; Buddha.

968 good spirit

n. good spirit, angel, ministering spirit, seraph, cherub, host, principalities, authorities, powers, thrones, dominions; archangel.

adj. angelic, ministering, heavenly, celestial.

969 evil spirit

n. devil, Satan, fallen angel, father of lies, Beelzebub, prince of this world, prince of darkness; demon, evil spirit, unclean spirit, powers of darkness; imp, fiend, vampire; adversary.

adj. satanic, devilish, diabolic, diabolical, wicked.

see also 984

970 mythical being

n. fairy, spirit, elf, brownie, goblin, hob, bogle, body, kobold, hobgoblin, dryad, pixie, gnome, peri; sprite, genie, jinnee; nymph; wood-nymph, hamadryad; mountain-nymph, oread; water-nymph, naiad; sea-nymph, nereid; siren, mermaid, water-spirit, water-elf, nix, nixie, kelpie; imp, puck,

leprechaun, gremlin, urchin; changeling; sylph; dwarf, troll.

adj. fairy, mythical, imaginary, fabulous; elfin, elfish, impish.

971 ghost

n. ghost, spectre, spook (*inf.*), apparition, vision, phantom, phantasm, appearance, shade, presence, poltergeist, wraith, *doppelgänger*, double, fetch, visitant, spirit, departed spirit, zombie.

adj. ghostly, spooky (*inf.*), supernatural, evil, haunted, eerie, weird, uncanny, phantom.

vb. haunt, visit, walk, return from the dead.

972 heaven

n. heaven, paradise, bliss, glory, kingdom of heaven, Abraham's bosom, heavenly city, next world, world to come, eternal rest, kingdom-come (*sl.*), happy hunting ground, Elysium; rapture, resurrection, translation, ascension, glorification.

adj. heavenly, celestial, blessed, glorious, glorified, empyrean.

973 hell

n. hell, perdition, underworld, lower world, nether regions, bottomless pit, abyss, inferno, everlasting fire, lake of fire and brimstone, place of the lost, place of torment, pandemonium; Sheol, Gehenna.

adj. hellish, infernal.

974 religion

n. religion, belief, faith, dogma, teaching, doctrine, creed, tenet, revelation, articles of faith, confession; theology.

deism, theism, monotheism, polytheism, pantheism; animism; gnosticism.

Christianity, Judaism; Islam,

Buddhism, Hinduism, Brahmanism, Taoism, Confucianism.

teacher; prophet, apostle; preacher, lay-preacher, exponent, interpreter, commentator, evangelist, missionary.

adj. religious, spiritual, divine, holy, sacred; theological, doctrinal; devout, godly, believing, practising, faithful, regenerate, converted.

see also 980

975 irreligion

n. irreligion, ungodliness, godlessness, unholiness, unspirituality, wickedness, sinfulness; idolatry, heathenism, paganism; atheism, unbelief; disbelief, scepticism, doubt, agnosticism; heresy, antichristianity, rationalism, free thinking, materialism.

unbeliever, atheist; agnostic, doubter, sceptic, doubting Thomas; idolater; heathen, pagan; infidel, heretic, dissenter.

adj. irreligious, ungodly, godless, wicked, sinful, idolatrous, heathen, pagan; unbelieving, atheistic; heretical, unorthodox; disbelieving, sceptical, agnostic; materialistic, secular, worldy, profane; unregenerate, unconverted, lost, damned.

see also 981

976 revelation

n. revelation, disclosure; inspiration, afflatus, prophecy, vision; signs, foreshadowing; Scripture, Bible, Word of God, canon; Talmud, Torah, Ten Commandments; Law, Gospel. Koran, Vedas.

adj. revelational, inspirational, inspired, revealed, prophetic, biblical, scriptural, canonical; evangelical; authoritative.

977 orthodoxy

n. orthodoxy, soundness, faithfulness, strictness, truth, adherence, observance.

the Church, body of Christ, Church invisible, Church militant, Church triumphant, Christendom; believer, true believer, Christian, practising Christian, church member, the saints, the faithful.

adj. orthodox, sound, correct, right, pure, true, faithful; evangelical, conservative, strict, literal, fundamentalist; practising, believing.

978 heresy

n. heresy, heterodoxy; divergence, aberration, distortion, perversion, unorthodoxy, unauthenticity, apostasy, infidelity.

adj. heretical, heterodox, divergent, different, unorthodox, unsound, unscriptural, unbiblical.

979 sectarianism

n. sectarianism, partisanship, schismatism, separatism; denominationalism; party-spirit.

sect, schism, split, section, faction, division, branch; denomination, communion, tradition; off-shoot, secession; sectarian, party-man, seceder, dissident, non-conformist, rebel.

adj. sectarian, partisan, schismatic, party-minded; denominational; dissident, non-conformist; separatist, secessionist, break-away; exclusive.

980 piety

n. piety, devoutness; devotion, single-mindedness; trust, faith; loyalty, submission, dedication, commitment, faithfulness, adherence, perseverance, allegiance, zeal, ardour, earnestness; adoration, worship, reverence, fear, awe, prayerfulness; holiness, sanctity, consecration, godliness, saintliness, humility, spirituality.

saint, believer, convert, man of prayer, man of God; follower, disciple, pilgrim; pietist.

adj. pious, devout, devoted, faithful, loyal, dedicated, committed, single-minded, zealous, earnest; believing, practising, holy, godly, saintly, spiritual, sanctified, consecrated, otherworldly, humble, meek.

vb. be pious, repent and believe, have faith, trust, fear God; keep the faith, persevere; worship, pray; sanctify, consecrate, make holy, dedicate, hallow.

981 impiety

n. impiety, godlessness, irreverence, unrighteousness, unholiness, sinfulness, disobedience; worldliness; blasphemy, sacrilege, desecration, defilement, violation.

hypocrisy, sanctimoniousness, false piety, self-righteousness, religiosity, formalism, hallowness, churchianity (*inf.*), religious show, façade, lip service, cant.

sinner, blasphemer; scoffer, mocker; materialist, worldling; hypocrite, Pharisee, scribe.

adj. impious, irreligious, ungodly, godless, irreverent, unholy, unrighteous, sinful, wicked, disobedient; unbelieving, atheistic, agnostic, non-practising; unhallowed, unsanctified, unregenerate, hardened; blasphemous, sacrilegious, profane; sanctimonious, hypocritical, pharasaical, false, deceitful, insincere, dishonest.

vb. be impious, sin, blaspheme; desecrate, profane, pay lip service.

982 worship

n. worship, honour, reverence, praise, adoration, exaltation, homage, veneration; service, devotions; prayer, private devotion, quiet time, meditation; confession; thanksgiving, grace; supplication, request, entreaty, appeal, petition, intercession, rogation; hymn, song, psalm, chant, anthem, canticle, chorus.

worshipper, church-goer, Christian, communicant; supplicant, petitioner, intercessor, man of prayer; congregation, church, flock, assembly.

adj. worshipping, devoted, reverent, religious, devout, prayerful, on one's knees, supplicant; worshipful, reverential, solemn, holy, serious, dignified, sublime, majestic, glorious.

vb. worship, adore, praise, glorify, bless, exalt, honour, magnify, revere, venerate, pay homage to, laud, bow down, humble oneself; idolize; pray to, seek; confess; thank, give thanks, ask, invoke, entreat, petition, implore, intercede, say one's prayers, beseech; sing; meditate, contemplate, consider, reflect.

see also 977

983 idolatry

n. idolatry, idolism, idol worship, irreligion, heathenism, paganism, fetishism, demonism, devil-worship, hero-worship, iconolatry, image-worship, mumbo-jumbo; idolization, deification, apotheosis.

idol, false god, image, graven image, icon, statue, golden calf, totem, fetish.

idolater, idolizer, pagan, heathen, image-maker.

adj. idolatrous, heathen, pagan, idol-worshipping.

vb. idolatrize, idolize, worship, enshrine, deify; sing the praises of, put on a pedestal, admire, dote on, treasure.

984 sorcery

n. sorcery, magic, superstition, witchcraft, diabolism, black magic, occultism, cabbala, exorcism, divination; miracle-working, thaumaturgy; spell, incantation, bewitchment, enchantment, influence, possession, trance, hocus-pocus, mumbo-jumbo, open sesame, abracadabra; charm, amulet, talisman, mascot, fetish, good-luck charm.

spiritism, spiritualism, spirit communication; séance, sitting; ouija board, planchette, automatic writing; levitation.

sorcerer, wizard, witch, enchanter, spell-binder, magician, conjurer; soothsayer, clairvoyant; astrologer; shaman, witch-doctor, medicine-man; voodoo; thaumaturgist, miracle-worker; diviner; exorcist; occultist, necromancer, spiritualist.

adj. sorcerous, devilish, diabolical, occult, necromantic; spell-binding; magical, supernatural, weird, uncanny, eerie; charmed, bewitched, enchanted; mystic, esoteric, transcendental.

vb. divine, conjure; wave a wand; exorcise, lay ghosts; call up spirits; bewitch, enchant, charm, fascinate, mesmerize, obsess, possess, put under a curse; hold a séance; go into a trance; materialize, dematerialize.

see also 447

985 churchdom

n. churchdom, Christendom, the church, ministry; call, vocation; office, holy orders; pastorship, pastorate, priesthood, clerical order, cure of souls, spiritual guidance, pastoral case, service, preaching, administration of the sacraments, prayer; fellowship communion.

adj. ecclesiastical, ministerial, pastoral, cleric, priestly, sacerdotal.

vb. call, ordain, consecrate, present, nominate; take holy orders.

986 clergyman

n. clergyman, servant of God, shepherd; pastor, preacher, minister, incumbent, priest, vicar, parson, rector; curate, chaplain, cleric, padre, father, reverend; abbot, prelate, bishop, archbishop, prior, dean, archdeacon, canon, primate, Pope; metropolitan, patriarch, cardinal; monk, friar; nun, sister; rabbi, teacher.

adj. clerical, ordained.

vb. be ordained, enter the ministry.

987 laity

n. laity, layman, lay people, parish, congregation, church, fold, flock, assembly, church member, parishioner, brethren; elder, deacon; lay-preacher, lay-reader.

adj. lay, unordained, non-clerical, secular, temporal, of the world, civil, profane, unholy, unconsecrated, unsacred.

vb. laicize, secularize, deconsecrate.

988 religious service

n. ceremony, ordinance, rite, ritual, custom, institution, observance; order, form, litany; administration, celebration, officiation.

service, divine worship, service of worship, morning service, matins, evening service, evensong, vespers, compline, fellowship, prayer meeting, Bible Study, Sunday School; Holy Communion, Lord's Supper, mass, Eucharist; baptism.

adj. ritual, ceremonial, customary, formal, liturgical.

vb. observe, keep, celebrate, minister, administer, officate, perform, dedicate, bless, pray, baptize, worship; encourage, share, fellowship.

989   vestment

n. vestment, cloth, clerical dress, canonicals, robes, surplice, gown, mantle, cassock, rochet, chasuble, cape, hood; mitre, staff, crook, crosier.

990   church building

n. church, chapel, sanctuary, house of prayer, house of God, Lord's house, bethel, kirk, tabernacle; mission, house-church, meeting-house; cathedral, minster, abbey; monastery, priory, friary, convent, nunnery; synagogue; mosque, shrine, temple.

Index

The index does not list every word or phrase in the main part of the book. In particular, many words derived from other related words, e.g. adverbs ending in -*ly* derived from adjectives, have been excluded. If you want to look up a word that is not in the index, you should therefore look up the word closest to it, and refer to the categories in the main part of the book, looking at the part of speech of the word you originally wanted. Further, a reference to a particular entry does not necessarily mean that the word looked up will appear at that entry — but since you are interested in other words related to this one, the fact that it does not occur at the entry is of no consequence.

Numbers printed in darker, bold type show the main categories for the particular words. The titles of the categories are also printed in the bolder typeface. For further help on finding the word you want, see the section 'How to use this thesaurus' at the front of the book.

Index

accolade *n.* 663, 965

accommodate *vb.* 105, 302, 545, 652

accommodation *n.* 191

accompaniment *n.* 60, 792

accompany *vb.* 60, 122, 882

accomplice *n.* 640

accomplish *vb.* 159, 609, 659, 661

accomplished *adj.* 581, 627, 659

accomplishment *n.* 609, 659, 661

accord *n.* 24, 643; *vb.* 16, 24, 105, 180

account *n.* (description) 460, 465, 483, 525; (money) 736, 742; *vb.* (describe) 157, 456, 483, 525; (pay) 742

accountable *adj.* 679, 919

accountant *n.* 733, 742

accounts *n.* 742

accretion *n.* 40, 41

accrue *vb.* 36, 40, 705, 716

accumulate *vb.* 36, 40, 94, 567, 705

accurate *adj.* 430, 476, 915

accursed *adj.* 892

accusation *n.* 930

accuse *vb.* 930

accustom *vb.* 105, 545

ache *n.* 828; *vb.* 828

achieve *vb.* 609, 659, 661

achievement *n.* 89, 609, 659, 661

achromatism *n.* 806

acid *n.* 773; *adj.* 773

acknowledge *vb.* 395, 424, 468, 692, 909, 925, 941

acme *n.* 212, 581

acoustics *n.* 778

acquaintance *n.* 882

acquiesce *vb.* 424, 654, 673, 692

acquire *vb.* 472, 705, 716, 720, 726

acquisition *n.* 705, 716, 726

acquisitive *adj.* 705, 750

acquit *vb.* 601, 680, 911, 921, 961

acquit oneself well *vb.* 919, 935

acquittal *n.* 601, 911, 961

acrimonious *adj.* 893, 900

act *n.* 609, 852, 954; *vb.* 172, 529, 609, 621

acting *n.* 529; *adj.* 689

action *n.* 172, 266, 609, 651, 960

activate *vb.* 88, 266, 282

active *adj.* 172, 368, 611

activism *n.* 611

activist *n.* 611; *adj.* 611

activity *n.* 266, 557, 609, 611

actor *n.* 529, 619

actress *n.* 529

actual *adj.* 1, 3, 120, 430

actuary *n.* 742

acumen *n.* 434

acute *adj.* 255, 434

acute angle *n.* 246

adage *n.* 432

Adam *n.* 379

adapt *vb.* 24, 105, 125, 142, 602, 606

adaptable *adj.* 105, 151

adaptation *n.* 456, 545, 792

add *vb.* 36, 40

addendum n. 41

addict *n.* 545

addition *n.* 38, 40, 41, 705

additional *adj.* 6, 40

additive *n.* 307

address *n.* 191, 518, 523, 695; *vb.* 514

addressee *n.* 523, 716

adept *n.* 629; *adj.* 627

adequate *adj.* 570, 579

adhere *vb.* 50

adherent *n.* 474, 640

adhesive *n.* 49; *adj.* 50

ad infinitum adv. 78

adjacent *adj.* 199, 238

adjective *n.* 499

adjoin *vb.* 199, 201

adjournment *n.* 89, 135

adjudicate *vb.* 415, 960

adjudicator *n.* 415, 653

adjunct *n.* 41, 60

adjure *vb.* 468, 695

adjust *vb.* 24, 105, 142, 403, 704

ad lib adj. 544; *vb.* 544

administer *vb.* 621, 622, 956, 988

administration *n.* 622, 667, 956

administrator *n.* 558, 623

admirable *adj.* 579

admire *vb.* 868, 888, 922, 925

admissible *adj.* 302

admission *n.* 98, 300, 302, 420, 462, 468, 716

admit *vb.* 98, 262, 300, 302, 424, 462, 468, 716, 833

admit defeat *vb.* 654

admonish *vb.* 597, 624, 926, 963

adolescent *n.* 131; *adj.* 129, 131

adopt *vb.* 540, 575, 606, 702, 720

adopted *adj.* 40, 100, 171, 606

adoption *n.* 171, 540, 606

adorable *adj.* 827

adore *vb.* 889, 982

adorn *vb.* 509, 844, 846

adroit *adj.* 627

adulation *n.* 927

adult *n.* 133; *adj.* 133

adulterate *vb.* 45, 477, 582, 952

adulterer *n.* 953

adultery *n.* 952

adulthood *n.* 133

adumbrate *vb.* 798

advance *n.* 288, 292, 587, 645, 693, 718, 890; *adj.* 236; *vb.* 288, 292, 587, 645, 661, 718

advanced *adj.* 125

advantage *n.* 34, 550, 575

advantageous *adj.* 550, 575, 577, 661, 965

adventure *n.* 153, 269

adventurer *n.* 270

adventurous *adj.* 605

adverb *n.* 499

adversary *n.* 638, 883, 969

adverse *adj.* 14, 665

adversity *n.* 445, 665

advertisement *n.* 464

advertising *n.* 727

advice *n.* 460, 597, 624, 636

advisable *adj.* 577

advise *vb.* 460, 597, 624, 636

advisor *n.* 473, 624

advisory *adj.* 597, 624

advocate *n.* 959; *vb.* 959

aerate *vb.* 344, 348, 775

aerial *adj.* 273, 318, 348

aerodynamics *n.* 348

aeronautical *adj.* 273, 278

aeronautics *n.* 273

aeroplane *n.* 278

aesthetic *adj.* 848

affable *adj.* 884

affair *n.* 153, 557, 889, 952

affect *vb.* 177, 752, 755

affectation *n.* 510, 852

affected *adj.* 510, 751, 752, 852

affection *n.* 752, 882, 889, 890

affections *n.* 751

affidavit *n.* 401, 468, 960

affiliate *vb.* 11, 52, 639, 641

affinity *n.* 18, 105, 218, 294

affirm *vb.* 401, 413, 424, 468, 514

affirmation *n.* 413, 424, 468, 690

affirmative *n.* 424; *adj.* 468

affix *n.* 499; *vb.* 40, 47

afflict *vb.* 830

affliction *n.* 551, 586, 592, 665, 828

affluence *n.* 664, 734

afford *vb.* 568, 715, 734

affront *n.* 923; *vb.* 887, 923

affronted *adj.* 893

afloat *adj.* 153

aforementioned *adj.* 84

afraid *adj.* 856

after *adj.* 119; *adv.* 85

after-effect *n.* 87, 156

afterlife *n.* 123

aftermath *n.* 87, 156

afternoon *n.* 128

afterthought *n.* 87, 441, 538

afterwards *adv.* 85

again *adv.* 62, 77

age *n.* 109, 130; *vb.* 130

aged *adj.* 130

ageless *adj.* 114, 129

agency *n.* 172, 563, 685

agenda *n.* 83, 441

agent *n.* 149, 155, 564, 619, 689

aggravation *n.* 835

aggregate *n.* 54; *adj.* 54

aggressive *adj.* 173, 175, 645, 651

aggressor *n.* 645

aghast *vb* *adj.* 866

agile *adj.* 280, 611, 627

agitation *n.* 80, 326, 755, 756

agitator *n.* 142, 148

agnostic *n.* 975; *adj.* 409, 975, 981

agnosticism *n.* 409, 421, 975

ago *adv.* 124

agonize *vb.* 830

agonizing *adj.* 828

agony *n.* 756, 828

agrarian *adj.* 378

agree *vb.* 24, 105, 180, 424, 692, 925

agreeable *adj.* 692, 829

agreed *adj.* 24

agreement *n.* 24, 105, 424, 643, 650, 692, 699, 704, 925

agriculture *n.* 378

ahead *adv.* 236, 286

ahead of *adj.* 118

aid *n.* 563, 636, 640, 834, 899; *vb.* 563, 636

ailment *n.* 586

aim *n.* 178, 284, 450, 552; *vb.* 178, 284, 552

aimless *adj.* 158, 399, 451, 553

air *n.* 329, 344, 348, 621, 792; *vb.* 348, 350

air conditioning *n.* 348

aircraft *n.* 278

airing *n.* 348

air in motion *n.* 359

airman *n.* 273

air-pipe *n.* 361

airport *n.* 298
airs *n.* 852
air travel *n.* 273
airy *adj.* 4, 331, 333, 344, 348
ajar *adj.* 262
akin *adj.* 11
alacrity *n.* 611
alarm *n.* 482, 598, 856
alarming *adj.* 594
album *n.* 441
alcoholism *n.* 950
alcove *n.* 254
alert *n.* 597, 598; *adj.* 392, 602, 611; *vb.* 597, 598
algebra *n.* 38
alias *n.* 497
alibi *n.* 549
alien *n.* 100; *adj.* 100
alienate *vb.* 883, 892
alight *adj.* 759; *vb.* 298
alike *adj.* 13, 18
alive *adj.* 368, 611, 753
all *n.* 54; *adj.* 54, 56
Allah *n.* 967
allegation *n.* 401, 930
allege *vb.* 549, 959
alleged *adj.* 448, 549, 825
allegiance *n.* 679, 919, 980
allegory *n.* 397, 455, 525
all-embracing *adj.* 54, 98
allergic *adj.* 862
alleviate *vb.* 176, 652, 834
alley *n.* 559
alliance *n.* 641, 699, 896
allied *adj.* 11, 47, 180, 641
all-inclusive *adj.* 54, 98
allocation *n.* 717
allot *vb.* 55, 717
allotment *n.* 378, 717

allow *vb.* 690, 692, 744, 925
allowance *n.* 31, 690, 715, 717, 718, 738, 744, 965
allow for *vb.* 31, 403
alloy *n.* 45; *vb.* 45
all right *adj.* 579, 585; *adv.* 79
all-round *adj.* 627
allure *vb.* 547, 829, 889
allusion *n.* 455, 459
ally *n.* 640
ally with *vb.* 47
almanac *n.* 116, 483
Almighty *n.* 967
almighty *adj.* 159, 966
almost *adv.* 199
alms *n.* 715, 899
aloft *adv.* 208
alone *adj.* 48, 59
alongside *adv.* 238
aloof *adj.* 198, 517, 754, 757, 885
alphabet *n.* 493
also *adv.* 40
alter *vb.* 142, 146
alternate *vb.* 12, 140, 142, 325
alternative *n.* 149, 540; *adj.* 149
altitude *n.* 208
altogether *adv.* 54, 56
altruistic *adj.* 899, 903
always *adv.* 114
amalgamate *vb.* 45, 52
amass *vb.* 94, 567
amateur *n.* 630; *adj.* 628
amaze *vb.* 866
ambassador *n.* 460, 467, 688, 689
ambience *n.* 8, 229
ambiguity *n.* 409, 412, 451, 453, 454, 503
ambition *n.* 552, 854, 861

ambitious *adj.* 605, 611, 854
ambivalent *adj.* 454
amble *n.* 269; *vb.* 269
ambrosia *n.* 770
ambulate *vb.* 269
ambush *n.* 463, 596; *vb.* 463
amelioration *n.* 587
amenable *adj.* 179, 654
amend *vb.* 589
amendment *n.* 587
amends *n.* 31, 589, 721, 943
amiable *adj.* 886
amicable *adj.* 643, 882
amity *n.* 643, 882
amnesia *n.* 442
amnesty *n.* 911
among *prep.* 230
amorous *adj.* 889
amorphous *adj.* 243
amount *n.* 26, 731, 743; *vb.* 743
amphibian *n.* 373; *adj.* 373
amphitheatre *n.* 658
ample *adj.* 32, 75, 182
amplify *vb.* 36, 196, 481, 505
amplitude *n.* 32, 194, 204, 400
amputate *vb.* 42
amulet *n.* 984
amuse *vb.* 829, 840
amusement *n.* 829, 840
amusing *adj.* 840, 842, 851
anachronism *n.* 117
anachronistic *adj.* 117, 126
anaemic *adj.* 162, 806, 807
analogy *n.* 9, 18, 397
analysis *n.* 38, 48, 53, 394, 396
analyst *n.* 456
analytical *adj.* 38, 456

anarchist n. 148, 167, 672

anarchistic adj. 148, 644, 672

anarchy n. 80, 148, 668

anathema n. 892

anatomy n. 366, 375

ancestor n. 11, 86

anchor n. 330; vb. 152

ancient adj. 124, 126

ancillary n. 640; adj. 35, 60

and adv. 40

anecdote n. 525

anew adv. 77, 125

angel n. 467, 891, 905, 939, **968**

angelic adj. 935, 968

anger n. **893**; vb. 755, 893

angle n. 246, 420; vb. 219, 246

angry adj. 893

anguish n. 551, 828

angular form n. **246**

animal n. 175, 373, adj. 373

animality n. 373

animal sound n. **789**

animate adj. 366; vb. 173, 368, 618, 755, 836

animate matter n. **366**

animism n. 974

animosity n. 425, 883, 900

annals n. 116, 483

annex vb. 40

annexe n. 41

annihilate vb. 164, 370, 963

anniversary n. 140, 878; adj. 878

annotate vb. 456, 482

announce vb. 458, 460, 464

announcement n. 458, 460, 464, 465

announcer n. 460

annoy vb. 830, 835, 887, 893

annoyed adj. 893, 894

annually adv. 140

annulment n. **686**, 898

anoint vb. 342, 365

anonymous adj. 497

answer n. 283, **395**, 402, 468, 523; vb. 395

answerable adj. 179, 679, 737, 919

answer back vb. 395, 880

antagonism n. 181, 637, 883, **892**, 893

antagonist n. 638, 883

antagonistic adj. 637, 883, 892

antecede vb. 118

antecedent n. 86, 118, 155; adj. 84, 118

antedate vb. 117

antediluvian adj. 126

anterior n. 236; adj. 84, 118, 236

anthem n. 982

anthology n. 527

anthropoid n. 379

anthropology n. 375, 379

anticipate vb. 134, 154, 443, 446, 854

anti-climax n. 445

antidote n. 181

antinomianism n. 955

antiquated adj. 126

antique adj. 126

antiquity n. 124, 126

antisocial adj. 885, 904

anxious adj. 828, 856, 894

any adj. 26

anyhow adv. 80

apart adj. 48

apartheid n. 99

apartment n. 191

apathy n. 281, 389, 393, 612, 754, 841, 863

ape n. 20

aperitif n. 306

aperture n. 254, 262

aphasia n. 515

apocalypse n. 462

apolegetics n. 410

apologetic adj. 833, 941

apologize vb. 538, 549, 833, 941, 943

apology n. 549, 833, 943

apostasy n. 147, 538, 590, 978

apostle n. 974

appal vb. 856

appalling adj. 830, 856

apparatus n. 565, 568

apparent adj. 458, 634, 823, 825

apparently adv. 825

apparition n. 4, 458, 971

appeal n. 518, 695, 960; vb. 695, 829

appear vb. 188, 298, 458, 621, **825**

appearance n. 222, 242, 298, 458, 621, **825**

appease vb. 335, 652, 831, 943

append vb. 40, 85

appendage n. 41 60, 87, 89

appendix n. 41

appertain vb. 707

appertaining adj. 9

appetite n. 861

appetizer n. 306

appetizing adj. 306, 767, 770

applause n. 838, 878, 888, 909, 925

appliance n. 565, 568

applicable adj. 9, 105, 575

applicant n. 697

application n. 172, 472, 575, 606, 611, 695

apply vb. 9, 575, 606, 695

appoint vb. 540, 557, 685

appointment n. 557, 685, 884

apportionment n. 717

apposite adj. 9, 577

appraise vb. 384, 400, 415

appreciate vb. 415, 770, 827, 888, 889, **909, 922**

appreciative adj. 909

apprehend vb. 426, 452, 681, 720

apprehensive adj. 326, 443, 856

apprentice n. 474, 619

apprise vb. 597

approach n. 154, 292, 298, 559, 602, 693; vb. 123, 154, 199, 292, 298, 693

approachable adj. 292

appropriate adj. 105, 499, 510, 577, 915; vb. 705, 720

approval n. 424, 690, 692, **925**, 954

approximate vb. 18, 199, 292

approximately adv. 199

apricot n. 816

apt adj. 179, 915

aptitude n. 627

aquarium n. 377

aquatic adj. 347

aquatics n. 271

aqueduct n. 360

arbiter n. 653

arbitrary adj. 10

arbitrate vb. 415, 653, 960

arc n. 247

arcade n. 247, 559, 730

arch n. 247; vb. 247, 252

archaic adj. 126

archaism n. 124, 494

archbishop n. 870, 986

archetype n. 23

architect n. 166, 491, 558

archives n. 483, 567

archivist n. 484

arctic adj. 760

ardent adj. 506, 759, 889

ardour n. 752, 759, 861, 889, 980

arduous adj. 615, 633

area n. 26, 182, 183, 194, 234, 400, 557

arena n. 234, **658**

arguable adj. 929

argue vb. 410, 414, 420, 514, 642, 959

argument n. 25, 387, 410, 525, 642, 893, 960

argumentative adj. 410

arid adj. 350

arise vb. 88, 153, 318, 825

aristocracy n. 870

arithmetic n. 38

arm n. 353; vb. 159, 646

armistice n. 144, 650

armour n. 646, 657

arms n. **657**

army n. 75, 655

aroma n. 776

around adv., prep. 229

arouse vb. 155, 618, 755

arraign vb. 930

arrange vb. 58, 81, 242, 558, 602, 699, 792

arrangement n. 9, 79, **81**, 244, 602, 699, 792, 884

array n. 79, 655; vb. 81, 846

arrears n. 737

arrest n. 635; vb. 89, 144, 635, 681, 681, 755, 930

arrival n. 292, **298**

arrive vb. 153, 298

arrogant adj. 875, 880

arrow n. 290, 482

arsenal n. 657

art n. 486, 488

artful adj. 631

article n. 163, 327, 499

articles n. 192, 729

articulate adj. 512; vb. 512

artifice n. 478, 631

artificial adj. 510, 849, 852

artillery n. 655

artist n. **491**, 793

artistic adj. 510

artlessness n. 508, **632**, 951

asbestos n. 762

ascend vb. 316

ascent n. **316**

ascertained adj. 408

ascetism n. **946**

ascribe vb. 157

ashamed adj. 874

ashen adj. 806, 807

aside n. 460, 520; adv. 567

ask vb. 394, 695

askance adj. 219

askew adj. 219, 245

asleep adj. 267

as long as adv., prep. 111

aspect n. 5, 7, 55, 825

aspersion n. 928

asphalt n. 365

asphyxiate vb. 370

aspirate vb. 512

aspire vb. 552, 604, 854, 861

aspiring adj. 605

ass n. 437

assail vb. 645

assassin n. 370, 906

assassinate vb. 370

assault n. 175, 645, 952; vb. 645, 952

assemblage n. 47, **94**

assemble vb. 47, 58, 94, 242, 568

assembly n. 59, 94, 625, 982, 987

assent n. **424**, 692; vb. 24, 424, 692

assert vb. 450, 468

assert oneself vb. 649

assess vb. 400, 415, 743

assessor n. 415, 653

assets n. 564, 566, 711, 734, 741

asseverate vb. 468

assiduous adj. 390, 392, 535

assign vb. 685, 714, 717

assignable adj. 157

assignment n. 470, 557

assignment of cause n. 157

assimilate vb. 302, 472

assist vb. 636

assistance n. 563, 636, 639

assistant n. 640, 676, 689

assizes n. 957

associate n. 640; vb. 9, 47, 94, 157, 397

associated adj. 60, 157, 639

association n. 52, 60, 397, 641

assorted adj. 45

assuage vb. 176, 652, 834

assume vb. 448, 720, 852

assumption n. 420, 918

assurance n. 408, 420, 854

assure vb. 420, 468, 701, 857

asthmatic adj. 359

astigmatism n. 820

astonish vb. 444, 866

astonishing adj. 444, 579, 866

astrologer n. 447, 984

astrology n. 329, 447

astronaut n. 274

astronomy n. 329

astute adj. 434

asylum n. 595

asymmetry n. 17, 219, 245

atavism n. 147

at hand adj. 123, 188; adv. 199

atheism n. 421, 975

atheist n. 975

athlete n. 270

athletic adj. 161

at home n. 884

atlas n. 329

at last adv. 89

atmosphere n. 8, 229, 329, 348, 488

atoll n. 357

atom n. 33, 195, 327

atomic adj. 195

atomic bomb n. 657

atomize vb. 53, 164, 340

atonal adj. 791

at once adv. 115

atonement n. 31, 652, 911, **943**

atrocious adj. 856, 936

atrocity n. 900

attach vb. 40, 47

attaché n. 688

attached adj. 47, 889

attachment n. 41, 50, 60, 889, 890

attack n. 326, 439, 586, **645**, 651; vb. 645, 648, 651, 928, 930

attacker n. 645, 723

attain vb. 472, 661

attainable adj. 292, 404

attainments n. 426, 472

attempt n. **604**; vb. 552, 604, 615

attend vb. 188, 287, 591, 676

attendant n. 60, 287, 683; adj. 60, 188

attending adj. 60, 676

attend to vb. 593, 795

attention n. 390, 702

attentive adj. 390, 922

attenuate vb. 205, 333

attest vb. 401, 408, 413, 468

attested adj. 408, 430

at the same time adv. 122

attire n. 227

attitude n. 7, 420, 621, 818

attorney n. 959

attract vb. 224, 291, 294, 390, 547, 889

attract attention vb. 755

attraction n. 294, 330, 547

attractive adj. 579, 829, 844, 889

attributable adj. 157

attribute n. 5; vb. 157

atypical adj. 19

auburn adj. 810, 811

auction n. 727; vb. 727

audacious adj. 857, 887

audacity n. 857, 880

audible adj. 452, 778

audience n. 519, 795, 821

audition n. 795

auditorium n. 475, 795

augment vb. 36, 196

augur n. 447; vb. 447

augury n. 447, 597

aunt n. 11

aurora n. 127, 800

auspicious adj. 136, 447, 664, 854

austere adj. 669, 946

austerity n. 169, 669, 743, 946

authentic *adj.* 21, 430

authenticate *vb.* 408, 413, 424

author *n.* 155, 166, 521, 524

authoritarian *n.* 669; *adj.* 669

authoritative *adj.* 177, 408, 667, 671, 976

authority *n.* 177, 436, 629, 667, 675, 685, 690, 956

authorize *vb.* 424, 667, 685, 690, 954

autocrat *n.* 669

autograph *n.* 482; *vb.* 482

automatic *adj.* 125, 411, 531, 544, 565

automaton *n.* 565

automobile *n.* 276

autonomous *adj.* 678

autumn *n.* 128; *adj.* 128

auxiliary *n.* 35, **640**; *adj.* 35, 40, 563, 636, 679

avail *vb.* 570, 575, 720

available *adj.* 188, 404, 464, 575, 705, 727

avalanche *n.* 572, 760

avant-garde n. 125; *adj.* 125

avarice *n.* 750

avenge *vb.* 647, 912

avenger *n.* 912

avenue *n.* 559

aver *vb.* 468

average *n.* 30, 90, 871; *adj.* 30, 90, 101, 666, 871; *vb.* 30, 400

averse *adj.* 533, 637, 862, 892

aviary *n.* 234

aviation *n.* 273

avid *adj.* 750

avoid *vb.* 555, 600, 862, 924

avoidance *n.* 555, 600

avow *vb.* 462

avowal *n.* 420, 468

avuncular *adj.* 11

await *vb.* 443

awake *adj.* 392, 753

award *n.* 663, 715, 960, 965; *vb.* 715, 965

aware *adj.* 426, 753

awash *adj.* 349

away *adj.* 189; *adv.* 198

awe *n.* 856, 866, 922, 980

awful *adj.* 580, 830, 856

awfully *adv.* 32

awkward *adj.* 129, 511, 628, 633, 852

awl *n.* 264

awning *n.* 225, 801

awry *adj.* 219, 245

axe *n.* 964

axiom *n.* 432

axiomatic *adj.* 408

axis *n.* 217

azure *n.* 815; *adj.* 815

B

baa *vb.* 789

babble *vb.* 451, 516

babe *n.* 131, 429, 632

Babel *n.* 492

baby *n.* 131, 163; *adj.* 131

babyish *adj.* 131

baby-sit *vb.* 392

baby-sitter *n.* 683

bachelor *n.* 897

back *n.* 217, 237; *adj.* 237; *vb.* 217, 553, 667, 701, 718

back and forth *adv.* 325

back-bencher *n.* 625

backbiting *n.* 869, 928

backbone *n.* 217, 535, 857

back-breaking *adj.* 615

back down *vb.* 538

backer *n.* 217, 553, 640, 905

backfire *n.* 147; *vb.* 283

background *n.* 8, 198, 229, 237, 456

backhanded *adj.* 454

back-handed compliment *n.* 923

backing *n.* 217, 401, 636

backlash *n.* 147, 156, 283, 647

backlog *n.* 567

back of beyond *n.* 198, 885

back on to *vb.* 237

back out *vb.* 289, 293, 538, 556, 858

backrest *n.* 217

backside *n.* 237

backslide *vb.* 147, 590

backsliding *n.* 147, 538

backstage *n.* 237

back-to-front *adj.* 220

back up *vb.* 217, 636

backward *adj.* 289, 427, 435, 603, 876

backwardness *n.* 135

backwash *n.* 358

backwoods *n.* 885

bad *adj.* 53, 551, 580, 855, 932, 936

badge *n.* 482, 663

badge of office *n.* 677

bad luck *n.* 158, 665

bad-mannered *adj.* 887

badness *n.* 580, 932

bad news *n.* 445

bad person *n.* **940**

bad taste *n.* 511, **849**

bad temper *n.* 893, 894, 895

baffle *vb.* 445, 633

bag *n.* 193, 275, 732

baggage *n.* 711

bail out *vb.* 273, 701

bait *n.* 294, 547

bake *vb.* 306, 350, 759

balance *n.* 28, 31, 44,
152, 244, 330, 400, 731;
vb. 28, 31, 152, 330,
397, 742
balance sheet *n.* 742
bald *adj.* 228
balderdash *n.* 451
balk at *vb.* 533
ball *n.* 249, 884
ballad *n.* 528
ballast *n.* 31, 152, 330
ballerina *n.* 793
ballet *n.* 792
ballistics *n.* 657
balloon *n.* 249, 278
ballot *n.* 540
ballyhoo *n.* 451
balm *n.* 176, 342, 365,
591, 776
balustrade *n.* 234
bamboozle *vb.* 478
ban *n.* 99, 681, 691, 694;
vb. 99, 691
banality *n.* 432, 843
band *n.* 49, 94, 207, 250,
641, 793; *vb.* 47
bandage *n.* 49, 207
bandit *n.* 885
bane *n.* 551, 580, 592
bang *n.* 782; *vb.* 282,
782, 787
banish *vb.* 99, 303, 963
bank *n.* 352, 718, 732
banker *n.* 718, 733
bank on *vb.* 443, 854
bankrupt *adj.* 571, 706,
735, 739; *vb.* 739
banner *n.* 482
banquet *n.* 306, 829,
840; *vb.* 306
banter *vb.* 842, 853
baptism *n.* 302, 988
baptize *vb.* 302, 496,
988
bar *n.* (inn) 191;
(restraint) 681; (tri-
bunal) 957; *vb.* 99,
263, 635; *prep.* 42, 99

barb *n.* 255; *vb.* 255
barbarian *n.* 175
barbarism *n.* 495, 500,
511, 849
barbarous *adj.* 175, 900,
908
barbecue *n.* 306, 840
bard *n.* 528, 793
bare *adj.* 189, 228, 753;
vb. 228
barely *adv.* 33
bargain *n.* 699, 746; *vb.*
699, 725, 726
bargain for *vb.* 443
bargaining *n.* 704, 725
barge *n.* 277
bark *vb.* 789
barman *n.* 676
baron *n.* 870
barrack *n.* 191
barrage *n.* 645
barrel *n.* 249
barren *adj.* 160, 169,
350, 612
barricade *n.* 635; *vb.*
635
barrier *n.* 234, 235, 635,
681
barrister *n.* 959
barrow *n.* 276, 372, 730
barter *n.* 150, 725; *vb.*
150, 725
base *n.* 89, 213, 217;
adj. 869, 924, 936
basement *n.* 213
bash *vb.* 282
bashful *adj.* 876
basic *adj.* 88, 155, 213,
573
basin *n.* 193, 213, 254,
354
basis *n.* 23, 155, 547
basket *n.* 193, 275
bastard *n.* 171, 955
baste *vb.* 306
bastion *n.* 646
batch *n.* 26, 94
bathe *vb.* 271, 349, 583

battle *n.* 649, 651
battleground *n.* 658
battlement *n.* 646
battleship *n.* 277
bawl *vb.* 788, 839
bay *n.* 353; *adj.* 810; *vb.*
789
bazaar *n.* 727, 730
be *vb.* 1, 185, 188, 368
beach *n.* 352
beacon *n.* 467, 482, 598,
800
beaker *n.* 193
be-all and end-all *n.*
573
beam *n.* 217, 797, 838;
vb. 797, 838
beanfeast *n.* 306
bear *vb.* 217, 275, 368,
828
bearer *n.* 275, 467
bearing *n.* 9, 217, 284,
621, 825
bearings *n.* 185
bear in mind *vb.* 384
bear malice *vb.* 893
bear out *vb.* 413, 929
bear upon *vb.* 9
bear witness to *vb.* 401
beast *n.* 175, 373, 906
beastly *adj.* 900
beast of burden *n.* 275
beat *n.* 140, 325, 528;
vb. 140, 282, 325, 340,
661, 783, 963
beat about the bush *vb.*
412, 505
beat off *vb.* 295, 646,
885
beat one's breast *vb.*
837
beat up *vb.* 645
beautiful *adj.* 844
beautify *vb.* 587, 844,
846
beauty *n.* 510, 844
becalm *vb.* 267
beck *n.* 358

beckon *vb.* 482
becloud *vb.* 798, 799
become *vb.* 1, 142, 288
become of *vb.* 156
becoming *n.* 1; *adj.* 848
bed *n.* 206, 213, 360; *vb.* 378
bed and breakfast *n.* 191
bedaub *vb.* 584
bedeck *vb.* 846
Bedlam *n.* 80
bedlamite *n.* 440
bed of roses *n.* 661, 664, 827
bedouin *n.* 270
bedraggled *adj.* 584
bed-ridden *adj.* 586
be drunk *vb.* 950
be dry *vb.* 861
bedsitter *n.* 191
beefy *adj.* 161, 194
bee-line *n.* 248
Beelzebub *n.* 969
beer *n.* 309
be excited *vb.* 756
be excused *vb.* 310
befall *vb.* 153
before *adj.* 118; *adv.* 84, 286
beforehand *adj.* 117
be found *vb.* 1, 185
befriend *vb.* 636, 882
befuddled *adj.* 950
beg *vb.* 695
beget *vb.* 163, 368
begetter *n.* 170
beggar *n.* 697, 735, 940
beggarly *adj.* 881
begin *vb.* 88, 605
begin again *vb.* 88
beginner *n.* 474, 630
beginning *n.* 88, 155
begrudge *vb.* 914
beg the question *vb.* 412
beguile *vb.* 391, 478, 547

beguiler *n.* 480
behave oneself *vb.* 621, 886, 935
behead *vb.* 48, 370, 963
behest *n.* 671
behind *adj.* 135; *adv.* 85, 237
behind bars *adj.* 681
behindhand *adj.* 135
behind someone's back *adj.* 478
behind the scenes *adj.* 461
behind the times *adj.* 126
beholder *n.* 821
behove *vb.* 919
beige *n.* 810; *adj.* 810
being *n.* 1, 5, 327, 368; *adj.* 1
being according to external form *n.* 6
being according to internal form *n.* 5
being around *n.* 229
being between *n.* 230
being exterior *n.* 222
being horizontal *n.* 215
being interior *n.* 223
being oblique *n.* 219
being opposite *n.* 239
being vertical *n.* 214
belated *adj.* 135
belie *vb.* 469
belief *n.* 415, 420, 974
believable *adj.* 420
believe *vb.* 420, 448, 854
believer *n.* 146, 977, 980
believing *adj.* 420, 974, 977, 980
belittle *vb.* 924, 926, 928
bell *n.* 482, 598, 784; *vb.* 789
belle *n.* 844
belligerent *adj.* 651

bellow *vb.* 780, 788, 789
belong *vb.* 9, 58, 60, 202, 707
belonging *adj.* 9, 60
belongings *n.* 60, 568, 711
beloved *n.* 891; *adj.* 889
below *adv.* 209
below average *adj.* 580
below par *adj.* 35
below the belt *adj.* 916
belt *n.* 49, 207, 250, 964; *vb.* 963
bemoan *vb.* 833
bench *n.* 957
bencher *n.* 959
bend *n.* 219, 247; *vb.* 105, 219, 246, 285
bend over *vb.* 319
bend over backwards to help *vb.* 899
beneath *adv.* 209
beneath contempt *adj.* 924
beneath the surface *adj.* 459
benediction *n.* 909
benefactor *n.* 905
beneficial *adj.* 550, 575, 585, 636, 661
beneficiary *n.* 716
beneficient *adj.* 747
benefit *n.* 550, 575, 636, 705, 829, 899; *vb.* 575, 577, 579, 661, 705, 899
benevolence *n.* 636, 747, 899, 907
bent *n.* 178, 545, 751; *adj.* 219, 247, 252
bequeath *vb.* 714
bequest *n.* 714, 715
bereave *vb.* 898
bereavement *n.* 369, 706, 828
bereft *adj.* 706
berry *n.* 306
berserk *adj.* 439
berth *n.* 191, 298

beryl *adj.* 812
beseech *vb.* 695, 982
beset *vb.* 633
besetting *adj.* 545
besetting sin *n.* 592, 936
beside onself *adj.* 756
besides *adv.* 40
besiege *vb.* 645
be situated *vb.* 1, 185
besmirched *adj.* 584
best *adj.* 34, 579
best friend *n.* 882
bestow *vb.* 715, 965
bestseller *n.* 524
best wishes *n.* 888
be subject to *vb.* 179, 679
bet *n.* 553; *vb.* 553
bête noire *n.* 892
be the duty of *vb.* 919
bethel *n.* 990
betoken *vb.* 447, 450, 482
betray *vb.* 458, 462, 478, 932
betrayer *n.* 480
betrothal *n.* 698
betrothed *adj.* 698
better *n.* 34, 553; *adj.* 34; *vb.* 587
better half *n.* 896
betterment *n.* 550, 587
between *prep.* 230
between ourselves *adv.* 466
between the lines *adj.* 459
be up to *vb.* 159
beverage *n.* 309
bewail *vb.* 833
bewilder *vb.* 409, 866
bewitch *vb.* 829, 984
bewitched *adj.* 984
be worth *vb.* 743
beyond compare *adj.* 34, 581
beyond hope *adj.* 855
bi- *adj.* 61

bias *n.* 178, 416, 545, 751, 916; *vb.* 416
biased *adj.* 416, 916
Bible *n.* 524, 976
biblical *adj.* 976
bibliography *n.* 83, 524
bicker *vb.* 642
bicycle *n.* 276
bid *n.* 693, 695; *vb.* 394, 671, 693
bidder *n.* 697
bide one's time *vb.* 443, 610, 612
bifurcate *vb.* 63, 297
big *adj.* 32, 161, 194, 509
bigheaded *adj.* 873
big-hearted *adj.* 747
big-mouthed *adj.* 879
big name *n.* 868
bigot *n.* 537
bigoted *adj.* 416
big-sounding *adj.* 509
big talk *n.* 879
bigwig *n.* 675, 868
bike *n.* 276; *vb.* 269
bilateral *adj.* 61
bilious *adj.* 812, 813
bill *n.* 464, 482, 742, 960
billet *n.* 191
billion *n.* 70
bill of fare *n.* 306
billow *vb.* 358
billy-goat *n.* 380
bin *n.* 193
binary *adj.* 39, 61
bind *vb.* 47, 378, 681, 698, 919
binding *adj.* 919
binoculars *n.* 822
biographer *n.* 484, 524
biology *n.* 366
bipartite *adj.* 61
birch *n.* 964
bird *n.* 373
bird's eye view *n.* 818
bird-watching *n.* 375
birth *n.* 88, 155, 870

birthday *n.* 140, 878
biscuit *n.* 306
bisection *n.* 63
bishop *n.* 870, 986
bit *n.* 33, 55, 59
bit by bit *adv.* 55
bitch *n.* 381
bite *n.* 306, 306, 769; *vb.* 304
bite someone's head off *vb.* 893
biting *adj.* 255, 760, 773
bitter *adj.* 769, 773, 893, 900
bitter-sweet *adj.* 772
bitumen *n.* 365
bizarre *adj.* 139, 433
blabber *vb.* 462
black *n.* 808; *adj.* 798, 808; *vb.* 99
blacken *vb.* 798, 808, 928
blackguard *n.* 940
black hole *n.* 329
blackish *adj.* 808
blacklist *vb.* 99
black magic *n.* 984
blackmail *n.* 902; *vb.* 902
black-market *adj.* 955
black out *vb.* 485, 798
blackout *n.* 463, 466, 779, 798
black sheep *n.* 940
black spot *n.* 596
blame *n.* 926, 930, 938; *vb.* 157, 926, 930, 962
blameless *adj.* 937
blameworthy *adj.* 926
blanch *vb.* 806, 807
bland *adj.* 768, 771
blank *n.* 2; *adj.* 2, 385, 451, 754
blank cheque *n.* 678, 690
blanket *n.* 225; *adj.* 54, 101, 399
blankness *n.* 442, 867

blare *vb.* 780
blasé *adj.* 757
blaspheme *vb.* 901, 981
blast *n.* 359, 780, 782;
 vb. 175, 359
blatant *adj.* 877
blather *n.* 451, 516; *vb.*
 451
blaze *n.* 759, 797; *vb.*
 797
blazon *vb.* 464
bleach *vb.* 806, 807
bleached *adj.* 350
bleak *adj.* 760, 798
bleat *vb.* 789
bleed *vb.* 301, 358, 745
blemish *n.* 582, 660,
 845, **847**; *vb.* 847
blend *n.* 45, 495; *vb.* 52
bless *vb.* 899, 982, 988
blessed *adj.* 972
blessing *n.* 550, 715,
 909
blessings *n.* 664
blight *n.* 53, 167, 592,
 665
blind *n.* 225, 463, 801;
 adj. 754, 819; *vb.* 797
blinded *adj.* 819
blindfold *adj.* 819; *vb.*
 819
blindness *n.* **819**
blind spot *n.* 819
blink *vb.* 797, 818
blinker *vb.* 801, 819
blinkers *n.* 801
bliss *n.* 827, 972
blithe *adj.* 827
blitz *n.* 645; *vb.* 164
blizzard *n.* 175, 359,
 760
bloat *vb.* 196
bloated *adj.* 252
block *n.* 490, 681, 964;
 vb. 263, 265, 635
blockade *n.* 99, 681; *vb.*
 234, 265, 645
blockage *n.* 263, 635

blockhead *n.* 429, 437,
 630
blonde *adj.* 807
blood *n.* 11, 870
blood relationship *n.*
 11
bloodshed *n.* 370, 649
bloom *n.* 374
bloomer *n.* 431
blossom *n.* 374; *vb.*
 163, 168, 664
blot *n.* 584, 845, 847,
 869; *vb.* 584, 847, 869
blotch *n.* 847
blot out *vb.* 164, 485,
 911
blow *n.* 282, 444, 609,
 828, 900, 963; *vb.* 359,
 749
blowout *n.* 48, 306
blow up *vb.* 196, 359,
 782, 893
blubber *n.* 306, 365; *vb.*
 839
blue *n.* **815**; *adj.* 815,
 837, 901, 952
blue blood *n.* 870
blue-eyed boy *n.* 891
blueprint *n.* 23, 558
blues *n.* 792, 837
bluff *vb.* 549
blunder *n.* 431, 500; *vb.*
 431
blunt *adj.* 256, 476, 508;
 vb. 162, 256, 754
bluntness *n.* **256**
blur *n.* 847; *vb.* 799
blurb *n.* 464
blurred *adj.* 243, 503,
 799, 803, 824
blurt out *vb.* 462, 544
blush *n.* 811; *vb.* 811,
 876
bluster *n.* 879
blustery *adj.* 359
board *n.* 217, 305, 625,
 688
boarder *n.* 190

boast *n.* 879; *vb.* 873,
 875, 879
boaster *n.* 873, 879
boastful *adj.* 481, 509,
 875, 879
boasting *n.* 879
boat *n.* 193, 277
bode *vb.* 447, 450
bode well *vb.* 854
bodiless *adj.* 4, 328
bodily *adj.* 327, 827,
 945
body *n.* 3, 327, 368, 371
body-building *adj.* 585
bodyguard *n.* 593, 683
body odour *n.* 777
boffin *n.* 396, 448
bog *n.* 355
bogie *n.* 217
bogus *adj.* 477
boil *n.* 252; *vb.* 175,
 306, 363, 759, 893
boil down *vb.* 203, 527
boiler *n.* 763
boil over *vb.* 756
boisterous *adj.* 175,
 756, 780
bold *adj.* 458, 506, 534,
 644, 854, 857
boldness *n.* 534, 857,
 880
bolshie *adj.* 642
bolster *vb.* 217, 636
bolt *n.* 49, 613; *vb.* 47,
 263, 304
bolt down *vb.* 948
bomb *n.* 657; *vb.* 280,
 613, 645
bombard *vb.* 164, 645
bombast *n.* 509, 879
bombastic *adj.* 481, 877
bomber *n.* 278
bombshell *n.* 444
bonanza *n.* 75, 572
bond *n.* 49, 681, 701
bondage *n.* 679
bone *n.* 337
bone to pick *n.* 893

bonus *n.* 41, 965

boo *vb.* 788, 853, 926

booby prize *n.* 663

booby-trap *n.* 596

book *n.* 464, 524; *vb.* 83

bookishness *n.* 426

bookkeeping *n.* 742

booklet *n.* 464, 524

bookmaker *n.* 553

bookworm *n.* 428, 474, 524

boom *n.* 168, 217, 664, 780, 782, 784; *vb.* 780, 782, 784

boomerang *n.* 147, 283

boon *n.* 550

boorish *adj.* 887

boost *vb.* 36, 196, 318, 857

booster *n.* 173

booth *n.* 730

booty *n.* 663, 724

booze *vb.* 950

boozer *n.* 950

border *n.* 232, 233, 235; *vb.* 199, 201, 233, 236

bore *n.* 204, 437; *vb.* 254, 264, 617, 841

boredom *n.* 841

borer *n.* 264

boring *adj.* 77, 841, 843

borough *n.* 183

borrow *vb.* 719

borrowed *adj.* 100, 495

borrower *n.* 737

borrowing *n.* 495, 719

boss *n.* 34, 675

botany *n.* 366, 374, 376

botch *vb.* 628

both *adj.* 61

bother *n.* 326; *vb.* 578, 695, 830, 856, 893

bothered *adj.* 856

bothersome *adj.* 633, 830

bottle *n.* 193; *vb.* 234, 599

bottleneck *n.* 205, 635

bottle up *vb.* 681

bottom *n.* 89, 210, 213, 237; *adj.* 213, 237

bottomless *adj.* 210

bough *n.* 374

bounce *n.* 173, 283, 326, 336; *vb.* 283, 320, 326, 336, 879

bouncer *n.* 303

bound *n.* 320; *vb.* 231, 235

boundary *n.* 89, 231, 232, 233, 235

boundless *adj.* 78, 202

bounteous *adj.* 168, 747

bounty *n.* 168, 572, 715, 747, 965

bouquet *n.* 776, 888, 925

bourgeois *adj.* 871

bout *n.* 586

boutique *n.* 730

bow *n.* 247, 319, 922; *vb.* 247, 319, 654, 673, 922

bow down *vb.* 982

bowl *n.* 193, 250, 254

bowl over *vb.* 444

box *n.* 193, 225; *vb.* 282, 963

boy *n.* 131, 380

boycott *n.* 99, 691; *vb.* 99, 144, 555, 691

boy-friend *n.* 882, 889

brace *n.* 217; *vb.* 161, 217

bracing *adj.* 585, 618

brag *vb.* 879

braid *n.* 49

brain *n.* 382, 428

brain-child *n.* 163

brainwash *vb.* 470, 547

braise *vb.* 306

brake *n.* 281; *vb.* 281

bramble *n.* 255

branch *n.* 55, 97, 358, 374, 620, 979; *vb.* 297

brand *n.* 97, 800, 869; *vb.* 482

brand-new *adj.* 125

brash *adj.* 859, 887

brass *n.* 794, 880; *adj.* 816

brat *n.* 131

brave *adj.* 857; *vb.* 644, 857

brawler *n.* 672

brawn *n.* 161

brawny *adj.* 161

bray *vb.* 789

brazen it out *vb.* 880

breach *n.* 703; *vb.* 703

bread *n.* 306

breadth *n.* 26, 204, 400

break *n.* 92, 200, 262, 614, 616; *vb.* 48, 92, 144, 164, 338, 703, 920

breakable *adj.* 338

break-away *adj.* 979

break down *vb.* 53, 588, 662, 839, 856

breakdown *n.* 48, 53, 586, 662

breaker *n.* 167, 358

breakfast *n.* 306

break in *vb.* 300

break in on *vb.* 137

breakneck *adj.* 859

break off *vb.* 89

break out *vb.* 88, 175, 600

break the law *vb.* 916, 955

breakthrough *n.* 661

break up *vb.* 53, 144, 588, 642

breakwater *n.* 217

break with *vb.* 556

breath *n.* 4, 359, 368, 512, 781

breathe *vb.* 359, 368

breather *n.* 92, 612, 614, 616

breathing space *n.* 144, 182

breathless *adj.* 369

breed *n.* 11, 97; *vb.* 163, 377, 470

breeding *n.* 377, 886

breeze *n.* 359

breezy *adj.* 348, 836

brevity *n.* 195, 203, 504

brewing *adj.* 154

bribe *vb.* 547

brickbat *n.* 926

bride *n.* 896

bridge *n.* 49; *vb.* 47

bridle *vb.* 681

brief *n.* 483; *adj.* 113, 203, 432, 504, 527

briefcase *n.* 193

briefing *n.* 460

brier *n.* 255

bright *adj.* 434, 759, 797, 805

brighten *vb.* 797, 836

brighten up *vb.* 840, 846

brilliant *adj.* 434, 581, 797, 805, 844

brim *n.* 233

brine *n.* 351

bring *vb.* 294

bring about *vb.* 155, 172, 609

bring back *vb.* 441

bring out *vb.* 464, 522

bring round *vb.* 420, 618

bring together *vb.* 94, 201, 652

bring to mind *vb.* 441

bring up *vb.* 303, 470

brink *n.* 233

brisk *adj.* 173, 280, 760

bristly *adj.* 258

brittleness *n.* 162, 338

broach *vb.* 605

broad *adj.* 101, 182, 204

broadcast *n.* 460, 464; *vb.* 95, 378, 460, 464, 465

broadcaster *n.* 460

broaden *vb.* 36, 101, 204

broad-minded *adj.* 288

brochure *n.* 464

broil *vb.* 306

broke *adj.* 735

broken *adj.* 833

broken down *adj.* 576

broken-hearted *adj.* 837

broken in *adj.* 602

broker *n.* 688

bronze *adj.* 810, 816

brood *n.* 94; *vb.* 384, 837

brook *n.* 358; *vb.* 757

broth *n.* 306

brother *n.* 11, 987

brotherhood *n.* 11, 639, 641

brow *n.* 212

brown *n.* 810; *adj.* 810

browned off *adj.* 832

browse *vb.* 472

bruise *n.* 588; *vb.* 282

bruised *adj.* 753

brunt *n.* 282

brush *n.* 649; *vb.* 201, 211, 341, 583, 649

brush aside *vb.* 393, 542

brush up *vb.* 472

brusque *adj.* 517, 887

brutal *adj.* 175, 900, 908

brute *n.* 175, 906

brutishness *n.* 900

bubble *n.* 249, 363; *vb.* 363

bubbling over *adj.* 827

bucket *n.* 193

buckle *n.* 245, 247

buckle down *vb.* 615

bud *n.* 374

Buddha *n.* 967

Buddhism *n.* 974

budding *adj.* 125, 129, 134

buddy *n.* 882

budget *n.* 447, 742; *vb.* 742

buff *adj.* 810, 813

buffet *n.* 191, 306; *vb.* 359

buffoon *n.* 437, 842

buffoonery *n.* 433

bug *n.* 586; *vb.* 795

buggy *n.* 276

build *vb.* 36, 163, 242

builder *n.* 166

building *n.* 163

building society *n.* 718

build up *vb.* 36, 161

built-in *adj.* 55

bulb *n.* 252, 374, 800

bulbous *adj.* 252

bulge *n.* 252; *vb.* 56, 252

bulk *n.* 32, 75, 204, 330, 567

bulkiness *n.* 194

bull *n.* 380, 671

bulldog *n.* 535

bullet *n.* 290

bulletin *n.* 465, 483

bulletproof *adj.* 593

bull's eye *n.* 224

bully *n.* 175, 940; *vb.* 902

bump *n.* 141, 252, 282, 326, 785; *vb.* 282, 785

bunch *n.* 94

bundle *n.* 94, 567; *vb.* 567

bung *n.* 265; *vb.* 265

bungalow *n.* 191

bungle *vb.* 431, 628

bungler *n.* 630

bunion *n.* 252

bunk *n.* 451

bunker *n.* 193

bunting *n.* 482, 846

buoy *n.* 331

buoyant *adj.* 331, 336

burden *n.* 387, 665, 828, 919; *vb.* 330, 635

burdensome *adj.* 330, 633

bureau, *n.* 620

bureaucracy *n.* 667

bureaucrat *n.* 623

bureaucratic *adj.* 622, 667

burglar *n.* 723

burglary *n.* 722

burial *n.* 372

buried *adj.* 210, 372, 461

burlesque *n.* 487, 842, 853

burly *adj.* 161

burn *n.* 828; *vb.* 759, 761, 797, 828, 893

burning *n.* 370, 761; *adj.* 752, 759, 811

burnish *vb.* 257, 341, 797

burr *vb.* 512

burrow *n.* 254

bursar *n.* 733

burst *n.* 48, 280, 613; *vb.* 48, 338, 782

burst forth *vb.* 88

burst into flames *vb.* 759

burst into tears *vb.* 839

burst out *vb.* 600

bury *vb.* 311, 372, 461, 472

bus *n.* 276

bush *n.* 374

business *p.* 557, 605, 725

businesslike *adj.* 79, 557

businessman *n.* 728

bust *n.* 489; *adj.* 739

bustle *n.* 611; *vb.* 611, 613

busy *adj.* 557, 611

busy-body *n.* 388

butcher *n.* 370; *vb.* 370

butler *n.* 676

butt *n.* 853; *vb.* 282

butter *n.* 306

buttercup *n.* 813

butterfingers *n.* 630; *adj.* 628

butterflies *n.* 326, 856

butter up *vb.* 927

buttress *n.* 217

buy *vb.* 547, 705, 726

buyer *n.* 710, 726, 737

buzz *n.* 783, 786; *vb.* 783, 784, 786, 789

by accident *adv.* 158

by chance *adv.* 158

bygone *adj.* 124

by-law *n.* 954

by-pass *n.* 322, 559, 561; *vb.* 322

by-product *n.* 87, 156

bystander *n.* 821

by the way *adv.* 10

C

cab *n.* 276

cabal *n.* 461, 558

cabaret *n.* 529

cabinet *n.* 625, 688

cable *n.* 49, 207, 460, 467; *vb.* 460

cackle *n.* 783, 838; *vb.* 783, 789

cacophony *n.* 787, 791

cad *n.* 849

cadge *vb.* 719

cadger *n.* 697

café *n.* 191

cage *n.* 234, 682

cajole *vb.* 478, 547, 927

cajoler *n.* 927

cake *n.* 306

calamity *n.* 153, 551, 665

calculate *vb.* 38, 400, 552

calculation *n.* 38, 400

calculator *n.* 38, 400

calculus *n.* 38

calendar *n.* 116

calibrate *vb.* 27, 400

calibre *n.* 204, 400

call *n.* 788, 789, 884; *vb.* 482, 496, 788

call away *vb.* 391

call by *vb.* 884

caller *n.* 884

call for *vb.* 562

call forth *vb.* 155, 547

call-girl *n.* 953

calligraphy *n.* 521

call in *vb.* 731

calling *n.* 557

call of duty *n.* 919

call on *vb.* 695

callous *adj.* 754, 900, 942

callow *adj.* 129

call up *vb.* 94, 441, 651

call upon *vb.* 394, 919

calm *n.* 267; *adj.* 176, 616, 681, 757; *vb.* 652, 779

calm down *vb.* 757

calque *n.* 495

calumny *n.* 869, 928

camber *n.* 247

cameo *n.* 489

camera *n.* 822

cameraman *n.* 491

camouflage *n.* 18, 461, 463; *vb.* 146, 461, 646

camp *n.* 191; *vb.* 186

campaign *n.* 605, 621, 651; *vb.* 649

campus *n.* 658

can *n.* 193; *vb.* 404, 599

canal *n.* 261, 360

cancel *vb.* 485, 686, 955

cancel out *vb.* 181, 402

cancer *n.* 167, 252, 592

candid *adj.* 476, 632, 931

candidate *n.* 395, 638, 697, 854

candle *n.* 800

candour *n.* 476
cane *n.* 964; *vb.* 963
canister *n.* 193
cannon *n.* 657
canoe *n.* 277
canoeing *n.* 271
canon *n.* 420, 626, 671, 976, 986
canonical *adj.* 976
canonicals *n.* 989
canopy *n.* 225, 801
cant *n.* 495, 981
cantankerous *adj.* 894
canteen *n.* 191
canticle *n.* 982
canvas *n.* 488
canvass *vb.* 394, 464, 695
canvasser *n.* 394, 697
canyon *n.* 254
cap *n.* 212; *vb.* 34, 212
capable *adj.* 159, 404, 627
capacious *adj.* 182, 194
capacity *n.* 26, 159, 194
cape *n.* 989
capillary *adj.* 207
capital *n.* 493, 711, 731; *adj.* 34, 212, 579
capitalist *n.* 728, 734
capitalize *vb.* 136, 606, 705
capital punishment *n.* 963
capitulate *vb.* 654
caprice *n.* 449, 539
capricious *adj.* 141, 151, 449, 539
capsize *vb.* 220, 317
capsule *n.* 193, 279, 591
captain *n.* 272, 675
captivate *vb.* 420, 547, 829, 889
captivation *n.* 755
captive *n.* 676, 684, 701
capture *n.* 663, 720, 724; *vb.* 705, 720
car *n.* 276

caravan *n.* 291
carcass *n.* 371
card *n.* 482
cardinal *n.* 986; *adj.* 34
cardinal point *n.* 284
care *n.* (carefulness) 392, 860; (worry) 828, 830; *vb.* 593, 676, 889
career *n.* 557
carefree *adj.* 831, 836
careful *adj.* 392, 398, 748, 860
careless *adj.* 391, 393, 703, 749, 859, 920
caress *vb.* 758, 890
caretaker *n.* 683
cargo *n.* 192
caricature *n.* 20, 22, 487, 853; *vb.* 20, 487, 853
carnage *n.* 370, 649
carnal *adj.* 827, 945
carnival *n.* 529, 840
carnivore *n.* 373
carouse *vb.* 840
carpet *n.* 225
carrel *n.* 475
carriage *n.* 217, 268, 276, 621
carried away *adj.* 827
carrier *n.* 275, 460, 467
carrot *n.* 547, 816
carry *vb.* 217, 268, 275
carry on *vb.* 91, 145, 535
carry out *vb.* 609, 659, 702
cart *n.* 276; *vb.* 268
carte blanche *n.* 678, 690
cartel *n.* 641, 681
cartilage *n.* 337
carton *n.* 193
cartoon *n.* 488
cartoonist *n.* 491
carve *vb.* 48, 163, 242, 489, 490
carver *n.* 491

cascade *n.* 358; *vb.* 358
case *n.* 7, 193, 401, 499, 930, 960
cash *n.* 731
cash-book *n.* 742
cash box *n.* 732
cashier *n.* 733, 742
cash in on *vb.* 136, 606, 705
cash register *n.* 732
casserole *vb.* 306
cassette-recorder *n.* 484, 794
cassock *n.* 989
cast *n.* 22, 94, 489, 529; *vb.* 242, 489
castaway *n.* 885
cast down *vb.* 321, 837
caste *n.* 97
castle *n.* 191, 595, 646
castles in the air *n.* 449
cast lots *vb.* 447
cast off *vb.* 228, 271, 556
castoffs *n.* 44
castrate *vb.* 160, 169
casual *n.* 655; *adj.* 139, 158, 393, 409
casuistry *n.* 631
catacomb *n.* 372
catalogue *n.* 83, 483; *vb.* 83, 483
catalyst *n.* 142, 173
cataract *n.* 358, 820
catastrophe *n.* 153, 551, 665, 900
catastrophic *adj.* 148, 551, 665
catch *n.* 635; *vb.* 478, 720, 795
catch-all *n.* 54; *adj.* 54
catch in the act *vb.* 419, 444, 938
catch on *vb.* 452, 545, 850
catch sight of *vb.* 818
catch up *vb.* 280
catchy *adj.* 790

catechism *n.* 420, 470

categorize *vb.* 97

category *n.* 97

catenary *n.* 247

cater *vb.* 568

catering *n.* 306, 568

cathedral *n.* 990

catholic *adj.* 101

cattle *n.* 373

cattleherd *n.* 377

catty *adj.* 900

cauldron *n.* 193

causal *adj.* 155

causation *n.* 155

cause *n.* 155, 547, 605; *vb.* 155, 547

caustic *adj.* 773, 900

caution *n.* 392, 597, 624, **860**; *vb.* 597

cautionary *adj.* 597

cautious *adj.* 681, 856, 860

cavalry *n.* 655

cave *n.* 254, 317, 353

caveat *n.* 597

cave in *vb.* 254

cavity *n.* 319

caw *vb.* 787, 789

cease *vb.* 89, 144, 267, 826

ceasefire *n.* 144

ceaseless *adj.* 145

ceiling *n.* 225, 235

celebrate *vb.* 838, 878, 888, 988

celebrated *adj.* 868

celebration *n.* 838, **878**

celebrity *n.* 868

celestial *adj.* 329, 966, 968, 972

celestial body *n.* 329

celibacy *n.* **897**

celibate *n.* 897; *adj.* 169, 897, 951

cell *n.* 234, 366, 682

cement *n.* 49; *vb.* 47

cemetery *n.* 372

cenotaph *n.* 372, 483

censor *vb.* 466

censorious *adj.* 926

censorship *n.* 681, 779

censure *n.* 466, 926, 930; *vb.* 926, 930

census *n.* 38

centenary *n.* 70, 109, 878

central *adj.* 5, 90, 223, **224**

centrality *n.* **224**

centralize *vb.* 224

centre *n.* 90, 96, 183, 560; *adj.* 90, 224; *vb.* 96, 224

centrifugal *adj.* 297

century *n.* 70

ceramics *n.* 489

ceramist *n.* 491

cereal *n.* 306, 374

ceremonial *adj.* 878, 988

ceremony *n.* 878, 896, 988

certain *adj.* **408**, 413, 420, 531, 534

certainly *adv.* 408, 531

certainty *n.* **408**, 420, 531, 534

certificate *n.* 483, 690

certified *adj.* 408

certify *vb.* 408, 690

cessation *n.* 89, **144**, 267

chafe *vb.* 341

chain *n.* 49, 85, 635, 681; *vb.* 635, 681

chalet *n.* 191

chalky *adj.* 807

challenge *n.* 394, 644, 649; *vb.* 394, 425, 644, 649

challenger *n.* 638

chamber *n.* 210

champ *vb.* 304

champagne *n.* 309

champion *n.* 579, 646, 661, 905; *adj.* 661

chance *n.* 158, 406, **553**; *adj.* 139, 553; *vb.* 158, 553

chance upon *vb.* 158

chancy *adj.* 409

change *n.* **142**, 731; *vb.* 15, 142

changeable *adj.* 15, 142, 151, 536, 539

changeableness *n.* 151

change of mind *n.* 538

change over *vb.* 714

channel *n.* 261, 262, 360, 564; *vb.* 261

chant *n.* 982; *vb.* 788, 792

chaos *n.* 80, 243, 668, 955

chap *n.* 380

chapel *n.* 990

chaperon *vb.* 392

chaplain *n.* 986

character *n.* 5, 58, 493, 529, 751, 868, 931

characteristic *n.* 102; *adj.* 5, 102, 486

characterize *vb.* 525

charcoal *n.* 765

charge *n.* 557, 622, 626, 645, 671, 685, 743, 930; *vb.* 159, 645, 671, 685, 736, 743, 930

charismatic *adj.* 294

charitable *adj.* 715, 747, 899, 965

charity *n.* 636, 715, 747, 899, 907

charlatan *n.* 480, 852

charm *n.* 547, 829, 844, 889, 984; *vb.* 547, 829, 889, 984

charming *adj.* 547, 829, 844, 889

chart *n.* 460, 486, 558

charter *n.* 690, 699; *vb.* 690, 718, 719, 954

charwoman *n.* 676

chary *adj.* 750

chase *n.* 554; *vb.* 287, 490, 554, 882, 890

chaser *n.* 554

chasm *n.* 200, 254, 317

chassis *n.* 217

chaste *adj.* 876, 935, 951

chastened *adj.* 874

chastise *vb.* 963

chat *n.* 516, 519; *vb.* 514, 516, 519

chatter *n.* 516, 519; *vb.* 326, 388, 516, 760

chatterbox *n.* 388, 516

chatty *adj.* 460, 516

chauffeur *n.* 676

chauvinist *n.* 903; *adj.* 379

cheap *adj.* 746

cheapen *vb.* 746, 924

cheapness *n.* 746

cheat *n.* 480, 631, 940; *vb.* 478, 631, 722, 916, 932

cheater *n.* 723

check *n.* 396, 635, 648, 681; *vb.* 37, 144, 394, 396, 408, 413, 635, 681

checker *vb.* 817

checklist *n.* 83

cheeky *adj.* 880, 887

cheer *n.* 827; *vb.* 618, 788, 834, 836, 840, 925

cheerfulness *n.* 836, 854

cheerless *adj.* 837, 895

cheers *n.* 838, 878

cheese *n.* 306

cheesed off *adj.* 832

cheese-paring *n.* 750

cheque *n.* 731

chequer *vb.* 817

cherish *vb.* 441, 712, 889, 890

cherub *n.* 968

chest *n.* 193

chestnut *n.* 842; *adj.* 810

chew *vb.* 304

chicanery *n.* 631

chicken *adj.* 858

chicken out *vb.* 858

chide *vb.* 926

chief *n.* 34, 675; *adj.* 34, 573

child *n.* 11, 131, 171

childhood *n.* 129

childish *adj.* 129, 131, 435

childless *adj.* 169

childlike *adj.* 129, 131, 632

chill *n.* 760; *vb.* 762

chilly *adj.* 760, 883

chime *n.* 784; *vb.* 783, 784

chimney *n.* 361

chink *n.* 200, 797

chip *n.* 33, 55, 482; *vb.* 48, 377

chip in *vb.* 738

chip on one's shoulder *n.* 832

chirp *vb.* 789

chirpy *adj.* 836

chirrup *vb.* 789

chisel *n.* 312, 480; *vb.* 163, 312, 478, 489, 490

chit *n.* 523

chit-chat *n.* 465, 516, 519

chivalry *n.* 857, 886

chocolate *adj.* 810

choice *n.* 398, 530, 540; *adj.* 579, 770

choiceless *adj.* 541

choir *n.* 793

choke *vb.* 265, 370, 572, 762

choleric *adj.* 894

choose *vb.* 398, 530, 532, 540, 861

choosy *adj.* 398, 540, 864

chop *vb.* 48, 319

chop and change *vb.* 151

choppy *adj.* 258

choral *adj.* 792

chord *n.* 247

chorister *n.* 793

chortle *vb.* 838

chorus *n.* 528, 792, 793, 982

christen *vb.* 496

Christendom *n.* 977, 985

Christian *n.* 977, 982

Christianity *n.* 974

chromatic *adj.* 805

chronicle *n.* 116, 483; *vb.* 483

chronicler *n.* 484

chronological *adj.* 116

chronometer *n.* 116

chronometry *n.* 116

chuck *vb.* 290, 556

chuckle *n.* 783, 838; *vb.* 783, 789, 838

chum *n.* 882

chunky *adj.* 203, 204

church *n.* 977, 982, 985, 987, 990

church building *n.* 990

churchdom *n.* 985

church-goer *n.* 982

church member *n.* 977, 987

churchyard *n.* 372

churlish *adj.* 895

cigar *n.* 308

cigarette *n.* 308

cinema *n.* 529, 840

cipher *n.* 39, 466

circle *n.* 94, 247, 250, 323; *vb.* 229, 322, 323

circuit *n.* 140, 232, 250, 269, 322, 323, 561

circular *n.* 464, 523; *adj.* 250

circulate *vb.* 322, 323, 460

circulation *n.* 322

circumambulate *vb.* 231, 322

circumference *n.* 232, 250

circumlocution *n.* 505

circumscription *n.* **231**

circumspect *adj.* 392, 434, 860

circumstance *n.* **8**, 153

circumstances *n.* 8, 229

circumstantial *adj.* 8

circumvent *vb.* 231, 555

circus *n.* 250, 559, 658

cistern *n.* 193

citadel *n.* 646

citation *n.* 663, 925

citizen *n.* 190, 871

city *n.* 183

city-dweller *n.* 190

civic *adj.* 379

civil *adj.* 379, 886, 987

civilian *n.* 871

civility *n.* 886

civilization *n.* 379

civilized *adj.* 379

clad *adj.* 227

claim *n.* 671, 737; *vb.* 549, 671, 917

claimant *n.* 697

clairvoyant *n.* 447, 984

clamber *vb.* 316

clammer *n.* 175

clamorous *adj.* 695, 780, 788

clamour *n.* 780, 788; *vb.* 695, 788

clamp *vb.* 47

clamp down on *vb.* 669

clan *n.* 11

clandestine *adj.* 461

clang *n.* 783; *vb.* 783, 784, 787

clanger *n.* 431

clanging *n.* 784; *adj.* 784, 787

clap *vb.* 282, 838, 878, 925

clarify *vb.* 456

clarity *n.* 452, 502, 823

clash *n.* 175, 282; *vb.*

14, 282, 642, 787, 791, 805, 883

clasp *n.* 49, 712; *vb.* 50, 712, 720, 758, 890

class *n.* 7, 55, **97**, 122, 206, 470, 472, 474; *vb.* 97

classified *adj.* 81, 466

classify *vb.* 81, 83, 97, 496

classroom *n.* 475

clatter *vb.* 783, 787

clause *n.* 498

clean *adj.* 46, **583**, 937, 951; *vb.* 341, **583**, 775, 807

cleaner *n.* 676

cleanliness *n.* 583, 585, 951

cleanness *n.* 583, 951

cleanse *vb.* 583

cleanser *n.* 775

clear *adj.* 46, 413, 452, 458, 502, 512, 678, 797, 802, 823, 921; *vb.* 320, 583, 921, 961

clearance *n.* 182, 200, 690, 727

clear-cut *adj.* 452, 823

clear-headed *adj.* 949

clearmindedness *n.* 438

cleavage *n.* 48

cleave *vb.* 48, 50

cleft *n.* 200, 259

clemency *n.* 670, 907

clergyman *n.* **986**

cleric *n.* 986; *adj.* 985

clerical *adj.* 986

clerical dress *n.* 989

clerk *n.* 484

clever *adj.* 426, **434**, 627, 631

cliché *n.* 495, 498

click *vb.* 24, 452, 782

client *n.* 545, 716, 726

cliff *n.* 214

climate *n.* 8, 229, 348

climax *n.* 89, 212

climb *vb.* 273, 316

climb down *vb.* 538

clinch *n.* 712; *vb.* 47, 50, 408, 712

clincher *n.* 414

cling *vb.* 50, 712

clip *vb.* 203

clipper *n.* 277

clippings *n.* 44

clique *n.* 94, 641

cloak *n.* 461, 463, 549; *vb.* 461

clock *n.* 116

clog *vb.* 265

cloister *n.* 885

clonk *n.* 785; *vb.* 785

close *n.* 89, 184, 559; *adj.* 47, 50, 154, 199, 419, 759, 882; *vb.* 144, 263, 461

closed book *n.* 427, 453

closed shop *n.* 99, 681

close-fisted *adj.* 750

close friend *n.* 882

close in on *vb.* 292

close-lipped *adj.* 517

close shave *n.* 600

closure *n.* 89, 144, 263

clot *vb.* 332

cloth *n.* 989

clothe *vb.* 227

clothes *n.* 227

cloud *n.* 363, 803; *vb.* 461, 799, 803

cloudburst *n.* 175, 358

cloudless *adj.* 664, 797

cloudy *adj.* 358, 363, 503, 799, 803, 824

clout *n.* 963; *vb.* 282, 963

clown *n.* 842

clowning *n.* 433

cloy *vb.* 56, 865

club *n.* 96, 191; *vb.* 282, 639

cluck *vb.* 787, 789

clue *n.* 401, 447, 482

clumsy *adj.* 511, 628

cluster *n.* 94

clutch *vb.* 712, 758

clutter *n.* 80

coach *n.* 276, 473; *vb.* 470

coagulate *vb.* 332, 334

coagulated *adj.* 362

coal *n.* 367, 765, 800

coalesce *vb.* 13, 52

coalition *n.* 641

coarse *adj.* 258, 511, 849, 887, 952

coastline *n.* 352

coat *n.* 206, 225; *vb.* 225, 342, 805

coating *n.* 206, 225

coat of arms *n.* 482

coax *vb.* 547, 695

cock *n.* 380

cocktail *n.* 309

cock-up *n.* 628

cocky *adj.* 875

coddle *vb.* 306

code *n.* 103, 466, 954

codification *n.* 954

coerce *vb.* 175, 674

coexist *vb.* 60, 122

coextensive *adj.* 28, 218

coffee *n.* 309; *adj.* 810

coffee-bar *n.* 191

coffee-break *n.* 616

coffer *n.* 193, 732

coffin *n.* 372

cog *vb.* 259

cogitation *n.* 384, 410

cognition *n.* 426

cognitive *adj.* 382

cognizability *n.* 452

cognizant *adj.* 426

cohabit *vb.* 889

cohabitant *n.* 889

cohere *vb.* 50

coherence *n.* 50, 337

cohesive *adj.* 50

coil *n.* 251; *vb.* 249

coin *vb.* 449, 731

coinage *n.* 495

coincide *vb.* 13, 24, 28, 60, 122

coincidence *n.* 24, 60, 105, 122, 553

coincidental *adj.* 60, 158

coke *n.* 765

cold *n.* 760; *adj.* 754, 760, 806, 863

cold-blooded *adj.* 754, 908

cold feet *n.* 856, 858

cold shoulder *n.* 924; *vb.* 885

cold war *n.* 650

coliseum *n.* 658

collaborate *vb.* 180, 639

collaborator *n.* 640

collage *n.* 488

collapse *n.* 164, 588, 617, 662; *vb.* 254, 588, 617

collate *vb.* 397

collateral *n.* 701; *adj.* 11

colleague *n.* 640

collect *vb.* 94, 567, 705, 716

collective *n.* 709; *adj.* 24

collectively *adv.* 60

college *n.* 475

collide *vb.* 282

collision course *n.* 296

colloid *n.* 362; *adj.* 362

colloquial *adj.* 495

colloquialism *n.* 494, 495

colonist *n.* 190

colonize *vb.* 191

colony *n.* 94

coloration *n.* 805

colossal *adj.* 32

colour *n.* 509, 805, 811; *vb.* 403, 509, 805

colour-blind *adj.* 819, 820

colourful *adj.* 805

colourlessness *n.* 806, 843

colours *n.* 482

column *n.* 91, 208, 217

coma *n.* 754

combat *n.* 651; *vb.* 637, 649

combatant *n.* 655

combination *n.* 45, 52

combine *vb.* 45, 47, 52, 639

combustible *n.* 765; *adj.* 761, 765

combustion *n.* 761

come *vb.* 298

come about *vb.* 153, 430

come across *vb.* 186, 419

come after *vb.* 85, 119, 287

comeback *n.* 147, 395, 589

come back to *vb.* 395

come before *vb.* 84, 118

come by *vb.* 716

come clean *vb.* 462

comedian *n.* 842

come down *vb.* 273, 317

come-down *n.* 874

come down on *vb.* 669, 963

comedy *n.* 529

come first *vb.* 286

come forward *vb.* 292, 693

come home *vb.* 298, 755

come in *vb.* 300, 716

come into *vb.* 705

come into conflict with *vb.* 25

come into sight *vb.* 292, 823

come into view *vb.* 823, 825

comely *adj.* 844

compel *vb.* 177, 531, 562, 674, 755

compelling *adj.* 674, 755

compendious *adj.* 54, 527

compendium *n.* 527

compensation *n.* 31, 721, 738, 917, 965

compensatory *adj.* 31, 721, 943, 965

compete *vb.* 649

competence *n.* 159, 627, 956

competent *adj.* 159, 579, 627, 956

competition *n.* 649

competitive *adj.* 649

competitor *n.* 638, 854

compile *vb.* 58

complacency *n.* 831

complain *vb.* 642, 788, 832, **926**, 930

complainer *n.* 832

complaint *n.* 586, 696, 926, 930

complement *n.* 28, 60

complete *adj.* 54, **56**, 581, 659; *vb.* 581, 609, **659**, 661

completely *adv.* 54, 56

completeness *n.* 54, **56**

completion *n.* 89, 581, **659**, 661

complex circularity *n.* 251

complexion *n.* 805

complexity *n.* 503

compliance *n.* 532, 673, 692, 702

compliant *adj.* 532, 654, 919

complicate *vb.* 835

complicated *adj.* 453, 503, 633

compliment *n.* 886, 888, 925, 927; *vb.* 886, 888, 925

comply *vb.* 105, 570, 654, 673, 702

component *n.* 55, 192, 327

compose *vb.* 58, 81, 163, 521, 528, 792

composed *adj.* 757

composer *n.* 166, 491, 528, 793

composite *adj.* 45

composition *n.* 45, **58**, 81, 339, 488, 521, 522, 526, 528, 792

compositor *n.* 522

composure *n.* 757

compound *n.* 45, 184; *vb.* 36, 52

comprehend *vb.* 58, 98, 452

comprehensible *adj.* 452

comprehension *n.* 410, 452

comprehensive *adj.* 54, 56, 98, 101

compress *vb.* 37, **197**, 205, 332, 504

compressed *adj.* 332, 504

compressor *n.* 197

comprise *vb.* 58, 98

compromise *n.* 30, 699, **704**; *vb.* 704

compulsion *n.* 439, 531, 562, **674**

compulsive *adj.* 674

compulsory *adj.* 531, 674, 919

compunction *n.* 833

compunctious *adj.* 941

compute *vb.* 38, 400

computer *n.* 38, 400, 565

comrade *n.* 640, 882

con *n.* 631, 684; *vb.* 631

concatenation *n.* 47, 85

concavity *n.* **254**

conceal *vb.* 225, **461**, 466

concealment *n.* **461**, 824

concede *vb.* 424, 462, 690, 692

conceited *adj.* 873, 875

conceivable *adj.* 404

conceive *vb.* 88, 163, 368, 382, 449

concentrate *vb.* 96, 296, 334, **384**, **390**

concentration *n.* 296, 332, **384**, **390**, 611

concept *n.* 386

conception *n.* 382, 386, 420

concern *n.* 387, 392, 557, 605, 620; *vb.* 9, 526, 609, 856

concerned *adj.* 388, 392

concerning *adv., prep.* 9

concert *n.* 180, 643, 790, 792, 840

concerto *n.* 792

concession *n.* 690, 704, 744

conciliation *n.* 650, 652

concise *adj.* 203, 432, **504**, 527

conciseness *n.* 504

conclude *vb.* 56, 89, 410, 530

conclusion *n.* 89, 144, 235, 410, 659

conclusive *adj.* 408, 413, 430, 659

concoct *vb.* 163, 477, 558, 930

concomitant *n.* 60; *adj.* 60

concord *n.* 24, **643**, 790

concordance *n.* 494, 524

concordat *n.* 699

concrete *adj.* 3, 327, 332

concur *vb.* 24, **180**, 424, 692

concurrence *n.* 24, **180**, 296, 692

concurrent *adj.* 24, 60, 122, 180, 296

condemn *vb.* 892, 926, **962**

condemnation *n.* **962**

condemned *adj.* 938

condemned cell *n.* 964

condensation *n.* 346

condense *vb.* 203, 332, 345, 504, 527

condescend *vb.* 869, 874, 886

condiment *n.* **307**

condition *n.* 7, 562, 825; *vb.* 470, 545

conditional *adj.* 403, 700

conditioning *n.* 470, 545

conditions *n.* 8, **700**

condolence *n.* 907

conduce *vb.* 155

conducive *adj.* 178, 563

conduct *n.* 172, 606, **621**, 622; *vb.* 268, 606, 609, **621**, 622

conduit *n.* 360

confectionery *n.* 306

confederate *n.* 640; *adj.* 641; *vb.* 47

confederation *n.* 641

confer *vb.* 159, 519, 715, 965

conference *n.* 94, 519, 625

confess *vb.* 420, 462, 941, 982

confession *n.* 420, 941, 974, 982

confidant *n.* 624, 882

confide *vb.* 462, 624

confidence *n.* 408, 420, 443, 466, 854

confident *adj.* 420, 443, 854, 857

confidential *adj.* 466

confine *vb.* 205, 234, 681, 712

confirm *vb.* 401, 408, 413, **468**, 699, 929

confiscate *vb.* 720

conflict *n.* 649; *vb.* 637, 642, 805, 883

confluence *n.* 221, 296

conform *vb.* 16, 24, **105**, 702

conformist *n.* 20, 105

conformity *n.* 16, **105**, 244, 643

confound *vb.* 82, 399, 414, 869

confront *vb.* 239, 637, 644, 649

confrontation *n.* 637, 649

confuse *vb.* 82, 187, 399

confused *adj.* 80, 399, 439

confusedly *adv.* 80

confusion *n.* 80, 326

confuted *adj.* 414

congeal *vb.* 332, 334, 762

congelation *n.* 760

congenial *adj.* 827

congenital *adj.* 5

congestion *n.* 332, 572

conglomerate *n.* 332

conglomeration *n.* 45

congratulate *vb.* 838, 878, **888**

congratulate oneself *vb.* 879

congratulation *n.* 838, **888**

congregate *vb.* 50, 94

congregation *n.* 94, 982, 987

congress *n.* 94, 519, 625, 641

congressman *n.* 625

congruity *n.* 16, 24, 105

conjecture *n.* 386, 396, 447, **448**; *vb.* 448

conjugal *adj.* 896

conjugate *vb.* 499

conjunction *n.* 499

conjunctivitis *n.* 820

conjure *vb.* 449, 984

conjurer *n.* 984

con man *n.* 480, 631, 906

connect *vb.* 47, 81

connected *adj.* 9, 47, 52, 60, 81

connection *n.* 9, 47, 49, 201

connoisseur *n.* 304, 436, 848

connotation *n.* 450, 459

conquer *vb.* 316, 661, 679

conqueror *n.* 661

conscience *n.* 382, 919

conscience-stricken *adj.* 833, 941

conscientiousness *n.* 392, 864, 931

conscious *adj.* 382, 426, 753

conscript *n.* 655; *vb.* 651

conscription *n.* 674

consecrate *vb.* 980, 985

consecration *n.* 715, 980

consecutive *adj.* 85, 91

consensus *n.* 24, 424, 643

consent *n.* 424, 690, **692**, 698; *vb.* 690, 692, 698

consequence *n.* 60, 85, 87, 156, 573

consequent *adj.* 85, 156

consequential *adj.* 119, 156, 573

conservation *n.* 374, 392, 599

215

conservatism *n.* 143

conservative *n.* 105, 143; *adj.* 143, 977

conserve *n.* 306; *vb.* 599, 748

consider *vb.* 384, 390, 415, 420, 526, 982

considerable *adj.* 32, 75, 573

considerate *adj.* 390, 392, 434, 886

consideration *n.* 384, 390, 392, 415, 886

consign *vb.* 268, 714

consignee *n.* 688

consignment *n.* 268

consist *vb.* 1, 58, 98

consistency *n.* 50, 105, 143

consistent *adj.* 16, 24, 105

consolation *n.* 176, 834, 907

consolation prize *n.* 663

console *vb.* 176, 834, 907

consolidate *vb.* 52, 334

consolidation *n.* 332

consonance *n.* 24, 643, 790

consonant *n.* 493, 512; *adj.* 24, 105

conspicuous *adj.* 253, 458, 462, 823, 877

conspiracy *n.* 558

conspire *vb.* 558

conspirer *n.* 558

constable *n.* 956

constancy *n.* 16, 91, 114, 140, 143, 152, 535

constant *n.* 152; *adj.* 91, 140, 143, 145, 152, 535

constellation *n.* 329

consternation *n.* 856

constituency *n.* 183, 540

constituent *n.* 55, 192; *adj.* 55, 73

constitute *vb.* 58, 98

constitution *n.* 5, 58, 339, 954

constitutional *n.* 269; *adj.* 954

constrain *vb.* 531, 674

constraint *n.* 674, 681

constrict *vb.* 197

construct *vb.* 58, 163, 242, 477, 930

construction *n.* 163, 242, 494

constructor *n.* 166

consul *n.* 688

consult *vb.* 624

consultant *n.* 624

consultative *adj.* 624

consultation *n.* 519

consume *vb.* 304, 569, 575, 740, 761

consumer *n.* 304, 726

consummate *adj.* 89, 581; *vb.* 56, 581, 659, 896

consummation *n.* 89, 156, 212, 581, 896

consumption *n.* 569

contact *n.* 47, 201, 758; *vb.* 201

contagious *adj.* 586

contain *vb.* 98, 234, 707, 712

container *n.* 193, 275

contaminate *vb.* 584, 588, 952

contemplate *vb.* 384, 415, 552

contemplative *adj.* 384, 434

contemporaneous *adj.* 120, 122

contemporary *n.* 122; *adj.* 60, 120, 122, 125

contempt *n.* 853, 869, 924

contemptible *adj.* 580, 869, 924

contemptuous *adj.* 853, 924

contend *vb.* 414, 615, 649, 651

contender *n.* 655

content *n.* 450, 831; *adj.* 831

contented *adj.* 827, 831

contentious *adj.* 409, 651

contents *n.* 192, 223

contest *n.* 649; *vb.* 604, 649

contestant *n.* 638; *adj.* 649

context *n.* 8

contiguity *n.* 199, 201

continent *n.* 352; *adj.* 944, 951

contingencies *n.* 700

contingent *adj.* 8, 403, 679, 700

contingent duration *n.* 111

continual *adj.* 114, 138, 143, 145

continuance *n.* 91, 107, 145, 535

continue *vb.* 91, 107, 112, 138, 145, 535

continuity *n.* 50, 91, 143

continuous *adj.* 91, 257

contort *vb.* 245, 251

contour *n.* 232, 242

contraband *n.* 724; *adj.* 955

contraception *n.* 169

contract *n.* 24, 468, 698, 699, 919; *vb.* 197, 203, 205 557, 698, 699

contraction *n.* 197, 205, 504

contractual *adj.* 699

contradict *vb.* 14, 25,

181, 402, 414, 425, 469, 637

contradiction n. 14, 181, 239, 412, 414, 469, 637

contraption n. 565

contrary n. 239; adj. 14, 15, 239, 402, 469, 883

contrast n. 106, 239, 397; vb. 14, 397, 805

contravene vb. 469, 703, 955

contribute vb. 40, 155, 639, 715, 738

contribution n. 41, 917

contributor n. 715, 905

contributory adj. 563

contrite adj. 833, 941

contrivance n. 565

contrive vb. 477, 631

control n. 159, 177, 235, 622, 667, 681, 707, 956; vb. 177, 622, 667, 681, 707, 956

controller n. 623

control oneself vb. 681, 757, 944

controversial adj. 409, 410

conurbation n. 183

convalescence n. 589, 618

convene vb. 94

convenience n. 575, 827

convenient adj. 136, 575, 577, 748

convent n. 990

convention n. 94, 103, 519, 545, 625, 699

conventional adj. 103, 143, 545, 699, 843

converge vb. 47, 94, 96, 224, 296

convergence n. 224, 296

conversation n. 410, 519

converse n. 239; vb. 410, 514, 519

conversely adv. 14

conversion n. 142, 146, 606, 714

convert n. 146, 941, 980; vb. 142, 146, 606, 714

convexity n. 252

convey vb. 268, 275, 450, 460, 714, 715

conveyance n. 268, 276

conveyancing n. 714

convict n. 684; vb. 681, 960, 962

convicted adj. 941

conviction n. 408, 420, 530, 534, 962

convince vb. 177, 420, 470

convincing adj. 547

convivial adj. 827

conviviality n. 884

convocation n. 94, 625

convolution n. 251

convoy vb. 268

convulsion n. 326, 586

coo vb. 789

cook n. 306, 759

cooker n. 763

cookery n. 306

cook up vb. 163

cool adj. 391, 579, 754, 757, 760, 883; vb. 348, 762

cooling apparatus n. 764

cooling-off period n. 135

coolness n. 391, 757, 837, 883

cooperate vb. 52, 180, 636, 639, 709

cooperation n. 60, 180, 639, 709

cooperative n. 641, 709; adj. 180, 639, 641, 709

co-opt vb. 540

coordinate vb. 81, 81

coordinated adj. 81

co-ownership n. 709

cop n. 956

copious adj. 32, 168

copper n. 956; adj. 810, 816

copse n. 374

copulate vb. 889

copy n. 20, 22, 62, 77, 486, 488, 521, 522, 524; vb. 20, 62, 77, 165, 488, 521

copyist n. 521

coral n. 816; adj. 811

cord n. 49, 207

cordial adj. 884

cordiality n. 747, 882, 884

core n. 5, 90, 224, 527

cork n. 265, 331; vb. 265

corn n. 252, 374

corner n. 184, 233, 246, 254; vb. 707

corner-stone n. 217

cornucopia n. 168, 572

corona n. 250, 800

coronation n. 685

corporality n. 3, 327

corporal punishment n. 963

corporation n. 956

corpse n. 371

corpulent adj. 194

correct adj. 430, 499, 510, 915, 977; vb. 587, 589, 963

correction n. 587, 963

corrective adj. 585, 589, 591, 963

correlate n. 22; vb. 12

correlation n. 9, 12, 18

correspond vb. 12, 24, 150, 218, 523

correspondence n. 9,

217

12, 18, 24, 105, 397, 521, 523

correspondent *n.* 395, 460, 523

corroborate *vb.* 217, 401, 408

corroborative *adj.* 401

corrode *vb.* 588

corrosion *n.* 53

corrugate *vb.* 260, 261

corrupt *adj.* 431, 477, 869, 932, 936; *vb.* 547, 580, 584, 588, 936

corruption *n.* 495, 551, 588, 932, 936

cosmetic *adj.* 211, 846

cosmetics *n.* 844

cosmic *adj.* 329

cosmology *n.* 329

cosmonaut *n.* 274

cosmopolitan *n.* 903; *adj.* 101

cosmos *n.* 329

cost *n.* 743; *vb.* 743

costly *adj.* 745

costs *n.* 31, 740, 963

costume *n.* 227

cosy *adj.* 827

cottage *n.* 191

cough *n.* 359; *vb.* 359

cough up *vb.* 738

council *n.* 94, 519, 625, 641

councillor *n.* 625

counsel *n.* 597, 624, 959; *vb.* 470, 519, 597, 624

counsellor *n.* 473, 624

count *n.* 38, 870; *vb.* 38, 400

countable *adj.* 38

count against *vb.* 588

countdown *n.* 274

countenance *n.* 236, 825

counter *n.* 482; *adj.* 181; *vb.* 637, 647

counteract *vb.* 31, 181, 648, 686

counteraction *n.* 181

counterattack *n.* 647

counterbalance *n.* 31, 152; *vb.* 31, 181, 330

counter-evidence *n.* 402

counterfeit *n.* 20, 487; *adj.* 20, 431, 477; *vb.* 20, 477

counterfoil *n.* 482

countermand *n.* 686, 691; *vb.* 686

countermeasure *n.* 181

counterpart *n.* 18, 20, 22, 28

counterpoise *vb.* 330

counter-productive *adj.* 576

counterweight *n.* 152, 181, 330

countless *adj.* 75, 78

count on *vb.* 443

country *n.* 183

countryman *n.* 871

county *n.* 183

coup n. 148

coup de grâce n. 659

coupé *n.* 276

couple *n.* 61; *vb.* 47, 61

couplet *n.* 61

coupling *n.* 47, 49

courage *n.* 857

courier *n.* 460, 467

course *n.* 269, 306, 358, 360, 470, 559

course of action *n.* 558

course of time *n.* 110

court *n.* 234, 559, 658, 870, 957; *vb.* 882, 890

court danger *vb.* 859

courteous *adj.* 392, 886, 922

courtesy *n.* 886, 899

courtship *n.* 890

cousin *n.* 11

cove *n.* 353

covenant *n.* 698, 699, 701; *vb.* 698, 699

cover *n.* 193, 225, 306, 463, 595; *vb.* 206, 225, 461, 646, 798, 801

cover for *vb.* 149

covering *n.* 211, 222, 225, 461, 801

covert *n.* 254, 374, 463, 595

covet *vb.* 861, 914

covetous *adj.* 750, 861, 914

covetousness *n.* 750, 861, 914

cow *n.* 381

coward *n.* 162, 858

cowardice *n.* 858

cowardly *adj.* 858

co-worker *n.* 640

coy *adj.* 876

crack *n.* 200; *vb.* 264, 456, 782

crack down on *vb.* 669, 963

cracker *n.* 306

crackle *n.* 782

crack up *vb.* 439, 856, 925

cradle *n.* 325

craft *n.* 277, 557, 631

craftsman *n.* 619

crafty *adj.* 478, 631, 932

cram *vb.* 56, 470, 472

crank *n.* 106, 440

cranky *adj.* 439

crash *n.* 282, 739, 782; *vb.* 282, 739, 780, 782, 787

crash-land *vb.* 273, 317, 321

crass *adj.* 849

crate *n.* 193

crater *n.* 254

crave *vb.* 695, 861, 914

craven *adj.* 858

craving *n.* 861

crawl *vb.* 281, 881

crawl with *vb.* 75
crayon *vb.* 488
craze *n.* 125, 439, 539, 850, 861
crazy *adj.* 433, 435, 439, 861, 889
creak *vb.* 781, 787
cream *n.* 306, 342, 365, 579, 813; *adj.* 807, 813; *vb.* 342
creamy *adj.* 362, 365
crease *n.* 260; *vb.* 260
create *vb.* 155, 163, 242, 449, 558
creation *n.* 21, 163, 329, 366
creative *adj.* 21, 163, 449
creator *n.* 155, 166, 491, 966
creature *n.* 366, 368, 373, 379
crèche *n.* 475
credence *n.* 420
credible *adj.* 404, 406, 420
credit *n.* 420, 718, 731, 736, 868, 909, 925; *vb.* 736, 742
creditable *adj.* 925
credit card *n.* 718, 731, 736
creditor *n.* 718, 736
credulous *adj.* 422
creed *n.* 420, 974
creek *n.* 354, 358
creep *vb.* 316, 461
cremate *vb.* 372, 761
cremation *n.* 372
crematorium *n.* 372, 763
crescent *n.* 247, 559; *adj.* 36, 247
crest *n.* 212, 358, 482, 872
crestfallen *adj.* 837, 874
cretin *n.* 437, 440
crevasse *n.* 254

crew *n.* 94, 272
crib *n.* 22; *vb.* 20
crier *n.* 467
crime *n.* 938, 955
criminal *n.* 684, 906, 940; *adj.* 932
criminality *n.* 932, 938
crimp *n.* 260; *vb.* 251, 260
crimson *adj.* 811
cringe *vb.* 856
cringing *adj.* 881
cripple *vb.* 245, 588
crisis *n.* 80, 136, 665
crisp *adj.* 760; *vb.* 306
crispy *adj.* 338
criterion *n.* 23, 27, 103, 400
critic *n.* 456, 524, 526, 848, 928
critical *adj.* 136, 382, 398, 415, 573, 594, 926
criticism *n.* 456, 624, 926
criticize *vb.* 696, 832, 893, 926, 962
critique *n.* 398, 456, 526
croak *vb.* 787, 789
crocodile *n.* 91
crocus *n.* 813
croft *n.* 378
crook *n.* 247, 480, 723, 906, 940, 989; *vb.* 247
crooked *adj.* 29, 219, 245
crop *n.* 374, 567, 705; *vb.* 203
crop up *vb.* 153, 825
cross *n.* 221, 592, 830, 964; *adj.* 893, 895; *vb.* 45, 221, 313, 478
cross-examination *n.* 394, 960
cross-eyed *adj.* 820
crossing *n.* 221, 313
cross purposes *n.* 642
crotchety *adj.* 539
crouch *vb.* 209, 319

crow *vb.* 789
crowd *n.* 75, 94, 821, 871; *vb.* 75, 94
crown *n.* 212, 250, 659, 663, 677; *vb.* 212, 685, 868, 878
crucial *adj.* 136, 573
crucifix *n.* 221
crucifixion *n.* 370, 828, 963
crucify *vb.* 830, 963
crude *adj.* 511, 887
cruel *adj.* 669, 900, 908
cruise *n.* 271; *vb.* 269, 271
crumb *n.* 33, 340
crumble *vb.* 162, 164, 338, 340, 588
crumple *vb.* 258
crunch *vb.* 340
crush *n.* 94, 889; *vb.* 164, 340, 364, 414, 661, 874
crushed *adj.* 837, 874
crushing *n.* 874
crustacean *n.* 373
crutch *n.* 217
crux *n.* 221
cry *n.* 597, 782, 788, 789, 839; *vb.* 788, 789, 833, 839
cry-baby *n.* 162, 858
cry out for *vb.* 531, 562
cry over *vb.* 833
cryptic *adj.* 466
crystal *adj.* 802
crystal-clear *adj.* 458
crystallize *vb.* 332, 334
cry wolf *vb.* 478, 598
cube *n.* 246
cuckoo *vb.* 789
cuddle *vb.* 890
cudgel *vb.* 282
cuff *n.* 963
cuisine *n.* 306
cul de sac *n.* 635
culinary *adj.* 306
cull *vb.* 540

culminate *vb.* 56, 212, 659

culmination *n.* 89, 581

culpable *adj.* 157, 938

culprit *n.* 684

cultivate *vb.* 378, 470

cultivated *adj.* 848, 886

cultivator *n.* 378

culture *n.* 426, 848, 886

cultured *adj.* 426, 848, 886

culvert *n.* 360

cumbersome *adj.* 330, 628

cumulative *adj.* 36

cuneiform *n.* 493; *adj.* 246

cunning *n.* 631, 932; *adj.* 478, 631

cup *n.* 193, 663

curate *n.* 986

curative *adj.* 589, 591

curator *n.* 593, 683

curb *n.* 281, 635, 681; *vb.* 37, 235, 281, 681

curdle *vb.* 332, 773

cure *n.* 176, 181, 589, 591, 834; *vb.* 589, 591, 599

curfew *n.* 128, 681

curiosity *n.* 388, 866

curious *adj.* 388, 394

curl *n.* 247, 251; *vb.* 247, 251, 260

currency *n.* 731

current *n.* 140, 358, 359; *adj.* 120, 125, 153, 464, 492, 545

current affairs *n.* 465

curriculum *n.* 470

curried *adj.* 769

curry *vb.* 306

curry favour *vb.* 881

curse *n.* 592, 665, 901; *vb.* 892, 901, 962

cursory *adj.* 113, 211

curt *adj.* 203, 504, 517, 887

curtail *vb.* 37, 197, 203

curtain *n.* 216, 461, 801

curtsy *n.* 319, 922; *vb.* 319, 922

curve *n.* 219, 247; *vb.* 219, 247

curved form *n.* 247

cushion *n.* 217; *vb.* 176, 834

custodian *n.* 593, 683

custody *n.* 593, 681, 707

custom *n.* 545, 726, 743, 988

customary *adj.* 126, 138, 545, 988

customer *n.* 716, 726

cut *n.* 43, 55, 259, 717, 744; *vb.* 48, 259, 264, 490, 744

cut back *vb.* 37, 42, 203, 748

cut down *vb.* 203, 319

cut out *vb.* 312

cut out for *adj.* 627

cut-price *adj.* 746

cut-throat *n.* 370

cutting *adj.* 255, 760, 773, 923

cut up *adj.* 828, 837; *vb.* 837

cycle *n.* 109, 140, 276, 323; *vb.* 269, 323

cyclic *adj.* 109, 140, 250

cycling *n.* 269

cyclone *n.* 323, 359

cyclopedia *n.* 524

cylinder *n.* 249

cylindrical *adj.* 249

cynic *n.* 904, 928

cynical *adj.* 904, 928

cynicism *n.* 904

D

dabble *vb.* 349

dad *n.* 170

daffodil *n.* 813

daily *adv.* 140

dainty *n.* 770, 848; *adj.* 331, 770

dally *vb.* 135

dam *vb.* 265

damage *n.* 588; *vb.* 164, 582, 588, 847

damages *n.* 31, 963

damaging *adj.* 580

damn *vb.* 901, 962

damned *adj.* 975

damp *n.* 349; *adj.* 349; *vb.* 762

dampen *vb.* 349, 548, 837

dampness *n.* 347, 349

dance *n.* 792, *vb.* 320, 838

dancer *n.* 793

dandy *n.* 852

danger *n.* 594

dangerous *adj.* 594

dangle *vb.* 216

dank *adj.* 349

dapple *vb.* 817

dare *n.* 644; *vb.* 644

daredevil *n.* 859

daring *n.* 857, 859; *adj.* 644, 857

dark *n.* 798; *adj.* 798, 803, 808

darken *vb.* 798, 803, 808

darkness *n.* 427, 798, 803, 808

darling *n.* 891

darn *vb.* 589

dart *n.* 290; *vb.* 273, 280

dash *n.* 33, 173, 613; *vb.* 280, 282, 613

dashing *adj.* 611, 613

dastardly *adj.* 858

data *n.* 38, 401, 460

date *n.* 107, 116, 884; *vb.* 116

dated *adj.* 107, 126

daub *n.* 847; *vb.* 342, 584, 847

daughter *n.* 171

daunt *vb.* 856

dauntless *adj.* 857

dawdle *vb.* 135, 281

dawn *n.* 127, 797; *vb.* 797

day *n.* 109, 116

daybreak *n.* 127, 797

day-dream *n.* 449; *vb.* 391, 449

daylight *n.* 797

dazzle *n.* 797; *vb.* 797

dazzling *adj.* 509, 797

deacon *n.* 987

dead *adj.* 2, 174, 369, 754, 785, 843

deaden *vb.* 513, 754, 779, 785

deadlock *n.* 144

deadly *adj.* 164, 370, 580, 586, 592

deaf *adj.* 796

deafen *vb.* 780, 796

deafening *adj.* 780, 796

deafness *n.* 796

deal *n.* 26, 699; *vb.* 9, 526, 606, 699, 717, 725

dealer *n.* 728

dealings *n.* 557

deal out *vb.* 715

dean *n.* 986

dear *n.* 891; *adj.* 745, 889

dearness *n.* 745

dearth *n.* 315, 571

death *n.* 89, 369

death chamber *n.* 964

deathly *adj.* 369, 371

death sentence *n.* 963

débâcle *n.* 148, 662

debar *vb.* 691

debase *vb.* 209, 584, 608, 869

debasement *n.* 209, 319, 608, 928

debatable *adj.* 409

debate *n.* 410, 519; *vb.* 414, 519

debauched *adj.* 945, 952

debilitate *vb.* 162

debility *n.* 162

debit *vb.* 742

debonair *adj.* 836

debrief *vb.* 460

debris *n.* 44

debt *n.* 737, 919

debts *n.* 737, 739

début *n.* 88

decade *n.* 70, 109

decadent *adj.* 588

decamp *vb.* 600

decant *vb.* 358

decapitate *vb.* 164, 370, 963

decay *n.* 53, 126, 588; *vb.* 53, 164, 588

decaying *adj.* 777

deceased *n.* 369; *adj.* 369

deceit *n.* 412, 463, 478, 631

deceitful *adj.* 431, 932, 981

deceive *vb.* 431, 471, 477, 478, 631, 932

deceiver *n.* 480

deceleration *n.* 281

decent *adj.* 848, 951

decentralize *vb.* 53, 95, 667, 714

deception *n.* 463, 477, 478, 631

deceptive *adj.* 431, 478, 631

decide *vb.* 415, 530, 534, 552, 622

decided *adj.* 408, 534

decimal *n.* 39; *adj.* 39, 70

decimate *vb.* 164, 370

decipher *vb.* 456

decipherable *adj.* 452

decision *n.* 415, 540, 960

decisive *adj.* 136, 413, 573

deck *vb.* 227, 568, 602, 846

declaim *vb.* 468

declaimer *n.* 514

declaration *n.* 460, 464, 468

declare *vb.* 413, 450, 460, 462, 468, 651, 698, 960, 961

declension *n.* 37, 499, 694

decline *n.* 37, 126, 219, 317, 495; *vb.* 37, 130, 162, 197, 317, 319, 499, 542, 588

declining *adj.* 37, 586

decode *vb.* 456

decollate *vb.* 48

decompose *vb.* 48, 53, 588

decomposition *n.* 53, 588

deconsecrate *vb.* 987

decorate *vb.* 587, 844, 846

decoration *n.* 509, 663, 677, 846, 872

decorum *n.* 848

decoy *n.* 294; *vb.* 463

decrease *n.* 37, 42, 43, 57, 197; *vb.* 37, 176, 197, 746

decree *n.* 415, 671, 898, 954, 960; *vb.* 415, 671

decrepit *adj.* 126, 130, 162

decry *vb.* 928

dedicate *vb.* 534, 980, 988

dedicated *adj.* 709, 980

dedication *n.* 715, 980

deduce *vb.* 410, 448

deduction *n.* 42, 43, 87, 410, 744

deed *n.* 609

deem *vb.* 420, 448

deep n. 351; adj. 148, 182, 210, 805

deepen vb. 36, 210, 835

deep-freeze n. 764; vb. 762

deep-seated adj. 210, 545

deface vb. 845, 847

defamation n. 869, 928

defamatory adj. 926, 928, 930

default n. 315, 739; vb. 739

defeat n. 445, 660, 662; vb. 414, 661

defeatist adj. 855

defecate vb. 310

defect n. 43, 57, 582, 660, 662, 847

defection n. 189, 538, 920, 932

defective adj. 55, 57, 580, 582, 847

defence n. 402, 593, 595, 646, 648, 929, 960

defenceless adj. 160

defend vb. 410, 593, 646, 647, 648, 929, 959

defendant n. 684, 960

defer vb. 135, 424, 654, 920

deference n. 654, 922

defiance n. 637, 644, 672, 880

deficiency n. 29, 35, 57, 189, 315, 571, 660

deficient adj. 29, 35, 57, 315, 582, 660

deficit n. 57, 315, 737

defile vb. 584, 588, 608, 928, 936

defilement n. 584, 588, 608, 928

define vb. 102, 235, 496, 525

defining adj. 456

definite adj. 408, 823

definite article n. 499

definite space n. 183

definition n. 235, 450

deflate vb. 874

deflated adj. 874

deflation n. 197, 874

deflect vb. 285

deformed adj. 243, 245, 845

deformity n. 245, 582, 845, 847

defraud vb. 478, 722

defrost vb. 345, 761

deft adj. 280, 627

defunct adj. 369

defy vb. 25, 331, 637, 644, 672

degenerate n. 940; adj. 147, 936; vb. 53, 147, 588, 590, 936

degradation n. 608, 686, 869, 928

degrade vb. 588, 686, 869

degree n. 7, 27, 93, 400, 766

dehydrate vb. 350, 599

de-ice vb. 761

deification n. 983

deign vb. 874

deism n. 974

deity n. 966

déjà vu n. 441

dejection n. 837

delay n. 135, 281; vb. 135, 281

delegate n. 149, 625, 688, 689; vb. 685, 714

delete vb. 42, 485

deliberate adj. 410, 530, 543, 552; vb. 384

deliberation n. 384, 410, 860

delicacy n. 162, 205, 306, 338, 770, 848

delicate n. 753; adj. 162, 205, 331, 338, 510, 594, 735, 848, 864

delicatessen n. 306

delicious adj. 306, 767, 770, 772, 829

delight n. 306, 770, 827, 829; vb. 755, 829, 840, 889

delighted adj. 756, 827

delightful adj. 755, 770, 827, 829

delineate vb. 232, 486, 525

delirious adj. 827

delirium n. 756

deliver vb. 268, 601, 680, 714

deliverance n. 600, 601, 680

delivery n. 268, 512, 514, 621, 715

delude vb. 478

deluge n. 358, 572; vb. 349

delusion n. 412, 457, 478

demand n. 562, 671, 695; vb. 562, 671, 695, 727, 743

demarcation n. 48, 231, 235

dematerialize vb. 2, 328, 826, 984

demeanour n. 621

demented adj. 439

demise n. 89, 369

democracy n. 667, 678

demolish vb. 164, 319

demolition n. 164

demon n. 969

demonism n. 983

demonstrate vb. 401, 413, 456, 458, 696

demonstration n. 413, 458, 696, 825

demonstrator n. 106, 148

demoralize vb. 837, 936

demote vb. 686

demur n. 533; vb. 533, 696

demure adj. 876, 951

den n. 234, 463, 595

dendrochronology n. 116

denial n. 414, 469, 542, 694

denigrate vb. 928

denomination n. 496, 641, 979

denominational adj. 979

denominator n. 39

denote vb. 450, 482

dénouement n. 89

denounce vb. 892, 928, 930, 962

dense adj. 75, 332, 334, 435

density n. 204, 332, 400

dent n. 254, 847

denude vb. 228

denunciation n. 901, 926, 930, 962

deny vb. 402, 414, 469, 542, 637, 691, 694, 944

deodorant n. 775

depart vb. 151, 285, 293, 299, 600, 687, 826

department n. 55, 97

departure n. 285, 293, 299, 369, 600, 687, 826

depend vb. 420, 679, 854

dependable adj. 392, 702, 868, 931

dependant n. 132, 287, 676

dependence n. 9, 420, 679

dependent adj. 420, 679, 700

depict vb. 20, 486, 488

deplete vb. 358, 569

depleted adj. 57, 569, 588

deplore vb. 941

deport vb. 99, 963

deposit n. 55, 367, 567, 701, 738; vb. 567

depository n. 193, 567, 732

depot n. 567

deprave vb. 588, 608

depreciate vb. 696, 744, 746, 928

depreciation n. 37, 43, 744, 928

depress vb. 209, 254, 319, 837, 841

depression n. 37, 169, 209, 210, 254, 259, 319, 837

deprive vb. 706, 720

deprived adj. 435, 706

depth n. 26, 209, 210, 400

deputation n. 685, 688

deputize vb. 685, 689

deputy n. 149, 688, 689; adj. 689

derail vb. 187

deranged adj. 439

derelict adj. 607

dereliction n. 393, 920

deride vb. 838, 853, 924, 928

derivation n. 155, 410, 494

derivative n. 494; adj. 156

derive vb. 156, 157, 410, 716

derogatory adj. 928

descend vb. 317, 869

descendant n. 11, 171

descent n. 11, 171, 317, 870

describe vb. 413, 460, 496, 525

description n. 460, 465, 486, 496, 525

descriptive adj. 456, 525

desecrate vb. 608, 981

desert adj. 350; vb. 556, 607, 898

deserter n. 538, 555, 672, 858

desertion n. 189, 556, 600, 672, 898, 920

deserts n. 917

deserve vb. 573, 917, 963

desiccate vb. 350

design n. 23, 58, 242, 482, 488, 552, 558; vb. 58, 488, 543, 552, 558

designate adj. 119, 123; vb. 102, 450, 482, 486, 496

designer n. 491, 558

desirable adj. 577, 579

desire n. 388, 530, 552, 854, 861; vb. 530, 532, 854, 861, 914

desist vb. 89, 144

desolate adj. 169, 588, 837

desolation n. 164, 569

despair n. 828, 837, 855, 856; vb. 828, 855

desperate adj. 706

desperation n. 855

despise vb. 542, 923, 924

despondency n. 445, 837, 855

despotism n. 669, 900

dessert n. 306

destination n. 235, 284, 298, 552

destined adj. 154, 531, 543

destiny n. 154

destitute adj. 708, 735

destroy vb. 82, 164, 370, 569

destroyer n. 167, 277

destruction n. 2, 53, 164, 370

destructive adj. 164, 175, 370, 580

detach *vb.* 48, 51

detached *adj.* 48, 391, 757

detachment *n.* 48, 391, 757, 933

detail *n.* 8, 55, 460

detailed *adj.* 8, 525

detain *vb.* 681, 712

detect *vb.* 419, 774, 795

détente n. 643

detention *n.* 681

deter *vb.* 548, 635

deteriorate *vb.* 37, 164, 588, 590

deterioration *n.* 126, 142, 569, 588, 590

determination *n.* 400, 415, 530, 534, 540, 857

determine *vb.* 89, 155, 177, 400, 413, 530, 534, 543, 552

determined *adj.* 534, 535, 857

determinism *n.* 531

deterrent *n.* 548

detest *vb.* 862, 892

detonate *vb.* 782

detonator *n.* 765

detour *n.* 285, 322, 561

detract *vb.* 42, 391

detriment *n.* 580, 588

detrimental *adj.* 164, 578, 580

devastate *vb.* 164

devastation *n.* 569

develop *vb.* 36, 196, 242, 288, 324, 587

developing *adj.* 36, 129, 603

development *n.* 36, 153, 196, 288, 324, 587

deviate *vb.* 15, 219, 247, 285, 505

deviation *n.* 15, 29, 142, 285, 431

device *n.* 565

devil *n.* 969, 984

devilish *adj.* 900, 969, 984

devious *adj.* 932

devise *vb.* 58, 163, 449, 558

devolution *n.* 667, 685, 714

devolve *vb.* 667, 685, 714, 919

devoted *adj.* 673, 702, 882, 889, 982

devotee *n.* 545

devote oneself to *vb.* 605

devotion *n.* 673, 702, 889, 980

devour *vb.* 304, 569, 948

devout *adj.* 974, 980, 982

dew *n.* 349

dexterity *n.* 240

dexterous *adj.* 627

diabolical *adj.* 900, 969, 984

diabolism *n.* 984

diagnosis *n.* 396, 398, 456

diagonal *n.* 219; *adj.* 219

diagram *n.* 486

dial 999 *vb.* 591, 598

dialect *n.* 492

dialectical materialism *n.* 327

dialogue *n.* 394, 410, 519

diameter *n.* 204, 400

diametrical *adj.* 14

diamond *n.* 246

diarrhoea *n.* 310

diary *n.* 116, 441, 483

dice *vb.* 48, 306

dichotomy *n.* 63

dictate *vb.* 671; *vb.* 531, 671, 674

dictator *n.* 623, 669

dictionary *n.* 83, 494, 524

didactic *adj.* 470

die *n.* 23; *vb.* 2, 89, 293, 369, 588, 826

die-hard *n.* 143, 537

diet *n.* 625, 947; *vb.* 205, 947

differ *vb.* 14, 15, 19, 151, 425, 642

difference *n.* 10, 15, 19, 104, 106, 425, 642

different *adj.* 14, 15, 19, 104, 106

differentiate *vb.* 15, 398

different time *n.* 121

differing *adj.* 25, 425

difficult *adj.* 405, 615, 633, 887

difficulty *n.* 633, 665, 830

diffuse *adj.* 505; *vb.* 95, 297, 346, 464

diffuseness *n.* 505

dig *n.* 254; *vb.* 210, 254, 378

digest *n.* 527; *vb.* 304, 472, 527

digestible *adj.* 306

digger *n.* 312

digit *n.* 39

dignified *adj.* 510, 848, 868, 870, 873, 982

dignity *n.* 510, 868, 870, 873

dig one's heels in *vb.* 537

digression *n.* 285, 505, 561

digs *n.* 191

dilapidated *adj.* 126

dilapidation *n.* 569, 588

dilated *adj.* 196

dilatory *adj.* 135

dilemma *n.* 136, 409, 633

diligent *adj.* 390, 392, 535, 611, 702

dilute vb. 37, 162
diluted adj. 162, 507
dim adj. 798, 799, 806, 820, 895; vb. 799
dimension n. 26, 194, 400
diminish vb. 37, 76
diminutive adj. 33, 195
dimness n. 128, 799, 806
dimple n. 254
din n. 780, 791
dine out vb. 304
dingy adj. 805, 809
dinner n. 306
diocese n. 183
dip n. 254, 319, 321; vb. 319, 321, 349
diplomat n. 688
diplomatic adj. 392, 886
dipsomania n. 950
direct adj. 248, 476, 502, 508; vb. 284, 290, 470, 529, 622, 624, 667, 671, 956
direction n. 103, 178, 269, 284, 392, 470, 559, 622, 626, 671, 956
directive n. 671; adj. 622
director n. 558, 623, 675
directory n. 83
dirge n. 839
dirt n. 584, 952
dirty adj. 584, 952; vb. 584
disable vb. 160, 162
disabled adj. 160, 586
disadvantage n. 551, 578
disadvantageous adj. 137, 576, 578
disagree vb. 25, 425, 586, 637, 642, 696, 771, 926

disagreeable adj. 771, 830, 862, 895
disagreeing adj. 25, 425, 642
disagreement n. 15, 25, 106, 425, 642, 926
disallow vb. 691, 694
disappear vb. 2, 113, 826
disappearance n. 189, 600, 826
disappeared adj. 189, 826
disappoint vb. 445, 832
disappointing adj. 445, 571
disappointment n. 445, 662, 830
disapproval n. 425, 542, 696, 926
disapprove vb. 425, 542, 637, 696, 926
disarm vb. 160
disarrangement n. 80, 82
disaster n. 551, 662, 665, 900
disastrous adj. 551, 662, 665, 855
disband vb. 53, 82, 95
disbelief n. 409, 421, 975
disbelieving adj. 421, 975
disc n. 250, 484, 794
discard vb. 542, 556, 607, 713
discarded adj. 126
discern vb. 398, 426, 434, 818
discerning adj. 384, 398, 426, 434
discharge n. 301, 303, 310, 680, 911, 961; vb. 290, 301, 303, 310, 601, 680, 738, 740, 911, 921, 961

disciple n. 146, 287, 428, 474
disciplinarian n. 669
discipline n. 79, 470, 681, 963; vb. 470, 669, 681, 963
disciplined adj. 81, 681, 944
disclaim vb. 469, 538, 542
disclosure n. 419, 458, 462, 464, 976
discoloration n. 582, 806
discomfort n. 828; vb. 830
disconcert vb. 82, 391, 445, 832
disconnect vb. 48, 92
disconnected adj. 51, 80, 92
discontent n. 445, 828, 832, 926
discontinue vb. 89, 92, 144, 546, 556
discontinuity n. 92
discord n. 25, 425, 642, 787, 791
discount n. 42, 43, 744
discourage vb. 548, 633, 832, 837
discourse n. 514, 518, 526
discourteous adj. 887, 923
discourtesy n. 887, 923
discover vb. 186, 419, 472
discoverer n. 155, 166
discovery n. 419, 460
discredit vb. 414, 588, 869, 928
discreet adj. 392, 434
discrepancy n. 15, 25
discrete adj. 48
discretion n. 530, 860
discriminate vb. 15, 398, 540, 916

225

discriminating *adj.* 392,
398, 434, 540, 848, 864
discrimination *n.* 15,
398, 848, 916
discuss *vb.* 410, 514,
519, 526, 624, 700
disdain *n.* 853, 924; *vb.*
924
disease *n.* 586
disembark *vb.* 298
disembodied *adj.* 4, 328
disentangle *vb.* 46, 48,
81, 248
disfigure *vb.* 245, 845,
847
disfigurement *n.* 582,
845, 847
disfranchise *vb.* 918
disgrace *n.* 869; *vb.*
588, 869
disgraceful *adj.* 869
disgruntle *vb.* 832
disgruntled *adj.* 832
disguise *n.* 18, 461, 463;
vb. 20, 146, 461
disgust *n.* 892; *vb.* 771,
892
dish *n.* 306
dishearten *vb.* 832
dishevel *vb.* 82
dishevelled *adj.* 584
dishonest *adj.* 477, 478,
631, 932
dishonour *n.* 869, 923;
vb. 588, 869, 923
dish out *vb.* 717
disillusion *vb.* 445
disinclination *n.* 389,
533, 862
disinfect *vb.* 583
disingenuous *adj.* 477
disinherit *vb.* 720
disintegrate *vb.* 48, 53,
164, 328
disintegration *n.* 48, 53,
164, 588
disinter *vb.* 372

disinterested *adj.* 541,
757, 915, 933
disinterestedness *n.* 933
dislike *n.* 637, 862, 883,
892; *vb.* 771, 862, 892
dislocate *vb.* 48, 82, 187
dislodge *vb.* 187, 312
disloyal *adj.* 431, 672,
920
disloyalty *n.* 703, 920,
932
dismal *adj.* 798, 837,
895
dismantle *vb.* 164
dismay *vb.* 837, 856
dismembered *adj.* 48
dismiss *vb.* 99, 295, 303,
389, 542, 686, 920, 961
dismount *vb.* 298
disobedience *n.* 644,
672, 703, 981
disobey *vb.* 644, 672,
703, 955
disorder *n.* 80, 175, 584,
586, 668, 955; *vb.* 82
disorderly *adj.* 82, 887
disorganized *adj.* 80, 82
disorientate *vb.* 285
disown *vb.* 469, 538,
542
disparage *vb.* 418, 548,
926, 928
disparagement *n.* 928
disparate *adj.* 15, 19,
29, 104
dispassionate *adj.* 757,
863, 915, 933
dispatch *n.* 268, 460,
465, 523; *vb.* 268, 523,
613
dispatch bearer *n.* 467
dispel *vb.* 95
dispensation *n.* 713,
921
dispense *vb.* 95, 715,
717
disperse *vb.* 48, 82, 95,
297

dispersion *n.* 95
dispirited *adj.* 837
displace *vb.* 85, 187,
312, 706
displacement *n.* 187,
686
display *n.* 413, 825; *vb.*
413, 458
displeasure *n.* 445, 893,
926
disposal *n.* 81, 713, 727
dispose *vb.* 81, 717
disposed *adj.* 81, 179,
532, 751
dispose of *vb.* 89, 303,
609, 713, 717
disposition *n.* 5, 532,
545, 751
dispossession *n.* 706,
720, 918
disproof *n.* 414
disproportion *n.* 10, 29,
245
disproportionate *adj.*
25, 29, 245
disprove *vb.* 414
dispute *n.* 25, 410, 642;
vb. 25, 410, 414, 637,
642, 649
disqualify *vb.* 99, 160,
918
disquiet *n.* 828; *vb.* 856
disregard *n.* 391, 393,
672, 703, 920; *vb.* 99,
389, 391, 393, 555, 644,
672, 703, 887, 924
disreputable *adj.* 869,
932
disrepute *n.* 869
disrespect *n.* 869, 887,
923, 924
disrespectful *adj.* 880,
887, 923, 924
disrupt *vb.* 82
disruption *n.* 175
dissatisfaction *n.* 445,
828, 832, 862, 926
dissect *vb.* 48, 53

dissemble vb. 461, 477

disseminate vb. 95, 378, 460, 464

dissension n. 25, 425, 637, 642

dissent n. 425, 696; vb. 151, 425, 642

dissenter n. 106, 425, 975

dissertation n. 526

dissident n. 979; adj. 106, 425, 672, 979

dissimilarity n. 19, 25, 29, 106

dissimulation n. 19

dissipate vb. 95, 346, 569, 749

dissipation n. 95, 569, 945

dissociation n. 10, 48

dissolute adj. 936, 952

dissolution n. 48, 53, 164, 345, 369, 686, 898

dissolve vb. 2, 53, 164, 345, 686, 826

dissonance n. 25, 787, 791

dissuade vb. 548, 624

dissuasion n. 548, 624

distance n. 194, 198, 400, 885; vb. 198

distant adj. 198, 517, 781, 885

distaste n. 862

distemper n. 225

distend vb. 196

distil vb. 346

distinct adj. 48, 102, 452, 512, 778, 823

distinction n. 398, 868, 870

distinctive adj. 5

distinguish vb. 15, 398, 452

distinguished adj. 208, 573, 868, 870

distort vb. 245, 457, 471, 477, 487, 588, 845

distorted adj. 245, 477, 582

distortion n. 245, 416, 457, 477, 487, 845

distracted adj. 391, 442

distraught adj. 756

distress n. 445, 665, 828; vb. 830

distressed adj. 735

distressing adj. 551, 830

distress signal n. 598, 902

distribute vb. 95, 464, 715, 717

distribution n. 81, 717

district n. 183

distrust n. 421, 913; vb. 423

disturb vb. 82, 137, 187, 326, 856

disturbance n. 80, 137, 175, 326

disunite vb. 48, 51

disunity n. 17

disuse n. 546, 569, 607; vb. 607

ditch n. 261, 360, 646; vb. 556

dither n. 326, 756

ditto adv. 77

dive n. 321; vb. 271, 273, 321

diverge vb. 15, 48, 95, 151, 219, 297

divergence n. 285, 297

divergent adj. 15, 219, 285, 297, 978

diverse adj. 15, 104

diversified adj. 17, 104

diversify vb. 817

diversion n. 142, 285, 449, 840

diversity n. 15, 17, 19, 104, 817

divert vb. 391

diverting adj. 840

divest vb. 228, 720

divide vb. 38, 48, 55, 63, 95, 97, 717

dividends n. 741

divination n. 447, 984

divine adj. 966, 974; vb. 447, 448, 984

divinity n. 966

divisibility n. 51

division n. 25, 38, 48, 55, 97, 425, 655, 717

divisive adj. 642

divorce n. 48, 713, 898; vb. 48, 898

divulge vb. 458, 462

do n. 878; vb. 570, 577, 605, 609, 673, 702

do away with vb. 370

docile adj. 654, 673

dock n. 298, 957; vb. 298

docket n. 482; vb. 482

doctor n. 428, 436, 473; vb. 477

doctrine n. 420, 626, 974

document n. 401, 483, 521; vb. 401, 483, 521

dodge n. 478, 631; vb. 533, 555

dodger n. 480, 600

doe n. 381

doer n. 609, 619

dog n. 380, vb. 287, 554

doggedness n. 534, 535

dogma n. 420, 974

dogmatic adj. 468, 537

do-gooder n. 899, 903, 905

do in vb. 370

doing n. 609, 702; adj. 609

do-it-yourself adj. 628

doldrums n. 837

doleful adj. 837

dole out vb. 95, 715, 717

doll up vb. 844

doltish adj. 435

227

domain *n.* 956
dome *n.* 225, 252
domestic *n.* 676; *adj.*
190
domestic animal *n.* 373
domesticate *vb.* 377
domesticated *adj.* 190
domestic science *n.* 306
domicile *n.* 191
dominance *n.* 34, 159,
177
dominant *adj.* 159, 177,
667
dominate *vb.* 177, 208,
667, 669, 679
domineer *vb.* 667, 669
dominion *n.* 667
don *n.* 428, 473; *vb.* 227
donate *vb.* 715
donor *n.* 715, 905
doom *n.* 543; *vb.* 962
door *n.* 262
doorman *n.* 676
do over *vb.* 645
dormancy *n.* 459, 610,
612
dorsal *adj.* 237
dose *n.* 26, 591
dot *n.* 33
dotage *n.* 130
dote on *vb.* 889, 983
double *n.* 28, 149, 971;
adj. 62; *vb.* 62, 149,
260
double-cross *vb.* 478,
932
double dealing *n.* 477,
631, 932; *adj.* 477, 932
double entendre *n.* 454,
842
double-sidedness *n.* 61
doubt *n.* 409, 421, 975;
vb. 409, 421, 423
doubtful *adj.* 407, 409,
421
dough *n.* 364, 731
douse *vb.* 762
dove *n.* 656

dovetail *vb.* 24, 47
dowager *n.* 870, 898
dowdiness *n.* 849
down *adj.* 837; *adv.* 209
down-and-out *n.* 697;
adj. 735
downcast *adj.* 837
downfall *n.* 164, 317,
662
downgrade *vb.* 686
down-hearted *adj.* 837
down-payment *n.* 55,
738
downpour *n.* 358
downward *adj.* 219, 317
doze *n.* 612, 617; *vb.*
612
dozen *n.* 70
drab *adj.* 805, 809, 843
draft *n.* 558, 602; *vb.*
521, 558
drag *n.* 181, 635; *vb.*
181, 291, 294
drag up *vb.* 441
drain *n.* 360; *vb.* 319,
358, 569, 806
drained *adj.* 617
drake *n.* 380
dram *n.* 309
drama *n.* 529, 866
dramatic *adj.* 529, 752,
755, 866
dramatis personae *n.*
529
drape *n.* 801; *vb.* 216
draught *n.* 309, 359
draught animal *n.* 291
draughtsman *n.* 491
draughty *adj.* 348, 359
draw *n.* 28, 294, 553;
vb. 28, 291, 294, 308,
312, 390, 486, 488, 525,
705, 889
drawback *n.* 582
drawer *n.* 491
drawing *n.* 291, 488
drawl *n.* 515; *vb.* 515
draw up *vb.* 558

dread *n.* 856; *vb.* 856
dreadful *adj.* 830, 856
dream *n.* 4, 449, 552,
854; *vb.* 391, 449, 552,
612, 854, 861
dream up *vb.* 558
dreamy *adj.* 384
dreary *adj.* 798, 841,
843
dredge *vb.* 312
dredge up *vb.* 441
dregs *n.* 44, 576, 871
drench *vb.* 349, 572
dress *n.* 227; *vb.* 227,
568, 844
dressage *n.* 269
dress down *vb.* 926, 963
dressing *n.* 227
dribble *vb.* 319, 358
dried *adj.* 350
drift *n.* 178, 450; *vb.*
178, 257, 612
drill *n.* 264; *vb.* 264,
378, 470
drink *n.* 309, 343; *vb.*
304, 950
drinker *n.* 304, 950
drink in *vb.* 390, 472
drinking *n.* 304
drip *n.* 349, 841; *vb.*
319, 358
drip-dry *vb.* 350
drive *n.* 173, 269, 282,
290, 559, 645, 674; *vb.*
173, 269, 282, 290, 295,
377, 547, 674
drive at *vb.* 450
drivel *n.* 451
driver *n.* 270
driving *n.* 269; *adj.* 674
drizzle *n.* 358; *vb.* 358
droll *adj.* 851
drone *vb.* 783, 784, 789
droop *vb.* 216, 317, 319,
837, 841
drop *n.* 37, 210, 249,
254, 309, 317, 321; *vb.*

37, 317, 319, 358, 556, 617, 706

drop anchor *vb.* 271, 298

drop in *vb.* 300

drop out *vb.* 660

droppings *n.* 310

drought *n.* 350, 861

drown *vb.* 321, 349, 370, 963

drowsy *adj.* 612, 617, 841

drudge *n.* 615, 619, 676; *vb.* 615

drug *n.* 173, 591; *vb.* 754

drum *n.* 249

drumming *n.* 325

drunk *n.* 950; *adj.* 950

drunkard *n.* 304, 950

dry *adj.* 350, 773, 787, 843, 949; *vb.* 306, 350

dryness *n.* 350, 843

dualism *n.* 61

duality *n.* 61

dub *vb.* 496, 497

dubious *adj.* 407, 421, 932

duchess *n.* 870

duchy *n.* 183

duck *n.* 74, 381; *vb.* 321, 349, 555

duct *n.* 360

dud *n.* 662

due *n.* 737, 917; *adj.* 737, 917

duel *n.* 649

dueness *n.* 917

dues *n.* 716, 743, 917

dug-out *n.* 254

duke *n.* 870

dull *adj.* 174, 256, 435, 666, 754, 768, 771, 785, 798, 799, 806, 843; *vb.* 256, 754, 785, 799

dullness *n.* 174, 435, 768, 806, 843

dumb *adj.* 435, 513, 517

dumbfound *vb.* 513, 866

dummy *n.* 22, 23, 149; *adj.* 149

dump *vb.* 727

dumpy *adj.* 195, 203, 204

dunce *n.* 429, 437, 630

dung *n.* 310

dungeon *n.* 234, 682

duo *n.* 792

dupe *n.* 479, 853; *vb.* 478

duple *adj.* 61

duplicate *n.* 22; *adj.* 13, 62; *vb.* 62, 165

duplication *n.* 62, 77, 165

duplicity *n.* 477, 932

durability *n.* 143, 337

durable *adj.* 112, 161, 337

duration *n.* 107, 145

duress *n.* 674

during *adv., prep.* 107

dusk *n.* 128, 799, 809

dust *n.* 340, 371, 576

duster *n.* 485

dusty *adj.* 340, 350, 584, 809

dutiful *adj.* 673, 919

duty *n.* 557, 685, 737, 743, 919

dwarf *n.* 195, 970; *adj.* 203

dwell *vb.* 191

dwindle *vb.* 37, 197, 569

dye *n.* 805

dying *n.* 369; *adj.* 130, 861

dynamic *adj.* 159, 173, 611

dynamite *n.* 657

dysentry *n.* 310

E

eager *adj.* 443, 532, 756, 861

earl *n.* 870

earlier *adj.* 84, 118; *adv.* 121

earliness *n.* 134

early *adj.* 117, 134

early warning *n.* 597

earmark *vb.* 482

earn *vb.* 705, 917

earner *n.* 716

earnest *n.* 701; *adj.* 532, 752, 837

earnings *n.* 705, 738, 741

earring *n.* 216

earshot *n.* 199, 795

earth *n.* 329, 352

earthquake *n.* 325

earthworks *n.* 646

earthy *adj.* 352

ease *n.* 616, 634, 827, 831, 834; *vb.* 335, 634, 834

ease off *vb.* 281, 616

east *n.* 284

easy *adj.* 634, 952

easy-going *adj.* 670, 757

eat *vb.* 304, 569, 767

eat away *vb.* 569, 588

eating *n.* 304

eavesdropping *n.* 460, 795

ebb *vb.* 37, 358

eccentric *n.* 106, 440; *adj.* 106, 439

ecclesiastical *adj.* 985

echo *n.* 22, 283, 778, 784; *vb.* 77, 283, 784

eclipse *n.* 798; *vb.* 34, 314, 461, 798

ecology *n.* 366, 376

economical *adj.* 392, 748

economics *n.* 622

economize *vb.* 37, 748

economy *n.* 392, 748; *adj.* 746

ecstasy *n.* 756, 827

eddy *n.* 323, 358; *vb.* 323, 358

edge *n.* 233, 235, 255, 769; *vb.* 233, 255

edgy *adj.* 756, 856, 894

edible *adj.* 306

edict *n.* 626, 671, 954

edifice *n.* 163

edify *vb.* 470, 550, 579

edit *vb.* 456

edition *n.* 524

editor *n.* 456, 524

educate *vb.* 470

educated *adj.* 426

education *n.* 426, 470

educational *adj.* 460, 470

eerie *adj.* 971, 984

efface *vb.* 485

effect *n.* 87, 156, 877; *vb.* 155, 163, 609, 659

effective *adj.* 159, 172, 563, 627

effeminate *adj.* 162, 381

effervesce *vb.* 363, 786

efficacy *n.* 159, 575

efficient *adj.* 159, 557

effluent *n.* 301, 358

effort *n.* 604, 615

effortless *adj.* 634

effrontery *n.* 880

egg *n.* 250, 306

egg-timer *n.* 116

ego *n.* 382

egoist *n.* 904, 934

egotism *n.* 875, 904

ego-trip *n.* 873

eight *n.* 70; *adj.* 70

eject *vb.* 301, 303

ejection *n.* 99, 303, 310, 312

elaborate *adj.* 509; *vb.* 196

elapse *vb.* 107, 110

elasticity *n.* 336

elated *adj.* 756, 827, 838

elbow *n.* 246

elder *n.* 34, 132; 987; *adj.* 130

eldest *adj.* 130

elect *adj.* 119; *vb.* 540

election *n.* 540

electorate *n.* 540

electric chair *n.* 964

electricity *n.* 159, 765

electrify *vb.* 159, 755

electrocute *vb.* 370, 963

electronic *adj.* 125

elegance *n.* 510, 844, 848

elegy *n.* 372, 839

element *n.* 5, 55, 155, 327

elementary *adj.* 88

elements *n.* 192, 348

elevated *adj.* 208, 318, 868, 873

elevation *n.* 208, 318

elevator *n.* 316

eleven *n.* 70

elevenses *n.* 306

eleventh hour *n.* 136

elf *n.* 970

elicit *vb.* 155, 547

eligible *adj.* 896, 897

eliminate *vb.* 46, 99, 164, 303

elite *n.* 579, 870

elixir *n.* 591

ellipse *n.* 247, 250

ellipsis *n.* 504

elliptic *adj.* 504

elocution *n.* 518

elongated *adj.* 202

elope *vb.* 600, 896

eloquent *adj.* 514, 516

elsewhere *adj.* 189

elucidate *vb.* 413, 456

elude *vb.* 555, 600

emaciated *adj.* 205, 588

emanation *n.* 156, 301, 774

emancipation *n.* 601, 680

emasculate *vb.* 160, 169

embalm *vb.* 372, 599, 776

embankment *n.* 559, 646

embargo *n.* 99, 681, 691

embarkation *n.* 299

embark on *vb.* 605

embarrass *vb.* 578, 633, 869, 874

embarrassed *adj.* 811, 830, 874, 876

embassy *n.* 685, 688

embed *vb.* 311

embellish *vb.* 509, 844, 846

ember *n.* 800

embezzle *vb.* 722

embezzler *n.* 723, 739

embittered *adj.* 893

emblazon *vb.* 482

emblem *n.* 482, 677, 872

embody *vb.* 52, 98, 222, 486

emboss *vb.* 482, 489

embrace *n.* 886, 890; *vb.* 50, 98, 702, 886, 890

embrocation *n.* 365

embroider *vb.* 481, 509, 846

embryology *n.* 375, 376

embryonic *adj.* 88

emerald *adj.* 812

emerge *vb.* 301, 313, 324, 600, 825

emergence *n.* 298, 301

emergency *n.* 136, 153, 562

emigrant *n.* 100, 270

emigration *n.* 299

eminent *adj.* 34, 208, 573, 868, 870

emissary *n.* 460, 467, 688

emit *vb.* 301, 303, 774, 778

emollient *n.* 365

emolument *n.* 705, 738

emotion *n.* 326, 752, 756, 889

empathy *n.* 752

emperor *n.* 675

emphasize *vb.* 417, 456, 468, 481, 512, 573

employ *vb.* 107, 557, 575, 606, 685

employee *n.* 619, 676

emporium *n.* 730

empower *vb.* 159, 161, 667, 685, 954

emptiness *n.* 2, 189, 333, 875

empty *adj.* 189, 333, 451; *vb.* 301, 358, 569

empty-handed *adj.* 735

empty-headed *adj.* 383, 427, 435

emulate *vb.* 20

emulsion *n.* 362

enable *vb.* 159, 404

enact *vb.* 529

enactment *n.* 486, 954

enamel *n.* 225

enamoured *adj.* 889

encampment *n.* 186

enchant *vb.* 827, 829, 889, 984

encircle *vb.* 231, 250

enclose *vb.* 98, 225, 229, 234

enclosure *n.* 184, 234, 378

encompass *vb.* 182, 229, 231

encore *n.* 62, 77; *adv.* 77

encounter *n.* 296, 649; *vb.* 649, 857

encourage *vb.* 217, 547, 618, 624, 636, 836, 857, 907

encroachment *n.* 314, 645, 918, 955

encrust *vb.* 226

encumbrance *n.* 635, 711

encyclopedia *n.* 426, 524

end *n.* 89, 156, 235, 237, 369, 552, 659; *vb.* 89, 659

endanger *vb.* 594

endearment *n.* 890

endeavour *n.* 604; *vb.* 604

endemic *adj.* 586

endless *adj.* 78, 91, 114

endless duration *n.* 114

endorsement *n.* 408, 424, 468, 690, 963

endow *vb.* 568, 715

endowment *n.* 5, 627, 714

endurance *n.* 112, 114, 143, 152, 337, 535, 757

endure *vb.* 91, 112, 145, 535, 648, 752, 757, 828

enemy *n.* 638, 645, 883

energetic *adj.* 32, 159, 161, 173, 368, 585, 611

energize *vb.* 161, 173, 618, 755

energy *n.* 159, 161, 173, 368, 611

enfeeble *vb.* 130, 162, 507

enforce *vb.* 954

enfranchise *vb.* 678, 680

engage *vb.* 557, 605

engaged *adj.* 698

engage in battle *vb.* 649, 651

engagement *n.* 557, 605, 649, 698, 890

engine *n.* 276, 565

engineer *n.* 558

engrave *vb.* 490, 521, 522

engraver *n.* 491

engraving *n.* 490

engrossed *adj.* 384

enhance *vb.* 36, 318, 509, 846

enigma *n.* 409, 453, 466

enjoy *vb.* 752, 770, 827, 861

enjoyable *adj.* 827, 829

enjoy immunity *vb.* 921

enjoy oneself *vb.* 827, 840

enlarge *vb.* 36, 40, 196, 202, 505

enlighten *vb.* 460, 470, 797

enlist *vb.* 83, 302, 557, 651

enliven *vb.* 173, 368, 618, 836, 840

enmity *n.* 883

ennoble *vb.* 318, 868, 870

ennui *n.* 841

enormous *adj.* 32, 194

enough *adj.* 75, 570

enquire *vb.* 388, 394

enquiry *n.* 394, 526

enrage *vb.* 893

enrapture *vb.* 547, 827, 829, 889

enrich *vb.* 509, 587

enrol *vb.* 83, 483, 641

ensconce *vb.* 461

ensemble *n.* 54, 793

enshrine *vb.* 372, 983

enshroud *vb.* 225

ensign *n.* 482

enslave *vb.* 679

ensnare *vb.* 463, 478

ensue *vb.* 85, 119, 153, 156, 287

ensure *vb.* 408

entail *vb.* 98, 459

entangle *vb.* 82, 221

entente *n.* 643, 699

enter *vb.* 298, 300, 483, 742

enterprise *n.* 173, 288, 604, **605**, 611, 627, 857

entertain *vb.* 840, 884.

enter upon *vb.* 88, 605

enthralling *adj.* 547, 829, 866

enthrone *vb.* 685, 868

enthusiasm *n.* 532, 611, 752

enthusiastic *adj.* 532, 611, 756, 827

entice *vb.* 547, 770

entire *adj.* 54, 56, 581, 659

entirety *n.* 54, 56, 59

entitled *adj.* 917

entity *n.* 1, 3, 59

entomb *vb.* 372

entomology *n.* 375

entrance *n.* 262, 298, **300**, 559

entrant *n.* 638

entrap *vb.* 478

entreat *vb.* 695, 982

entrée *n.* 306

entrench *vb.* 152, 186

entrepreneur *n.* 728

entrust *vb.* 685, 714, 718

entry *n.* 298, 300

entwine *vb.* 251

enumerate *vb.* 38, 83, 102

enunciate *vb.* 512, 514

envelop *vb.* 225, 229, 234, 461

envelope *n.* 193, 234

envious *adj.* 914

environment *n.* 8, 183, 229

envisage *vb.* 449

envoy *n.* 460, **467**, 685, 688

envy *n.* **914**; *vb.* 914

ephemeral *adj.* 113

epic *n.* 525, 528

epicure *n.* 304, 945, 948

epigram *n.* 432, 842

epilogue *n.* 87, 89

episode *n.* 153

epistle *n.* 523

epitaph *n.* 372

epithet *n.* 496

epitome *n.* 527

epitomize *vb.* 203

epoch *n.* 109

equal *n.* 28; *adj.* 13, **28**, 159

equality *n.* 13, **28**, 244

equalize *vb.* 28, 31

equate *vb.* 13, 218, 397

equation *n.* 28, 397

equator *n.* 63, 250

equestrianism *n.* 269

equidistant *adj.* 90, 218

equilibrium *n.* 28, 152

equip *vb.* 227, 564, 568, **602**

equipment *n.* 568, 711

equity *n.* 711, 915

equivalence *n.* 12, 28, 450

equivalent *n.* 18, 28, 456; *adj.* 12, 13, 18, 28

equivocal *adj.* 409, 453, 454

equivocate *vb.* 454, 477

era *n.* 109

eradicate *vb.* 164, 303, 485

erase *vb.* 485

erect *adj.* 214, 248, 318; *vb.* 214, 318

erection *n.* 163, 318

erode *vb.* 37, 53, 164, 341, 569, **588**

Eros *n.* 889, 967

erotic *adj.* 952

err *vb.* 285, 431, 936

errand *n.* 685

errand-boy *n.* 467

erratic *adj.* 151, 539

erring *adj.* 409

erroneous *adj.* 412, 431, 916

error *n.* **431**, 457, 471

erudite *adj.* 426, 472

eruption *n.* 148, 175, 301, 782

escalate *vb.* 36, 196

escalator *n.* 316

escape *n.* 293, 301, 555, 595, **600**, 826; *vb.* 293, 555, **600**, 826

escapism *n.* 449

escarpment *n.* 208

escort *n.* 683; *vb.* 268

esoteric *adj.* 453, 984

especial *adj.* 34, 102

Esperanto *n.* 492

espouse *vb.* 896

essay *n.* 526, 604

essence *n.* 1, 5, 450

essential *n.* 5, 531, 562; *adj.* 1, 5, 531, 562, 573

establish *vb.* 81, 88, 152, 161, 413, 685, 929, 954

established *adj.* 126, 152, 413, 545

establishment *n.* 88, 152, 191, 413, 620, 641, 667, 730

estate *n.* 7, 378, 711

esteem *n.* 922, 925; *vb.* 384, 861, 868, 889, 925

estimate *n.* 447, 743; *vb.* 38, 400, 415, 448, 743

estrange *vb.* 883, 892

estuary *n.* 353

etcher *n.* 491

etching *n.* 490

eternal *adj.* 78, 114, 966

eternity *n.* 78, 108, 112, **114**

ethereal *adj.* 4, 328, 333

ethics *n.* 935

ethnic *adj.* 11, 379

etiquette *n.* 545

etymology *n.* 492, 494

Eucharist *n.* 988

eunuch *n.* 160

euphemism *n.* 455, 509

euphoria *n.* 827
euthanasia *n.* 370
evacuate *vb.* 293, 299, 310, 600
evacuee *n.* 885
evade *vb.* 393, 412, 533, 555, 600, 920
evaluation *n.* 400, 415, 456, 743
evanescent *adj.* 113, 799, 826
evangelical *adj.* 976, 977
evangelist *n.* 974
evangelize *vb.* 146
evaporate *vb.* 2, 95, 346, 350, 826
even *adj.* 16, 28, 39, 140, 244, 248, 257; *vb.* 215, 257
evening *n.* 128; *adj.* 128
event *n.* 153, 465, 649
eventful *adj.* 611
eventuality *n.* 153
everlasting *adj.* 114, 966
every *adj.* 54
everybody *n.* 54, 101
everything *n.* 54
eviction *n.* 99, 303
evidence *n.* 401, 458, 460, 482, 483; *vb.* 401
evident *adj.* 413, 458, 823
evil *n.* 551, 592, 932, 936; *adj.* 551, 592, 932, 936
evildoer *n.* 906, 940
evil spirit *n.* 969
evocative *adj.* 441, 450
evoke *vb.* 155, 547
evolution *n.* 142, 288, 324, 366
ewe *n.* 381
ex- *adj.* 118, 124
exacerbate *vb.* 36, 588, 835

exact *adj.* 392, 430, 864; *vb.* 671, 743
exacting *adj.* 392, 398, 669, 864
exactness *n.* 392, 502
exaggeration *n.* 417, 477, **481**, 487, 879
exalt *vb.* 318, 868, 982
exalted *adj.* 32, 208, 318, 868
examination *n.* 394, 415, 526
examine *vb.* 384, 390, 394, 396, 415, 526
examinee *n.* 395
example *n.* 23, 597
exasperation *n.* 835, 893, 894
excavate *vb.* 210, 254, 312
exceed *vb.* 32, 34, 314
excel *vb.* 34, 314
excellence *n.* 34, 579, 581, 935
excellent *adj.* 34, 579, 844, 935
except *vb.* 99; *prep.* 99
excepting *adv., prep.* 42
exception *n.* 403, 921
exceptional *adj.* 21, 32, 573, 579
excerpt *n.* 55
excess *n.* 44, 569, 572, 945, 948
excessive *adj.* 481, 572, 691, 745, 945
exchange *n.* 142, 149, 150, 410, 714, 725, 730; *vb.* 142, 149, 150, 714, 725
exchequer *n.* 732
excise *n.* 743
excitability *n.* 753, **756**
excitation *n.* 326, 755
excite *vb.* 752, 755, 829
excited *adj.* 756, 759, 827
exclaim *vb.* 788

exclude *vb.* 42, **99**, 542, 691, 694
exclusion *n.* **99**, 542, 694
exclusive *adj.* 99, 641, 707, **979**
exclusively *adv.* 56
excommunicate *vb.* 99, 885
excrement *n.* 310
excrescent *adj.* 252
excrete *vb.* 303, 310
excretion *n.* 310
excruciating *adj.* 828
excursion *n.* 269, 840
excuse *n.* 549, 929; *vb.* 549, 911, 929
execration *n.* 901
execution *n.* 172, 370, 609, 621, 963
executive *n.* 623, 675, 956; *adj.* 172, 622, 667, 956
executor *n.* 619, 688
exegetical *adj.* 456
exemplary *adj.* 456, 579
exemplify *vb.* 23, 456, 458, 486
exempt *adj.* 921; *vb.* 403, 713, 921, 961
exemption *n.* 678, 713, 921
exercise *n.* 396, 470, 605, 606; *vb.* 470, 575
exercise self-control *vb.* 944
exertion *n.* 615
exert oneself *vb.* 615
exhale *vb.* 301, 346, 359, 774
exhaust *n.* 600; *vb.* 162, 169, 569, 617, 841
exhaustive *adj.* 56
exhibit *n.* 401, 458; *vb.* 413, 458
exhibition *n.* 413, 458, 529

exhibitionist *n.* 875, 877; *adj.* 875

exhilarate *vb.* 618, 755, 827

exhilaration *n.* 756

exhort *vb.* 518, 597, 624

exhume *vb.* 372

exile *n.* 303, 963; *vb.* 303, 963

existence *n.* 1, 368

existent *adj.* 120

existentialism *n.* 1

exit *n.* 262, 299, 369, 600

exodus *n.* 299

exonerate *vb.* 601, 911, 929, 961

exorbitant *adj.* 572, 745, 749

exorcise *vb.* 984

exotic *adj.* 100

expand *vb.* 36, **196**

expand on *vb.* 456

expanse *n.* 26, 182, 204, 356

expansion *n.* 36, 182, **196**

expatriot *n.* 100

expect *vb.* 154, 443, 552, 854

expectation *n.* 406, 443, 552, 854, 867

expected *adj.* 123, 138, 406, 443, 447, 545, 867

expecting *adj.* 163, 854

expedience *n.* 136, 577

expedite *vb.* 613

expedition *n.* 269, 280

expel *vb.* 99, 301, 303, 310, 542, 885, 963

expend *vb.* 569, 715, 738, 740

expenditure *n.* **740**

expense *n.* 743, 745

expenses *n.* 636, 738, 740, 965

experience *n.* 130, 153,

426, 434, 602, 627, 752; *vb.* 153, 426, 472, 752

experiment *n.* 394, **396**, 604; *vb.* 396

expert *n.* 428, 436, **629**, 848; *adj.* 130, 627

expertise *n.* 426, 627

expiation *n.* 943

expiration *n.* 89, 144, 359, 369

explain *vb.* 157, 410, 413, 456, 470, 525, 526

explanation *n.* 155, 157, 413, 450, 456, 525

expletive *n.* 901

explicit *adj.* 452, 458, 502

explode *vb.* 175, 756, 782, 893

exploit *n.* 605, 609; *vb.* 136, 575, 606, 745

exploration *n.* 269, 271, 419

exploratory *adj.* 86, 394

explore *vb.* 269, 396, 758

explorer *n.* 270

explosive *n.* 657; *adj.* 594, 765

exponent *n.* 456, 974

exponential *adj.* 39

export *vb.* 268

exporter *n.* 728

expose *vb.* 228, 262, 414, 419, 458, **462**

exposed *adj.* 228, 348, 414, 462, 753, 823

expose oneself to *vb.* 179

expositor *n.* 456, 514, 526

expostulate *vb.* 696

expound *vb.* 456, 470

express *adj.* 458; *vb.* 242, 450, 458, 460, 514, 525

expression *n.* 242, 458, 468, 492, 494, 498, 825

expressionless *adj.* 451, 754, 843

expulsion *n.* 99, 303, 310, 312, 542

expunge *vb.* 485

expurgate *vb.* 583

exquisite *adj.* 579, 770, 829, 844

extant *adj.* 1

extemporize *vb.* 544

extend *vb.* 6, 182, 196, 202, 208, 253, 693

extended *adj.* 202, 204, 253, 455

extension *n.* 36, 41, 196, 202, 253

extensive *adj.* 32, 54, **182**, 202

extent *n.* 26, 27, 107, 182, 194, 198, 202, 400, 956

extenuating *adj.* 403, 929

exterior *n.* 222, 236; *adj.* 6, 222

exterminate *vb.* 164, 369, 370

external *n.* 6; *adj.* 6, 100, 222, 825

extinct *adj.* 2, 126, 369

extinguish *vb.* 164, 369, 762

extol *vb.* 922

extort *vb.* 312, 720, 722, 745

extra *n.* 529; *adj.* 40, 572, 607; *adv.* 40

extract *n.* 55, 306; *vb.* 187, 312

extraction *n.* **312**

extradite *vb.* 303

extramarital *adj.* 952

extraneousness *n.* 6, 40, **100**, 222

extraordinary *adj.* 407, 573, 866

extrapolate *vb.* 6, 222

extra-sensory perception
n. 411, 447, 753
extraterrestrial adj. 329
extravagance n. 481,
569, 572, 745, 749, 945
extravagant adj. 481,
509, 569, 572, 745, 749,
877
extreme n. 89; adj. 89,
148, 175, 669, 828, 830
extremely adv. 32
extremist n. 148, 672
extremity n. 89, 233,
235
extricate vb. 312, 601,
678, 680
extrinsic adj. 6, 100,
222
exuberant adj. 168, 572,
836
exudation n. 310
exude vb. 301, 358
exultation n. 827, 838
eye n. 818; vb. 818
eye for an eye n. 647
eyelash n. 207
eyesight n. 818
eyesore n. 845
eye-witness n. 821

F

fable n. 455, 525
fabric n. 221, 339
fabrication n. 163, 465,
477, 631
fabulous adj. 449, 481,
525, 970
façade n. 211, 222, 236,
477, 852
face n. 222, 236, 825;
vb. 226, 239, 857
face-lift n. 587, 589, 844
facet n. 7, 55
facetiousness n. 842
face value n. 743, 825

facility n. 514, 568, 627,
634
facsimile n. 20, 22
fact n. 1, 401, 426, 430,
460
fact-finding adj. 394
faction n. 641, 979
factious adj. 25, 642,
672
factor n. 8, 55, 155, 327
factory n. 620
factual adj. 1, 430
faculties n. 382
faculty n. 159
fad n. 125, 850
fade vb. 162, 588, 806,
826
fade out vb. 799
faeces n. 310
failing n. 819, 936
failure n. 315, 393, 431,
445, 571, 660, 662
faint vb. 162, 617
faint-hearted adj. 162,
858
faintness n. 162, 507,
617, 781, 799, 806
fair n. 840; adj.
(average) 30, 666; (of
weather) 759;
(whitish) 807; (good-
looking) 844; (just)
915, 931, 933
fairy n. 953, 970
fairy story n. 525
faith n. 420, 854, 974,
980
faithful adj. 430, 456,
673, 702, 882, 977
faithless adj. 409, 421
fake n. 20; adj. 20, 477,
478; vb. 20, 477, 852
fall n. 37, 317, 321, 358;
vb. 37, 317, 321, 588,
936
fallacy n. 412, 431
fall apart vb. 51
fall away vb. 538, 588

fall.back vb. 289, 293
fall back on vb. 606
fall down vb. 431, 662
fallen adj. 662
fallen angel n. 969
fallen woman n. 953
fall for vb. 422, 889
fallible adj. 431, 582
fall ill vb. 586
fall in vb. 254
falling star n. 329
fall in love vb. 889
fall on vb. 153, 179
fallow adj. 603, 612
fall short vb. 29, 35,
315, 571, 582, 662
fall through vb. 662
fall to vb. 716, 919
false adj. 2, 477, 478
falsehood n. 431, 477
false reasoning n. 412
falsification n. 457, 471,
477, 487
falter vb. 325, 515, 536,
662
fame n. 868
familiar adj. 138, 426,
545, 882
familiarize vb. 470, 545
family n. 11, 55, 97, 171
famished adj. 861, 947
famous adj. 573, 868
fan n. 764; vb. 348
fanatic n. 148, 537, 611
fanciful adj. 449, 539
fancy n. 448, 449, 539,
861; adj. 509, 846; vb.
448, 449, 540, 861, 889
fan out vb. 297
fantastic adj. 433, 449,
851, 866
fantasy n. 449, 481
far adj. 198
farce n. 433, 529, 851
fare n. 306, 743
farewell n. 299
far-flung adj. 198

farm *n.* 377, 378; *vb.* 377

farm out *vb.* 717

far-reaching *adj.* 32, 182

far-sighted *adj.* 434

farthest *adj.* 198

fascinate *vb.* 294, 547, 755, 889

fascinating *adj.* 547, 755, 829

fascism *n.* 669

fashion *n.* 125, 242, 545, 559, **850**

fast *n.* 947; *adj.* 280, 613, 805; *vb.* 947; *adv.* 280

fasten *vb.* 47, 50, 152, 263

fastidiousness *n.* 392, 540, **864**

fasting *n.* **947**; *adj.* 947

fat *n.* 306; *adj.* 194

fatal *adj.* 164, 369, 370

fatalism *n.* 531

fate *n.* 123, 154, **158**, 531, 543, 553

fat-head *n.* 437

father *n.* 11, 170

fathom *vb.* 452

fathomless *adj.* 210

fatigue *n.* **617**, 841

fatten *vb.* 204, 377

fatty *adj.* 365

fault *n.* 200, 315, 431, 582

faultless *adj.* 581, 937

faulty *adj.* 582

fauna *n.* 366, 373

faux pas *n.* 431

favour *n.* 636, 670, 715, 886, 899, 907, 922; *vb.* 540, 925

favourable *adj.* 854, 925

favourite *n.* **891**

favouritism *n.* 916

fawning *n.* 927; *adj.* 881

fear *n.* **856**, 858, 980; *vb.* 856

fearless *adj.* 857

feasible *adj.* 404, 406

feast *n.* 306; *vb.* 304

feat *n.* 605, 609

feathery *adj.* 331

feature *n.* 5, 8, 55, 825

fecundity *n.* 168

federal *adj.* 379, 641

federation *n.* 641

fed up with *adj.* 862

fee *n.* 738, 743, 917

feeble-minded *adj.* 435

feebleness *n.* 160, 162, 507, 666, 781

feed *vb.* 304, 377

feedback *n.* 395

feeder *n.* 559

feel *n.* 339, 398, 758; *vb.* 411, 752, 758

feel better *vb.* 834

feeler *n.* 394, 396

feel for *vb.* 758, 907

feeling *n.* 411, **752**, 758; *adj.* 752

feel like *vb.* 532

feel small *vb.* 874

fees *n.* 917

feign *vb.* 477, 852

felicitate *vb.* 888

felicitous *adj.* 510

fell *n.* 208; *vb.* 48

fellow *n.* 11, 122, 131, 380, 473

fellow-feeling *n.* 899, 907

fellowship *n.* 60, 639, 641, 988; *vb.* 988

fellow-worker *n.* 640

female *n.* 381; *adj.* 381

femininity *n.* 162, 381

feminism *n.* 381

fen *n.* 355

fence *n.* 230, 234

fend for oneself *vb.* 678

fend off *vb.* 646

ferment *n.* 80, 175; *vb.* 331, 363, 773

ferry *n.* 277; *vb.* 271

fertile *adj.* 163, 168

fertilize *vb.* 378

fervour *n.* 506, 752, 759

festive *adj.* 878

festivity *n.* 838, 840

festoon *n.* 846

fetch *vb.* 705, 718, 743

fete *n.* 840

fetid *adj.* 777

fetish *n.* 967, 983, 984

fetter *n.* 681; *vb.* 635, 681

feud *n.* 642, 649

fever *n.* 326, 439, 586

few *adj.* 33, 76, 139

fewness *n.* 33, **76**

fiancée *n.* 698, 889

fiasco *n.* 662

fib *vb.* 477

fibber *n.* 480

fibre *n.* 207, 339

fibrous *adj.* 337

fickle *adj.* 151, 536, 538, 539

fiction *n.* 525

fictitious *adj.* 2, 449

fiddle *n.* 478; *vb.* 722, 742

fidelity *n.* 673, 931

fidgety *adj.* 151, 611, 756, 856

field *n.* 184, 352, 356, 378, 557, 658

fiend *n.* 175, 969

fierce *adj.* 175, 900

fiery *adj.* 506, 759, 893

fiesta *n.* 840

fifth columnist *n.* 480

fight *n.* 642, 649, 651; *vb.* 25, 615, **637**, 642, 645, 649

fight back *vb.* 647

fighter *n.* 645, 655

figurative *adj.* 455

figure *n.* 39, 489; *vb.* 38

figure-head n. 253

figure of speech n. 455, 498

figure out vb. 452

filament n. 207

filch vb. 722

file n. 83, 202; vb. 83, 91, 255, 257, 341

filial adj. 171

filibuster n. 135; vb. 135

fill n. 865; vb. 56, 107, 265, 865

fill in vb. 149, 460, 483

fillip n. 173; vb. 613

fill up vb. 568

filly n. 381

film n. 225, 363, 483, 803; vb. 483

filter vb. 319

filth n. 584, 952

final adj. 89, 237, 408, 659

finality n. 543

finance n. 731; vb. 636, 718

financier n. 718, 728

find vb. 415, 419, 960

find fault with vb. 832, 926, 930, 962

fine n. 963; adj. 205, 255, 333, 340, 579, 844; vb. 963

finesse n. 631

finger vb. 758

fingerprint n. 482

finicky adj. 392, 864

finish n. 56, 89, 257, 510, 659; vb. 89, 144, 414, 581, 659

fiord n. 353

fire n. 506, 759, 763; vb. 645, 686, 755, 761, 765

firearm n. 657

fireproof adj. 762

fireside n. 191, 763

fireworks n. 800

firing squad n. 963

firm n. 620, 641; adj. 143, 152, 161, 334, 337, 534, 535, 669

first adj. 34, 88

first-class adj. 34, 579

first hand adj. 21

firth n. 353

fish n. 306, 373

fishy adj. 373, 932

fissure n. 254

fit n. 326, 439, 586, 893; adj. 585, 915; vb. 47, 105, 568, 602

fitful adj. 141, 539

fit in with vb. 24

fit out vb. 227, 602

fitting adj. 577, 915

fittings n. 568

five and over n. 70

fix n. 633; vb. 47, 152, 311, 589

fixation n. 439

fixative n. 49

fixed adj. 47, 143, 152, 543

fixtures n. 152, 568, 711

fizz n. 363; vb. 363, 786

fizzle out vb. 144, 162, 662

flabbergasted adj. 866

flabby adj. 668

flaccid adj. 507

flag n. 467, 482, 677; vb. 617, 841

flagellant n. 946

flagon n. 193

flagrant adj. 458, 877

flail vb. 282

flake n. 33, 206, 340; vb. 206

flake out vb. 617

flamboyant adj. 877

flame n. 797, 800; vb. 759

flammable adj. 761, 765

flank n. 238; vb. 238

flap n. 225, 326; vb. 216, 326, 359, 756

flare n. 797, 800; vb. 756, 797

flash n. 115, 539, 797, 800; vb. 797

flashback n. 147, 441

flashlight n. 800

flashy adj. 509, 805, 849, 877

flask n. 193

flat n. 191, 356; adj. 215, 257, 768, 791, 843

flat out adv. 280

flattery n. 881, 886, 927

flaunt vb. 877

flavour n. 767; vb. 307

flavourless adj. 768, 771

flaw n. 431, 582, 847

flawless adj. 54, 581

flay vb. 228, 963

fleck n. 33

fledgling n. 125

flee vb. 555, 600, 826

fleece n. 377, 478, 722

fleeting adj. 113

flesh n. 306, 327, 379

flesh and blood n. 3, 327

fleshly adj. 945

fleshy adj. 194, 364

flex vb. 247

flexible adj. 151, 335, 336, 668

flexuous adj. 251

flicker vb. 326, 759, 797

flickering adj. 141

flick through vb. 472, 818

flight n. 273, 293, 299, 555, 600, 826

flighty adj. 151, 539

flimsy adj. 162, 205, 335, 338

flinch vb. 283, 555, 856

fling vb. 359

flint n. 765

flippancy n. 842

flirt n. 953; vb. 890

flirtation *n.* 889, 890

flit *vb.* 113

float *vb.* 216, 257, 331

flock *n.* 75, 94, 982, 987; *vb.* 75, 94

flog *vb.* 963

flood *n.* 358, 572; *vb.* 349, 358, 572

floodlight *n.* 800

floor *n.* 206, 209, 213

flop *n.* 662

flora *n.* 366

floral *adj.* 374

florid *adj.* 846, 849

flounder *vb.* 409, 633, 662

flourish *n.* 877; *vb.* 36, 168, 585, 661, 664, 877

flout *vb.* 644

flow *n.* 85, 91, 301, 313, 343, 358

flower *n.* 374; *vb.* 163

flowering *n.* 127; *adj.* 129

flowery *adj.* 509

fluctuate *vb.* 141, 142, 151, 325, 536

flue *n.* 361

fluency *n.* 501, 514, 516

fluffy *adj.* 331, 335

fluid *n.* 243, 309, 343; *adj.* 343, 347

fluidity *n.* 343, 345

fluke *n.* 158, 553

flurry *n.* 359, 611, 613

flush *adj.* 28, 215; *vb.* 811

fluster *n.* 756

fluted *adj.* 261

flutter *vb.* 325, 326, 359

flux *vb.* 345

fly *vb.* 110, 113, 273, 280

foam *n.* 363; *vb.* 363, 893

focal *adj.* 90, 96, 224

focalize *vb.* 296

focus *n.* 90, 96, 224; *vb.* 96, 224, 390

fodder *n.* 305; *vb.* 377

foe *n.* 638, 883

fog *n.* 363, 409, 427, 799

foil *vb.* 445, 635, 648, 662

fold *n.* 206, 260; *vb.* 251, 260, 739

foliage *n.* 374

folk *n.* 379

follow *vb.* 85, 105, 119, 237, 287, 452, 673, 702

follower *n.* 119, 287, 424, 474, 554, 640, 821

following *n.* 85, 287; *adj.* 85, 119, 156, 554

follow up *vb.* 392, 554

follow-up *n.* 87

folly *n.* 385, 433, 435

fond *adj.* 861, 889

fondle *vb.* 758, 890

fondness *n.* 861, 889, 890

food *n.* 305, 306

fool *n.* 429, 437, 440, 479; *vb.* 478

fool around *vb.* 433, 435

foolhardy *adj.* 613, 859

foolish *adj.* 385, 433, 435, 451

foot *n.* 213, 528

footing *n.* 93

footpath *n.* 559

footprint *n.* 482, 483

fop *n.* 852

foray *n.* 645

forbearance *n.* 670, 757, 907, 911

forbears *n.* 11, 86

forbid *vb.* 99, 635, 691, 955

forbidding *adj.* 669, 691

force *n.* 159, 161, 175, 177, 506, 674; *vb.* 175, 282, 531, 562, 674

forced *adj.* 507, 511

force in *vb.* 300, 311

force oneself *vb.* 533

forces *n.* 655

ford *vb.* 313

fore *adj.* 236

foreboding *n.* 447, 597; *adj.* 447

forecast *n.* 154, 348, 447; *vb.* 154, 443, 446, 447, 558

foregoing *adj.* 84, 118

foreground *n.* 199, 236

foreign *adj.* 100, 222

foreknowledge *n.* 447

foreman *n.* 623, 958

foremost *adj.* 236, 573

foreordain *vb.* 531, 543

forerun *vb.* 84, 118

forerunner *n.* 86, 467

foresee *vb.* 443, 446, 447

foreshadow *vb.* 447, 976

foresight *n.* 134, 434, 446, 447, 860

forest *n.* 374

forestall *vb.* 134

foretaste *n.* 55, 118

foretell *vb.* 447, 543

forethought *n.* 392, 446, 447, 860

forever *adv.* 114

forewarn *vb.* 447, 597

foreword *n.* 86, 88

forfeit *n.* 43, 701; *vb.* 706

forge *vb.* 477

forge ahead *vb.* 288

forgery *n.* 20, 22

forget *vb.* 385, 393, 442

forgiveness *n.* 601, 670, 907, 911

forgo *vb.* 556

forgotten *adj.* 124, 126, 442

fork *n.* 246, 255, 297, 358; *vb.* 63, 297

fork out *vb.* 738

forlorn *adj.* 837

form *n.* 242, 339, 474, 482, 825; *vb.* 58, 242

formal *adj.* 511, 988

formalism *n.* 981

formalize *vb.* 81

formation *n.* 242, 655

formative *adj.* 129, 242

former *adj.* 84, 118, 124, 126

formless *adj.* 243

formula *n.* 39, 103, 498, 626

formulate *vb.* 81, 468, 498

fornicate *vb.* 952

fornicator *n.* 953

forsake *vb.* 556

forswear *vb.* 477

forte *n.* 627

forthcoming *adj.* 154, 292

forthright *adj.* 476, 632

forthwith *adv.* 115

fortification *n.* 646

fortify *vb.* 161, 173, 646, 857

fortitude *n.* 534, 857

fortress *n.* 595, 646

fortuitous *adj.* 136, 158, 553

fortunate *adj.* 661

fortune *n.* 158, 447, 550, 553, 734

forum *n.* 96, 625, 658

forward *adj.* 236, 288, 880; *vb.* 268; *adv.* 288

forward-looking *adj.* 125, 288

fossilize *vb.* 334

foster *vb.* 470, 636

foul *adj.* 584, 777; *vb.* 584

foul play *n.* 551, 900, 916, 932

found *vb.* 88

foundation *n.* 88, 155, 213, 217, 401, 602

founder *n.* 155; *vb.* 588

foundry *n.* 620

fountain *n.* 358, 567

four *n.* 67; *adj.* 67

fourfold *adj.* 68

fowl *n.* 306, 373

fracas n. 80

fraction *n.* 39, 73, 717

fracture *n.* 48; *vb.* 48

fragile *adj.* 162, 338

fragment *n.* 33, 55, 73, 717; *vb.* 48, 338

fragrance *n.* 774, 776

frail *adj.* 162, 338, 507, 586

frame *n.* 5; *vb.* 558, 930

frame of mind *n.* 751

frame of reference *n.* 700

framework *n.* 5, 232

franchise *n.* 540; *vb.* 690

frangible *adj.* 338

frank *adj.* 476, 508, 632, 931

fraternity *n.* 11, 882

fraud *n.* 478, 631, 722

fraudulent *adj.* 477, 478, 631, 932

freak *n.* 440, 539, 866

freckled · *adj.* 817

free *adj.* 10, 530, 600, 678, 708, 715, 897, 911; *vb.* 48, 600, 601, 678, 680, 921

freedom *n.* 600, 678, 690, 921

freedom from mixture *n.* 46

free thinking *n.* 975

free time *n.* 614

free will *n.* 530, 678

freeze *vb.* 332, 334, 599, 760, 762

freight *n.* 192, 268

frenzied *adj.* 439, 859

frenzy · *n.* 80, 175, 439, 861

frequency *n.* 27, 138, 140, 400

frequent *adj.* 138, 545; *vb.* 188

fresh *adj.* 125, 359, 599, 760

freshen *vb.* 348, 583

fret *vb.* 837

fretting *n.* 828

friable *adj.* 338, 340

friar *n.* 986

friary *n.* 990

friction *n.* 181, 341, 642

fridge *n.* 764

friend *n.* 640, 882

friendless *adj.* 885

friendly *adj.* 643, 882, 884, 886

friendship *n.* 643, 650, **882**

frighten *vb.* 856, 902

frightful *adj.* 845

frigid *adj.* 160, 169, 754, 760

frill *n.* 509, 846

fringe *n.* 233, 235

frisky *adj.* 320

fritter away *vb.* 749

frivolous *adj.* 539

front *n.* 222, 236, 658, 852; *adj.* 236

frontier *n.* 233, 235

frost *n.* 760; *vb.* 762

frosted *adj.* 804, 807

froth *n.* 363

frown *n.* 895; *vb.* 895

frown on *vb.* 926

frozen *adj.* 332, 760, 762

frugal *adj.* 392, 748, 944

fruit *n.* 156, 163, 306

fruitful *adj.* 163, 168, 661

fruitless *adj.* 169, 576, 662

frustrate *vb.* 181, 445, 635, 648, 662

fry *vb.* 306, 759

fuel *n.* 765; *vb.* 765
fugitive *n.* 555, 600
fulcrum *n.* 217
fulfil *vb.* 56, 659, 661, 673, 702
fulfilment *n.* 659, 827
full *adj.* 54, 56, 204, 570, 865
fullness *n.* 32, 56, 567
fulminate *vb.* 780
fulsome *adj.* 168
fumble *vb.* 409, 758
fumbler *n.* 630
fume *n.* 344, 777; *vb.* 175, 346, 756, 759, **893**
fumigate *vb.* 583, 775
fun *n.* 829, 836, 840, 842
function *n.* 39, 172, 557, 878; *vb.* 172, 609
functional *adj.* 172, 575
functionary *n.* 623
fundamental *adj.* 5, 88, 155, 213, 573
fundamentalist *adj.* 977
funds *n.* 731
funeral *n.* 372
fungus *n.* 167, 592
funk *n.* 858; *vb.* 856, 858
funny *adj.* 842, 851
furious *adj.* 175, 893
furlough *n.* 614
furnace *n.* 763
furnish *vb.* 163, 568, 715
furniture *n.* 711
furrow *n.* 254, 261
further *adj.* 40; *vb.* 217 288, 587; *adv.* 40
furthest *adj.* 89, 198
furtive *adj.* 461, 478
fury *n.* 175, 756, 893
fuse *n.* 765; *vb.* 45, 47, 52, 345
fusion *n.* 45, 47, 52, 639
fuss *n.* 326, 756, 877; *vb.* 756, 864
fussy *adj.* 392, 864

futile *adj.* 576, 662, 855
future *n.* **123**; *adj.* 123
future events *n.* **154**
futuristic *adj.* 125
fuzzy *adj.* 243, 503, 824

G

gabble *vb.* 516
gad about *vb.* 269
gadget *n.* 565
gag *n.* 842; *vb.* 681
gaiety *n.* 836
gain *n.* 288, 550, 705; *vb.* 36, 116, 705, 720
gala *n.* 840
galaxy *n.* 329
gale *n.* 175, 359
gallant *adj.* 857, 886
gallery *n.* 818
galley *n.* 522
gallivant about *vb.* 269
gallows *n.* 964
galore *adj.* 75
galvanize *vb.* 755
gamble *n.* 158, 553; *vb.* 158, 553
gambler *n.* 553
game *n.* 306, 373, 649, 840; *adj.* 532, 857
gamekeeper *n.* 683
gamut *n.* 182
gang *n.* 94
gangster *n.* 370, 906
gang up against *vb.* 639
gaol *n.* 682
gap *n.* 92, 200, 262
gape *vb.* 262, 818, 866
garb *n.* 227
garbage *n.* 44
garble *vb.* 487, 515
garden *n.* 234, 374, 378
gardener *n.* 378
garish *adj.* 805, 846, 877
garment *n.* 227
garnish *vb.* 846

garrison *n.* 646
garrulous *adj.* 516
gas *n.* 159, 344, 765; *vb.* 963
gaseity *n.* **344**
gash *n.* 588
gasify *vb.* 344, 346
gasp *n.* 359; *vb.* 359
gastronomy *n.* 304
gate *n.* 262
gatecrash *vb.* 300
gate-crasher *n.* 884
gather *n.* 260; *vb.* **94**, 196, 260, 296, 448, 567
gaudy *adj.* 805, 846, 877
gauge *n.* 400, 482; *vb.* 400, 482
gay *n.* 106, 953; *adj.* 836, 952
gaze *vb.* 818
gazette *n.* 483, 524
gear *n.* 227
geld *vb.* 160, 169
gem *n.* 579, 846
gene *n.* 5
genealogy *n.* 170
general *adj.* 101
generality *n.* **101**
generalize *vb.* 101
generally *adv.* 138, 545
generate *vb.* 11, 155, 163
generation *n.* 11, 109, 163, 171
generative *adj.* 163, 170
generic *adj.* 101
generosity *n.* 747, 886
generous *adj.* 715, 747, 899, 965
genetics *n.* 366
genial *adj.* 827, 836, 884
genius *n.* 382, 428, 434, 627, 629
genocide *n.* 370, 963
gentle *adj.* 176, 670, 907
gentleman *n.* 380
gentlemanly *adj.* 380, 886

gentleman's agreement n. 698, 699

gentry n. 870

genuine adj. 1, 21, 430, 632

geography n. 329

geology n. 367

geometry n. 38

gesticulate vb. 482

gesture n. 482, 549; vb. 482

get vb. 705, 716, 720, 726

get across vb. 460

get along with vb. 24, 643

get around vb. 464

get at vb. 460, 547, 893

get-at-able adj. 292

getaway n. 600

get away with vb. 600, 722, 921

get back vb. 647, 705, 721

get by vb. 661, 666

get down vb. 298, 837

get down to vb. 605

get dressed vb. 227

get even with vb. 647, 912, 963

get in with vb. 177, 882

get on vb. 661, 664

get one's own back vb. 647, 912

get on one's nerves vb. 787, 893

get on with vb. 24, 643

get over vb. 460, 659

get ready vb. 602

get rid of vb. 303, 607, 634, 680

get the hang of vb. 452, 472

get to vb. 298

get-together n. 884

get up vb. 318, 472, 477

get-up-and-go n. 173, 611

get used to vb. 545

get well vb. 589

ghastly adj. 856

ghost n. 328, 971

ghostly adj. 4, 328, 971

ghost-writer n. 149, 524

giant n. 194; adj. 208

gibberish n. 453

gibe vb. 853

gift n. 627, 652, 715, 829

gifted adj. 627

gift of the gab n. 514, 516

giggle vb. 838

gild vb. 846

ginger adj. 816

gipsy n. 447

gird vb. 322

girder n. 217

girdle n. 49; vb. 229

girl n. 131, 381

girl-friend n. 882, 889

girth n. 204

gist n. 224

give vb. 335, 568, 715, 965

give and take n. 150, 639, 704

give away vb. 462, 717, 896

give in vb. 654

given adj. 1, 715

give off vb. 301, 774

give out vb. 301, 774, 778

giver n. 715, 905

give up vb. 556, 654, 855

give up office vb. 687

give way vb. 162

giving n. 636, 715, 747

glaciate vb. 762

glacier n. 760

glad adj. 827, 836

gladden vb. 829, 836

gladly adv. 532

glamorous adj. 829, 844

glamour n. 547, 829, 844

glance n. 818; vb. 818

glare n. 797; vb. 797, 818

glaring adj. 458, 805, 823

glass n. 193, 257, 822

glasses n. 822

glassy adj. 257, 802

glaze n. 225; vb. 225, 369, 257

gleam n. 797; vb. 797

glean vb. 378, 540, 705

glee n. 827, 836

glib adj. 516

glide vb. 257, 273

glider n. 278

glimmer n. 460, 797; vb. 326, 797

glimpse n. 818; vb. 818

glint n. 797

glisten vb. 797

glitter n. 797; vb. 797

global adj. 101

globe n. 249, 329

globe-trotter n. 270

globule n. 249, 363

gloom n. 798, 799, 837

gloomy adj. 798, 799, 837, 843, 895

glorification n. 925, 972

glorify vb. 318, 868, 982

glorious adj. 664, 972, 982

glory n. 868, 972; vb. 873

gloss n. 211, 225, 257, 456, 797; vb. 225, 257, 456

glossary n. 83, 494

gloss over vb. 393

glossy adj. 257, 797

glow n. 759, 797, 805; vb. 759, 797, 811

glue n. 49, 362; vb. 50

glum adj. 895

glut n. 572, 865

glutton   *n.* 304, 948

gluttony   *n.* 304, 750, 945, **948**

gnome   *n.* 970

go   *vb.* 172, **266**, **299**

goad   *vb.* 547, 613

go after   *vb.* 85, 119, 287, 554, 882

go-ahead   *n.* 424, 690; *adj.* 605, 611

goal   *n.* 89, 298, 552

go along with   *vb.* 424, 639

go around   *vb.* 322

go around with   *vb.* 882

go away   *vb.* 299, 826, 896

go back   *vb.* 147, 289, 441

go back on   *vb.* 556

go bad   *vb.* 588

gobble   *vb.* 304, 789, 948

go before   *vb.* 84, 118, 286

go behind   *vb.* 85

go-between   *n.* 467, 653

go beyond   *vb.* 314

goblin   *n.* 970

God   *n.* 966, **967**

goddess   *n.* 967

God-forsaken   *adj.* 198, 885

godhead   *n.* 966

godless   *adj.* 975, 981

godly   *adj.* 966, 974, 980

go down   *vb.* 317, 321, 586, 662

godsend   *n.* 550

go for   *vb.* 284, 540, 552, 743, 861

goggles   *n.* 801, 822

go in   *vb.* 300

go in for   *vb.* 472, 605

go into   *vb.* 394, 472

go it alone   *vb.* 678

gold   *adj.* 813, 816

golden   *adj.* 664, 813

golden age   *n.* 664, 827

golden calf   *n.* 967, 983

golden   handshake   *n.* 687, 715

golden rule   *n.* 899

gold-mine   *n.* 567

go mad   *vb.* 439

gondola   *n.* 277

gone   *adj.* 124, 706, 855

gone off   *adj.* 771

gone on   *adj.* 889

gong   *n.* 784

good   *n.* **550**; *adj.* 550, 579, 585, 673, 899, 931

goodbye   *n.* 518

good deed   *n.* 899

good example   *n.* 939

good-for-nothing   *n.* 612, 940

good health   *n.* 585

good humour   *n.* 836

good-looking   *adj.* 844

good luck   *n.* 158

good manners   *n.* 886

good memory   *n.* 441

good name   *n.* 868

good neighbour   *n.* 899, 905

goodness   *n.* **579**, 907, 931, 935

good person   *n.* **939**

goods   *n.* 163, 711, 729

good spirit   *n.* **968**

good taste   *n.* **848**

good time   *n.* 840

good turn   *n.* 550, 886, 899

goodwill   *n.* 643

go off at a tangent   *vb.* 285, 505

go off with   *vb.* 722

go on   *vb.* 1, 138, 145, 535

go on about   *vb.* 516, 832

go on strike   *vb.* 696

goose   *n.* 381

go out   *vb.* 144, **301**

go out of control   *vb.* 326

go out with   *vb.* 882, 890

go over   *vb.* 77

gorge   *n.* 200, 210, 254; *vb.* 56, 304, 865

gorgeous   *adj.* 844

go round   *vb.* 250

go shopping   *vb.* 726

go-slow   *n.* 144, 281

gospel   *n.* 430, 976

gossamer   *n.* 207

gossip   *n.* 388, **516**, 516, 869, 928; *vb.* 388, 516

go   through   *vb.* 313, 752, 828

go through the motions   *vb.* 477, 852

go through with   *vb.* 659

go together   *vb.* 60, 882

go to law   *vb.* 960

go to pieces   *vb.* 588, 856

go to press   *vb.* 522

go to the bottom   *vb.* 321

gouge   *n.* 259, 261, 312; *vb.* 254, 312

go under   *vb.* 321, 662, 665, 739

go up   *vb.* 316, 745

gourmand   *n.* 304, 848, 948

gourmandise   *n.* 304

gourmet   *n.* 304

govern   *vb.* 177, 622, 667, 681

governess   *n.* 473, 675, 683

government   *n.*   621, 622, 625, 667

governmental   *adj.* 622, 667

governor   *n.* 623, 675

go with   *vb.* 24, 60, 882

go wrong   *vb.* 431

grab   *vb.* 705, 720, 758

grace n. 844, 848, 907,
911

graceful adj. 510, 844,
848

gracious adj. 510, 899,
907, 966

gradation n. 27

grade n. 27, 93, 400,
474; vb. 27, 97

gradual adj. 27

graduate n. 474; vb. 27,
400

graft vb. 378

grain n. 33, 306, 340,
374

grammar n. 492, **499**

grammarian n. 492

grammatical adj. 492,
499

granary n. 193

grand adj. 509, 844,
868, 870

grandeur n. 870, 877

grandiloquent adj. 509

grandiose adj. 509, 877

grandstand n. 818

grange n. 191, 378

grant n. 636, 715; vb.
424, 690, 692, 715

grant permission vb.
424

granular adj. 339

granulate vb. 340

granule n. 340

grapevine n. 465

graphic adj. 488, 506,
521, 525

graphics n. 488

grapple vb. 758

grasp n. 410, 707, 712;
vb. 50, 426, 452, 472,
707, 712, 720, 758

grasping adj. 705, 720,
750

grass n. 356, 374, 460

grassland n. 356, 378

grassy adj. 374, 812

grate n. 763; vb. 341,
787, 805

grateful adj. 909

gratify vb. 829, 831, 865

grating adj. 787, 791

gratitude n. **909**

gratuity n. 715, 965

grave n. 372; adj. 573,
837

graven image n. 983

gravestone n. 372

gravitate towards vb.
178

gravity n. 294, 330, 573,
837

graze vb. 201, 341, 377,
758

grease n. 306, 342, 365,
584; vb. 342, 365

greasy adj. 365, 584

great adj. 32, 573, 579,
868, 870

greater adj. 34

greatness n. 26, 32, 194,
579, 868, 870

greedy adj. 720, 750,
861, 934, **948**

greedy-guts n. 948

green n. 559, **812**; adj.
129, 422, 427, 812, 913

greenhorn n. 429, 479,
630

greenhouse n. 378

greet vb. 886, 922

greeting n. 518, 886,
922

gregarious adj. 884

gremlin n. 970

grey n. **809**; adj. 30,
130, 363, 799, 809

grey matter n. 434

grid n. 159, 221

grief n. 828, 837, 839

grievance n. 916

grieve vb. 830, 833, 837,
839

grill n. 221; vb. 306,
394, 759

grim adj. 669, 830

grimace n. 895; vb. 245,
895

grimy adj. 584

grin n. 838; vb. 838

grin and bear it vb. 757,
836

grind vb. 341, 615, 787

grip n. 193, 712; vb. 50,
712, 720, 758

gripping adj. 755

gristle n. 337

groan n. 788; vb. 696,
788

groceries n. 305

groggy adj. 586, 950

groom vb. 377, 470

groove n. 184, 261, 545;
vb. 261

grope vb. 409, 758

gross n. 70; adj. 54, 56,
849, 936

grotesque adj. 245, 845

grotto n. 254

grouch n. 832; vb. 895

ground n. (reason) 155,
401, 547, 929; (land)
213, 352, 658; vb. 319,
470

groundwork n. 213, 602

group n. 55, 94, 97, 641,
793; vb. 52, 94, 97

grovel vb. 209, 881, 922

grow vb. 36, 168, 196,
242, 288, 316, 324

growl vb. 783, 789, 895

grown-up n. 133; adj.
133

growth n. 36, 196, 252,
288, 324

grow up vb. 133

grudge n. 832, 893; vb.
914

grudgingly adv. 533

gruelling adj. 615

gruff adj. 787, 887, 894

grumble vb. 783, 832

grumbler n. 832

grumpy *adj.* 894

grunt *vb.* 789

guarantee *n.* 424; *vb.* 408, 468, 698, 701

guard *n.* 593, 646, 683; *vb.* 392, 593, 646

guardian *n.* 593, 683, 905

guardroom *n.* 682

guerdon *n.* 965

guerrilla *n.* 148

guess *n.* 386, 396, 447, 448; *vb.* 396, 411, **448**

guest *n.* 100, 884

guffaw *vb.* 838

guidance *n.* 470, 624

guide *n.* 103, 217, 473, 623; *vb.* 470, 621, 622, **624**

guidebook *n.* 460, 524

guile *n.* 477, 478, 631, 932

guileless *adj.* 422, 476, 632, 937, 951

guillotine *n.* 964; *vb.* 370, 963

guilt *n.* **938**

guilty *adj.* 938

guinea pig *n.* 396, 716, 828

guise *n.* 227, 463, 549

gulf *n.* 200, 254, 353

gullibility *n.* 422

gully *n.* 254, 360

gulp *n.* 309; *vb.* 304, 948

gum *n.* 365; *vb.* 50

gun *n.* 657; *vb.* 370

gunman *n.* 167, 370

gunpowder *n.* 657

gurgle *vb.* 358

guru *n.* 473

gush *vb.* 301, 358, 532

gust *n.* 359

gusto *n.* 827

gusty *adj.* 359

guts *n.* 535, 857

gutter *n.* 261, 360

guzzle *vb.* 304, 948, 950

gypsy *n.* 270

gyration *n.* 323

H

habit *n.* 79, 138, **545**

habitat *n.* **191**, 229

habitation *n.* 188, **191**

hack *n.* 524, 619, 676

hackneyed *adj.* 426

haggard *adj.* 205, 617

hail *n.* 760; *vb.* 886, 925

hair *n.* 207

hair-dressing *n.* 844

hairless *adj.* 228

hairy *adj.* 207, 258

halcyon days *n.* 664, 827

hale *adj.* 585

half *n.* 63; *adj.* 63

half a dozen *n.* 70

half-and-half *adj.* 45

half-done *adj.* 55, 57, 660

half-hearted *adj.* 533, 863

half-price *adj.* 746

half-remembered *adj.* 441

halfway *n.* 30, 704; *adj.* 30, 90, 560; *adv.* 90

half-wit *n.* 437

half-witted *adj.* 435

hall *n.* 191, 529

hallmark *n.* 482

hallow *vb.* 980

hallucination *n.* 478

halo *n.* 250, 800

halt *n.* 144; *vb.* 144, 267, 691

halve *vb.* 63

hamlet *n.* 183

hammer *vb.* 282

hammer out *vb.* 659, 699

hamper *n.* 193; *vb.* 635, 681, 691

hand *n.* 238, 521

handbook *n.* 524

hand down *vb.* 714

handful *n.* 26, 76, 633

handicap *vb.* 162

hand in one's notice *vb.* 687

handiwork *n.* 163

handle *n.* 872; *vb.* 172, 606, 609, 622, 725

hand out *vb.* 715, 717

hand-out *n.* 464, 465, 715

hand over *vb.* 268

handshake *n.* 886

handsome *adj.* 844

handwriting *n.* 521

handy *adj.* 575, 627

handyman *n.* 629

hang *vb.* 216, 370, 963

hang around *vb.* 188, 612

hanger-on *n.* 287, 640, 881

hanging *n.* 216, 370, 963

hangman *n.* 370, 963

hangover *n.* 44, 950

hanker *vb.* 861, 914

haphazard *adj.* 158, 399, 409, 553

happen *vb.* 1, 107, 153, 825

happening *n.* 153

happiness *n.* 550, 661, 664, 831, **836**

happy *adj.* 827, 831, **836**, 950

happy medium *n.* 30

happy returns *n.* 888

harangue *n.* 518

harass *vb.* 830, 893

harbour *n.* 298, 353, 595; *vb.* 461, 593, 712

hard *adj.* 334, 337, 537, **633**, 669, 942

harden *vb.* 332, 334, 337, 754

hardened *adj.* 537, 942

hard-hearted *adj.* 648, 754, 908

hard labour *n.* 963

hardly *adv.* 33, 139

hardness *n.* 334, 537, 633, 669, 754

hardship *n.* 633, 665, 735

hard-working *adj.* 611, 615

hardy *adj.* 161

harlot *n.* 953

harm *n.* 551, 900; *vb.* 580, 608, 900, 916

harmful *adj.* 164, 580, 592, 916

harmonious *adj.* 24, 79, 105, 244, 643, 790

harmony *n.* 24, 244, 510, 643, 650, 790

harness *n.* 49; *vb.* 47

harrow *vb.* 378, 830

harrowing *adj.* 828, 856

harsh *adj.* 258, 642, 669, 787, 900, 908

harsh sound *n.* 787

harvest *n.* 128, 163, 567; *vb.* 378, 567

haste *n.* 280, 613

hasty *adj.* 393, 544, 603, 613

hatch *n.* 262; *vb.* 449, 477, 558

hatchway *n.* 262

hate *n.* 862, 892, 900; *vb.* 862, 892

hatred *n.* 862, 883, 892

haughty *adj.* 873, 875, 924

haul *n.* 291, 724; *vb.* 268, 291

haunt *vb.* 188, 441, 830, 971

have *vb.* 707

have a go *vb.* 604

have fun *vb.* 840

have in mind *vb.* 552

have it in for *vb.* 892, 900

haven *n.* 595

have nothing to do with *vb.* 10, 542, 862

have no time for *vb.* 923

have-nots *n.* 871

have on *vb.* 227, 478

have one's own way *vb.* 530

have one's say *vb.* 468

have on one's mind *vb.* 384

havoc *n.* 164

hawk *vb.* 695, 727

hawker *n.* 697, 728

hazard *n.* 553, 594; *vb.* 553

hazel *adj.* 810

hazy *adj.* 363, 799, 824

H-bomb *n.* 657

head *n.* 89, 236, 675; *vb.* 212, 236, 284, 286

headache *n.* 633, 950

headlines *n.* 465

headlong *adj.* 613, 859

headmaster *n.* 473

headquarters *n.* 96

head start *n.* 34

headstone *n.* 372

headstrong *adj.* 537, 859

headway *n.* 288

heal *vb.* 589, 591

health *n.* 585

heap *n.* 567; *vb.* 567, 747

hear *vb.* 778, 795, 960

hearing *n.* 795, 960

hearsay *n.* 465

heart *n.* 223, 224, 368, 751, 857

heart-broken *adj.* 828, 837

heartening *adj.* 836, 857

hearth *n.* 191, 763

heartlessness *n.* 908

heart-to-heart *n.* 519

heartwarming *adj.* 836

hearty *adj.* 585

heat *n.* 759, 763; *vb.* 306, 761

heath *n.* 356

heathen *n.* 975, 983

heating *n.* 761

heatwave *n.* 759

heave *vb.* 291, 303, 318, 834

heaven *n.* 329, 972

heavenly *adj.* 770, 966, 972

heavy *adj.* 330, 332, 511, 573, 617, 841

heavy drinker *n.* 950

heavy-handed *adj.* 628, 669

heavy-laden *adj.* 828

heavyweight *adj.* 573

heckle *vb.* 425, 696

hedge *n.* 234; *vb.* 555

hedonistic *adj.* 827, 945

heed *n.* 390, 392, 860; *vb.* 390, 392, 673, 702

heedless *adj.* 391, 442, 859

hefty *adj.* 161

height *n.* 26, 208, 400, 581

heighten *vb.* 36, 318, 481, 835

heinous *adj.* 936

heir *n.* 171, 710, 716

helicopter *n.* 278

helix *n.* 251

hell *n.* 828, 973

helmsman *n.* 272

help *n.* 563, 636, 639, 834; *vb.* 563, 575, 577, 636, 639, 676

helper *n.* 624, 640, 905

helpful *adj.* 550, 575, 636

helping *n.* 305, 717

holy orders   n. 985
Holy Spirit   n. 967
homage   n. 982
home   n. 11, 191, 595;
   adj. 190
homecoming   n. 298
homeless   adj. 59, 187
homely   adj. 508, 827
home-made   adj. 628
homesickness   n. 861
homestead   n. 191, 377,
   378
homework   n. 470, 472
homicide   n. 370
homogeneity   n. 13, 16,
   46, 59
homo sapiens   n. 379
homosexual   n.   106,
   953; adj. 952
honest   adj. 430, 476,
   915, 931
honey   n. 772, 891
honeymoon   n.   829,
   896; vb. 896
honour   n. 663, 868,
   872, 909, 922, 982; vb.
   868, 878, 922, 982
honourable   adj.   868,
   931
hood   n. 225, 801, 989
hooded   adj. 225
hoodwink   vb. 478, 819
hook   n. 49; vb. 47, 896
hooligan   n. 906
hoop   n. 250; vb. 788
hoot   vb. 482, 788, 853
hooter   n. 116, 482
hop   n. 320; vb. 320
hope   n. 406, 420, 443,
   854; vb. 406, 443, 552,
   854
hopeful   adj. 443, 854
hopelessness   n.   405,
   576, 855
horizon   n. 198
horizontal   adj. 215, 248
horn   n. 598
horn of plenty   n. 168

horology   n. 116
horoscope   n. 329, 447
horrible   adj. 580, 771
horrid   adj. 580, 845
horrifying   adj. 856
horror   n. 845, 856
horse   n. 275
horsemanship   n. 269
horse-power   n. 159
horse-racing   n. 269
horse-rider   n. 270
horticultural   adj. 374,
   376, 378
hospitable   adj. 716, 884
hospitality   n. 302, 747,
   884
host   n. 75, 968
hostage   n. 701
hostel   n. 191
hostile   adj. 637, 665,
   883, 892
hostilities   n. 649, 651
hot   adj. 759, 769
hotel   n. 191
hour   n. 109
hour-glass   n. 116
hourly   adv. 140
house   n. 191, 620
household   n. 11; adj.
   426
householder   n. 190
housekeeper   n.   676,
   683
housekeeping   n.   622,
   748
hover   vb. 154, 216
hovercraft   n. 278
howl   vb. 359, 788, 789,
   839
hub   n. 96, 224
huddle   n. 94; vb. 94
hue   n. 805
hug   n. 712, 886; vb. 50,
   712, 886, 890
huge   adj. 32, 194
hull   n. 225
hum   n. vb. 781, 783,
   784, 789

human   n. 368; adj. 379
human being   n. 379
humane   adj. 903
humanitarian   adj. 899,
   903
humanity   n. 379
human rights   n. 917
human sound   n. 788
humble   adj. 35, 654,
   833, 871, 874, 941, 980;
   vb. 869, 874, 922
humble oneself   vb. 833,
   874, 941, 982
humid   adj. 349, 759
humiliate   vb. 869, 874,
   923
humility   n. 654, 874,
   980
humorous   adj. 842
humour   n. 5, 751, 842
hump   n. 252
hunch   n. 134, 411; vb.
   319
hunchbacked   adj. 245
hundred   n. 70
hunger   n. 861, 947; vb.
   861
hunger strike   n. 696
hungry   adj. 735, 861,
   947
hunt   n. 554; vb. 394,
   554
hurdle   n. 230, 235, 320,
   635
hurricane   n. 175, 359
hurried   adj. 613, 859
hurry   n. 280, 611, 613;
   vb. 280, 613
hurt   n. 828; adj. 893;
   vb. 580, 608, 830, 900,
   916
hurtful   adj. 164, 551,
   580, 828, 830
husband   n. 896; vb.
   377, 748
husbandry   n. 378, 622,
   748

247

hush n. 779, 781; vb. 267, 779

hush-hush adj. 461, 466

hush up vb. 466

husk n. 225

husky adj. 787

hut n. 191

hybrid n. 45, 495

hydrated adj. 347

hydro- adj. 347

hydro-electricity n. 159, 765

hydrogen bomb n. 657

hygienic adj. 585

hymn n. 792, 982

hyperbole n. 481

hyper-critical adj. 832, 864

hyper-sensitive adj. 753

hypnosis n. 754

hypochondriac n. 440

hypocrisy n. 477, 981

hypocrite n. 480, 631

hypothesis n. 157, 386, 396, 448

hypothetical adj. 2, 396, 448

hysteria n. 439, 756

hysteric n. 440

I

ice n. 347, 760; vb. 762

iceberg n. 754, 760

icon n. 983

icy adj. 760, 762

idea n. 386, 415, 420, 449, 552

ideal n. 581, 939; adj. 449, 581

idealist n. 449, 864, 903

identical adj. 13

identification n. 397, 419, 482, 496

identify vb. 482, 496

identity n. 13

idiom n. 492, 498

idiosyncratic adj. 102

idiosyncrasy n. 5, 102, 501

idiot n. 437, 440, 630

idiotic adj. 435

idle adj. 174, 610, 612; vb. 107, 174, 281, 612

idler n. 281, 612, 940

idol n. 967, 983

idolatry n. 975, 983

idolize vb. 982, 983

idyllic adj. 528

ignite vb. 761

ignited adj. 759

ignoble adj. 871

ignominious adj. 869

ignoramus n. 429, 437, 630

ignorance n. 385, 427

ignorant adj. 427

ignore vb. 385, 389, 393, 672, 694, 887, 911

ill n. 551, 900; adj. 586

illegal adj. 691, 916, 955

illegality n. 955

illegible adj. 453

illegitimate adj. 171, 916, 955

ill feeling n. 642, 883

ill health n. 586

ill-humoured adj. 895

illicit adj. 691, 916, 952, 955

illiterate adj. 427

illness n. 586, 828

illogical adj. 412, 451

illuminate vb. 456, 797

illusion n. 4, 449, 478

illustrate vb. 413, 456, 486, 488, 525

illustration n. 23, 397, 413, 456, 486, 488, 525

illustrative adj. 456, 486

illustrious adj. 573, 868

image n. 386, 486, 489, 525, 983

imagery n. 455

imaginable adj. 404

imaginary adj. 2, 449, 970

imagination n. 449

imagine vb. 448, 449

imbecile n. 437, 440; adj. 435

imbecility n. 383, 435, 439

imitate vb. 18, 20

imitation n. 20, 486, 719; adj. 149

immaculate adj. 581, 583, 935

immanent adj. 5, 966

immateriality n. 4, 328, 574

immaturity n. 129, 427, 582, 603

immeasurable adj. 78

immediate adj. 115, 134

immensity n. 194

immerse vb. 311, 321, 349

immersed adj. 210

immigrant n. 100, 190, 270; adj. 100

immigration n. 300

imminent adj. 123, 134, 154, 902

immobile adj. 152, 174, 267

immoderate adj. 32, 393, 572, 749, 918, 945

immoral adj. 932, 936, 952

immortal adj. 114, 966

immortalize vb. 114, 868

immovable adj. 143, 152, 267, 669, 757

immunity n. 593, 678, 921

immutability n. 152

imp n. 969, 970

impact n. 282

impair vb. 160, 588

inattention *n.* 385, **391,**
703

inattentive *adj.* 389,
391, 393, 442, 863

inaudibility *n.* 453, 779,
781, 796

inaugural *adj.* 88

inaugurate *vb.* 88, 685

inauspicious *adj.* 137

inborn *adj.* 5, 223

incandescent *adj.* 761

incantation *n.* 984

incapable *adj.* 160

incapacitate *vb.* 160

incapacity *n.* 169

incense *vb.* 893

incentive *n.* 173, 547

incessant *adj.* 114, 138,
145

incest *n.* 952

inch *vb.* 281

incident *n.* 153

incidental *adj.* 8, 60,
139

incineration *n.* 372, 761

incinerator *n.* 763

incise *vb.* 490

incision *n.* 259

incisive *adj.* 255, 506

incite *vb.* 175, 755, 893

inclination *n.* 178, 219,
532, 861

incline *vb.* 178, 219,
319, 530, 861

include *vb.* 58, **98**

inclusion *n.* **98**

inclusive *adj.* 54, 55, 98

incoherence *n.* 51, 453

incoherent *adj.* 80, 453

incombustibility *n.* **762**

income *n.* 705, 741

incomparable *adj.* 21,
579

incompatibility *n.* 14,
106, 637

incompetent *adj.* 160,
576, 628

incomplete *adj.* 55, 57,
315, 582, 660

incompleteness *n.* 57

incomprehensible *adj.*
385, 453, 503

incomprehension *n.*
427

incompressibility *n.*
332

inconceivable *adj.* 405,
856

inconclusive *adj.* 409

incongruence *n.* 25

incongruent *adj.* 10, 19

incongruous *adj.* 15, 17,
25, 106

inconsequential *adj.* 10,
574

inconsiderable *adj.* 33,
574

inconsiderate *adj.* 391,
393, 887, 900

inconsistent *adj.* 14, 17,
25, 51, 106, 412

inconspicuous *adj.* 824

inconstant *adj.* 142,
151, 536, 538, 539

incontinence *n.* 952

incontrovertible *adj.*
408

inconvenience *n.* 578,
635; *vb.* 578, 633, 830

inconvenient *adj.* 137,
576, 578

incorporate *vb.* 52, 58,
98, 302

incorrect *adj.* 431, 500,
511

incorrigible *adj.* 942

incorruptible *adj.* 114

increase *n.* 36, 40, 196;
vb. 36, 40, 196, 664,
745

incredible *adj.* 579, 866

incredulity *n.* 409, 421,
423, 866

increment *n.* 41

incriminate *vb.* 926,
930

incumbency *n.* 557

incumbent *n.* 190, 986;
adj. 919

incur *vb.* 179

incurable *adj.* 855

incuriosity *n.* **389**

incursion *n.* 300, 645

indebted *adj.* 737, 909

indecent *adj.* 901, 952

indecipherable *adj.* 453

indecision *n.* 151, 409,
536

indefinite *adj.* 243, 453

indefinite space *n.* **182**

indemnification *n.* 31,
721

indemnify *vb.* 31, 721,
943

indent *vb.* 254, 259

independent *n.* 653;
adj. 10, 644, 678

indeterminate *adj.* 243,
409

index *n.* 83, 482, 494,
524

indicate *vb.* 401, 450,
458, **482**

indication *n.* 401, 447,
460, **482,** 597

indication of danger *n.*
598

indicative *adj.* 401, 450,
482

indicator *n.* 482, 800

indictment *n.* 930, 960

indifference *n.* 391, 393,
541, 612, 754, **863,** 933

indifferent *adj.* 389,
391, 393, 533, 541, 612,
666, 754, 863, 933

indigenous *adj.* 190

indignant *adj.* 893

indigo *n.* 815; *adj.* 814,
815

indirect *adj.* 561

indiscernible *adj.* 824

indiscretion *n.* 435. 859

indiscriminate *adj.* 15, 54, 399

indiscrimination *n.* 399

indispensable *adj.* 531, 562

indisputable *adj.* 408

indissoluble *adj.* 54

indistinct *adj.* 243, 503, 515, 781, 799, 824

indistinguishable *adj.* 13

individual *n.* 368, 379; *adj.* 59, 102, 139, 379

individualist *n.* 934

indivisibility *n.* 50, 59

indivisible *adj.* 50, 54, 59, 332

indoctrinate *vb.* 470

indolent *adj.* 174, 612

indubitable *adj.* 408

induction *n.* 300, 410, 685

indulge *vb.* 831, 945

indulgence *n.* 827, 948

industrialist *n.* 728

industrious *adj.* 472, 535, 611

industry *n.* 472, 611, 620

inebriated *adj.* 950

inedible *adj.* 771

ineffable *adj.* 453

ineffably *adv.* 32

ineffective *adj.* 160, 169, 576, 662

inefficient *adj.* 160, 628

inelegance *n.* 511, 845, 849

inept *adj.* 160, 427, 628

inequality *n.* 14, 29

inequity *n.* 14, 916

inerrant *adj.* 408

inertia *n.* 174, 610, 612

inertness *n.* 174

inescapable *adj.* 154, 531

inevitable *adj.* 123, 154, 408, 531, 543

inexact *adj.* 19, 431, 453

inexcitability *n.* 754, 757

inexcusable *adj.* 916

inexhaustible *adj.* 145

inexpedience *n.* 137, 578

inexpensive *adj.* 746

inexperience *n.* 129, 427, 603, 628

inexperienced *adj.* 125, 129, 422, 546, 628, 937

inexplicable *adj.* 158, 453

infallible *adj.* 408, 430

infamous *adj.* 426, 869

infancy *n.* 88, 129

infant *n.* 131; *adj.* 129

infantry *n.* 655

infatuated *adj.* 439, 889

infatuation *n.* 439, 889

infect *vb.* 45, 584, 588

infection *n.* 586

infectious *adj.* 586

infer *vb.* 101, 410, 448, 459

inferable *adj.* 413

inference *n.* 410, 448, 459

inferiority *n.* 29, 35, 580, 679

infernal *adj.* 973

inferno *n.* 973

infertile *adj.* 160, 169

infest *vb.* 314

infidel *n.* 975

infidelity *n.* 703, 952, 978

infiltrate *vb.* 45, 300

infinite *adj.* 78, 114

infinitely *adv.* 78

infinitesimal *adj.* 33, 195

infinity *n.* 78, 114

infirm *adj.* 130, 160, 586

infirmity *n.* 126, 130, 162, 586

inflammation *n.* 252, 835

inflate *vb.* 196, 359

inflated *adj.* 879

inflation *n.* 196

inflect *vb.* 499

inflection *n.* 499, 512

inflexible *adj.* 152, 334, 537, 908

inflict *vb.* 674

influence *n.* 155, 159, 177, 294, 547; *vb.* 155, 177, 547, 573, 755

influential *adj.* 177, 573

influx *n.* 300

in force *adj.* 172, 606

inform *vb.* 460, 470, 597, 624

informal *adj.* 495

informant *n.* 460, 624

information *n.* 401, 426, 460, 465, 525, 624

informative *adj.* 460, 470

informed *adj.* 426

informer *n.* 460, 480, 883

infrequency *n.* 139, 407

infringement *n.* 672, 703, 955

infuriate *vb.* 893

infusion *n.* 309, 311

ingenuity *n.* 21

ingenuous *adj.* 476, 632

ingratiating *adj.* 881, 886, 927

ingratitude *n.* 910

ingredient *n.* 55, 192, 327

inhabit *vb.* 188, 191

inhabitant *n.* 190

inhale *vb.* 308, 359

inharmonious *adj.* 791

inhere *vb.* 5

inherent *adj.* 5, 55, 459

inherit *vb.* 705

inheritance n. 711

inheritor n. 710

inhibition n. 876

inhuman adj. 900, 904

inimical adj. 25, 883

iniquity n. 936

initial adj. 88, 155, 602;
vb. 482

initiation n. 88, 300,
302, 470

initiative n. 173, 611,
857

inject vb. 264, 311

injection n. 181, 311,
591

injudicious adj. 393,
416

injunction n. 626, 671,
691

injure vb. 580, 588, 608,
830, 900, 916

injured adj. 582

injury n. 551, 588, 828,
916

injustice n. 916, 955

ink vb. 488, 808

inkling n. 448

inland n. 352; adj. 223,
352

inland revenue n. 743

inlay n. 226; vb. 226

inlet n. 353

in lieu adv. 149

in love adj. 889

inmate n. 684

in memoriam n. 372

inn n. 191

innate adj. 5, 223

inner adj. 223, 224

innermost adj. 223

inner self n. 751

innocence n. 632, 935,
937, 961

innocent adj. 632, 935,
937, 951

innovation n. 125, 142

innuendo n. 928

inoculation n. 591

inodorousness n. 775

inoffensive adj. 757

in operation adj. 172,
609

inoperative adj. 576,
610

inopportune adj. 137,
578

in order adv. 79, 605

inordinate adj. 572, 945

inordinately adv. 32

inorganic matter n. 367

in part adv. 55

in progress adj. 57; adv.
288

inquire vb. 695

inquirer n. 697

inquiry n. 394, 695

inquisition n. 963

inquisitive adj. 388, 394

inroad n. 645

insalubrious adj. 586

insane adj. 435, 439

insanitary adj. 586

insanity n. 439

inscription n. 483, 490,
521

inscrutable adj. 453

insect n. 373

insecure adj. 409, 594

insensible adj. 754

insensitive adj. 754, 942

insensitivity n. 754, 863

inseparable adj. 47, 50,
54, 882

insert n. 230; vb. 40,
230, 311, 483

insertion n. 311

inside n. 223, 226; adj.
223, 681

insidious adj. 459, 932

insight n. 410, 411, 434

insignia n. 482, 677

insignificant adj. 451,
574

insincere adj. 477, 852,
927, 932, 981

insinuate vb. 311, 459,
460

insinuation n. 311, 928,
930

insipid adj. 162, 507,
666, 768, 843

insist vb. 547, 669, 700

insistent adj. 506

insobriety n. 950

insolence n. 644, 672,
873, 880, 924

insoluble adj. 332, 405

insolvent adj. 706, 735,
739

inspect vb. 390, 394,
818

inspection n. 390, 392,
394, 396, 818

inspector n. 623

inspiration n. 411, 755,
976

inspire vb. 547, 755,
836, 854, 857

inspired adj. 411, 449,
506, 756, 976

instability n. 17, 151,
536, 756

install vb. 186, 302, 311,
685

installation n. 620, 685

instalment n. 55, 738

instance n. 23, 456

instant n. 115; adj. 602

instantaneous adj. 115

instantly adv. 115

instead adv. 149

instigate vb. 547

instigator n. 166, 547

instill vb. 470

instinct n. 382, 411,
531, 545

instinctive adj. 411,
531, 544

institute n. 475; vb. 88

institution n. 475, 620,
988

in store adj. 154; adv.
567

instruct *vb.* 470, 514
instructed *adj.* 426
instruction *n.* 103, 426, **470**, 624, 626
instructive *adj.* 460, 470, 597
instructor *n.* 473
instrument *n.* **565**, 609, 619
instrumental *adj.* 563, 565
instrumentalist *n.* 793
instrumentality *n.* 172, **563**
insubordinate *adj.* 644, 672
insubstantial *adj.* 4, 328, 331, 333, 451
insufficiency *n.* 315, **571**
insular *adj.* 183, 416
insulate *vb.* 226, 761
insult *n.* 869, 923; *vb.* 644, 887, 923
insulting *adj.* 880, 923
insuperable *adj.* 405
insurance *n.* 701
insurgence *n.* 672
insurgent *n.* 672; *adj.* 148, 672
insurmountable *adj.* 405
insurrection *n* 148
insurrectionist *n.* 148, 672
insusceptible *adj.* 754
intact *adj.* 54, 599
intangible *adj.* 4, 328, 824
integer *n.* 39
integral *adj.* 5, 39, 54, 55, 56, 223
integrate *vb.* 52, 105
integration *n.* 24, 45, 52, 56, 59
integrity *n.* 56, 476, 931, 935, 937
intellect *n.* **382**, 434

intellectual *n.* 428; *adj.* 382, 384, 426
intelligence *n.* 382, 426, **434**, 460
intelligent *adj.* 382, 426, **434**
intelligibility *n.* **452**, 502
intemperance *n.* **945**, 948, 950
intend *vb.* 552
intended *n.* 698; *adj.* 552
intense *adj.* 173, 752, 759, 805
intensification *n.* 196, 835
intensify *vb.* 36, 173, 196, 481, 835
intensity *n.* 27, 32, 506, 759, 805
intention *n.* 284, 530, 552
intentional *adj.* 530
interact *vb.* 12, 150
intercession *n.* 230, 653, 695, 982
intercessor *n.* 653, 982
interchange *n.* 12, **150**, 519, 714; *vb.* 150
interdiction *n.* 691
interest *n.* 41, 388, 755; *vb.* 294, 547, 755, 829
interested *adj.* 388
interesting *adj.* 755
interfere *vb.* 181, 635, 653
interior *n.* 223, 352; *adj.* 223, 352
interjection *n.* 230, 499
interlude *n.* 144
intermediary *n.* 653; *adj.* 230
intermediate *adj.* 30, 90, 230, 560, 563
interminable *adj.* 78, 114, 202
intermingle *vb.* 45

intermission *n.* 92, 144
intermittent *adj.* 92, 139
internal *adj.* 5, 223
international *adj.* 101
internationalism *n.* 903
internecine *adj.* 164, 370
internee *n.* 684
internment camp *n.* 682
interplay *n.* 12, *vb.* 12
interpose *vb.* 230, 653
interpret *vb.* 456
interpretation *n.* 450, **456**
interpreter *n.* 456, 974
interrogate *vb.* 394
interrupt *vb.* 92, 137, 144, 230, 887, 923
interruption *n.* 92, 230
intersect *vb.* 221, 246
intersperse *vb.* 230
interval *n.* 92, 109, 144, 200, 267
intervention *n.* 92, 230, 563, 635, 653
interview *n.* 394, 410, 519, 884; *vb.* 394
interviewer *n.* 394
intimacy *n.* 882
intimate *n.* 882; *adj.* 199, 882; *vb.* 450, 459, 460, 482
intimation *n.* 448, 460, 482, 597
intimidate *vb.* 856, 902
intolerance *n.* 537, 900
intonation *n.* 501, 512, 778
intoxicate *vb.* 950
intractable *adj.* 537, 672
intransigent *adj.* 537
intrepid *adj.* 857
intricate *adj.* 251, 453, 503, 633
intrigue *n.* 558, 631; *vb.* 755

intrinsic *adj.* 1, **5**, 223
introduce *vb.* 84, 88, 300, 302, 311
introductory *adj.* 86, 88, 602
introspective *adj.* 384
intrude *vb.* 137, 300, 388, 645
intruder *n.* 388, 645
intrusive *adj.* 137, 388
intuition *n.* **411**, 531, 753
inundate *vb.* 349, 358, 572
in use *adj.* 606
inutility *n.* **576**
invade *vb.* 314, 645, 651
invader *n.* 100, 645, 883
invalid *adj.* 412, 586
invalidate *vb.* 414, 469, **686**
invariability *n.* 13, 16, 143, 152
invasion *n.* 300, 314, 645
inveigle *vb.* 927
invent *vb.* 163, 449, 477, 930
invention *n.* 88, 163, 419, 449
inventive *adj.* 21, 449, 627
inventor *n.* 155, 166
inventory *n.* 83
inversion *n.* **220**
invertebrate *n.* 373
invest *vb.* 159, 568, 715, 726, 740
investigate *vb.* 388, 394, 396, 818
investigation *n.* 394, 526, 818
investigator *n.* 394
investiture *n.* 685
investment *n.* 718, 726, 740
inveterate *adj.* 152, 545
in view *adj.* 823

invigorate *vb.* 161, 173, 618
invigorating *adj.* 173, 585, 618
invincible *adj.* 161, 661
invisibility *n.* **824**
invitation *n.* 394, 695
invite *vb.* 562, 695, 884
invocation *n.* 518, 695
invoice *n.* 742
invoke *vb.* 901, 982
involuntary *adj.* 411, 531, 544
involve *vb.* 9, 98, 155, 450
involved *adj.* 9, 251, 503, 709
inward *adj.* 5, 223
iota *n.* 33
irate *adj.* 893
iron *vb.* 257, 583
ironical *adj.* 455, 853
iron out *vb.* 485
irony *n.* 455, 842, 853
irrational *adj.* 39, 385, 412
irreconcilability *n.* 10, 14
irreconcilable *adj.* 883
irredeemable *adj.* 855, 942
irrefutable *adj.* 408
irregular *adj.* 17, 80, 92, 104, 106, 141, 151, 245
irregularity *n.* 17, 106, 141, 151, 245, 258, 285, 916
irrelevant *adj.* 10, 451, 574
irreligion *n.* **975**, 983
irreligious *adj.* 936, 975, 981
irreproachable *adj.* 581, 935, 937
irresistible *adj.* 531, 674, 889
irresolution *n.* 421, **536**, 538

irresponsible *adj.* 955
irretrievable *adj.* 706
irreverent *adj.* 923, 981
irreversibility *n.* 152, 855
irrevocable *adj.* 855
irrigate *vb.* 378
irritability *n.* 756, 893, **894**
irritate *vb.* 830, 835, 893
irritation *n.* 341, 830, 835
Islam *n.* 974
island *n.* 357
isolate *vb.* 48, 102
isolated *adj.* 885
isolation *n.* 59, 461, 885
issue *n.* 11, 87, 156, 171, 301, 387; *vb.* 358, 464, 522, 600, 731
italic *adj.* 521
itch *vb.* 326, 758
itching *adj.* 443, 861
item *n.* 59, 192, 327
itinerant *n.* 270
itinerary *n.* 269, 460, 559
ivory *adj.* 807
ivory tower *n.* 595, 885

J

jab *n.* 591; *vb.* 282
jacket *n.* 225
jaded *adj.* 617, 841, 865
jagged *adj.* 246, 258, 259
jail *n.* 682; *vb.* 234, 963
jailer *n.* 683
jam *n.* 306
jangle *vb.* 787
janitor *n.* 676, 683
jar *n.* 193, 326; *vb.* 282, 326, 787, 791
jargon *n.* 492, 494

jaundice *vb.* 416, 813

jaunt *n.* 269, 840

jazz *n.* 792

jealousy *n.* 913, 914

jeer *vb.* 696, 853

jell *vb.* 332

jelly *n.* 306, 364

jeopardize *vb.* 594

jerk *n.* 92, 141, 326, 437; *vb.* 326

jest *n.* 433, 539, 842; *vb.* 842

jet *n.* 278, 358; *vb.* 358

jettison *vb.* 331, 542, 607, 713

jewel *n.* 846, 891

jilt *vb.* 556

jittery *adj.* 326, 756, 856, 894

job *n.* 557, 605, 609, 722

jockey *n.* 270

jocular *adj.* 836, 842

jog *n.* 326; *vb.* 282, 441

join *vb.* 40, 45, 47, 52, 639, 709

joint *n.* 49; *adj.* 180, 709

joint possession *n.* 709

joke *n.* 842; *vb.* 842

jolly *adj.* 827, 836

jolt *n.* 282, 326, 444; *vb.* 282, 326

jot *n.* 33

jot down *vb.* 441, 483

journal *n.* 116, 441, 464, 483, 524

journalist *n.* 460, 484, 521

journey *n.* 269, 313; *vb.* 269

jovial *adj.* 836

joy *n.* 827, 829, 836

J.P. *n.* 958

jubilant *adj.* 838

jubilee *n.* 109, 878

Judaism *n.* 974

judge *n.* 415, 653, **958**; *vb.* 382, **415**, 540, 653, 956, 960

judgment *n.* 382, 398, 410, **415**, 434, 627, 926

judicious *adj.* 392, 398, 415, 434

jug *n.* 193, 682

juice *n.* 309, 343

jumble *n.* 45; *vb.* 45, 82, 399

jump *n.* 316, 320, 321; *vb.* 320, 321

jump at *vb.* 532

jump the queue *vb.* 134

jumpy *adj.* 756, 856, 894

junction *n.* 47, 49, 201, 221

jungle *n.* 374

junior *n.* 35, 131; *adj.* 35, 129, 679

junk *n.* 277

jurisdiction *n.* 622, **956**

jurisprudence *n.* 954

jurist *n.* 959

juror *n.* 958

jury *n.* 958

just *adj.* 915, 917, 954, 966

just deserts *n.* 647, 917

justice *n.* 915, 954, 958

justification *n.* 401, 413, 549, 911, 929

justify *vb.* 410, 413, 911, 929, 961

jut *vb.* 252, 253

juvenile *n.* 131; *adj.* 129, 131

juxtaposition *n.* 94, 199, 201, 238, 397

K

kaleidoscope *n.* 817

keel over *vb.* 220

keen *adj.* 255, 434, 611, 760, 842, 861

keenness *n.* 611

keen on *adj.* 889

keep *n.* 646; *vb.* 377, 567, 593, 599, 673, 702, 707, 712

keep apart *vb.* 48, 200

keep away *vb.* 198, 555, 885

keep back *vb.* 681

keeper *n.* 593, **683**

keep in with *vb.* 24, 922

keep off *vb.* 555

keep on *vb.* 145, 516

keep one's temper *vb.* 757

keep order *vb.* 593, 956

keepsake *n.* 441

keep up *vb.* 217, 460

kernel *n.* 90, 224, 306

key *n.* 357; *adj.* 136

keyed up *adj.* 756

kick *n.* 769, 827; *vb.* 282

kick against *vb.* 644

kid *n.* 131; *vb.* 478, 842

kidnap *vb.* 720, 722

kidnapper *n.* 720, 723

kill *vb.* 370, 963

killing *n.* 370; *adj.* 370, 851

killjoy *n.* 548

kill time *vb.* 612

kiln *n.* 763

kind *n.* 97; *adj.* 882, 886, 899, 903, 935

kindergarten *n.* 475

kindhearted *adj.* 899

kindle *vb.* 755, 761

kindness *n.* 670, 747, 886, 899, 935

kindred relations *n.* 11

king *n.* 675

kingdom *n.* 183

kingdom of heaven *n.* 972

kink *n.* 251

kinship *n.* 11

kiosk *n.* 730

kip down *vb.* 612

kiss n. 886, 890; vb. 758, 886, 890

kitty n. 709

kleptomaniac n. 440

knack n. 627

knead vb. 335

kneel vb. 319, 922

knell n. 372

knife n. 255; vb. 370

knight n. 870; vb. 868

knit vb. 47, 221

knock n. 282, 782; vb. 282, 782, 926, 928

knock down vb. 164

knock off vb. 144, 370, 659, 722, 744

knot n. 49

know vb. 426, 452, 882

know-all n. 428, 436, 875

know-how n. 426, 627

knowing n. 410, 426; adj. 426, 434

knowledge n. 426, 460, 472

knowledgeable adj. 426, 434, 472

knuckle down vb. 615

Koran n. 976

L

label n. 482, 496, 743; vb. 482, 496

laboratory n. 620

laborious adj. 615, 633

labour n. 615, 619; vb. 615

laboured adj. 511

labourer n. 378, 619

lace n. 49, 846

lack n. 57, 76, 189, 315, 571, 582, 706, 708; vb. 35, 57, 76, 189, 562, 571

lacklustre adj. 806

laconic adj. 504, 517

lacquer n. 225, 365

lactescent adj. 807

lad n. 131

ladder n. 316

laden adj. 56

lady n. 381, 870

lady-like adj. 381, 886

lag behind vb. 287, 315

lagoon n. 353, 354

laid up adj. 586

lair n. 595

laissez-faire n. 610

laity n. 987

lake n. 354, 805

lame vb. 588

lamellar adj. 206

lament n. 839; vb. 839

lamentation n. 839

lamina n. 206

laminate n. 206; adj. 206; vb. 206

lamp n. 800

lance vb. 264

lancet n. 264

land n. 352, 378, 711, 711; vb. 273, 298, 317

landed gentry n. 870

landlady n. 710

landlord n. 710

landscape n. 488

landscape gardener n. 378

landslide n. 317, 662

land travel n. 269

lane n. 559

language n. 492, 512, 514

languish vb. 162, 174, 586, 612, 617, 837

lanky adj. 205, 208

lantern n. 800

lap n. 322; vb. 260, 322

lapel n. 260

lapidary n. 491

lapse n. 110, 144, 147, 315, 431, 938; vb. 110, 147, 869, 936

lap up vb. 390

larceny n. 722

lard vb. 306

larder n. 305

large adj. 26, 32, 194, 204

largesse n. 715, 747

lark about vb. 435

larynx n. 512

lascivious adj. 952

laser n. 797

lash n. 964; vb. 175

lass n. 131

lassitude n. 617, 841

last adj. 89, 659; vb. 107, 112, 143, 145

last-minute adj. 135

last resort n. 595

last rites n. 372

last straw n. 659

last word n. 89, 667, 939

late adj. 117, 124, 135, 369

lately adv. 125

latency n. 459, 824

lateness n. 135

later adj. 85, 119, 123; adv. 121

lateral adj. 238

latest adj. 120, 850

lather n. 363; vb. 583

latitude n. 182, 204, 678

lattice n. 221

laud vb. 982

laudable adj. 925

laugh n. 838; vb. 644, 827, 838, 851, 853, 924

laugh off vb. 393, 477

launch n. 277; vb. 271, 290

launch into vb. 605

launder vb. 583

laurel n. 663

lavender n. 814; adj. 814

lavish adj. 509, 745,

747, **749**; *vb.* 569, 740, 747

law *n.* 103, 626, 671, 954, 976

lawful *adj.* 667, 915, 954

lawless *adj.* 80, 644, 668, 672, **955**

lawn *n.* 374, 812

lawsuit *n.* **960**

lawyer *n.* **959**

laxity *n.* 51, 335, 393, **668**

lay *adj.* 628, **987**

layabout *n.* 906

lay at *vb.* 157, 693

lay bare *vb.* 419, 456, 458, 462

lay claim to *vb.* 917

lay down *vb.* 671

layer *n.* 206; *vb.* 206

lay hold of *vb.* 705, 720

lay in wait *vb.* 463

lay it on *vb.* 481, 509, 927

layman *n.* 630, 987

lay-off *n.* 686

lay on *vb.* 805

lay out *vb.* 372, 740

lay-preacher *n.* 974, 987

lay siege to *vb.* 645

lay waste *vb.* 164, 645

lazy *adj.* 393, 612

lead *n.* 286, 529; *vb.* 34, 84, 236, 284, **286**, 573, 622

lead astray *vb.* 431, 936

leader *n.* 125, 253, 623, 675

leading *n.* (printing) 522

lead to *vb.* 155

leaf *n.* 374, 812

leaflet *n.* 464

league *n.* 641, 699

leak *n.* 600; *vb.* (es-

cape) 301, 358; (disclosure) 462

lean *adj.* 205; *vb.* (tend) 178; (incline) 219

lean on *vb.* 679, 854

leap *n.* 200, **320**, 321; *vb.* 320

leapfrog *n.* 320; *vb.* 320

leap year *n.* 109

learn *vb.* 441, 472

learner *n.* 428, 474

learning *n.* 426, 472

lease *n.* 708, 714; *vb.* 718, 719

leave *n.* 614, 690, 921; *vb.* **299**, 556, 600, 660, 687

leave alone *vb.* 555, 610

leaven *n.* 142, 331; *vb.* 318

leave of absence *n.* 614

leave out *vb.* 99

leave-taking *n.* 299

leave undone *vb.* 393, 660

leavings *n.* 44

lechery *n.* 952, 953

lecture *n.* 470, 518, 926; *vb.* 470, 514, 926

lecturer *n.* 473, 514

lecture theatre *n.* 475

ledge *n.* 217

ledger *n.* 742

leer *n.* 818; *vb.* 818

leeway *n.* 182, 200, 678

left *n.* 241; *adj.* 44, 241

legacy *n.* 714, 715

legal adviser *n.* 959

legality *n.* 915, **954**

legalize *vb.* 424, 690, 954

legal proceedings *n.* 960

legal tender *n.* 731

legation *n.* 685

legend *n.* 525

legerdemain *n.* 478

legible *adj.* 452

legion *n.* 75; *adj.* 75

legislation *n.* 622, 954

legislative *adj.* 103, 622

legislator *n.* 623

legist *n.* 959

legitimacy *n.* 915, 954

leisure *n.* **614**, 840

leisurely *adj.* 281, 614

leitmotif *n.* 387

lemon *n.* 813

lend *vb.* 568, **718**, 736

lending *n.* **718**

length *n.* 26, 198, **202**, 400

lengthen *vb.* 36, 202

lengthy *adj.* 202, 505

lenience *n.* 670

lenient *adj.* **670**, 690, 907

lens *n.* 247, 822

Lent *n.* 947

leper *n.* 885

leprechaun *n.* 970

lesbian *n.* 106, 953; *adj.* 952

lesion *n.* 588

lessee *n.* 710

lessen *vb.* 37, 76, 197, 333, 403

lesser *adj.* 35, 209

lesson *n.* 470, 472, 597

let *vb.* 690, 718

let down *vb.* 445, 874

let fall *vb.* 319

let go *vb.* 556, 713

lethal *adj.* 164, 370

lethargy *n.* 174, 281, **612**, 754

let off *vb.* 601, 911, 961

let on *vb.* 462

let out *vb.* 196, 462, 680, 718

let pass *vb.* 911

let slip *vb.* 680, 706, 920

letter *n.* 493, 522, 523; *vb.* 482, 493

lettering *n.* 521, 846

letter of the law   n. 669, 908

let up   vb. 144, 176, 281, 616

level   n. 27, 93, 206, 215; adj. 28, 215, 248, 257; vb. 16, 257, 400

level-headed   adj. 757

lever   n. 217

leviathan   n. 194

levitation   n. 331, 984

levity   n. 331, 836, 859

levy   n. 743, 917; vb. 716, 743

lewdness   n. 952

lexical   adj. 494

lexicography   n. 492, 494

lexicology   n. 494

lexicon   n. 83, 494

liability   n. 179, 701, 737, 919, 938

liaison   n. 889, 952

liar   n. 480, 940

libel   n. 928; vb. 928, 930

liberal   adj. 570, 715, 747, 965

liberated   adj. 678, 680, 961

liberation   n. 601, 680, 921

liberator   n. 905

libertine   n. 953

liberty   n. 678, 690

library   n. 475, 524, 567

librate   vb. 325

licence   n. 690

license   vb. 690, 954

licentiousness   n. 952

lick   vb. 758, 963

lick into shape   vb. 470, 570

lid   n. 225

lie   n. 431; vb. 185, 477, 932

lie down   vb. 215

lie low   vb. 209, 459, 461, 593

lieutenant   n. 675

life   n. 107, 159, 368, 557, 611

life-blood   n. 368

life-giving   adj. 170

life-guard   n. 593

lifeless   adj. 174, 369, 507, 612, 843

lifelike   adj. 18, 525

life-line   n. 600

life peer   n. 870

life science   n. 375

lifetime   n. 112

life-work   n. 557

lift   n. 316, 318; vb. 318

lift restrictions   vb. 713, 921

ligature   n. 49

light   n. 797, 800; adj. (not heavy) 331, 333, 344; (of colour) 797, 807

lighted   adj. 797

lighten   vb. 634, 797, 834

lighter   n. 277, 765

light-hearted   adj. 836

lighthouse   n. 800

lighting   n. 797

light music   n. 792

lightness   n. 331, 797, 807

lightning   n. 800

light up   vb. 755, 797

like   adj. 13, 18; vb. 540, 770, 827, 861, 889

like clockwork   adv. 140

likely   adj. 123, 404, 406, 447; adv. 406

likely to   adj. 179

like-minded   adj. 24, 424

liken   vb. 18, 397

likeness   n. 18, 20, 22, 486, 488

like to   vb. 532

liking   n. 178, 861, 922

lilac   adj. 814

lily-livered   adj. 858

limb   n. 374

limber   adj. 335

lime   adj. 812

limerick   n. 528

limit   n. 89, 233, 235, 400, 659; vb. 231, 235, 403, 681

limitation   n. 231, 235, 403, 681

limitations   n. 700

limited   adj. 195, 205, 235

limited space   n. 184

limitless   adj. 78, 202

limp   adj. 335, 507; vb. 281

limpid   adj. 502, 802

line   n. 11, 170, 202, 655, 729; vb. 81, 226

lineage   n. 11, 170, 171

lineal   adj. 171

linearity   n. 202

liner   n. 277

linger   vb. 112, 135, 281

lingua franca   n. 492

linguist   n. 456, 492

linguistic   adj. 450, 492

lining   n. 226

link   n. 9, 49; vb. 9, 47, 52, 157, 397

lip reading   n. 796

lip service   n. 981

liquefaction   n. 345

liquefied   adj. 343, 345

liquefy   vb. 343, 345, 761

liquescent   adj. 343

liquid   n. 309, 343, 347; adj. 343, 347

liquidate   vb. 164, 370, 739

liquidize   vb. 164

liquor   n. 343

lisp   n. 515; vb. 515

list *n.* **83**, 97; *vb.* 38, 83, 483

listen *vb.* 390, 778, 792, 795

listless *adj.* 174, 281, **612**, 863

lit *adj.* 759, 797

litany *n.* 988

literal *n.* 431; *adj.* 456, 493, 494, 977

literature *n.* 528

lithe *adj.* 335

lithographer *n.* 491

lithography *n.* 490

litigation *n.* 960

litter *n.* 576

little *adj.* 33, 195, 203; *adv.* 33

little by little *adv.* 27

liturgical *adj.* 988

live *adj.* 172; *vb.* 1, 188, 191, 368

live apart *vb.* 898

live comfortably *vb.* 734

lively *adj.* 173, 368, **506**, 611, 836

livery *n.* 227, 677

livestock *n.* 373

live together *vb.* 889

live up to *vb.* 28, 570

live wire *n.* 611

live with *vb.* 889

llama *n.* 275

llano *n.* 356

load *n.* 26, 192, 330, 830; *vb.* 192, 268, 330

loaf about *vb.* 612

loafer *n.* 281, 612, 697, 940

loan *n.* 718, 719, 736; *vb.* 718

loan-word *n.* 495

loath *adj.* 533

loathe *vb.* 771, 862, 892

loathsome *adj.* 862, 892

lobby *n.* 547, 697; *vb.* 177, 547

local *n.* 191; *adj.* 183, 190, 199

locality *n.* 183, 199

locate *vb.* 186, 284

location *n.* 185, **186**

loch *n.* 353, 354

lock *n.* 207; *vb.* 263, 461

locker *n.* 193

locket *n.* 216

lock out *vb.* 144

lock-out *n.* 99, 144

lock up *vb.* 234, 681

lock-up *n.* 682

locomotive *n.* 276; *adj.* 276

locust *n.* 167

lodge *n.* 191; *vb.* 186, 191

lodger *n.* 190, 710

lodging *n.* 186

lodgings *n.* 191

loftiness *n.* 208

lofty *adj.* 208, 318, 870

log *n.* 116, 483, 742, 765; *vb.* 83

logic *n.* 410

logo *n.* 482

loiter *vb.* 281, 612

lone *adj.* 59

loneliness *n.* 59, 885

long *adj.* 182, 202; *vb.* 443, 854, 861, 889

long-distance *adj.* 198

long duration *n.* **112**

longhand *n.* 521

longing *n.* 854, 861; *adj.* 861, 889

long-lasting *adj.* 112

longness *n.* 202

long-range *adj.* 198

longsighted *adj.* 820

long-standing *adj.* 112

long-suffering *n.* 757; *adj.* 670

long-term *adj.* 112

long-winded *adj.* 505, 516, 843

look *n.* 242, 818, 825; *vb.* 818, 825

look after *vb.* 392, 593, 599, 676

look back *vb.* 441

look down on *vb.* 923, 924

looker-on *n.* 821

look for *vb.* 394, 554

look forward to *vb.* 443

look in *vb.* 884

looking glass *n.* 822

look like *vb.* 18

look out *vb.* 860

lookout *n.* 593, 683, 818

look over *vb.* 208, 818

look through *vb.* 818

look to *vb.* 390, 919

loom *n.* 221; *vb.* 154, 221, 292, 902

loop *n.* 250, 251, 322; *vb.* 251, 273, 323

loophole *n.* 582, 600

loose *adj.* 335, 453, 500, 668, 680, 952; *vb.* 48, 680

loosen *vb.* 262, 319, 601

loot *n.* 663, 724; *vb.* 722

lopsidedness *n.* 29, 245

loquacious *adj.* 516

lord *n.* 675, 870, 967

lord it over *vb.* 34, 667, 669

Lord's Day *n.* 616

Lord's Supper *n.* 988

lore *n.* 472

lorgnette *n.* 822

lorry *n.* 276

lose *vb.* 116, 187, 662, **706**

lose consciousness *vb.* 617

lose face *vb.* 869

lose ground *vb.* 289, 315

lose heart *vb.* 837, 855

M

make amends *vb.* 31,
589, 721, 943

make a mess of *vb.* 628

make a mistake *vb.* 431,
500

make an example of *vb.*
963

make a noise *vb.* 778

make a speech *vb.* 514

make-believe *n.* 477;
adj. 449, 477

make certain *vb.* 408

make clear *vb.* 452, 456

make do *vb.* 149, 606,
666

make exceptions *vb.*
403

make excuses *vb.* 549

make eyes at *vb.* 890

make for *vb.* 271, 284

make friends with *vb.*
882

make fun of *vb.* 842,
853

make headway *vb.* 288

make it *vb.* 661

make it up *vb.* 652, 911

make known *vb.* 460,
462, 464

make light of *vb.* 393,
418, 574

make love to *vb.* 889

make nothing of *vb.*
574

make off with *vb.* 722

make one jump *vb.* 444,
856

make one think of *vb.*
441

make out *vb.* 288, 441,
452

make over *vb.* 714

make passes *vb.* 890

make peace *vb.* 652

make plain *vb.* 456,
458, 462

make possible *vb.* 404

make preparations *vb.*
602

make progress *vb.* 288,
587

maker *n.* 166, 967

make sense *vb.* 410,
452, 456

makeshift *adj.* 149, 162,
603

make the best of *vb.*
757

make too much of *vb.*
417, 481

make up *vb.* 58, 163,
449, 477

make-up *n.* 5, 58, 339,
751, 844

make up for *vb.* 31

make up one's mind
vb. 530, 540

malady *n.* 586

malapropism *n.* 433,
497, 500

male *n.* 380; *adj.* 380

malevolence *n.* 900,
936

malformed *adj.* 245,
582

malice *n.* 893, 900

malign *vb.* 608, 900,
928, 936

malleable *adj.* 151

maltreat *vb.* 588, 608,
900, 916

mammal *n.* 373

man *n.* 133, 368, 373,
379, 380

manage *vb.* 392, 605,
606, 621, 622, 661, 666,
748

manageable *adj.* 634

management *n.* 392,
606, 609, 621, 622, 675

management of animals
n. 377

manager *n.* 623, 675,
728

manage to *vb.* 661

mandate *n.* 626, 671,
685

mangled *adj.* 245

manhood *n.* 133, 380

mania *n.* 439

maniac *n.* 175, 440

manifest *adj.* 458, 825;
vb. 401, 413, 458, 482,
823, 825

manifestation *n.* 419,
458, 462

manipulate *vb.* 477, 758

mankind *n.* 379

manliness *n.* 380, 857

manner *n.* 501, 559,
621, 825

mannerism *n.* 501

manners *n.* 886

man of learning *n.* 428,
436, 524

man of many talents *n.*
629

man of means *n.* 734

man of the world *n.* 629

manor *n.* 191

manpower *n.* 619

mansion *n.* 191

manslaughter *n.* 370

manual *n.* 460, 524

manufacture *n.* 163; *vb.*
163

manufacturer *n.* 166

manure *n.* 310; *vb.* 378

manuscript *n.* 483, 521,
524

many *adj.* 72, 75

many-coloured *adj.* 817

many-sided *adj.* 151

map *n.* 269, 460, 486;
vb. 400

mar *vb.* 847

march *vb.* 91, 269, 696

mare *n.* 381

margarine *n.* 306

margin *n.* 44, 182, 200,
233; *vb.* 233

marine *n.* 272; *adj.* 271,
277, 351

mariner n. 272
marital adj. 896
maritime adj. 271, 277, 351
mark n. 97, 202, 235, 400, 441, 483, 521, 522; vb. 382, 390, 482, 483
mark down vb. 743, 746
marker n. 482
market n. 96, 559, 726, 730; vb. 377, 725, 727
mark up vb. 743
maroon adj. 810, 811
marooned adj. 713
marquee n. 225
marquis n. 870
marred adj. 588
marriage n. 47, 896
marrow n. 224
marry vb. 47, 896
marsh n. 355
marshal n. 958; vb. 81
marsupial n. 373
martial adj. 651
martyr n. 980; vb. 830, 963
martyrdom n. 828
marvel n. 866; vb. 866
marvellous adj. 32, 579, 844, 866
Marxism n. 327
mascot n. 984
masculine adj. 380
mash vb. 335, 364
mask n. 225, 461, 463, 549; vb. 146, 225, 819
mass n. 26, 75, 94, 194, 327, 330, 332, 567, 988; vb. 75, 192
massacre n. 370, 963
massage vb. 341, 758
masses n. 26, 32, 871
massive adj. 32, 204
mast n. 208
master n. 34, 131, 436, 629, 675; vb. 441, 472, 679
masterly adj. 579

masterpiece n. 488, 581, 844
master-plan n. 558
mastery n. 501, 707
masticate vb. 304
mat n. 225
match n. 397, 649, 765, 800, 896; vb. 24, 28, 61, 218, 397, 896
matchless adj. 34
mate n. 882, 896; vb. 61, 889
material n. 192, 327; adj. 3, 327
material existence n. 3
materialist n. 981
materialistic adj. 327, 975
materiality n. 3, 327
materialize vb. 242, 327, 825, 984
materials n. 566
maternal adj. 11, 170
mathematics n. 38
matriculate vb. 83, 483
matt adj. 805
matter n. 3, 153, 327, 387, 573; vb. 573
matter in hand n. 605
matter-of-fact adj. 508
matter of life and death n. 562
mature adj. 133, 426; vb. 130, 133, 288, 324, 587, 659
maturity n. 126, 130, 133, 581
mauve adj. 814
maxim n. 103, 432, 498, 626
maximize vb. 417, 481
maximum n. 212
mayor n. 675
maze n. 409
meadow n. 356, 378
meagre adj. 33, 57, 205, 507, 571
meal n. 306, 840

mean n. 30, 90, 560; adj. (average) 30, 90; (stingy) 748, 750; (disreputable) 869, 871, 924, 936; (selfish) 934; vb. 450, 459, 482, 552
meander vb. 247, 251
meaning n. 450, 552
meaningful adj. 450, 514
meaninglessness n. 451, 453
meanness n. 750, 887, 934, 936
means n. 155, 172, 559, 564, 566, 711, 734
means of punishment n. 964
meanwhile adv., prep. 107
measure n. 26, 27, 400, 559, 609; vb. 26, 27, 330, 397, 400
measure for measure n. 647
measurement n. 27, 194, 397, 400
meat n. 306
Mecca n. 96
mechanic n. 619
mechanical adj. 411, 531, 545, 565
mechanism n. 565
medal n. 482, 663, 872
meddle vb. 388, 635, 653
meddler n. 388, 821
medial adj. 90, 560
median n. 30, 90
mediation n. 230, 563, 653
mediator n. 653
medicine n. 181, 591
mediocre adj. 30, 35, 580, 666, 843
mediocrity n. 35, 580, 666, 843
meditate vb. 384, 982

medium *n.* 30, 447, 563, 564, 619; *adj.* 30

medley *n.* 45, 104

meekness *n.* 654, 673, 757, 874, 876

meet *vb.* 94, 153, 201, 296, 419

meet half-way *vb.* 704

meeting *n.* 94, 201, 296, 884

meeting place *n.* 96

melancholy *n.* 828, 837; *adj.* 837

mellow *adj.* 335, 790; *vb.* 130, 587

melodious *adj.* 790

melodrama *n.* 326, 529

melody *n.* 790

melt *vb.* 345, 761

member *n.* 55, 709

member of parliament *n.* 625

membership *n.* 639

memo *n.* 441, 483

memoirs *n.* 116, 441

memorable *adj.* 441, 790

memorial *n.* 372, 441, 483, 663; *adj.* 441

memorize *vb.* 441, 472

memory *n.* 124, 441

menace *n.* 154, 594, 892, 902; *vb.* 154, 902

mend *vb.* 146, 587, 589

menial *n.* 676; *adj.* 35, 881

meniscus *n.* 247

mensuration *n.* 400

mental *adj.* 382

mental block *n.* 442

mental illness *n.* 439

mention *n.* 460, 663; *vb.* 460, 514

menu *n.* 306

mercantile *adj.* 725

mercenary *n.* 655

merchandise *n.* 163, 729

merchant *n.* 728

merciful *adj.* 670, 899, 907, 966

merciless *adj.* 908

mercury *n.* 766, 967

mercy *n.* 670, 715, 907, 911

mere *n.* 354; *adj.* 1, 46

merge *vb.* 45, 47, 52, 639

merger *n.* 36, 45, 52, 639

meridian *n.* 127

merit *n.* 575, 579, 917; *vb.* 919

mermaid *n.* 970

merry *adj.* 827, 836

merrymaking *n.* 838

mesh *n.* 221; *vb.* 221

mesmerize *vb.* 984

mess *n.* 80, 204, 628, 845

message *n.* 460, 465, 523

messenger *n.* 275, 460, 467

Messiah *n.* 967

mess up *vb.* 584, 588, 628

messy *adj.* 584

metal *n.* 367

metallic *adj.* 787

metallurgy *n.* 367

metamorphosis *n.* 142

metaphor *n.* 397, 455, 509

metaphysics *n.* 1

meteor *n.* 329, 800

meteorologist *n.* 447

meteorology *n.* 348

mete out *vb.* 715

meter *n.* 400

method *n.* 79, 81, 558, 559, 606

methodical *adj.* 79, 81, 140

meticulous *adj.* 392, 864

metre *n.* 528

metric system *n.* 400

metropolis *n.* 183

metropolitan *n.* 986

mettle *n.* 534, 857

mew *vb.* 789

miaow *vb.* 789

microscope *n.* 822

microscopic *adj.* 195

mid *adj.* 90

mid-course *n.* 560

midday *n.* 127

middle *n.* 30, 90, 224; *adj.* 30, 90, 224, 560

middle age *n.* 130

middle class *n.* 871

middleman *n.* 688, 728

middle of the road *adj.* 560

middling *adj.* 30, 579, 666

midget *n.* 195

midnight *n.* 128

midpoint *n.* 30, 90

midsummer *n.* 127

midway *adj.* 560; *adv.* 90

midwinter *n.* 128

mien *n.* 621, 825

might *n.* 32, 159, 161

mighty *adj.* 32, 159, 161

migrant *n.* 100, 270

mild *adj.* 176, 670, 757, 759

mildew *n.* 53, 167, 592

mileage *n.* 198

milieu *n.* 8, 183, 229

militant *n.* 611; *adj.* 148, 611, 644, 651

militate against *vb.* 181

milk *n.* 309; *vb.* 377

milk product *n.* 306

milky *adj.* 804, 807

millenium *n.* 70, 109

million *n.* 70

millionaire *n.* 734

mime *n.* 529

mimic *n.* 20; *vb.* 20

mix *vb.* **45**, 52, 58, 82, 399

mixed up *adj.* 80, 453

mixer *n.* 884

mixture *n.* **45**, 52, 104, 591

mix-up *n.* 80

mnemonic *n.* 441

moan *vb.* 788, 832

moat *n.* 234, 261, 360, 646

mob *n.* 75, 94; *vb.* 175, 888

mobile *adj.* 142, 151, 266

mobilization *n.* 94, 651

mob rule *n.* 668, 955

mock *adj.* 18, 20, 149; *vb.* 853, 869, 924, 928

mocker *n.* 928, 981

mockery *n.* 477, 853

mock-up *n.* 23

modal *adj.* 8

mode *n.* 7, 545, 850

model *n.* 22, 486, 581, 939; *vb.* 23, 242, 489

modeller *n.* 491

moderate *adj.* 176, 560, 746, 757, 944; *vb.* 142, **176**, 403, 652

moderation *n.* 176, 944

modern *adj.* 120, 125, 850

modernization *n.* 125, 587, 589

modest *adj.* 33, 176, 418, 508, 517, 874, **876**

modesty *n.* 508, 517, 874; **876**

modify *vb.* 15, 142, 335, 403

modulation *n.* 142

module *n.* 279

moist *adj.* 347, 349, 358

moisten *vb.* 349

moisture *n.* 346, **349**

molecule *n.* 327

mollify *vb.* 176, 335, 652

molten *adj.* 343, 345, 759

moment *n.* 115, 573

momentary *adj.* 113

momentous *adj.* 136, 177, 573

momentum *n.* 282

monarchic *adj.* 870

monastery *n.* 990

money *n.* **731**, 734

money lender *n.* 718

mongol *n.* 440

mongrel *n.* 45; *adj.* 45

monitor *vb.* 394

monk *n.* 885, 986

monocle *n.* 822

monograph *n.* 526

monologue *n.* **520**

monopolize *vb.* 707

monopoly *n.* 681

monotony *n.* 16, 91, 841

monsoon *n.* 358

monster *n.* 175, 194, 906

monstrous *adj.* 845, 936

month *n.* 109

monthly *adv.* 140

monument *n.* 372, 441, 483

moo *vb.* 789

mooch about *vb.* 612

mood *n.* 5, 751

moody *adj.* 756, 894, 895

moon *n.* 329, 800

moor *n.* 208, 355, 356; *vb.* 186, 271, 298

moot *adj.* 409

moot point *n.* 387

mop *vb.* 583

mope *vb.* 837, 895

moral *n.* 432; *adj.* 931, 935

moralize *vb.* 470

moral obligation *n.* 919

moratorium *n.* 135

more *adj.* 72

moreish *adj.* 770

moreover *adv.* 40

more than enough *n.* 572

morgue *n.* 372

moribund *adj.* 130, 369

morning *n.* **127**; *adj.* 127

moron *n.* 437, 440

moroseness *n.* 895

morphology *n.* 242, 499

morsel *n.* 33, 306

mortal *n.* 368, 379; *adj.* 369, 370, 379

mortgage *n.* 701, 718

mortgagee *n.* 736

mortgagor *n.* 737

mortification *n.* 874, 946

mortuary *n.* 372

mosaic *n.* 817

mosque *n.* 990

motel *n.* 191

moth *n.* 167

mothball *vb.* 135

moth-eaten *adj.* 126

mother *n.* 11, 170; *vb.* 676

motion *n.* **266**; *vb.* 482

motionless *adj.* 174, 267

motivate *vb.* 155, 547

motivator *n.* 547

motive *n.* 8, 155, **547**

motley *adj.* 17, 45, 104, 817

motor *n.* 276; *vb.* 269

motorcycle *n.* 276

motoring *n.* 269

motorist *n.* 270

motorway *n.* 559

mottled *adj.* 817

motto *n.* 432

mould *n.* 23, 53, 339, 592; *vb.* 146, 242, 489

mouldable *adj.* 242, 335, 654

mount *n.* 316; *vb.* 32, 208, 316

mountain *n.* 208, 316

mourn *vb.* 828, 833, 837

mournful *adj.* 372, 828, 839, 895

mouth *n.* 262, 353

mouthful *n.* 26, 306

mouthpiece *n.* 514, 689

mouth-watering *adj.* 770

movable *adj.* 142, 266, 268

move *n.* 266, 609; *vb.* 172, 187, 266, 268, 282, 290, 299, 693, 752, 755

moved *adj.* 189, 752, 756

movement *n.* 266, 268, 641, 792

move on *vb.* 288

mover *n.* 166

moving *adj.* 752, 755

mow *vb.* 378

mow down *vb.* 370

Mr. X *n.* 497

much *adj.* 75; *adv.* 32

muck *n.* 576, 584

muckraker *n.* 516, 928

mucky *adj.* 584

mud *n.* 355

muddle *n.* 80; *vb.* 82, 399

muddler *n.* 630

muddle through *vb.* 666

muddy *adj.* 355, 584, 803

mud-slinging *n.* 928

muffle *vb.* 513, 779, 785

muffled *adj.* 781, 785

mugging *n.* 645, 722

muggy *adj.* 349, 759

mulch *n.* 364

mule *n.* 537

mull *vb.* 384

multi-coloured *adj.* 817

multifarious *adj.* 104

multilateral *adj.* 246

multiple *n.* 730; *adj.* 39, 72

multiplication *n.* 38

multiplicity *n.* 72, 75

multiply *vb.* 36, 38, 163, 165, 835

multisection *n.* 71

multi-storey *adj.* 208

multitude *n.* 75

mum *n.* 170; *adj.* 513, 517

mumble *vb.* 515

mumbo-jumbo *n.* 967, 983, 984

mummify *vb.* 372, 599

mundane *adj.* 327, 329

municipal *adj.* 183

munificent *adj.* 747

munitions *n.* 657

mural *n.* 488

murder *n.* 370; *vb.* 370

murderer *n.* 167, 370, 906

murky *adj.* 363, 798, 803, 808

murmur *n.* 781; *vb.* 696, 781

muscle *n.* 159, 161

muse *vb.* 384, 449

museum *n.* 567

mush *n.* 364

music *n.* 790, 792

musical instrument *n.* 794

musician *n.* 793

must *n.* 531, 562

mustard *n.* 307

muster *vb.* 94, 651, 857

musty *adj.* 777

mutability *n.* 151

mutation *n.* 142

mute *adj.* 513, 517, 781; *vb.* 513, 779

muteness *n.* 513

mutilate *vb.* 164, 845

mutineer *n.* 672

mutiny *n.* 644, 672, 920; *vb.* 672, 920

mutter *n.* 781; *vb.* 515, 781

mutual *adj.* 9, 12, 150, 180

muzzle *vb.* 681

myriads *n.* 75

mystery *n.* 427, 453, 466

mystic *adj.* 984

myth *n.* 525

mythical being *n.* 970

N

nag *vb.* 893

nail *n.* 255; *vb.* 47

naive *adj.* 131, 422, 632

naked *adj.* 228, 594

name *n.* 482, 494, 496, 868, 872; *vb.* 482, 496

nanny *n.* 683

nanny-goat *n.* 381

nap *n.* 612

narcissism *n.* 875, 934

narrate *vb.* 460, 525

narrative *n.* 525; *adj.* 525

narrow *adj.* 205, 416, 681, 934; *vb.* 27, 681

narrow-mindedness *n.* 416, 537

narrowness *n.* 205, 416, 934

narrows *n.* 205, 353

nasalization *n.* 515

nasty *adj.* 580, 777, 887

nation *n.* 379

national *n.* 190; *adj.* 190, 379

nationality *n.* 379

nationalization *n.* 709

native *n.* 190; *adj.* 5, 190

nativity n. 155
natural adj. 3, 508, 632, 955
natural history n. 366
naturalized adj. 100, 190
nature n. 5, 58, 329, 366, 751
naturism n. 228
naughty adj. 672, 901
nausea n. 303
nautical adj. 271, 277
naval adj. 271, 277
navigate vb. 271
navy n. 655
near adj. 154, 199, 419; vb. 154, 292
nearby adj. 199; adv. 199
nearly adv. 199
nearness n. 199, 292
nearside adj. 241
neat adj. 79, 392, 579, 583
nebula n. 329
nebulous adj. 363, 798, 824
necessary adj. 531, 562, 674, 919
necessities n. 8
necessity n. 408, 531, 543, 562, 674
neck n. 205, 352; vb. 890
nectar n. 770
need n. 57, 189, 315, 562, 674, 861; vb. 76, 315, 531, 562, 571, 861
needle n. 255, 264, 482; vb. 830, 893
needlework n. 846
needy adj. 735, 917
negation n. 469
negative n. 23, 425; adj. 39, 469
neglect n. 385, 391, 393, 546, 610, 660, 662, 672, 703, 920; vb. 391, 393,

546, 607, 660, 662, 672, 703, 920
negligent adj. 391, 393, 703, 920
negligible adj. 76
negotiable adj. 714
negotiate vb. 519, 653, 700, 704, 725
neigh vb. 789
neighbour n. 882
neighbourhood n. 183, 199
neighbouring adj. 199
neighbourly adj. 884, 899
neologism n. 494, **495**
nephew n. 11
nerve n. 880
nerveless adj. 160
nerves n. 439, 856
nervous adj. 326, 756, 856, 894
nervousness n. 439, 856, 876, 894
nest n. 595
net n. 221, 463
nether adj. 209
netting n. 221
network n. 221
neurotic n. 440
neutral n. 653, 656; adj. 90, 541, 560, 863
neutrality n. 541, 863, 933
neutralize vb. 31, 181, 648
never adv. 108
new adj. 40, 125, 134, 603
newborn adj. 131
newcomer n. 100, 474
newest adj. 120
newly adv. 125
newly-wed adj. 896
newness n. 21, **125**
news n. 460, 465
newspaper n. 464, 483
next adj. 85, 119, 199

nibble n. 304, 306
nice adj. 770, 829, 864
niche n. 184, 254
nick n. 259, 682; vb. 259, 722
nickname n. 496, 497; vb. 497
nicotine n. 308
niece n. 11
niggardly adj. 750
nigh adv. 199
night n. 128, 798; adj. 128
nightfall n. 128, 798
nightmare n. 449, 830
nihilist n. 167
nil n. 74
nimble adj. 280, 611, 842
nimbus n. 800
nine n. 70
nip n. 760; vb. 197, 203
no n. 425
nobility n. 34, **870**
noble adj. 32, 318, 868, 870
nobody n. 74
nocturnal adj. 128
nod n. 424, 482, 612, 690; vb. 325, 482
node n. 49
nod off vb. 612
noise n. 778, 780, 788, 791
noiseless adj. 779
noisome adj. 777
nomad n. 270
nomadic adj. 266
nom de plume n. 497
nomenclature n. 496
nominal adj. 496
nominate vb. 496, 540, 685, 985
nominee n. 688
non-acceptance n. 425, 926
non-adhesive adj. 51
non aggressive adj. 650

nonce *adj.* 495
nonchalant *adj.* 757
non-combatant *n.* 656
non-completion *n.* 660
nonconformist *n.* 106, 425, 979; *adj.* 25, 106, 979
none *n.* 74
nonentity *n.* 2, 574
non-existence *n.* 2
non-expectation *n.* 444
non-flammable *adj.* 762
non-imitation *n.* 21
non-material existence *n.* 4
non-observance *n.* 672, 703, 920
non-payment *n.* 739
non-possession *n.* 708
non-preparation *n.* 603
non-resonance *n.* 785
non-retention *n.* 713
nonsense *n.* 433, 451, 516
non sequitur n. 412
non-starter *n.* 662
non-stop *adj.* 138
non-uniformity *n.* 17, 29
noon *n.* 127
no one *n.* 74
noose *n.* 463, 964
norm *n.* 30, 103
normal *adj.* 438, 545
normalize *vb.* 16
normative *adj.* 103
north *n.* 284
nostalgia *n.* 861
nosy *adj.* 388, 394
notable *adj.* 32, 573, 868
notary *n.* 959
notation *n.* 39
notch *n.* 259; *vb.* 258, 259
note *n.* 41, 441, 456, 460, 482, 483, 523, 778; *vb.* 382, 390, 483

nothing *n.* 74
notice *n.* 390, 460, 464, 482, 597, 624, 818; *vb.* 390, 818
noticeable *adj.* 458, 823
notify *vb.* 460, 464, 597, 624
notion *n.* 386, 420, 448, 449
notorious *adj.* 426, 869
nought *n.* 74
noun *n.* 499
nourish *vb.* 304
nourishing *adj.* 585
novel *n.* 525; *adj.* 125
novelist *n.* 521, 524, 525
novelty *n.* 21, 125, 142
novice *n.* 474, 630
now *adv.* 120
nowadays *adv.* 120
no way *adv.* 405
noxious *adj.* 777
nuance *n.* 27
nucleus *n.* 224
nude *n.* 228; *adj.* 228
nudge *n.* 482; *vb.* 482
nuisance *n.* 551, 830
null *adj.* 74
nullify *vb.* 2, 164, 469, 686
numb *adj.* 754; *vb.* 754
number *n.* 26, 39, 72, 499; *vb.* 38, 482
numbering *n.* 38
numbing *adj.* 760
numeral *n.* 39
numeration *n.* 38
numerous *adj.* 32, 72, 75
nun *n.* 986
nunnery *n.* 990
nuptial *adj.* 896
nurse *n.* 676, 683; *vb.* 304, 589, 676
nursery *n.* 378, 475
nurture *vb.* 304, 470, 712
nut *n.* 49, 306, 440

nutrition *n.* 304, 306
nutritious *adj.* 306, 585
nymph *n.* 970

O

oaf *n.* 437
oafish *adj.* 435
oath *n.* 468, 901
obdurate *adj.* 537, 942
obedience *n.* 654, 673, 702, 874
obedient *adj.* 654, 673, 702, 919
obesity *n.* 194
obey *vb.* 105, 654, 673, 874
obituary *n.* 369, 372
object *n.* 327, 552, 716; *vb.* 25, 425, 637, 642, 696, 892, 926
objection *n.* 425, 696, 926
objectionable *adj.* 862, 926
objective *n.* 298, 552; *adj.* 3, 6, 327, 430, 933
obligation *n.* 531, 562, 605, 674, 737, 919
oblige *vb.* 674, 919
obliged *adj.* 909, 919
obliging *adj.* 886, 899
oblique *adj.* 219; *vb.* 531
obliteration *n.* 164, 485
oblivion *n.* 442
oblivious *adj.* 393, 442, 754
oblong *n.* 246
obscene *adj.* 901, 952
obscure *adj.* 453, 503, 798, 799, 824; *vb.* 461, 798, 799
obscurity *n.* 453, 503, 799, 803, 824

obsequious *adj.* 881, 886

observable *adj.* 458, 823

observance *n.* 702, 878, 977, 988

observant *adj.* 390, 702, 818

observation *n.* 101, 384, 386, 390, 396, 818

observatory *n.* 329

observe *vb.* 105, 390, 392, 673, 702, 818, 878, 988

observer *n.* 460, 821

obsess *vb.* 830, 984

obsessed *adj.* 439

obsolete *adj.* 2, 126

obstacle *n.* 635, 681

obstinacy *n.* 537, 644

obstinate *adj.* 143, 535, 537

obstruct *vb.* 265, 635, 637, 648, 691

obtain *vb.* 1, 661, 705, 716, 720, 726

obtainable *adj.* 292, 404, 464, 705

obtrusive *adj.* 253, 877

obtuse *adj.* 256

obtuse angle *n.* 246

obvious *adj.* 452, 458, 502, 634, 823

occasion *n.* 136, 155, 878; *vb.* 155

occasionally *adv.* 138, 139

occult *adj.* 984

occupancy *n.* 188, 707

occupation *n.* 557, 605

occupier *n.* 190, 710

occupy *vb.* 107, 188, 191, 557, 707

occur *vb.* 1, 107, 153, 384, 430, 825

ocean *n.* 351

octagon *n.* 70, 246

octave *n.* 70

octet *n.* 70

odd *adj.* 29, 39, 439

oddity *n.* 439, 866

odds *n.* 158

ode *n.* 528

odious *adj.* 892

odorous *adj.* 774, 776

odour *n.* 774

of course *adv.* 408

off *adj.* 53, 240; *adv.* 614

offal *n.* 310

offence *n.* 923, 938, 955

offend *vb.* 892, 923

offender *n.* 906

offensive *n.* 645; *adj.* 295, 777, 845, 869, 880, 887, 892, 923, 936

offer *n.* 693, 695; *vb.* 532, 693, 715

offering *n.* 715, 943

offertory *n.* 715

offhand *adj.* 544, 887

office *n.* 557, 620, 985

office-boy *n.* 467

officer *n.* 625, 675, 956

official *n.* 623, 675, 683; *adj.* 430, 557, 622, 667

officious *adj.* 880

offset *n.* 31; *vb.* 31

off-shoot *n.* 979

offside *adj.* 240

offspring *n.* 11, 171

often *adv.* 138

ogle *vb.* 818, 890

oil *n.* 306, 342, 365, 765; *vb.* 342, 365, 547

oiliness *n.* 365, 886

oily *adj.* 257, 365, 477

ointment *n.* 342, 365, 591

O.K. *adj.* 579; *adv.* 79

old *adj.* 124, 126, 130, 606

old-fashioned *adj.* 126

old maid *n.* 897, 951

old master *n.* 488

oldness *n.* 126, 130

olive *adj.* 812

olive branch *n.* 652

omen *n.* 447, 597

ominous *adj.* 154, 447, 594, 902

omission *n.* 57, 99, 393, 431, 662, 703, 920

omitted *adj.* 189

omnibus *n.* 524; *adj.* 54

omnipotent *adj.* 159, 966

on *adv.* 288; *adv., prep.* 9

on and on *adv.* 114

once *adj.* 124

one *n.* 59; *adj.* 13, 59

on edge *adj.* 443, 856

on end *adj.* 214

oneness *n.* 13, 59

onerous *adj.* 615

one-sided *adj.* 416

one-time *adj.* 118, 124, 687

ongoing *adj.* 288

onlooker *n.* 821

only *adj.* 46, 59

onomatopoeia *n.* 455

onset *n.* 88, 298

onslaught *n.* 175, 645, 649

on time *adj.* 134, 136

ontological *adj.* 1

onus *n.* 919

onward *adv.* 288

ooze *vb.* 301, 319

opacity *n.* 803

opal glass *n.* 804

opaque *adj.* 799, 803

open *adj.* 262, 348, 409, 458, 462, 476, 508, 632, 753, 823; *vb.* 88, 182, 262, 348

open-handed *adj.* 747, 965

opening *n.* 88, 254, 262, 462, 518; *adj.* 88

openness *n.* 476, 594

open up *vb.* 462

opera n. 529, 792

opera glasses n. 822

operate vb. 159, **172**, 575, 591, 609

operation n. 172, 396, 591, 605, 609, 651

operative n. 619; adj. 172, 609

ophthalmic adj. 818

opinion n. 386, 415, 420, 624

opponent n. **638**, 655, 883

opportune adj. 136

opportunity n. 136, 406, 678

oppose vb. 14, 25, 181, 239, 414, 425, 637, 644, 648, 649, 696, 926

opposed adj. 533, 883

opposite n. 239; adj. 14, 220, 239, 883; adv., prep. 239

opposition n. 181, 239, 397, 637, 926

oppress vb. 669, 837, 900

oppressive adj. 330, 669, 759, 900

opt vb. 540

optical adj. 818

optical illusion n. 4

optical instrument n. **822**

optimism n. 417, 854

optimum adj. 579

option n. 540

opulence n. 734

opus n. 163, 792

oracle n. 436, 447

oral adj. 512, 514

orange n. **816**; adj. 816

oration n. 518

orator n. 514

orb n. 249, 329

orbit n. 250, 322, 323; vb. 274

orchard n. 378

orchestra n. 793

ordain vb. 671, 685, 985

ordeal n. 828

order n. 79, 81, 85, 93, 103, 622, 663, 872; vb. 79, 248, 622, 671, 902

orderliness n. 79, 583

orderly n. 676; adj. 79; adv. 79

ordinance n. 103, 671, 954, 988

ordinary adj. 508, 574, 580, 666, 867, 871

ordure n. 310

ore n. 367

organ n. 563

organic adj. 366

organism n. 366, 368

organization n. 58, 79, 81, 564, 622, 641

organize vb. 58, 79, 81, 558, 622

organizer n. 558, 623

orgy n. 306, 950

orientate vb. 284, 545

orifice n. 262

origin n. 88, 155, 170

original n. 23; adj. 21, 88, 102, 125, 155, 430

originality n. 21, 102, 449

ornament n. **509**, 844; vb. 844

ornamentation n. 509, **846**

ornate adj. 509, 846

ornithology n. 375

orphan n. 885

orthodox adj. 545, 977

orthodoxy n. 977

orthography n. 493

oscillation n. 140, **325**

ostentation n. 875, 877

ostracize vb. 99

other adj. 40

otherworldly adj. 328, 980

ought vb. 919

oust vb. 686

out adj. 189, 600

outbreak n. 88, 175, 645

outburst n. 175, 645, 756, 893

outcast n. 885; adj. 44

outclass vb. 29

outcome n. 87, 156

outcry n. 780, 788

outdated adj. 126

outdistance vb. 280, 314

outdo vb. 314

outer adj. 222

outer space n. 329

outfit n. 227, 568

outflow n. 301, 301

outgoing adj. 687

outgoings n. 740

outgrowth n. 252

outing, n. 269, 840

outlast vb. 112

outlaw n. 885; vb. 963

outlay n. 740

outlet n. 262

outline n. **232**, 242, 488, 558, 602, 825; vb. 232, 525, 558

outlive vb. 112

outlook n. 154, 284, 420, 443

outlying adj. 222

outmanoeuvre vb. 478

outmatch vb. 34

outmoded adj. 126

outnumber vb. 75

out of date adj. 126

outpace vb. 198, 280

outpost n. 198

outpour n. 301

output n. 163, 705

outrage n. 608, 900; vb. 830, 887

outrageous adj. 175, 433, 851, 869, 880, 936

outright adj. 54

outrun vb. 198

outset n. 88

outside *n.* 222, 232; *adj.*
  6, 100, 222, 921
outskirts *n.* 198
outspeed *vb.* 198
outspoken *adj.* 887
outstanding *adj.* 44,
  573, 737, 917
outstay *vb.* 112
outstretched *adj.* 202
outstrip *vb.* 29, 198,
  280, 314
outward *adj.* 6, 100,
  222, 825
outwit *vb.* 478, 631
oval *n.* 250; *adj.* 250
ovation *n.* 878, 925
oven *n.* 763
over *adj.* 44
over again *adv.* 77
over against *adv., prep.*
  239
overall *adj.* 98, 101
over and above *adv.* 40
overawe *vb.* 922
overbalance *vb.* 317
overbearing *adj.* 669
overcast *adj.* 363, 798
overcharge *vb.* 745
overcome *vb.* 661
overcompensate *vb.* 31
overdo *vb.* 481, 572,
  611, 615, 617
overdraft *n.* 739
overdrawn *adj.* 706,
  737
overdue *adj.* 117, 135,
  737, 917
overeat *vb.* 945, 948
overestimation *n.* 416,
  417
overfeed *vb.* 865
overfill *vb.* 865
overflow *n.* 600; *vb.* 56,
  358
overflowing *adj.* 75,
  865
over-generous *adj.* 749
overgrown *adj.* 194

overhanging *adj.* 216
overhaul *vb.* 280
overhear *vb.* 795
overjoyed *adj.* 827
overlap *n.* 206, 260; *vb.*
  206, 260
overlay *n.* 206; *vb.* 206,
  226
overload *vb.* 330
overlook *vb.* 208, 391,
  393
overlord *n.* 34
overplay *vb.* 481
overrate *vb.* 416, 417
overrun *vb.* 314
overseer *n.* 623, 675
oversensitive *adj.* 753,
  894
overshadow *vb.* 34,
  154, 208, 798
overshoot *vb.* 314
oversight *n.* 392, 621,
  622
overstatement *n.* 417,
  481
overstepping *n.* 314,
  918
overtake *vb.* 280
overthrow *n.* 148, 164,
  662; *vb.* 148, 164, 220,
  414, 686
overture *n.* 693, 792
overturn *vb.* 82, 164,
  220, 414
overvalue *vb.* 416, 417
overwhelm *vb.* 414,
  572, 661, 866, 922
overwhelming *adj.* 32
overwork *vb.* 611
owe *vb.* 737
owing *adj.* 737, 917
own *vb.* 707
owner *n.* 710
ownership *n.* 707
own up *vb.* 462, 833,
  941
ox *n.* 380

oxygen *n.* 348
ozone *n.* 348

P

pace *n.* 269; *vb.* 269
pacesetter *n.* 125
pacification *n.* 176, 650,
  652
pacifist *n.* 656; *adj.* 650
pack *n.* 94; *vb.* 56, 75,
  192
package *n.* 193; *vb.* 234
packet *n.* 193, 277
pact *n.* 698, 699
pad *vb.* 226
padding *n.* 226, 505
paddle *vb.* 271
paddock *n.* 184
padre *n.* 986
pagan *n.* 975, 983
page *n.* 467, 522
pageant *n.* 458, 529, 825
pageantry *n.* 877
pail *n.* 193
pain *n.* 551, 586, **828**,
  830; *vb.* 830
painful *adj.* 551, 753,
  805, 828
painfulness *n.* **830**
pain in the neck *n.* 592,
  841
pains *n.* 392
painstaking *adj.* 392,
  615
paint *n.* 225, 805; *vb.*
  225, 488, 525, 805
painter *n.* 491
painting *n.* 486, **488**
pair *n.* 61; *vb.* 61
pal *n.* 880
palatable *adj.* 306, 767,
  770
palatalize *vb.* 512
palate *n.* 767
palatial *adj.* 827

palaver *n.* 516

pale *adj.* 371, 806, 807, 812

palindrome *n.* 220

paling *n.* 234

pall *n.* 372

palliate *vb.* 591

pallid *adj.* 806

pally *adj.* 882

palm *n.* 663

palmist *n.* 447

palpable *adj.* 758

palpitate *vb.* 326, 756, 783

palpitation *n.* 325

palsy *n.* 326

paltry *adj.* 574, 580

pampa *n.* 356

pamphlet *n.* 464

panacea *n.* 591

pandemonium *n.* 780, 973

panel *n.* 206, 625, 688, 958

pang *n.* 828, 833

panic *n.* 615, 856; *vb.* 856

pannier *n.* 193

panoply *n.* 657

panorama *n.* 54, 818

pansy *n.* 162, 814, 953

pant *n.* 359; *vb.* 359, 756

pantheism *n.* 974

pantheon *n.* 967

pantomime *n.* 529

pantry *n.* 305

pap *n.* 364

paper *n.* 460, 518, 521, 526; *vb.* 225

paperback *n.* 524

par *n.* 30

parable *n.* 455, 525

parabola *n.* 247

parabolic *adj.* 455, 525

parachute *vb.* 273, 317

parade *n.* 458, 825, 877; *vb.* 91, 458, 877

paradise *n.* 449, 827, 972

paragon *n.* 581, 939

parallel *n.* 397; *adj.* 28, 218; *vb.* 218, 397

parallelism *n.* 218, 397

parallelogram *n.* 218, 246

paralysis *n.* 754

paralyze *vb.* 160, 754

paramount *adj.* 34, 573

paranoid *n.* 440

paranormal *adj.* 447

paraphernalia *n.* 568, 711

paraphrase *vb.* 20, 456

parapsychology *n.* 447

parasite *n.* 373, 612, 881

parasol *n.* 225, 801

parcel *n.* 193, 717; *vb.* 234, 717

parch *vb.* 350, 759

parchment *n.* 521

pardon *vb.* 601, 670, 680, 907, 911, 961

pare *vb.* 203, 228

parent *n.* 11, 86, 170

parenthood *n.* 170

parish *n.* 183, 987

parishioner *n.* 987

parity *n.* 28

park *n.* 234, 559; *vb.* 186

parliament *n.* 625

parochial *adj.* 183

parody *n.* 20, 487, 853

parrot *n.* 20; *vb.* 20

parse *vb.* 499

parsimony *n.* 748, 750

parson *n.* 986

part *n.* 55, 73, 327, 529, 717; *vb.* 48, 55, 637, 642, 898

partake *vb.* 304, 709

partial *adj.* 55, 73, 660, 861, 916

participant *n.* 619, 709

participate *vb.* 605, 639, 709

participation *n.* 188, 639, 709

participle *n.* 499

particle *n.* 33, 195, 340, 499

particular *adj.* 5, 8, 102, 392, 398, 864

particularize *vb.* 102

particularly *adv.* 34

parting *n.* 48, 299, 369, 642

partisan *adj.* 641, 916, 979

partition *n.* 230; *vb.* 48

partly *adv.* 55

partner *n.* 640, 709, 710, 896

partnership *n.* 60, 180, 639, 709

part of speech *n.* 499

part with *vb.* 556, 713

party *n.* 94, 641, 655, 840, 884, 896, 950, 960

party-minded *adj.* 979

pass *n.* 200, 690, 890; *vb.* 107, 110, 310, 313, 424, 427, 954

passable *adj.* 579, 666

passage *n.* 200, 262, 266, 313, 360, 559, 792

pass away *vb.* 369

passé *adj.* 126

passenger *n.* 270

passer-by *n.* 821

pass for *vb.* 18

passing *n.* 369

passion *n.* 752, 889, 893

passionate *adj.* 506, 752, 759, 889

passive *adj.* 499; *adj.* 174

pass on *vb.* 714

pass out *vb.* 617

pass over *vb.* 393, 670, 920

passport *n.* 690

pass sentence *vb.* 960

password *n.* 690

past *n.* 124; *adj.* 118, 124

paste *n.* 49, 362, 364; *vb.* 50

pastel *adj.* 805

pasteurize *vb.* 583

pastime *n.* 840

pastor *n.* 986

pastry *n.* 306

pasturage *n.* 305

pasture *n.* 305, 352, 356, 374

pasty *adj.* 806

pat *vb.* 758, 890

patch *n.* 183, 378; *vb.* 589

patched *adj.* 126, 817

patent *adj.* 458, 823

paternal *adj.* 11, 170

path *n.* 559

patience *n.* 757, 911

patient *adj.* 654, 757

patio *n.* 184

patisserie *n.* 306

patriarch *n.* 11, 132, 986

patrimony *n.* 11

patriotic *adj.* 903

patrol *n.* 593, 655, 683; *vb.* 593

patron *n.* 217, 545, 640, 726, 905

patronage *n.* 636, 726

patronize *vb.* 636, 726

patronizing *adj.* 873, 886

patter *vb.* 358, 783

pattern *n.* 23, 58, 79, 339, 488; *vb.* 81

pauper *n.* 735

pause *n.* 92, 144, 267, 612, 614, 616; *vb.* 92, 144, 267, 610, 612

pave *vb.* 225

paw *vb.* 758

pawn *n.* 701; *vb.* 701, 719

pawnbroker *n.* 718

pay *n.* 731, 738, 965; *vb.* 726, 738, 740, 965

payable *adj.* 737, 917

pay attention *vb.* 390

pay back *vb.* 647

payee *n.* 716

paymaster *n.* 733

payment *n.* 726, 738, 740, 965

payroll *n.* 619, 738

peace *n.* 267, 650, 779, 831

peaceful *adj.* 267, 616, 643, 650, 831

peace-maker *n.* 653, 656

peace-offering *n.* 652

peace of mind *n.* 757, 831

peach *n.* 816, 844

peak *n.* 89, 212

peal *vb.* 780, 783

pearly *adj.* 804, 807

peasant *n.* 378, 871; *adj.* 378

pebble *n.* 352

peculiar *adj.* 102, 106, 439

pedagogics *n.* 470

pedagogy *n.* 470

pedant *n.* 537, 864

pedantic *adj.* 392, 702, 864

peddle *vb.* 727

pedestal *n.* 213

pedestrian *n.* 270

pedlar *n.* 270, 697, 728

peek *n.* 818

peel *n.* 225; *vb.* 228

peel off *vb.* 51

peep *n.* 818; *vb.* 818

Peeping Tom *n.* 795, 821

peer *n.* 28, 122, 870

peg out *vb.* 617

pejorative *adj.* 923, 928

pellucid *adj.* 502, 802

pelt *vb.* 280

pen *n.* 184, 234; *vb.* 521

penalty *n.* 963

penance *n.* 943

penchant *n.* 178, 545

pencil *n.* 797; *vb.* 488

penda..t *n.* 216, 482

pendulum *n.* 216, 325

penetrability *n.* 335

penetrate *vb.* 300, 313, 441, 452

penetrating *adj.* 384, 434, 769, 787

penetration *n.* 300, 434

pen-friend *n.* 523

peninsula *n.* 352

penitence *n.* 833, 941

pennant *n.* 482

penniless *adj.* 708, 735

penny-pinching *n.* 750; *adj.* 750

pen-pal *n.* 523

pension *n.* 191, 687

pension off *vb.* 686

pensive *adj.* 384, 837

pentagon *n.* 70, 246

pent-up *adj.* 681

penumbra *n.* 798

people *n.* 379, 871; *vb.* 191

pep *n.* 173

pepper *n.* 307; *vb.* 307

perceive *vb.* 382, 419, 426, 452, 795, 818

perceptible *adj.* 458, 823

perception *n.* 382, 384, 752, 818

perceptive *adj.* 398, 426, 434

perch *vb.* 319

percolate *vb.* 300, 319

percussion *n.* 794

perennial *adj.* 114, 138

perfect *adj.* 581, 659, 937, 951; *vb.* 56, 581, 659

perfection n. 581, 659, 937, 951

perfectionist n. 864

perforation n. 262, 264

perforator n. 264

perform vb. 163, 172, 529, 609, 659, 702, 792, 919, 988

performance n. 163, 172, 529, 609, 659, 702

performer n. 529, 609, 619, 793

perfume n. 776; vb. 776

peril n. 594

perimeter n. 232, 250

period n. 109

periodic adj. 109, 138, 140

periodical n. 464, 524; adj. 140

peripatetic adj. 269

periphery n. 232, 250

periphrastic adj. 505

perish vb. 164, 369, 826

perishable adj. 113

perjury n. 477

perk up vb. 618, 836

permanence n. 112, 143, 152

permeable adj. 264

permeate vb. 45, 319

permissible adj. 954

permission n. 424, 690, 692, 921, 925

permissive society n. 952

permit n. 690; vb. 690, 954

permutation n. 142

pernickety adj. 864

perpendicular adj. 214, 248

perpetual adj. 78, 91, 114

perpetuate vb. 114

perpetuation n. 91, 145

perpetuity n. 78, 91, 114

perplex vb. 409, 633

perplexing adj. 409, 633

persecute vb. 900

perseverance n. 534, 535, 611, 980

persevere vb. 145, 535, 611, 648, 980

persist vb. 112, 143, 145, 535, 695

persistence n. 145, 534, 535

person n. 368, 379, 499

personal adj. 379, 966

personal effects n. 711

personality n. 5, 58, 382, 751

personification n. 455, 486

personnel n. 619, 676

perspective n. 488, 818

perspicacity n. 434

perspicuity n. 502

perspiration n. 310

persuade vb. 177, 420, 547, 624

persuasion n. 420, 547

perturb vb. 82

peruse vb. 394

perverse adj. 936

perversion n. 412, 457, 471, 477, 487, 608, 978

perversity n. 936

pervert n. 953; vb. 431, 457, 487, 588, 608

perverted adj. 936

pessimism n. 418, 443, 855

pest n. 892

pester vb. 695, 830

pestilence n. 167

pestilent adj. 592

pet n. 373, 891; vb. 890

petal n. 374

peter out vb. 37

petition n. 394, 695, 982; vb. 394, 695, 982

petitioner n. 697, 982

petrify vb. 332, 334, 856

petrol n. 342, 765

petty adj. 416, 574

phantom n. 971; adj. 971

Pharisee n. 981

pharmaceutical n. 591

phase n. 109; vb. 558

phasing n. 140

phenomenal adj. 866

phenomenon n. 153, 825, 866

philanthropy n. 899, 903

philosopher n. 428

philosophic adj. 757

philosophize vb. 384, 410

phlegmatic adj. 757

phobia n. 439

phoneme n. 512

phonetics n. 492, 512, 778

phoney n. 480; adj. 20

phosphorescence n. 797

photograph n. 483, 486; vb. 483

photographer n. 491

photography n. 486

phrase n. 494, 498, 792; vb. 498

phraseology n. 501

physical adj. 3, 327, 827

physiognomy n. 236

physiology n. 366, 375

piazza n. 559

pick vb. 378, 398, 540

picket vb. 144, 696

pickle n. 307, 633; vb. 599

pick-me-up n. 173, 591

pick on vb. 830

pick-pocket n. 723; vb. 722

pick up vb. 318, 472, 587, 589, 618

picnic n. 269, 306, 840

pictogram n. 493

pleasure   n. **827**, 840
pleasure trip   n. 840
pleat   n. 260; vb. 260
plebeian   n. 871; adj. 849, 871
plebiscite   n. 540
pledge   n. 468, **698**, 699, 701, 919; vb. 468, **698**, 699, 701
plenary   adj. 56
plenipotentiary   n. 688
plenitude   n. 32, 56
plentiful   adj. 32, 75, 572
plenty   n. 75, 168, 572; adj. 168, 570, 572
plethora   n. 168, 572, 865
pliable   adj. 335
pliant   adj. 335, 336
plight   n. 633
plight one's troth   vb. 896
plod   vb. 281, 535, 615
plonk   vb. 782, 785
plop   n. 785; vb. 782, 785
plot   n. 148, 184, 234, 378, 525, 558, 631; vb. 558, 631
plough   vb. 261, 378
pluck   n. 857; vb. 228, 312, 378
pluck up courage   vb. 857
plucky   adj. 857
plug   n. 265, 464; vb. 265, 464, 468
plug away   vb. 615
plumb   n. 330; adj. 214
plummet   n. 321; vb. 273
plump   n. 785; adj. 194, 204; vb. 540, 785
plunder   n. 663, 722, 724; vb. 164, 722
plunderer   n. 723
plunge   n. 317, 321; vb. 210, 273, 317, 321, 605

plural   n. 72; adj. 72
plurality   n. 72
ply   n. 206; vb. 268, 271, 695
pneumatic   adj. 348
poach   vb. 306
pocket   n. 254; vb. 705
pocket money   n. 731
pod   n. 225
podgy   adj. 194
poem   n. 528
poet   n. 528
poetic justice   n. 915
poet laureate   n. 528
poetry   n. **528**
poignant   adj. 769
point   n. 184, 233, 246, 255, 387, 400; vb. 178, 255, 284, 482
pointer   n. 482
pointless   adj. 576, 843
point of time   n. 115
point of view   n. 284, 420
poise   n. 514; vb. 216, 330
poison   n. 167, 592; vb. 370, 963
poisoner   n. 370
poisonous   adj. 164, 580, 586, 592
poke fun at   vb. 838
poker-faced   adj. 754
polar   adj. 760
polarity   n. 14, 181, 239, 637
pole   n. 217
polemical   adj. 410
police   n. 956; vb. 593, 956
policeman   n. 593, 956
police station   n. 682
policy   n. 558, 621
polish   n. 225, 257, 510, 797, 848; vb. 257, 341, 587, 797
polished   adj. 257, 510, 583, 848, 886

polish off   vb. 304, 659
polite   adj. 886, 922
politic   adj. 392, 577, 886
political   adj. 379, 667
politician   n. 623
politics   n. 379
poll   n. 540; vb. 38, 540
pollen   n. 340
pollster   n. 394
pollution   n. 584, 588, 608, 952
poltergeist   n. 971
polygon   n. 246
polytechnic   n. 475
pomp   n. 877
pompous   adj. 509, 875, 877
pond   n. 354
ponder   vb. 384
ponderous   adj. 330, 511, 573, 843
pooh-pooh   vb. 393, 924
pool   n. 354, 709; vb. 639
poor   adj. 169, 507, 571, 666, 735
poorly   adj. 586
pop   n. 170; vb. 782
Pope   n. 986
pop music   n. 792
popular   adj. 190, 868, 925
populate   vb. 191
population   n. 190, 379
pop up   vb. 825
pore over   vb. 472
pornography   n. 952
porous   adj. 264
port   n. 241, 298, 595
portable   adj. 268, 331
portentous   adj. 447
porter   n. 275, 676, 683
portfolio   n. 557
porthole   n. 262
portion   n. 55, 73, 305, 306, 717

portrait *n.* 20, 22, 488, 525

portray *vb.* 20, 486, 488, 525

portrayal *n.* 20, 486, 525

pose *n.* 825; *vb.* 23, 394, 621, 852

position *n.* 7, 93, 184, 185, 186, 420, 557; *vb.* 186

position in a series *n.* 93

positive *adj.* 39, 468

possess *vb.* 707, 720, 984

possession *n.* 707, 720, 729, 984

possessive *adj.* 707, 750, **913**

possessor *n.* 710, 720

possibility *n.* **404**, 406

possible *adj.* 404, 409, 459

post *n.* 217, 467, 523, 557; *vb.* 268, 523

postdate *vb.* 117

poster *n.* 464

posterior *n.* 237; *adj.* 85, 119, 237

posteriority *n.* **119**

posterity *n.* 171

postgraduate *n.* 474

post office *n.* 467

postpone *vb.* 89, 135, 920

postscript *n.* 41, 87, 89

postulate *n.* 386, 410, 448; *vb.* 448, 700

posture *n.* 7, 621, 825

pot *n.* 193

pot-bellied *adj.* 194

potent *adj.* 159, 173

potential *n.* 159, 564; *adj.* 159, 404, 459

pothole *n.* 254

potion *n.* 309, 591

pot luck *n.* 158

potter *n.* 491

pottery *n.* 489

pouch *n.* 193

poultry *n.* 306, 373

pounce *n.* 320; *vb.* 321

pound *n.* 184, 234, 325; *vb.* 282, 325, 340, 783

pound of flesh *n.* 669, 908

pour *vb.* 343, 358

pour out *vb.* 301

poverty *n.* 571, 735

powder *n.* 340

powderiness *n.* **340**

power *n.* **159**, 173, 177, 506, 530, 564, 622, 667; *vb.* 159, 765

powerful *adj.* 159, 161, 173, 177, 506, 667, 671

powerless *adj.* 160, 162

power station *n.* 159

practicable *adj.* 404, 406, 575

practical *adj.* 404, 577

practical joke *n.* 433

practically *adv.* 199

practice *n.* 396, 545, 602, 627, 702

practise *vb.* 470, 591, 602, 702

practised *adj.* 606

practising *adj.* 702, 974, 977, 980

practitioner *n.* 619

pragmatic *adj.* 575

prairie *n.* 356

praise *n.* 909, 922, **925**, 982; *vb.* 868, 909, 922, 925, 982

praiseworthy *adj.* 579, 925

pram *n.* 276

prank *n.* 433, 539, 932

prattle *vb.* 451, 516

pray *vb.* 695, 980, 982, 988

prayer *n.* 695, 909, 982, 985, 988

prayerful *adj.* 695, 980, 982

preach *vb.* 470, 514

preacher *n.* 456, 514, 974, 986

preaching *n.* 518, 985

preamble *n.* 86; *vb.* 84

precarious *adj.* 409, 594

precaution *n.* 392, 860

precede *vb.* 84, 118, 134, 286

precedence *n.* **84**, **286**

precedent *n.* 23, 84, 86, 118, 545, 960; *adj.* 84

preceding *adj.* 84, 118, 134

precept *n.* 103, **626**

precinct *n.* 184

precious *adj.* 139

precious stone *n.* 846

precipice *n.* 214

precipitate *adj.* 544, 613

precipitation *n.* 349, 358, 613

precipitous *adj.* 859

precis *n.* 527

precise *adj.* 392, 504, 864

preclude *vb.* 99, 691

precocious *adj.* 134

preconception *n.* 412, 416, 446

precursor *n.* 86, 467

predate *vb.* 117

predecessor *n.* 86

predestination *n.* 531, 543

predetermination *n.* **543**

predicament *n.* 153, 633

predict *vb.* 443, 447, 543

predictable *adj.* 447

prediction *n.* 154, **447**, 543

predilection *n.* 178, 861

printer n. 491, 522
printing n. 490, 521, 522
prior n. 986; adj. 84, 118, 134
priority n. 84, 118, 286, 573
priory n. 990
prism n. 246, 805
prison n. 234, 682
prisoner n. 684, 701
privacy n. 461, 885
private adj. 466
privilege n. 34, 678, 872, 917, 921
prize n. 663, 715, 724, 965; vb. 573, 861, 889
pro n. 953; adj. 689
probability n. 158, 406
probable adj. 404, 406
probationary adj. 396, 604
probationer n. 474
probe n. 394, 396; vb. 394
probity n. 931, 937
problem n. 387, 409, 410, 633, 828, 830
problematical adj. 409
procedure n. 103, 545, 558, 559
proceed vb. 110, 266, 288, 313, 558, 661
proceedings n. 483
proceeds n. 705, 716, 741
process n. 172, 559
processed adj. 602
processing n. 146, 163
procession n. 91, 458
proclaim vb. 458, 460, 464, 671
procrastinate vb. 135, 920
procreation n. 163
procuration n. 705
procure vb. 705
prod n. 547; vb. 547

prodigal n. 749, 940; adj. 569, 749
prodigality n. 569, 749
prodigal son n. 941
prodigy n. 866
produce n. 163, 705; vb. 155, 163, 172, 458, 529
producer n. 155, 166
product n. 38, 156, 163, 729
production n. 163, 529
productive adj. 163, 168, 705
productiveness n. 168
profanation n. 608, 901
profane adj. 901, 975, 981, 987; vb. 608, 981
profess vb. 420, 468, 549, 702
profession n. 468, 557
professional n. 629; adj. 557
professor n. 428, 473
proffer vb. 693
proficiency n. 426, 627
proficient n. 629; adj. 627
profile n. 232, 242, 525, 825
profit n. 550, 575, 705, 734, 741; vb. 136, 575, 587, 661, 705
profitable adj. 575, 705, 965
profitless adj. 169, 662
profit-sharing n. 709; adj. 709
profligate n. 953; adj. 749, 952
profound adj. 210, 453
profuse adj. 32, 56, 75, 168, 505
profusion n. 26, 32, 75, 168, 567, 572
prognosis n. 447
prognosticate vb. 154, 447

programme n. 83, 558, 605, 621
progress n. 266, 288, 550, 587, 661; vb. 130, 145, 266, 288, 324, 587, 661
progression n. 36, 85, 91, 288
progressive adj. 91, 125, 148, 288, 587, 605
prohibit vb. 99, 635, 691
prohibition n. 99, 635, 691, 949
prohibitive adj. 99, 691, 745
project n. 558, 605; vb. 6, 222, 252, 253, 552, 558
projectile n. 290
projection n. 6, 253
prolegomena n. 86
proletariat n. 871
proliferate vb. 36, 165, 168
prolific adj. 163, 168
prolix adj. 505
prologue n. 86
prolongation n. 36, 112, 145, 202
promenade n. 269
prominence n. 253, 573, 823, 868
prominent adj. 177, 253, 458, 573, 823, 868
promiscuous adj. 399, 952
promise n. 698, 699, 701, 854; vb. 698, 699, 854
promised adj. 406, 698
promised land n. 96
promontory n. 253
promote vb. 217, 288, 458, 464, 587, 636
promotion n. 464, 587, 636, 727
prompt adj. 115, 134,

280, 557; *vb.* 441, 547, 597, 624

prompter *n.* 441, 547

promptly *adv.* 115

promulgate *vb.* 460, 464

prone *adj.* 178, 179, 215

prong *n.* 255

pronoun *n.* 499

pronounce *vb.* 415, 464, 468, 512, 514, 960

pronounced *adj.* 458, 823

pronouncement *n.* 415, 468, 960

pronunciation *n.* 512, 514

proof *n.* 396, 413, 460, 482, 522

proofreader *n.* 522

prop *n.* 213, 217; *vb.* 217, 318

propagandism *n.* 470

propagate *vb.* 95, 163, 165

propel *vb.* 266, 282, 290

propellant *n.* 290

propensity *n.* 178, 545

proper *adj.* 499, 510, 848, 876, 915, 935

proper noun *n.* 499

property *n.* 711, 729

prophecy *n.* 447, 976

prophesy *vb.* 443, 446, 447

prophet *n.* 447, 449, 467, 974

prophetic *adj.* 976

propitiation *n.* 652, 943

propitious *adj.* 136

proportion *n.* 27, 244, 510, 717

proportions *n.* 194

proposal *n.* 552, 558, 693, 695, 890

proposition *n.* 103, 410, 448, 468, 605, 693, 695

proprietor *n.* 710

propriety *n.* 510, 577

propulsion *n.* **290**

prosaic *adj.* 843

proscribe *vb.* 962

prose *n.* **528**

prosecution *n.* 930, 959, 960

prosecutor *n.* 930

proselytize *vb.* 146, 470

prosody *n.* 528

prospect *n.* 123, 154, 406, 443

prospective *adj.* 123, 443, 558

prospectus *n.* 83

prosperity *n.* 168, 550, 661, **664**, 734

prostitute *n.* 953; *vb.* 608, 952

prostrate *adj.* 215, 319, 922; *vb.* 215

protect *vb.* 225, 392, 593, 599, 646, 801

protection *n.* 392, 593, 595, 599, 646

protectionism *n.* 681

protector *n.* 593, 646, 905

protest *n.* 425, 533, **696**; *vb.* 425, 644, 696

protester *n.* 425, 832

protocol *n.* 545

prototype *n.* **23**

protract *vb.* 196, 202

protrude *vb.* 252, 253

protuberance *n.* 252, 253

proud *adj.* 644, 877

prove *vb.* 396, 396, 408, **413**, 420, 929

proverb *n.* 432

proverbial *adj.* 426, 432

provide *vb.* 163, 304, 564, **568**, 602, 715

providence *n.* 550, 748, 966

providential *adj.* 136

province *n.* 183, 557

provincial *adj.* 183

provincialism *n.* 492, 494

provision *n.* **568**

provisional *adj.* 149, 396, 403, 700

provisionally *adv.*, *prep.* 111

provisions *n.* 305, 306, 564, 700

proviso *n.* 403, 700

provocation *n.* 755

provocative *adj.* 459, 547

provoke *vb.* 155, 459, 547, 755, 883, 893

prowess *n.* 857

prowl *vb.* 461

proximity *n.* 199

proxy *n.* 149, 688, 689, 689

prudent *adj.* 392, 434, 748, 860

prudish *adj.* 951

prune *vb.* 203

pry *vb.* 388, 394

psalm *n.* 982

pseudo- *adj.* 20, 497

pseudonym *n.* 497

psyche *n.* 382, 751

psychiatry *n.* 382

psychic *adj.* 328, 382, 447

psychology *n.* 382

psychopath *n.* 440

psychotherapy *n.* 382

psychotic *n.* 440

pub *n.* 191

puberty *n.* 129

public *n.* 379, 821; *adj.* 379, 464

publication *n.* **464**, 524

public house *n.* 191

publicity *n.* 464

publicize *vb.* 458, 464

public records *n.* 483

public-spirited *adj.* 903

pylon *n.* 159
pyramid *n.* 246
pyre *n.* 372

Q

quack *vb.* 787, 789
quadrangle *n.* 67, 184
quadratic *adj.* 67
quadrilateral *n.* 67, 246
quadrisection *n.* **69**
quadruped *n.* 373
quadruple *adj.* 68; *vb.* 68
quadruplet *n.* 67
quadruplication *n.* **68**
quagmire *n.* 355
quail *vb.* 858
quake *n.* 326; *vb.* 325, 326, 856
qualification *n.* 41, 142, **403**
qualifications *n.* 627
qualified *adj.* 130, 602, 627
qualify *vb.* 142, 403, 570
quality *n.* 5, 58, 579, 935
qualm *n.* 421, 533, 833
quandary *n.* 409, 633
quantify *vb.* 26, 400
quantitative *adj.* 26
quantity *n.* **26**, 32, 75, 400
quarrel *n.* 25, 642, 893; *vb.* 25, 642
quarrelsome *adj.* 642, 883
quarry *vb.* 312
quart *n.* 69
quarter *n.* 69, 183; *vb.* 69
quartet *n.* 67, 792
quasar *n.* 329
quash *vb.* 681, 686

quasi- *adj.* 497
quaternity *n.* 67
queen *n.* 675
Queen's English *n.* 492
queer *n.* 106, 953; *adj.* 952
quell *vb.* 37, 89, 652, 681
quench *vb.* 762
query *n.* 394
quest *n.* 269, 388, 394, 554; *vb.* 554
question *n.* 387, **394**, 695; *vb.* 388, **394**, 421
questionable *adj.* 407, 409, 421, 869, 932
questioner *n.* 388, 394
questionnaire *n.* 394
queue *n.* 91; *vb.* 91
quibble *vb.* 454
quick *adj.* **280**, 434, **613**, 842
quicken *vb.* **280**, 368, 613, 752, 755
quicksand *n.* 355, 596
quick-tempered *adj.* 756
quick-witted *adj.* 842
quiescent *adj.* 267, 459
quiet *n.* 267, 616, 779; *adj.* 517, 616, 650, 779, 781, 876; *vb.* 652, 779
quieten *vb.* 176
quiet time *n.* 982
quilt *vb.* 226
quintessence *n.* 5
quintet *n.* 70
quintuple *adj.* 70
quintuplet *n.* 70
quip *n.* 842
quirk *n.* 539
quisling *n.* 480
quit *vb.* 299, **556**, 687
quite *adv.* 56
quiver *n.* 325; *vb.* 325, 326, 756, 760, 856
Quixote *n.* 449
quiz *n.* 394; *vb.* 394

quoit *n.* 250
quota *n.* 305, 717
quotation *n.* 743
quote *vb.* 20
quotient *n.* 38

R

rabbi *n.* 986
rabble *n.* 871
rabid *adj.* 148, 439
race *n.* 11, 554, 613, 649; *vb.* 280, 649
racialist *adj.* 379
rack *n.* 217, 964
racket *n.* 780, 791
raconteur *n.* 525
racy *adj.* 506, 769
radiate *vb.* 297
radiation *n.* 297
radiator *n.* 763
radical *n.* 148, 672, 832; *adj.* 56, 148, 155
radio *n.* 467, 840
radius *n.* 400
rafter *n.* 217
rag *n.* 33; *vb.* 842
rage *n.* 439, 756, 850, 893; *vb.* 756, 893
ragtime *n.* 792
raid *n.* 300, 645; *vb.* 645, 720, 722
rail *n.* 234
railing *n.* 234
railway *n.* 559
rain *n.* 347, 349, 358; *vb.* 358
rainbow *n.* 247, 817
rainfall *n.* 358
rainproof *adj.* 350
raise *vb.* 214, 318, 331, 377
rake *n.* 953
rally *n.* 649, 696; *vb.* 94, 587, 589
ram *vb.* 265

Ramadan *n*. 947

ramble *n*. 269; *vb*. 269, 439, 505

rambler *n*. 270

rambling *adj*. 505

ramification *n*. 297

rampart *n*. 646

ramshackle *adj*. 588

ranch *n*. 377, 378

rancid *adj*. 53, 584, 777

rancorous *adj*. 912

random *adj*. 141, 158, 399, 409, 553

range *n*. 27, 182, 198, 400, 678, 795, 956; *vb*. 81, 182

ranger *n*. 683

rank *n*. 7, 93, 97, 870; *adj*. 777; *vb*. 27, 97

rankle *vb*. 893

ransack *vb*. 722

ransom *n*. 601; *vb*. 601, 680, 721

rant *vb*. 514

rap *n*. 282, 782, 963; *vb*. 282, 782

rape *vb*. 645, 952

rapidity *n*. 280

rapids *n*. 358

rapist *n*. 645, 953

rapport *n*. 643

rapprochement n. 643

rapture *n*. 827, 972

rare *adj*. 21, 33, 139, 333

rarefied *adj*. 333

rarely *adv*. 139

rarity *n*. 76, 139, 333, 770

rascal *n*. 940

rashness *n*. 393, 544, 613, **859**

rasp *vb*. 341, 787

rat *n*. 480, 538, 940

rate *n*. 27; *vb*. 743

rates. *n*. 743

ratify *vb*. 408, 424, 468, 699

ratio *n*. 27, 400

ration *n*. 305, 717; *vb*. 717

rational *adj*. 39, 382, 410

rationale *n*. 157

rationalism *n*. 410, 975

rationality *n*. 410, 438

rat-race *n*. 611

rattle *n*. 783; *vb*. 780, 783

raucous *adj* 787

ravage *n*. 164; *vb*. 164, 228, 314, 645

ravaged *adj*. 588

rave *vb*. 439, 827, 925

ravenous *adj*. 720, 861, 948

ravine *n*. 200, 210, 254

raw *adj*. 129, 603, 753, 760

raw deal *n*. 551, 916

raw materials *n*. 566

ray *n*. 297, 797

raze *vb*. 164, 319, 485

re *adv., prep*. 9

reach *n*. 182, 198, 202; *vb*. 182, 280, 298, 661

reaction *n*. 147, 156, 283, 647

reactionary *n*. 143, 672, 832; *adj*. 143, 289

read *vb*. 456, 472, 482

readable *adj*. 452

reader *n*. 473, 522, 524

reading *n*. 456, 472, 518

read into *vb*. 457

readjustment *n*. 142

ready *adj*. 188, 532, 602

ready reckoner *n*. 38

real *adj*. 1, 3, 327, 430

realistic *adj*. 18

realize *vb*. 327, 382, 419, 426, 452, 486, 659

really *adv*. 1

realm *n*. 183, 557

reanimate *vb*. 368, 589

reap *vb*. 48, 378, 661, 705

reappear *vb*. 77, 147

rear *n*. 237; *adj*. 237; *vb*. 377, 470

rearguard *n*. 237

rearrange *vb*. 142, 220

reason *n*. 8, 155, 401, 410, 438, 456, 547; *vb*. 382, 410

reasonable *adj*. 176, 406, 410, 746

reasoning *n*. 382, 384, 410; *adj*. 410, 434

reawaken *vb*. 589, 618

rebate *n*. 43, 744; *vb*. 744

rebel *n*. 106, 148, 425, 672; *vb*. 644, 672

rebellion *n*. 148, 644, 672

rebellious *adj*. 148, 644, 668, 672

rebirth *n*. 146, 589

rebound *n*. 147, 283; *vb*. 147, 283

rebuff *n*. 283, 295, 542, 694, 923; *vb*. 295, 542, 694, 923

rebuild *vb*. 165, 589

rebuke *n*. 926; *vb*. 926, 962, 963

rebuttal *n*. 395, 402, 414

recalcitrant *adj*. 537, 648

recall *n*. 441; *vb*. 441, 686

recantation *n*. 538

recapitulate *vb*. 77

recede *vb*. 37, 289, 293

receipts *n*. 705, 716, 741

receive *vb*. 302, 705, 716, 720, 884

receiver *n*. 467, 716, 733

receiving *n*. 716; *adj*. 716

recency *n*. 134

recent *adj.* 125, 134
receptacle *n.* 193
reception *n.* 94, 98, 302, 716, 795, 884, 896
receptive *adj.* 302, 716, 753
recess *n.* 144, 254, 614
recession *n.* 169, 197, 293, 317
recipe *n.* 626
recipient *n.* 523, 716
reciprocal *adj.* 9, 12, 28, 39, 150, 647
recital *n.* 518, 792
recite *vb.* 77, 460, 525
reckless *adj.* 393, 613, 749, 859
reckon *vb.* 38, 400, 743
reckoning *n.* 38, 400, 738, 742
reclaim *vb.* 589, 721
recline *vb.* 215
recluse *n.* 885, 946
recognition *n.* 426, 818, 909, 925
recognize *vb.* 426, 441, 452, 818, 909, 925
recoil *n.* 147, **283**; *vb.* 147, 283
recollect *vb.* 441
recommend *vb.* 415, 624
recompense *n.* 31, 721, 738, 965; *vb.* 31, 589, 738, 965
reconcile *vb.* 24, 105, 652, 653, 704, 831, 911, 943
reconciled *adj.* 643, 654, 911
reconciliation *n.* 24, 650, 652, 911, 943
recondite *adj.* 453
reconditioning *n.* 147, 589
reconsider *vb.* 384
reconsideration *n.* 441

reconstruct *vb.* 142, 146, 165, 589
record *n.* 83, 441, **483**, 484, 525, 792, 794; *vb.* 83, 483, 525
recorder *n.* **484**, 958
recount *vb.* 525
recoup *vb.* 31, 721, 738
recourse *n.* 595
recover *vb.* 589, 618, 720, 721, 834
recovery *n.* 147, 589, 618, 705, 720, 721
recreation *n.* 614, 649, 840
recriminate *vb.* 647, 930
recruit *n.* 287, 474, 655; *vb.* 557, 651
rectangle *n.* 246
rectify *vb.* 587, 589
rector *n.* 986
recuperate *vb.* 589, 618
recur *vb.* 77, 138, 140, 441
recurrent *adj.* 109, 138
red *n.* **811**; *adj.* 811, 876
redeem *vb.* 31, 146, 601, 721, 726, 911, 943
redeemer *n.* 905, 967
rediscover *vb.* 165
red-letter day *n.* 878
redress *n.* 943, 965; *vb.* 589, 943, 965
reduce *vb.* 37, 76, 197, 203, 588, 743, 744
reduction *n.* 37, 42, 195, 197, 527, 744
redundancy *n.* 505, 686
redundant *adj.* 505, 572
reduplication *n.* 62, 165
re-echo *vb.* 784
reef *n.* 357, 596
reek *n.* 777; *vb.* 759, 777
re-entry *n.* 274
re-establish *vb.* 589
refer *vb.* 9, 157, 450

referee *n.* 415, 653
reference *n.* 157, 401, 450
reference book *n.* 524
referendum *n.* 450, 540
refill *n.* 56
refine *vb.* 142, 333, 587
refined *adj.* 398, 510, 805, 844, 848, 886
reflect *vb.* 384, 486, 797, 982
reflection *n.* 22, 384, 441, 797
reflector *n.* 822
reflex *adj.* 411, 531, 544
reform *n.* 587; *vb.* 142, 146, 587, 589
reforming *n.* 165; *adj.* 903
refractory *adj.* 537, 672
refrain *n.* 528, 792; *vb.* 89, 144, 555, 610, 944
refresh *vb.* 161, 348, 472, 589, 618
refresher *n.* 591
refreshment *n.* 147, 306, 618, 829
refresh one's memory *vb.* 441
refrigeration *n.* 599, **762**
refrigerator *n.* 305, **764**
refuge *n.* 463, 595, 885
refugee *n.* 270, 600, 885
refund *n.* 31, 721, 738; *vb.* 31, 589, 721, 738
refurbish *vb.* 125, 587, 589
refusal *n.* 469, 542, 691, **694**
refuse *n.* 576; *vb.* 425, 469, 533, 542, 691, **694**
refutation *n.* 414
refute *vb.* 402, 686
regain *vb.* 705, 721
regal *adj.* 870
regalia *n.* 482, 677
regard *n.* 388, 390, 392,

868, 922; *vb.* 390, 420, 868, 889

regarding *adv., prep.* 9

regenerate *adj.* 146, 974; *vb.* 165, 589

regent *n.* 675

reggae *n.* 792

region *n.* 183

register *n.* 83, 116, 302, 483; *vb.* 83, 483

registrar *n.* 484

regress *n.* 147, 289; *vb.* 147, 289, 590

regression *n.* 37, 147, 289, 590

regret *n.* 445, 828, 832, 833; *vb.* 828, 833, 837, 941

regular *n.* 545; *adj.* 16, 79, 81, 91, 138, 140, 244, 545

regularity *n.* 16, 79, 138, 140, 244, 257, 545

regulate *vb.* 81, 140, 621, 622

regulation *n.* 81, 103, 622, 954

rehabilitate *vb.* 589, 721

rehearse *vb.* 77, 525, 602

reign *vb.* 667

reigning *adj.* 870

reimburse *vb.* 31, 721, 738, 965

reinforce *vb.* 161, 173, 226, 468, 646

reinforcement *n.* 196, 217

reinstate *vb.* 147, 589, 721

reissue *n.* 77; *vb.* 77, 125, 464

reiterate *vb.* 77, 140

reject *vb.* 25, 99, 393, 425, 469, 542, 694

rejection *n.* 99, 421, 542, 694, 926

rejects *n.* 44

rejoice *vb.* 829, 838

rejoicing *n.* **838**

rejoin *vb.* 395

rejuvenation *n.* 147, 589

rekindle *vb.* 589

relapse *n.* 147, 586, 590; *vb.* 147, 590

relate *vb.* 9, 397, 460, 525

related *adj.* 9, 11, 60

relation *n.* 9, 11, 12, 397

relationship *n.* 9, 889, 952

relative *n.* 11; *adj.* 9, 12, 27

relative quantity *n.* 27

relax *vb.* 144, 176, 267, 335, 612, 614, 840, 907

relaxation *n.* 614, 616, 834, 840

relay *n.* 268; *vb.* 268

release *n.* 460, 465, 600, 601, 680, 713, 911, 921, 961; *vb.* 601, 634, 680, 713, 921, 961

relegate *vb.* 303

relent *vb.* 335, 907

relentless *adj.* 900, 908

relevant *adj.* 9, 573

reliable *adj.* 152, 408, 868, 931

reliance *n.* 408, 420, 854

relic *n.* 44, 371, 441, 483

relief *n.* 149, 176, 181, 253, 489, 591, 601, 618, 636, 834, 899

relieve *vb.* 149, 176, 591, 601, 618, 634, 636, 686, 834, 899

religion *n.* 974

religious *adj.* 392, 974, 982

religious service *n.* **988**

relinquishment *n.* 546, 556, 607, 687, 713

relish *n.* 307, 767, 827, 861; *vb.* 767, 770, 827, 861

relocate *vb.* 268

reluctant *adj.* 281, 533, 694, 876

rely *vb.* 420, 443, 854

remain *vb.* 91, 112, 143, 145, 535

remainder *n.* 44

remains *n.* 44, 371, 483

remake *vb.* 77, 165, 589

remark *vb.* 395, 456

remarkable *adj.* 32, 866

remedy *n.* 365, 591, 834; *vb.* 591

remember *vb.* 441, 878

remembrance *n.* 483

remind *vb.* 441

reminiscences *n.* 441

reminiscent *adj.* 441

remiss *adj.* 393, 668

remission *n.* 43, 144, 601, 744, 911, 961

remit *vb.* 268, 601, 715, 911

remittance *n.* 268, 738

remnant *n.* 44, 76

remodel *vb.* 77, 146, 589

remonstrate *vb.* 696

remorse *n.* 833, 941

remote *adj.* 198, 885

remould *vb.* 165

removal *n.* 42, 48, 142, 268, 293, 299, 303, 312

remove *vb.* 42, 99, 187, 228, 268, 293, 303, 312, 485, 680, 720, 722, 826

remuneration *n.* 31, 721, 738, 965

remunerative *adj.* 705, 738, 965

renaissance *n.* 165, 589

rend *vb.* 48

render *vb.* 456, 486, 715, 792

rendezvous *n.* 96, 884;
vb. 94
renegade *n.* 538
renew *vb.* 77, 125, 142,
165, 589
renounce *vb.* 469, 542,
556, 713
renovate *vb.* 125, 142,
165, 589
renown *n.* 868
rent *n.* 743; *adj.* 48,
262; *vb.* 191, 719
renunciation *n.* 469,
538, 542, 556, 713
reoccurrence *n.* 77, 138
reorganization *n.* 81,
142
reorganize *vb.* 142, 587,
589
repair *n.* 589; *vb.* 589,
721
reparation *n.* 31, 589,
721, 943, 965
repartee *n.* 395, 519,
842
repatriation *n.* 721
repay *vb.* 647, 721, 738,
943
repeal *n.* 686; *vb.* 686
repeat *n.* 77; *vb.* 20, 62,
77, 138, 140, 165
repeated and prolonged
sound *n.* 783
repel *vb.* 295, 648, 885,
892
repent *vb.* 833, 907, 941
repercussion *n.* 156,
283
repetition *n.* 62, 77,
140, 505
repetitive *adj.* 77, 841
replace *vb.* 147, 149,
187, 686
replay *n.* 77
replenish *vb.* 56, 568
replete *adj.* 56, 570, 865
replica *n.* 20, 22

reply *n.* 283, 395, 402,
523; *vb.* 395
report *n.* 415, 460, 465,
468, 483, 523, 525, 778,
782; *vb.* 460, 465, 483,
521, 525
reporter *n.* 460, 524
repose *n.* 612, 616; *vb.*
215
repository *n.* 732
reprehensible *adj.* 926
represent *vb.* 20, 486,
488, 525, 685, 689
representation *n.* 20,
22, 486, 488, 489, 525,
558, 685
representative *n.* 625,
688, 689; *adj.* 18, 101,
482, 486
repress *vb.* 679, 681,
691, 779
reprieve *n.* 135, 601,
911, 961; *vb.* 907, 911,
961
reprimand *n.* 926, 963;
vb. 926, 963
reprint *n.* 20, 22, 77,
524; *vb.* 165, 464
reprisal *n.* 647, 912
reproach *n.* 869, 926;
vb. 926
reproduce *vb.* 20, 163,
165, 486
reproduction *n.* 22, 77,
163, 165, 486
reprove *vb.* 926, 930,
963
reptile *n.* 373
repudiate *vb.* 414, 469,
542, 686, 694
repugnance *n.* 637, 862,
883, 892
repugnant *adj.* 862,
892, 936
repulse *vb.* 295, 694
repulsion *n.* 295, 892
repulsive *adj.* 295, 777,
892

reputable *adj.* 177, 868,
931
reputation *n.* 177, 868
repute *n.* 868
request *n.* 394, 671, 695,
982; *vb.* 394, 671, 695
requiem *n.* 372, 839
require *vb.* 531, 562,
571, 671, 674
requirement *n.* 8, 315,
562, 671
requital *n.* 31, 647, 912,
943
rescue *n.* 589, 600, 601,
680; *vb.* 589, 601, 636,
680
research *n.* 396; *vb.* 396
researcher *n.* 394, 396,
428
resemblance *n.* 18, 105,
397
resentful *adj.* 883, 893,
900, 913
resentment *n.* 832, 893,
913, 914
reservation *n.* 403, 421,
425, 700
reserve *n.* 149, 198, 517,
568, 681, 876; *adj.* 149;
vb. 712
reserves *n.* 564, 567,
731
reservoir *n.* 193, 354,
567
reside *vb.* 188, 191
residence *n.* 188, 191,
707
resident *n.* 190, 710;
adj. 188
residual *adj.* 44
residue *n.* 44
resign *vb.* 654, 687
resignation *n.* 654, 687,
757
resilience *n.* 336
resin *n.* 365; *vb.* 365
resist *vb.* 295, 537, 637,
644, 648, 694

resistance n. 181, **648**

resistant adj. 337

resolute adj. 152, 534, 857

resolution n. 415, 530, **534**, 611, 857

resolve n. 534; vb. 53, 530, 534, 552

resonance n. 778, **784**

resort to vb. 606

resounding n. 784; adj. 780

resourceful adj. 449

resources n. 564, 566, 711, 734

respect n. 868, 886, **922**; vb. 868, 922

respectful adj. 673, 922

respiration n. 359

respite n. 135, 144, 614

respond vb. 283, 395, 752, 909

responsibility n. 179, 557, 701, 917, 919, 956

responsible adj. 133, 179, 702, 919, 956

responsive adj. 395, 909

rest n. 44, 92, 144, 213, 217, **267**, 610, 612, 614, 616; vb. 144, 267, 612, 614, 616

restate vb. 77, 456

restaurant n. 191

restitution n. 31, 147, 589, 721, 738, 943

restless adj. 266, 611, 756, 832

restoration n. 147; **589**, 618, 721

restorative n. 591; adj. 585, 589, 591

restore vb. 147, 589, 591, 618, 680, 721, 911

restrain vb. 37, 144, 176, 403, 635, **681**, 691

restrained adj. 176, 508, 517, 681, 876, 944

restraint n. 37, 176, 281, 548, 635, **681**, 876, 944

restrict vb. 99, 231, 235, 403, 635, 681, 691

restrictions n. 700

result n. 44, 87, 156, 163, 460; vb. 85, 119, 156

resumé n. 527; vb. 589

resumption n. 77, 589

resurgence n. 589

resurrection n. 147, 165, 589, 972

resuscitate vb. 589, 618

retail vb. 727

retailer n. 727, 728

retain vb. 441, 707, 712

retaliate vb. 647, 912, 963

retaliation n. 395, **647**, 912

retard vb. 135, 281, 635

retarded adj. 435

retch vb. 303

retention n. 441, **712**

reticent adj. 466, 517, 681, 876

retinue n. 91

retire vb. 289, 293, 299, 687

retired adj. 118, 124, 687

retirement n. 89, 293, 687, 826

retiring adj. 517, 876, 885

retort n. 395, 647; vb. 395, 647

retrace vb. 441

retraction n. 538, 686

retreat n. 289, 293, 299, 463, 595, 600, 885; vb. 289, 293, 556

retribution n. 647, 943, 963

retrieve vb. 589, 601, 705, 720, 721

retrograde adj. 289

return n. 147, 289, 298, 721; vb. 147, 163, 298, 589, 647, 721

reunion n. 47, 884

revalue vb. 745

reveal vb. 228, 262, 419, 456, 458, 462

revealed adj. 976

revealing adj. 228, 802

revel vb. 827, 838, 840

revelation n. 419, 420, 458, 462, 464, 974, **976**

revenge n. 647, **912**; vb. 647

revengeful adj. 908, 912

revenue n. 741

reverberate vb. 283, 784

reverberation n. 283, 778

revere vb. 868, 922, 982

reverence n. 922, 980, 982

reverend n. 986

reversal n. 147, 220, 289, 538, 686

reverse n. 237, 239; adj. 14, 289; vb. 147, 220, 686

reversion n. 147, 220, 590

review n. 394, 415, 456, 524, 526; vb. 394, 415, 441, 472, 526

reviewer n. 456, 524, 526

revile vb. 853, 901, 928

revise vb. 142, 472, 587

revitalize vb. 589

revival n. 147, 165, 589

revive vb. 77, 165, 368, 441, 589, 618

revoke vb. 538, 686

revolt n. 148, 644, 672; vb. 148, 644, 672

revolting adj. 148, 771, 892

revolution n. **148**, 323, 644, 672

revolve vb. 140, 323

revolver n. 657

revue n. 529

reward n. 663, 705, 909, 917, **965**; vb. 738, 909, 965

reword vb. 77, 456, 498

rhetorical adj. 455, 509

rhetorician n. 514

rhombus n. 246

rhyme n. 528; vb. 528

rhythm n. 140, 510, 512, 528

rhythmical adj. 790

rib vb. 842

ribbon n. 49, 207, 663, 846, 872

rich adj. 163, 168, 509, 664, 734, 770, 772, 790, 805

riches n. 664, 711, 734

rickshaw n. 276

rid vb. 634

riddle n. 466; vb. 264

ride n. 269; vb. 269

rider n. 41, 270

ridge n. 252, 357

ridicule n. 853, 924; vb. 788, 842, 853, 869, 924, 928

ridiculousness n. 433, 851

riding n. 269

rifle n. 657; vb. 722

rift n. 200, 642

rig vb. 568

right n. 240, 667, **915**, 917, 929, 954, 956; adj. 240, 430, 915, 931, 954, 977

right angle n. 246

righteous adj. 915, 935

right-hand man n. 624, 640, 676, 689

right side n. 240

rigid adj. 334, 669, 946

rigorous adj. 392, 669, 864, 946

rigour n. 669

riled adj. 893, 894

rim n. 233, 250; vb. 233

rind n. 225

ring n. 250; vb. 231, 322, 460, 482, 784

ringing n. 778, 784; adj. 780, 784

riot n. 80, 672

ripe adj. 364

ripen vb. 659

ripple n. 325, 358, 781; vb. 251, 358, 783

rise n. 36, 41, 208, 316, 320; vb. 32, 34, 36, 88, 214, 252, 273, 316, 320

risk n. 553, 594; vb. 158, 553, 594, 604, 718, 857

risqué adj. 952

rite n. 988

ritual n. 16, 545, 988; adj. 988

rival n. 638, 883; vb. 28

rivalry n. 642, 913

river n. 358

riverside adj. 352

road n. 559

roamer n. 270

roaming n. 269

roar n. 780, 838; vb. 175, 359, 780, 789, 838, 893

roast vb. 306, 759

rob vb. 645, 722

robber n. 723

robbery n. 722

robe n. 225

robes n. 989

robot n. 565

robust adj. 143, 161, 337, 585

rock n. 152, 330, 352, 367, 792; vb. 325, 326

rocket n. 279; vb. 316

rod n. 677, 677, 964

rodent n. 373

rogue n. 480, 723, 906, 940

roguish adj. 477

role n. 529, 557

roll n. 83, 249, 306, 323, 325, 783; vb. 249, 323, 325, 358, 783

roller n. 197, 358

roman adj. 521

romance n. 449, 889

romantic adj. 752

roof n. 225; vb. 225

room n. 182, 678

roomy adj. 182, 204

roost vb. 319

root n. 39, 88, 155, 213, 306, 374, 494

rooted adj. 47

rope n. 49, 207, 964

roster n. 83

rosy adj. 585, 811

rot n. 53, 451, 592; vb. 53, 584, 588

rota n. 83, 140

rotary adj. 323

rotate vb. 323

rotation n. 140, 323

rotten adj. 53, 162, 580, 584, 588

rotund adj. 249

rough adj. 57, 175, 258, 887, 908

roughage n. 305

roughness n. **258**

round n. 249, 649, 792; adj. 249, 250; vb. 249, 256

roundabout adj. 505, 561

rounded adj. 247, 249

round form n. 249

rouse vb. 611, 889

rousing adj. 547

rout n. 662

route n. 269, 559

routine n. 16, 79, 91,

140, 545; *adj.* 16, 140,
545
rove *vb.* 269
row *n.* 85, 202, 206, 642
rowdy *adj.* 780, 887
rowing *n.* 271
royal *adj.* 870
rub *vb.* 341, 342, 758
rubber *n.* 485
rubbish *n.* 451, 576
rub in *vb.* 468
ruby *adj.* 811
rude *adj.* 511, 849, 880,
887, 910, 923
rudiment *n.* 155
rudimentary *adj.* 88
rue *vb.* 833
ruffian *n.* 175, 906
ruffle *vb.* 82, 258, 260,
893
rug *n.* 225
rugged *adj.* 258
ruin *n.* 164, 551, 569,
588, 662, 739; *vb.* 164,
588, 628, 735
rule *n.* 103, 400, 522,
626, 667, 671, 954; *vb.*
415, 653, 667, 671
ruler *n.* 400, 675
rumble *vb.* 783
ruminate *vb.* 384
rumour *n.* 465
run *n.* 613; *vb.* 110, 172,
266, 280, 343, 345, 358,
622
run away *vb.* 293, 299,
896
runaway *n.* 555, 600
run down *vb.* 160, 853,
926, 928
run-down *n.* 460; *adj.*
586, 612, 617
rung *n.* 93
run in *vb.* 681
run into *vb.* 282
runner *n.* 270, 275, 467
running *n.* 172; *adj.* 91,
172, 343

runny *adj.* 51, 345, 358
run off with *vb.* 722,
896
run out *vb.* 89, 301
rupture *n.* 48; *vb.* 48
rural *adj.* 183, 378
ruse *n.* 478, 631
rush *n.* 280, 282, 358,
611, 613; *adj.* 603; *vb.*
280, 358, 359, 613, 645
russet *adj.* 810, 811
rust *n.* 167, 588, 592,
847; *adj.* 810, 811; *vb.*
53, 584
rustic *n.* 871; *adj.* 378,
871, 885
rustle *n.* 781, 783, 786;
vb. 781, 783, 786
rusty *adj.* 126, 810, 811
rut *n.* 261, 545
ruthless *adj.* 900

S

Sabbath *n.* 616
sabbatical *n.* 614; *adj.*
616
sable *adj.* 808
sabotage *n.* 164
saboteur *n.* 480
saccharin *n.* 772
sack *n.* 193, 303, 686;
vb. 164, 303, 686, 722
sackcloth and ashes *n.*
941
sacred *adj.* 974
sacrifice *n.* 652, 715,
943; *vb.* 652, 693, 715
sacrilege *n.* 901, 981
sad *adj.* 828, 837, 839,
895
sadden *vb.* 837
saddle *n.* 217; *vb.* 330,
919
safari *n.* 269

safe *n.* 732; *adj.* 54, 593,
646
safe-blower *n.* 723
safeguard *n.* 595; *vb.*
593, 646
safekeeping *n.* 567, 593
safety *n.* 593
safety curtain *n.* 762
sag *vb.* 216, 319
saga *n.* 525
sage *n.* 428, 436
sail *vb.* 271
sailing *n.* 271, 299
sailing ship *n.* 277
sailor *n.* 272
saint *n.* 939, 977, 980
saintly *adj.* 935, 980
salacious *adj.* 952
salad days *n.* 129
salary *n.* 705, 731, 738,
741
sale *n.* 714, 727
salesman *n.* 727
sales talk *n.* 727
salient *adj.* 253, 458,
573
sallow *adj.* 806, 807,
813
sally *n.* 645, 842; *vb.*
645
salmon *n.* 811, 816
saloon *n.* 276
salt *n.* 307; *vb.* 307, 599
salt away *vb.* 567
salt of the earth *n.* 579,
939
salubrious *adj.* 585
salutation *n.* 518, 922
salute *n.* 878, 922; *vb.*
888
salvage *n.* 44, 589; *vb.*
589, 601
salve *n.* 342, 365, 591
same *adj.* 13, 16, 28
sample *n.* 767
sanctify *vb.* 980
sanctimonious *adj.* 981

sanction *vb.* 690, 925, 954

sanctity *n.* 935, 980

sanctuary *n.* 595, 990

sand *n.* 352; *adj.* 813; *vb.* 257

sandbags *n.* 152, 330

sandbank *n.* 357, 596

sandwich *n.* 306

sane *adj.* 438

sanguine *adj.* 854

sanitation *n.* 585

sanity *n.* 438, 585

sap *n.* 309; *vb.* 162

sapling *n.* 374

sapphire *adj.* 815

sarcasm *n.* 842, 853

sarcophagus *n.* 372

sash *n.* 207

Satan *n.* 969

sated *adj.* 56, 865

satellite *n.* 60, 279, 329; *adj.* 679

satiety *n.* 865

satire *n.* 455, 842, 853

satirist *n.* 842, 928

satisfaction *n.* (pacification) 652, 721, 943; (enjoyment) 827, 831

satisfactory *adj.* 570

satisfied *adj.* 827, 831, 865

satisfy *vb.* (of food) 304, 865; (enjoy) 829, 831

satisfying *adj.* 306, 827, 943

saturation *n.* 56, 349, 572, 865

sauce *n.* 307, 880

saunter *n.* 269; *vb.* 135, 281

savage *n.* 175; *adj.* 175, 900, 908; *vb.* 588

save *vb.* 567, 601, 680, 748, 961

saving *n.* 567, 599, 601, 748

Saviour *n.* 967

savour *n.* 767; *vb.* 767, 770

savouriness *n.* 770

savoury *n.* 306; *adj.* 770

saw *n.* 259; *vb.* 48, 787

say *vb.* 460, 514

saying *n.* 432, 498

scaffold *n.* 964

scald *vb.* 759, 761

scale *n.* 27, 206, 400; *vb.* 206, 316

scales *n.* 330, 400

scallywag *n.* 940

scalp *vb.* 228

scamp *n.* 940

scan *vb.* 472, 528, 818

scandal *n.* 465, 516, 869, 928

scandalmonger *n.* 388, 460, 928

scandalous *adj.* 869, 936

scant *adj.* 76, 507

scanty *adj.* 33, 139, 571

scapegoat *n.* 149, 828, 943

scarce *adj.* 139

scarcity *n.* 33, 76, 139, 571, 735

scare *n.* 598, 856; *vb.* 856, 902

scared *adj.* 856, 858

scarf *n.* 207

scarlet *adj.* 811

scatter *vb.* 82, 95, 297

scene *n.* 185, 186, 658

scenery *n.* 185

scenic *adj.* 488

scent *n.* 483, 774, 776; *vb.* 774, 776

scented *adj.* 774, 776

sceptic *n.* 975

sceptical *adj.* 409, 421, 423, 975

sceptre *n.* 677

schedule *n.* 83, 116, 558; *vb.* 83

scheme *n.* 558, 602, 631; *vb.* 558, 631

schemer *n.* 558

schism *n.* 106, 642, 979

scholar *n.* 428, 436, 474, 524, 629

scholarly *adj.* 426, 472

scholarship *n.* 426, 472

school *n.* 94, 475; *vb.* 470

schoolchild *n.* 131, 428, 474

schooling *n.* 470

school-teacher *n.* 473

scientist *n.* 396, 428, 448

scintillate *vb.* 797, 842

scintillating *adj.* 509

scissors *n.* 255

scoff *n.* 924; *vb.* 853, 928

scoffer *n.* 928, 981

scold *vb.* 926

scoop *n.* 312, 465

scooter *n.* 276

scope *n.* 182, 557, 558, 678, 956

scorch *vb.* 350, 759, 761

scorcher *n.* 759

score *n.* 70, 737; *vb.* 38, 482, 792

scorn *n.* 853, 892, 924; *vb.* 644, 694, 923, 924

scornful *adj.* 923, 924

scoundrel *n.* 940

scour *vb.* 341, 583

scourge *n.* 592, 665, 964; *vb.* 963

scout *n.* 86, 593, 683

scowl *n.* 895; *vb.* 245, 895

scraggy *adj.* 205, 246

scram *vb.* 299

scramble *n.* 613; *vb.* 45, 306, 316

scrap *n.* 55, 649; *vb.* 607, 649

scrapbook *n.* 441

scrape n. 633; vb. 257, 341

scrape out vb. 210

scrape through vb. 666

scrappy adj. 57

scratch adj. 628; vb. 482, 758

scratch the surface vb. 211

scratchy adj. 787

scrawl n. 521; vb. 521

scream n. 788; vb. 787, 788

screech vb. 787, 788, 789

screen n. 461, 595, 801; vb. 461, 593, 646, 801

screw n. 49, 251

scribble n. 441, 521; vb. 521

scribe n. 484, 521, 981

script n. 521

Scripture n. 976

scroll n. 251, 483, 521

scrounger n. 697

scrub vb. 341, 583

scrumptious adj. 306, 770

scruple n. 533, 833

scrupulous adj. 392, 702, 864, 931

scrutinize vb. 390, 394, 396, 818

scrutiny n. 394, 818

sculptor n. 491

sculpture n. 486, 489; vb. 489

scum n. 44, 871

scurrilous adj. 901

scurry n. 613; vb. 613

scythe vb. 378

sea n. 351

seaboard n. 352

seafaring n. 271

sea-food n. 306

seagoing adj. 277

seal n. 482; vb. 265, 408, 424, 461, 482

sealed book n. 427, 453

seam n. 49, 206

seaman n. 272

séance n. 984

sear vb. 754

search vb. 394, 396, 554

searching adj. 388

searchlight n. 800

seared conscience n. 942

seaside n. 352; adj. 352

season n. 107, 109; vb. 307, 545, 599

seasoned adj. 130, 545, 602

seat n. 186, 217

secede vb. 289, 425, 556

secession n. 425, 979

secluded adj. 466, 885

seclusion n. 461, 824, 885

second n. 109, 115; adj. 62

secondary adj. 35

secondhand adj. 126, 606

second nature n. 545

second-rate adj. 580

second thoughts n. 87, 538

secrecy n. 459

secret n. 466; adj. 427, 461, 466

secret agent n. 460

secretary n. 484, 521, 623

secrete vb. 301, 310, 461

secretive adj. 466, 517, 876

sect n. 641, 979

sectarian n. 979; adj. 641, 979

sectarianism n. 979

section n. 55, 73, 97, 183, 717

sectional adj. 73

sector n. 55, 183

secular adj. 975, 987

secure adj. 47, 161, 593; vb. 47, 152, 408, 646, 705, 712

security n. 593, 646, 701

sedateness n. 757, 837

sedative n. 591

sedentary adj. 319

sediment n. 44

seditious adj. 148

seducer n. 953

seduction n. 952

seductive adj. 829

see vb. 419, 426, 818, 882

see ahead vb. 446

seed n. 155, 306, 374; vb. 95, 378

see double vb. 820, 950

seedy adj. 586

see fit vb. 530

see it through vb. 535

seek vb. 388, 394, 554, 604, 982

seem vb. 18, 621, 825

seeming adj. 406, 825

seemly adj. 510, 577, 848

seep vb. 301, 319, 349, 358

seer n. 447, 449

see-saw n. 325; vb. 325

seethe vb. 175, 759, 893

see through vb. 659, 802

segment n. 55, 73

segregate vb. 99, 540

segregation n. 48, 99

seismic adj. 325

seize vb. 326, 705, 720, 722

seizure n. 326, 586, 720

seldom adv. 139

select adj. 579; vb. 398, 540, 557

selection n. 398, 527, 540

291

selective adj. 398, 540, 864

self n. 382

self-abasement n. 874

self-assurance n. 757, 873

self-centred adj. 875, 934

self-control n. 534, 681, 757, 944

self-deception n. 478

self-denial n. 933, 944

self-destruction n. 370

self-determination n. 678

self-discipline n. 681, 944

self-effacing adj. 874, 933

self-esteem n. 873

self-evident adj. 408, 458

self-forgetful adj. 933

self-glory n. 879

self-important adj. 875

self-improvement n. 472

self-indulgent adj. 827, 934, 945

self-instruction n. 472

self-interest n. 934

selfishness n. 904, 934

selfless adj. 933

self-love n. 873

self-made adj. 472

self-portrait n. 488

self-possessed adj. 392, 438, 757

self-regard n. 873

self-reliance n. 534, 857

self-respect n. 873

self-sacrifice n. 933

selfsameness n. 13

self-satisfied adj. 831, 873

self-seeking n. 934; adj. 934

self-styled adj. 497

self-taught adj. 472

sell vb. 464, 714, 727

sell-out n. 727, 932

semantic adj. 450

semantics n. 492

semaphore n. 467

semblance n. 22, 236

semi- adj. 63

semiliquidity n. 362

seminar n. 519

seminary n. 475

semitransparency n. 804

senator n. 625

send vb. 268, 523

send for vb. 671

send forth vb. 301, 464

send-off n. 299

send up vb. 20

senility n. 126, 130

senior n. 34, 132; adj. 130

sensation n. 465, 752, 866

sensational adj. 755, 866, 877

sense n. 398, 411, 434, 450, 752; vb. 382, 411, 452, 752

senseless adj. 433, 451

sense of duty n. 919

sense of hearing n. 795

sense of smell n. 774

sensibility n. 753

sensible adj. 434, 575, 753

sensitive adj. 398, 716, 753, 756, 828, 894

sensitivity n. 398, 752, 753, 894

sensory adj. 753

sensual adj. 945, 952

sensuality n. 827, 945, 952

sentence n. 498, 960; vb. 960, 962, 963

sententious adj. 504

sentient adj. 753

sentiment n. 411, 420, 752, 889

sentimental adj. 752, 889

sentry n. 593, 646

separability n. 48, 51

separate vb. 48, 55, 95, 398, 540, 898

separation n. 48, 898

separatism n. 979

separatist n. 106, 425; adj. 979

sepia adj. 810

septet n. 70

sepulchre n. 372

sequel n. 87, 119, 156

sequence n. 85, 91

seraph n. 968

serenity n. 267, 757, 827, 831

serf n. 378, 676, 871

serfdom n. 679

serial adj. 85, 91, 140

serial position n. 93

series n. 85

serious adj. 534, 573, 594, 837, 982

seriousness n. 573, 837

sermon n. 470, 518

serrate vb. 246, 258, 259

servant n. 35, 676

serve vb. 636, 676, 679

serve as vb. 486

service n. 550, 575, 679, 982, 988

service of worship n. 988

services n. 655

servility n. 679, 881

serving n. 717

session n. 957

set n. 94, 474, 850; adj. 152, 185, 235; vb. 47, 81, 152, 186, 235, 332, 334

set about vb. 88, 605

set apart vb. 48, 398

setback n. 445, 635

set fire to vb. 761

set forth vb. 456, 460, 525

set free adj. 961; vb. 48, 961

set great store by vb. 573

set in motion vb. 88, 266, 282

set in order vb. 81

set no store by vb. 421

set off vb. 782, 805, 846

set one's heart on vb. 861

set one's teeth on edge vb. 773, 787

set out vb. 299, 458

set sail vb. 271

setting n. 8, 185, 229, 792

settle vb. 186, 191, 319, 408, 413, 652, 659, 699, 738

settle down vb. 191

settlement n. 699, 704, 738

settler n. 190

settle up vb. 647

set to vb. 605, 649

set up vb. 186, 522

seven n. 70; adj. 70

sever vb. 42, 48

several adj. 75

severe adj. 175, 508, 669, 828, 908, 946

severity n. 508, 669, 900

sew vb. 221, 589

sewer n. 360

sex-appeal n. 889

sextet n. 70

sexuality n. 827

sexy adj. 952

shabby adj. 580, 869

shackle n. 681; vb. 635

shade n. 225, 463, 595, 798, 801; vb. 799, 801

shadow n. 4, 328, 798; vb. 287, 554

shadowy adj. 4, 328, 798, 799, 824

shady adj. 631, 798, 801, 869, 932

shaft n. 213, 254, 361, 797

shake vb. 45, 51, 326, 756, 856

shake hands vb. 408, 652, 699, 886

shake off vb. 680

shake-up n. 148

shaky adj. 141, 326, 338, 594

shallow adj. 211, 435, 507, 852

shallowness n. 211, 383, 427, 435

sham n. 20, 852; adj. 20, 431, 478; vb. 477, 852

shambles n. 80

shame n. 869, 874; vb. 874

shameful adj. 869, 924

shameless adj. 887

shampoo vb. 583

shanty n. 191

shape n. 242, 339, 825; vb. 489

shapeless adj. 243

shapely adj. 244, 844

share n. 55, 305, 709, 717; vb. 55, 639, 709, 988

shareholder n. 709

share out vb. 717

sharing n. 709, 717

shark n. 718

sharp adj. 255, 434, 769, 773, 787, 791, 828

sharpen vb. 255

sharpness n. 255, 434, 769, 773

sharp practice n. 478

shatter vb. 164, 338

shattering adj. 148, 164

shave vb. 203, 257

shaving n. 228

shear vb. 203, 377

shears n. 255

sheath n. 225

shed vb. 95, 228, 319, 556

shed light on vb. 797

sheep n. 20

sheer adj. 46, 214

sheet n. 206, 225, 522

shelf n. 217

shell n. 23, 225, 290, 885; vb. 228

shellac n. 365

shelter n. 191, 225, 463, 595, 801; vb. 225, 461, 593, 646, 801

shelve vb. 135

Sheol n. 973

shepherd n. 377, 986

shield n. 595, 801; vb. 225, 593, 646, 801

shift n. 149, 187, 268; vb. 142, 149, 151, 187, 268, 285

shifty adj. 478, 631

shilly-shally vb. 135, 536, 612

shimmer n. 797; vb. 797

shine n. 797; vb. 257, 341, 797

shine at vb. 627

ship n. 277; vb. 192, 268

shipment n. 268

shipper n. 728

shirk vb. 533, 555, 920

shirker n. 555, 858

shirty adj. 893, 894

shiver vb. 326, 760

shoal n. 94, 211

shock n. 282, 444, 828; vb. 856, 892

shockable adj. 951

shocked adj. 856, 926

shocking *adj.* 830, 845, 869, 936

shoddy *adj.* 580, 849, 869

shoot *n.* 374; *vb.* 290, 370, 645, 963

shooting star *n.* 329, 800

shop *n.* 620, 730

shop assistant *n.* 727

shop-lifter *n.* 723

shop-lifting *n.* 722

shopper *n.* 726

shopping. *n.* 726

shopping centre *n.* 730

shopping spree *n.* 749

shore *n.* 352; *vb.* 217

short *adj.* 57, 113, 203, 315, 504

shortage *n.* 57, 315

shortcoming *n.* 29, 35, 43, 57, 315, 662

short duration *n.* 113

shorten *vb.* 37, 42, 197, 203, 504, 527

shortfall *n.* 57, 315

shorthand *n.* 521

short-lived *adj.* 113

shortness *n.* 33, 195, 203

short-sighted *adj.* 416, 435, 820

short-sightedness *n.* 435, 820

short-tempered *adj.* 894

short-term *adj.* 113

shot *n.* 173, 290, 782

shoulder *n.* 238; *vb.* 217, 605, 636

shout *n.* 482, 597, 782, 788; *vb.* 482, 788

shout down *vb.* 425, 788, 887

shove *n.* 282; *vb.* 282, 290

show *n.*
(manifestation) 458;
(drama) 529; (vanity)

852, 875; *vb.* (be visible) 458, 802, 823, 825; (demonstrate) 413; (indicate) 482

show-down *n.* 462

shower *n.* 358; *vb.* 349, 358

show-jumper *n.* 270

show-jumping *n.* 269

showman *n.* 877

showmanship *n.* 529, 877

show off *vb.* 419, 875, 877, 879

show-off *n.* 875, 877

show one's colours *vb.* 462

showpiece *n.* 458, 581, 844

show through *vb.* 802, 823

show up *vb.* 188, 298, 414, 825, 869

show willing *vb.* 532

showy *adj.* 509, 852, 875, 877

shred *n.* 33, 207

shrewd *adj.* 434, 631

shrewd idea *n.* 448

shrewdness *n.* 398, 434, 631

shriek *n.* 787, 788

shrill *adj.* 333, 787; *vb.* 787

shrine *n.* 483, 990

shrink *vb.* 37, 197, 205, 283, 533, 555, 856, 858

shrivel *vb.* 197, 350, 588

shroud *vb.* 461

shrub *n.* 374

shrug off *vb.* 921

shudder *vb.* 326, 760, 856

shuffle *vb.* 82, 149, 281, 756

shun *vb.* 555, 694, 924

shut *vb.* 263

shut down *vb.* 144

shut-eye *n.* 612

shut in *vb.* 234

shut oneself up *vb.* 885

shut out *vb.* 691

shutter *n.* 801

shuttle *n.* 278, 325; *vb.* 268

shut up *vb.* 144, 234, 681

shy *adj.* 856, 858, 876, 885

shy away *vb.* 533

shyness *n.* 858, 876, 885

sibilant *adj.* 786

sick *adj.* 369, 586

sicken *vb.* 162, 586

sickly *adj.* 812

sickness *n.* 303, 586, 828

side. *n.* 11, 233, 238

side by side *adv.* 238

sidedness *n.* 238

side-splitting *adj.* 851

sideways *adj.* 219, 238; *adv.* 238

side with *vb.* 641

sidle up to *vb.* 292

siege *n.* 645

siesta *n.* 612

sieve *n.* 264

sift *vb.* 46, 415, 540

sigh *vb.* 359, 781

sight *n.* 753, 818

sightly *adj.* 844

sightseeing *n.* 269

sightseer *n.* 270, 821

sign *n.* 401, 447, 458, 482, 597; *vb.* 424, 482, 699, 701, 714, 726

signal *n.* 482; *vb.* 482

signatory *n.* 424

signature *n.* 482, 496

significance *n.* 450, 456, 573

significant *adj.* 136, 450, 573

signify *vb.* 450, 482

sign of authority *n.* 677

signpost *vb.* 284

silence *n.* 267, 513, 517, 779; *vb.* 414, 513, 779

silent *adj.* 513, 517, 779, 895

silhouette *n.* 232, 488; *vb.* 488

silky *adj.* 257

silly *adj.* 433, 435

silver-haired *adj.* 809

silvery *adj.* 807

similarity *n.* 18, 105, 218, 397

simile *n.* 397, 455

simmer *vb.* 306

simmer down *vb.* 757

simple *adj.* (not mixed) 46; (gullible) 422, 632, 937, 951; (foolish) 427, 435; (easy to understand) 452, 502, 508; (easy) 634

simple circularity *n.* 250

simple-minded *adj.* 435, 632

simpleton *n.* 429, 437, 479

simplify *vb.* 46, 53, 456

simulate *vb.* 20, 477, 852

simultaneous *adj.* 60, 122

sin *n.* 431, 672, 703, 938; *vb.* 672, 981

sincere *adj.* 430, 476, 931

sine qua non *n.* 60, 700

sinew *n.* 207

sinful *adj.* 916, 936, 938, 952, 975, 981

sing *vb.* 528, 789, 792, 982

singer *n.* 793

single *adj.* 54, 59, 139, 897

single-minded *adj.* 534, 980

single out *vb.* 102

singular *adj.* 59

sinister *adj.* 665

sinistral *n.* 241

sink *vb.* 209, 210, 317, 319, 321, 588

sink back *vb.* 590

sinker *n.* 330

sinless *adj.* 951

sinner *n.* 906, 940, 981

sinuate *vb.* 251

sip *n.* 309; *vb.* 767

siphon *n.* 360

sir *n.* 380

siren *n.* 116, 482, 598, 970

sirupy *adj.* 772

sister *n.* 11, 986

sit *vb.* 23, 185

sit down *vb.* 319

site *n.* 185, 186

sit-in *n.* 144, 696

sit on *vb.* 466, 679

sit on the fence *vb.* 409, 541

sit pretty *vb.* 831

sitting *n.* 984

sitting duck *n.* 479

situation *n.* 8, 93, 153, 185, 229, 557

six *n.* 70; *adj.* 70

sixth sense *n.* 411, 753

size *n.* 26, 27, 32, 194, 362, 400

size up *vb.* 415

sizzle *vb.* 306, 759, 786

skeleton *n.* 232, 371, 527

sketch *n.* 232, 486, 488, 525, 558; *vb.* 232, 488, 525, 558

sketchy *adj.* 57

skew *adj.* 219

skewer *n.* 264

skilful *adj.* 627

skill *n.* 159, 426, 501, 627

skilled *adj.* 579, 602

skilled worker *n.* 619, 629

skim *vb.* 211, 257

skimp *vb.* 393, 750

skimpy *adj.* 57

skin *n.* 225; *vb.* 228

skinny *adj.* 205

skip *vb.* 320, 393

skirmish *n.* 645, 649

skirt *n.* 233; *vb.* 233, 238

skunk *n.* 777

sky *n.* 329, 348, 815

skyjacking *n.* 722

skyline *n.* 198

skyscraper *n.* 191, 208

slab *n.* 206

slack *adj.* 391, 612, 668, 920, 952

slacken *vb.* 281

slacker *n.* 858

slag *n.* 44

slam *vb.* 782, 926

slander *n.* 869, 928; *vb.* 928, 930

slanderer *n.* 928

slang *n.* 494, 495; *adj.* 495

slant *vb.* 219

slap *n.* 782, 963; *vb.* 282, 782, 963

slap in the face *n.* 694, 923

slapstick *n.* 529

slash *vb.* 203

slate *n.* 206

slaughter *n.* 164, 370, 963; *vb.* 370, 963

slave *n.* 35, 619, 676

slavery *n.* 679

slavish *adj.* 881

slay *vb.* 370

sleek *adj.* 257

sleep *n.* 612; *vb.* 612

sleep around *vb.* 952

sleep together *vb.* 889

sleep with *vb.* 889

sleepy *adj.* 612, 617

sleet *n.* 760
sleight of hand *n.* 478
slender *adj.* 33, 205
slice *n.* 55, 305, 717
slide *n.* 219, 486; *vb.* 257, 588
slide-rule *n.* 400
slight *n.* 869, 923, 924; *adj.* 33, 195, 203, 571; *vb.* 418, 923, 928
slim *adj.* 33, 205; *vb.* 205, 947
slime *n.* 584
slimy *adj.* 362
slink *vb.* 461
slip *n.* 431, 500, 522, 741, 938
slip back *vb.* 590
slippery *adj.* 51, 257, 594, 631
slipshod *adj.* 393, 500
slip-up *n.* 431
slit *n.* 261, 262; *vb.* 48, 264
sliver *n.* 55
slogan *n.* 432, 494, 498
slog away *vb.* 535, 615
slope *n.* 208, 219; *vb.* 219
sloppy *adj.* 584
slot *n.* 261, 262; *vb.* 261
slothful *adj.* 612
slough *n.* 355
slovenly *adj.* 500, 584, 920
slow *adj.* 174, 281, 435; *vb.* 281, 616
slowcoach *n.* 281
slowness *n.* 135, 281, 435, 843
sluggard *n.* 612
sluggish *adj.* 174, 281, 612, 843
slum *n.* 845
slumber *vb.* 174, 612
slump *n.* 169, 317; *vb.* 317, 588

slur *n.* 869, 928, 930; *vb.* 515, 928, 930
slush *n.* 760
slushy *adj.* 355, 362
slut *n.* 953
sly *adj.* 461, 631, 932
smack *vb.* 282, 782
smack one's lips *vb.* 767
small *adj.* 33, 195, 203, 331
small arms *n.* 657
small change *n.* 731
smallholding *n.* 378
smallness *n.* 33, 195
small talk *n.* 516
smarmy *adj.* 927
smart *adj.* 125, 631; *vb.* 828
smart aleck *n.* 875
smash *vb.* 164, 282, 645
smash-and-grab-raid *n.* 722
smash hit *n.* 661
smash-up *n.* 282
smattering *n.* 76, 427
smear *n.* 584, 928, 930; *vb.* 342, 847, 869, 928
smell *n.* 753, 774, 777; *vb.* 774, 776, 777
smell out *vb.* 394, 554, 774
smelly *adj.* 777
smelt *vb.* 761
smile *n.* 838, 886; *vb.* 838, 886
smirch *n.* 847; *vb.* 847
smirk *n.* 838; *vb.* 838
smite *vb.* 282
smitten *adj.* 889
smog *n.* 363
smoke *n.* 344, 346, 803; *vb.* 308, 346, 599, 759, 803
smoke-signal *n.* 467
smoking *adj.* 759
smoky *adj.* 803, 809
smooth *adj.* 228, 257,

335, 364, 477, 631, 927; *vb.* 16, 215, 257, 341, 758
smoothness *n.* 257
smother *vb.* 513, 759, 762
smoulder *vb.* 759
smudge *vb.* 584, 847
smuggle *vb.* 722
smuggled *adj.* 955
smuggler *n.* 723
smut *n.* 952
snack *n.* 306
snack bar *n.* 191
snag *n.* 582, 635
snail *n.* 281
snake in the grass *n.* 459, 596
snake-like *adj.* 251
snap *vb.* 338, 782, 789, 893
snap out of it *vb.* 836
snapshot *n.* 486
snare *n.* 463, 596
snarl *vb.* 789
snatch *vb.* 720
sneak *n.* 858; *vb.* 461
sneer *n.* 895, 924, 926; *vb.* 696, 853, 895, 924, 926
sneeze *vb.* 359, 786
sniff *vb.* 774
sniff out *vb.* 394, 554
snigger *n.* 838; *vb.* 838
snip *vb.* 48
sniper *n.* 645
snivel *vb.* 839
snobbish *adj.* 875, 924
snoop *n.* 388, 460, 821; *vb.* 388, 394
snooty *adj.* 875, 924
snooze *n.* 612; *vb.* 612
snort *vb.* 789
snow *n.* 760; *vb.* 807
snowball *n.* 36; *vb.* 36
snowdrift *n.* 760
snowflake *n.* 760
snowstorm *n.* 760

snub n. 295, 694, 923;
vb. 887, 923, 926
snuff n. 308; vb. 762
snug adj. 827
snuggle vb. 890
soak vb. 56, 349
soak up vb. 350
so-and-so n. 497
soapy adj. 363
soar vb. 32, 208, 273,
316
sob n. 839; vb. 788, 839
sober adj. 837, 848, 944,
949
soberness n. 848, 949
so-called adj. 497
sociability n. 882, 884
social n. 884; adj. 379
social conscience n.
903
socialism n. 709
social services n. 903
society n. 379, 641, 850,
870
sociology n. 379
socket n. 184
sod n. 374
sodden adj. 349
sodomy n. 952
soft adj. 257, 331, 335,
670, 781, 805, 889
soft drink n. 309
soften vb. 267, 335, 513,
652, 834
soft-hearted adj. 670,
907
softness n. 335, 364,
670, 778, 781
soft nothings n. 890
soft soap n. 927
sog vb. 349
soggy adj. 364
soi-disant adj. 497
soil n. 352, 378; vb. 584,
847
soirée n. 884
sojourn n. 269; vb. 191
solace n. 831, 907

solar adj. 329
solar energy n. 159, 765
solder vb. 50
soldier n. 655
soldier on vb. 535
sole adj. 59
solecism n. 412, **500**
solemn adj. 468, 573,
837, 982
solicit vb. 695
solicitor n. 959
solicitous adj. 392
solid n. 3, 332; adj. 3,
50, 161, 332, 334, 337
solidarity n. 50, 639
solidify vb. 332, 334
solidity n. 3, 152, 204,
332, 334
soliloquize vb. 520
soliloquy n. 520
solitary adj. 885
solitude n. 59, 461
solo n. 792
soloist n. 793
soluble adj. 345
solution n. 343
solve vb. 157, 456
solvent n. 343, 345
sombre adj. 798, 809,
895
some adj. 26, 72
somebody n. 868
somersault n. 220; vb.
220
something n. 327
sometime adj. 124, 687;
adv. 121
sometimes adv. 138
somnolence n. 612, 617
son n. 171
sonata n. 792
song n. 528, 792, 982
sonnet n. 528
sonorous adj. 778
soothe vb. 176, 591, 834
soothing adj. 589, 790,
834
soothsayer n. 447, 984

sooty adj. 584, 808
sophism n. 412
sophisticated n.   848;
adj. 423, 848
sophistry n. 412
soporific adj. 841
sorcery n. 984
sore n. 588; adj. 753,
828, 893
sore point n. 893
sorrow n. 828, 830, 833,
837, 839, 941; vb. 837,
839
sorry adj. 833, 907, 941
sort n. 97; vb. 97, 540
sortie n. 645; vb. 645
SOS n. 598
soul n. 223, 368, 382,
751
sound n. 353, 512, 778,
795; adj. 410, 438, 581,
585, 977; vb. 512, 778
sounding board n. 396
sound out vb. 396
soundproof adj. 779
soup n. 306
soupçon n. 33
sour adj. 769, 773, 895
source n. 88, 155
source of light n. **800**
sourness n. 773, 895
souvenir n. 441, 483
sovereign n. 675; adj.
667
sow n. 381; vb. 95, 378
space n. 182, 198, 200,
202, **329**
space-age adj. 125
spaceman n. 274
spaceship n. 279
space travel n. 274
space traveller n. 274
spacious adj. 32, 182,
204
spade vb. 254
spadework n. 602
span n. 109, 182, 202;
vb. 47, 182, 313

spank *vb.* 963

spanner in the works *n.* 580, 635

spare *adj.* 44, 607; *vb.* 670, 907

spare time *n.* 614

sparing *adj.* 748, 750, 944

spark *n.* 797

sparkle *n.* 506, 759, 797, 836; *vb.* 326, 797, 842

sparse *adj.* 33, 76, 139, 333

spasm *n.* 141, 326, 586, 828

spasmodic *adj.* 92, 141

spatial *adj.* 182

spatter *vb.* 817

spay *vb.* 160, 169

speak *vb.* 460, 512, 514, 788

speak against *vb.* 25, 696

speaker *n.* 514

speak for itself *vb.* 401

speak one's mind *vb.* 476, 632

speak out *vb.* 468

speak out against *vb.* 832

speak volumes *vb.* 401

spear *vb.* 264

special *adj.* 59, 102

specialist *n.* 629

speciality *n.* 102, 557

specialize *vb.* 472, 609

species *n.* 97

specific *adj.* 5, 59, 102

specification *n.* 97, 525

specifications *n.* 102, 700

specify *vb.* 102, 482, 496, 525

specimen *n.* 458

specious *adj.* 412, 549, 825

speck *n.* 33, 847 .

speckle *vb.* 817

spectacle *n.* 529, 825, 866

spectacles *n.* 822

spectacular *adj.* 529, 877

spectator *n.* **821**

spectre *n.* 971

spectrum *n.* 805, 817

speculation *n.* 396, 448, 553

speculator *n.* 396, 448, 553, 728

speech *n.* 492, 512, 514, 518

speech defect *n.* 515

speechless *adj.* 513, 866

speech-making *n.* 518

speed *n.* 27, 266, **280**, 400; *vb.* 280

speed up *vb.* 280, 613

speedy *adj.* 134, 280, 613

spell *n.* 109, 586, 984; *vb.* 450, 493

spell-binder *n.* 984

spellbound *adj.* 866

spelling *n.* 493

spell out *vb.* 456

spend *vb.* 575, 715, 738, 740

spendthrift *n.* 749; *adj.* 569

spend time *vb.* 107

spew *vb.* 303, 358

sphere *n.* 249, 329, 658

spice *n.* 776; *vb.* 307, 599

spick and span *adj.* 583

spicy *adj.* 769, 776, 952

spike *n.* 255; *vb.* 264

spill *n.* 800; *vb.* 319, 358

spin *n.* 269, 323; *vb.* 221, 273, 323

spine *n.* 255

spineless *adj.* 160, 162

spinney *n.* 374

spin-off *n.* 87, 156

spin out *vb.* 202

spinster *n.* 897

spiral *n.* 251, 322, 323; *adj.* 251; *vb.* 323

spire *n.* 208, 212

spirit *n.* 4, 368, 382, 506, 611, 751, 966, 968, 969

spirited *adj.* 280, 368

spiritism *n.* 984

spiritless *adj.* 757

spiritual *adj.* 4, 328, 382, 966, 974, 980

spiritualist *n.* 984

spirituality *n.* 328, 980

spit *n.* 253; *vb.* 306, 358

spiteful *adj.* 900, 912

splash *n.* 786; *vb.* 349, 358, 786

splash down *vb.* 274, 317, 321

spleen *n.* 895

splendid *adj.* 579, 844

splendour *n.* 797, 844, 877

splice *n.* 49; *vb.* 47, 896

splint *n.* 217

splinter *n.* 55; *vb.* 338

splinter-group *n.* 641

split *n.* 642, 717, 979; *adj.* 48; *vb.* 48, 63, 200, 338

split hairs *vb.* 864

spoil *n.* 663, 724; *vb.* 588, 628, 635, 847

spoilsport *n.* 548

spoke *n.* 297

spokesman *n.* 460, 467, 514, 689

sponge *n.* 264, 364, 485; *vb.* 349, 583

sponger *n.* 612, 697, 881

spongy *adj.* 264, 335, 364

sponsor *vb.* 636

spontaneity *n.* 531, **544**

spontaneous *adj.* 115, 131, 411, **544**

spooky adj. 971

spoonerism n. 433, 500, 842

spoon-feeding n. 470

spoonful n. 26, 306

sporadic adj. 139, 141

sport n. 649, 840, 939

sporting adj. 915

spot n. 33, 184, 584, 847; vb. 419, 482

spotless adj. 581, 583, 807, 937, 951

spotlight n. 800

spotted adj. 584, 817

spouse n. 896

spout n. 301, 358, 360; vb. 358, 514

sprachgefühl n. 501

sprawl vb. 95

spray n. 363, 374; vb. 225

spread n. 36, 182, 196, 306; vb. 95, 182, 196, 297, 460

sprig n. 374

spring n. (season) 127; (cause) 155, 547; (recoil) 283, 336; (leap) 320; (water) 358; adj. 127; vb. 156, 283, 320, 336

sprinkle vb. 95, 349, 583

sprinkling n. 76, 583

sprint n. 613; vb. 280, 613

sprout vb. 316

spry adj. 611

spur n. 253, 547; vb. 547

spurious adj. 431, 477

spurn vb. 542, 644, 694, 892, 924

spur of the moment n. 544

spurt vb. 280, 301, 358, 613

sputnik n. 279

spy n. 460, 821; vb. 394, 396

squabble n. 642; vb. 642

squad n. 94, 655

squalid adj. 584

squall n. 359

squander vb. 107, 569, 608, 706, 740, 749

squanderer n. 749

square n. 67, 183, 184, 246, 730; adj. 67, 931; vb. 24, 28, 105, 400

square deal n. 915

square one n. 88

squash vb. 215, 319, 402, 874

squat adj. 195, 204, 209; vb. 191, 209, 319

squatter n. 100, 190

squawk n. 787; vb. 787, 789

squeak vb. 781, 787, 788

squeal vb. 460, 787, 788, 789

squealer n. 460

squeamish adj. 862, 864, 951

squeeze n. 37, 743; vb. 37, 197, 712, 758

squelch vb. 786

squelchy adj. 355

squint n. 219, 818, 820; vb. 820

squirm vb. 251

squirt vb. 301, 358

stab vb. 264

stability n. 16, 143, 152, 757

stabilizer n. 152

stable adj. 16, 143, 152, 257, 612, 757

stack n. 567; vb. 378, 567

stadium n. 658

staff n. 619, 676, 677, 989

stag n. 380

stage n. 27, 527; vb. 529

stagger vb. 326

staggering adj. 444

stagnate vb. 169, 174, 610, 666

stain n. 225, 582, 584, 805, 847, 869; vb. 805, 847, 869

stainless adj. 581, 583

staircase n. 316

stake n. 217, 553, 701, 964; vb. 701

stalactite n. 216

stale adj. 612, 617, 666, 768, 841

stalemate n. 28

stalk n. 374; vb. 554

stall n. 730; vb. 144

stallion n. 380

stalwart n. 640, 857; adj. 161

stamina n. 161, 535, 857

stammer n. 515; vb. 515

stamp n. 23, 482, 522; vb. 242, 482, 490, 522

stance n. 420

stand n. 7, 184, 186, 213, 217, 420, 648, 730; vb. 1, 185, 318, 738

standard n. 23, 27, 103, 400, 482, 531, 939; adj. 492, 746

standardize vb. 16, 81

stand by vb. 217, 636, 702

stand-by n. 149

stand down vb. 687

stand fast vb. 534, 648

stand for vb. 424, 486, 693, 701

stand-in n. 149, 689

stand in for vb. 149, 685, 689

standing n. 7, 93

stand-offish adj. 875, 885

stand out vb. 253, 823

standpoint *n.* 284, 818

standstill *n.* 144, 267

stand together *vb.* 639

stand up *vb.* 318

stand up for *vb.* 217

stand up to *vb.* 648

stanza *n.* 528

star *n.* 329, 529, 684, 800, 868

starboard *n.* 240

starch *n.* 306; *vb.* 334, 583

stare *vb.* 818, 866

starless *adj.* 798

start *n.* 34, **88**, 298, 444; *vb.* **88**, 282, 605

startle *vb.* 444, 856

start out *vb.* 299

starve *vb.* 205, 735, 861, 947

stash away *vb.* 567

state *n.* 7, 183, 379; *adj.* 379; *vb.* 468, 498, 525

statehood *n.* 379

stately *adj.* 32, 873

statement *n.* 83, 401 **468**, 483, 525, 742

statesman *n.* 625

station *n.* 7, 93, 185, 186, 620, 868

stationary *adj.* 152

statistics *n.* 38, 460

statue *n.* 483, 489, 983

stature *n.* 208

status *n.* 7, 93, 868

status quo *n.* 143

statute *n.* 626, 954

statutory *adj.* 954

staunch *adj.* 882

stay *n.* 135, 213, 217, 884; *vb.* (of time) 112, 135, 143, 145; (dwell) 191; (support) 217; (resist) 648

stay-at-home *n.* 885; *adj.* 612

stay away *vb.* 189

staying power *n.* 535, 857

stay up *vb.* 135

steadfast *adj.* 112, 143, 152, 534, 535

steady *n.* 889; *adj.* 16, 140, 143, 145, 152, 534, 535; *vb.* 152

steal *vb.* 461, 720, 722

stealing *n.* 722

stealthy *adj.* 461

steam *n.* 159, 344, 347; *vb.* 306, 346

steam engine *n.* 276

steamer *n.* 277

steep *adj.* 214, 745; *vb.* 349

steeple *n.* 208

steer *vb.* 271, 284, 622

steer clear of *vb.* 555, 924

stem *n* 374

stench *n.* 774, 777

stenography *n.* 521

step *n.* 269, 400, 602, 609; *vb.* 269

step by step *adv.* 27

step down *vb.* 687

step in *vb.* 300

stepmotherly *adj.* 900

step on it *vb.* 280, 613

steppe *n.* 356

steps *n.* 316, 559

stereogram *n.* 794

stereo-recorder *n.* 484

stereotyped *adj.* 16, 152, 545, 843

sterile *adj.* 160, 169

sterilization *n.* 169, 583

stern *adj.* 669, 837, 946

stew *n.* 756; *vb.* 306

steward *n.* 623, 676, 733; *vb.* 622, 748

stewardship *n.* 392, 622, 748

stick *n.* 964; *vb.* 47, 50, 264

stick by *vb.* 217

stick-in-the-mud *n.* 143

stick it out *vb.* 535, 648, 757

stickler *n.* 537, 864

stick one's heels in *vb.* 648

stick one's neck out *vb.* 859

stick out *vb.* 253, 823

stick out for *vb.* 535

stick to *vb.* 712

stick together *vb.* 639

stick to one's guns *vb.* 534, 537, 648

stick-up *n.* 722

stick up for *vb.* 217

sticky *adj.* 50, 362, 759, 772

stiff *n.* 371; *adj.* 334, 337, 511, 745

stiffen *vb.* 332, 334, 337

stiff-necked *adj.* 537

stiff upper lip *n.* 535, 836

stifle *vb.* 466, 548, 762, 779, 785

stifled *adj.* 781

stifling *adj.* 759

stigma *n.* 847, 869

still *adj.* 174, 257, 267, 612, 779; *vb.* 176, 267, 513, 652, 779

still-life *n.* 488

stilt *n.* 217

stilted *adj.* 511

stimulant *n.* 173, 591

stimulate *vb.* 173, 547, 618, 755, 829

stimulus *n.* 173, 547

sting *n.* 255, 828; *vb.* 255, 758, 828

stinginess *n.* 748, 750

stink *n.* 777; *vb.* 777

stint *n.* 109; *vb.* 750

stipend *n.* 636, 738

stipendiary *n.* 958

stipple *vb.* 817

stipulate *vb.* 699, 700

strong *adj.* 32, 159, **161**, 173, 337, 506, 534, 585, 769, 774

stronghold *n.* 595, 646

strong point *n.* 627

strongroom *n.* 732

strong-smelling *adj.* 777

strong-willed *adj.* 534

structure *n.* 5, 47, 163, 242, 339

struggle *n.* 649; *vb.* 615, 642, 649

strum *n.* 783; *vb.* 783

strut *n.* 217

stub *n.* 482

stubborn *adj.* 143, 537, 672, 942

stubby *adj.* 203, 204

stuck up *adj.* 875

stud *vb.* 817

student *n.* 131, **428**, 474

studious *adj.* 384, 390, 472, 611

study *n.* 390, 394, 472, 475, 488, 526; *vb.* 384, 390, 394, 472, 602

stuff *n.* 3, 327, 566, 729; *vb.* 56, 75, 226, 265, 304, 865, 948

stuffing *n.* 192, 226, 265

stuffy *adj.* 843

stumble *vb.* 317, 515

stumble on *vb.* 158

stumbling-block *n.* 635

stun *vb.* 754, 796, 922

stunner *n.* 844

stunted *adj.* 195, 203

stupefy *vb.* 754, 866

stupendous *adj.* 32, 866

stupid *adj.* 427, 433, 435

stupidity *n.* 383, 427, 433, 435

stupor *n.* 754

stutter *n.* 515; *vb.* 515

sty *n.* 184

style *n.* 242, 492, **501**, 510, 850; *vb.* 496

stylish *adj.* 125, 850

subconscious *adj.* 382

subdivide *vb.* 48

subdue *vb.* 335, 679, 681, 779

subdued *adj.* 654, 781, 805

subject *n.* 387, 499, 525; *vb.* 679

subjection *n.* 35, 179, 679, 874

subject to *adj.* 35, 179, 679, 700, 919

subjugate *vb.* 679

sublimation *n.* 318, 346

sublime *adj.* 32, 208, 318, 868, 966, 982

subliminal *adj.* 382

sublimity *n.* 34

submarine *n.* 277

submerge *vb.* 321, 349

submerged *adj.* 210

submission *n.* 654, 673, 757, 874

submissive *adj.* **654**, 673, 679, 757, 874

submit *vb.* 468, 654, 673, 693, 757, 874

subnormal *adj.* 435

subordinate *n.* 35, 676; *adj.* 35, 679; *vb.* 679

subpoena *n.* 671, 960

subscribe *vb.* 424, 641

subscriber *n.* 424

subsequent *adj.* 85, 119, 156

subservient *adj.* 563, 673, 679, 874, 881

subside *vb.* 37, 197, 317

subsidiary *adj.* 563, 679

subsidize *vb.* 636, 715, 738

subsidy *n.* 636, 715, 738, 744

subsist *vb.* 1, 368

subsistence *n.* 1, 305

substance *n.* 3, 5, 223, 332, 450, 573

substandard *adj.* 35

substantial *adj.* 1, 3, 327, 450

substantiate *vb.* 161, 401, 413

substitute *n.* 149, 540, 688, 99, 943; *vb.* 142, 149, 689

substitution *n.* 142, **149**

substratum *n.* 206, 213

subsume *vb.* 98

subterfuge *n.* 478

subterranean *adj.* 210

subtle *adj.* 333, 459, 631

subtraction *n.* 38, **42**, 744

suburb *n.* 183

suburban *adj.* 183

subversion *n.* 148, 164

subversive *adj.* 148, 580

subvert *vb.* 148, 580

succeed *vb.* 85, 119, 287, 659, 661

success *n.* 550, **661**

successful *adj.* 661, 664

succession *n.* 85, 91, 119, 287

successor *n.* 119

succinct *adj.* 203, 504, 527

succour *n.* 636

succulence *n.* 364

succulent *adj.* 306, 364

succumb *vb.* 179, 369

suck *vb.* 308

sucker *n.* 479

suckle *vb.* 304

suckling *n.* 131

suck up to *vb.* 881, 927

sudden *adj.* 115, 444, 544, 859

sudden and violent sound *n.* **782**

suds *n.* 363

sue *vb.* 960

suffer *vb.* 586, 590, 648, 752, **828**, 963
suffer defeat *vb.* 662
sufferer *n.* 828
suffice *vb.* 28, 570, 831
sufficiency *n.* **570**
sufficient *adj.* 75, 570
suffix *n.* 41, 87, 499; *vb.* 40
suffocate *vb.* 370, 759
suffrage *n.* 540
sugar *n.* 772, 891; *vb.* 772
sugary *adj.* 772
suggest *vb.* 155, 401, 441, 450, 459, 460, 597, 624, 693
suggestion *n.* 441, 459, 460, 482, 624, 693
suggestive *adj.* 401, 450, 459, 482
suicide *n.* 370
sui generis adj. 59, 102
suit *n.* 227, 960; *vb.* 105, 577
suitable *adj.* 136, 302, 575, 577, 896, 915
suitcase *n.* 193
suite *n.* 91, 191, 792
suitor *n.* 889, 960
sulk *vb.* 895
sullenness *n.* **895**
sullied *adj.* 584, 952
sully *vb.* 584, 847, 869, 928, 952
sultry *adj.* 759
sum *n.* 26, 54, 731; *vb.* 40
summarize *vb.* 203, 504, 525, 527
summary *n.* 441, 525, 527; *adj.* 504
summer *n.* 127, 664, 759; *adj.* 127
summer time *n.* 116, 127
summery *adj.* 127, 759
summing up *n.* 527, 960

summit *n.* 89, 208, **212**, 519, 581
summon *vb.* 94, 671, 695, 857, 901
summons *n.* 671, 960
sum up *vb.* 527, 960
sun *n.* 329, 800
Sunday School *n.* 988
sunder *vb.* 63
sundown *n.* 128
sunglasses *n.* 801, 804
sunken *adj.* 209, 210, 254
sunny *adj.* 664, 759
sunrise *n.* 127, 797
sunset *n.* 128
sunshine *n.* 797
sup *vb.* 304
super *adj.* 579
superabundance *n.* 32, 572
superannuated *adj.* 130
superannuation *n.* 687
superb *adj.* 579
supercilious *adj.* 875, 924
superficial *adj.* 211, 435, 574, 825, 852
superfluity *n.* 32, 572
superimpose *vb.* 225
superintend *vb.* 392, 622
superintendent *n.* 623
superior *n.* 34, 675; *adj.* 34, 579, 868
superiority *n.* 34, 84, 579, 868
superlative *n.* 499; *adj.* 34, 481, 579
supermarket *n.* 730
supernatural *adj.* 447, 971, 984
superpose *vb.* 225
supersede *vb.* 85
superstition *n.* 984
supervision *n.* 392, 593, 621, 622, 956
supervisor *n.* 623, 675

supper *n.* 306
supplant *vb.* 85
supple *adj.* 335
supplement *n.* 40, 41, 87; *vb.* 40, 196, 568
supplementary *adj.* 40
supplicant *n.* 697, 982; *adj.* 982
supplication *n.* 695, 982
supplies *n.* 564, 566, 729
supply *n.* 568; *vb.* 564, 568, 602, 715
support *n.* 213, 217, 401, 424, 636, 929; *vb.* 152, 217, 392, 401, 410, 424, 636, 907
supporter *n.* 217, 287, 424, 640, 821, 905
suppose *vb.* 416, 420, **448**, 449
supposed *adj.* 448, 459, 825
supposition *n.* **448**
suppress *vb.* 164, 461, 466, 513, 679, 681, 691
supreme *adj.* 34, 579, 581, 667, 966
sure *adj.* 152, 408, 531
surety *n.* 420, 593, 701
surf *n.* 363; *vb.* 271
surface *n.* 182, 211, 222; *adj.* 211; *vb.* 225, 331
surfeit *n.* 572, 865; *vb.* 865
surge *vb.* 316, 320, 325, 358
surgery *n.* 591
surly *adj.* 887, 895
surmise *n.* 448; *vb.* 420, 448
surmount *vb.* 316
surname *n.* 496
surpass *vb.* 6, 34, 314
surpassing *adj.* 32, 34, 579
surplice *n.* 989
surplus *n.* 44, 572

surprise n. 444, 829,
866; vb. 444, 866

surrender n. 556, 687,
708; vb. 556, 654

surround vb. 229, 231,
231

surroundings n. 8, 183,
229

surveillance n. 392, 622

survey n. 456, 526, 527,
818; vb. 400, 415, 526,
527, 818

surveyor n. 415

survive vb. 112, 145,
368, 661, 898

surviving adj. 44, 112,
368

survivor n. 898

susceptibility n. 179,
753

susceptible adj. 753,
894

suspect vb. 409, 421,
448

suspend vb. 89, 99, 135,
216, 607, 686, 920

suspended sentence n.
961

suspense n. 144, 409,
443

suspension n. 99, 135,
216, 607, 610

suspicion n. 409, 421,
423, 460, 860, 913

sustain vb. 91, 143, 145,
152, 217, 304, 636

sustenance n. 217, 305

swab vb. 583

swag n. 724

swallow vb. 302, 304,
757

swamp n. 355; vb. 56,
349

swampy adj. 355

swank n. 873, 879

swan song n. 89, 369

swap vb. 150, 725

swarm n. 94; vb. 75, 94,
168, 314, 572

swarthy adj. 808

swastika n. 221

sway n. 159, 177, 667;
vb. 177, 216, 325, 326,
547, 667

swear vb. 468, 698, 901

swearword n. 901

sweat n. 310, 615 vb.
615

sweep n. 182, 247; vb.
182, 358, 359, 583

sweeping adj. 32, 54,
56, 98

sweet n. 306, 772, 891;
adj. 772, 776, 790, 889

sweeten vb. 772

sweetener n. 772

sweetheart n. 891

sweetmeat n. 306

sweetness n. 772

swell n. 358, 780; adj.
844; vb. 36, 196, 252,
343, 358, 359

swelter vb. 759

swerve vb. 247, 285

swift adj. 280, 613

swim vb. 271, 331

swindle n. 478; vb. 478,
722, 932

swindler n. 480, 723

swing n. 140, 325; vb.
140, 216, 323, 325, 326

swirl vb. 323, 358

swish vb. 783, 786

switch n. 149, 964; vb.
149

switched off adj. 385

switch off vb. 89, 754,
798

switch on vb. 755, 797,
829

swivel vb. 323

swollen adj. 196, 252

swollen-headed adj.
875

swoop n. 317, 321; vb.
317

sword n. 677

swot n. 474

sycophancy n. 881

syllable n. 493, 494

syllabus n. 83, 527

syllogism n. 410

symbol n. 482, 493, 677

symbolic adj. 455, 482

symbolism n. 455

symbolize vb. 450, 482,
486

symmetry n. 16, 28, 244

sympathetic adj. 24,
302, 670, 882, 899, 907

sympathize vb. 907

sympathy n. 24, 752,
907

symphony n. 792

symphony orchestra n.
793

symposium n. 94, 410,
519

symptom n. 447, 482,
597

symptomatic adj. 60,
401, 482

synagogue n. 990

synchronism n. 122

synchronize vb. 24, 52,
122

syndicate n. 641

synod n. 625

synonym n. 28, 450,
494

synopsis n. 83, 527

syntactic adj. 499

syntax n. 492, 499

synthesis n. 52

syrup n. 362, 772

system n. 59, 79, 81,
103, 221

systematic adj. 79, 81,
140

systematize vb. 58, 81,
97

T

tab *n.* 482; *vb.* 482
table *n.* 83, 217, 306
tablet *n.* 591
taboo *n.* 691; *adj.* 691
tacit *adj.* 459
taciturnity *n.* 517
tackle *vb.* 88, 605
tack on *vb.* 40
tacky *adj.* 362
tactful *adj.* 398
tactical *adj.* 621
tactics *n.* 559, 621
tactless *adj.* 887
tag *n.* 482, 496; *vb.* 482, 496
tail *n.* 87, 89, 91, 237; *adj.* 237; *vb.* 37, 287, 554
taint *n.* 847; *vb.* 584, 952
take *vb.* 268, 720, 722
take action *vb.* 609
take advantage of *vb.* 136, 478, 575, 606, 952
take after *vb.* 18, 20
take away *vb.* 42, 720
take back *vb.* 31, 538
take care *vb.* 860
take care of *vb.* 392
take charge of *vb.* 593
take exception *vb.* 425, 893
take for granted *vb.* 443, 867, 880, 910
take from *vb.* 720
take heart *vb.* 836, 857
take in *vb.* 98, 302, 304, 452, 716, 795
take into account *vb.* 390
take it out of *vb.* 617
take it out on *vb.* 149, 900
take liberties *vb.* 918
take life *vb.* 370

take measures *vb.* 602
take notice *vb.* 390
take off *vb.* 20, 228, 273, 744
take on *vb.* 557, 605, 649
take out *vb.* 882
take over *vb.* 667
take pains *vb.* 615
take part in *vb.* 605, 639, 709
take place *vb.* 1, 153
take precautions *vb.* 860
take sides *vb.* 408, 639
take steps *vb.* 602, 609
take to *vb.* 545, 861
take umbrage *vb.* 893
take up *vb.* 540, 575, 716
take upon oneself *vb.* 605
taking *n.* 720
takings *n.* 724, 741
tale *n.* 460, 465, 525
talent *n.* 434, 627
talisman *n.* 984
talk *n.* 470, 492, 514, 518, 519; *vb.* 514
talkativeness *n.* 516
talk down *vb.* 273
talker *n.* 514
talk into *vb.* 547
talk out of *vb.* 548
talk over *vb.* 624
tall *adj.* 32, 202, **208**, 318
tally *vb.* 24, 38
tame *adj.* 507, 654; *vb.* 377, 679
tan *n.* 810, 813; *adj.* 813; *vb.* 963
tandem *n.* 61, 276
tang *n.* 767, 769
tangency *n.* 201
tangent *n.* 285
tangerine *n.* 816
tangible *adj.* 3, 327, 758

tangle *n.* 45, 82; *vb.* 221
tangy *adj.* 769
tanker *n.* 277
tantalize *vb.* 547, 755
tantamount *adj.* 28; *adv.* 199
tantrum *n.* 893
tap *n.* 265, 360, 782; *vb.* 282, 358, 758, 782
tape *n.* 207; *vb.* 483
tape-measure *n.* 400
taper *n.* 800; *vb.* 37, 205, 255
tape-recorder *n.* 484, 794
tape-recording *n.* 483
tardy *adj.* 135
target *n.* 552, 716, 853
tariff *n.* 743
tarnish *n.* 847; *vb.* 584, 847, 869, 928
tarpaulin *n.* 225
tarry *vb.* 135, 281
tart *adj.* 769, 773
tartan *n.* 817
tart up *vb.* 844
task *n.* 557, 605
tassel *n.* 846
taste *n.* 339, 398, 753, 767; *vb.* 767
tasteful *adj.* 398, 510, 848, 876
taste good *vb.* 770
tasteless *adj.* 511, 768, 771, 849
tastelessness *n.* 399, 511, **768**, 771, 849
tasty *adj.* 767, 770, 829
taunt *n.* 926; *vb.* 644, 853, 926
taut *adj.* 334
tautological *adj.* 451
tautology *n.* 505
tavern *n.* 191
tawdry *adj.* 849
tax *n.* 743
taxi *n.* 276; *vb.* 273
taxonomy *n.* 97, 375

tea *n.* 306, 309
tea-break *n.* 616
teach *vb.* 420, 470
teacher *n.* 428, 473, 624, 974, 986
teaching *n.* 470
team *n.* 94
team-mate *n.* 640
team up with *vb.* 639
teamwork *n.* 639
tear *vb.* 48, 280, 613
tea-room *n.* 191
tears *n.* 839
tease *vb.* 755, 830, 842
technique *n.* 488, 606
tedious *adj.* 841, 843
teem *vb.* 75, 572
teenager *n.* 131
teens *n.* 70, 129
teeter *vb.* 325
teeth *n.* 159
teetotalism *n.* 944, 949
telecommunications *n.* 467
telegram *n.* 460, 467
telegraphic *adj.* 504
telepathy *n.* 447
telephone *n.* 467; *vb.* 460
telescope *n.* 329, 822; *vb.* 203
television *n.* 467, 840
tell *vb.* 38, 460, 465, 514, 525, 624
tell apart *vb.* 398
teller *n.* 733
tell fortunes *vb.* 447
telling *adj.* 525
tell off *vb.* 926
tell on *vb.* 460
tell-tale *n.* 460; *adj.* 462
tell tales *vb.* 516
tell the future *vb.* 447
temerity *n.* 859
temper *n.* 5, 751; *vb.* 142, 176, 334, 335, 403
temperament *n.* 5, 751

temperamental *adj.* 756, 894
temperance *n.* 935, **944**, 949
temperate *adj.* 176, 759, 944, 949
temperature *n.* 400, 759
tempest *n.* 175, 359
tempestuous *adj.* 359
temple *n.* 990
temporal *adj.* 107, 116, 987
temporary *adj.* 113, 149, 396
tempt *vb.* 547
temptation *n.* 547
tempting *adj.* 306, 770
tempt providence *vb.* 594, 859
ten *n.* 70; *adj.* 70
tenable *adj.* 420
tenacious *adj.* 50, 337, 534, 535, 537
tenancy *n.* 707
tenant *n.* 190, 710
tend *vb.* 178, 284, 377, 392
tendency *n.* 178, 284, 545, 751
tender *n.* 693; *adj.* 129, 335, 670, 752, 753, 889; *vb.* 693
tenderize *vb.* 335
tendril *n.* 207, 251
tenement *n.* 191
tenet *n.* 420, 974
tenor *n.* 178, 284, 450, 778
tense *n.* 499; *adj.* 756, 856
tension *n.* 25, 615, 642, 832
tent *n.* 225
tentative *adj.* 396, 448, 604
tenuous *adj.* 333
tenure *n.* 707
tepid *adj.* 759

tergiversation *n.* 538
term *n.* 93, 109, 494; *vb.* 496
terminal *n.* 89; *adj.* 89, 237
terminate *vb.* 89, 144, 164, 659
terminology *n.* 494, 496
terminus *n.* 89, 235, 298
terms *n.* 700
terms of reference *n.* 557
terrace *n.* 559
terra firma *n.* 352
terrain *n.* 352
terrestrial *adj.* 329, 352
terrible *adj.* 580, 856
terrific *adj.* 579
terrify *vb.* 856
territory *n.* 183, 956
terror *n.* 856
terrorism *n.* 955
terrorist *n.* 167, 175, 370
terse *adj.* 203, 432, 504
test *n.* 394, 396; *vb.* 408, 413
testify *vb.* 401, 413, 468
testimonial *n.* 441, 483
testimony *n.* 401, 468, 483
tether *vb.* 47
text *n.* 432, 524
textbook *n.* 524
textile *n.* 221
textural *adj.* 339
texture *n.* 339
thank *vb.* 909, 965
thankful *adj.* 909
thankless *adj.* 576, 910
thanks *n.* 909
thanksgiving *n.* 838, 982
thaw *vb.* 345, 761
theatre *n.* 529, 840
theatrical *adj.* 529, 852, 877
theft *n.* 722

theism n. 974
theme n. 387
theology n. 974
theorem n. 410
theoretical adj. 448
theorist n. 448
theorize vb. 448
theory n. 157, 386, 448
therapeutic adj. 585, 589, 591
thermal adj. 759
thermometer n. 759, 766
thermostat n. 766
thesaurus n. 83, 494
thesis n. 387, 410, 448, 526
thick adj. 204, 332, 364, 435
thicken vb. 204, 332
thicket n. 374
thickness n. 204, 206, 332
thickset adj. 203, 204
thick-skinned adj. 754
thief n. 723, 906
thin adj. 33, 76, 205, 333, 507, 571; vb. 27, 333
thing n. 3, 163, 327, 609
thing added n. 41
thing subtracted n. 43
think vb. 384, 420, 448
thinkable adj. 404
think about vb. 552
think ahead vb. 558
thinker n. 448
think-tank n. 624
thinness n. 76, 205, 333
third n. 66; adj. 65
third party n. 653
thirst n. 350, 388, 861; vb. 861
thirst-quencher n. 309
thirsty adj. 350
thorn n. 255, 255
thorn in the flesh n. 592
thorny adj. 255, 633

thorough adj. 56, 148, 392
thoroughfare n. 313
thought n. 384, 386, 392, 420, 441
thoughtful adj. 384, 392, 410, 434, 837, 886
thoughtless adj. 385, 391, 393, 603, 859, 887, 900, 910
thousand n. 70
thrall n. 679
thrash vb. 282, 963
thread n. 49, 207; vb. 313
threadbare adj. 228
threadlike adj. 205, 207
threat n. 154, 594, 902
threatening adj. 154, 594, 651, 902
three n. 64; adj. 64
thresh vb. 378
threshold n. 233, 235
thrifty adj. 392, 748
thrill n. 756, 827; vb. 752, 755, 756, 829
thrive vb. 36, 168, 661, 664
throat n. 262
throaty adj. 515, 787
throb n. 325, 783; vb. 140, 325, 783, 828
throne n. 957
throng n. 75, 94; vb. 75, 94
throughout adv., prep. 107
throw vb. 290
throw away vb. 556, 713, 749
throwaway adj. 544
throw in vb. 311
throw in the towel vb. 556, 654
throw light on vb. 456
throw off vb. 295, 546
throw out vb. 607
throw up vb. 303

thrust n. 173, 178, 282, 290, 645; vb. 290, 645
thud vb. 782, 785
thug n. 723, 906
thumb through vb. 472, 818
thump vb. 282, 783, 785
thunder n. 325, 784; vb. 780, 782
thunderbolt n. 444
thunderstorm n. 175, 358
thunderstruck adj. 444, 866
thundery adj. 358
thwart vb. 445, 635, 637, 648, 662
tick vb. 783
ticket n. 482, 483, 743
tickle vb. 758, 829
tick off vb. 926
tide n. 358
tidy adj. 79, 392, 583; vb. 583
tie n. 28, 49; vb. 28, 47, 681
tier n. 93, 206
tie-up n. 47
tight adj. 47, 334, 950
tight-fisted adj. 750
tight-lipped adj. 517
till n. 732; vb. 378
tilt vb. 219, 220, 317
timber n. 217
timbre n. 512, 778
time n. 107, 109, 116, 400; vb. 116
time-honoured adj. 126, 922
timekeeping n. 116
timelessness n. 108, 114
timeliness n. 136
timepiece n. 116
time-saving adj. 748
time-server n. 538, 934
timetable n. 116, 460
timid adj. 856, 858, 876
timing n. 116, 140

timorous *adj.* 856

tin *n.* 193; *vb.* 599

tincture *n.* 45, 805

tinder *n.* 765

tinge *n.* 805; *vb.* 805

tingle *vb.* 752, 756

tininess *n.* 33, 195

tinker *n.* 728

tinkle *n.* 784

tinny *adj.* 787

tinsel *n.* 846

tint *n.* 27, 805; *vb.* 488

tinted *adj.* 805

tiny *adj.* 33, 195, 203

tip *n.* 212, 233, 255, 715, 965; *vb.* 212, 220, 909

tip-off *n.* 460, 597

tipple *vb.* 304, 950

tipsy *adj.* 950

tirade *n.* 518

tire *vb.* 617, 841

tired *adj.* 612, 617, 841

tiresome *adj.* 830, 841

tissue *n.* 339

titbit *n.* 770, 829

tit for tat *n.* 150, 647

titillate *vb.* 758, 829

title *n.* 496, **872**

titled *adj.* 870

title-holder *n.* 661

titter *n.* 838

titular *adj.* 496

tizzy *n.* 326, 756

toady *n.* 881, 927; *vb.* 881

to and fro *adv.* 325

toast *n.* 309, 888; *vb.* 306, 888

tobacco *n.* **308**

today *n.* 120

toddler *n.* 131

to-do *n.* 80, 756

toe *n.* 213

together *adj.* 47; *adv.* 60

togetherness *n.* 60

toil *n.* 615; *vb.* 615

toilet *n.* 227

token *n.* 4, 441, 482, 701

tolerable *adj.* 579, 666

tolerant *adj.* 288, 670, 690

tolerate *vb.* 670, 690, 911

toll *n.* 716, 743; *vb.* 783

tomb *n.* 372

tomorrow *n.* 123; *adv.* 121, 123

tone *n.* 488, 512, 778, 805

tone down *vb.* 176, 779

toneless *adj.* 806

tongue *n.* 253, 492, 512, 767

tongue in cheek *adj.* 852

tongue-tied *adj.* 513

tonic *n.* 591

tonsure *n.* 228

too *adv.* 40

tool *n.* 565

tooth *n.* 255; *vb.* 259

toothless *adj.* 130, 256

top *n.* 89, 208, 212, 222; *adj.* 212; *vb.* 34, 212, 316

top-heavy *adj.* 29, 330

topic *n.* **387**

topical *adj.* 125

top-notch *adj.* 573, 579

topple *vb.* 220, 317, 319

topsy-turvy *adj.* 220

top up *vb.* 56

Torah *n.* 976

torch *n.* 765, 800

torment *n.* 828; *vb.* 830, 856, 900, 902

torn *adj.* 48, 262

tornado *n.* 175, 323, 359

torpedo *n.* 290

torpid *adj.* 174, 612

torrent *n.* 358, 572

torrential *adj.* 358

tortoise *n.* 281

tortuous *adj.* 251

torture *n.* 828, 900, 963; *vb.* 830, 900, 963

toss *vb.* 290, 326

toss-up *n.* 553

tot *n.* 131

total *n.* 40, 54; *adj.* 54; *vb.* 38, 40

totalitarian *adj.* 669

totality *n.* 54

totem *n.* 967, 983

totter *vb.* 325, 326

touch *n.* 753, 758, 805; *vb.* 201, 752, 755, **758**

touch-and-go *adj.* 553

touch down *vb.* 273, 298, 317

touched *adj.* 752, 756

touch on *vb.* 211, 450

touch up *vb.* 587, 589, 805

touchy *adj.* 756, 894

tough *adj.* 161, 334, 337, 506, 633, 857

toughen *vb.* 334, 337

toughness *n.* 161, 334, 337

tour *vb.* 269, 322

tourism *n.* 269

tourist *n.* 270

tournament *n.* 649

tout *n.* 697, 728; *vb.* 695

tow *vb.* 291

towards *adv.* 284

tower *n.* 208; *vb.* 32, 34, 208, 316

towering *adj.* 32, 208

tower of strength *n.* 640

town *n.* 183

townsman *n.* 190

toxic *adj.* 164, 580, 586

trace *n.* 33, 401, 483, 774; *vb.* 157, 232, 525

tracing *n.* 22, 232

track *n.* 559, 658; *vb.* 287, 554

track down *vb.* 419

tractable *adj.* 654, 919

tractor *n.* 291

trade *n.* 150, 557, 725;
    vb. 150, 725, 727
trader *n.* 728
tradition *n.* 126, 545,
    641, 979
traditional *adj.* 126, 143
traditionalist *n.* 105,
    143
traffic *n.* 313, 725; *vb.*
    725
trafficker *n.* 728
traffic warden *n.* 956
tragedy *n.* 529, 551
tragic *adj.* 551, 830
trail *n.* 483, 774; *vb.*
    287, 291, 554
trailer *n.* 276, 291
train *n.* 85, 91, 276, 291;
    vb. 377, 470, 545, 602
trained *adj.* 426, 627
trainee *n.* 474
trainer *n.* 473
training *n.* 470, 472,
    545, 602, 627
traitor *n.* 148, 480, 538,
    940
tramp *n.* 269, 270, 612,
    697, 940
trance *n.* 754, 984
tranquil *adj.* 616, 757
tranquillize *vb.* 652
tranquillizer *n.* 176, 591
transact *vb.* 609, 727
transaction *n.* 153, 699,
    725
transcend *vb.* 6, 32, 34,
    314
transcribe *vb.* 456, 521
transcriber *n.* 521
transcript *n.* 22, 521
transcription *n.* 456,
    521, 792
transfer *n.* 22, 149, 150,
    714; *vb.* 142, 149, 268,
    275, 714
transferable *adj.* 268,
    714
transferal *n.* 268

transference *n.* 142,
    149, 268, 455, 714
transfix *vb.* 152
transform *vb.* 142, 146
transformer *n.* 142
transfusion *n.* 45
transgression *n.* 672,
    936, 955
transgressor *n.* 906, 940
transient *adj.* 113
transit *n.* 268
transition *n.* 142
transitional *adj.* 266
transitory *adj.* 113
translate *vb.* 20, 142,
    456
translation *n.* 456, 495,
    972
translator *n.* 456
transliterate *vb.* 456
translucent *adj.* 802,
    804
transmission *n.* 460
transmit *vb.* 268
transmutation *n.* 142
transmute *vb.* 146
transparency *n.* 452,
    486, 502, 802
transparent *adj.* 802,
    806
transpire *vb.* 107, 153
transplant *vb.* 268, 378
transport *n.* 268, 756,
    827; *vb.* 187, 275, 963
transpose *vb.* 149, 187,
    220
transverse *adj.* 219
transvestite *n.* 953
trap *n.* 276, 463, 478,
    596, 631; *vb.* 463, 478,
    631, 720
trappings *n.* 711
trash *n.* 451
trashy *adj.* 580
traumatic *adj.* 856
travail *n.* 615
travel *vb.* 269
traveller *n.* 270

traverse *vb.* 269, 313
travesty *n.* 22, 487
treacherous *adj.* 478,
    594, 932
treachery *n.* 478, 932
treacle *n.* 772
tread *vb.* 269
treason *n.* 478, 932
treasure *n.* 567, 579,
    891; *vb.* 441, 889, 983
treasurer *n.* 733
treasury *n.* 732
treat *n.* 770, 829; *vb.*
    526, 589, 591, 606, 738
treated *adj.* 602
treatise *n.* 526
treatment *n.* 488, 591,
    606
treaty *n.* 24, 650, 699
treble *adj.* 65; *vb.* 65
tree *n.* 374
trek *n.* 313; *vb.* 269
tremble *vb.* 326, 756,
    856
tremendously *adv.* 32
tremor *n.* 325, 326, 856
tremulous *adj.* 326
trench *n.* 210, 234, 254,
    259, 261, 360
trenchant *adj.* 255, 506
trenches *n.* 646, 658
trend *n.* 178, 850
trepidation *n.* 856
trespass *n.* 703, 938,
    955; *vb.* 300, 314
trial *n.* 551, 592, 604,
    828; *adj.* 396, 396, 604
triality *n.* 64
triangle *n.* 64, 246
tribe *n.* 11
tribulation *n.* 828
tribunal *n.* 957, 958
tributary *n.* 358
tribute *n.* 743, 909
trick *n.* 433, 478, 631,
    932; *vb.* 431, 478, 478,
    631
trickery *n.* 478

trickle *vb.* 358
trickster *n.* 480, 631
trifle *n.* 33, 574; *vb.* 478
trigonometry *n.* 38
trill *vb.* 512, 783, 789
trim *vb.* 37, 203, 538, 844
trimming *n.* 846
trimmings *n.* 44
trimness *n.* 583
trinity *n.* 64, 967
trio *n.* 64, 792
trip *n.* 269, 909; *vb.* 478
triplication *n.* 65
trisection *n.* 66
trite *adj.* 432, 451, 843
triumph *n.* 153, 661
trivial *adj.* 451, 574
troll *n.* 970
trolley *n.* 276
troop *n.* 94, 655
trophy *n.* 441, 663, 965
tropical *adj.* 759
trot out *vb.* 514
troubadour *n.* 528
trouble *n.* 615, 633, 642, 665, 830; *vb.* 82, 578, 580, 633, 830, 856
troubled *adj.* 665, 828, 837, 856
trouble-maker *n.* 596, 672, 906
trouble-shooter *n.* 653
troublesome *adj.* 164, 330, 633, 642, 830
trouble spot *n.* 596
trough *n.* 259, 360
truancy *n.* 189, 920
truant *n.* 555, 600
truce *n.* 144, 650
truck *n.* 217; *vb.* 268
true *adj.* 1, 430, 450, 882, 915
true-to-life *adj.* 525
truism *n.* 432, 451
trump up *vb.* 477, 930
truncate *vb.* 203
trunk *n.* 193

truss *n.* 217
trust *n.* 408, 420, 443, 685, 736, 854; *vb.* 420, 854, 980
trustee *n.* 688, 733
trusteeship *n.* 685
trustworthy *adj.* 408, 420, 868, 931
truth *n.* 1, 408, 430, 432, 977
truthful *adj.* 430, 476
truthfulness *n.* 476, 931
try *n.* 604; *vb.* 604, 615, 767, 960
trying *adj.* 633, 830
tube *n.* 360, 361, 559
tuck *n.* 260, 306; *vb.* 304
tug *n.* 277, 291; *vb.* 291
tuition *n.* 470
tumble *vb.* 317, 358
tumid *adj.* 252
tumour *n.* 252
tumult *n.* 80, 175, 326, 780
tumultuous *adj.* 80
tundra *n.* 356
tune *n.* 792
tuneful *adj.* 528, 790, 792
tunnel *n.* 254, 360; *vb.* 254, 264
turbulence *n.* 80, 175, 326
turf *n.* 374, 812
turmoil *n.* 80, 175, 326, 668
turn *n.* 251, 260, 323; *vb.* 142, 177, 247, 251, 256
turn around *vb.* 289
turn aside *vb.* 285
turn away *vb.* 295, 391, 555
turn back *vb.* 147
turn down *vb.* 694
turn in *vb.* 556, 612, 681
turning *n.* 285

turning point *n.* 136
turn inside out *vb.* 220, 394
turn into *vb.* 146
turn off *vb.* 754, 771
turn on *vb.* 755, 829
turn out *vb.* 153, 227
turn-out *n.* 821
turn over *vb.* 220, 317
turn-over *n.* 741
turn to *vb.* 575, 624
turn up *vb.* 153, 188, 298, 444, 825
turn upside down *vb.* 220
turquoise *adj.* 815
tussle *n.* 649
tutor *n.* 473
twaddle *n.* 451, 516
twang *n.* 515
tweet *vb.* 789
twice *adv.* 62
twig *n.* 374; *vb.* 419, 452
twilight *n.* 128, 799
twin *n.* 11, 28; *adj.* 13, 18, 61, 62; *vb.* 62
twine *n.* 207, 251; *vb.* 221, 251
twinge *n.* 828
twinkle *n.* 797, 818; *vb.* 326, 797, 818, 838
twinkling *n.* 115
twirl *n.* 323; *vb.* 251, 323
twist *n.* 245, 251; *vb.* 219, 221, 245, 247, 251, 323
twitch *vb.* 326
twitter *vb.* 789
two *n.* 61
two-edged *adj.* 454
two-faced *adj.* 477, 932
two-time *vb.* 932
tycoon *n.* 728
type *n.* 23, 97, 482, 522; *vb.* 521
typescript *n.* 521

typhoon *n.* 359
typical *adj.* 18, 30, 101, 482, 486
typify *vb.* 23, 486
typist *n.* 521
typography *n.* 522
tyrannical *adj.* 669, 908
tyrannize *vb.* 669, 900
tyranny *n.* 669, 900
tyrant *n.* 669

U

ubiquitous *adj.* 101, 188
UFO *n.* 279
ugliness *n.* 245, **845**, 849
ultimate *n.* 581, 939; *adj.* 89, 198
ultimatum *n.* 671
umbra *n.* 798
umbrella *n.* 225, 595, 801
umimaginable *adj.* 405
umpire *n.* 415, 653; *vb.* 653
unable *adj.* 160, 405
unacceptable *adj.* 500, 571
unaccompanied *adj.* 59
unaccustomed *adj.* 546
unacknowledged *adj.* 910
unadorned *adj.* 508
unadulterated *adj.* 46, 430, 581, 951
unadventurous *adj.* 612
unaffected *adj.* 508, 632, 754, 921
unamazed *adj.* 867
unambiguous *adj.* **408**, 450, 452, 502
unambitiousness *n.* 863
unanimity *n.* 24, 424, 643

unappealing *adj.* 771
unappetizing *adj.* 771
unappreciative *adj.* 910
unapproachable *adj.* 198, 885
unashamed *adj.* 942
unasked *adj.* 532
unassailable *adj.* 408, 593
unassuming *adj.* 874, 876
unattached *adj.* **48**, 678, 897
unattested *adj.* 409
unauthenticity *n.* 431, 978
unauthorized *adj.* 955
unavailable *adj.* 189, 405, 576
unavoidable *adj.* 154, 531, 674
unaware *adj.* 427, 754, 796
unbalanced *adj.* 439, 916
unbeaten *adj.* 661
unbecoming *adj.* 845, 887
unbelief *n.* 409, 421, 866, 975
unbending *adj.* 334, 534, 669
unbiased *adj.* 415, 541, 915, 933
unbind *vb.* 48, 601, 680
unblemished *adj.* 54, 581, 583, 935
unbolt *vb.* 262
unbosom *vb.* 462
unbound *adj.* 708, 921
unbreakable *adj.* 334, 337
unbroken *adj.* 54, 91, 145
unburden oneself *vb.* 462
uncanny *adj.* 971, 984
unceasing *adj.* 114, 145

uncertainty *n.* 325, **409**, 421, 454, 553
uncertified *adj.* 409
unchangeable *adj.* 13, 143, 152
unchanging *adj.* 16, 143, 669
uncharitable *adj.* 900
uncharted *adj.* 427
unchaste *adj.* 952
unclassified *adj.* 35
uncle *n.* 11
uncleanness *n.* **584**, 586, 777, 952
unclear *adj.* 409, 453, 503, 633, 803
uncoil *vb.* 81, 248
uncomfortable *adj.* 187
uncommon *adj.* 139
uncommunicative *adj.* 517, 863, 885
uncomplaining *adj.* 757, 831
uncompleted *adj.* 660
uncomplicated *adj.* 46, 632, 634
uncomplimentary *adj.* 926
uncompromising *adj.* 537, 669
unconcerned *adj.* 389, 391, 393, 863, 933
unconditional *adj.* 56, 408
unconfirmed *adj.* 409
unconformity *n.* **106**
unconnected *adj.* 10, 48, 92
unconscious *n.* 382; *adj.* 427, 531, 754
unconsecrated *adj.* 987
unconsidered *adj.* 544
unconstitutionality *n.* 955
uncontrolled *adj.* 668, 672, 921
unconventional *adj.* 106

311

ungracious *adj.* 887
ungrammatical *adj.* 500
ungrateful *adj.* 910
unguarded *adj.* 393, 603
unguent *n.* 342, 365;
 adj. 365
unhallowed *adj.* 981
unhappy *adj.* 665, 828,
 832, 837
unharmed *adj.* 593
unhealthy *adj.* 586
unheard of *adj.* 407,
 444, 869
unheeding *adj.* 393
unhelpful *adj.* 576
unhesitating *adj.* 534
unhindered *adj.* 678
unhitch *vb.* 48
unholy *adj.* 975, 981
unhurt *adj.* 593
unhygienic *adj.* 586
unidentified *adj.* 497
uniform *n.* 227, 677;
 adj. 16, 46, 140, 152,
 257
uniformity *n.* 13, 16, 24,
 28, 79
unify *vb.* 47, 52, 59
unilateral *adj.* 10
unimaginative *adj.* 508
unimpaired *adj.* 54
unimpeded *adj.* 678
unimportance *n.* 451,
 574
unimpressed *adj.* 867
uninhabited *adj.* 189,
 885
uninspired *adj.* 507, 843
uninspiring *adj.* 841
unintelligibility *n.* 453,
 503
unintended *adj.* 451
unintentional *adj.* 158,
 531, 553
uninterested *adj.* 389,
 612
uninteresting *adj.* 771,
 841, 843

uninterrupted *adj.* 91,
 143, 145
uninvited *adj.* 532
uninviting *adj.* 771, 805
uninvolved *adj.* 10, 863
union *n.* 47, 52, 180,
 296, 641, 896
unique *adj.* 21, 59, 102
unison *n.* 24, 790
unit *n.* 59, 655
unite *vb.* 45, 47, 180,
 296, 639, 896
unity *n.* 16, 54, 59, 643
universal *adj.* 32, 54,
 56, 101, 329
universe *n.* 329
university *n.* 475
unjust *adj.* 916, 918
unjustifiable *adj.* 916
unkempt *adj.* 584
unkind *adj.* 887, 900
unknown *n.* 427; *adj.*
 427, 466, 497
unlawful *adj.* 691, 952,
 955
unlearned *adj.* 427
unlike *adj.* 15, 19
unlikely *adj.* 407, 409
unlit *adj.* 798
unload *vb.* 42, 187, 331
unlocked *adj.* 262
unlovely *adj.* 845, 849
unloving *adj.* 900
unlucky *adj.* 665
unman *vb.* 160
unmarried *adj.* 897
unmask *vb.* 458, 462
unmelodious *adj.* 791
unmentioned *adj.* 459
unmerited *adj.* 918
unmindful *adj.* 393,
 427, 442, 910
unmistakable *adj.* 408,
 458, 823
unmix *vb.* 46
unmixed *adj.* 430
unmotivated *adj.* 158

unmoved *adj.* 535, 754,
 863, 908
unmusical *adj.* 791
unnatural *adj.* 852
unnecessary *adj.* 576,
 918
unnerve *vb.* 837, 856
unobservant *adj.* 391
unobtainable *adj.* 405
unobtrusive *adj.* 876
unoccupied *adj.* 189,
 612, 614, 708
unoffending *adj.* 937
unopened *adj.* 263
unorganized *adj.* 80,
 603
unoriginal *adj.* 431
unorthodox *adj.* 106,
 975, 978
unpack *vb.* 42, 187
unpaid *adj.* 737, 917
unparalleled *adj.* 866
unpatriotic *adj.* 904
unpitying *adj.* 908
unpleasant *adj.* 828,
 830, 887
unpolished *adj.* 849
unpolluted *adj.* 583
unpopular *adj.* 862
unprecedented *adj.* 59,
 866
unpredictable *adj.* 139,
 158, 409, 539
unprejudiced *adj.* 415,
 915, 933
unpremeditated *adj.*
 544
unprepared *adj.* 444,
 603
unprepossessing *adj.*
 845
unpretentious *adj.* 508,
 874
unprincipled *adj.* 932
unprivileged *adj.* 918
unproductiveness *n.*
 160, 169
unprofessional *adj.* 628

313

unwise *adj.* 393, 416, 435, 578

unworthy *adj.* 918

unwrap *vb.* 324

unyielding *adj.* 112, 161, 334, 337, 534, 537

up *adv.* 208

update *vb.* 125, 587

upgrade *vb.* 587

upheaval *n.* 80, 148

uphill *adj.* 615, 633

uphold *vb.* 143, 145, 217, 929

upland *n.* 356

uplands *n.* 208

uplift *vb.* 318, 836

upper *adj.* 34

upper classes *n.* 870

uppermost *adj.* 212

upraised *adj.* 318

upright *adj.* 214, 248, 430, 915, 931, 935

uprising *n.* 358

uproar *n.* 80, 175, 780

uproot *vb.* 187, 312

upset *n.* 220, 414; *adj.* 837; *vb.* 82, 148, 830, 893

upshot *n.* 87, 156

upside-down *adj.* 220; *adv.* 80

upstanding *adj.* 214, 318

upstart *n.* 125, 880

upsurge *vb.* 36

uptight *adj.* 756, 894

up-to-date *adj.* 125

upward *adj.* 219, 316

urban *adj.* 183

urchin *n.* 970

urge *n.* 547, 861; *vb.* 468, 547, 613, 624, 674, 695

urgency *n.* 506, 562, 573, 613, 674, 695

urinate *vb.* 303, 310

urn *n.* 193, 372

usage *n.* 499, 501, 545, 606

use *n.* 606; *vb.* 575, 606, 707, 719

used *adj.* 126, 606

used to *adj.* 545

useful *adj.* 550, 575, 577

useless *adj.* 576, 662

usher in *vb.* 84

usual *adj.* 138, 545, 867

usurer *n.* 718

usurp *vb.* 918

utensil *n.* 565

utilitarian *adj.* 575

utilitarianism *n.* 903

utility *n.* 575, 606

utilize *vb.* 575, 606

utmost *n.* 235

utopia *n.* 449

utter *adj.* 56; *vb.* 512, 514, 788

utterance *n.* 492, 494, 498, 512, 514, 788

V

vacant *adj.* 189, 385, 435, 451

vacate *vb.* 187

vacation *n.* 144, 612, 614

vaccine *n.* 591

vacillate *vb.* 151, 325, 536

vacuity *n.* 2, 189

vacuum *n.* 2, 189, 333

vagabond *n.* 270, 697

vagrant *n.* 270

vague *adj.* 4, 243, 409, 454, 503, 799, 824

vain *adj.* 576, 662, 855, 875

valentine *n.* 523, 890

valiant *adj.* 857

valid *adj.* 413, 430, 915, 954

validate *vb.* 413, 954

validity *n.* 430, 954

valley *n.* 200, 209, 254

valour *n.* 857

valuable *adj.* 573, 575, 579

valuables *n.* 711

value *n.* 575, 579, 743; *vb.* 573, 743, 889, 922

valuer *n.* 415

valve *n.* 265

vampire *n.* 906, 969

van *n.* 276

vandal *n.* 167

vandalism *n.* 722

vanished *adj.* 2, 189, 706, 826

vanity *n.* 576, 873, 875, 934

vaporization *n.* 346

vaporous *adj.* 4, 344, 346

vapour *n.* 4, 343, 344, 346

variable *n.* 39; *adj.* 15, 17, 104, 142, 151

variance *n.* 15, 425, 642

variant *n.* 15; *adj.* 15

variation *n.* 15, 19, 104, 142

variegation *n.* 817

variety *n.* 19, 72, 104, 529

various *adj.* 104

varnish *vb.* 225, 257, 365

vary *vb.* 15, 142, 151

vase *n.* 193

vast *adj.* 32, 78, 182, 194

vastly *adv.* 32

vat *n.* 193

vault *n.* 252, 320, 329, 372, 732; *vb.* 320

vaulted *adj.* 247

vaunt *vb.* 879

veer *vb.* 142, 247, 285

vegetability *n.* 374

315

vegetable *n.* 306

vegetate *vb.* 169, 174, 612, 666

vegetation *n.* 374

vehement *adj.* 173, 175, 506, 759

vehicle *n.* 276, 563

veil *n.* 461, 463, 549, 801; *vb.* 225, 461, 801

veiled *adj.* 225, 459

velocity *n.* 266, **280**

vendetta *n.* 425, 642

vendor *n.* 697, 727

veneer *n.* 211, 225; *vb.* 206, 225

venerable *adj.* 126, 130

venerate *vb.* 922, 982

vengeance *n.* 647, 912

venomous *adj.* 164, 580, 592

vent *n.* 262, 361, 600

ventilate *vb.* 348, 583

ventilation *n.* 348, 775

ventilator *n.* 361, 764

venture *n.* 269, 553, 604, **605**; *vb.* 158, 553, 604, 918

veracity *n.* 476

verb *n.* 499

verbal *adj.* 450, 494, 514

verbalize *vb.* 498

verbose *adj.* 505, 516

verdict *n.* 415, 960

verge *n.* 233; *vb.* 233

verge on *vb.* 292

verify *vb.* 396, 401, 408, 413

veritable *adj.* 430

vermin *n.* 373

vernacular *n.* 492; *adj.* 190, 492

versatile *adj.* 151, 627

verse *n.* 528

versed *adj.* 602

version *n.* 456

vertebrate *n.* 373

vertical *adj.* 214, 248

verve *n.* 173, 368, 506, 611

very *adj.* 13; *adv.* 32

vespers *n.* 128, 988

vessel *n.* 193, 277

vestige *n.* 44

vestment *n.* 227, **989**

vet *n.* 377

veteran *n.* 132, 629, 655; *adj.* 627

veterinary science *n.* 377

veto *n.* 681, 691, 694; *vb.* 691

vexed *adj.* 828, 893

via *adv.* 284

viable *adj.* 404

vibration *n.* 325, 326, 778, 784

vicar *n.* 689, 986

vicarious *adj.* 149, 685, 943

vicarious authority *n.* **685**

vice *n.* **936**; *adj.* 689

vicinity *n.* 199, 229

vicious circle *n.* 412

vicissitude *n.* 142

victim *n.* 479, 716, 828, 853

victimize *vb.* 478, 900

victor *n.* 661

Victorian *adj.* 126, 951

victorious *adj.* 661

victory *n.* 661

video-recorder *n.* 484

videotape *n.* 483

view *n.* 415, 420, 624, 818; *vb.* 818

viewer *n.* 821

vie with *vb.* 649

viewpoint *n.* 818

vigilant *adj.* 390, 392, 818, 860

vigilante *n.* 593

vigour *n.* 159, 161, 173, 368, **506**, 585, 611

vile *adj.* 580, 777, 892

vilify *vb.* 901, 928

villa *n.* 191

village *n.* 183

villain *n.* 906, 940

vindicate *vb.* 647, 912, 929, 961

vindication *n.* **929**

vindictive *adj.* 908, 912

vinegar *n.* 773

vineyard *n.* 378

violate *vb.* 314, 608, 672, 703, 920, 952, 955, 981

violence *n.* 175, 674

violent *adj.* 175, 642

violet *n.* 814; *adj.* 814

VIP *n.* 868

viper *n.* 906

virgin *n.* 897; *adj.* 125, 427, 603, 897, 951

virgin territory *n.* 427

virile *adj.* 161, 380

virtual *adj.* 404

virtually *adv.* 199

virtue *n.* 876, 931, **935**, 951

virtuoso *n.* 793

virtuous *adj.* 931, 935, 951

virus *n.* 167, 586, 592

visa *n.* 690

viscosity *n.* 362, 400

viscount *n.* 870

visibility *n.* **823**

visible *adj.* 3, 458, 823, 825

vision *n.* 449, 458, **818**, 854, 971, 976

visionary *n.* 449, 903; *adj.* 4, 449

visit *n.* 269, 884; *vb.* 188, 269, 300, 971

visitor *n.* 100, 270, 884

visual *adj.* 488, 818

visualize *vb.* 449

vital *adj.* 368, 562

vitality *n.* 161, 173, 368, 506, 585, 836

vitalize *vb.* 173, 368
vitreous *adj.* 802
vivacious *adj.* 368, 836
vivacity *n.* 514
vivid *adj.* 441, 506, 509, 525
vivisection *n.* 370
vocabulary *n.* 494, 501
vocal *adj.* 512, 792
vocalist *n.* 793
vocalize *vb.* 512, 514
vocation *n.* 557, 985
vociferous *adj.* 780, 788
vogue *n.* 125; *adj.* 495
voice *n.* 492, 512; *vb.* 512, 514
void *n.* 2, 74, 189; *adj.* 2, 333, 451; *vb.* 955
volatile *adj.* 151, 344, 346
volition *n.* 530
volte-face n. 147, 220, 289, 538
voluble *adj.* 509, 514, 516
volume *n.* 26, 194, 400, 524
voluntary *adj.* 530, 532
volunteer *vb.* 532, 693
voluptuous *adj.* 827, 945
vomit *vb.* 303
voodoo *n.* 984
voracity *n.* 750, 861, 948
vortex *n.* 323, 358
vote *n.* 540, 909; *vb.* 424, 540
voted *adj.* 424
voter *n.* 190, 540
vouch *vb.* 468
voucher *n.* 482, 741
vow *n.* 468, 698; *vb.* 468, 698
vowel *n.* 493, 512
voyage *n.* 271, 313; *vb.* 271
voyager *n.* 270

vulgar *adj.* 511, 849, 887, 952
vulnerable *adj.* 594, 753

W

wadding *n.* 226
wade *vb.* 271
wafer *n.* 306
waffle *vb.* 516
waft *vb.* 359
wag *n.* 842; *vb.* 325
wager *n.* 553
wages *n.* 731, 738, 741
wagon *n.* 276
wail *n.* 788, 839; *vb.* 788, 839
wait *vb.* 443, 610
wait and see *vb.* 135, 610
waiter *n.* 676
wait on *vb.* 287, 676
waive *vb.* 556, 713
wake *n.* 237
walk *n.* 269, 559; *vb.* 269
walk away with *vb.* 661
walker *n.* 270
walkie-talkie *n.* 467
walk out *vb.* 144, 556, 687
walkout *n.* 144
walk-over *n.* 634, 661
wall *n.* 217, 230, 234
wallet *n.* 193, 732
wallop *vb.* 282, 963
wan *adj.* 807
wand *n.* 677
wander *vb.* 269, 285, 505
wanderer *n.* 270
wandering *n.* 391
wane *n.* 37; *vb.* 37, 799
want *n.* 57, 562, 706, 861; *vb.* 57, 189, 530, 532, 562, 571, 861

wanted *adj.* 562, 600
wanton *adj.* 936, 952
war *n.* 649, 651
warble *vb.* 789
ward *n.* 183, 540
warden *n.* 593, 683
warder *n.* 683
ward off *vb.* 646
wardrobe *n.* 227
wardship *n.* 129
warehouse *n.* 567
wares *n.* 729
warfare *n.* 649, 651
warlike *adj.* 651
warm *adj.* 419, 759, 805; *vb.* 306, 761, 836
warm-hearted *adj.* 882, 899
warmth *n.* 506, 752, 759, 805, 882
warm up *vb.* 306
warning *n.* 447, 460, 597, 902; *adj.* 597
warp *vb.* 219, 247, 416, 487
warrant *n.* 424, 671, 685; *vb.* 690, 698, 917
warranty *n.* 701
warren *n.* 234, 254
warrior *n.* 655
wart *n.* 252
wary *adj.* 390, 860
wash *n.* 358, 805; *vb.* 583, 805
washed out *adj.* 612, 617, 806
wash-out *n.* 662
waste *n.* 44, 164, 569, 576; *vb.* 569, 608, 749
waste away *vb.* 53, 586, 588
wasted *adj.* 205, 569
wasteful *adj.* 393, 569, 749
waste-pipe *n.* 600
waste time *vb.* 612
wastrel *n.* 612, 749, 940

watch *n.* 116, 646; *vb.* 392, 818

watchdog *n.* 593

watcher *n.* 821

watchful *adj.* 392, 443, 818, 860

watchman *n.* 683

watchword *n.* 432

water *n.* 309, 347; *vb.* 378

water channel *n.* **360**

water down *vb.* 45, 162

waterfall *n.* 358

water in motion *n.* **358**

waterlogged *adj.* 349, 355

waterproof *adj.* 350, 593

watershed *n.* 230

water sports *n.* 271

watertight *adj.* 265, 350

water travel *n.* **271**

waterway *n.* 358

watery *adj.* 343, 347

wave *n.* 325, 358, 482; *vb.* 325, 482, 886

wavering *n.* 142, 151, 325, 409, 536; *adj.* 141, 151, 326, 536

wavy *adj.* 251

wax *n.* 342, 800; *vb.* 36, 225

way *n.* 198, 313, **559**

wayfarer *n.* 270

way out *n.* 301, 600

wayward *adj.* 151, 672

weak *adj.* 162, 507, 586, 617, 628, 781, 858

weak-minded *adj.* 162, 435

weakness *n.* **162**, 178, 315, 507, 586, 617, 858, 936

weak spot *n.* 582, 594

wealth *n.* 168, 664, 711, 731, **734**

wean from *vb.* 546, 548

weapons *n.* 657

wear *vb.* 227

wear and tear *n.* 569

wear away *vb.* 341

wear down *vb.* 160, 547

weariness *n.* 612, 617, **841**

wearisome *adj.* 633, 841

wear out *vb.* 569, 617

weather *n.* 348

weave *n.* 339; *vb.* 221, 313

web *n.* 221, 339

wed *adj.* 47; *vb.* 896

wedding *n.* 896

wedge *n.* 230, 246, 265

weed *n.* 374; *vb.* 378

weedy *adj.* 205

week *n.* 109

weep *vb.* 301, 833, 839, 907

weigh *vb.* 330, 397, 415

weight *n.* 26, 177, 194, **330**, 400, 573; *vb.* 330

weighting *n.* 31

weightless *adj.* 331

weigh up *vb.* 384

weird *adj.* 971, 984

welcome *n.* 302; *adj.* 827; *vb.* 302, 884, 886

welcoming *adj.* 716

weld *n.* 49; *vb.* 50

welfare *n.* 550, 664

well *n.* 254, 567; *adj.* 585; *vb.* 301, 358

well-behaved *adj.* 673

well-being *n.* 550, 585, 664

well-dressed *adj.* 227

well-formed *adj.* 499, 844

well grounded *adj.* 426

well-meaning *adj.* 899

well-off *adj.* 664, 734

well-proportioned *adj.* 244, 510, 844

well-read *adj.* 426, 472

well thought of *adj.* 868, 922

well-turned *adj.* 510

well-versed *adj.* 426, 627

weltschmerz *n.* 837

west *n.* 284

wet *n.* 347, 349; *adj.* 347, 349; *vb.* 349

wet blanket *n.* 548, 841

whack *n.* 782; *vb.* 282, 782, 963

whacked *adj.* 617

whale *n.* 194

what's-its-name *n.* 497

wheedle *vb.* 547, 927

wheel *n.* 250

wheeled *adj.* 276

wheeze *vb.* 359, 786

when *adv., prep.* 107

whereabouts *n.* 185

wherewithal *n.* 564, 566

whet *vb.* 255, 755

while *adv., prep.* 107

while away *vb.* 107, 612

whim *n.* 449, 539

whimper *vb.* 788, 839

whimsical *adj.* 449, 539, 842, 851

whine *vb.* 784, 788, 789, 839

whip *n.* 964; *vb.* 282, 963

whip up *vb.* 175, 755

whirl *n.* 323; *vb.* 323, 358, 359

whirlpool *n.* 323, 358

whirlwind *n.* 323, 359

whirr *n.* 783, 786; *vb.* 783, 784, 786

whisk *n.* 359; *vb.* 359

whisper *n.* 460, 781; *vb.* 781

whistle *n.* 482, 786, 787; *vb.* 482, 786, 787, 789

white *n.* 807, 951; *adj.* 583, 806, 807

white flag n. 652
whittle vb. 203
whiz vb. 280, 786
whizz-kid n. 629
whole n. 26, 54, 59; adj. 39, 54, 56, 581, 585
wholehearted adj. 534
wholesale adj. 54, 56, 98
wholesome adj. 438, 585
whoop vb. 788, 840
whore n. 953
wicked adj. 551, 580, 900, 916, 932, 936, 981
wickerwork n. 221
wide adj. 101, 182, 204
widen vb. 36, 182, 204
widespread adj. 32, 54, 101, 182
widow n. 898; vb. 898
widowhood n. **898**
width n. 26, 204, 400
wife n. 896
wiggle vb. 251
wild adj. 175, 433, 439, 859, 889
wilful adj. 530
will n. **530**; vb. 530, 714
willies n. 856
willingness n. 532, 692
willpower n. 530, 534
wilt vb. 837
wily adj. 478, 631
win vb. 661, 705, 720
wince n. 283
wind n. 359; vb. 251, 322
windfall n. 550, 715
window n. 262
wind up vb. 89, 116, 739
windy adj. 344, 348, 359
wine n. 309
wink n. 482, 818; vb. 482, 818
winner n. 661

winnings n. 724
winnow vb. 46, 48, 378
win over vb. 547
winsome adj. 829, 889
winter n. **128**; adj. 128
wintry adj. 128, 760
wipe vb. 341
wipe out vb. 164, 485, 911
wire n. 207, 460, 467; adj. 611; vb. 460
wireless n. 467
wiry adj. 207
wisdom n. 382, 392, 426, **434**
wisecrack n. 842
wish n. 530, 854, 861; vb. 530, 854, 861
wishful thinking n. 449, 478, 854
wishy-washy adj. 162, 507, 666, 768
wisp n. 4, 207
wit n. 434, **842**
witchcraft n. 984
withdraw vb. 42, 289, **293**, 299, 312, 538, 556, 600, 687, 731, 826
withdrawn adj. 681, 885
wither vb. 350, 588
withhold vb. 461, 694, 712
within hearing adv. 199
within reach adj. 404
without adv., prep. 42; prep. 571
with reference to adv., prep. 9
withstand vb. 646, 648
with strings attached adj. 700
with the exception of adv., prep. 42
with young adj. 163
witness n. 401, 483; vb. 401, 413
witty adj. 840, 842

wizard n. 447, 984
wizened adj. 197, 205
wobble n. 326; vb. 325, 326
woe n. 580
wold n. 356
woman n. 133, 381
woman-hater n. 904
womanizer n. 953
women's rights n. 917
wonder n. **866**; vb. 866
wonderful adj. 32, 579, 844
wont n. 545
woo vb. 882, 889, 890
wood n. 374, 765
woodwind n. 794
word n. **494**, 698; vb. 498
wording n. 501
Word of God n. 976
word order n. 499
wordy adj. 505
work n. 163, 488, 521, 524, 557, 605, 615, 792; vb. 172, 557, 615, 676
workable adj. 406
work against vb. 181
worked up adj. 893
worker n. 609, 619, 676
work off vb. 149
work oneself up vb. 756
work one's way up vb. 316
work out vb. 38, 452, 552, 558, 659
workshop n. **620**
work together vb. 52, 180
work up vb. 755
world n. 329, 379
worldliness n. 327, 329, 981
world-weariness n. 837, 841
worldwide adj. 32, 101

X, Y, Z

List of categories

I Abstract Relations

A Existence

1 existence
2 non-existence
3 material existence
4 non-material existence
5 being according to internal form
6 being according to external form
7 absolute state
8 circumstance

B Relation

9 relation
10 absence of relation
11 kindred relations
12 correlation
13 identity
14 absolute difference
15 variance
16 uniformity
17 non-uniformity
18 similarity
19 dissimilarity
20 imitation
21 non-imitation
22 copy
23 prototype
24 agreement
25 disagreement

C Quantity

26 quantity
27 relative quantity
28 equality
29 inequality
30 mean
31 compensation
32 greatness
33 smallness

34 superiority
35 inferiority
36 increase
37 decrease
38 numeration
39 number
40 addition
41 thing added
42 subtraction
43 thing subtracted
44 remainder
45 mixture
46 freedom from mixture
47 junction
48 separation
49 bond
50 coherence
51 incoherence
52 combination
53 decomposition
54 whole
55 part
56 completeness
57 incompleteness
58 composition
59 unity
60 accompaniment
61 duality
62 duplication
63 bisection
64 triality
65 triplication
66 trisection
67 quaternity
68 quadruplication
69 quadrisection
70 five and over
71 multisection
72 plurality
73 fraction
74 zero
75 multitude

76 fewness
77 repetition
78 infinity

D Order

79 order
80 disorder
81 arrangement
82 disarrangement
83 list
84 precedence
85 sequence
86 precursor
87 sequel
88 beginning
89 end
90 middle
91 continuity
92 discontinuity
93 position in a series
94 assemblage
95 dispersion
96 focus
97 class
98 inclusion
99 exclusion
100 extraneousness
101 generality
102 speciality
103 rule
104 diversity
105 conformity
106 unconformity

E Time

107 time
108 absence of time
109 period
110 course of time
111 contingent duration
112 long duration
113 short duration
114 endless duration

321

243	absence of form	288	progression	**B**	**Inorganic matter**
244	symmetry	289	regression	332	density
245	asymmetry	290	propulsion	333	rarity
246	angular form	291	pulling	334	hardness
247	curved form	292	approach	335	softness
248	straight form	293	retreat	336	elasticity
249	round form	294	attraction	337	toughness
250	simple circularity	295	repulsion	338	brittleness
251	complex circu-larity	296	convergence	339	texture
		297	divergence	340	powderiness
252	convexity	298	arrival	341	friction
253	prominence	299	departure	342	lubrication
254	concavity	300	entrance	343	fluidity
255	sharpness	301	emergence	344	gaseity
256	bluntness	302	reception	345	liquefaction
257	smoothness	303	ejection	346	vaporization
258	roughness	304	eating: drinking	347	water
259	notch	305	provisions	348	air
260	fold	306	food	349	moisture
261	furrow	307	condiment	350	dryness
262	opening	308	tobacco	351	ocean
263	closure	309	drink	352	land
264	perforator	310	excretion	353	gulf
265	stopper	311	insertion	354	lake
		312-	extraction	355	marsh
	D Motion	313	passage	356	plain
266	motion	314	overstepping	357	island
267	rest	315	shortcoming	358	water in motion
268	transference	316	ascent	359	air in motion
269	land travel	317	descent	360	water channel
270	traveller	318	elevation	361	air-pipe
271	water travel	319	depression	362	semiliquidity
272	mariner	320	leap	363	bubble; cloud
273	air travel	321	plunge	364	pulpiness
274	space travel	322	circulation	365	unctuousness
275	carrier	323	rotation		
276	vehicle	324	evolution	**C**	**Organic matter**
277	ship	325	oscillation	366	animate matter
278	aircraft	326	agitation	367	inorganic matter
279	spaceship			368	life
280	velocity			369	death
281	slowness	**III Matter**		370	killing
282	impulse			371	corpse
283	recoil	**A**	**Matter in general**	372	burial
284	direction	327	materiality	373	animality; animal
285	deviation	328	immateriality	374	vegetability; plant
286	precedence	329	universe	375	zoology
287	following	330	weight	376	botany
		331	lightness		

879 boasting	**E Moral**	954 legality
880 insolence	915 right	955 illegality
881 servility	916 wrong	956 jurisdiction
	917 dueness	957 tribunal
	918 undueness	958 judge
	919 duty	959 lawyer
D Sympathetic	920 neglect of duty	960 lawsuit
882 friendship	921 exemption	961 acquittal
883 enmity	922 respect	962 condemnation
884 sociability	923 disrespect	963 punishment
885 unsociability	924 contempt	964 means of punishment
886 courtesy	925 approval	
887 discourtesy	926 disapproval	965 reward
888 congratulation	927 flattery	
889 love	928 disparagement	**F Religious**
890 endearment	929 vindication	966 divinity
891 darling; favourite	930 accusation	967 God
892 hate	931 probity	968 good spirit
893 resentment; anger	932 improbity	969 evil spirit
894 irritability	933 disinterestedness	970 mythical being
895 sullenness	934 selfishness	971 ghost
896 marriage	935 virtue	972 heaven
897 celibacy	936 vice	973 hell
898 divorce;	937 innocence	974 religion
widowhood	938 guilt	975 irreligion
899 benevolence	939 good person	976 revelation
900 malevolence	940 bad person	977 orthodoxy
901 curse	941 penitence	978 heresy
902 threat	942 impenitence	979 sectarianism
903 philanthropy	943 atonement	980 piety
904 misanthropy	944 temperance	981 impiety
905 benefactor	945 intemperance	982 worship
906 evildoer	946 asceticism	983 idolatry
907 pity	947 fasting	984 sorcery
908 pitilessness	948 gluttony	985 churchdom
909 gratitude	949 soberness	986 clergyman
910 ingratitude	950 drunkenness	987 laity
911 forgiveness	951 purity	988 religious service
912 revenge	952 impurity	989 vestment
913 jealousy	953 libertine	990 church building
914 envy		